Modern Ireland

2nd EDITION

GERA   **H**

Gill & Macmillan

Gill & Macmillan Ltd
Hume Avenue
Park West
Dublin 12
with associated companies throughout the world
www.gillmacmillan.ie

© Gerard Brockie and Raymond Walsh 2004 and 2008
978 07171 4375 7
Design, illustrations and print origination in Ireland by Designit
Colour reproduction by Typeform Repro, Dublin

The paper used in this book is made from the wood pulp of managed forests. For every tree felled, at least one tree is planted, thereby renewing natural resources.

Contents

Course Outline

PART 4: POLITICS AND SOCIETY IN NORTHERN IRELAND, 1949–93

Course Outline

Note
The sections of this book, parts 1 to 4, cover Topics 2, 3, 5 and 6 of the syllabus. They will be labelled Topic 2, Topic 3, Topic 5 and Topic 6 on your exam paper.

Topic 2: Movements for Political and Social Reform, 1870–1914

PERSPECTIVE	ELEMENTS	CASE STUDIES
Politics and administration	The Home Rule movement: • Origins • Development • Leadership – Butt, Parnell, Redmond The suffrage movement The first Sinn Féin Party The Irish Volunteers Unionism and the Ulster Question	The elections of 1885 and 1886: issues and outcomes
Society and economy	Land agitation and land reform Unionisation of the working classes The co-operative movement Industrial development in Belfast: the shipyards Educational reforms: schools and universities	Dublin 1913 – strike and lockout
Culture and religion	The GAA Cultural revivals: the Gaelic League, the Anglo-Irish Literary Revival The consolidation of Catholic identity	The GAA to 1891

In their study of the topic, students should become aware of the role of certain key personalities.

Another 'key' to developing understanding will be learning to identify the main issues through a familiarity with certain key concepts.

KEY PERSONALITIES

Students should be aware of the contribution of the following to the developments listed under the elements above:

C.S. Parnell, John Redmond, Edward Carson, Isabella Tod, Hanna Sheehy-Skeffington, James Connolly, Michael Davitt, James Larkin, Douglas Hyde, W.B. Yeats

KEY CONCEPTS

Democracy, Home Rule, separatism, militarism, socialism, feminism, political agitation, anglicisation/de-anglicisation, Irish Ireland, Anglo-Irish, suffragette

Topic 3: The Pursuit of Sovereignty and the Impact of Partition, 1912–49

PERSPECTIVE	ELEMENTS	CASE STUDIES
Politics and administration	The Third Home Rule Bill, 1912–14 The impact of World War I; the 1916 Rising; the rise of the Second Sinn Féin Party; the 1918 election; the War of Independence; partition, treaty and civil war State building and the consolidation of democracy; from Free State to Republic Northern Ireland – the Unionist Party in power The impact of World War II, North and South Anglo-Irish relations	The Treaty negotiations, October–December 1921
Society and economy	Impact of partition on economy and society; impact of world economic crisis; from free trade to protectionism; impact of World War II	Belfast during World War II
Culture and religion	State and culture, North and South: language, religion and education; promotion of cultural identity	The Eucharistic Congress, 1932

In their study of the topic, students should become aware of the role of certain key personalities.

Another 'key' to developing understanding will be learning to identify the main issues through a familiarity with certain key concepts.

KEY PERSONALITIES

Students should be aware of the contribution of the following to the developments listed under the elements above:

Patrick Pearse, Éamon de Valera, Arthur Griffith, Michael Collins, Countess Markievicz, W.T. Cosgrave, James J. McElligott, James Craig, Richard Dawson Bates, Evie Hone

KEY CONCEPTS

Sovereignty, partition, Ulster unionism, allegiance, physical force, IRB/IRA, 'blood sacrifice', dominion status, republic, free trade, protectionism, neutrality, discrimination, conformity/censorship

Topic 5: Politics and Society in Northern Ireland, 1949–93

PERSPECTIVE	ELEMENTS	CASE STUDIES
Politics and administration	From Brookeborough to O'Neill; the civil rights movement; emergence of the provisional IRA; the fall of Stormont; direct rule; republican and loyalist terrorism; Sunningdale and power-sharing; the Anglo-Irish Agreement, 1985. The Republic - responses to the Troubles	The Sunningdale Agreement and Power-Sharing Executive, 1973–74
Society and economy	Impact of Welfare State: education, health, housing. Social and economic developments prior to 1969. Impact of the Troubles: (a) the economy (b) society - education, health, housing.	The Coleraine University Controversy
Culture and religion	Religious affiliation and cultural identity; ecumenism; cultural responses to the Troubles.	The Apprentice Boys of Derry

In their study of the topic, students should become aware of the role of certain key personalities.

Another 'key' to developing understanding will be learning to identify the main issues through a familiarity with certain key concepts.

KEY PERSONALITIES

Students should be aware of the contribution of the following to the developments listed under the elements above:

Terence O'Neill; Conn and Patricia McCluskey; Bernadette Devlin; Ian Paisley; Brian Faulkner; John Hume; James Molyneaux; Margaret Thatcher; Gerry Adams; Seamus Heaney

KEY CONCEPTS

Civil rights; gerrymandering; terrorism; power-sharing; sectarianism; bigotry; tolerance and intolerance; cultural traditions; cultural identity, ecumenism, propaganda

NOTE: The topic 'Politics and Society in Northern Ireland, 1949–93' will be prescribed for the compulsory documents study section of the Leaving Certificate Examination in 2010 and 2011. Questions will be based on the case studies in this topic and on a wider knowledge of the topic overall.

Topic 6: Government, Economy and Society in the Republic of Ireland, 1949–89

PERSPECTIVE	ELEMENTS	CASE STUDIES
Politics and administration	Alternating governments and their economic and social policies, 1948–59 Economic planning; the move to free trade Changes in education, health and social welfare provision; economic and social challenges of the 1970s and 1980s Anglo-Irish relations, 1949–89; increasing international involvement – the UN and the EEC	The First Programme for Economic Expansion, 1958–63
Society and economy	Demographic change Social change – status of women, housing, schools, amenities Economic change and its social consequences; the impact of EEC membership	The impact of the EEC on fisheries
Culture/religion/science	Changing attitudes towards Irish language and culture: the impact of television the impact of Vatican II the impact of the communications revolution	The impact of RTÉ, 1962–72

In their study of the topic, students should become aware of the role of certain key personalities.

Another 'key' to developing understanding will be learning to identify the main issues through a familiarity with certain key concepts.

KEY PERSONALITIES

Students should be aware of the contribution of the following to the developments listed under the elements above:

T.K. Whitaker, Seán Lemass, Archbishop J.C. McQuaid, Jack Lynch, Charles Haughey, Garret FitzGerald, Sylvia Meehan, Mary Robinson, Breandán Ó hEithir, Gay Byrne

KEY CONCEPTS

Economic planning, free trade, Common Market, equality of opportunity, ecumenism, secularisation, balance of payments, discrimination, censorship, pluralism, liberalisation

PART 1:
MOVEMENTS FOR POLITICAL AND SOCIAL REFORM, 1870–1914

Government and Politics

The nature of government and politics in Ireland in 1870 was determined largely by the Act of Union (1800). Under this Act, the old Dublin-based Parliament was abolished, and Ireland was ruled directly by the British Government in London. From then on, the 103 Irish Members of Parliament (MPs) attended the British Parliament in Westminster. In addition to the MPs who sat in the House of Commons, 28 Irish noblemen, or peers, sat in the House of Lords. As well as political union, the Act of Union inaugurated a period of economic integration: there was to be free trade and a common currency between Great Britain and Ireland.

Although Ireland was ruled directly from Westminster, a number of key officials in Ireland were responsible for government and administration:

1 The **Viceroy**, also called the **Lord Lieutenant**, represented the British monarch in Ireland. He lived in the Vice-Regal Lodge in the Phoenix Park in Dublin and performed ceremonial functions such as hosting state receptions in Dublin Castle.

2 The **Chief Secretary** was a member of the British Government who was in charge of Irish affairs. From his headquarters in Dublin Castle, he implemented the policies of the British Government throughout the country and also answered questions concerning Ireland in the Westminster Parliament.

3 Unlike the Chief Secretary, the **Under-Secretary** was not a politician but a permanent civil servant who was in charge of government departments in Dublin Castle.

Law and Order

Against a background of political and social agitation, the maintenance of law and order was a priority for successive British administrations in Ireland. In order to maintain control over Ireland, the British Government stationed large numbers of soldiers in army garrisons throughout the country. Many Irishmen joined the British army and served both at home in Ireland, in Britain and throughout the British Empire.

The everyday maintenance of law and order was left in the

Dublin Castle: headquarters of British rule in Ireland

hands of the police force, known as the **Royal Irish Constabulary** (RIC). In addition to carrying out normal policing duties, members of the RIC reported all suspicious activity to Dublin Castle. Because they helped to defeat rebellions and assisted at evictions, they were frequently unpopular among ordinary people. Dublin city was not policed by the RIC. Instead it had its own force, known as the **Dublin Metropolitan Police** (DMP). Whereas members of the RIC carried guns, the DMP was an unarmed force.

The courts were responsible for the administration of justice. At local level most cases were dealt with by **magistrates**. These unpaid judges were usually landlords who dealt with a range of small offences, including poteen making, petty theft, drunkenness and fighting. More serious offences, including murder, were tried in the **assizes**, courts presided over by travelling judges. The most important court of all was the **High Court** in Dublin, which dealt with serious cases.

Members of the Royal Irish Constabulary with a woman under arrest beside her illegal poteen still

Political Divisions in Ireland

Nationalism and **unionism** were the two main political traditions in nineteenth-century Ireland. These contrasting traditions emerged from totally opposing views on the Act of Union (1800). While nationalists desired varying degrees of independence from Britain, unionists wished to maintain the Act of Union in its entirety.

NATIONALISM

All nationalists desired some degree of freedom from Britain. However, they held widely differing views on the extent of this freedom and the means that should be used to achieve it. Two forms of Irish nationalism developed in the nineteenth century:

- **Constitutional nationalists** wanted the Act of Union abolished and the establishment of a parliament in Ireland. They sought **limited self-government**: although Ireland would have its own parliament, it would remain within the British Empire. Constitutional nationalists were committed to achieving their aims through **peaceful parliamentary means**. The first great leader of constitutional nationalism was Daniel O'Connell, who championed the causes of Catholic Emancipation and repeal of the Act of Union. O'Connell paved the way for later developments in constitutional nationalism, such as the Home Rule movement. Under

Irish MPs at the Westminster Parliament

the leadership of Parnell, this was to become the most powerful expression of constitutional nationalism in nineteenth-century Ireland.

- **Physical force nationalists** desired complete separation from Britain and the establishment of an **Irish republic**. They believed that this could be achieved only by an **armed uprising** against British rule in Ireland. This tradition began with Wolfe Tone and the United Irishmen's rebellion of 1798. It continued during the nineteenth century, with rebellions by Robert Emmet (1803), the

A new member of the Irish Republican Brotherhood (IRB) being sworn into the organisation

Young Ireland movement (1848) and the Fenians (1867). The Fenian movement, or Irish Republican Brotherhood (IRB), was the most powerful and enduring example of physical force nationalism. It continued to exist after the failure of the 1867 rebellion, and its members ultimately went on to plan the Easter Rising of 1916.

The two traditions of Irish nationalism, although distinct, frequently existed side by side. In the promotion of Irish interests, there was some co-operation between both traditions. However, for the most part one tradition tended to be strong and dominant while the other was in decline. By and large, most Irish nationalists throughout the nineteenth century supported the constitutional rather than the physical force tradition.

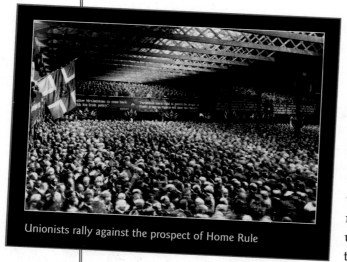

Unionists rally against the prospect of Home Rule

UNIONISM

Unionists fully supported the existing Union between Britain and Ireland. They believed that their interests were best served and safeguarded by the system of direct rule by the British Government. Most unionists were Protestants and were especially concentrated in north-east Ulster. As the nineteenth century progressed, unionists viewed with alarm the growing strength of Irish nationalism. As they perceived the Union to be under threat, they began to organise themselves in a more disciplined and effective manner. The rise of unionism from the 1880s onwards coincided with the threat posed to the Union by the Home Rule movement.

Economy and Society

The Great Famine (1845–50) had far-reaching social and economic consequences. A sustained decline in population took place because of falling marriage and birth rates and continued emigration. This occurred at a time when the populations of most other European countries were rising rapidly. The vast majority of Irish people continued to live in the countryside and earned their living from farming. The land, therefore, remained the central issue in nineteenth-century Ireland.

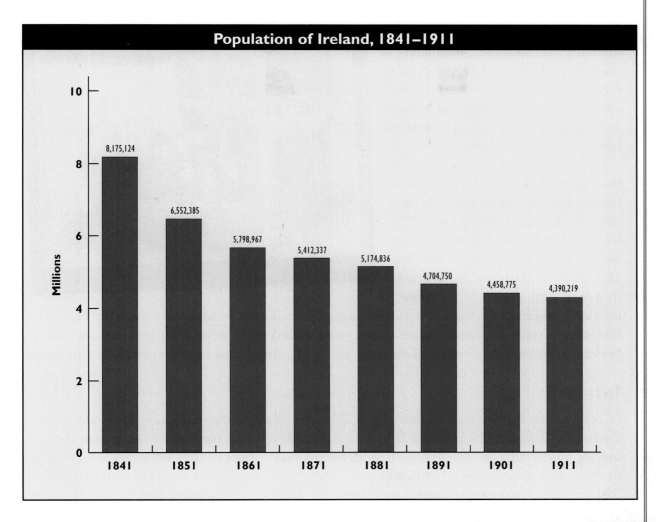

Population of Ireland, 1841–1911

Millions

- 1841: 8,175,124
- 1851: 6,552,385
- 1861: 5,798,967
- 1871: 5,412,337
- 1881: 5,174,836
- 1891: 4,704,750
- 1901: 4,458,775
- 1911: 4,390,219

THE LAND QUESTION

In 1870 the land of Ireland was owned by around 4,000 **landlords**. Most landlords were Anglo-Irish Protestants – they were descended from English and Scottish settlers and supported the Union between Britain and Ireland. Although some landlords lived in mansions on their Irish estates, others were absentees who left the running of their estates in the hands of agents. Between 1870 and 1922 the landlord class in Ireland was to experience dramatic decline both in numbers and in influence.

A landlord's mansion

Tenant farmers rented their holdings from the landlords. A minority of tenants had written agreements (leases) with their landlords. Most, however, were tenants-at-will, who rented their farms from year to year without any written agreement. There were sharp differences in prosperity among Irish tenant farmers. Large farmers with over a hundred acres lived prosperous lives and employed labourers on the farm. However, many small farmers had fewer than fifteen acres of poor land and continued to survive by growing potatoes. In the years after the Famine, the number of smallholdings declined, and that of larger farms increased. By 1870 the average family farm was around thirty acres. The tenant farmers ensured that the family farm would remain intact by passing it on to a named heir, usually the eldest son.

In the decades after the Famine a dramatic shift took place not merely in the size of farms but in the type of farming practised. Farmers moved away from tillage in favour of pasture, and the number of agricultural labourers decreased greatly.

Landlord–tenant relations were at the heart of the Land Question in Ireland. During a period of prosperity from the mid-1850s to the mid-1870s, large rent increases and evictions were rare. However, from the late 1870s, at a time of agricultural depression, conflict between landlords and tenants over rents and evictions became acute. Indeed, the ownership of the land itself became one of the major issues in late nineteenth-century Ireland. By 1914 the vast majority of farmers had become owners of the land, and the landlord class had been virtually eliminated.

A tenant farmer family

INDUSTRY

In contrast to Britain and western Europe, where rapid industrialisation was taking place around 1870, Ireland remained a largely agricultural country. North-east Ulster was the only industrialised area in an otherwise underdeveloped economy. Ireland's lack of industrial development was due to a combination of factors, including scarcity of raw materials such as coal and iron, inadequate capital investment, a declining population and competition from cheap British imports. Many traditional smaller industries went into serious decline during the nineteenth century. They included the manufacture of furniture, pottery, shoes and leather because small-scale producers were unable to compete with mass-produced imports from England. There were, however, some successful industries, most notably brewing, distilling and milling.

The industrialisation of Belfast and the Lagan Valley was in marked contrast to the rest of the country. This area had a long tradition of textile manufacture, including linen and cotton. These industries were converted from domestic to factory production. Along with this industrial tradition, north-east Ulster was helped by other factors, such as the availability of labour and investment, and proximity to British raw materials and markets. The most successful industries in late nineteenth-century Belfast included textiles, engineering and shipbuilding.

Part of the Harland & Wolff shipyard in Belfast

The centre of Belfast around 1900

Urbanisation in Ireland followed the same patterns as industrialisation. Whereas Dublin and Belfast grew substantially between 1870 and 1914, smaller cities such as Cork, Limerick and Galway remained stagnant. Belfast in particular experienced huge growth, and for a time it outclassed Dublin as the biggest city in Ireland. This was in large part due to the migration of people from the countryside to work in the new factories. Much of this employment was provided in shipyards such as that of Harland & Wolff. Many of the workers in Belfast were able to rent newly built terraced houses which contrasted with the tenements of Dublin.

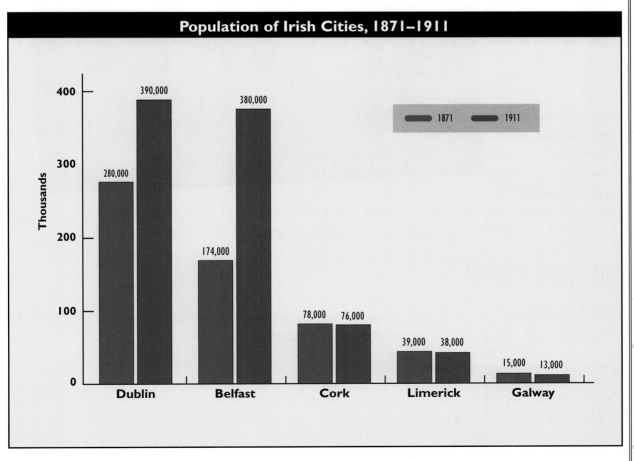

Population of Irish Cities, 1871–1911

Thousands

City	1871	1911
Dublin	280,000	390,000
Belfast	174,000	380,000
Cork	78,000	76,000
Limerick	39,000	38,000
Galway	15,000	13,000

Economy and Society

Dublin's population also grew substantially between 1870 and 1914. However, this was primarily due to growth in government and business jobs rather than to industrial development. One of the main industries in Dublin was the Guinness brewery, which produced stout for both domestic and foreign markets. The vast majority of workers in Dublin were unskilled labourers. They were in insecure, poorly paid jobs and lived with their families in overcrowded tenements. The middle classes of Belfast and Dublin, by contrast, lived in comfortable houses outside city centres in the growing suburbs.

One of the most important developments in Irish towns from around 1900 was the unionisation of the unskilled

Coopers making barrels in the Guinness brewery

The thriving Dublin suburb of Rathmines around 1900

workers. Under the influence of James Connolly and James Larkin, workers became organised for the first time in pursuit of higher wages and better working conditions.

Religious Identity

There were three main religious denominations in Ireland in 1870: the Roman Catholic Church, the Anglican Church of Ireland and the Presbyterian Church.

THE CATHOLIC CHURCH

Over 77 per cent of people in Ireland belonged to the Catholic Church. The vast majority of people in Munster, Leinster and Connaught were Catholics. However, in Ulster, Catholics numbered 50 per cent of the population. Although most Catholics were ordinary farmers or

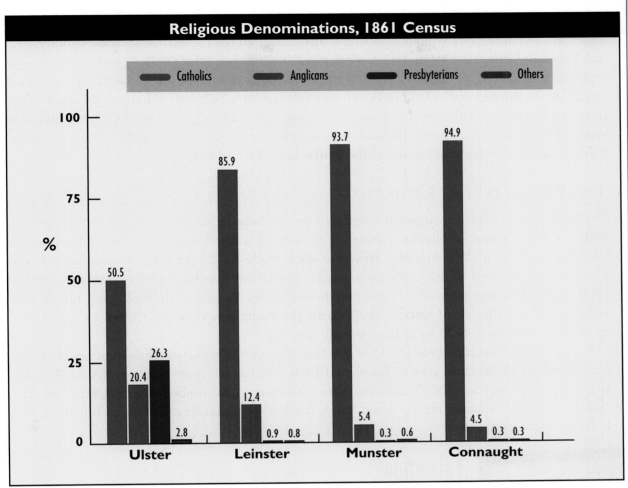

Religious Denominations, 1861 Census

Legend: Catholics, Anglicans, Presbyterians, Others

	Catholics	Anglicans	Presbyterians	Others
Ulster	50.5	20.4	26.3	2.8
Leinster	85.9	12.4	0.9	0.8
Munster	93.7	5.4	0.3	0.6
Connaught	94.9	4.5	0.3	0.3

workers, a small but increasing minority of Catholics were rich businessmen and professionals. In 1870 the Catholic Church in Ireland was dominated by Cardinal Paul Cullen, who was Archbishop of Dublin from 1852 to 1878. Under his leadership the Catholic bishops and priests became more powerful, and the authority of the Pope was strongly emphasised. The numbers of priests, nuns and religious brothers increased, and many new Catholic churches, hospitals and schools were built. While this expansion continued at home, Irish missionaries were sent abroad, especially to countries with large numbers of Irish emigrants. Whereas Irish Catholics were proud of the growing wealth and power of their Church, many Protestants felt threatened because of the overwhelming majority of Catholics in Ireland.

Mass in a Connemara cabin, 1883

THE CHURCH OF IRELAND

The second-largest religious denomination in Ireland in 1870 was the Church of Ireland, which was Protestant. Members of this Church were also known as Anglicans because of their close connection with the Church of England. Up to 1869 the Church of Ireland had been the established – or state – Church, with the British monarch at its head. Its bishops were appointed and paid by the British Government, and it enjoyed many privileges. However, in 1869 the Government of William Gladstone disestablished the Church of Ireland. Although the link between Church and state was broken, most members of the Church of Ireland were very loyal to the Queen of England and were committed unionists. Most landlords and rich businessmen throughout Ireland in 1870 were members of the Church of Ireland. Whereas in the province of Ulster Anglicans accounted for 20 per cent of the population, in the country as a whole they stood at 12 per cent. Because of their dominant position in the political and economic life of Ireland, they became known as the **Protestant Ascendancy.**

THE PRESBYTERIAN CHURCH

The Presbyterian Church promoted a stricter form of Protestantism than the Church of Ireland. Unlike Catholics and Anglicans, Presbyterians formed a small minority of the population in Leinster, Munster and Connaught. However, they made up 26 per cent of the population in Ulster and 9 per cent in the island as a whole. The Ulster Presbyterians were descendants of Scottish planters and were often extremely hostile to the Pope and the Catholic Church. Like members of the Church of Ireland, they feared the rising power of the Catholic Church, and most Presbyterians in 1870 were also strongly unionist.

It is clear, therefore, that between 1870 and 1914 the main religious division in Ireland between Catholics and Protestants was accompanied by a political division between nationalists and unionists. The vast majority of Catholics were nationalists who wished to weaken the link with Britain. Most Protestants, on the other hand, were determined to maintain in full the Union between both countries.

Education

Nuns supervise a lace-making class at a convent in Kenmare in the late 1890s

PRIMARY EDUCATION

One of the main achievements in education in nineteenth-century Ireland was the substantial increase in the rate of literacy. At the time of the Great Famine, only half the population could read and write. By 1900 only 16 per cent of the Irish population was illiterate. The National School system established in 1831 was the most important vehicle in increasing literacy throughout the country. By 1900 half a million children received their primary education in National Schools. These were originally intended to be non-denominational, catering for Protestants and Catholics in the same school. However, the vast majority of National Schools quickly became divided along religious lines, with Catholic and Protestant children attending separate schools controlled by the local clergy.

SECONDARY EDUCATION

In 1870 only a small minority of children went beyond primary education. Unlike the National School system, secondary education received no state aid until 1878. Secondary schools charged fees and were strictly divided on religious grounds. Here students were prepared for entry to university or for careers in business or the professions. With increasing prosperity, the participation of Catholics in secondary education expanded steadily after 1870.

UNIVERSITY EDUCATION

As with primary and secondary education, religious divisions were prominent in university education. Trinity College, Dublin was the oldest university in Ireland. It was closely linked to the Protestant Church of Ireland, and most of its students belonged to that Church. The Queen's Colleges at Cork, Galway and Belfast were set up by the British Government in 1845 to provide non-denominational university education. However, the Catholic bishops wanted a purely Catholic university; they condemned the Queen's Colleges and advised Catholics not to attend them. Instead they set up the Catholic University in Dublin in 1854. This was not a successful venture, mainly because the Government refused to recognise its degrees. The University Question in Ireland was not settled until 1908.

The improvements in educational provision in nineteenth-century Ireland led to greater involvement in public affairs. As more and more people read newspapers, they became increasingly aware of political developments at local and national level. This heightened political consciousness and played a significant role in the struggle between unionists and nationalists in the years leading up to 1914.

Culture

THE DECLINE OF THE IRISH LANGUAGE

The most significant cultural development in nineteenth-century Ireland was the dramatic decline in

Trinity College, Dublin, which had close links with the Protestant Ascendancy

the use of the Irish language. Irish was associated with poverty and backwardness in the minds of ordinary people. Many Irish-speaking parents, for reasons of social advancement, insisted that their children speak English. This trend was further strengthened by the high level of emigration to English-speaking countries such as Britain and America. Concern at the decline of the Irish language and the growing influence of English culture led to the establishment of various cultural movements, such as the Gaelic League.

DEVELOPMENTS IN SPORT

English influence was also increasing in the area of sport. Around 1870 English games such as soccer and rugby were becoming increasingly popular in Ireland. In 1884 the Gaelic Athletic Association (GAA) was set up to counter this development and to promote native Irish games such as hurling and Gaelic football.

From the late nineteenth century onwards, members of cultural and sporting organisations such as the Gaelic League and the GAA were to play a prominent role in the development of Irish nationalism.

This chapter has provided an overview of the main political, economic and cultural features of late nineteenth-century Ireland. The following chapters will explore in greater depth the principal developments in Irish history between 1870 and 1914.

ORDINARY LEVEL

1. Write a paragraph on how Ireland was governed in 1870.

2. Describe the two main types of nationalism in Ireland at the time.

3. Write a paragraph on unionism in Ireland around 1870.

4. State what you understand by the expression 'the Land Question' in Ireland around 1870.

5. Write a short account of Irish industry around 1870.

6. Examine the chart on population change 1841–1911 on page 11 and describe and explain the population changes.

7. Write a paragraph on the growth of Irish towns in the late nineteenth century, referring to the chart on page 13.

8. With reference to the chart on page 15, describe the religious divisions in Ireland around 1870.

9. Write an account of the Catholic Church in Ireland around 1870.

10. What do you understand by the term 'Protestant Ascendancy'?

11. Explain briefly why the Irish language declined in the nineteenth century. What organisation was formed to reverse this decline?

12. How were traditional Irish games under threat in the late nineteenth century?

HIGHER LEVEL

1. Assess the relative importance of agriculture and industry in Ireland around 1870.

2. Discuss religion and education in Ireland between 1870 and 1914.

3. 'Political divisions in nineteenth-century Ireland were based on opposing views of the Act of Union.' Discuss this statement.

4. Explain the relationship between political and religious divisions in nineteenth-century Ireland.

William Gladstone and Ireland

In 1868 William Gladstone, the leader of the British Liberal Party, became Prime Minister for the first time. Bringing peace to Ireland was to be one of his priorities. When he realised that he had won the general election, he remarked, 'My mission is to pacify Ireland.' Following the unsuccessful Fenian rising of 1867, the country was unsettled and discontented. Fenian activities also extended to England, where bombings and shootings occurred. Gladstone's reaction to Fenian violence differed significantly from the traditional English view. Most English politicians believed that strict law and order was the only solution to Irish discontent. Gladstone, however, while agreeing that violence should be suppressed, also considered the causes of Irish grievances. He believed that problems on the land and difficulties over religion were among the major causes of discontent in Ireland. Therefore, his first efforts at reform centred on these two areas of Irish life.

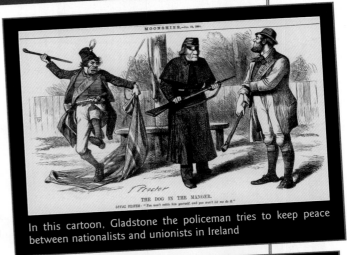

In this cartoon, Gladstone the policeman tries to keep peace between nationalists and unionists in Ireland

Fenian prisoners exercising inside Mountjoy Jail in Dublin

The Disestablishment of the Church of Ireland (1869)

The privileged position of the Protestant Church of Ireland was resented by the Catholic majority. According to the census of 1861, only 11.8 per cent of the population belonged to the Church of Ireland. Despite this, the Church of Ireland was the state – or established – Church, with the Queen of England at its head and its bishops appointed and paid by the Government. This privileged position was guaranteed by the Act of Union of 1800. Taxes for the support of the Church of Ireland were known as tithes. These had to be paid by all farmers, including Catholics and Presbyterians, who resented paying for the upkeep of clergy of another religion. The Catholic Church, under the leadership of Cardinal Paul Cullen, called for ending the privileged position of the Church of Ireland.

In 1869 Gladstone introduced the Disestablishment Bill in the British Parliament. This Bill contained the following provisions:

1. From 1 January 1871 the Church of Ireland was to become a voluntary body.
2. The legal connection between Church and state in Ireland was completely broken.
3. Church property was confiscated and given over to the Church Temporalities Commission. This body would look after the interests of clergy and teachers who were on the payroll of the disestablished Church.

cont'd

William Gladstone and Ireland

4   A land purchase clause gave tenants on Church lands the option of buying their own holdings. They could borrow three-quarters of the purchase price at an interest rate of 4 per cent.

The link between the state and the Church of Ireland was broken. However, the Church received financial assistance as compensation. Gladstone resisted calls to hand over ancient cathedrals in Ireland to the Catholic Church. Although Catholics and Presbyterians in Ireland supported Disestablishment, many members of the Church of Ireland regarded it as an act of betrayal by the British Government.

Having successfully implemented Disestablishment in 1869, Gladstone attempted to tackle the vexed question of the Irish land system the following year.

Christchurch — one of two Church of Ireland cathedrals in Dublin

GLADSTONE'S FIRST LAND ACT (1870)

Gladstone realised that reform of the land system in Ireland was long overdue. Many tenant farmers throughout the country desired the level of tenant security that prevailed in Ulster. Here tenants enjoyed a tradition known as the Ulster Custom, or the three Fs – fair rent, fixity of tenure and freedom of sale. Fair rent meant a rent that the tenant could afford to pay. Under fixity of tenure a tenant could not be evicted as long as the rent was paid. Freedom of sale involved compensation for improvements made on the farm. The demand for the extension of the Ulster Custom was known as **tenant right.**

Under Gladstone's First Land Act (1870), the following reforms were introduced:

1   The Ulster Custom was legalised wherever it existed.

2   Under the Bright Clause, tenants wishing to purchase their farms would be lent two-thirds of the price by the British Government.

A tenant farmer outside his cottage

In practice, the Land Act made no difference to the lives of most tenant farmers. Only a small number (eight hundred) purchased their farms under the Bright Clause. The Act did not define the Ulster Custom, and tenant farmers would have to go to court to prove that it existed in their area. However, Gladstone's First Land Act had important symbolic significance. By intervening in the relationship between landlords and tenants, the British Government had attempted for the first time to reduce the power of landlords in Ireland.

REACTIONS TO GLADSTONE'S POLICIES

Those who supported tenant right were deeply disappointed by the limited provisions of Gladstone's First Land Act. In addition, many members of the Protestant Ascendancy, already dismayed by Gladstone's Disestablishment of the Church of Ireland, felt further undermined by the provisions of his First Land Act. Having witnessed the gradual erosion of their privileged position, which had been guaranteed under the Act of Union, they began to wonder whether their interests might be better protected by some new arrangement outside the Union. In this reaction to Gladstone's policies lay the genesis of the Home Rule movement. Support for Home Rule was advocated most strongly by an Irish lawyer and Member of Parliament named Isaac Butt.

Isaac Butt and the Origins of Home Rule

Isaac Butt was born in Co. Donegal in 1813, the son of a Church of Ireland clergyman. A lawyer by profession, he started his political career in 1852, when he was elected MP for Harwich in England. He served this constituency for thirteen years before returning to Ireland. In Ireland he was elected MP for Youghal, Co. Cork, a constituency he represented until his death in 1879. As well as a politician, Butt was a distinguished barrister. In 1848 he defended in the courts some of those who had taken part in the Young Ireland Rebellion of that year, and in 1868 he set up the Amnesty Association to defend Fenian prisoners.

Initially Butt supported the Act of Union as the best means of protecting the interests of the Protestant Ascendancy in Ireland. However, he shared with other members of the Church of Ireland a deep concern about the policies of Disestablishment and land reform introduced by Gladstone after he became Prime Minister in 1868. He now came to believe that the interests of the Protestant Ascendancy might best be served by a Dublin-based parliament, which would look after Irish domestic affairs, combined with continued Irish representation at Westminster, where matters of foreign policy and defence would be dealt with. Butt established a new organisation in order to promote this **federal** proposal of **Home Rule** for Ireland.

THE HOME GOVERNMENT ASSOCIATION

At a meeting in Dublin on 19 May 1870, Isaac Butt founded the **Home Government Association** to advance his policy of Home Rule. This meeting was attended by people of very diverse points of view. Members of the Protestant Ascendancy attended because they shared Butt's deep distrust of Gladstone's policies; supporters of tenant right joined the new organisation because they were deeply disappointed with the recent Land Act; constitutional nationalists saw an opportunity to advance their demand for an Irish parliament; and some Fenians joined in the hope of using the organisation for their own purposes. However, from the beginning the Home Government Association was weakened by its lack of any clear programme of action and by the diversity of its membership. It was considerably undermined by Butt's determination that the organisation would not develop into a political party. Instead the Home Government Association became an umbrella organisation that included Catholics and Protestants, constitutional nationalists and Fenians. By 1873 many Protestants, alarmed by the dominance of Catholic nationalists, had left the movement. Butt now reconstituted the Home Government Association and replaced it with a much more political organisation called the **Home Rule League**. In the same year he established the **Home Rule Confederation of Great Britain** in order to promote his ideas among the Irish in England, Scotland and Wales.

The Home Rule League and the 1874 General Election

The Home Rule League attempted to become a national organisation by opening its membership to all who paid an annual subscription of £1. The first electoral test for the Home Rule League came in 1874, when Gladstone called a general election. The League put forward candidates who, in order to make their policies acceptable, combined support for Home Rule with other issues relating to land and education. The League candidates were also helped by the **Secret Ballot Act** (1872), which for the first time enabled tenant farmers entitled to vote to do so independently of their landlords.

In the 1874 general election the Home Rule League won 59 out of the 105 Irish seats at the Westminster Parliament. These 59 members now organised themselves into a separate political party – the Home Rule Party – at Westminster. However, from the outset the new party was to be undermined by poor organisation, ineffective tactics and weak leadership.

The Home Rule Party at Westminster

Organisation and Tactics

The Home Rule Party suffered from lack of unity, as many of those elected for the party had used the Home Rule issue as a means of securing election and were now quick to abandon it. In the absence of a pledge binding its members to vote always as a group, the party was very undisciplined. Butt himself was a traditional parliamentarian whose tactics in the House of Commons were always moderate and gentlemanly. In addition, his leadership was marred by severe personal gambling debts, which amounted to £12,000 by 1871. Pursued by creditors, he frequently returned to his work as a barrister in order to earn money and was therefore regularly absent from the House of Commons.

In addition to poor organisation, tactics and leadership, the fortunes of the Home Rule Party were not helped by the nature of the political landscape in Britain itself. The general election of 1874 had returned a Conservative Government under the leadership of Benjamin Disraeli. Disraeli's Government was especially concerned with international issues, and in general, English MPs and the English electorate showed little interest in Irish affairs. Indeed, an amendment to the Queen's speech at the opening of Parliament in March 1874 calling for an investigation into Irish dissatisfaction with the Union was defeated by 314 votes to 50. A more specific motion in favour of Home Rule was defeated by 458 votes to 61 votes in June 1874.

Members of Butt's own party were becoming increasingly dissatisfied with the party's lack of success in the House of Commons and, more specifically, with the gentlemanly and parliamentary tactics employed by their leader. They believed that a more extreme approach was required in order to force the British Parliament to take notice of Irish grievances. The tactic they advocated was called **parliamentary obstruction.**

Parliamentary Obstruction

Parliamentary obstruction was first advocated by Joseph Biggar, a Belfast merchant and Fenian who played a leading part in the establishment of the Home Rule League and was first elected to Parliament in 1874. Becoming increasingly dissatisfied with the futility of Butt's polite and co-operative approach, he and other Home Rule MPs engaged in disrupting the business of the

House of Commons in order to draw attention to the Irish Question. When a bill was introduced in Parliament, the 'obstructionists' would speak about it at great length, often engaging in prolonged, irrelevant discussion so that Parliament, which only met for a limited time each year, could not conduct its business properly. On one occasion Biggar used the rules of the House of Commons to force the Prince of Wales to leave the public gallery during a debate. Butt was horrified by these tactics, which he regarded as ungentlemanly and unparliamentary.

In Ireland the general public, including Fenians, supported the new tactic of parliamentary obstruction. In 1875 the obstructionists received another supporter when a young Home Rule MP was elected in a by-election to represent Co. Meath in the House of Commons. His name was Charles Stewart Parnell, and he was to dominate and transform the Irish political scene over the following years.

Irish MPs being removed from the House of Commons for obstructing its business

Charles Stewart Parnell (1846–91)

The son of a Protestant landowner, Charles Stewart Parnell was born in Avondale, Co. Wicklow, in 1846. From an early age the young Parnell, although born into the Ascendancy class, was intensely anti-English. This he inherited in part from his mother, Delia Stewart, herself the daughter of an American admiral who had fought against England in the war of 1812. His anti-English views were further intensified by his experiences in Cambridge University, where a clash with the authorities forced him to leave without receiving his degree.

On the surface Parnell seemed an unlikely type of person to enter politics. He was shy in personality and hesitant in speech. He was later to state that Fenianism and the memories of the 1798 United Irishmen's rebellion in his native Wicklow generated his interest in Irish nationalism. In 1875, at the age of twenty-eight, he was elected Home Rule MP for Co. Meath. Although a poor and reticent orator, Parnell soon drew attention to himself in Parliament. In a speech he asserted that the Fenians who had killed the two policemen in Manchester in 1867 while attempting to rescue their comrades were not murderers but martyrs. He quickly adopted the obstructionist tactics associated with Joseph Biggar and a small number of other Home Rule MPs.

Parnell was highly ambitious, and his rise within the Home Rule Party was to be dramatic and meteoric. His speeches and obstructionist tactics drew him to the attention of Fenians and ex-Fenians in England. As a result, in 1877 he replaced Butt as leader of the Fenian-dominated Home Rule Confederation of Great Britain. Butt's position as leader of the Home Rule Party was becoming increasingly weak. However, when he died in 1879, Parnell was not yet in a strong enough position to become leader of the party. This position was filled by William Shaw. Following the general election in 1880, Parnell's supporters were in a dominant position, and he was elected chairman of the Home Rule Party. Over the next ten years, he was to fashion it into a unified and disciplined organisation. However, although the achievement of Home Rule for Ireland was to be Parnell's primary political objective, the Land Question was to dominate the early years of his political career.

Charles Stewart Parnell (1846–91)

ORDINARY LEVEL

1. The following passage was written by Isaac Butt, the founder of the Home Rule movement. Read it carefully and answer the questions that follow.

> The Federal arrangement which I contemplate is one which would preserve the Imperial Parliament in its present form . . . It would leave it still the power of providing by Imperial taxation for Imperial necessities, including an Army and a Navy such as it judged necessary for the safety of the country, either in peace or war – imposing only a guarantee in the nature of the taxation that the levy should be one to which each member of the United Kingdom should contribute in proportion to its ability and its means.
>
> The Irish Parliament consisting, be it always remembered, of the Queen, Lords and Commons of Ireland, would have supreme control in Ireland, except in those matters which the federal Constitution might specifically reserve to the Imperial Assembly.
>
> That which is important is that Ireland would send, as we do now, 105 representatives to vote in an Imperial Parliament on all questions of Imperial concern, and in return we would submit, as we do now, to be taxed, but only for certain definite purposes and in a certain definite manner.
>
> At home in Ireland we would have our own Parliament controlling all the affairs of our internal administration.
>
> *Isaac Butt, Irish Federalism:*
> *Its Meaning, Its Objects and Its Hopes,*
> *Dublin: John Falconer, 1870; 4th ed.,*
> *Dublin: Irish Home Rule League 1874*

   (i) Would Irish taxpayers still have to pay for the British army and navy?

   (ii) What body would control Irish affairs?

   (iii) How many MPs from Ireland would continue to go to the Westminster Parliament?

   (iv) On which issue could they vote?

2. How did Gladstone view the problem of violence and unrest in Ireland?

3. Write a paragraph on the Disestablishment of the Church in Ireland.

4. What were the provisions of Gladstone's First Land Act (1870)? What was the significance of this Act?

5. Why were members of the Protestant Ascendancy dissatisfied with Gladstone's Irish policies?

6. Write a paragraph on the early career and beliefs of Isaac Butt up to the formation of the Home Government Association.

7. What was Isaac Butt's solution to the Irish Question, and how did he set about promoting it?

8. What were the weaknesses of the Home Government Association, and how did it differ from the Home Rule League?

9. Describe the weaknesses of the Home Rule Party at Westminster under the leadership of Butt.

10. Write a paragraph on parliamentary obstruction.

11. Write an account of the early life and career of Charles Stewart Parnell.

HIGHER LEVEL

1. Discuss the Irish policy of Gladstone's First Government, 1868–74.

2. Discuss the origins and early development of the Home Rule movement, 1870–74.

3. Assess the strengths and weaknesses of Isaac Butt as leader of the Home Rule movement between 1874 and 1879.

3. The Land War, 1879–82

The Land Question

The rise of Isaac Butt and the Home Rule Party constituted a significant development in Irish nationalism in the 1870s. However, for most people in Ireland at the time, Home Rule was not the most important issue. Instead, they were more interested in the Land Question because it affected their everyday lives.

The Land Question revolved around the issue of relations between landlords and tenants. In 1870 about 4,000 landlords owned most of the land of Ireland. Not only could they decide the level of rent on their estates, but they also had a wide influence in the local area. Unlike English landlords, they generally did not invest much of their wealth towards the improvement of their property. Instead, once rent was paid, most tenants were left undisturbed on their holdings.

Between 1852 and 1877 Irish agriculture was mostly prosperous. Demand for Irish food exports was growing in Britain, where the population was rising rapidly because of the Industrial Revolution. The prices paid to Irish farmers were therefore rising, and most tenants could afford to pay their rents. During this period rents did not rise as much as prices – in fact, they lagged about 20 per cent behind them. As a result, tenants enjoyed increasing prosperity. In these years evictions ran at a very low rate.

Workers on a landlord's estate

Taking a break from the harvest

In contrast to the economic prosperity of the early 1870s, the political climate was beginning to change for landlords. We have seen in Chapter 2 how they resented Gladstone's Disestablishment of the Church of Ireland (1869) and his First Land Act (1870). In 1872 the passing of the Secret Ballot Act further reduced their power in the countryside. Before that, voting took place in public, and landlords could therefore influence the way tenants voted. In 1874 the Home Rule Party, which most landlords opposed, won 59 seats in the general election. Significantly, the number of Irish MPs who were landlords dropped from 73 to 52. Therefore, in any future conflict between landlords and tenants, the self-confidence and prestige of landlords were already undermined. Tenants, on the other hand, had already secured some concessions in Gladstone's First Land Act (1870). With a strong Home Rule Party in Westminster, they could be confident of securing more concessions in the future.

THE CRISIS OF 1877–80

The long period of agricultural prosperity came to a sudden halt in 1877. Even before this there were signs of trouble ahead. In 1873 a period of economic decline known as the Great Depression began in Britain and lasted until 1896. This not only involved sharp falls in the prices of agricultural exports from Ireland, it also led to a reduction in the demand for seasonal Irish labourers on farms in England and Scotland. These jobs were vital to poor farming families in the west and north-west of Ireland. Between 1873 and 1879 emigration to the United States of America dropped because of an economic depression there also.

Poverty in the West of Ireland

By the 1870s Irish farmers had to compete with an increasing number of cheaper imports from countries such as Denmark, Argentina and the USA. The invention of refrigeration and the modernisation of agriculture in these countries enabled them to produce cheaper food. As a result the prices for Irish farm exports fell. In addition to these other setbacks, the weather was disastrous in 1877, 1878 and 1879. A succession of bad harvests had a far greater impact on Irish farmers than did foreign competition. Potato crops in particular were badly hit by the wet weather. This in turn led to serious losses of pigs and poultry.

Whereas in other parts of the country the crisis led to a serious reduction in farmers' incomes, in Connaught in particular the threat of starvation loomed. Here tenant farmers had good reason to fear mass evictions if they could not pay their rents. In the short term, food and financial assistance were sent to the West of Ireland from other parts of Ireland, and from England, Europe and America. However, in the long term the future of farmers in Connaught and throughout the country depended on a solution to the Land Question. This in turn required leadership and organisation. That leadership was soon to emerge in the person of Michael Davitt, himself the son of an evicted tenant farmer from Co. Mayo.

MICHAEL DAVITT: THE EARLY YEARS

Michael Davitt was born during the Great Famine in March 1846 in Straide, Co. Mayo. The Davitt family was evicted from a small farm in 1852 and moved to Lancashire in England. Here Michael began to work in a cotton mill at the age of nine. Two years later he lost his right arm in a factory accident. He then returned to school for a further four years. While working in a printing company, he continued to educate himself by attending evening classes and reading widely, especially in the area of politics and economics. In 1865 he joined the Fenian movement and became responsible for acquiring arms and ammunition in England and Scotland. He was arrested in May 1870 in London, found guilty of treason and sentenced to fifteen years' penal servitude.

Michael Davitt pictured on an anti-landlord banner

The Land Question

Having served over seven years in prison, he was released on ticket of leave (parole) in December 1877.

On his release he visited his native Mayo, where he was shocked by the conditions of the tenant farmers. He met Parnell on a number of occasions and was impressed by him. He hoped that the Fenians and the Home Rule movement would agree that a solution to the Land Question should be their first objective. In July 1878 Davitt set sail for New York. Here he was to meet John Devoy, the leader of the American Fenian movement, Clan na Gael. These two men were to reach an important understanding concerning the solution of the Land Question.

THE NEW DEPARTURE

Like Davitt, John Devoy had been imprisoned for Fenian activities and had gone to the United States on his release in 1871. He worked in journalism in New York and became leader of Clan na Gael, the American Fenian organisation. He and Michael Davitt travelled around America in 1878, meeting Irish exiles and seeking support for tenant farmers in Ireland. They agreed that a new approach was required that would place the Land Question in the forefront of Irish nationalism. Devoy called this approach the 'New Departure' because it required a departure from traditional Fenian tactics, with Fenians now agreeing to support land reform before the struggle for Irish independence.

Both Davitt and Devoy sailed for Europe in order to convince the Fenian leadership and Parnell to support the New Departure. Devoy met with the Fenian leader Charles J. Kickham in Paris. Kickham and the Supreme Council of the IRB refused to support the change in Fenian tactics. However, the rising star of the Home Rule movement, Parnell, gave the New Departure a guarded welcome.

In effect, the New Departure involved co-operation between three different elements:

1 Fenian supporters of rebellion against British rule in Ireland.
2 Constitutional nationalists in the Home Rule Party.
3 Supporters who wanted reform of the land system.

Parnell, Davitt and Devoy believed that all groups should work together to solve the Land Question. By land reform they ultimately meant peasant proprietorship, that is that the landlords should be forced to sell their estates to the tenants, who would borrow the cost from the British Government. However, the immediate aim of the New Departure was more limited. Given the developing agricultural crisis throughout Ireland, its supporters pressed for a reduction in rents and an end to eviction. In order to achieve these aims, a new and powerful tenants' organisation was required. This was soon to be provided by Michael Davitt.

THE FOUNDATION OF THE LAND LEAGUE

The impetus for the foundation of a new tenants' movement came from Davitt's native Co. Mayo. In April 1879 James Daly, the editor of the *Connaught Telegraph*, organised a meeting of tenants at Irishtown, Co. Mayo, to protest against increases in rents imposed by the local landlord. About 10,000 people attended, although neither Davitt nor Parnell were present. As a result of this protest meeting, some tenants in Galway and Mayo had their rents reduced.

Parnell now realised that in order to achieve leadership of the Home Rule Party and gain popular support, he needed to identify himself with the protests in Mayo. On 8 June 1879, therefore, he joined Davitt in addressing a meeting of tenant farmers in Mayo. In a stirring speech Parnell recalled the memory of the Great Famine and urged the tenants to resist eviction:

A fair rent is a rent that the tenant can reasonably pay according to the times, but in bad times a tenant cannot be expected to pay as much as he did in good times, three or four years ago . . . You must show the landlord that you intend to keep a firm grip on your homesteads and lands. You must not allow yourselves to be dispossessed as you were dispossessed in 1847.

Parnell's strong words were widely reported in the newspapers and increased his standing in Ireland and among Irish emigrants abroad.

Meanwhile, the economic crisis continued to worsen; the summer of 1879 was the coldest and wettest on record. In August, Davitt set up the Land League of Mayo, and on 21 October the National Land League was established in Dublin. The Land League had the following aims:

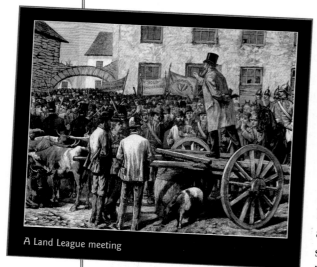

A Land League meeting

- To put an end to rack-renting, evictions and landlord oppression.
- To achieve the three Fs (fair rent, fixity of tenure, freedom of sale).
- To establish a peasant proprietorship, i.e. to ensure that every tenant in Ireland would become the owner of his land.

Although Davitt had founded the movement, he agreed that Parnell should be its leader, as a combination of local agitation and parliamentary pressure would be more likely to succeed. Parnell himself saw the Land League as a means of increasing his own popularity. Soon after the foundation of the Land League, Parnell left for a fund-raising tour of the United States. He collected over £70,000 for famine relief and for the newly established Land League. His tour was also a political triumph. It was widely reported in American and Irish newspapers and placed him in a strong position to become the leader of Irish nationalism.

The Land War, 1879–82

Although the Land League supported the use of peaceful means to achieve its aims, its leaders could not control the violent actions of the more extreme tenant farmers. Traditionally, attacks on landlords and agents, the maiming of cattle and the burning of homes and barns had been the methods of protest at times of crisis on the land. There was a long tradition of violent agrarian, or rural, secret societies, such as the Whiteboys. Now for the first time in 1879, tenant farmers' concerns were at the heart of a major social and political movement. Historians explain this by pointing to better education, the availability of newspapers and rising expectations. Having enjoyed the boom years up to 1876, farmers were unwilling to allow themselves to be evicted on a vast scale, as had happened during the Great Famine. However, old attitudes, such as the resort to agrarian violence, were difficult to eradicate. The number of land-related crimes rose from 236 in 1877 to 2,585 in 1880 and 4,439 in 1881. These crimes took place against a background of steadily rising evictions as more and more tenants were unable to pay their rents.

A commemoration of Parnell's triumphant tour of the United States which included a speech to the House of Representatives in 1880

BOYCOTTING

The most effective tactic used by the Land League during this period was proposed by Parnell in a speech at Ennis, Co. Clare, in September 1880. He advised the tenant farmers as follows:

> When a man takes a farm from which another has been evicted, you must show him on the roadside when you meet him – you must show him on the streets of the town – you must show him in the shop – you must show him in the fair green and the market place, and even in the house of worship, by leaving him severely alone, by putting him into a moral Coventry, by isolating him from his kind as if he were a leper of old – you must show him your detestation of the crime he has committed.

Captain Boycott thanking Orange labourers who had come from Ulster to save his harvest

Soon after Parnell's Ennis speech a Mayo land agent named Captain Charles Boycott became the first victim of the new policy. Boycott was deserted by his servants, shopkeepers refused to serve him, and his crops were left to rot in the fields. Although the Orange Order sent fifty labourers from Ulster to save his harvest, the cost of the soldiers and police who were protecting them was several times the value of the crops. Boycott left Ireland soon afterwards. A new word – 'boycotting' – entered the English language, and the Land League won a significant moral victory.

THE REACTION OF THE BRITISH GOVERNMENT

After the victory of the Liberal Party in the general election of 1880, Gladstone became Prime Minister for the second time. As in 1868, he once again gave priority to Irish affairs. He faced a formidable opponent in Parnell, who had been chosen as the leader of the Irish Home Rule Party after the election.

Gladstone's approach to Ireland contained two main elements. Although he wished to maintain law and order, he was also willing to introduce reforms into the Irish land system. However, dismayed by the rising level of agrarian violence that characterised the **Land War**, he insisted on restoring order first. This policy, known as 'coercion', was enthusiastically implemented by the new Chief Secretary, W.E. Forster. In his view, the Land League was taking the law into its own hands by encouraging tenants to pay reduced rents. Against this background, Gladstone's Government introduced stern coercive measures in the spring of 1881. When Parnell and other Irish MPs engaged in obstruction in Parliament, they were suspended. The rules of the House of Commons were then changed to prevent obstruction occurring again.

When Michael Davitt was re-arrested and his parole cancelled, Parnell led a walk-out of his followers from Parliament. Although urged to return to Ireland and lead the struggle from there, Parnell insisted on returning to Parliament. Historians regard this as an illustration of his commitment to constitutional politics.

Having implemented coercion in an effort to restore law and order, Gladstone was now ready to engage in conciliation by introducing the reforms that were eagerly awaited by the Land League and its supporters. This policy of conciliation took the form of a Second Land Act.

GLADSTONE'S SECOND LAND ACT (1881)

On 7 April 1881 Gladstone introduced his Second Land Bill in the House of Commons. It was a considerable improvement on his First Land Act (1870). The Bill contained the following new provisions:

> 1 The Ulster Custom (three Fs) was introduced throughout the country.
> 2 A land court was established to decide the level at which fair rents should be set.
> 3 A scheme was established to allow tenants to buy their farms if they could raise a quarter of the cost themselves.

From Gladstone's point of view, this was a major concession to tenant farmers and should lead to the end of the Land War. Indeed, at a time when the rights of private property owners were very strong, the 1881 Land Act was a huge interference by the state in the rights of landlords. Gladstone justified this in the hope that it would bring peace and prosperity to Ireland. In effect the new law introduced a form of **dual ownership** in that both landlord and tenant shared practical control of the farms.

However, from the point of view of the tenants, the 1881 Act contained some major flaws:

1 It did not include those tenants who had written agreements or leases with their landlords.
2 It did nothing to help those tenants in arrears with their rent.

Given the advantages and disadvantages of the new law, Parnell and the Land League had difficult decisions to make. Parnell's supporters were deeply divided in their reactions. Many MPs, most Catholic bishops and priests, better-off farmers and shopkeepers supported the measure. They wanted to return to totally peaceful conditions in the countryside, and they stood to gain from the provisions of the Land Act. However, it was opposed by many poorer farmers who were in arrears with their rents and gained nothing from it. A small number of more extreme Home Rule MPs felt that it did not go far enough. In the background the Fenians were also opposed to it.

Parnell now faced a dilemma. By supporting the Act he would alienate smaller farmers and many supporters of the Land League among Irish exiles in Britain and America. These exiles were a valued source of financial assistance, and Parnell could not afford to lose their support. However, by opposing the Act he would run the risk of alienating people of moderate views within his own party. Parnell had to try to find a middle course between the two opposing points of view.

A hostile cartoon shows Parnell threatening Gladstone

THE ARREST OF PARNELL

Parnell's solution to his difficulties involved two stages. First, the Home Rule Party abstained from voting on the Land Bill during its passage through Parliament. Parnell also called a convention of the Land League in Dublin, which did not support or oppose the Land Act but decided to wait in order to test individual cases in the land court to see if rents were fair. The second stage in Parnell's strategy was to have himself arrested and thereby appeal to the more extreme elements in the land movement. He knew that there would be trouble during the winter of 1881–2 as smaller farmers unable to benefit from the Land Act engaged in violent protests. He could then claim that the disorder was due to his absence. Therefore, he made some violent speeches denouncing Gladstone and succeeded in having himself and other leaders of the Land League imprisoned in Kilmainham Gaol in Dublin in October 1881.

Cartoons of Parnell's career: entering Parliament in 1875, becoming leader of the Home Rule Federation in 1879 and President of the Land League

THE 'NO RENT' MANIFESTO

From Kilmainham Gaol the leaders of the Land League issued a **'No Rent'** manifesto. In this they called on all members of the Land League to refuse to pay rent until the prisoners were released. The British Government responded by declaring the Land League an illegal organisation. Parnell had warned that if he were arrested, **Captain Moonlight** would take his place. By this he meant violent agrarian incidents, such as attacks on landlords, animals and property. Indeed, while he was in gaol between October 1881 and April 1882, a huge increase occurred in violent incidents in the countryside.

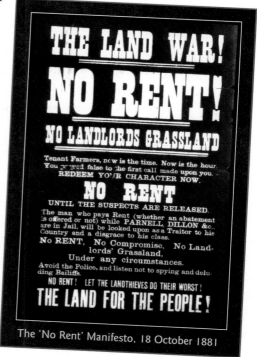

The 'No Rent' Manifesto, 18 October 1881

THE LADIES' LAND LEAGUE

After the Land League was banned, its work was continued by the Ladies' Land League, which had been founded in January 1881 by Parnell's sister Anna. Michael Davitt encouraged its members because he believed that they could fill the vacuum if the male leaders of the Land League were arrested. Parnell himself, being more conservative in outlook than Davitt, was more doubtful and thought that a Ladies' Land League might be a source of ridicule. At the time, women's role in public life was quite restricted – they could not vote or become Members of Parliament. However, educational opportunities for women were improving significantly, and the Ladies' Land League was to be a forerunner of increased female participation in public life from 1900 onwards.

Police raid a meeting of the Ladies' Land League

After the imprisonment of the Land League leaders in October 1881, the Ladies' Land League took over the running of the movement. At that time the Ladies' Land League had about 300 branches throughout the country. The members collected money to help the families of evicted tenants and of prisoners. They organised protests and spread propaganda in favour of the tenants.

The Catholic Archbishop of Dublin, Dr Edward McCabe, who was opposed to the Land League, was highly critical of the Ladies' Land League. He believed that women should remain in the background and that their proper place was in the home. The Government vigorously pursued a campaign against the Ladies' Land League. Several of its members were arrested and sentenced to terms of imprisonment.

In the circumstances of the time the contribution of the Ladies' Land League was necessarily of short duration. A conclusion to this most critical phase of the Land War could only be reached by an agreement between the leaders of both sides, Gladstone and Parnell.

THE 'KILMAINHAM TREATY' (1882)

By the spring of 1882 Gladstone realised that he needed Parnell's help in restoring calm throughout the Irish countryside. He was therefore willing to compromise and grant further concessions to the tenant farmers.

Parnell also had a number of reasons which impelled him to come to an agreement with Gladstone. He realised that the power of the Land League was broken. It had been banned by the Government, and many better-off farmers had defied the 'No Rent' manifesto. Instead they hastened to the new land courts in order to have their rents reduced. It would also suit Parnell to have a settlement to the Land Question. He could then concentrate on achieving his main ambition – the introduction of Home Rule in Ireland. Finally, he had a personal reason for wishing to be released from prison. Katherine O'Shea, the woman with whom he was having an affair, had given birth to their child while Parnell was in Kilmainham Gaol. The baby had died, and he longed to travel to England to be with Mrs O'Shea.

Secret negotiations began between Captain William O'Shea, Katherine's husband, who represented Parnell, and Joseph Chamberlain, a government minister, who represented Gladstone. An agreement was reached, and Parnell and the other prisoners were released on 2 May 1882. Although not a formal written document, the agreement has become known as the 'Kilmainham Treaty'. Under this arrangement Gladstone and the British Government agreed:

- To admit leaseholders to the benefits of the 1881 Land Act.
- To assist tenants in arrears with their rents and admit them to the land courts.
- To drop coercion and release Land League prisoners.

In return Parnell promised:

- To help restore law and order throughout the country.
- To co-operate with the Liberal Government in the British Parliament.

The 'Kilmainham Treaty' was a major turning point not only in the career of Parnell but also in the development of the Land Question. After 1882, Parnell concentrated on Home Rule. Even when difficulties arose over land from 1886 onwards, he left the matter in the hands of other leading party members such as John Dillon and William O'Brien. By extending the benefits of the 1881 Land Act to all tenants, the 'Kilmainham Treaty' satisfied some of the main demands of the Land League. Fair rent was established, and security of tenure was guaranteed as long as the rent was paid. The introduction of effective dual ownership was to be merely a halfway stage on the journey, however. The tenants continued to aspire to eventual full ownership of their farms. We shall see in Chapter 5 how this other objective of the Land League came to be realised under a series of Conservative governments.

Parnell in Kilmainham Gaol

Exercises

ORDINARY LEVEL

1. The following passage was written by Michael Davitt, the founder of the Land League. Read it and answer the questions that follow.

> Almost my first remembered experience of my own life and of the existence of landlordism was our eviction in 1852, when I was about five years of age. That eviction and the privations of the preceding famine years, the story of the starving peasantry of Mayo, of the deaths from hunger and the coffin-less graves on the roadside – everywhere a hole could be dug for the slaves who died because of 'God's providence' – all this was the political food seasoned with a mother's tears over unmerited sorrows and sufferings which had fed my mind in another land, a teaching which lost none of its force or directness by being imparted in the Gaelic tongue, which was almost always spoken in our Lancashire home. My first knowledge and impressions of landlordism were got in that school, with an assistant monitor of a father who had been the head of some agrarian secret society in Mayo in 1837, and who had to fly to England in that year to escape a threatened prosecution for Ribbonism.

> *Michael Davitt,*
> *The Fall of Feudalism in Ireland,*
> *London/New York: Harper 1904, 222*

   (i) What happened to Davitt in 1852?

   (ii) Give two examples of suffering in Famine times that the young Davitt heard about.

   (iii) What language was spoken in his home in Lancashire, England?

   (iv) Who gave Davitt his first knowledge of landlordism?

2. Compare and contrast the various portrayals of Parnell in the poster on page 29 and the cartoons on pages 31 and 32. Show how political sympathies are conveyed in each case.

3. What was the state of Irish agriculture between 1852 and 1877?

4. How was the political climate for landlords beginning to change at this time?

5. Explain why a crisis developed in Irish agriculture in the late 1870s.

6. Write a paragraph on the early life and activities of Michael Davitt.

7. State what you understand by the expression 'the New Departure'.

8. Write a paragraph on the foundation and aims of the Land League.

9. Write a paragraph on boycotting.

10. What were the two elements in Gladstone's approach to the Land League in Ireland?

11. Outline the main provisions of Gladstone's Second Land Act (1881), and state the flaws that existed in it.

12. Explain Parnell's reaction to Gladstone's Second Land Act.

13. Write a paragraph on the Ladies' Land League.

14. Explain the 'Kilmainham Treaty' (1882).

15. Write a detailed account of the role of Parnell in the land struggle, 1879–82.

16. Examine the chart and answer the questions that follow.

Number of agrarian outrages reported in Cork, 1881–4

| YEAR | OFFENCES AGAINST | | | |
	PERSONS	PROPERTY	PUBLIC PEACE	TOTAL
1881	52	82	517	651
1882	14	62	252	328
1883	5	22	71	98
1884	2	38	68	108

Source: J.R. Donnelly Jr.,
The Land and the People of Nineteenth Century Cork,
London: Routledge & Kegan Paul 1975, 295

(i) In which year did the highest number of offences against persons occur in Co. Cork? Can you suggest why?

(ii) Would you consider that the 'Kilmainham Treaty' had an influence on the reduction in offences against property between 1882 and 1883? Explain your answer.

(iii) In what year did the greatest reduction in offences against public peace occur in Co. Cork?

(iv) Write a short account on the total reduction in agrarian offences in Co. Cork between 1881 and 1884.

HIGHER LEVEL

1. Discuss the part played by Michael Davitt in the evolution of the Land Question up to 1882.

2. The following is an extract from a speech made by Charles Stewart Parnell at Ennis, Co. Clare, in September 1880. Read it carefully and answer the questions that follow.

> Depend upon it that the measure of the Land Bill of next session will be the measure of your activity and energy this winter. It will be the measure of your determination not to pay unjust rents; it will be the measure of your determination to keep a firm grip of your homesteads; it will be the measure of your determination not to bid for farms from which others have been evicted, and to use the strong force of public opinion to deter any unjust men amongst yourselves, and there are many such, from bidding for such farms. If you refuse to pay unjust rents, if you refuse to take farms from which others have been evicted, the Land Question must be settled, and settled in a way that will be satisfying to you. It depends therefore, upon yourselves, and not upon any Commission or any Government. When you have made this question ripe for settlement, then and not till then will it be settled . . . Now, what are you to do to a tenant who bids for a farm from which another tenant has been evicted? I think I heard somebody say shoot him. I wish to point out to you a very much better way, a more Christian and charitable way, which will give the lost sinner an opportunity of repenting. When a man takes a farm from which another had been evicted, you must shun him on the roadside when you meet him, you must shun him in the streets of the town, you must shun him in the shop, you must shun him on the fair green and in the market place, and even in the place of worship, by leaving him alone, by putting him into a moral Coventry, by isolating him from the rest of his country, as if he were the leper of old, you must show him your detestation of the crime he has committed . . .

The Times, 20 September 1880

(i) List three measures that Parnell advises the tenants to adopt.

(ii) How does he justify his statement that a settlement of the Land Question depends on the actions of the tenants?

(iii) What tactic does he advise the tenants to employ against people taking over the farms that have been vacated because of eviction?

(iv) Was Parnell's advice followed by the tenants? Explain your answer.

3. Consider in detail the response of the British Prime Minister, W.E. Gladstone, to the land crisis in Ireland between 1880 and 1882.

4. Assess the role of Charles Stewart Parnell during the Land War.

4. PARNELL AND THE HOME RULE MOVEMENT, 1882–91

The Phoenix Park Murders

On 2 May 1882 Parnell was released from Kilmainham Gaol. Having secured a satisfactory agreement on the subject of the Land Question (the 'Kilmainham Treaty'), he was ready to turn his attention to the issue of Home Rule for Ireland. However, within a few days of his release an event occurred in Dublin that almost led to his resignation as leader of the Home Rule Party.

Some members of the Liberal Party had opposed any compromise with Parnell and the Land League. They included the Irish Chief Secretary, W.E. Forster. When the 'Kilmainham Treaty' was agreed, therefore, Forster resigned from Gladstone's Government. He was replaced by Lord Frederick Cavendish, a son of the Duke of Devonshire and a relation of Gladstone's through marriage.

The Phoenix Park murders

On the day of his arrival in Dublin, 6 May 1882, the new Chief Secretary was walking towards the Vice-Regal Lodge in the Phoenix Park. He was accompanied by the Under-Secretary, T.H. Burke. They were both attacked and murdered with butchers' knives by members of a secret society called the Invincibles. This extreme group had broken away from the Irish Republican Brotherhood (IRB) and had been trying for a long time to kill W.E. Forster and T.H. Burke. The Phoenix Park murders led to a deep sense of shock throughout Great Britain and Ireland. Irish people living in Britain suffered particularly as anti-Irish feeling swept the country. Parnell was dismayed and believed that it would wreck all that he had achieved so far, including the 'Kilmainham Treaty'. He wrote to Gladstone, offering to resign as leader of the Home Rule Party. However, Gladstone advised him to stay on, as his influence could help to restore calm in Ireland. In the long run Parnell was strengthened after the Phoenix Park murders. The Fenians were discredited, and many of their members became completely committed to the peaceful approach of the Home Rule Party. Within months of the murders in the Phoenix Park, Parnell set about strengthening and reviving the Home Rule Party both at Westminster and throughout Ireland.

The Revival of the Home Rule Party

Historians see the 'Kilmainham Treaty' and the Phoenix Park murders as important turning points in the political career of Parnell. Up to then he had to devote much of his energy to the Land Question. This was not a distraction from the search for Home Rule, however. It provided Parnell and his party with a vital element of mass support in Ireland and among Irish emigrants abroad. From the middle of 1882, Parnell could build on that support and pursue his principal political goal, the achievement of Home Rule.

In one important respect, he was assisted by the British Government. By banning the Land League, Gladstone paved the way for the emergence of a new organisation. Although Michael Davitt favoured a revival of the Land League, Parnell had other plans. In October 1882 he

An Irish National League banner

replaced it with a new organisation called the **Irish National League**. Whereas the local branches of the Land League had a lot of power, the Irish National League was controlled from the centre by Parnell. The Fenians had a greater influence over the Land League. Their influence in the Irish National League was almost eliminated. The main functions of the new movement were to raise funds for the Home Rule Party and to accept the candidates that Parnell had chosen to stand for election to Parliament. As the Home Rule movement became stronger after 1882, the involvement of the Catholic Church increased.

The Catholic Church and the Home Rule Movement

During the Land War between 1879 and 1882, most Catholic bishops and many priests had distanced themselves from Parnell and the Land League. However, from 1882 onwards this situation changed. With the return of relatively peaceful conditions to the countryside, priests and bishops took a more active role in the Home Rule Party.

At local level, parish priests were often chairmen of branches of the Irish National League and presided over conventions to select parliamentary candidates. Archbishop Thomas Croke of Cashel was Parnell's strongest supporter among the bishops. In 1883, when a public fund known as the **Parnell Testimonial Fund** was launched to help pay Parnell's expenses, Archbishop Croke was one of the leading subscribers. The British Government complained secretly to Pope Leo XIII, and Dr Croke had to go to Rome to explain his actions. However, more and more bishops came to support the Home Rule Party, and in 1884 the Irish Catholic bishops asked the Home Rule Party to campaign for the needs of Catholic education in the British Parliament.

Archbishop Croke of Cashel

Although involvement by Catholic bishops and priests appeared to strengthen the Home Rule movement, it also contained dangers for Parnell's party. Protestants throughout Ireland were deeply suspicious of the closer identification between the Catholic Church and the cause of Home Rule. Although the first two leaders of the party, Butt and Parnell, were Protestants and the young Home Rule Party had attracted a certain degree of Protestant support in the early 1870s, by the mid-1880s Protestants constituted a small minority of the Home Rule Party. However, they were untypical of most of their co-religionists, who were solidly in favour of the Union between Great Britain and Ireland. The increasing power of the Catholic Church in the Home Rule Party strengthened the conviction of Protestant unionists throughout Ireland that the Catholic Church would wield great influence in any Home Rule Parliament in Ireland.

Finally, by facilitating an enhanced role for Catholic clerics in the affairs of his party, Parnell ran the risk that they would be in a powerful position to oppose him if ever a conflict emerged between himself and the Catholic Church in the future.

Preparing for Electoral Success

Between 1882 and 1885 Parnell spent much of the time in England, where he succeeded in persuading Gladstone's Government to introduce more reforms, such as a Labourers' Dwellings Act to provide cottages for landless labourers and a Tramways Act to help build rail networks in the West of Ireland. His domestic life also kept him in England, where his secret affair with Katherine O'Shea continued and two children were born to the couple.

During this period the work of building up the Irish National League in Ireland was undertaken by Parnell's leading followers, known by historians as his 'lieutenants'. These included John Dillon, Timothy Harrington, William O'Brien, editor of the party's newspaper, *United Ireland*, and Timothy Healy. By 1885 the League had over 1,000 branches throughout Ireland.

While his 'lieutenants' built up a strong organisation at home, Parnell imposed strict discipline on members of his parliamentary party. Once chosen to stand for election, a candidate had to take the **party pledge**. By taking this pledge, a candidate promised to vote at all times the way the party decided. Should he fail to do this, he promised to resign his seat in Parliament. The emergence of a disciplined, united party was a great source of strength to Parnell. It would strengthen his hand when he came to negotiate with the British Government. Furthermore, it would be extremely important if in the future Parnell held the **balance of power** between the two main British political parties in Parliament – in other words, if they were both fairly similar in size and Parnell could decide which to support. In Parliament, Parnell's Home Rule MPs became known as the **Irish Parliamentary Party**.

In 1884 Parliament passed an electoral reform law called the Third Reform Act. In Ireland it increased the number of voters from 220,000 to over 700,000. Most of the new voters were small farmers who would be likely to support the Home Rule Party. Realising that a general election could not be very far off, Parnell returned to Ireland at the beginning of 1885 and launched a public campaign for Home Rule.

By the start of the momentous year 1885, Parnell had huge popular appeal and was widely regarded as 'the uncrowned king of Ireland'. In a major speech in Cork in January (Document 1), Parnell argued that the restoration of an Irish parliament was a minimal requirement of the Irish nation.

In this speech Parnell was appealing to more radical sections of his own party supporters by hinting that Home Rule might not be a final settlement to the Irish Question; he was leaving the door open for future generations to achieve complete independence from Great Britain. This stance pleased his Irish-American and Fenian supporters. However, it alarmed Irish unionists and most British politicians. The enemies of Home Rule pointed out that the establishment of a parliament in Dublin would inevitably lead to complete separation between Ireland and Great Britain and thereby threaten the unity of the British Empire.

> ### Document 1
>
> I come back to the great question of national self-government for Ireland (*cheers*). I do not know how this great question will be eventually settled . . . We cannot ask for less than the restitution of Grattan's parliament (*loud cheers*), with its important privileges and wide and far-reaching constitution. We cannot under the British constitution ask for more than the restitution of Grattan's parliament (*renewed cheers*), but no man has the right to fix the boundary to the march of a nation (*great cheers*). No man has the right to say to his country 'Thus far shalt thou go and no further', and we have never attempted to fix the *ne plus ultra* to the progress of Ireland's nationhood, and we never shall (*cheers*) . . . and while we struggle today for that which may seem possible for us with our combination, we must struggle for it with the proud consciousness, that we shall not do anything to hinder or prevent better men who may come after us from gaining better things than those for which we now contend.
>
> *United Ireland*, 30 January 1885

THE COLLAPSE OF GLADSTONE'S LIBERAL GOVERNMENT

By the spring of 1885, Gladstone's Government had been in office for five years and was troubled by deep divisions between various ministers. There were differences on the treatment of British possessions in Africa and India and also on the future government of Ireland. The Liberal Party contained two opposing sides: the Whigs, or right wing, led by Lord Hartington, and the Radicals, or left wing, led by Joseph Chamberlain.

The Whigs wanted to maintain the policy of coercion in Ireland. Many of them were landlords with Irish estates. Hartington himself was the son and heir of the Duke of Devonshire, owner of Lismore Castle and of huge estates in the south of Ireland.

Chamberlain and the Radicals disliked coercion and called for reforms in Ireland. At this stage Chamberlain was drawing up his own plan for Ireland – the Central Board Scheme. This was a step in the direction of Home Rule, involving a Central Board chosen by elected county councils. This Board would have limited power over internal Irish affairs. Chamberlain communicated secretly with Parnell, using Captain William O'Shea, Katherine O'Shea's husband, as a go-between. Parnell was prepared to accept the scheme as a step on the road to Home Rule. However, Chamberlain misunderstood this and thought Parnell had accepted his scheme as an alternative to Home Rule. When

A scene from the House of Commons at Westminster, showing, from left to right, Joseph Chamberlain, Charles Stewart Parnell, William Gladstone, Lord Randolph Churchill and Lord Hartington

the truth became known, he turned against Parnell and the Irish Parliamentary Party. In any event Joseph Chamberlain was becoming more devoted to the British Empire and would oppose Home Rule because it threatened imperial unity.

As disunity within his party increased, Gladstone's Government was defeated in the House of Commons on 9 June 1885, when the Home Rule Party MPs joined with the Conservative Opposition on a financial issue. Gladstone immediately placed his resignation in the hands of Queen Victoria. Because of delays due to the introduction of new constituencies under the 1884 Reform Act, a general election could not be held until the following November. In the meantime, the leader of the Conservative Opposition, Lord Salisbury, agreed to become Prime Minister until the election could be held.

THE CONSERVATIVES AND PARNELL

In order to pass laws in Parliament, Lord Salisbury's minority Government needed the votes of the Irish Parliamentary Party. To secure them, a number of concessions were made to Parnell and his followers. The Coercion Act was not renewed, although when in opposition the Conservatives had been strong supporters of harsh law and order measures in Ireland. The new Viceroy was Lord Carnarvon, who was believed to be sympathetic to Irish demands for Home Rule. A major measure of land reform known as the Ashbourne Act was passed. It provided money to allow 25,000 tenants to buy their farms. You will read about this measure in Chapter 5.

Although Parnell was pleased to obtain various reforms, he never lost sight of the main aim of Home Rule for Ireland. With this in mind, he held secret talks with Lord Carnarvon in London. If the Conservatives could be persuaded to support Home Rule, it would stand a much better chance of succeeding than if proposed by a Liberal Government. This was because the Conservatives had a permanent massive majority in the House of Lords. At this time the House of Lords could block any measure passed by the Commons. However, Parnell's relationship with the Conservative Government was based on very insecure foundations. Lord Carnarvon was exceptional in his pro-Home Rule views. The vast majority of Conservatives, including the Prime Minister, Lord Salisbury, were strongly unionist in their political outlook. Yet as long as neither of the two British political parties committed themselves openly on the Home Rule issue, Parnell's aim was to win as many seats as possible in the general election and play one party off against the other.

THE GENERAL ELECTION OF 1885

Confident that he would gain many extra seats on account of the Reform Act (1884), Parnell hoped to be in a position to hold the balance of power in Parliament after the general election. Because he thought that the Liberals would win more seats than the Conservatives, he set out to redress the balance. He decided to advise the Irish people living in Great Britain to vote Conservative. He was fortunate that an issue existed to justify this seemingly strange choice. Because the Conservatives were more generous than the Liberals to Catholic and other religious-run schools, the leader of the Catholic Church in England, Cardinal Manning, called on Catholics, many of whom were Irish, to support the Conservatives. For his own political advantage, Parnell endorsed this call in his 'Manifesto to the Irish Electors in Great Britain' (Document 2).

Central to the message contained in the manifesto is the notion of the strength of Joseph Chamberlain's Radical wing of the Liberal Party. It is no coincidence that these were also the strongest opponents of concessions to Catholic schools in England. The mention of 'a halting measure of self-government' is a clear reference to Chamberlain's Central Board Scheme. It is not possible to know for certain the impact of Parnell's manifesto. However, historians have estimated that it could have deprived the Liberals of over twenty seats, which went to the Conservatives instead.

Cartoon showing Irish voters in Britain ditching Gladstone in the 1885 election

1885 GENERAL ELECTION	
Conservatives	249
Liberals	335
Home Rule Party	86

When the results of the 1885 general election became known, Parnell was in a very strong position. In Ireland the election resulted in a massive triumph for Parnell. Out of 103 seats, his party won 85 and also picked up a seat in Liverpool, where T.P. O'Connor was elected a Home Rule MP largely by the votes of Irish emigrants. The overall result in the United Kingdom was less favourable to Parnell. By combining with the Conservatives, he could barely keep Lord Salisbury's Government in power. However, as governments usually lose by-elections, the administration could soon be undermined. Consequently, Parnell was likely to be of little use in sustaining the Conservatives in power. They in turn were even less likely to grant concessions to the Irish party. The initiative therefore passed to Gladstone and the Liberals, who could hope to form a stable government with the support of Irish MPs in the House of Commons. By this stage, however, the price of such support would be high – nothing short of a commitment on the central issue of Home Rule itself.

GLADSTONE'S CONVERSION TO HOME RULE: THE 'HAWARDEN KITE'

Following the general election, William Gladstone was content to leave the Conservatives in power for the time being. He hoped that they would attempt to solve the Irish Question with his support. However, he could not ignore the results of the general election. Although the Liberals had done quite well in Great Britain, they had not won a single seat in Ireland. The overwhelming victory of the Home Rule Party there could not be ignored, in Gladstone's view. Apart from the 2 Unionists elected for Trinity College, Dublin, Parnell's party had won every seat in Munster, Leinster and Connaught. In north-east Ulster the Unionists won 17 seats. However, the Home

Rule Party won 18 seats in the rest of Ulster. Gladstone therefore decided that he would have to tackle the Irish Question once more if Salisbury's Government failed to do so.

On 17 December 1885 Gladstone's son Herbert announced to the press that his father had been converted to the cause of Irish Home Rule. He based this statement on a conversation he had had with Gladstone at the family home, Hawarden Castle. It is not clear whether he had his father's consent to do this or not. Gladstone may have been testing public opinion by 'flying a kite', that is, putting out information to see the public reaction. For this reason the announcement became known as 'flying the Hawarden Kite'. Once the issue was made public, Gladstone had to defend his position. In a letter to Lord Hartington (Document 3) he made his position clear.

Gladstone need not have worried over the possibility of 'rival biddings'. Salisbury and the Conservatives were greatly relieved by the Liberal leader's conversion to Home Rule. They could now position themselves as strong unionists and ardent defenders of the unity of the British Empire.

> **Document 3**
>
> The conditions of an admissible plan are:
> 1. Union of the Empire and due supremacy of parliament.
> 2. Protection for the minority.
> 3. Fair allocation of imperial charges.
> 4. A statutory basis seems to me better and safer than the revival of Grattan's Parliament.
> 5. Neither as opinions nor as intentions have I to any one alive promulgated these ideas as decided on by me.
> 6. As to intentions, I am determined to have none at present, to leave space to the government – I should wish to encourage them if I properly could – above all, on no account to say or do anything which would enable the nationalists to establish rival biddings between us.
>
> **Gladstone to Hartington, 17 December 1885**

GLADSTONE'S RETURN TO POWER

Parnell's ability to bargain with both Conservatives and Liberals had now disappeared. After the 'Hawarden Kite', the Irish Parliamentary Party was committed to supporting the Liberals, because they alone were willing to introduce Home Rule. This 'Liberal Alliance' on the part of the Home Rule Party was destined to continue up to 1918. Thus, when Parliament assembled in January 1886, Parnell was waiting for the earliest opportunity to combine with the Liberals and vote Salisbury's Government out of office. He succeeded on 27 January, and Gladstone returned to become Prime Minister for the third time. His first objective was the introduction of a Home Rule Bill for Ireland.

THE FIRST HOME RULE BILL, 1886

Gladstone was just as committed to the unity of the British Empire as the Conservatives were. However, unlike them, he believed that Ireland under Home Rule would actually draw closer to Great Britain, and that the granting of Home Rule would

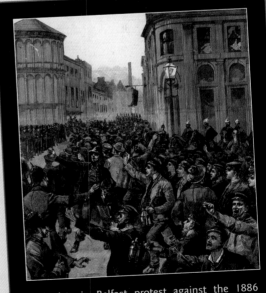

Unionists in Belfast protest against the 1886 Home Rule Bill

make most Irish people loyal to the Crown and content to take their place in the British Empire. In this belief he was underestimating one of the strongest political forces of the nineteenth century – nationalism. His opponents among Conservatives and unionists declared that given the strength of Irish nationalist feeling, a certain degree of autonomy would only make Irish nationalists look for more, and total separation would eventually occur.

Gladstone, however, believed that coercion had failed and that law and order could only be secured in Ireland by the granting of Home Rule. On 8 April 1886, therefore, he introduced the First Home Rule Bill in the House of Commons. It provided for the following changes:

> 1 A law-making body, or legislature, containing two houses would be set up in Dublin.
> 2 The Lower House would be directly elected, but the Upper House would consist of lords and other landowners.
> 3 The Viceroy would be the nominal head of the executive, or government.
> 4 Irish MPs and lords would no longer sit in the Westminster Parliament.
> 5 Ireland would pay one-fifteenth of overall imperial charges.
> 6 The Westminster Parliament would continue to control foreign affairs, customs and land defence.

Parnell broadly welcomed the Bill but sought to have certain changes made, such as a reduction in the Irish contribution to the imperial budget. However, a huge wave of opposition emerged throughout Great Britain and Ireland to the threat posed to the Union by Gladstone's First Home Rule Bill.

OPPOSITION TO HOME RULE

Unionists throughout Ireland, but especially in Ulster, began a strong campaign to prevent the introduction of Home Rule. Their objections can be summarised under three main headings:

> - *Political*: They believed that their loyalty to Queen and Empire could be protected only by the existing Union and single imperial Parliament in London.
> - *Religious*: As most unionists were Protestant, they feared for their future in an Ireland ruled by the Catholic majority. Their fear of the influence of the Catholic Church was summed up in the phrase 'Home Rule is Rome Rule'.
> - *Economic*: Ulster unionists in particular feared that the economic prosperity of the Belfast region, Ireland's only industrialised area, would be totally undermined by the existence of a Home Rule Parliament.

These fears were very real and deep-seated. For hundreds of years the descendants of English settlers had relied on the British Government to protect their interests in Ireland. They were determined to do all in their power to stop Home Rule in its tracks, as they regarded it as the ultimate form of betrayal. In the midst of the Home Rule crisis, the Irish unionists received powerful support from one of the leading Conservative politicians in England, Lord Randolph Churchill.

In a letter (Document 4) to an Irish unionist, Gerald Fitzgibbon, he outlined his position.

Document 4

I decided some time ago, that if the G.O.M. [Grand Old Man = Gladstone] went for Home Rule, the Orange Card would be the one to play. Please God it may turn out the ace of trumps and not the two . . .

It may be that this dark cloud which is now impending over Ireland, will pass away without breaking. If it does I believe you and your descendants will be safe for a long time to come. Her Majesty's Government hesitates. Like Macbeth before the murder of Duncan, Mr Gladstone asks for time. Before he plunged the knife into the heart of the British Empire he reflects, he hesitates . . . The Loyalists of Ulster should wait and watch – organise and prepare. Diligence and vigilance ought to be your watchword; so that the blow, if it does come, may not come upon you like a thief in the night and may not find you unready and taken by surprise . . .

I do not hesitate to tell you most truly that in that dark hour there will not be wanting to you those of position and influence in England who would be willing to cast in their lot with you and who, whatever the result, will share your fortunes and your fate.

Lord Randolph Churchill to Gerald Fitzgibbon, 22 February 1886

By the 'Orange Card', Lord Randolph meant that the Conservatives should use the Ulster unionists in order to defeat Gladstone's Government on the Home Rule issue. A week after writing this letter, Lord Randolph went to Belfast. Addressing a meeting of unionists, he declared that if Home Rule were passed, 'Ulster will fight and Ulster will be right.' This was the beginning of an alliance between the unionists and the Conservative Party that lasted for the following century.

Along with the Conservatives, many members of the Liberal Party were not prepared to support Gladstone on the issue of Home Rule. In particular the Whigs, led by Lord Hartington, and the Radicals, led by Joseph Chamberlain, were determined to vote against it, as they believed that it threatened the unity of the British Empire. In the following extracts from the parliamentary debates on Home Rule (Document 5), these points are clearly made.

Document 5

Gladstone: Can anything stop a nation's demand? Ireland stands at your bar expectant, hopeful, almost suppliant . . . We hail the demand of Ireland for what I call a blessed oblivion of the past.

Parnell: You must give up the idea of protecting the Protestants either as a body or as a majority by the establishment of a separate legislature either in Ulster or in any portion of Ulster. No, Sir, we cannot give up a single Irishman.

Parnell: I accept this bill as a final settlement of our national question and I believe the Irish people will accept it.

William Johnston, an Ulster Unionist: If Home Rule were introduced the dictates of the Irish Parliament would be resisted by the people of Ulster at the point of a bayonet.

G. Goschen, Liberal: If this bill is passed it will mean that every subject race, that India, that Europe would know that we were no longer able to cope with resistance, if resistance were offered.

Joseph Chamberlain: This proposal is tantamount to separation. It would set up a temporary and unstable form of government, which would be a perpetual source of irritation and agitation until the full demands of the Nationalist Party were conceded.

Lord Hartington: The Parliament which would be restored would not be a Protestant, but would be a Roman Catholic Parliament. The Established Church has been swept away, and instead of a Roman Catholic priesthood which at the time of the Union was without political influence at all, we have a Roman Catholic clergy wielding a large political influence.

Hansard, Reports of British Parliamentary Debates, 1886

As can be seen from the parliamentary debates, a strong fear existed in Great Britain that Home Rule could lead to total separation. Most British politicians opposed this for reasons of national security. In the event of war, an enemy of Britain could attempt to invade Ireland and launch an attack from there. Indeed the Spaniards in 1601 and the French in 1798 had succeeded in landing armies in Ireland. This fear for their safety in times of war was a strong argument among British people against Irish Home Rule. Many people also shared the fear, mentioned in the debates, that other peoples in the British Empire would follow the Irish example and seek greater autonomy for themselves, thereby paving the way for the decline of the Empire. Given the strength, therefore, of British opposition to the First Home Rule Bill, it was unlikely to have a successful passage through Parliament.

THE DEFEAT OF THE FIRST HOME RULE BILL

The First Home Rule Bill was defeated on its third reading in the House of Commons on 8 June 1886. The vote was 311 in favour to 341 against. Those voting against included the Conservatives, the Ulster Unionists and 93 members of Gladstone's Liberal Party, including Whigs and Radicals. Those Liberals who voted against Home Rule, such as Hartington and Chamberlain, became known as Liberal Unionists. In order to prevent further attempts to introduce Home Rule, they allied themselves with the Conservative Party.

Three cartoons which appeared at the time of the 1886 Home Rule Bill

The defeat of Gladstone's First Home Rule Bill was a major turning point in the political development not merely of Ireland but of Great Britain also. The split in the Liberal Party between Gladstonian Liberals and Liberal Unionists started a period of long-term decline for that party. Over the following twenty years, the Liberals would be in government only between 1892 and 1895. In contrast, the Conservatives under Salisbury were greatly strengthened and remained in power for most of the period between 1886 and 1906.

THE GENERAL ELECTION OF 1886

After the defeat of Home Rule, Gladstone advised Queen Victoria to dissolve Parliament and call a general election for July 1886. It was clear from the results of the 1886 election that Irish Home Rule was very unpopular in Great Britain. Clearly, Gladstone and the Irish Parliamentary Party had a difficult task ahead of them to convince the ordinary British voters of the merits of granting Home Rule to Ireland.

1886 GENERAL ELECTION	
Conservatives and Liberal Unionists	317
Gladstonian Liberals	191
Home Rule Party	85

In Ireland the 1886 election was a mirror image of that of 1885. The election of 85 Home Rule MPs made the intentions of most Irish voters clear. Salisbury's incoming Conservative Government would therefore have a difficult task in governing the country.

Although the Ulster unionists had seen Home Rule defeated for the time being, they were not reassured. Serious riots broke out in Belfast throughout the summer of 1886 in protest against Home Rule. The Home Rule Crisis led directly to the formation of the Irish Unionist Party, which was allied to the Conservatives. Unionists continued to fear that Gladstone might achieve a majority in a future election and attempt to introduce another Home Rule Bill with the help of the Irish Parliamentary Party in Parliament.

Although the defeat of the Home Rule Bill and the results of the 1886 general election in Great Britain represented a setback for Parnell, he was far from despondent. He had succeeded in persuading Gladstone to support Home Rule. The Home Rule Party was stronger than ever in Ireland, and Parnell looked forward to the day when Gladstone might return to power.

COMPREHENSION

1. In Document 1, what does Parnell mean when he says, 'No man has the right to fix the boundary to the march of a nation'?

2. How can you tell from Document 1 that Parnell's speech was popular with his audience?

3. What is the attitude of the writer of Document 2 to the Liberal Party?

4. Give two examples of the type of measures taken under the policy of coercion, as outlined in Document 2.

5. How does the author of Document 2 advise the Irish electors in Great Britain to treat the Liberal Party?

6. What is the first condition in Gladstone's list in Document 3?

7. To whom is he referring in the second condition?

8. Explain what Gladstone meant by 'rival biddings' in point no. 6 of Document 3.

9. Explain the term 'Orange Card' in Document 4.

10. Who was responsible for coining this expression?

11. What does the author of Document 4 mean by the expression 'plunge the knife into the heart of the British Empire'?

12. What advice does he give to the loyalists of Ulster?

13. Explain the assistance that the author of this document believes the loyalists of Ulster might receive from people in England.

14. At the start of Document 5, what does Gladstone declare the Irish nation's demand to be?

15. Explain what Parnell meant by the statement 'No, Sir, we cannot give up a single Irishman.'

16. Explain the threat made by William Johnston in Document 5.

17. What fear was expressed by G. Goschen?

18. What do you think Joseph Chamberlain meant by the words 'the full demands of the Nationalist Party'?

COMPARISON

1. Read Documents 4 and 5. Draw a link between references to powerful people in England (Document 4) and the views of Goschen and Hartington (Document 5).

2. Documents 3 and 4 are private letters. Which do you think is more persuasive? Why?

3. Compare the attitude of Parnell to the Irish nation, as expressed in Documents 1 and 5.

4. Is there a similarity between the views of the author of Document 4 and those of William Johnston in Document 5?

5. Compare the arguments of Goschen and Chamberlain in Document 5.

CRITICISM

1. Would you consider Document 1 to be an unbiased source? Explain your answer.

2. Give two reasons why Document 2 might be considered a form of propaganda.

3. Gladstone appears anxious to justify himself in Document 3. Would you agree with this statement? Give reasons for your answer.

4. What, in your view, is the main purpose behind the writing of Document 4?

5. Would you agree that Lord Hartington was making a powerful and emotive point in Document 5? Give reasons for your answer.

CONTEXTUALISATION

1. Write an account of Parnell's political leadership during 1885 and 1886.

2. What was Gladstone's main motivation in agreeing to Home Rule for Ireland?

3. Explain in detail the unionist objections to Home Rule.

4. Write a paragraph on the First Home Rule Bill (1886).

5. Explain how Home Rule was defeated in Parliament in 1886.

The Times and Parnell

Unknown to Parnell, the prestigious London newspaper *The Times* started a secret campaign to discredit him. In 1887 it published a series of articles entitled 'Parnellism and Crime' that tried to link Parnell and other members of his party with agrarian crimes in Ireland. This was part of an attempt to show that the Irish were unfit for self-government. One of the articles contained a startling allegation, namely that Parnell had supported the Phoenix Park murders. Parnell claimed that the letter he was supposed to have signed was a forgery. When the matter was raised in Parliament, the Conservative Government reluctantly agreed to a Commission of Enquiry to investigate any possible evidence connecting Parnell and other Home Rule MPs to crimes in rural Ireland. During the public hearings of the Commission, Parnell was completely vindicated. The forger of his signature, Richard Pigott, broke down during cross-examination and later fled to Madrid, where he committed suicide. Parnell was exonerated, and *The Times* had to pay him £5,000 in damages. On his return to the House of Commons, he received a standing ovation. It appeared that he had reached a high point in his career. However, a year later his private life was to be made public in circumstances that led to the ruin of his political career.

The Fall of Parnell

On 17 November 1890 Parnell was found to be the guilty party in a case before the divorce court in London. Although Captain William O'Shea had condoned the affair between his wife, Katherine, and Parnell for years, he had finally sued for divorce. He did this when he realised that he had little chance of getting some of the money left to his wife by her rich

Parnell addresses a meeting of the Irish Parliamentary Party at the time of the divorce scandal

aunt, Mrs Wood, as other relatives had contested the will.

Parnell was anxious for the divorce to go through so that he could marry Katherine O'Shea. However, Captain O'Shea and other enemies of Parnell could now portray him as a wrecker of another man's marriage. Because the marriage between William and Katherine O'Shea existed only in name, Parnell refused to accept that he had done anything wrong.

Once the divorce case became public, there were calls for Parnell's resignation in Great Britain and Ireland. Initially, even the Catholic bishops were wary of becoming involved. However, the intervention of Gladstone changed the situation dramatically. Because he received much of his support from Nonconformists (Protestants such as Baptists, Presbyterians or Methodists, who were not members of the Church of England), he had to take a stance on a moral issue such as adultery. He therefore declared that on moral grounds he could not introduce Home Rule in the future as long as Parnell remained leader of the Irish Parliamentary Party. Thereafter, Parnell lost support rapidly. Even his former ally, Archbishop Croke of Cashel, called for his resignation for the sake of the Liberal Alliance and Home Rule.

During the first week of December 1890 the Irish Parliamentary Party met in Committee Room 15 of the House of Commons to discuss Parnell's leadership. Days of bitter wrangling ensued. Parnell, as chairman, refused absolutely to put the issue to a vote. His supporters argued that the English political leader, Gladstone, should not decide the leadership of the Irish party. Parnell's opponents said that if he retired, even temporarily, it would show that he was not putting himself before the cause of Home Rule and the greater good of Ireland. Seeing no solution in sight, a majority of 54 of the party followed the deputy leader, Justin McCarthy, out of Committee Room 15. Parnell was left with 31 followers. However, he refused to concede defeat or be reconciled with his opponents in the party.

During 1891 Parnell fought a number of bitter by-elections against anti-Parnellite Home Rulers. In each case his candidate lost. In some cases he was attacked by angry crowds. His health was deteriorating all the time. On 27 September he received a bad soaking at a meeting in the West of Ireland. He then returned to Katherine O'Shea at Brighton, where he died on 6 October 1891.

There was universal grief in Ireland when news of his death was published. His funeral to Glasnevin Cemetery in Dublin was one of the largest ever seen. Members of the newly founded Gaelic Athletic Association were present as a guard of honour, and in death Parnell came to symbolise people's aspirations for national freedom and self-respect.

Floral tributes in the form of national symbols on Parnell's grave

The Legacy of Charles Stewart Parnell

Much of Parnell's success was linked to his personal charisma. He towered above his leading followers, and his somewhat aristocratic and distant personality created an aura of mystery and uniqueness. His involvement in the Land League was crucial to the advances gained by the tenant farmers during the Land War and afterwards. His formation of the Irish National League and the creation of a pledge-bound, disciplined parliamentary party greatly advanced the struggle for Home Rule.

Unlike some other Irish politicians, Parnell had no feelings of inferiority when dealing with leading British statesmen. In his view, England and Ireland were both kingdoms, and he believed that an Englishman only respected you when you stood up to him.

Despite certain hints in his early speeches and in his statements after the party split, Parnell distanced himself from the Fenians and would never have countenanced the withdrawal of Irish MPs from the British Parliament. As a superb parliamentarian, he used the House of Commons to great effect to gain concessions for the Irish people.

Like many Irish nationalists both before and after, he failed to understand the depth of unionist, especially Ulster unionist, attachment to the full Union with Great Britain. When he claimed, in his argument against the exclusion of Ulster from the Home Rule Bill, that he could not afford to lose a single Irishman, was he perhaps denying many of his fellow Protestants the right to be fully British?

The fall of Parnell was a personal tragedy for both himself and Katherine O'Shea, but also a public tragedy for all the people of Ireland. During this crisis, he displayed a weakness of character in refusing to put the interests of the country before his own views. It was significant that, apart from John Redmond, all the major 'lieutenants', such as John Dillon, William O'Brien, Timothy Healy and even Michael Davitt, sided against him. It was the tragedy of his final year that he left behind a deeply divided party that ultimately disillusioned many young people and turned them against parliamentary politics altogether.

KEY PERSONALITY: CHARLES STEWART PARNELL (1846–91)

Charles Stewart Parnell was born in Avondale, Co. Wicklow, in 1846. His father, John Henry Parnell, was a Protestant landlord who also served as the local magistrate. His mother, Delia Stewart, was the daughter of an American admiral who had fought against Britain in the the war of 1812. At an early age, Charles inherited from his mother a pronounced hostility towards England. This hostility was deepened by his early educational experiences. He attended Cambridge University, where he particularly resented the condescending attitudes displayed by the English towards the Irish. After three and a half years at Cambridge, the young Parnell was expelled for his involvement in a drunken brawl.

Parnell first entered politics in 1874, when he stood for election as a Home Rule League candidate. He was badly defeated but secured a seat at Westminster the following year, when he successfully contested a by-election in Meath. Parnell, although a shy and hesitant speaker, impressed the Fenians by his defence of the 'Manchester Martyrs' in his maiden speech at Westminster in 1875. His popularity grew when, disillusioned with the parliamentary and gentlemanly tactics of Isaac Butt, he joined obstructionists such as Joseph Biggar in disrupting the business of the House of Commons.

Parnell was an intensely ambitious politician, and in 1877 he replaced Isaac Butt as leader of the Fenian-dominated Home Rule Confederation of Great Britain. The following year he adopted the strategy known as the New Departure with Michael Davitt of the land movement and John Devoy, leader of the Irish-American Fenian organisation, Clan na Gael. This was a very significant development, as it marked an agreement between constitutional and physical force nationalists to work together to solve the Irish Land Question.

When Isaac Butt died in May 1879, he was replaced by William Shaw as leader of the Home Rule Party. The following year Parnell replaced Shaw as leader. However, by then Parnell had come to realise that conditions on the land would have to be improved before the question of Home Rule could be tackled. In 1879 he had become president of the newly formed Land League. In 1880, during a speech at a meeting in Ennis, Co. Clare, he proposed the Land League's most famous tactic, boycotting.

During the Land War (1879–82), Parnell played a very important role in marshalling public opinion in Ireland behind the cause of land reform and agitating for change in the Westminster Parliament. In October 1881 Parnell was imprisoned in Kilmainham Gaol for his criticism of Gladstone's Second Land Act (1881) and for personal remarks he made about Gladstone himself. From Kilmainham he issued the 'No Rent' manifesto, inciting tenants not to pay their rents until their grievances were addressed.

In May 1882 Parnell was released from gaol when he and Gladstone agreed to the 'Kilmainham Treaty'. Gladstone agreed to improve the Land Act, and Parnell agreed to accept the improved terms. The 'Kilmainham Treaty' was very significant, as it marked the end of the New Departure and Parnell's involvement in the Land Question. He was now going to concentrate on his main political aim of achieving Home Rule for Ireland.

Between 1882 and 1885 Parnell created a unified, disciplined and pledge-bound Home Rule Party in the Westminster Parliament. He used the Irish National League, which replaced the Land League, to build up a strong local organisation in Ireland. In the House of Commons he supported the political party that gave most concessions to Ireland. In the beginning this was the Conservative Party. After the general election of 1885, the 86 Home Rule MPs held the balance of power at Westminster, and they helped the Conservatives to form a government.

In December 1885 Gladstone's son Herbert, speaking at the family's country home in Hawarden, announced his father's conversion to the cause of Home Rule. This move was seen as an attempt to gauge public opinion and was known as 'flying the Hawarden Kite'. For the Home Rule Party, this marked the beginning of the Liberal Alliance. Gladstone, with the help of the Irish party, became Prime Minister of a Liberal Government in February 1886 and introduced the First Home Rule Bill in the House of Commons in April 1886. Although the Bill was defeated, Parnell maintained the Liberal Alliance in the hope that Home Rule would be passed at a future date.

In 1887 the Pigott Forgeries failed to discredit Parnell. However, his career came to a dramatic end through his involvement in a divorce scandal in 1890, when his love affair with a married woman, Katherine O'Shea, became public. Gladstone and the Liberals withdrew support from Parnell, and the Irish Parliamentary Party split bitterly into Parnellite and anti-Parnellite factions. These divisions remained for almost a decade after Parnell's death in October 1891.

Parnell had achieved much in the course of his short political career. Through his involvement in the land movement, he secured improvements for tenant farmers and advanced the quest to achieve a final resolution of the Land Question. He built up huge popular support in Ireland for Home Rule and converted a major British political party – the Liberals – to the cause. His greatest political achievement lay in transforming Home Rule from an aspiration with little support to a realistic and achievable aim with support in Ireland and Westminster.

EXERCISES

ORDINARY LEVEL

1. The following passage appeared in the London *Times* on 11 December 1890, during the Parnell Split. Read it carefully and answer the questions that follow.

> Mr Parnell speaks as if he were an injured man, but the facts cannot be forgotten. Mr Parnell is responsible, and he alone, for the present deplorable situation. He pledged himself, again and again, to repel the charge against him. His pledges were accepted in good faith. When the time for speaking came, he remained silent. The pledges were broken. The charge was not repelled. Upon these facts a strong opinion was formed by multitudes of Englishmen, true friends of the liberty of Ireland. Mr Parnell does not hesitate to denounce them as 'English wolves'. But the fact remains that the 'English wolves' and the Irish bishops express the same opinion about him, and he cannot mend the matter by calling nicknames . . .
>
> *The Times, 11 December 1890*

   (i) How does Parnell speak, according to the writer?

   (ii) What pledge or promise did Parnell repeatedly make?

   (iii) In what way did Parnell denounce his enemies in England?

   (iv) What other group shared the opinions of Parnell's English enemies?

2. Write a paragraph on the Phoenix Park murders.

3. Explain how the 'Kilmainham Treaty' and the Phoenix Park murders were turning points in the political career of Parnell.

4. What was the attitude of the leaders of the Catholic Church in Ireland to the Home Rule Party up to 1885?

5. Outline the development of the Home Rule Party between 1882 and 1885.

6. Why did Parnell support the Conservative Party in the 1885 general election?

7. Explain what is meant by 'flying the Hawarden Kite', and show how this brought about a change of direction in the Home Rule Party.

8. What were the provisions of the First Home Rule Bill (1885)? Explain why it was defeated.

9. Explain why Irish unionists opposed Home Rule.

10. Write a paragraph on the Piggot Forgeries.

11. Outline the causes, course and consequences of the Parnell Split.

12. Write a paragraph on the strengths and weaknesses of Parnell as leader of the Home Rule movement.

HIGHER LEVEL

1. Analyse critically Parnell's leadership of the Home Rule movement between 1882 and 1891.

2. Discuss unionists' opposition to Home Rule up to 1891.

3. Discuss the view that Parnell was the cause of his own downfall.

4. Discuss the political strategies adopted by Parnell and his party in the critical years of 1885 and 1886.

5. 'Parnell effectively used the Land Question as a means of promoting Home Rule.' Discuss.

6. Evaluate critically the contribution of Charles Stewart Parnell to Irish politics between 1875 and 1891.

5. Conservative Policy Towards Ireland: Constructive Unionism

The Conservative Party and Ireland

Before the rise of the Home Rule Party, the traditional policy of Conservative governments towards Ireland consisted of supporting landlords and defending the existing state of affairs. However, the prominent role of the Home Rule Party under Parnell compelled both Liberals and Conservatives to reconsider their Irish policies. We have seen already in Chapter 4 how the Conservatives under Lord Salisbury appeared to be friendly to the Home Rule Party in the second half of 1885. This was only a temporary manoeuvre, however, to secure the support of the Home Rule Party in Parliament and the votes of Irish people in Britain in the election of 1885. As soon as Gladstone announced his conversion to Home Rule, the Conservatives came out strongly in favour of the Union between Great Britain and Ireland. Indeed the Prime Minister and Conservative leader, Lord Salisbury, was absolutely opposed to Home Rule under any circumstances.

A group of tenants with their landlord

After the heavy defeat suffered by Gladstone in the general election of 1886 that followed the failure of the First Home Rule Bill, Salisbury and the Conservatives returned to power. For the next twenty years until 1906, the Conservatives were almost continuously in power, except for a short Liberal interlude between 1892 and 1895. However, under Salisbury, Conservative policy towards Ireland was to contain important positive as well as negative elements. While opposing Home Rule and insisting on the maintenance of law and order, Conservative Governments also introduced a series of significant and long-awaited reforms.

KILLING HOME RULE WITH KINDNESS

The Conservative policy of introducing reforms in Ireland became known as 'Killing Home Rule with Kindness'. This approach involved improving the living conditions of people in the hope that they would be content to live under the Union and cease to desire Home Rule. Although the policy was to fail in the aim of reducing support for Home Rule, it contributed to alleviating hardship in people's lives. Reforms were introduced in various areas, including measures to improve local government and increase employment opportunities for people in the West of Ireland. However, the most significant reforms of all under the policy of 'Killing Home Rule with Kindness' occurred in the area of land tenure.

THE CONSERVATIVES TACKLE THE LAND QUESTION: THE ASHBOURNE ACT (1885)

During the short-lived Conservative administration of 1885–6, a very important measure of land reform was passed at Westminster. It was known as the Ashbourne Act, after Lord Ashbourne, the Lord Chancellor at the time. Unlike previous land acts, the Ashbourne Act allowed tenants to borrow the entire purchase price of their farms from the British Government. Tenants buying

The Conservative Party and Ireland

under the Ashbourne Act were given forty-nine years to repay the money they had borrowed. The Act proved highly popular, and within three years over 25,000 tenant farmers bought their farms under its provisions.

In the following year of 1886, however, the political issue of Home Rule again took centre stage. After the defeat of the First Home Rule Bill and the Conservative electoral victory, positions became polarised. When economic conditions deteriorated in rural Ireland, Salisbury's Government was unsympathetic and prepared to pass new coercion laws strengthening the powers of the courts and police in case tenant farmers began to engage in agitation once again. Many of the leading figures in the Home Rule Party were more than willing to challenge the Conservative Government and its landlord supporters in Ireland.

The Plan of Campaign

On 23 October 1886 an article appeared in the Parnellite newspaper, *United Ireland*, under the heading 'A Plan of Campaign'. It called for new tactics in the struggle to get landlords to reduce rents. The article was written by Timothy Harrington, one of Parnell's principal 'lieutenants'. The new campaign was also strongly supported by two other leading Home Rule MPs, John Dillon and William O'Brien. Parnell himself, however, remained aloof from the outset. He was now living permanently in England with Katherine O'Shea and was more interested in the issue of Home Rule than in the problems of tenant farmers in Ireland.

The Plan of Campaign was essentially a system of collective action by tenants. All tenants on

An eviction during the Plan of Campaign

a single estate were to approach their landlord and ask for a reduction in rent. If he refused, they should pay no rent at all but lodge the money in a special fund that would be used to campaign against the landlord and to assist evicted families.

By the end of 1886 the Plan of Campaign was in operation in more than a hundred estates. However, Parnell became concerned that it would alienate his Liberal allies in England. He tried to stop the new campaign but failed. However, a compromise was reached with Dillon and O'Brien. The Plan of Campaign could continue where it was already in existence but could not spread to other estates.

To deal with this new crisis in Ireland, the Prime Minister, Lord Salisbury, decided to appoint his own nephew, Arthur Balfour, as the new Irish Chief Secretary early in 1887.

Arthur Balfour and Ireland

Arthur Balfour (1848–1930) was appointed to his post in Ireland in March 1887. Between then and his departure from office in November 1891, he was to prove one of the most capable, but also one of the most controversial, of all Chief Secretaries.

From the start Balfour was determined to stamp out agrarian crime in Ireland and, in particular, to crush the Plan

Arthur Balfour

of Campaign. He piloted a tough new Coercion Act through Parliament in the summer of 1887. His willingness to put the new law into practice in Ireland was to earn him the hatred of nationalists and the nickname 'Bloody Balfour'. He encouraged the police to take a strong line with the Plan of Campaign protests. At one such public meeting in Mitchelstown, Co. Cork, in September 1887, matters got out of control, and two people were killed by the police, with many more being wounded. Although he admitted privately that the police had overreacted, he defended them vigorously in public.

Balfour did not rely on coercion alone to defeat the Plan of Campaign. He had two other approaches to the problem. He encouraged landlords to unite to defend their interests, and he tried to get the Pope to intervene in Ireland on the side of the British Government.

Balfour and Irish Landlords

In early 1889 Balfour began to encourage landlords to set up groups in opposition to the Plan of Campaign. He worked closely with a wealthy Cork-based landlord, Arthur Smith-Barry of Fota Island. When Smith-Barry's tenants in Tipperary refused to pay their rents because of his leading role against the Plan of Campaign, a prolonged landlord–tenant conflict broke out, centred on Tipperary town. When Smith-Barry evicted tenants, the Plan of Campaign leaders tried to found a new town nearby, named 'New Tipperary'. This proved a financial failure and came to an end in 1895 when Smith-Barry and his tenants reached an agreement.

While helping landlords like Smith-Barry to defeat the Plan of Campaign, Balfour was also encouraging secret contacts with the Vatican to enlist the support of the Pope.

A butter market in New Tipperary

Pope Leo XIII and the Plan of Campaign

Pope Leo XIII (1878–1903) was approached in secret by agents of the British Government, who asked him to denounce the Plan of Campaign. They stressed the unchristian nature of boycotting, the refusal to pay lawful rent and the frequent involvement of local priests in the land movement and in nationalist politics. While quite favourably disposed towards Ireland, Pope Leo also desired closer friendship with the British Government. At the time, the worldwide British Empire included Catholic populations in several different countries. In order to investigate the state of affairs in Ireland, the Pope sent a mission under Archbishop Ignaz Persico in the summer of 1887. Persico travelled throughout Ireland and recommended that the four Irish Catholic archbishops be called to Rome to discuss the situation.

However, without taking this action, the Pope issued a letter condemning the Plan of Campaign in April 1888. Most Catholics in Ireland regarded this as an interference in Irish political affairs, and they ignored the Pope's letter. John Dillon, in particular, was highly critical of this intervention. Even the majority of Catholic bishops avoided supporting the Pope's letter in public. Therefore, Balfour's attempt to influence events in rural Ireland by means of papal intervention was largely a failure.

THE END OF THE PLAN OF CAMPAIGN

By 1890 the Plan of Campaign was beginning to peter out. Deadlock continued on a mere seventeen estates. The tenants had succeeded on eighty-four estates; landlords had held out successfully in a further fifteen. Because of the difficulties during and after the Parnellite Split, the land movement was less effective, and many of the evicted tenants continued to suffer hardship. Not until 1907 were the last of the tenants who lost their farms during the Plan of Campaign restored to their holdings once more.

In political terms the Plan of Campaign contributed to the growing rift between Parnell and some of his leading followers, such as John Dillon and William O'Brien. Leaders of the Plan of Campaign such as these resented Parnell's opposition and the fact that he remained in London and did not become involved.

For Arthur Balfour, the Plan of Campaign was a complex experience. He could claim that he defended law and order and presided over a situation in which many supporters of the campaign, including over twenty Home Rule MPs, served terms in prison. However, his support for landlord groups and his approaches to the Pope were not successful policies. With the decline in the Plan of Campaign by 1890, he turned his attention once more to the constructive side of the Conservative policy of 'Killing Home Rule with Kindness'.

BALFOUR'S LAND ACT (1891) AND THE CONGESTED DISTRICTS BOARD

In 1891 Balfour had a new Land Act passed in the British Parliament. It contained two main elements:
- A land purchase scheme.
- A Congested Districts Board.

Under Balfour's Land Act the British Government advanced £33 million in loans to Irish farmers to enable them to purchase their holdings. As in the Ashbourne Act (1885), they were to be given forty-nine years to repay the loans. As a result of this Act, over 47,000 tenants were able to purchase their farms, almost double the 25,000 who had done so under the Ashbourne Act.

The Congested Districts Board was an official body set up by the British Government to improve the living conditions of people in the south-western and western regions of Ireland. 'Congested' implied that there were too many people living on poor land. The Board offered assistance in various ways:

1 It assisted the development of home industries such as knitting and weaving.
2 It provided advice and instruction to farmers to improve farming methods.
3 It helped redistribute land to poorer farmers.
4 It partly financed the construction of fishing harbours and railways.

Although well-intentioned and responsible for some improvements, the Congested Districts Board was powerless to eradicate the underlying causes of poverty in the West of Ireland: small, uneconomic farms leading to poverty and emigration. The Board continued in operation until it was finally abolished in 1923.

Although Arthur Balfour's term as Irish Chief Secretary ended in November 1891, he maintained his interest in the country. After the Liberal Government of 1892–5 lost power, the

A poor farming family in a congested district in the West of Ireland

The Congested Districts Board helped finance this new monorail system at Ballybunion, Co. Kerry

Conservatives returned again and remained in power until 1906. They continued to pursue a policy of 'Killing Home Rule with Kindness' and supported various reforms as long as these did not lead to Home Rule. Thus, when an Irish unionist and reformer, Sir Horace Plunkett, began a campaign to improve Irish agriculture, he received support from the Conservative Government.

Sir Horace Plunkett and the Co-operative Movement

Horace Plunkett, a member of the Anglo-Irish Protestant Ascendancy, was born in 1854. He was a younger son of Lord Dunsany, a Co. Meath landlord. As a young man he spent ten years in Wyoming in the western part of the United States of America. While there, he greatly admired the efficient methods of American agriculture and contrasted them with the situation back in Ireland.

After his return to Ireland on the death of his father in 1889, Plunkett attempted to improve the condition of agriculture in Ireland. In his view the main problem was not the relationship between landlords and tenants. In any case this was being resolved by a series of land acts that contained land purchase schemes. Rather, he identified serious faults at the primary level of production and the secondary level of distribution. Because many Irish farmers were producing poor-quality food, they received low prices on the English market and could not compete with countries such as Argentina and Denmark. In selling their produce farmers usually depended on middlemen, who paid low prices and made a profit for themselves by reselling the goods at a higher rate.

Horace Plunkett proposed two principal solutions to improve the lot of farmers in Ireland: education and co-operation.

THE IRISH AGRICULTURAL ORGANISATION SOCIETY

After 1891 Plunkett had a better opportunity to see at first hand the dreadful living conditions of poorer farmers when he was appointed a member of the Congested Districts Board. His influence increased in 1892, when he was elected to Parliament as a Unionist MP for South County Dublin. In his view, the Irish had shown themselves to be unfit for Home Rule during the Parnellite Split. He believed that people should accept the Act of Union and try to improve conditions in Ireland on a social and economic level. This attitude attracted the hostility of many Catholics and nationalists and thus hindered Plunkett's efforts from the outset. Nevertheless, he pressed ahead with his efforts to reform Irish agriculture.

In 1894 he gathered together thirty existing co-operatives to form one national society, known as the Irish Agricultural Organisation Society (IAOS). These co-operatives had begun in Doneraile, Co. Cork, in 1889. They consisted of

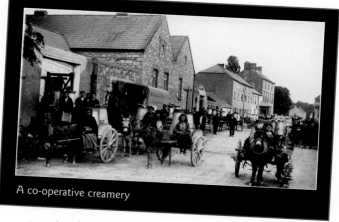

A co-operative creamery

groups of farmers who came together to organise the buying and selling of farm produce and to eliminate the middlemen. Many of the co-operatives also included creameries, which purchased farmers' milk for distribution and for conversion into butter and cheese.

The IAOS soon spread far and wide throughout the country. It published its own journal, the *Irish Homestead*, which was edited by the writer George Russell (Æ). Political and religious issues were excluded from the society, which included Catholics and Protestants, unionists and nationalists. Plunkett now used the support of the co-operative movement to press the British Government to offer greater support to the Irish agricultural sector.

THE DEPARTMENT OF AGRICULTURE

In 1895 Plunkett organised a group of Irish MPs to form a body known as the Recess Committee. They discovered that Ireland had been overtaxed in comparison with Great Britain and called for a number of reforms. One of these was the establishment of a special Department of Agriculture for Ireland. In 1899 the Conservative Government agreed and set up the Department of Agriculture and Technical Instruction. Sir Horace Plunkett was appointed as the

first head of the new department, which took over responsibility for agriculture and technical education in Ireland.

The new department sought to improve the standard of agriculture by sending qualified instructors around the country. Farmers and their wives were shown how to improve their crops, livestock and poultry. Schools that taught technical subjects were given special grants by the department. Plunkett continued at the Department of Agriculture and

Farmers selling their produce at Moy, Co. Tyrone, around 1900

Technical Instruction until 1907. By this time, however, he had become disillusioned with the attitudes of the majority of Irish people.

The Limits of the Co-operative Approach

Because of his attempts to bypass the Home Rule issue, Plunkett had made many enemies. Many Home Rule MPs, especially the anti-Parnellite leader John Dillon, believed that he was playing into the hands of the Conservative Government and supporting its policy of 'Killing Home Rule with Kindness'. At local level in Ireland he offended shopkeepers, merchants and moneylenders, who had made a profit from farmers and were deeply suspicious of the co-operative movement, as it would affect their income.

In 1904 he published a book entitled *Ireland in the New Century*. While much of the work was a thorough analysis of the social and economic shortcomings of Ireland as he saw them, one aspect in particular proved highly controversial. Like many Protestant commentators at the time, Plunkett believed that the Catholic Church hindered economic progress by its emphasis on following authority and waiting for one's reward in the next life. Most Catholics and nationalists, who blamed English rule for the backward state of the Irish economy, deeply resented Plunkett's criticism, and he became a marginalised figure in public life.

However, despite the difficulties he encountered, Horace Plunkett was an inspirational influence in Irish society. He found Irish agriculture in a backward state and was not afraid to state his views and attempt to remedy the situation. It is understandable that his remedy of co-operation would enjoy real, if limited, success. Rural society in Ireland was deeply conservative and slow to change. The deep divisions between unionists and nationalists could not be overcome on an economic level. Nevertheless, Sir Horace Plunkett proved himself a practical reformer in seeking to improve the welfare of all Irish people, irrespective of politics or religion.

The Arrival of Local Democracy

One of Horace Plunkett's main beliefs was that local people should take responsibility for the improvement of their lives. A further step in this direction was taken in 1898, when the British Government passed the **Local Government Act**. This set up a system of local democracy in Ireland based on county councils. Before this, local government in most of the country had been in the hands of unelected committees of landlords, known as grand juries.

The new county councils were to be elected by ratepayers, that is, people liable to pay local property taxes known as rates. As both men and women who paid rates could vote, this meant that for the first time in Ireland, women could vote in an election. The county councils had responsibility for local issues such as the building and maintenance of roads, the public water supply and sanitation.

From the outset the county councils became polarised along political lines. In most of the country they were controlled by Home Rule nationalists, whereas they were under unionist control in north-east Ulster. Because of this single-party control, corruption crept into many county councils: local party supporters were given jobs or contracts, and money changed hands over appointments to posts such as dispensary doctor.

Although frequently seen as part of the Conservative policy of 'Killing Home Rule with Kindness', the reform of local government served to undermine the unionist cause in most of Ireland. The vast majority of county councils were soon in nationalist hands, and the power of local landlords was further eroded with the passing of the grand juries. In addition, many nationalist politicians got their first political experience at local level. This included not merely Home Rule supporters but more radical separatists as well.

Having introduced reform in local government in Ireland in 1898, the Conservative Government went on to implement the final measure in its policy of 'Killing Home Rule with Kindness' – a final and comprehensive settlement of the Land Question.

The United Irish League and Land Reform

In 1898 William O'Brien, one of Parnell's former 'lieutenants', set up a new land organisation called the **United Irish League**. It began in Mayo and took its title from the centenary of the United Irishmen's rebellion of 1798, which was being celebrated that year. O'Brien objected to the existence in Connaught of large farms, or ranches, side by side with tiny holdings on poor ground where families were trying to eke out an existence. He called for the breaking up of ranches and the redistribution of the land among poorer farmers. By 1901 the new movement had over 100,000 members throughout Ireland. O'Brien called for a new land act, and the British Government, anxious to avoid a new land war, was prepared to explore the idea.

THE LAND CONFERENCE OF 1902–3

The Irish Chief Secretary since 1900 was George Wyndham, who had been Arthur Balfour's private secretary between 1887 and 1891. Balfour was now Prime Minister and gave Wyndham his full support in completing the process of land purchase in Ireland. Therefore, Wyndham responded favourably when in 1902 a Co. Galway landlord, Captain John Shawe-Taylor, called for a conference between landlords and tenants.

The Land Conference opened in December 1902 under the chairmanship of Lord Dunraven, a southern unionist. The tenants were represented by the Home Rule MPs John Redmond, William O'Brien and Timothy Harrington. It reached agreement on a fundamental and far-reaching system of land purchase, in effect the practical end of the landlord system itself.

THE WYNDHAM LAND ACT (1903)

The Land Act of 1903 was guided through Parliament by the Chief Secretary, George Wyndham. It contained several improvements on previous land acts:

> 1 The British Government provided £70 million in loans for Irish farmers.
> 2 Landlords received higher prices for their land than in earlier land acts.
> 3 Tenants could repay their loans over a period of sixty-eight years.
> 4 The Government agreed to pay the legal costs of land purchase.
> 5 Landlords who sold their whole estate would get a bonus payment.

In terms of the number of farms purchased, the Wyndham Act was a huge success. Between 1903 and 1909, when a further act – the Birrell Act – was passed, over 270,000 tenants bought their holdings. Although some Home Rule MPs, such as John Dillon and Michael Davitt, believed that the Wyndham Act was too generous to landlords, it was very popular in the country.

The Significance of the Change in Land Ownership

Thus, by 1909 a peaceful revolution in land ownership, which had begun with Gladstone's First Land Act of 1870, was almost complete. The much-condemned system of landlord tenure was a thing of the past, and most farmers owned the land that they worked. Michael Davitt's original vision of the land of Ireland for the people of Ireland had been achieved by largely peaceful means.

In economic terms, however, the change of land ownership in Ireland made little difference. Lack of investment in agriculture continued, as the new owners preferred to save money rather than re-invest it in their holdings. Farmers in Ireland remained distinctly conservative in their approach and suspicious of any innovations in agriculture.

The system of land purchase also failed to alter the social divisions in rural Ireland. Although landlord families disappeared from many areas, their influence was replaced by that of larger farmers and the Catholic clergy. Small farmers continued to endure lives of poverty, and little was done to improve the lot of landless labourers.

For the Conservative Government, however, the Wyndham Act (1903) was to be the final instalment of 'Killing Home Rule with Kindness'. Like all its predecessors, it failed in that respect. Throughout most of Ireland, nationalist farmers purchased their holdings but remained as committed as ever to the cause of Home Rule. In effect, Ireland remained a deeply polarised society, with nationalists and unionists unwilling to compromise on the primary issue of self-government. An incident towards the close of the long period of Conservative rule brought this home to nationalists and unionists alike.

A farm scene from around 1900, showing various pieces of equipment

The Twilight of Conservative Rule

A year after the passage of his successful Land Act, George Wyndham had to resign from office under a cloud of controversy. This was due to an incident known as the Devolution Crisis. Lord Dunraven, the southern unionist who had chaired the successful Land Conference of 1902, thought that other issues such as education could be solved by similar co-operation. He discussed the matter with the Under-Secretary at Dublin Castle, Sir Anthony McDonnell. He drew up a scheme of very limited self-government, known as devolution. This was very far removed from full Home Rule and stood no chance of acceptance by nationalists. However, unionists in Ireland became alarmed, and they urged their Conservative allies to disown the plan. Wyndham was forced to condemn the devolution plan, and he resigned shortly afterwards owing to ill health.

The Devolution Crisis marked the end of constructive unionism. It proved beyond all doubt that, although Conservative Governments could introduce other reforms, they would not touch the highly controversial area of Home Rule. By 1904, however, the Conservative Party, in government continuously since 1895, was beginning to look tired and divided. It fell from power late in 1905, and in the general election of 1906 the Liberals returned to power with a landslide victory.

Paradoxically, the Conservative programme of constructive unionism had served to weaken the Union rather than strengthen it. The Conservative policy of land reform had failed to weaken the attachment of most Irish farmers to Home Rule. While reforms in agriculture improved conditions to a certain extent, they did not strengthen support for the Union. The arrival of county councils served to weaken the power of the largely unionist landlord class still further throughout most of Ireland.

Therefore, when the long period of Conservative rule came to an end in 1906, the unionist cause was at a low ebb throughout Ireland, except in Ulster. With the power of landlords practically eliminated, nationalists looked to future British governments to meet their political demands by introducing Home Rule.

KEY PERSONALITY: MICHAEL DAVITT (1846–1906)

Michael Davitt was born in Straide, Co. Mayo, in 1846, the son of a small tenant farmer. In 1852, when he was six years old, the family was evicted for non-payment of rent. They emigrated to Lancashire, where, at the age of nine, Davitt began work in a cotton mill. Two years later, as a result of an industrial accident, he lost his right arm and was unfit for manual work. This allowed him to return to school and resume his education.

In 1865 he joined the IRB and in 1870 was convicted of gun-running. In 1877 he was released from prison on 'ticket of leave' and immediately renewed his involvement with the IRB. On his release, Davitt went to the USA, where he met John Devoy, the leader of Clan na Gael. The two men worked out the New Departure and then persuaded Parnell to work with them towards a resolution of the Land Question. Davitt was greatly influenced by the writings of the Young Irelander James Fintan Lalor. Like Lalor, he came to believe that tenant ownership of the land would be the first step in achieving national self-rule.

In April 1879 Davitt visited his native Mayo in the midst of the agricultural depression and was appalled by the conditions he witnessed. He set up the Mayo Land League and organised a demonstration at Irishtown, which resulted in a reduction in rents. Other meetings followed, and Parnell was invited to speak at one in Westport in June 1879. In October 1879 Davitt set up the National Land League, and Parnell became its president. The Land League aimed to secure the Ulster Custom (three Fs) for tenants in the short term and to make the farmers owners of their land in the longer term.

During the Land War, Davitt, considered by the British Government to be responsible for the excesses of the Land League, was imprisoned. Before this, he had been instrumental in setting up the Ladies' Land League, which took over the running of the Land League after its leaders were imprisoned. From prison,

Davitt strongly opposed Gladstone's Second Land Act. Although he was released from gaol in May 1882 under the terms of the 'Kilmainham Treaty', Davitt believed that this agreement was an act of betrayal.

With the establishment of the National League and its primary aim of promoting the cause of Home Rule, Davitt was to play a less prominent role in Irish affairs. No longer satisfied that the Land Question would be resolved through tenant ownership, he began increasingly to advocate land nationalisation. Under this system the state would take the land from the landlords and lease it to all farmers. This notion gained little support and in part accounted for Davitt's declining influence after 1882.

During the Parnellite Split, Davitt spoke out strongly against Parnell for putting his own career before the cause of Home Rule. He was elected as an anti-Parnellite MP in 1892 and was a founder member of the United Irish League in 1898.

Michael Davitt was a passionate advocate of social justice. He campaigned for improvements in the conditions of British workers, as well as for reform in education and the prison system. He read and wrote extensively, and some of his major works include *Leaves from a Prison Diary* (1885) and *The Fall of Feudalism* (1904). Davitt's greatest achievement was the foundation and organisation of the Land League. While peasant proprietorship had been effectively achieved by 1903, Davitt's aim of land nationalisation was to remain an aspiration.

EXERCISES

ORDINARY LEVEL

1. The following passage was written by Lord Dunraven, the chairman of the 1902–3 Land Conference. Read it carefully and answer the questions that follow.

> The story of the Irish Land Conference of 1902–1903 may be said to begin with the Land Bill, introduced by George Wyndham, the best Chief Secretary Ireland had had for many years, in the spring of 1902. This Bill was not a very great advance upon earlier Land Purchase Acts. It did not provide for the completion of purchase on anything like an adequate scale, nor did it afford any remedy for the sufferings of evicted tenants. It did not recognise the pressing problems of the Irish Land system, and it was condemned by the United Irish League and the great majority of the people . . .
>
> During the summer of 1902 a great deal of agitation and violent disturbance took place in Ireland. Large portions of the country, including the cities of Dublin, Cork, and Limerick, were proclaimed under the Crimes Act; public meetings were suppressed and a number of Members of Parliament were imprisoned.
>
> It is probable that the Conference idea was saved from an untimely death by a bold appeal in a letter from Captain Shawe-Taylor, which appeared in several of the leading Irish newspapers on September 3, and which after deploring the 200-year-long 'land war', with its resulting paralysis of commercial enterprise, and its hatred and bitterness, and warning against the impending renewed conflict between the United Irish League and the Irish Land Trust, put forth a strong plea for the convening of an early Conference in Dublin.
>
> *The Earl of Dunraven, 1922, cited in J. Carty, Ireland from the Great Famine to the Treaty, Dublin: Fallon 1951, 91–3*

(i) How did the story of the Land Conference of 1902–3 begin?

(ii) Who condemned the proposed land bill?

(iii) Describe the events of the summer of 1902.

(iv) What action was taken by Captain Shawe-Taylor?

2. Describe the traditional policy of the Conservative Party towards Ireland before the rise of the Home Rule movement.

3. Explain the Conservative policy of 'Killing Home Rule with Kindness'.

4. Write a paragraph on the Ashbourne Act (1885).

5. Write an account of the Plan of Campaign.

6. Describe how Arthur Balfour dealt with the Plan of Campaign.

7. What interventions were made by Pope Leo XIII during the Plan of Campaign? Were they successful?

8. Write a paragraph on Balfour's Land Act (1891).

9. How did the Congested Districts Board attempt to improve the living conditions of people in the West of Ireland?

10. Write an account of the achievements of Sir Horace Plunkett in Irish agriculture.

11. Write a paragraph on the reform of local government in Ireland that was introduced in 1898.

12. What happened at the Land Conference of 1902–3?

13. Write a paragraph on the Wyndham Act (1903).

14. Explain the significance of the change in land ownership in Ireland between 1870 and 1903.

15. Write a note on the Devolution Crisis.

16. How successful was the Conservative policy of constructive unionism?

17. Choose three photographs from this chapter which illustrate the lifestyle of people at the time. In each case state how the image furthers our knowledge of living and working conditions.

Higher Level

1. Analyse the policy of Conservative governments in Ireland between 1885 and 1906.

2. Discuss land purchase in Ireland, 1885–1903, and assess its impact.

3. The following passage is taken from Sir Horace Plunkett's *Ireland in the New Century*. Read it carefully and answer the questions that follow.

> It was hard and thankless work. There was the apathy of the people and the active opposition of the press and the politicians. It would be hard to say now whether the abuse of the Conservative *Cork Constitution* or that of the Nationalist *Eagle*, of Skibbereen, was the louder . . . Once when I thought I had planted a Creamery within the precincts of the town of Rathkeale, County Limerick, my co-operative apple cart was upset by a local solicitor who, having elicited the fact that our movement recognised neither political nor religious differences – that the Unionist-Protestant cow was as dear to us as her Nationalist-Catholic sister – gravely informed me that our programme would not suit Rathkeale. 'Rathkeale,' said he, pompously, 'is a Nationalist town – Nationalist to the backbone – and every pound of butter made in this Creamery must be made on Nationalist principles, or it shan't be made at all.' This sentiment was applauded loudly, and the proceedings terminated.

> *Horace Plunkett, Ireland in the New Century, London: John Murray 1904, 190–91*

(i) Why was Plunkett's task of spreading the notion of co-operation 'hard and thankless work'?

(ii) What objection had the solicitor in Rathkeale to Plunkett's movement?

(iii) Explain the humour employed by Plunkett regarding the religion and politics of cows.

(iv) How would you evaluate the worth of this primary source in conveying a sense of the times it describes?

4. Assess the role of Sir Horace Plunkett in Irish affairs.

5. 'The Local Government Act (1898) was an important milestone in the development of local democracy in Ireland.' Discuss this statement.

6. Read the following extract from a letter by the Chief Secretary, George Wyndham, and answer the questions that follow. He was discussing his efforts to reach a solution to the Land Question.

> I am disappointed and chagrined by recent events. Nor can I take the sanguine view that the Land Act will fulfil the objects of the Land Conference, if it is to be assailed daily by the Freemen, Davitt and Dillon. My power of usefulness to Ireland is already diminished and may be destroyed. I have convinced my colleagues...that it was right in itself to foster Union among Irishmen and to obliterate the vestiges of ancient feuds without troubling ourselves about the ultimate effect of social reconciliation on Ireland's attitude towards 'Home Rule' versus 'Union' controversy. And if this is set back, you cannot deal with the 'University Question' or the 'Labourers' question, if so large and beneficent a measure as the Land Act is to be used only to divide classes more sharply.

> *Letter of George Wyndham to Moreton Frewen, 14 November 1903, cited in J.W. Mackail & G. Wyndham, The Life and Letters of George Wyndham, London, 1925, ii, 472*

(i) Which leading members of the Home Rule Party were attacking the Land Act, according to Wyndham?

(ii) What exactly was the Land Conference referred to by Wyndham?

(iii) What points did he make to his colleagues in the Conservative Government concerning land policy in Ireland?

(iv) Explain what is meant by the phrase 'the ultimate effect of social reconciliation on Ireland's attitude towards the "Home Rule" versus "Union" controversy'.

(v) What accusation did Wyndham make against his critics at the end of the extract?

The Growing Power of the Catholic Church

From 1850 the position of the Catholic Church in Ireland strengthened considerably. Historians have identified several factors that contributed to this development.

1. The Role of Cardinal Paul Cullen

Dr Paul Cullen, Ireland's first cardinal, played a crucial role in strengthening the power of the Catholic Church in Ireland. A native of Co. Kildare, he went to Rome to study for the priesthood and remained there to take charge of the Irish College, where students from Ireland prepared

The splendid Catholic cathedral at Cobh, Co. Cork, which was opened in 1877

to become priests. Cullen was appointed Archbishop of Armagh in 1849 and transferred to Dublin in 1852. He was highly regarded by Pope Pius IX (1846–78) and in turn was determined that the Catholic Church in Ireland should be bound closely to the Pope. As such, Paul Cullen was one of the leading supporters of ultramontanism in Europe. This was a movement that advocated the end of many existing customs in various countries and the complete dependence of local Catholic communities on the Pope. In 1850 Cullen convened a church gathering known as the Synod of Thurles. Many new rules were drawn up to strengthen the power of the Pope and the bishops over the Catholic Church in Ireland. Old customs such as the celebration of Mass in private homes were condemned, and Catholics were ordered to avoid attending schools or colleges that were not controlled by the Church.

Until his death in 1878, Cullen wielded huge power over the Catholic Church in Ireland. He usually had a decisive input into the selection of new bishops throughout the country. He strongly supported the foundation of schools, colleges and hospitals run by priests, nuns or brothers. He understood the overriding importance of education and believed that the Church and not the British Government should be in control. In this regard, Cullen hoped not merely to ensure a Catholic upbringing for future generations but especially to control the expanding Catholic middle class. His hope that middle-class Catholics would compete with and outnumber Protestants in areas such as medicine and law was to be fulfilled in the years ahead.

2. Population Changes

Demographic, or population-based, trends were also of key importance in the rising power of the Catholic Church. The vast population decline during and after the Great Famine affected primarily the poorest sections of society. When the economy began to prosper from the mid-1850s onwards, the bishops, priests and religious were in a stronger position than before. Resources previously needed for the poor were now also available for a programme of church and school building. From the 1850s, the numbers of priests, brothers and nuns began to increase gradually.

3. Decline in the Power of Landlords

The sustained decline in the power of landlords in Ireland after 1870 was crucial to the rising power of the Catholic Church. For historical reasons such as the plantations and the Penal Laws, there were very few Catholic landlords in Ireland. When the power of the mostly Protestant landlords declined, Catholic bishops and priests frequently filled the vacuum and exerted strong influence in their local areas. This development was greatly feared by Protestants, who believed that their way of life could be under threat.

4. Decline of the Irish Language

The loss of the Irish language as the main means of communication in most of the country also strengthened the position of the Catholic Church. Although some Catholic priests claimed that the Irish language would protect people from foreign influences, many bishops and priests actively promoted the use of English. While nationalist propaganda condemned them for this in the past, many historians now believe that in this matter the Church was responding to the demands of its lay members, who turned their backs on Irish and learned the English language. At a deeper level, however, this development strengthened the bond between Church and people. Deprived of their language as a badge of identity, many Irish people at home and especially abroad stressed their Catholic identity as a means of distinguishing themselves from the English. Thus, by the 1870s there was a strong connection between the Catholic Church and Ireland, between faith and fatherland, in the minds of many bishops, priests and people.

Mass on the summit of Croagh Patrick around 1900

As the power of the Catholic Church increased, many Catholics showed a growing unwillingness to compromise with Protestant opinion. In this regard, Catholic bishops continued to insist on the provision of denominational education at first, second and third level. With regard to university education, they rejected all offers of a settlement by successive British governments until 1908.

During the pontificate of Pope Pius X (1903–14), the Catholic Church passed a law that was to be highly contentious for decades to come. Under the **Ne Temere Decree** (1907), the rules governing mixed marriages (marriages between Catholics and non-Catholics) were made much stricter. The old custom whereby the sons of such marriages followed their father's religion and the daughters that of their mother was banned. In future both the Catholic and non-Catholic marriage partner had to sign a written agreement that all children of the marriage would be brought up in the Catholic Church. Protestants regarded these provisions as an infringement of their rights as parents and feared that the decree would lead to a fall in the Protestant population in areas where they were in a minority. The passing of the *Ne Temere* Decree was one of the causes of friction between Catholics and other Christians in the period immediately before the Home Rule Crisis of 1912–14.

The Expansion of Education

Between 1870 and 1914 there were a number of developments in education that reflected the divisions and tensions in Irish society. Education was often a controversial matter because it was closely linked to two extremely sensitive areas: religion and politics. The main churches in Ireland took a close interest in education and exercised as much control as the British Government would permit. Various British governments believed that children should be taught loyalty to Queen Victoria and the British Empire at school. Nationalists, on the other hand, objected to this. They in their turn believed that schools should foster the Irish language, teach Irish history and promote other aspects of national identity. Thus, education at all three levels became the focus of rivalry between different interest groups.

PRIMARY EDUCATION

In 1870 the vast majority of children received their primary education in the local National School. These schools were part of the National School system administered by the Board of National Education in Dublin. The system was established in 1831 as a non-denominational one. Children of different religious backgrounds were supposed to be educated together in all subjects except religious instruction. However, the Catholic Church and the Protestant churches accepted the system only reluctantly. They constantly called for a denominational system, with separate schools for children of different religions. By 1870, however, the system was in effect highly denominational. The vast majority of primary school children attended schools in which all the pupils were of one religion only. The Board of Education laid down the subjects to be studied, printed textbooks, inspected schools and paid teachers' salaries. However, the local parish priest or minister was the school manager and exercised power over teachers and pupils alike. The curriculum in National Schools was based on the three Rs – reading, writing and arithmetic. The vast majority of children left school at the end of primary level, at around twelve years of age.

Although criticised by nationalists for neglecting the Irish language, the National Schools were largely responsible for the high levels

First Holy Communion class in a primary school in the late nineteenth century

of literacy in Ireland by 1900. In contrast to the situation at primary level, where state intervention began in 1831, it was 1878 before the British Government provided funds for secondary education.

SECONDARY EDUCATION

As a necessary qualification for a career in professions such as law or medicine, or for positions in offices or the civil service, secondary education was vitally important in better-off families. Traditionally, only the rich could afford this type of education, although a small number of scholarships were available for very clever poorer students.

Woodwork class in a Christian Brothers school around 1900

In Ireland as late as 1870 no state system of examinations existed, nor did the state pay teachers' salaries at second level. This situation continued largely because of disagreements between the British Government and the Catholic Church. Whereas the Catholic Church wanted a completely denominational system of secondary education, British politicians refused to commit taxpayers' money without certain guarantees. Although the Church of Ireland had certain long-established, well-endowed schools, the Presbyterian Church, like the Catholic Church, stood in need of state aid to expand its educational provision.

Finally, in 1878 a compromise solution was reached under the **Intermediate Education (Ireland) Act.** This established an Intermediate Education Board in Dublin to supervise secondary education in Ireland. The Board organised examinations in various subjects at different levels. The system was based on payment by results. Successful candidates were paid a certain amount, which then went to the school as a fee. There were no examinations in religious education. Although the Intermediate Act allowed parents to withdraw their children from religious classes, in effect most schools were denominational. Protestant secondary schools were either boarding or day schools under Protestant management. Catholic secondary schools were either diocesan colleges under the control of the local bishop or run by religious orders of priests, brothers or nuns.

The Intermediate education system, which lasted until 1924, had certain faults. Great emphasis was placed on a narrow range of learning in order to pass examinations, and cultural subjects such as music and art were frequently neglected. However, unlike in the National Schools, the Irish language was available as an examination subject from the outset, although few schools taught it until after the foundation of the Gaelic League in 1893.

Under the Intermediate system, the position of girls at second level improved enormously. Competing on equal terms with boys, many girls went on to university and to careers in the professions. By the 1880s, some Protestant girls' schools and certain Catholic convent schools became famous for the high calibre of their students.

Another vital contribution of the Intermediate system was the promotion of social mobility. Slowly but surely, more students from lower-middle-class backgrounds were able to remain on at school because of the incentives offered by the Intermediate system. By charging low fees or by forgoing fees completely in some cases, religious orders such as the Christian Brothers and the Sisters of Mercy enabled their students to aspire to better-paid employment than that of their parents. Many of those prominent in the cultural revival and, later, in the struggle for independence were educated under the Intermediate system.

THE UNIVERSITY QUESTION

As with secondary education, repeated efforts by various British governments to improve university education in Ireland failed because of religious objections. Until 1845 there had been only one university in Ireland – Trinity College, Dublin. This was controlled by the Church of Ireland and catered largely for members of that Church. In 1845 the British Government had set up Queen's Colleges at Cork, Belfast and Galway. Because they were non-denominational, the Catholic bishops condemned them as 'godless colleges'. Therefore, although the Belfast college, which catered largely for Presbyterians, was fairly successful, those at Cork and Galway never flourished and had low student numbers.

Women graduates of the Royal University of Ireland, 1883

In 1879, a year after the Intermediate Education Act, the Conservative Government of Disraeli introduced a similar scheme for the university sector. The old Queen's University, to which the Queen's Colleges had belonged, was abolished and replaced by the Royal University. Like the Intermediate Board, the Royal University was mainly an examination board that arranged examinations, awarded degrees and provided scholarships and grants for students and lecturers. Members of different religious groups received equal treatment. In this way, the majority of Catholic students could get degrees for the first time. The Catholic bishops had set up a Catholic university for the first time, but successive British governments refused to recognise its degrees. Under the Royal University system, students from any college could sit examinations, and several lecturers in the Catholic University were paid allowances. In this way the Royal University made degrees more widely available.

In the area of women's education, the Royal University of Ireland was to the forefront. It was one of the first universities in the world to admit women on equal terms with men. Soon some high-profile female graduates went on to become academics or to take a prominent part in public life.

By its very nature as an examining body, the Royal University was merely a stage on the road to the final settlement of the University Question. In 1908, after a number of royal commissions of enquiry, the Liberal Government finally resolved the issue. The Irish Chief Secretary, Augustine Birrell, was in charge of guiding the Act through Parliament. The University of Dublin (Trinity College) was left as it was, and two new universities were created. In Belfast, the old Queen's College became the fully independent Queen's University of Belfast. In the south, the National University of Ireland (NUI) was created. It consisted of the old Queen's Colleges of Cork and Galway, which changed their names to University Colleges, and the old Catholic University in Dublin, which became known as University College, Dublin. Although the new National University of Ireland was non-denominational and could not use its funds for the teaching of religion, in effect the vast majority of its students were Catholics, and a decidedly Catholic atmosphere existed in its colleges in the years ahead.

Therefore, while the University Question may have been solved in 1908, in many ways the solution reflected the deep divisions in Ireland at the time. Queen's University, Belfast, was proud to be British and was situated in a thriving industrial city. The National University stressed its Irish identity from the outset and catered for a largely rural population. Indeed its commitment to national identity was in keeping with the popularity of the Gaelic cultural revival, which had been in progress since the 1880s.

The Idea of Cultural Nationalism

Between 1884 and 1914, a number of powerful new organisations emerged in Ireland with the aim of strengthening the country's cultural heritage. As in the rest of Europe at the time, people began to take an increasing interest in their country's language, folklore, sport and other traditions. Organisations such as the Gaelic Athletic Association and the Gaelic League responded to these trends and fostered greater participation in, and appreciation of, Ireland's unique culture.

Although some members of the new organisations wished to avoid politics, for many others an interest in Gaelic games or the Irish language went hand in hand with a desire to see Ireland become an independent nation. Because of this linkage, these developments have often been discussed by historians under the title of 'cultural nationalism'. As we shall see, the cultural revival was to have a profound impact on the generation growing up in Ireland between 1890 and 1916. It began in effect with the successful attempts, initiated by Michael Cusack in 1884, to revive Gaelic games.

Case Study: The Foundation and Early Years of the GAA

On 1 November 1884 a momentous gathering took place at Hayes's Hotel in Thurles, Co. Tipperary. At a short meeting, attended by about twelve men, Michael Cusack founded the Gaelic Athletic Association (GAA) in order to preserve Gaelic games from extinction in Ireland. This was the culmination of a long period of planning on Cusack's part. For many years he had observed

Michael Cusack, founder of the GAA

with dismay the decline of hurling and other local Irish games due to increased competition from British sports. During the 1860s, soccer and rugby became organised in England, and they spread to Ireland. In Cusack's view, this was just one further example of the threat to Irish culture from the spread of English influence. He was also an enthusiast for the revival of the Irish language and had deep sympathy for the Fenians.

Cusack believed that an Irish organisation should control not only field games but athletics as well. At the time, athletics were controlled by British groups whose policies were strongly influenced by snobbery and class distinction. Ordinary workers were excluded. He made this clear in a newspaper article written less than a month before the foundation of the GAA (Document 1).

A week later, Maurice Davin, a farmer from Co. Tipperary and a leading athlete in Ireland at the time, wrote to the same newspaper to support the views of Michael Cusack and to offer his assistance (Document 2). Davin was as good as his word. He attended the inaugural meeting of the GAA and became its first president.

Document 1

A Word About Irish Athletics
No movement having for its object the social and political advancement of a nation from the tyranny of imported and enforced customs and manners, can be regarded as perfect, if it has not made adequate provision for the preservation and cultivation of the national pastimes of the people. Voluntary neglect of such pastimes is a sure sign of National decay and of approaching dissolution . . .

A so-called revival of athletics was inaugurated in Ireland. The new movement did not originate with those who have ever had any sympathy with Ireland or the Irish people. Accordingly, labourers, tradesmen, artisans, and even policemen and soldiers were excluded from the few competitions which constituted the lame and halting programme of the promoters . . .

We tell the Irish people to take the management of their games into their own hands, to encourage and promote in every way, every form of athletics that is peculiarly Irish and to remove with one sweep everything that is foreign and iniquitous in the present system. The vast majority of the best athletes in Ireland are Nationalists. These gentlemen should take the matter in hand at once, and draft laws for the guidance of promoters of meetings in Ireland next year . . .

It is only by such an arrangement that pure Irish athletics will be revived, and that the incomparable strength and physique of our race will be preserved.

Document 2

It is time that a handbook was published with rules for all Irish games. The English Handbooks of Athletics are very good in their way, but they do not touch on many of the Irish games . . .

Irish football is a great game and worth going a very long way to see, when played on a fairly laid-out ground and under proper rules. Many old people say that hurling exceeded it as a trial of men. I would not care to see either game now, as the rules stand at present. I may say that there are no rules, and, therefore, those games are often dangerous. I am anxious to see both games revived under regular rules . . .

If a movement such as you advise is made for the purpose of reviving or encouraging Irish games and drafting rules, I will gladly lend a hand, if I can be of any use.

THE FOUNDATION OF THE GAA

On 1 November 1884, Cusack, Davin and others interested in Gaelic games met in Thurles, Co. Tipperary, to found a new organisation. An account of the meeting at Hayes's Hotel, Thurles appeared two days later in the *Cork Examiner* under the heading 'Gaelic Association for National Pastimes' (Document 3).

ARCHBISHOP CROKE AND THE GAA

By inviting Archbishop Croke of Cashel to become a patron, the members of the new association were choosing one of the most outspoken supporters of Parnell among the Irish Catholic bishops. Archbishop Croke had been in trouble over his support for nationalist politicians and was called to Rome to explain his actions to Pope Leo XIII. Croke's public letter accepting his role as patron of the GAA is a famous historical document that amply illustrates nationalist resentment at the growing English influence in the Ireland of 1884 (Document 4).

The strong anti-English feelings expressed by Archbishop Croke were shared by Michael Cusack and other founders of the GAA. They saw themselves involved in a struggle between English and Irish cultures. Thus, from the outset the GAA sought not merely to promote Gaelic games but to reduce the influence of English or 'foreign' games at the same time.

THE IDEALS OF THE GAA

The twofold approach of the GAA soon became apparent. On the positive side, the organisers set about establishing branches throughout the country. In the first two years it spread rapidly, causing Michael Cusack to remark later that 'it spread like a prairie fire'. In 1887 All-Ireland Championships were held in hurling and Gaelic football for the first time.

Document 3

A meeting of athletes and friends of athletics was held on Saturday at three o'clock in Miss Hayes's Commercial Hotel Thurles for the purpose of forming an association for the preservation and cultivation of our national pastimes.

Mr Michael Cusack of Dublin and Mr Maurice Davin of Carrick-on-Suir had the meeting convened by the following circular: 'You are earnestly requested to attend a meeting, which will be held in Thurles on 1st of November, to take steps for the formation of a Gaelic Association for the preservation and cultivation of our national pastimes, and for providing rational amusements for the Irish people during their leisure hours' . . .

Mr Davin was called to the chair and Mr Cusack read the circular convening the meeting. The Chairman then said that many of the good old Irish games had been allowed to die out in the country, which he and many others would like to see revived . . .

On the motion of Mr Cusack, seconded by Mr Power, Archbishop Croke, Mr Parnell and Mr Davitt were appointed patrons of the new organisation . . .

Mr Cusack then proposed that Mr Maurice Davin – an athlete who had distinguished himself much both in Ireland and in England – should be the president of the association.

The Cork Examiner, 3 November 1884

Document 4

We are daily importing from England not only her manufactured goods . . . but together with her fashions, her accent, her vicious literature, her music, her dances and her manifold mannerisms, her games also and her pastimes, to the utter discredit of our own grand national sports, and to the sore humiliation, as I believe, of every genuine son and daughter of the old land.

Ball-playing, hurling, football, kicking, according to Irish rules, 'casting', leaping in various ways, wrestling, handy-grips, top-pegging, leap-frog, rounders, tip-in-the-heat, and all such favourite exercises and amusements among men and boys, may be said not only to be dead and buried, but in several localities to be entirely forgotten and unknown. And what have we got in their stead? We have got such foreign and fantastic field sports as lawn-tennis, croquet, cricket and the like – very excellent, I believe, and health-giving exercises in their way, still not racy of the soil, but rather alien, on the contrary, to it, as are indeed, for the most part, the men and women who first imported and still continue to patronise them . . .

Indeed if we continue travelling for the next score of years in the same direction that we have been going in for some time past . . . we had better at once and publicly, adjure our nationality, clap hands for joy at the sight of the Union Jack, and place 'England's bloody red' exultingly above 'the green'.

Archbishop T.W. Croke, November 1884

However, the young association also launched an offensive against 'foreign' games. In 1886 players of games such as soccer and rugby were barred from the GAA. In 1888 members of the police, the Royal Irish Constabulary, were barred. In 1902 and 1903 these bans were strengthened and extended to members of the British army. This approach, while popular with many nationalists, alienated many others, including Protestants and unionists. Protestants were also practically excluded from the GAA by the fact that most games were played on Sundays. This suited most working men, but the Protestant tradition disapproved of games on Sundays. Thus, although certain Protestants, such as Sam Maguire, the donor of the cup for the All-Ireland Football Championship, were members of the GAA, they were the exception rather than the rule.

By imposing a ban on policemen and soldiers who upheld British rule, the GAA was becoming involved in political issues. Members defended this by saying that it was a national organisation that favoured Irish independence. However, in the first decade of its existence, it was to learn a costly lesson concerning the dangers of political involvement. On two occasions such involvement did serious damage to the young organisation.

THE FENIAN THREAT AND THE PARNELLITE SPLIT

From the foundation of the GAA, members of the IRB belonged to the organisation. Some Fenians regarded it as a good training ground and a source of recruits for future Irish rebels. Others, however, actually tried to gain control of the organisation itself.

At a GAA convention held in Thurles in November 1887, the IRB gained substantial control of the organisation. Maurice Davin was removed from the presidency of the GAA and replaced by an IRB candidate. However, Archbishop Croke and Michael Davitt took the initiative to reverse this situation, and at another convention held in Thurles in January 1888, Maurice Davin was re-elected president, and IRB members were ousted from the most important positions in the GAA. Yet within two years the IRB succeeded in re-establishing control.

The Parnellite Split, which began in December 1890, almost ruined the GAA. The association was strongly Parnellite and took a prominent part in Parnell's funeral in October 1891. As a result, many anti-Parnellites left the GAA, and by the end of 1891 it was a mere shadow of its strength a year previously. It was to take over ten years before it eventually began to recover from this setback.

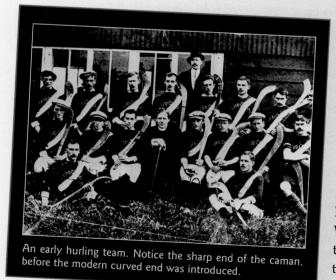

An early hurling team. Notice the sharp end of the caman, before the modern curved end was introduced.

THE GAA AND THE GROWTH OF SEPARATISM

The revival of the GAA after 1900 coincided with the revival of the IRB and the growing influence of other forms of cultural nationalism, such as the Gaelic League and the Abbey Theatre. Many of those active in the struggle for Irish independence between 1916 and 1921 were involved in the GAA at this time. In 1913 the GAA acquired the grounds at Jones's Road in Dublin that were later developed into Croke Park. Thus, by the outbreak of World War I in 1914, the GAA was established throughout the country and had a significant influence not merely in terms of promoting Gaelic sports but also in supporting the cause of Ireland's unique national identity.

COMPREHENSION

1. According to the author of Document 1, what does voluntary neglect of national pastimes signify?

2. Why is a recent growth in athletics called 'a so-called revival of athletics'?

3. What, according to the author, is the main fault of this movement?

4. What advice is given to the Irish people regarding control of athletics in Document 1?

5. According to the writer, what is the political viewpoint of 'the vast majority of the best athletes in Ireland'?

6. Explain the principal recommendation made at the end of Document 1.

7. According to Maurice Davin (Document 2), what is wrong with English handbooks of athletics?

8. How did he regard Irish football?

9. Why, according to Davin, were both football and hurling dangerous at the time?

10. What commitment does he make at the end of Document 2?

11. Explain the purpose of the meeting at Hayes's Hotel, Thurles, on 1 November 1884, as outlined in Document 3.

12. What unfortunate development does the chairman of the meeting refer to?

13. Name the three patrons of the new association.

14. Why was Maurice Davin invited to become the first president of the GAA, according to Document 3?

15. List any four items that Archbishop Croke believes the Irish people are importing from England (Document 4).

16. List the sports he calls 'foreign and fantastic'.

17. What was Dr Croke's main objection to these?

18. Explain the meaning of the final paragraph in Document 4.

COMPARISON

1. In all four documents there is one main theme. Identify it.

2. Compare the references to English-controlled athletics in Document 1 and English sports in Document 4.

3. Would you agree that the events described in Document 3 are a response to the wishes expressed in Document 1? Explain your answer.

4. List the similarities between the views expressed in Document 3 and those of Archbishop Croke in Document 4.

CRITICISM

1. Do you think that Document 1 is a biased source? Explain your answer.

2. Point out qualities in Document 3 that mark it out as a newspaper report.

3. What would you consider to be the main advantages of Document 4 as a primary source?

4. Document 4 is intended to persuade people to support the writer's opinions. Point out some elements in it that you consider especially useful for this purpose.

CONTEXTUALISATION

1. Write a paragraph on the reasons for the foundation of the Gaelic Athletic Association.

2. Explain the positive and negative aspects of the GAA attitude to sport in its early days.

3. Write an account of political influence in the GAA up to 1900.

The Gaelic League

In July 1893 an organisation was founded in Dublin to support the Irish language, just as the GAA cultivated Gaelic games. Known as the Gaelic League (Conradh na Gaeilge), it was to have a profound impact on Irish society, especially between the time of its foundation and the Easter Rising of 1916. Its two principal founders were Douglas Hyde and Eoin MacNeill. Hyde, the son of a Church of Ireland minister from Co. Roscommon, was interested in the Irish language and Gaelic culture from a young age. MacNeill, an Irish and history scholar from the Glens of Antrim, shared his enthusiasm for the Irish language. Unlike many Irish scholars at the time, who were interested in earlier written forms of Irish, Hyde and MacNeill were committed to saving Irish in the areas where it was still spoken and to reviving it throughout the country.

THE DECLINE OF THE IRISH LANGUAGE

By 1893 Irish was in serious decline as a spoken language. Most of those speaking it lived in poverty on the western seaboard. It had been declining significantly for over a hundred years. Even before the Great Famine, many parents refused to have their children brought up speaking Irish. They associated it with poverty and ignorance. Politics and trade were mostly conducted through English, and English was necessary for the huge numbers emigrating from Ireland. The Famine dealt a heavy blow to the language. The areas that were most severely affected by death and emigration were precisely those where Irish was strongest. From then on, the language appeared to be in terminal decline.

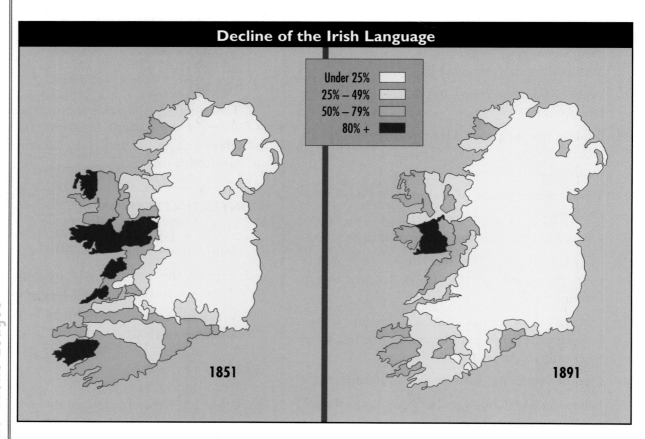

Decline of the Irish Language

Under 25%
25% – 49%
50% – 79%
80% +

1851

1891

THE AIMS OF THE GAELIC LEAGUE

For Douglas Hyde, far from being associated with poverty and ignorance, the Irish language was one of the most precious possessions of the Irish people. It was one of the oldest languages in Europe, with a rich literary tradition. In a famous essay written in 1892, entitled 'The Necessity for De-Anglicising Ireland', Hyde called for a revival of the Irish language and Irish culture. In his belief, the country was becoming 'anglicised', or English, and needed to reverse this trend.

Thus, from its foundation in 1893 the main aim of the Gaelic League was the revival of the Irish language. The main methods chosen were the teaching of Irish and the publication of books in the language. At that time there were very few books in print in Irish. Travelling teachers known as *timirí* travelled around the country teaching Irish.

In 1899 the Gaelic League began the publication of its own newspaper, *An Claidheamh Soluis*. Patrick Pearse edited it between 1903 and 1909. The Gaelic League also published new works in Irish by Pearse and other writers, such as an tAthair Peadar Ó Laoghaire and Pádraic Ó Conaire.

The Gaelic League also fostered an interest in Irish music and dancing. It organised *feiseanna* and *céilithe*, and the *Oireachtas*, an annual festival of Irish literature and music. Irish courses in the Gaeltacht were organised for teachers and other interested people.

An Claidheamh Soluis

After a slow start in the 1890s, the Gaelic League expanded rapidly after 1900. This expansion gave it renewed optimism to press for reforms in public life. It agitated for an improvement in the status of Irish at primary and secondary level. In 1903 it persuaded the British Government to make St Patrick's Day a public holiday and to close public houses on that day.

The involvement of the Gaelic League in the successful campaign to make Irish compulsory in order to attend the colleges of the National University was more controversial, however. Many people objected to compulsion, and the Catholic bishops opposed this campaign. As a result, many priests withdrew from involvement in the Gaelic League, and the organisation was weakened from 1910 onwards.

THE GAELIC LEAGUE AND IRISH FREEDOM

Like the GAA, the Gaelic League became involved in political issues. Some members, including Douglas Hyde, believed that it should stay outside of politics and that the Irish language belonged to all Irish people, Catholic and Protestant, nationalist and unionist alike. However, given the rising tide of national feeling, this was always a minority point of view.

For most ordinary members of the Gaelic League, love of the Irish language was combined with a desire to see Ireland win its independence from Great Britain. Indeed, many of the leaders of the independence movement from 1916 onwards, such as Patrick Pearse and Éamon de Valera, had strong connections with the Gaelic League.

Pearse in effect forced the political issue within the Gaelic League. He used emotive slogans, such as 'A country without a language is a country without a soul' or 'Ireland should not merely be free but Gaelic as well, not merely Gaelic, but free as well.' At a congress of the Gaelic League in 1915, a motion was passed supporting the cause of Irish freedom. Although in favour of Irish independence, Douglas Hyde resigned from the presidency of the League because of its connection with politics.

Thus, in the years leading up to 1916, the Gaelic League became more and more identified with the aspirations of those who desired complete separation between Great Britain and Ireland.

KEY PERSONALITY: DOUGLAS HYDE (1860–1949)

Born in Co. Roscommon in 1860, Douglas Hyde was the son of a Church of Ireland rector. He was educated at Trinity College, Dublin. A collector and translator of Irish folklore and poetry, he was co-founder of the Irish Literary Society in London in 1891 and became president of the National Literary Society in Dublin in 1892. In 1893 he published *Love Songs of Connacht* and in 1899 wrote *A Literary History of Ireland*.

Deeply concerned about the decline of the Irish language, Hyde spoke about the need for the 'De-anglicisation of Ireland'. In 1893, together with Eoin MacNeill, he founded the Gaelic League with the aim of reviving the Irish language and promoting the writing and publication of Irish literature. He became the League's first president.

Although the work of the League remained Hyde's main commitment, he continued to write, producing in 1901 the first modern play in the Irish language, *Casadh an tSúgáin*. He wrote under the pseudonym *An Craoibhín Aoibhinn*. His writings had an important influence on W.B. Yeats and other members of the newly established Irish Literary Theatre. He also sat on the Commission for Irish Intermediate and University Education.

Douglas Hyde became increasingly disillusioned with the involvement of the Gaelic League in separatist politics and resigned as its president in 1915 when the League, at a congress held in Dundalk, passed a resolution in favour of Irish independence. He was Professor of Modern Irish at the National University of Ireland from 1909 to 1932 and, for a short period (1925–6), was a member of the Senate of the Irish Free State. In 1938 he was chosen by all-party agreement as the first President of Ireland under the 1937 Constitution. He served a full term as president from 1938 to 1945. He died in 1949.

The Anglo-Irish Literary Revival

Along with the GAA and the Gaelic League, the third main cultural movement in Ireland around 1900 was the Anglo-Irish Literary Revival. Unlike the members of the Gaelic League, the members of this movement wrote about Ireland in the English language. The two greatest writers involved were the poet and playwright William Butler Yeats (1865–1939) and the playwright John Millington Synge (1871–1909).

Although the movement produced poetry and prose writing concerning Ireland in the English language, its main focus was the theatre, particularly the plays associated with the famous Abbey Theatre.

In 1898 the Irish Literary Theatre was established by Yeats and two members of the landlord class from Galway. These were Lady Augusta Gregory of Coole Park – like Yeats, a member of the Church of Ireland – and a local Catholic landlord, Edward Martyn. Like Douglas Hyde, Lady Gregory collected songs and stories from the local people. The aim of the new theatre group was to stage plays dealing with Irish subjects. Like many writers throughout Europe at the time, Yeats and Lady Gregory had developed an interest in the customs, traditions and folklore of the local country people. This was a reaction against plays that dealt with modern city life and that arrived in Ireland from England.

The first play put on by the new group was Yeats's *The Countess Cathleen*. This concerned an imaginary Irish lady who sold her soul to the devil in order to feed the starving poor. The beautiful Maud Gonne, with whom Yeats was in love, played the leading role in the next play, *Cathleen Ni Houlihan*, which was set in Mayo during the rebellion of 1798. Ireland was portrayed as a beautiful woman for whom young men would willingly die. It was in reference to this play that Yeats wrote, after the 1916 Rising,

Maud Gonne (on right) in the title role in Yeats's play *Cathleen Ni Houlihan*

> *Did that play of mine send out*
> *Certain men the English shot?*

Lady Gregory also wrote plays, including a famous one set in Fenian times, *The Rising of the Moon*.

THE ABBEY THEATRE

In 1904 the Irish Literary Theatre acquired a permanent home, owing to the generosity of a wealthy English supporter, Annie Horniman. She bought premises in Dublin's Abbey Street and had them converted into a theatre. Known as the Abbey Theatre, it became for a time one of the most exciting theatres in Europe.

The most gifted writer of plays in the early years of the Abbey was John Millington Synge. A native of Dublin, he went to the Aran Islands to study the life of the people there. In plays such as *The Shadow of the Glen* and *Riders to the Sea*, he was not afraid to depict the harsh realities of life in a loveless marriage or the harsh conditions of western fishing communities. His realistic portrayals caused some controversy. However, this was but a prelude to the riots that erupted when his most famous play, *The Playboy of the Western World*, was staged for the first time in the Abbey Theatre in 1907. The hero, Christy Mahon, thinks that he has killed his father, and the play contains a criticism of the narrow-minded behaviour of some country people of the time. Nationalists were outraged at a supposed slur on the Irish country people. When they rioted against the play, Trinity College students defended it. Yeats came on stage to condemn the rioters and called for the right of freedom of expression.

THE LITERARY REVIVAL AND THE CAUSE OF IRISH FREEDOM

The *Playboy* riots revealed some of the difficulties facing those involved in the Literary Revival. Was a writer's first duty to the art of writing or to Ireland? Whereas Yeats and the other leading figures stressed the importance of freedom of speech and devotion to the art of writing, many nationalists believed that plays should be part of a propaganda scheme praising Ireland and denigrating England, and indeed supporting the call for Irish independence.

As with the GAA and the Gaelic League, many of those involved in the Irish Literary Theatre were advanced nationalists. A notable Abbey actor, Seán Connolly, was killed in the attack on Dublin Castle on Easter Monday in 1916. Maud Gonne was to the forefront of the women's section of the independence movement during and after 1916. Consequently, while the Irish

Literary Theatre produced plays that were brilliant works of literature in their own right, at the same time the Literary Revival contributed to the rise of cultural nationalism. This in turn contributed to the increasing demand for self-determination in Ireland after 1900.

D.P. Moran and Irish Ireland

Irish identity was one of the main issues in the cultural revival from the 1880s onwards. Douglas Hyde and W.B. Yeats believed that all people living in Ireland belonged to the Irish nation. As we have seen, Hyde believed that the Irish language belonged to Catholics and Protestants alike, and Yeats considered Anglo-Irish literature the property of all Irish people. However, some people in Ireland at the time had a much narrower concept of Irishness. They believed that only Catholics and Irish speakers were truly Irish. The main spokesman for this point of view was a journalist named D.P. Moran.

Moran was born in Waterford in 1871 and later emigrated to London. Having returned to Ireland in 1898, he joined the Gaelic League and founded his own newspaper, *The Leader*, in 1900. In the pages of *The Leader* and in his book, *The Philosophy of Irish Ireland* (1905), Moran propagated his views. His main idea was that there was 'a battle of two civilisations' between Catholic Ireland and Protestant England. He therefore defended the Irish language and the Catholic religion and condemned Protestants living in Ireland, whom he regarded as part of the English occupation.

Moran particularly attacked the Irish Literary Theatre because some of its leaders, such as Yeats and Lady Gregory, were Protestants. He also detested the plays of Synge and supported the rioters against *The Playboy of the Western World*. In his view, works such as this did not portray Irish country people properly.

Moran's style of writing was characterised by satire and mockery. He invented sectarian and divisive terms such as 'Sourface' (for Protestant) and 'Shoneen' (for West Briton, a follower of England). His writings were popular among sections of the Catholic lower middle class, including priests, office workers and teachers. Many of these resented Protestant dominance of government positions and of office jobs in banking, insurance and industry. Moran conducted a newspaper campaign calling for an increase in Catholic participation in these sectors.

Although his appeal was limited, Moran's writings alarmed many Protestants. Indeed from around 1910 onwards, many of them began to withdraw from the cultural revival, and the sectarian nature of Moran's Irish Ireland philosophy was particularly unfortunate at a time when Protestants in most of Ireland were already feeling under threat owing to the expected arrival of Home Rule.

KEY PERSONALITY: W.B. YEATS (1865–1939)

William Butler Yeats was born in Dublin of a Sligo family in 1865. Two years later, his family moved to London, where his father earned a meagre living as a portrait painter. The family returned to Ireland in 1881, and Yeats attended the High School in Harcourt Street. He failed to gain entrance to Trinity College and in 1884 joined the Metropolitan School of Art, where he met George Russell. In the late 1880s Yeats came into contact with the Fenian John O'Leary and with the historian and folklorist Standish James O'Grady. Through them, he became increasingly interested in Irish history, tradition and folklore.

A key figure in the Anglo-Irish literary movement, Yeats, together with Lady Gregory and Edward Martyn, founded the Irish Literary Theatre in 1899. The first work staged by the theatre was Yeats's play *The Countess Cathleen*. In 1902 Yeats's revolutionary play, *Cathleen Ni Houlihan*, was staged. In this play, which stirred nationalist feelings, Ireland is portrayed as an old woman who is rejuvenated into a beautiful young girl who urges her young men to take up arms on her behalf. In later years, Yeats wondered about the emotional impact of his play when he wrote,

> Did that play of mine send out
> Certain men the English shot?

The title role was played by Maud Gonne, with whom Yeats had fallen passionately in love but who rejected his repeated offers of marriage.

In 1904 the Abbey Theatre became the home of the Irish Literary Theatre. The first play produced at the new theatre was Yeats's *On Baile's Strand* (1904), the first of his plays to feature the Celtic hero Cúchulainn. Yeats continued to write controversial plays with Irish themes, drawing extensively on Irish myth and folklore. He also encouraged new Irish playwrights, most notably J.M. Synge, whose *Playboy of the Western World* he vehemently defended during riots at the theatre in 1907.

As a poet and playwright, Yeats's contribution to the creation of a distinct Irish literature in the English language was enormous. While the Literary Revival inspired Irish patriotism, some nationalists criticised the movement as not truly Irish because it contained too many Protestants and was influenced by the Ascendancy class. Yeats himself became increasingly disillusioned with the apparent small-mindedness of the Irish, as illustrated during the *Playboy* riots and the refusal to build an art gallery to house the Hugh Lane art collection.

Yeats married Georgie Hyde-Lees in 1917. In 1922 he was made a senator of the Irish Free State and in 1923 was awarded the Nobel Prize for Literature. After travelling extensively in southern Europe, he settled in south Dublin with his wife and two children. In 1938 he visited the south of France, where he died on 28 January 1939. His remains were brought back to his beloved Sligo.

ORDINARY LEVEL

1. Write a paragraph on the influence of Cardinal Paul Cullen on the Catholic Church in Ireland.

2. Explain how each of the following developments helped to strengthen the position of the Catholic Church in Ireland after 1850:

   • Population changes.

   • Decline in the power of the landlords.

   • Decline of the Irish language.

3. Write an account of primary education in Ireland in the late nineteenth century.

4. Outline the development of secondary education in Ireland between 1870 and 1914.

5. What is meant by the expression 'the University Question'? Outline the efforts made by successive British governments to deal with this issue.

6. Write a paragraph on the part played by Michael Cusack in the development of Gaelic games.

7. Account for the foundation of the Gaelic League in 1893, and list its main aims.

8. Write a paragraph on Douglas Hyde.

9. Outline the role of William Butler Yeats in the Anglo-Irish Literary Revival.

10. Write a paragraph on D.P. Moran and Irish Ireland.

HIGHER LEVEL

1. Account for the growing power of the Catholic Church in Ireland in the late nineteenth century.

2. Consider the developments in education in Ireland at all three levels between 1870 and 1914.

3. Analyse critically the foundation and development of the Gaelic Athletic Association (GAA) up to 1900.

4. Consider the part played by the Gaelic League, the GAA and the Anglo-Irish Literary Revival in Irish life up to 1914.

5. Read the following contrasting views on Irish identity and answer the questions that follow.

   (a) D.P. Moran

   When we look out on Ireland we see that those who believe...in Ireland as a nation are, as a matter of fact, Catholics. When we look back on history we find also, as a matter of fact, that those who stood during the last three hundred years for Ireland as an Irish entity were mainly Catholics, and that those who sought to corrupt them and trample on them were mainly non-Catholics.

   The Leader, 27 July 1901

   (b) Douglas Hyde to Lady Gregory

   The fact is that we cannot turn our back on the Davis ideal of every person in Ireland being an Irishman, no matter what their blood and politics, for the moment we cease to profess that, we land ourselves in an intolerable position...The Gaelic League and *The Leader* aim at stimulating the old peasant, Papist aboriginal population, and we care very little about the others, though I would not let this be seen as Moran has done.

   Douglas Hyde to Lady Gregory, 7 January 1901, quoted in L.P. Curtis Jr., Anglo-Saxons and Celts, New York University Press: 1968, 147

   (i) According to D.P. Moran, which religious denomination contained true believers in the Irish nation?

   (ii) How does Moran use his version of the history of the preceding three hundred years to justify his connection between religion and Irish nationalism?

   (iii) According to Douglas Hyde, what was the 'ideal' of Thomas Davis?

   (iv) In Hyde's view which group in Ireland was targeted by the Gaelic League and *The Leader*?

   (v) What distinction does Hyde draw between himself and D.P. Moran?

7. INDUSTRIAL DEVELOPMENT AND SOCIAL CHANGE: TRADE UNIONS AND SUFFRAGETTES

Industrial Development in Ireland

Ireland in 1870 was a predominantly agricultural society. This absence of industrial development was due to a combination of factors:

> 1 Raw materials such as coal and iron were not available in sufficient quantity.
> 2 The population had declined substantially since the Famine.
> 3 Few entrepreneurs were willing to invest capital in Irish industry.
> 4 Competition from cheaper mass-produced imported goods undermined Irish industry.
> 5 Small Irish industries failed to modernise and adopt new technologies.

Throughout most of Ireland, towns and villages were heavily dependent on agriculture. In times of agricultural depression, local towns suffered and only recovered when farmers prospered once again.

In contrast to other European countries, most of Ireland actually experienced a period of industrial decline in the second half of the nineteenth century. Export-oriented industries such as brewing and distilling were an exception to this trend. The most famous of these companies was the Dublin-based firm of Arthur Guinness & Co., which exported beer throughout the world. The Guinness brewery, and distilleries such as Jameson's, provided well-paid, secure employment. However, because of new

The British Army on parade in Grafton Street, Dublin, around 1900. Ireland's principal city was a centre of government, law, trade and commerce, rather than of industrial development.

technology, the numbers employed were not large. In 1914 Guinness, which produced two-thirds of Ireland's beer, needed only 2,000 workers. In contrast to the situation in Guinness, most employment in Dublin was casual, unskilled and poorly paid. In reality, Dublin was a centre of trade and commerce, with little industrial development. Provincial cities such as Cork, Limerick and Waterford were even less developed. Their economic activity centred around the ports, and they provided markets for local agricultural produce.

The industrial decline experienced in most of the country was in marked contrast to the economic growth and prosperity enjoyed by north-east Ulster and the city of Belfast.

Belfast – City of Industry

Belfast was a thriving industrial city by the late nineteenth century. In this regard it had much more in common with cities such as Manchester and Glasgow than with Dublin or Cork. The industrial development of Belfast and the Lagan Valley was due to the following factors:

1 Coal and iron were readily available, as they could be imported from Britain.
2 Migration of people into Belfast provided labour for industries.
3 Entrepreneurs were willing to invest capital in industrial development.
4 Free trade between Ireland and the rest of the United Kingdom facilitated the import of raw materials and the export of finished products.
5 Industries were willing to adapt to new technologies.

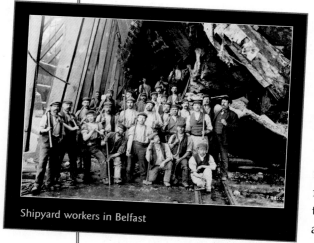
Shipyard workers in Belfast

The industrial prosperity of the north-east was based on a long tradition dating back to the eighteenth century and centred around the textile industry. Linen in particular was the main textile produced in Ulster. Flax was spun and woven in linen mills in Belfast, Derry and other Ulster towns. In 1900 over 60,000 workers were employed in the linen industry. The shirt-making industry, centred largely in the Derry area, was an offshoot of the linen industry. Shirt-making in 1900 employed around 20,000 full-time workers, mostly poorly paid women. At this stage textiles remained the largest single source of employment in Irish industry, accounting for around one-third of all workers.

Conditions in linen mills and shirt factories were quite harsh. Nearly 70 per cent of workers were women and children, who worked long hours for low wages. The damp, warm atmosphere, together with the presence of flax dust in the air, frequently led to tuberculosis and other lung diseases. Workers were fined for being late or for singing at work. However, compared with the rest of Ireland, where employment opportunities were scarce, many working-class families in Ulster counted themselves fortunate to have more than one wage-earner in the family.

Along with linen, the other major industry in Belfast was shipbuilding, which was a spectacular example of a successful Irish industry.

Shipbuilding in Belfast

Between 1870 and 1914 the city of Belfast was one of the greatest shipbuilding centres in the world. This position of strength developed from small beginnings when a shipyard was opened in 1853. The new industry owed its success to the insight and ability of the British businessman Edward Harland and his associate, G.W. Wolff. Harland attracted outside capital investment and won a crucial contract with a Liverpool shipping company. A key factor in the expansion of the Harland & Wolff shipyard was the adoption of the latest technology. Although the raw materials of coal and iron had to be imported, as time went on an increasing number of local companies emerged to supply the shipyard with materials such as engines and ropes.

Harland & Wolff supplied the famous White Star Line with luxury liners, one such being the ill-fated *Titanic*, which sank in 1912. By 1914 the company employed over 12,000 workers, and a second Belfast shipyard, Workman, Clark & Co., employed a further 3,000. However, the economic importance of the ship-building industry extended far beyond the shipyards themselves. The flourishing Belfast shipyards were responsible for the presence in the city of a host of ancillary industries, particularly in the area of engineering. The success of the industry also encouraged Ulster people to be proud of their industrial achievement. As unionists linked this to the economic conditions provided by the Act of Union, Belfast's industrial prosperity was to be a powerful argument in their campaign against Home Rule.

A ship under constuction at the Belfast shipyard of Harland & Wolff

The *Titanic* in dock before her first and only voyage across the Atlantic

Although north-east Ulster contained Ireland's only heavily industrialised area around 1900, it did not become the main focus of trade union activity as workers struggled for better wages and conditions. For various reasons the trade union movement began in the less industrialised city of Dublin.

LIVING AND WORKING CONDITIONS IN DUBLIN

Dublin around 1900 was a city of deep divisions between rich and poor. A minority of people, who made their wealth from business or the professions, lived lives of luxury and could afford to employ domestic servants. Although the majority of people were working-class, there were sharp contrasts between skilled and unskilled workers. Skilled workers or tradesmen enjoyed higher pay and more secure employment than the unskilled. In turn skilled workers enjoyed the protection of craft organisations and trade unions, which were frequently British-based.

Unskilled workers, however, were paid much lower wages than their counterparts in England. Because of the vast oversupply of unskilled labour in Dublin, employers could pay low wages and hire practically at will. For general labourers such as carters and dockers, short-time working was the norm; they were frequently employed on a casual day-by-day basis. Unlike in north-east Ulster and Britain, industrial employment for women and children was practically non-existent in Dublin.

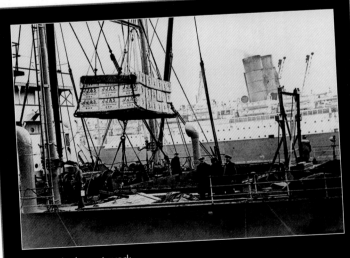

Dublin dockers at work

Most unskilled workers and their families in Dublin lived in one-room tenements. As late as 1914 over 20,000 families – amounting to one-third of the city's population – lived in these conditions. Weekly wages were barely sufficient to pay for rent and food. Because of the unsanitary conditions in the slums, death from diseases such as tuberculosis was a constant threat. Death rates among infants and children were among the highest of any city in Europe at the time.

A street in the Dublin slums around 1900

Unlike skilled workers, the unskilled labourers of Dublin were completely unorganised and unrepresented by trade unions. Two men set about the task of organising Irish labourers to struggle for better working and living conditions – James Connolly and James Larkin.

The Growth of the Irish Labour Movement

JAMES CONNOLLY AND IRISH SOCIALISM

James Connolly was born into a family of poor Irish immigrants in Edinburgh in 1868. Having worked at different odd jobs since the age of eleven, he joined the British army in 1882. As he was only fourteen at the time, he gave a false age to the authorities. Connolly's first visit to Ireland occurred when his regiment was stationed there. After his marriage in Dublin in 1890, he left the army and returned to Edinburgh, where he worked as a carter for the corporation.

Connolly was largely self-educated: he read widely in the area of politics and economics and learned foreign languages in order to broaden his knowledge. He followed the career of Parnell with interest and joined the Edinburgh branch of the Irish National League. Irish nationalism, defined as a belief in Ireland's right to independence, was one of Connolly's two principal interests throughout his life. The other was socialism.

Influenced by the deep inequalities in the society around him, James Connolly became a socialist at an early stage. He read the writings of Karl Marx and was convinced that the working classes could never prosper under the existing capitalist system. He was also strongly influenced by John Leslie, a leading Scottish socialist. When he stood as a socialist candidate for Edinburgh Corporation and failed to be elected, he was dismissed from his job as a corporation carter. He was considering emigrating to America when he was offered a position of organiser by the Dublin Socialist Society at a salary of £1 a week. He accepted the offer and returned to Dublin in 1896.

Although the salary was barely adequate for his young family, he persevered with the task of spreading socialism in Ireland. As he believed that the cause of workers in Ireland was linked to that of national independence, he set up the Irish Socialist Republican Party

An outing to the races by tram for Dubliners who could afford it

(ISRP) in 1896 with the aim of achieving a completely independent republic run on socialist principles, where the people would collectively own the land, factories, banks and means of transport. In 1898 Connolly founded a newspaper, the *Workers' Republic*, which was not a success. Although he was developing a reputation among socialists abroad, he gained few followers in Ireland. Indeed many people associated him more with nationalist protests against British royalty than with his socialist programme. Owing mainly to continuing poverty, he emigrated with his family to the USA in 1903. He was to remain there, working as a trade union organiser, until 1910.

Connolly longed to return to Ireland, however, and an opportunity arose when he was offered the position of secretary of the Belfast branch of the Irish Transport and General Workers' Union (ITGWU). He organised a successful dockers' strike in Belfast in 1911 and succeeded in bringing about better conditions for female workers in the linen mills. Because of his three years in Belfast, he returned to Dublin in 1913 with an enhanced reputation as a successful trade union organiser. At this stage Dublin was in the throes of a gigantic struggle between employers and workers that was the culmination of the efforts of one man – James Larkin.

James Larkin and the ITGWU

James Larkin was born in Liverpool of Irish parents in 1876. After a short spell at sea he worked as a docker in Liverpool. He had a natural gift for holding the attention of audiences by means of his powerful speeches. This helped him advance in the trade union movement, and in 1907 he was sent to Belfast as local leader of the British-based National Union of Dock Labourers. He soon organised a strike among dockers and transport workers. Here for the first time he used one of his most famous tactics – the sympathetic strike, in which workers not initially involved would come out in sympathy with their fellow workers who were on strike. Although the Belfast strike was a modest success, Larkin's bosses in England believed that his tactics were too costly, and they transferred him to Dublin.

The challenge facing Larkin in Dublin was a huge one. In 1900, out of an estimated 40,000 male manual workers, only 10,000 were skilled. Of the remainder, 7,000 were dockers or carters, and 23,000 were casual labourers. Because casual workers were often hired only on a daily basis, employers were extremely powerful. If they suspected a worker of attempting to organise others to struggle for improved conditions, he was 'blacklisted'. This meant that no employer would give him a job, and he and his family faced the workhouse or emigration. Against this background and in circumstances of widespread poverty, Larkin believed nevertheless that the workers' only hope lay in being organised in trade unions. When the British-based Dockers' Union suspended him, he set up his own trade union in 1908. Known as the **Irish Transport and General Workers' Union (ITGWU)**, it soon spread from Dublin and attracted members in Belfast, Cork and Limerick. Unlike most existing unions, which were British-based and catered for skilled workers, the ITGWU catered for both skilled and unskilled members. It was openly socialist in its aims, reflecting the fact that Larkin shared Connolly's belief that the working classes would always be exploited under the capitalist system. Both Connolly and Larkin approved of a socialist idea known as syndicalism, which was widely discussed at the time. According to the theory of syndicalism, workers should organise themselves into huge unions and call general strikes, which would lead to the collapse of the capitalist system in various countries. While this theory was far removed from the realities of everyday living, it gave the enemies of Connolly and Larkin an opportunity to claim that they were dangerous revolutionaries plotting to overthrow existing society.

The Foundation of the Irish Labour Party (1912)

At the start the ITGWU encountered difficulties and lost a number of strikes. Larkin was imprisoned for four months in 1910 after a strike in Cork. However, in 1911 his fortunes began to improve, and he organised a series of successful strikes involving carters and railway workers.

In 1912 Connolly and Larkin co-operated to found the Irish Labour Party. They believed that a Home Rule Parliament was on the way and that trade unions were only one part of the workers' movement. In the view of both labour leaders, a political struggle was also vital, and the new Irish Labour Party would have an important role to play in representing the workers' point of view.

As Larkin became more successful as a trade union organiser, the fortunes of the ITGWU improved. Its membership rose from 4,000 in 1911 to over 10,000 by 1913. This trend alarmed the employers, who had begun to organise a collective response to the challenges posed by Larkin and his union.

William Martin Murphy and the Dublin Employers

In response to the growing threat posed by Larkin and the ITGWU, in 1911 the employers of Dublin formed their own organisation, the Dublin Employers' Association. Its leader was

How one of William Martin's campaign papers reported Larkin's activities in August 1913

William Martin Murphy, a highly successful Catholic businessman. Murphy, from Bantry in Co. Cork, had earlier been a Home Rule MP at Westminster. In 1913 he was chairman of the Dublin United Tramway Company and owner of Clery's department store and the Imperial Hotel. He also controlled the *Irish Independent* newspaper. Although kind and charitable in his private life, Murphy was opposed to trade unions intervening between employers and workers. He particularly objected to Larkin, whom he regarded as a dangerous revolutionary.

In July 1913 Murphy presided over a meeting of 300 Dublin employers at which a decision was taken to force workers to sign the following undertaking:

> I hereby undertake to carry out all instructions given me by or on behalf of my employers, and further, I agree to resign immediately my membership of the Irish Transport and General Workers' Union, and I further undertake that I will not join or in any way support the Union.

Larkin responded to this threat by planning a general strike among the workers of Dublin.

CASE STUDY: DUBLIN, 1913 – STRIKE AND LOCKOUT

The first workers to be called out on strike by Larkin belonged to the Dublin United Tramway Company, of which William Martin Murphy was chairman. The date for the commencement of the strike, Tuesday, 26 August 1913, was chosen carefully. It was the beginning of Horse Show Week in Dublin, one of the busiest days of the year in the city's social calendar. Shortly before 10.00 a.m. on that day, trams were stopped in their tracks as members of Larkin's union went on strike. In all, around 700 out of 1,700 tram workers joined the strike. The response of William Martin Murphy and many other Dublin employers was immediate and drastic. They decided to close the doors of their businesses and lock out the workers. A total of about 20,000 workers and 300 employers were involved in the lockout.

That same evening, 26 August 1913, Larkin addressed a group of striking tramway workers outside Liberty Hall, the headquarters of the Irish Transport and General Workers' Union (Document 1).

Document 1

It is not a strike, it is a lockout of the men, who have been tyrannically treated by a most unscrupulous scoundrel. Murphy has boasted that he will beat Larkin . . . He said he would spend £100,000 to break Larkin, a man who is going to lead you out of bondage into the land of promise.

William Martin Murphy has stated that the cars are running, but I would ask, how many are running? I hope that no working-man will go into them. The cars are taken off the street at seven o'clock. Murphy is a coward . . .

If one of our class should fall then two of the others must fall in for that one. We must demonstrate in O'Connell Street. It is our street as well as William Martin Murphy's. We are fighting for bread and butter. We will hold our meetings in the street and if any one of our men fall, there must be justice. By the living God, if they want war, they can have it.

James Larkin, *Irish Times*, 27 August 1913

The following morning all of the Dublin newspapers contained an interview given by William Martin Murphy, in which he vigorously condemned his opponent, James Larkin (Document 2).

Document 2

Mr Larkin's so-called 'strike' today was the feeblest and most contemptible attempt that was ever made. I expected that when his strike came, if it came at all, it might last a day, but it was actually broken within half an hour after Larkin's 'orders' were issued . . .

I became aware six weeks ago that Larkin was getting some of the motormen and conductors . . . into his meshes by inducing them to attend midnight meetings and making violent addresses attacking the Tramway Company. I did not leave all the talking to Mr Larkin but invited the men to meet myself . . . That meeting checked Larkin's inroad on the men, and his influence amongst them has steadily waned since then . . .

Larkin has tried to hold up our coal supply without success, and even if there was a temporary stoppage, the stock we hold would last . . . months . . .

I think I have broken the malign influence of Mr Larkin and set him on the run. It is now up to the employers to keep him going.

Interview with William Martin Murphy, *Irish Times*, 27 August 1913

Document 3

My fight is not against trade unionism but against Larkinism . . . This is the most pestilential 'ism' that any community could be affected with. The so-called Transport Union is not a union at all. It is merely a rabble commanded by Larkin, who is the greatest enemy of trade unionism. He calls men out on strike when it suits his game, without asking whether they like it or not, and they are so terrorised by this man's mob that they blindly obey. He then telephones to the employer and if he can get recognised he will let the employer off very cheaply and order his dupes, whom he has betrayed, back again to work . . .

I never set eyes on him, but I am told that he is a big man wearing a slouched hat, and with a swaggering style, throwing downstairs any smaller than himself, and giving the impression of great physical courage. I notice, however, that whenever there is any trouble in the wind, he is not to be found where his skin would be in any danger.

Interview with William Martin Murphy,
Evening Herald, **27 August 1913**

Pleased with the response to his first newspaper interview, Murphy gave another to an *Evening Herald* reporter (Document 3). Larkin announced that he would address a public meeting in O'Connell Street on Sunday, 31 August. Although banned by the police, the meeting went ahead. Larkin, disguised with a beard, entered the Imperial Hotel, which was owned by William Martin Murphy. He briefly addressed the crowd from a first-floor balcony of the hotel before being arrested by the police. In the uproar that followed, the police panicked and made a number of heavy baton charges against the crowd, which resulted in the deaths of two people and injuries to hundreds.

The following photographs from 31 August 1913 show riots and the arrest of Larkin (Document 4).

DOCUMENT 4

Police charge protesting workers during the 1913 Lockout

James Larkin in disguise being arrested

One of those present that day in O'Connell Street was Ernie O'Malley, who later played a prominent role in the War of Independence. He has left an eyewitness account of the events of this day (Document 5).

Document 5

I was in O'Connell Street one evening when Jim Larkin, to keep a promise, appeared on the balcony of the hotel, wearing a beard as a disguise. He spoke amidst cheers, the hoots for the employers. Police swept down from many quarters, hemmed in the crowd, and used their heavy batons on anyone who came in their way. I saw women knocked down and kicked – I scurried up a side street; at the other end the police struck people as they lay injured on the ground, struck them again and again. I could hear the crunch as the heavy sticks struck unprotected skulls. I was in favour of the strikers.

Ernie O'Malley

Following the events of 31 August 1913, Dublin was plunged into a state of great unrest. Larkin was imprisoned following his arrest, and attitudes on both sides in the dispute became deeply entrenched. The struggle that followed involved 20,000 workers and their 80,000 dependants, who endured great hardship. Help for the workers came from trade unions in England, and local sympathisers such as Countess Markievicz set up food kitchens to feed the starving workers and their families. Many of the writers who led the cultural revival supported the workers in their struggle for better conditions. The letter written to the newspapers by George Russell (Æ) was a good example of this support (Document 6).

THE DISPUTE CONTINUES

As the dispute continued, supporters of Larkin in England offered to take starving Dublin children into their homes. Although Larkin was in favour of this, it led to fierce opposition from the Catholic Church. While Archbishop William Walsh of Dublin and many priests were sympathetic to the plight of the workers, they were strongly opposed to Connolly and Larkin because of their socialism. The Catholic Church regarded socialism as a serious threat to the wellbeing of society. The plan to send children to England led to fears that they might lose their Catholic faith. Archbishop Walsh wrote a public letter condemning the proposal (Document 7).

Document 6

It remained for the twentieth century and the capital city of Ireland to see four hundred masters deciding openly upon starving one hundred thousand people, and refusing to consider any solution except that fixed by their pride. You, masters, asked men to do that which masters of labour in any other city in these islands had not dared to do. You insolently demanded of those men who were members of a trade union that they should resign from that union: and from those who were not members you insisted on a vow that they would never join it.

You may succeed in your policy and ensure your own damnation by your victory. The men whose manhood you have broken will loathe you, and will always be brooding and scheming to strike a fresh blow. The children will be taught to curse you. The infant being moulded in the womb will have breathed into its starved body the vitality of hate. It is not they – it is you who are blind Samsons pulling down the pillars of the social order.

Letter of George Russell (Æ), 6 October 1913

Document 7

Dear Sir

I have read with nothing short of consternation in some of our evening newspapers that a movement is on foot, and has already made some progress, to induce the wives of the working men who are now unemployed by reason of the present deplorable industrial deadlock in Dublin, to hand over their children to be cared for in England by persons of whom they, of course, can have no knowledge whatsoever.

The Dublin women now subjected to this cruel temptation to part with their helpless offspring are, in the majority of cases, Catholics. Have they abandoned their Faith? Surely not. Well, if they have not, they should need no words of mine to remind them of the plain duty of every Catholic mother in such a case. I can only put it to them that they can be no longer held worthy of the name of Catholic mothers, if they so far forget that duty as to send away their little children to be cared for in a strange land, without security of any kind that those to whom the poor children are to be handed over are Catholics, or indeed are persons of any faith at all.

I am much mistaken if this recent and most mischievous development of our labour trouble in Dublin fails to appeal to all who are involved in the conflict, employers or employed as they may be, or fails to move them to strive with all earnestness to bring the conflict to an end.

Letter of Archbishop William J. Walsh, 20 October 1913

Archbishop Walsh's pious hope at the end of the letter – that the issue of the starving children would lead to a quicker resolution of the conflict – failed to be realised. In effect the children were victims not merely of the employer–worker conflict but also of rivalry between Catholics and Protestants. At the time proselytism, the attempt to convert people, especially children, was widespread. The issue of sending children to England was therefore an extremely sensitive one. The plan had to be dropped after violent scenes at the dockside and at railway stations, when groups of Catholic priests and their supporters prevented the departure of the children.

THE CITIZEN ARMY

As winter approached, deadlock had set in in the dispute. A Commission of Enquiry appointed by the British government failed to bring about a resolution when the employers ignored its recommendations. In November 1913 a workers' defence group known as the Irish Citizen Army was set up by James Connolly. Its purpose was to protect workers in clashes with the police, and it had its headquarters in Liberty Hall. It soon became a familiar sight on the streets of Dublin, with its special uniform and its own flag containing the plough and the stars.

THE END OF THE DISPUTE

Although the Citizen Army could help raise the morale of the workers, nothing could prevent their complete defeat. When British trade unions failed to come out in sympathetic strike with the Dublin workers, it was clear that the dispute could not last much longer. On 18 January 1914 Larkin and other leaders of the ITGWU held a secret meeting at which they decided to advise workers to return to work, without signing the employers' document, if that were possible. Over the next few weeks, workers drifted back to their jobs all over Dublin, mostly on the employers' terms. The following October James Larkin left Ireland for America, where he remained until 1923.

It appeared to be a total defeat for the workers, and Larkin and Connolly were very bitter at the time. In February 1914 Connolly wrote:

> And so we Irish workers must go down into Hell, bow our backs to the lash of the slave-driver . . . and eat the dust of defeat and betrayal.

THE CONSEQUENCES OF THE 1913 STRIKE AND LOCKOUT

However, the consequences of the Dublin strike and lockout of 1913 were far from being totally favourable to the employers. The horrific living conditions in the slums had been highlighted, leading to future attempts at slum clearance. Larkin and Connolly had instilled a spirit of self-respect in their followers in the face of overwhelming difficulties. Soon after the return to work in 1914, many employees drifted back into the ITGWU. Most employers chose to ignore this, as they could not risk another lengthy dispute. Never again would employers in Dublin be able to treat workers in such a fashion. The Citizen Army that was founded in the middle of the dispute was to play an important role in the Easter Rising of 1916.

In assessing the impact of the events in Dublin in 1913–14, it is important to see them in the context of the time. Widespread turmoil existed in other areas as well, where people adopted militant stances and were eager for confrontation with their opponents. This is very obvious in the political sphere, where unionists and nationalists confronted one another over the issue of Home Rule for Ireland. However, around 1910 a challenge to the existing order in society came from an unexpected source – women who were demanding their rights through direct action.

COMPREHENSION

1. What promise does James Larkin make to his followers in Document 1?

2. According to Larkin, what was William Martin Murphy willing to do to break the strike?

3. Give two examples of war imagery used by Larkin to describe the struggle of the Dublin workers (Document 1).

4. In Document 2, what evidence does William Martin Murphy give to prove his statement concerning the weakness of the strike?

5. What important step did Murphy take to reduce Larkin's influence over the workers?

6. What claim does William Martin Murphy make at the start of Document 3?

7. What accusation does he make concerning Larkin's power over the workers?

8. Explain how Murphy accuses Larkin of personal cowardice in Document 3.

9. What do you learn of the events in Dublin on 31 August 1913 from studying the photographs (Document 4)?

10. In Document 5 the writer remarks, 'I was in favour of the strikers.' Give two examples from the document to prove the truth of this assertion.

11. How did Larkin disguise himself?

12. Explain the accusation made by the writer at the opening of Document 6.

13. What was the demand made by the Dublin employers, according to the writer of Document 6?

14. The writer says that even if the employers win the dispute, they will regret it. Explain his reasoning.

15. Explain the reference to Samson in Document 6.

16. What led the author of Document 7 to write this public letter?

17. What, according to the writer, is the 'plain duty' of every Catholic mother?

18. What hope is expressed at the end of the letter?

COMPARISON

1. Compare the point of view expressed in Document 1 with the opposite viewpoint expressed in Documents 2 and 3.

2. Pick out examples of exaggeration used in these documents, and compare them.

3. Does the visual evidence in Document 4 agree with the verbal evidence in Document 5? Explain your answer.

4. Compare the tone and content of Document 1 and Document 6.

CRITICISM

1. Assess the value of the eyewitness account contained in Document 5.

2. How valuable is Document 1 as a primary source in conveying the tension and excitement of events as they occurred?

3. Would you regard Documents 2 and 3 as biased or partisan contributions? Explain your answer.

4. What evidence can you deduce that the writer of Document 6 was a poet?

5. Which of the documents did you find most informative? Explain your choice.

CONTEXTUALISATION

1. Outline the living and working conditions that existed in Dublin in 1913.

2. Write an account of the part played by James Larkin in Dublin in 1913.

3. Explain in detail the attitudes and actions of William Martin Murphy and the Dublin employers during the 1913 strike and lockout.

4. Write a paragraph on the conclusion of the strike and lockout and on the consequences that followed.

KEY PERSONALITY: JAMES LARKIN (1876–1947)

James Larkin was born in Liverpool in 1876 to Irish parents. He went to live with his grandparents in Newry in 1881. He returned to Liverpool in 1885 and began work as a labourer. He became a dock foreman and organiser of the National Union of Dock Labourers. In 1907 he organised a strike among the dockers in Belfast and founded a Dublin branch of the National Union of Dock Labourers. In both Belfast and Dublin, Larkin had established himself as a charismatic and fearless labour leader who was more than willing to use the strike weapon in his campaign for improved conditions for workers.

In his efforts to organise the workers in Dublin, he established the ITGWU in 1908. Along with James Connolly, he was a founder member in 1912 of the Independent Labour Party of Ireland. In the same year he was elected to Dublin Corporation. As the chief organiser of the 1913 strike and lockout, Larkin revealed his combative and aggressive style in his clashes with the employers and the authorities. He was an impassioned orator who incited the workers not to submit.

Although the strike and lockout ended in failure, it established Larkin as a major trade union leader. In October 1914, disillusioned by developments, he left for the USA, where he remained until 1923. While in the USA, he engaged in extensive trade union activities and was imprisoned for a brief period. From prison he denounced the Anglo-Irish Treaty, which brought the War of Independence to an end.

Larkin returned to Ireland in 1923 and struggled to regain control of the ITGWU, now under the leadership of William O'Brien. He lost this battle and was expelled from the union. In June 1924 he founded a rival union, the Workers' Union of Ireland, and remained its general secretary until his death in 1947. He was also in conflict with the Irish Labour Party, partly because of its close association with the ITGWU. The split in the Irish labour movement, centred on the personalities of Larkin and O'Brien, was to remain intensely bitter.

Larkin was elected to the Dáil as an Independent Labour TD in 1926–32 and 1937–8. He strongly opposed two government measures, a Wages Standstill Order and the Trade Union Act, which sought to limit the powers of trade unions. In the belief that labour must unite against these measures, he rejoined the Labour Party in 1941 and was elected Labour TD in 1943–4. His candidature had been strongly opposed by O'Brien, who left the Labour Party in 1944 to form his own group, National Labour.

The split in the labour movement was partly healed by the retirement of O'Brien from the ITGWU in 1946 and the death a year later of James Larkin. Larkin had been a leading voice in the Irish labour movement for forty years. His greatest strength during the early years of trade union activity – his uncompromising, combative style of leadership – was also his greatest weakness in the latter years, contributing in no small way to the bitter divisions within the labour movement.

KEY PERSONALITY: JAMES CONNOLLY (1868–1916)

James Connolly was born in Edinburgh to Irish parents in 1868. Growing up in poverty, Connolly started work at the age of eleven. After a variety of jobs, he joined the British army in 1882 and remained in the army until 1889. He was largely self-educated and read widely in history and economics. Connolly hated social injustice and at an early age became involved in socialist politics. He advocated the writings of Karl Marx and was greatly influenced by the Scottish socialist John Leslie.

In 1896 Connolly arrived in Dublin as organiser of the Dublin Socialist Society. Under Connolly's influence, the society was dissolved and replaced by a new organisation called the Irish Socialist Republican Party (ISRP). This new party espoused Connolly's twin principles of republicanism and socialism. He believed that socialist reforms would only succeed in Ireland following the overthrow of British rule.

However, despite Connolly's efforts, the ISRP received little support from Irish workers or other nationalist organisations. Nevertheless, during his seven years in Dublin from 1896 to 1903, he was actively involved in socialist and nationalist politics. His writings appeared in the *Workers' Republic*, a socialist newspaper he edited in 1898–9.

In 1903 Connolly accepted an invitation to work in the USA. During his stay in America from 1903 to 1910, he became involved in union and lecturing activities. He returned to Ireland in 1910 and the following year became organiser in Belfast for the ITGWU. While in Belfast, he was involved in the dockers' strike in 1911 and also succeeded in obtaining improved working conditions for the women in the linen mills.

Connolly worked closely with Larkin to develop the labour movement in Ireland. In 1912 the Irish Socialist Republican Party became the Independent Labour Party of Ireland, forerunner of the present Labour Party. Connolly played a very significant role in the 1913 strike and lockout in Dublin. In November 1913 he established the Irish Citizen Army, founded to protect the workers in clashes with the police. Following Larkin's departure to the USA in 1914, he became acting general secretary of the ITGWU and editor of the revived *Workers' Republic*.

Connolly vehemently opposed the outbreak of war in Europe because, as a socialist, he hated the prospect of workers fighting against one another. He was increasingly convinced of the need for rebellion against British rule in Ireland. After some initial disagreements, his Citizen Army joined forces with the Irish Volunteers to stage a rebellion in Dublin on Easter Monday 1916. As commander of the Dublin forces in the GPO, Connolly remained a huge driving force behind the Rising until he was gravely wounded. He was executed on 12 May 1916.

As a passionate advocate of social justice, Connolly played a major role in the development of the Irish labour movement. His most significant achievement was to combine in a single movement the two doctrines of socialism and nationalism.

The Status of Women

Women street traders

In 1870 Irish women, like their counterparts in Great Britain, had very few rights. Until they married, they were subject to the authority of their fathers; once married, they were expected to obey their husbands. Once a woman married, her husband gained control of her property. Except in Ulster, where women worked in factories, working-class women had few opportunities to earn a living outside the home. In factories and shops women's wages were always much lower than men's. In rural Ireland women were usually unpaid workers on the family farm.

For middle-class women, conditions were also difficult. They were expected to remain at home until married. If they did work at positions such as governess or typist, their salaries were very low.

Regardless of their wealth or level of education, women did not have the right to vote (suffrage) or stand for Parliament. This situation remained unchallenged until the 1870s, when movements developed in Dublin and Belfast to campaign for women's rights.

TWO PIONEERING WOMEN : ISABELLA TOD AND ANNA HASLAM

In 1870 a women's journal in England reported that many letters reached the British Parliament from Ireland seeking for married women the right to own their own property and to vote.

In Belfast the movement for women's rights was led by Isabella Tod (1836–96). Born in Scotland in 1836, she later moved to Belfast, where she founded the Belfast Ladies' Institute in 1867. In 1873 she was the first woman in Ireland to demand that women be admitted to Irish universities. As we have seen in Chapter 6, this demand was partly fulfilled when women were admitted to the new Royal University in 1879. Isabella Tod travelled throughout Ireland spreading the message of women's rights, especially the right to vote.

In Dublin the leader of the women's movement was Anna Haslam (1829–1922), a Quaker, who was born in Youghal, Co. Cork. She and her husband, Thomas, founded the Dublin Women's Suffrage Association in 1876 to demand votes for women. This organisation changed its name a few times until it finally became known from 1901 as the Irish Women's Suffrage and Local Government Association (IWSLGA). Its membership remained quite small and was largely Protestant and middle-class. It agitated for better educational opportunities for women. Whereas its ultimate aim was the attainment for women of the right to vote in parliamentary elections, in the short term it campaigned for women's right to vote in local elections. Anna Haslam and her association also contributed to the campaign for reform of women's property rights.

In 1882 a significant advance in the rights of women took place when Gladstone's Government introduced the Married Women's Property Act. From then on, married women were entitled to possess and inherit property in their own right. As part of the 1898 Local Government Act, which set up county councils in Ireland, female ratepayers were given the right to vote. After this the main outstanding issue was the right of women to vote in parliamentary elections. While the tactics of Anna Haslam's group were essentially peaceful, the impetus for a more militant campaign was to come from England after 1903.

Hanna Sheehy-Skeffington and the Irish Women's Franchise League

A new militancy entered the women's movement when Emmeline Pankhurst established the Women's Social and Political Union in Manchester in 1903. Unlike previous women's movements, which relied on peaceful tactics such as lectures, petitions to Parliament and pamphlets, the new movement was to resort to violent tactics against people and property in the struggle for women's suffrage.

An Irish campaigner for women's rights, Hanna Sheehy, was deeply influenced by Emmeline Pankhurst's movement. In 1903, when she married Frank Skeffington, a convinced supporter of women's rights, they both adopted the name Sheehy-Skeffington. Hanna was an eminent graduate of the Royal University and deeply resented not being able to vote. Like a number of other young, educated women, she joined the IWSLGA. She later commented on this period:

> I was then an undergraduate and was amazed and disgusted to learn that I was classed among criminals, infants and lunatics – in fact that my status as a woman was worse than any of these.

Postcard promoting the cause of votes for Irish women

Dissatisfied with the peaceful tactics and slow progress of the IWSLGA, Hanna Sheehy-Skeffington founded the **Irish Women's Franchise League** (IWFL) in 1908. From the beginning, this new organisation adopted militant tactics like those of the English suffragettes and concentrated on the single aim of achieving women's right to vote.

Violent Tactics

The question of votes for women in Ireland was to the forefront between 1910 and 1914 as suffragettes campaigned to have the right included in the Home Rule Bill. Although some Home Rule MPs were sympathetic, the party's leading figures, John Redmond and John Dillon, were strongly opposed because it could endanger the granting of Home Rule. At the same time, the Government of Prime Minister Herbert Asquith in London was strongly opposed to the campaign of Emmeline Pankhurst and the English suffragettes.

Between 1912 and 1914 Hanna Sheehy-Skeffington and her followers carried out a campaign of violence in support of votes for women. In June 1912 windows of government buildings were smashed, and leading suffragettes were arrested. Like their counterparts in England, some of them went on hunger strike. When Prime Minister Asquith visited Dublin in 1912, the IWFL organised various demonstrations. Unknown to the Irish suffragettes, three English militant campaigners travelled to Dublin, where they attacked Asquith with a hatchet and attempted to set fire to a theatre where he was due to speak. While the IWFL disowned the actions of the English suffragettes, it was associated in the popular mind with violent tactics and aroused much public hostility.

Despite its high profile, only a small minority of Irish women were involved in the suffrage movement. With the outbreak of World War I in 1914, the campaign for female suffrage in Great Britain and Ireland was suspended as the war effort took priority.

WOMEN ATTAIN THE RIGHT TO VOTE

Women finally achieved the right to vote in Great Britain and Ireland at the end of World War I in 1918. Initially only women over thirty could vote, whereas men could vote from the age of twenty-one. In the 1918 general election, the first in which women could participate, Countess Markievicz made history by becoming the first woman elected to the British Parliament. As a Sinn Féin MP, however, she followed the policy of parliamentary abstention and refused to take her seat in the British House of Commons. It was not until 1928 that women in Great Britain and Northern Ireland could vote along with men at the age of twenty-one. In the newly created Irish Free State, however, women could vote on equal terms with men from 1922 onwards.

The attainment of the right to vote was a major landmark in the campaign for women's rights. This campaign coincided with a period of political and social turmoil in Ireland. Many campaigners for women's rights were also involved in other political and cultural organisations of the time. Countess Markievicz took a leading part in the Irish Citizen Army and in the movement for Irish independence. Another prominent suffragette, Jenny Wyse-Power, was vice-president of Sinn Féin, while Maud Gonne, a strong advocate of women's rights, was prominent in the Abbey Theatre and in the struggle for independence. Although the Irish suffragette movement was limited in its immediate influence, it heralded the increased involvement of Irish women in public life, especially during the tumultuous years between 1916 and 1923.

KEY PERSONALITY: ISABELLA TOD (1836–96)

Born in Edinburgh in 1836, of Scots-Irish parentage, Isabella Tod moved to Belfast in the 1860s, where she became involved in campaigning for women's rights. Largely self-educated, in 1867 she founded the Belfast Ladies' Institute, which provided courses for women. Greatly committed to campaigning for greater educational opportunities for women, she was the first woman to demand that women be admitted to Irish universities.

Throughout her life, Isabella Tod remained a passionate advocate of women's rights. Mainly by organising lectures and petitions, she fought for the repeal of the Contagious Diseases Acts, for married women's property rights and for the right to vote (suffrage). She founded the first Irish Suffrage Society in Belfast in 1871 and was a pioneer in spreading the suffrage doctrine in Ireland.

While women's rights remained her primary concern, Isabella Tod also had other interests. She was a committee member of the Belfast Women's Temperance Association, vice-president of the British Women's Temperance Association between 1877 and 1892, and vice-president of the Irish Women's Total Abstinence Union from 1893 to 1896.

As well as a campaigner for women's rights, Isabella Tod was a passionate unionist. From the introduction of the First Home Rule Bill (1886), she defended the Union and vehemently opposed Home Rule. She was the only female member of the executive committee of the Ulster Liberal Unionist Association and in 1888 established the Ulster Women's Liberal Unionist Association.

Isabella Tod was one of the most prominent campaigners for women's rights in the late nineteenth century. However, her involvement as a woman in unionist politics was also highly significant.

Key Personality: Hanna Sheehy-Skeffington (1877–1946)

Born in Co. Tipperary in 1877, Hanna Sheehy-Skeffington was the daughter of David Sheehy, a Home Rule MP from 1885 to 1918. She was educated at the Dominican school in Eccles Street, Dublin, and later at the Royal University, where she received an MA degree. She married Francis Skeffington in 1903, with both adopting the joint name of Sheehy-Skeffington.

Hanna Sheehy-Skeffington and her husband were committed, lifelong campaigners for women's rights. One of a small group of female graduates of the Royal University, she founded the Women's Graduate Association in 1901, and in 1904 he resigned as registrar of the Royal University over a dispute concerning the non-recognition of women graduates.

Hanna Sheehy-Skeffington joined the Irish Women's Suffrage and Local Government Association (IWSLGA). Increasingly influenced by the more militant tactics adopted by the Women's Social and Political Union, founded by Emmeline Pankhurst in Manchester in 1903, she believed that a similar organisation should be founded in Ireland. Thus, in 1908 she co-founded the Irish Women's Franchise League and became its first secretary. Committed primarily to obtaining the vote for women, the new organisation from the beginning was militant and 'non-party' (independent of political parties). She was imprisoned for rioting when votes for women were excluded from the Third Home Rule Bill (1912).

Hanna Sheehy-Skeffington was an important influence in forging links between the suffrage and labour movements. She strongly supported the 1913 strike and lockout in Dublin and worked alongside Countess Markiewicz and others in the soup kitchen in Liberty Hall. Like many other women in the suffrage movement, she supported Irish republicanism and was a messenger to the GPO during the Easter Rising of 1916.

Following the murder of her husband in 1916, Hanna Sheehy-Skeffington visited the USA, where she interviewed President Woodrow Wilson. She was imprisoned on her return to Ireland in 1918 but was released when she began a hunger strike. She strongly opposed the Anglo-Irish Treaty and became a member of the first executive of Fianna Fáil, founded in 1926.

Hanna Sheehy-Skeffington regarded the granting of the vote to women over thirty in 1918 as merely the first step on the road to equality for women. She continued to campaign for women's rights, founding the Women's Social and Progressive League in 1938. Like many feminists of her generation, she successfully combined the causes of suffrage, labour and national independence.

ORDINARY LEVEL

1. The following passages are about life in Dublin in 1913. Document A was written by James Connolly, and Document B by a Mrs Maguire, who witnessed the scene she describes. Read them carefully and answer the questions that follow.

   Document A
   Ireland is a country of wonderful charity and singularly little justice. And Dublin being an epitome of Ireland, it is not strange to find that Dublin, a city famous for its charitable institutions and its charitable citizens, should also be infamous for the perfectly hellish conditions under which its people are housed, and under which its men, women and children labour for a living.

   James Connolly, cited in Curriculum Development Unit, Divided City: Portrait of Dublin, 1913; Dublin: O'Brien 1978, 38

   Document B
   A tenement collapses
   I was standing in the halldoor of the house, looking at the children playing in the streets. Other women were sitting on the kerb-stone so as to be in the air. Suddenly I heard a terrible crash and shrieking. I ran, not knowing why, but hearing as I did a frightful noise of falling bricks. When I looked back I saw that two houses had tumbled down. I do not know what I did then but I remembered rushing. There was a heap of bricks and stuff piled up on the street, where a moment or two before children were playing and women sitting, watching them.

   Curriculum Development Unit, Divided City: Portrait of Dublin, 1913, Dublin: O'Brien 1978, 38–40

   (i) What does Connolly mean by the first sentence of Document A?

   (ii) Why was Dublin infamous, according to the writer?

   (iii) In Document B, where was the writer when the crash was heard?

   (iv) What did she observe when she looked back?

   (v) Do you think that Document B is a good primary source? Explain your answer.

2. Account for the lack of industrial development in most parts of Ireland around 1870.

3. Write an account of Belfast's industrial development in the nineteenth century.

4. Describe in detail the Belfast shipbuilding industry.

5. Describe, with reference to photographic evidence, living and working conditions in Dublin around 1900.

6. Write an account of James Connolly and socialism in Ireland.

7. Outline the activities of James Larkin in Ireland up to 1912.

8. Why was the Irish Labour Party founded in 1912?

9. Write a paragraph on William Martin Murphy.

10. Write a detailed account of the Dublin strike and lockout of 1913–14.

11. Describe the status of women in Ireland in the late nineteenth century.

12. Write a paragraph on the achievements of Isabella Tod and Anna Haslam.

13. Write a detailed account of the activities of Hanna Sheehy-Skeffington in the cause of women's rights.

14. Outline the development of the women's suffrage movement in Ireland up to 1914.

HIGHER LEVEL

1. Compare and contrast the industrial development of the Belfast region and the rest of Ireland up to 1914.

2. Assess the contribution of James Connolly to the labour movement in Ireland.

3. Discuss the role played by James Larkin in the development of trade unionism in Ireland.

4. Consider the significance of the Dublin strike and lockout of 1913–14 in the social and political development of Ireland.

5. Analyse the rise of women's movements in Ireland up to 1914.

The Home Rule Movement After Parnell

The deep divisions between the Parnellites and the anti-Parnellites continued after Parnell's death in October 1891. The Parnellites were led by John Redmond, and the anti-Parnellites by Justin McCarthy. However, the anti-Parnellites soon began to quarrel among themselves. When John Dillon replaced Justin McCarthy as leader, he was continually challenged by T.M. Healy and William O'Brien. These divisions weakened the popular appeal of the party and damaged its cause.

Gladstone introducing the Second Home Rule Bill in the House of Commons in 1893

After the general election of 1892, Gladstone and the Liberals returned to power. At the age of eighty-three Gladstone now formed his fourth, and final, ministry. He was still committed to the cause of Home Rule for Ireland. In the following year, 1893, he introduced the **Second Home Rule Bill** in the House of Commons. This was very similar to the First Home Rule Bill of 1886, with the important difference that eighty Irish MPs would continue to sit in the Westminster Parliament. In 1886 it had been proposed to exclude them completely. The Second Home Rule Bill was passed by the House of Commons, but the House of Lords, which had the power of veto on legislation, rejected it overwhelmingly by 419 to 41 votes. Following this defeat, Gladstone retired from public life in March 1894. He was succeeded as Prime Minister and leader of the Liberal Party by Lord Rosebery, an imperialist who had little interest in Irish affairs.

In 1895 the Conservative Party under Lord Salisbury was returned to power with a huge majority. The Conservatives, who were to remain in power for over a decade, pursued the policy of constructive unionism, or 'Killing Home Rule with Kindness'.

The Reunification of the Home Rule Party

The divisions within the Home Rule Movement remained bitter throughout the 1890s. After 1895, with the return of the Conservatives to power and little hope of Home Rule in the near future, the tensions worsened. On the anti-Parnellite side there was intense rivalry between John

Dillon and T.M. Healy. Whereas Healy was closely associated with the Catholic clergy, Dillon wished to diminish the influence of the Catholic Church in political matters. In an effort to reunite the Parnellites and anti-Parnellites, a leading anti-Parnellite MP, William O'Brien, set up the United Irish League in 1898. Although it adopted a policy of land reform, O'Brien hoped that the new movement, which attracted support from both factions, would provide a basis for reuniting the Home Rule movement.

In 1900, after a decade of division, the Irish Parliamentary Party reunited under the leadership of John Redmond. Although John Dillon was leader of the larger, anti-Parnellite group, he agreed to step aside in favour of John Redmond, who had been leader of the Parnellite faction. Redmond was noted for his skills of oratory and negotiation. He was deeply committed to the Liberal Alliance as the best strategy for achieving Home Rule.

However, despite the unification of the party, the cause of Home Rule had been dealt a series of severe blows. Owing to disillusionment with the party following the fall of Parnell, popular enthusiasm had waned, and subscriptions from America had declined considerably. The long period of Conservative government frustrated the advancement of Home Rule. When the Liberals returned to power in 1906, they did not need the support of the Home Rule Party in Parliament, as they had an overwhelming majority of MPs. Against the background of a weakened Home Rule movement, new forms of nationalism began to emerge in Ireland around 1900.

New Forms of Nationalism

Many people who were looking for new ways of expressing their national identity began to emphasise Ireland's distinctive culture and traditions. As we have seen in Chapter 6, organisations such as the GAA and the Gaelic League flourished during this period. They were not merely cultural movements – they also frequently instilled in their members a desire for Irish independence. The year 1898, the centenary of the United Irish rebellion, became a focal point for those advocating a more radical vision of Irish nationalism. Commemorations took place throughout the country, and people were reminded of Wolfe Tone and the physical force republican tradition of Irish nationalism. For many of the organisers of these events, the Home Rule movement was conservative and ineffective. One leading supporter of this viewpoint was a recently returned emigrant and printer named Arthur Griffith.

Arthur Griffith (1871–1922)

ARTHUR GRIFFITH

Arthur Griffith was born in Dublin in 1871. He trained as a printer, but in 1897 he had to emigrate to South Africa because of unemployment. He returned to Ireland the following year to become editor of a weekly newspaper, the *United Irishman*. Griffith encouraged the cultural revival: W.B. Yeats and Douglas Hyde wrote articles for his newspaper. In 1900 he founded an organisation called Cumann na nGaedheal to bring together various nationalist and cultural activities, including promotion of the Irish language and music and encouragement of Irish industry. However, Griffith's main interest lay in the area of politics and economics.

GRIFFITH'S POLITICAL AND ECONOMIC VIEWS

Although Arthur Griffith was a republican who favoured total separation between Ireland and Britain, he realised that this was an unlikely prospect. However, he was also completely dissatisfied with the Home Rule Party. He believed that under Home Rule, Ireland would still be too much under the control of the British Government. In a book entitled *The Resurrection of Hungary*, published in 1904, Griffith set out an alternative solution to the Irish Question. He proposed a concept of **dual monarchy** that was modelled on the settlement of 1867 between Austria and Hungary. Under this scheme both Ireland and Britain would have separate parliaments but remain under a single monarch. Griffith also advocated a policy of **parliamentary abstention**: Irish MPs should withdraw from Westminster and set up a parliament in Dublin.

For Griffith, economic independence was as important as political autonomy. Heavily influenced by the views of the German economist Friedrich List, Griffith believed that Irish industries should be protected from foreign competition by high tariff barriers. Ignoring the success of export-oriented industries such as shipbuilding, brewing and distilling, Griffith believed that the Act of Union was responsible for Ireland's lack of industrial development.

THE FOUNDATION OF SINN FÉIN

In 1905 a new political movement known as **Sinn Féin** was founded by Arthur Griffith. This new organisation – its name means 'We Ourselves' – spread its founder's ideas on parliamentary abstention, economic independence and reform in the areas of education and the Poor Law. Although it had over one hundred branches by 1908 and was the first Irish political party to admit women as full members, in reality Sinn Féin had little impact. Although participating on local councils, the party failed to have members elected to the Westminster Parliament. In 1908 a former Home Rule MP, C.J. Dolan, stood as a Sinn Féin candidate in a by-election in North Leitrim. Although not elected, he succeeded in winning 25 per cent of the vote. The party did not contest another parliamentary election until 1917.

By 1910 Sinn Féin was in decline. Its name and organisation were to be transformed by the Irish Republican Brotherhood (IRB), which was itself experiencing a revival at this time.

THE REVIVAL OF THE IRB

The IRB, representing the physical force tradition of Irish nationalism, had undergone a steady decline since its bombing campaign of the 1880s. The success of the Home Rule movement under the leadership of Parnell in the 1880s and the development of new forms of nationalism in the 1890s contributed to this eclipse. However, from 1900 the IRB experienced a revival as the old guard was gradually replaced by younger, energetic leaders who imbued the organisation with a new spirit. This new spirit was seen in the work and dedication of three men:

- **Denis McCullagh** was born in Belfast in 1883, the son of a publican and Fenian. He became a member of the IRB in 1901 and immediately began a recruitment drive for the organisation. In 1906 he became a member of the Supreme Council of the IRB.
- **Bulmer Hobson** was born in Belfast in 1883 into a Quaker family. He joined the Gaelic League in 1901 and was recruited into the IRB by McCullagh in 1904. Both men were responsible for creating the Dungannon Clubs, which evoked memories of the Volunteer movement that had won legislative independence for Ireland in 1782

The committee which organised the Dublin funeral of the veteran Fenian Jeremiah O'Donovan Rossa in 1915. The committee included Éamon de Valera (fourth from left, back row), Thomas MacDonagh (first on left, third row), Arthur Griffith (seventh from left, third row), Countess Markievicz (second from left, second row) and Thomas Clarke (eighth from left, second row).

Others who were part of the younger generation within the IRB included Dr Patrick McCartan, P.S. O'Hegarty and Major John MacBride. Gradually replacing the old guard on the Supreme Council of the IRB, the younger generation of republicans was greatly helped by an older republican named Thomas Clarke, who formed a link with the Fenian past.

Thomas Clarke was born in the Isle of Wight in 1857 of Irish parents. He went to the USA at the age of twenty-one and joined the Irish-American Fenian movement, Clan na Gael. He was sentenced to life imprisonment in 1883 for his part in a bombing campaign in England. He was released in 1898 and emigrated the following year to the US, where he continued to work closely with Clan na Gael. Clarke returned to Ireland in 1907 and operated a tobacco and newsagent shop in North Great Britain Street, Dublin. His shop was to become a centre for the IRB organisation over the next decade. He was soon co-opted onto the Supreme Council of the IRB. Clarke was a republican zealot who worked energetically with the younger generation of republicans to revitalise the organisation.

The revived IRB remained alert and ready to exploit opportunities for its own gain. As part of its recruitment drive, its members were encouraged to infiltrate organisations such as the GAA and the Gaelic League. Although the reunited Home Rule Party was also to experience an improvement in its fortunes, the IRB remained poised to take advantage of any difficulties encountered by Redmond's party.

The Home Rule Party, 1906–10

With Gladstone's withdrawal from politics in 1894, the Home Rule movement had lost its greatest ally. Following his retirement, the Liberal Party, first under Rosebery and then under Henry Campbell-Bannerman, showed little interest in the cause of Home Rule for Ireland. However, Redmond, despite reservations within his party, remained personally committed to the Liberal Alliance as the best means of achieving Home Rule. After more than a decade of

Conservative government, the Liberals returned to power after securing a huge majority in the general election of 1906. They were not dependent on the support of the Irish Parliamentary Party in Westminster and showed little appetite for the cause of Home Rule. Even before returning to power, the Liberals had indicated that they now favoured a more gradual approach to the question of Home Rule – in November 1905 Campbell-Bannerman spoke of giving Ireland an 'instalment of representative control' that might eventually lead to Home Rule.

This policy was clearly seen in the Liberal Government's proposal of the **Irish Council Bill** in 1907. Under this proposed legislation, an executive council of 107 members would be created to advise and assist the Viceroy. The members of this council, most of whom would be elected, were to be given control of eight departments of the Irish administration. However, the Viceroy would retain wide powers of veto, and the council would remain strictly subject to the overall authority of the Westminster Parliament.

The Irish Council Bill was rejected by Redmond and the Irish Parliamentary Party as falling far short of the degree of legislative independence they sought. It appeared that the Home Rule movement was to remain, at least in the short term, beset by problems. In particular, the failure of the Liberal Alliance to advance the cause of Home Rule for Ireland exacerbated existing tensions within the party. The party's declining popularity was further dented by the threat from new movements such as Sinn Féin.

Although the Liberals displayed little interest in Home Rule, they proceeded to implement legislation that would benefit Ireland in a number of other ways. This included measures to improve rural and urban housing, the reinstatement of tenants formerly evicted from their homes and a resolution of the complex and problematic University Question. Much of this social legislation was the work of Augustine Birrell, who was appointed Chief Secretary for Ireland in 1907. However, by introducing a programme of social legislation that brought the House of Commons into conflict with the House of Lords, the Government unintentionally provided the Home Rule movement with the opportunity to improve its fortunes.

THE CRISIS OF 1910

By 1909 the Liberal Government, under the leadership of Asquith, had inaugurated a programme of social reform that included the introduction of old-age pensions and the extension of social insurance. Lloyd George, as Chancellor of the Exchequer, set down in his budget of 1909 how these measures were to be financed. He proposed to increase income tax, impose a supertax on incomes over a certain limit, introduce a series of land taxes and raise death duties. These radical budget proposals were intensely unpopular among the rich, who saw them as an attack on wealth and property. A constitutional crisis loomed when the hereditary House of Lords exercised its power of veto and rejected the budget passed by the elected House of Commons.

Asquith responded to the rejection of the budget proposals by calling a general election. The election of January 1910 was to present Redmond and the Irish Parliamentary Party with an unexpected advantage. With the Liberals winning 275 seats and the

John Redmond, leader of the Irish Parliamentary Party, seen here in London accompanied by his wife

Conservatives 273, the 71 Irish nationalist members were left holding the balance of power, a position of influence not enjoyed since Parnell's time. When attempts to resolve the conflict between the House of Lords and the House of Commons failed, a second election was called in December 1910. This yielded similar results to the January election, with the Liberals and Conservatives securing 272 seats each and the Irish nationalists returning 83 MPs. Redmond's commitment to the Liberal Alliance appeared to be yielding fruit when the Parliament Act of 1911 reduced the absolute veto of the House of Lords to a delaying power of two years. With Redmond and his party still holding the balance of power in the House of Commons, the Liberal Government was prepared to support Home Rule for Ireland.

THE THIRD HOME RULE BILL, 1912

In April 1912 Asquith introduced the Third Home Rule Bill. The Bill proposed to give Ireland a separate parliament with control over its own internal affairs. However, the Westminster Parliament would continue to be responsible for a number of key areas, including defence, war and peace, relations with the Crown, customs and excise, and land purchase. This Bill was very similar to the Second Home Rule Bill (1893) and proposed that forty-two Irish MPs continue to sit in the Westminster Parliament. Passed in the House of Commons, the bill was predictably rejected by the House of Lords. However, as the Lords could now delay a Bill for only two years, Home Rule was due to become law in 1914.

While the Liberal Alliance seemed on the verge of delivering Home Rule for Ireland, Asquith and Redmond now had to contend with the strength and determination of opposition to Home Rule from the Ulster unionists and their allies, the Conservative Party.

The Emergence of Unionist Resistance

Unionists wished to maintain in full the Union between Great Britain and Ireland. Although a minority lived in the south of Ireland, they were most numerous in the north-eastern region of the country. Unionists were strongly opposed to Home Rule for a combination of religious, economic and political reasons:

- Most unionists were Protestants who feared that, as a minority group in Ireland as a whole, they would be subjected to Catholic domination if Home Rule were granted. This **religious fear** was summed up by the unionist dictum 'Home Rule is Rome Rule'.
- North-east Ireland was the only industrial enclave in an otherwise underdeveloped country. As such, it had very close **economic links** with Britain, which supplied raw materials for its industries and provided markets for its manufactured goods. Protestant businessmen feared that a Home Rule Parliament might impose protective tariffs and thus interfere with the free trade established by the Act of Union between Britain and Ireland.
- The privileged position of the Protestant Ascendancy had been significantly eroded in the course of the nineteenth century. Many Protestants feared that their **political status** would be further diminished by a Home Rule Parliament dominated by the Catholic majority.

Although the origins of unionism may be traced back to the plantations of the seventeenth century, we must look to the 1880s to discover its emergence as an organised political force. The development of organised unionism was a direct response to the threat posed by the success of the Home Rule movement under the leadership of Parnell. In May 1886 a group of wealthy southern Irish unionists formed a new organisation named the **Irish Loyal and Patriotic Union**. This organisation, although seeking mainly to influence opinion in Great Britain, put up candidates in the general election. Its electoral efforts proved disastrous, and the only candidates returned were the two unopposed members representing Trinity College, Dublin. Ulster unionists seemed slower to act. However, the nationalist success in the general election of November 1885, together with Gladstone's conversion to Home Rule, convinced many Ulster unionists of the urgency of the need for action. In January 1886 they established the **Ulster Loyalist Anti-Repeal Union**. This organisation grew very rapidly and set about marshalling opposition to Gladstone's Home Rule proposals between April and June 1886. Under the shadow of the threat of Home Rule, a **Unionist Parliamentary Party** in the Westminster Parliament also began to emerge. Under the leadership of a wealthy Cavan landlord named E.H. Saunderson, the party was formed in January 1886 and had eighteen MPs in the Westminster Parliament. From the beginning the unionists were closely allied to the Conservative Party in Britain. The chief architect of this alliance was the Conservative MP Lord Randolph Churchill, who, on visiting Belfast in February 1886, pledged support in resisting Home Rule.

As the immediate threat of Home Rule lessened considerably with the defeat in the House of Commons of the First Home Rule Bill, unionist agitation also abated. However, in 1893, with the threat of the Second Home Rule Bill looming, unionist agitation resumed, with the organisation of mass demonstrations in Ulster in opposition to Home Rule. After the House of Lords used its veto to defeat the Second Home Rule Bill, the long period of Conservative rule that ensued gave the unionists a sense of security. Even the huge Liberal victory in the general election of 1906 did not seem a threat as long as the House of Lords retained its absolute power of veto. Nevertheless, unionist opposition to Home Rule continued to grow. The Devolution Crisis of 1904 had alarmed unionists, and in the following year the **Ulster Unionist Council** was founded as the central organising body to co-ordinate resistance to Home Rule. In Parliament the Unionist Party maintained its separate identity, although closely allied with the Conservative Party. From 1906 to 1910 it was led by an Englishman named Walter Long. He was succeeded in 1910 by one of the MPs representing Dublin University, Sir Edward Carson.

Unionist poster, 1912

EDWARD CARSON (1854–1935)

Edward Carson was born in Dublin in 1854, the son of an architect. He studied law at Trinity College and displayed his abilities as a prosecuting lawyer during the Plan of Campaign in the 1880s. In 1892 he was appointed Irish Solicitor-General and was first elected Unionist MP for Dublin University (Trinity College), which he continued to represent in the Westminster Parliament until 1918. He built up a very successful legal practice and acted as prosecutor in many successful cases, most notably that of Oscar Wilde in 1895. In 1900 he was appointed Solicitor-General of England and was knighted by Queen Victoria.

Carson was a southern unionist who was passionately opposed to Home Rule, once describing the maintenance of the Union as the 'guiding star' of his political life. He became leader of the Irish Unionist Parliamentary Party in February 1910 and marshalled unionist resistance to Home Rule at the time of the Third Home Rule Bill. In this task he was joined by an Ulster MP and businessman named **James Craig**. Born in Belfast in 1871, Craig was the son of a prosperous whiskey distiller. Having served against the Boers in South Africa, he was elected Unionist MP for East Down in 1906. Under the leadership of Carson and Craig, unionist resistance to Home Rule adopted a more militant guise.

Edward Carson addressing an anti-Home Rule rally

UNIONIST REACTION TO THE THIRD HOME RULE BILL

Unionists felt seriously threatened by the Parliament Act of 1911, which paved the way for the introduction of Home Rule. At a mass demonstration held at Craigavon in September 1911, Carson incited his followers to 'be prepared the morning Home Rule passes, ourselves to become responsible for the government of the Protestant Province of Ulster'. By these remarks he was advocating the establishment of a separate unionist government in Ulster should Home Rule be passed. Although a southern unionist who passionately believed in keeping all of Ireland within the Union, Carson now concentrated on resisting the imposition of Home Rule in Ulster. Ulster unionist resistance to Home

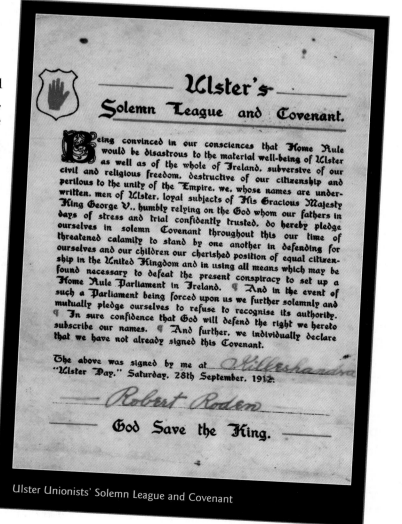
Ulster Unionists' Solemn League and Covenant

Rule was strongly supported by the Conservative Party. Bonar Law, the Conservative leader, who was of Ulster Presbyterian stock, visited Belfast in April 1912 and pledged his support for the unionist cause. Later, speaking at another meeting at Blenheim in England, Bonar Law stated: 'I can imagine no length of resistance to which Ulster will go which I shall not be ready to support.'

The unionist response to the threat of the Third Home Rule Bill took two forms. One was the signing of a mass petition pledging Ulster resistance to the introduction of Home Rule. The second was the establishment of a volunteer force threatening armed resistance in Ulster to the imposition of Home Rule.

Unionist women in Ulster signing a declaration against Home Rule in 1912

THE ULSTER SOLEMN LEAGUE AND COVENANT

On 28 September 1912, over 200,000 male Ulster unionists signed a petition pledging themselves to 'use all means which may be found necessary to defeat the present conspiracy to set up a Home Rule Parliament in Ireland'. Signed by unionists of all social classes, the petition went on to state that 'in the event of such a Parliament being forced upon us we further solemnly and mutually pledge ourselves to refuse to recognise its authority'. This defiance of the authority of the Government by a determined minority became more menacing with the establishment in 1913 of the Ulster Volunteer Force.

THE ULSTER VOLUNTEER FORCE

Unionists had begun military drilling in 1911. With the aim of co-ordinating the various military bodies in existence throughout the province, the Ulster Unionist Council set up the Ulster Volunteer Force in January 1913. A limit of 100,000 men was set on recruitment to the new force. Sir George Richardson, a retired general who had served with the British army in India, was appointed as its commander. Organised on military lines, the Ulster Volunteer Force made preparations for resisting Home Rule and continued to drill openly.

The militancy of Ulster unionism gave rise to the issue of excluding the province or part of it from the operation of Home Rule. Although as a southern unionist, Carson keenly desired to keep all of Ireland within the Union, he realised that the greater part of the island would have to be abandoned in favour of Ulster. Redmond had also come around to accepting that some form of exclusion from Home Rule for part of Ulster might be necessary. In the meantime, while discussions continued on a compromise solution for Ulster, Irish nationalists responded to unionist militancy by establishing a volunteer force of their own.

A battalion of the Ulster Volunteers drilling in Belfast in 1913

Nationalist Mobilisation: The Irish Volunteers

In November 1913 Eoin MacNeill, Professor of Early Irish History at UCD and one of the founders of the Gaelic League, wrote an article in the Gaelic League journal, *An Claidheamh Soluis*. In this article, entitled 'The North Began', MacNeill praised the Ulster unionists for their initiative in establishing the Ulster Volunteer Force and proposed that Irish nationalists should set up a volunteer force of their own to defend the cause of Home Rule. The renewed IRB, waiting for the right opportunity to promote the separatist cause, saw great merit in the establishment of an armed nationalist volunteer force, which they could use in the future to stage a rebellion against British rule. Bulmer Hobson approached MacNeill and persuaded him to call a meeting to further the idea of organising a volunteer force. At a meeting attended by thousands in the Rotunda, Dublin, on 25 November 1913, the Irish National Volunteers were set up. By May 1914 the Irish Volunteers, run by a provisional committee and under the command of Eoin MacNeill, had a membership of 75,000. A number of nationalist women set up Cumann na mBan as an auxiliary to the Volunteers. From the beginning the Irish Volunteers were infiltrated by the IRB, which was intent on using them at the earliest opportunity to strike another blow against British rule in Ireland.

The establishment of the Irish Volunteers posed a threat not only to Asquith's Government but also to John Redmond and the Irish Parliamentary Party. By June 1914 Redmond decided that it was time to assert his authority over the Volunteers. He demanded that twenty-five persons nominated by the Irish Parliamentary Party be included on the provisional committee of the Volunteers. MacNeill, despite the opposition of Bulmer Hobson and other members of the IRB, accepted this demand.

Ulster Volunteers landing guns at Bangor, Co. Down

1914: Year of Crisis

By 1914, therefore, two volunteer forces existed in the country, one pledged to defend Home Rule and the other pledged to resist it. The outlook for compromise seemed bleak when fifty-eight army officers in the Curragh Camp resigned in anticipation that they would be ordered to crush Ulster opposition to Home Rule.

Matters moved dangerously closer to crisis when the two volunteer forces illegally imported arms. On the night of 24–25 April 1914, the UVF successfully landed some 25,000 firearms and 3 million rounds of ammunition at the harbours of Larne, Bangor and Donaghadee. This was a daring and determined operation and posed an open challenge to the Government. Both the 'Curragh Mutiny' and the successful landing of arms by the UVF made the unionists more optimistic in their resolve to resist Home Rule.

Running guns into Howth, Co. Dublin, for the Irish Volunteers, in July 1914

The Irish Volunteers followed the example of the UVF. On 26 July 1914, guns and ammunition arrived at Howth Harbour on board Erskine Childers's yacht, the *Asgard*, in a mission as daring,

if not quite as grand, as that of the UVF. The arms were speedily unloaded by the Volunteers, who cunningly managed to escape the awaiting authorities. Later in the day British soldiers, marching down Bachelor's Walk in Dublin on their return to barracks, were jeered by a local crowd. The soldiers opened fire, killing three onlookers and wounding thirty-eight.

Any hope of compromise between unionists and nationalists over Ulster was dashed when the Buckingham Palace Conference ended in failure on 24 July 1914. This conference – attended by Asquith, Redmond, Bonar Law and Carson, among others – represented a last-ditch effort to arrive at a compromise on the place of Ulster in a Home Rule settlement.

Relatives of those shot dead at Bachelor's Walk after the Howth Gun-Running arrive at the Dublin City Mortuary to identify the bodies

With the arming of the two volunteer forces and the failure of the Buckingham Palace Conference to broker a compromise, tensions between unionists and nationalists might have exploded into crisis had not developments in Europe taken centre stage.

World War I and the Split in the Irish Volunteers

The Home Rule Crisis ended with the outbreak of World War I in August 1914. Carson and Redmond both pledged support for the war effort. The unionist community made an overwhelming commitment to the war effort, with many members of the Ulster Volunteer Force going off to fight for Britain.

Although the Home Rule Bill passed into law on 18 September 1914, Redmond agreed that it should not be implemented until after the war, when the question of Ulster would again be considered. He also believed that the war provided an opportunity for nationalists to show that Home Rule was fully compatible with loyalty to Empire. In a speech at Woodenbridge, Co. Wicklow, on 20 September 1914, Redmond urged the Volunteers to support the war effort wherever needed. This speech led to a split between moderate and advanced nationalists in the Volunteer movement. A large majority of around 170,000 accepted Redmond's view and renamed themselves the **National Volunteers**. About 25,000 of this group joined the British army.

John Redmond inspecting the National Volunteers in the Phoenix Park, Dublin in 1915

A minority of around 11,000, representing for the most part the IRB-dominated section of the organisation, retained the name **Irish Volunteers** and remained adamantly opposed to the British war effort. The revitalised IRB, controlled by a highly organised group of young zealots, was waiting for the right opportunity to use this group in staging a rebellion against British rule in Ireland.

KEY PERSONALITY: JOHN REDMOND (1856–1918)

John Redmond was born in Ballytrent, Co. Wexford, in 1856. Educated at Clongowes Wood College and at Trinity College, Dublin, he was called to the Irish Bar in 1886. Before that he had been elected Home Rule MP for New Ross in 1881 and from the beginning was a dedicated follower of Parnell. During a fund-raising trip to America and Australia between 1882 and 1884, he raised £30,000 for the Irish Parliamentary Party. At the time of the Parnellite Split in 1890–91, Redmond remained one of Parnell's most loyal supporters. After Parnell's death in 1891, he became leader of the Parnellite group in the House of Commons.

Redmond became leader of the reunited Irish Parliamentary Party in 1900. He remained committed to the Liberal Alliance, but while the Conservatives were in power the cause of Home Rule had little hope of advancement. He represented the tenants at the Land Conference of 1902 that resulted in the Wyndham Land Act (1903). When the Liberals returned to power in 1906, they showed little interest in Home Rule, and Redmond rejected their Irish Councils Bill (1907) as a totally inadequate measure.

Despite some criticism of his continuing commitment to the Liberal Alliance, Redmond believed that it was the only way of achieving Home Rule. His fortunes changed dramatically in 1910 when, in the course of two general elections, the Home Rule Party held the balance of power in the House of Commons. As the price for Redmond's continuing support, the Liberal Prime Minister, Herbert Asquith, agreed to introduce a Home Rule bill in Parliament.

On 11 April 1912 the Third Home Rule Bill was introduced by Asquith in the House of Commons. Under the Parliament Act (1911), the House of Lords could no longer reject a bill completely but could only delay it for a period of two years. Therefore, Home Rule would become law in 1914. However, neither Redmond nor Asquith fully realised the strength of unionist resistance to Home Rule. In an effort to resolve difficulties between nationalists and unionists, Redmond represented nationalists at the Buckingham Palace Conference in July 1914. The conference ended in failure.

The outbreak of World War I transformed the political situation in Ireland. Tensions were already high, with the formation the previous year of the Ulster Volunteer Force and the Irish Volunteer Force. With the outbreak of war, the Ulster Volunteer Force declared its loyalty to Britain, and many of its members joined the British forces. At a famous speech at Woodenbridge, Co. Wicklow, in September 1914, Redmond called upon the Irish Volunteers to do likewise. Although Home Rule was signed into law in September 1914, its implementation was suspended until the end of the war. Redmond hoped that, in demonstrating Irish support for the British war effort, he would ensure the early granting of Home Rule. This stance led to a split in the Irish Volunteers. The vast majority remained loyal to Redmond and became known as the National Volunteers. Many of these went off to fight on the side of Britain in the war.

Redmond was passionately opposed to the Easter Rising of 1916 and condemned it in the House of Commons. Redmond's popularity declined drastically, as the Home Rule Party appeared willing to accept partition and the prospect of Home Rule seemed increasingly distant. In addition, the emergence of a new, resurgent Sinn Féin after the 1916 Rising posed a serious threat to Redmond and his party. In an unsuccessful effort to reach compromise with unionists, he took part in the Irish Convention in 1917–18. His death in March 1918 spared him the humiliation of seeing the overwhelming defeat of his party in the general election later that year. By then, Home Rule was no longer regarded by most Irish nationalists as an adequate measure of independence.

While John Redmond was not regarded as an inspiring or charismatic leader, he brought a much-needed stability to the Irish Parliamentary Party after its reunification in 1900. He was moderate in his tactics and believed that Ireland's best interests lay in self-government within the British Empire. His failure to adapt to the changed political circumstances after 1916 contributed to the ultimate eclipse of the Home Rule Movement.

KEY PERSONALITY: EDWARD CARSON (1854–1935)

Born in Dublin in 1854, Edward Carson was educated at Portarlington School, Co. Laois, and Trinity College, Dublin. He was called to the Irish Bar in 1877 and was appointed Solicitor-General of Ireland in 1892. He soon gained a reputation as a brilliant advocate and acted on behalf of the Government during the Plan of Campaign in 1889–91. His most famous case was his successful defence of the Marquess of Queensberry in the libel proceedings brought by Oscar Wilde. He was knighted in 1900 and in the same year was appointed Solicitor-General of England by the Conservative Government.

Carson was an ardent unionist who served as MP for Trinity College from 1892 to 1918. In 1910 he became leader of the Irish Unionist Party in the Westminster Parliament. Joining forces with Belfast businessman James Craig, Carson incited Ulstermen to resist Home Rule and defeat the threat posed in 1912 by the Liberal Government's support for Home Rule. In 1911, at a major rally held in Craigavon, the home of James Craig, Carson told a huge audience, 'We will yet defeat the most nefarious conspiracy that has ever been hatched against a free people.' He was one of the main architects of the Ulster Solemn League and Covenant, a petition signed by 250,000 Ulstermen in September 1912 pledging resistance to Home Rule. He supported the formation of the Ulster Volunteer Force in 1913 and subscribed £10,000 to the new organisation.

While Carson wanted all of Ireland to be excluded from Home Rule, he was forced to accept a compromise solution that involved the exclusion of most Ulster counties from a Home Rule settlement. Carson represented unionists at the Buckingham Palace Conference in 1914, and although a final agreement was not reached, the principle of some form of exclusion for Ulster remained. Southern unionists felt abandoned by this turn of events.

The political scene in Ireland was transformed by the outbreak of World War I, the 1916 Rising and the resurgence of Sinn Féin. However, Carson's reluctant compromise of excluding a number of Ulster counties was eventually implemented when the Parliament of Northern Ireland was established in 1920.

Edward Carson served in the British wartime governments, first as Attorney-General and then as First Lord of the Admiralty. He resigned as unionist leader in 1921. He was then created a life peer as Baron Carson of Duncairn and served as Lord of Appeal from 1921 to 1929.

ORDINARY LEVEL

1. The following passage is taken from a speech by Andrew Bonar Law, the Conservative Party leader, at an anti-Home Rule rally on 28 July 1912. Read it and answer the questions that follow.

> In our opposition . . . we shall not be guided by the considerations or bound by the restraints which would influence us in an ordinary constitutional struggle . . . They may, perhaps they will, carry their Home Rule bill through the House of Commons, but what then? I said the other day in the House of Commons and I repeat here that there are things stronger than parliamentary majorities. . .
>
> Before I occupied the position I now fill in the party I said that, in my belief, if an attempt were made to deprive these men [Ulster Unionists] of their birth-right – as part of a corrupt parliamentary bargain – they would be justified in resisting such an attempt by all means in their power, including force. I said it then and I repeat it now with a full sense of the responsibility which attaches to my position, that, in my opinion, if such an attempt is made, I can imagine no length of resistance to which Ulster can go in which I should not be prepared to support them, and in which, in my belief, they would not be supported by the overwhelming majority of the British people.
>
> *The Times, 29 July 1912*

(i) What did the speaker mean by the phrase 'things stronger than parliamentary majorities'?

(ii) What do you think the speaker meant by the phrase 'a corrupt parliamentary bargain'?

(iii) When, according to Bonar Law, would the unionists be justified in using force?

(iv) What unconditional promise did he make in the final sentence?

2. Write a paragraph on the reunification of the Irish Parliamentary Party in 1900.

3. Write a note on the early life of Arthur Griffith.

4. What did Arthur Griffith mean by each of the following?

   (a) Dual monarchy

   (b) Parliamentary abstention

   (c) Economic protectionism

5. Write a paragraph on the foundation and beliefs of Sinn Féin.

6. Explain the revival of the IRB after 1900.

7. Explain why there was little progress towards Home Rule between 1906 and 1910.

8. What constitutional crisis occurred in Great Britain in 1910, and how did it change the fortunes of the Irish Home Rule Party?

9. Write a short account of the Third Home Rule Bill (1912).

10. State three reasons for unionist opposition to Home Rule, and explain the fears of unionists in each case.

11. Examine the pictures and documents concerning unionist opposition to Home Rule on pages 107–108, and answer the following questions.

    (a) What is the message contained in the cartoon on page 107?

    (b) How does the picture of Sir Edward Carson on page 108 convey the strength of unionist opposition to Home Rule?

    (c) From your reading of the Ulster Solemn League and Covenant on page 108, state the reasons given for the claim that Home Rule would be disastrous for Ulster and the rest of Ireland. What action is pledged in the event that Home Rule is forced on Ulster?

12. Write a paragraph on Sir Edward Carson.

13. Write a paragraph on the following.

    (i) The Ulster Volunteers.

    (ii) The Irish Volunteers.

14. Explain the split in the Irish Volunteers in 1914.

HIGHER LEVEL

1. 'The Home Rule movement after the fall of Parnell was deeply divided.' Discuss.

2. Discuss the political and economic ideas of Arthur Griffith.

3. Discuss the changing fortunes of the Home Rule Party between 1906 and 1914.

4. Evaluate unionist opposition to Home Rule up to 1914.

5. Read the following extract from a letter of Winston Churchill, a Cabinet minister in the Liberal Government, to the leader of the Home Rule Party, John Redmond, suggesting special treatment for Ulster. Answer the questions that follow.

> I do not believe there is any real feeling against Home Rule in the Tory Party apart from the Ulster Question, but they hate the government, are bitterly desirous of turning it out, and see in the resistance of Ulster an extra parliamentary force which they will not hesitate to use to the full. I have been pondering a great deal over this matter, and my general view is just what I told you earlier in the year – namely, that something should be done to afford the characteristically Protestant and Orange counties the option of a moratorium of several years before acceding to the Irish Parliament...Much is to be apprehended from a combination of the rancour of a party in the ascendant and the fanaticism of these stubborn and determined Orangemen.
>
> *Winston Churchill to John Redmond, 31 August 1913, Redmond Papers, National Library of Ireland, Dublin*

(i) From your study of the Home Rule issue, would you agree with Churchill's observation that there was not 'any real feeling against Home Rule in the Tory Party apart from the Ulster Question'?

(ii) How was the Conservative or Tory Opposition prepared to use the Ulster problem against the Liberal Government, according to Churchill?

(iii) What was Churchill's main suggestion in this letter to Redmond?

(iv) Was this proposal acceptable to Sir Edward Carson and the unionists? Explain your answer.

(v) Explain clearly the 'combination' of forces which Churchill regarded as a threat at the end of the letter.

(vi) How would you evaluate this primary source in terms of providing an insight into the thinking of a government minister during the Home Rule Crisis?

MOVEMENTS FOR POLITICAL AND SOCIAL REFORM, 1870–1914

During this section you became familiar with the following KEY CONCEPTS:

Democracy This involved the right of people to choose their own government.

Home Rule This referred to the creation, through peaceful means, of limited self-government for Ireland within the British Empire.

Separatism This involved the establishment, through the use of physical force, of an independent Irish republic.

Militarism This was the use of physical force to achieve political goals.

Socialism This referred to the pursuit of social justice through redistribution of wealth and state ownership of property.

Feminism This was the movement for women's rights, especially the right to vote.

Political Agitation This referred to the pursuit of objectives such as the right to vote through public meetings, demonstrations and petitions.

Anglicisation /De-anglicisation Anglicisation referred to the process through which the Irish language, literature and culture had been replaced by the English language, literature and culture. De-anglicisation referred to the process of reducing English influence by reviving Irish language and culture.

Irish Ireland This was a movement and philosophy that defined Irish identity very narrowly in terms of religion (Catholicism) and politics (nationalism).

Anglo-Irish This term referred to descendants of the Protestant Ascendancy who were born in Ireland. Anglo-Irish literature referred to writing in English containing Irish themes.

Suffragette The suffragette movement campaigned for women's right to vote.

PART 2:
THE PURSUIT OF SOVEREIGNTY AND
THE IMPACT OF PARTITION, 1912–49

The Home Rule Crisis

The introduction of the Third Home Rule Bill in the British Parliament in April 1912 was a milestone in the political development of modern Ireland. It was nearly twenty years since the defeat of Gladstone's Second Home Rule Bill by the House of Lords in 1893. This time nationalists throughout Ireland were distinctly hopeful that the Bill would pass and that Ireland would obtain its own parliament. Under the Parliament Act of 1911, the peers in the House of Lords could no longer reject a bill passed by the House of Commons – they could only delay its passage into law for two years.

Crowds in Dublin welcoming the British Prime Minister Herbert Asquith after his Government introduced the Third Home Rule Bill in April 1912

In 1912 a Liberal Government under Prime Minister Herbert Asquith was in power. Dependent on the votes of the Irish Parliamentary Party to stay in power, Asquith had drawn up the Home Rule Bill in consultation with John Redmond, the leader of the Irish Party. Therefore, the votes of Liberal, Irish Home Rule and Labour Party MPs would guarantee the passage of the Home Rule Bill in the House of Commons. The House of Lords; dominated by the Conservative Party, which was strongly unionist, was bound to reject it but could now delay it only for two years. This situation infuriated the unionists throughout Ireland, but especially in Ulster. The introduction of the Third Home Rule Bill in 1912 was a landmark in Irish history because it provoked massive opposition from Irish unionists determined to prevent the introduction of Home Rule at all costs. For nationalists also, it was a significant development. If the third attempt to achieve Home Rule by peaceful means failed, it was possible that the old physical force republican tradition of Irish nationalism might be revived once again.

The Third Home Rule Bill, 1912

The Bill itself was very like those defeated in 1886 and 1893. Ireland was to have a Home Rule Parliament with very limited powers. To preserve the link with Britain, Ireland would continue to elect forty MPs to the imperial Parliament at Westminster. The country was still under the British monarch and part of the Empire. The British army and navy would remain in Ireland. The Westminster Parliament was still responsible for foreign policy, issues of war and peace, taxation, coinage and the post office.

Despite the limited self-government involved, nationalists were willing to accept the Bill. The Home Rule Party leader, John Redmond, spoke eloquently in favour of it in the House of

Commons and declared that its passage into law would mark the beginning of a new era of friendship and co-operation between Great Britain and Ireland. Even certain more extreme separatists, such as Patrick Pearse, were prepared to accept the Home Rule settlement because it gave Irish people control over areas such as education and language policy.

However, unionists regarded the prospect of Home Rule as a deadly threat not only to their prosperity but to their very freedom and sense of identity. The passage of the Bill through the House of Commons in 1912 was a signal for the start of a campaign of unionist resistance.

John Redmond addressing a Home Rule rally

Unionist Opposition to Home Rule

Throughout Europe around 1912 national feeling was intense, as people of different races prided themselves on their distinctive identities. This situation was mirrored in Ireland. Just as nationalists prided themselves on being Irish, unionists were equally proud of their British identity. The fact that they were in a minority on the island of Ireland made them feel vulnerable and even more determined to resist threats to their identity. In their view, Home Rule would pose serious threats to unionist wellbeing. They opposed it on three fundamental grounds:

- *Political*: Unionists were loyal to the British monarch and were content to remain fully within the United Kingdom under a single parliament.
- *Economic*: North-east Ulster had prospered under the Act of Union (1800). Unionists feared that a Home Rule Parliament in Dublin would destroy this prosperity.
- *Religious*: Their slogan, 'Home Rule is Rome Rule', summed up their fears of being dominated by a Catholic-controlled parliament in Dublin.

Although unionists outside of Ulster, known as southern unionists, were in a small minority, they were quite powerful. They were usually Protestant landlords, professionals or businessmen. Some richer Catholics, such as landlords, judges, lawyers and businessmen, were also unionists. Many powerful officers in the British army, such as Lord Kitchener and Sir Henry Wilson, were from southern unionist families.

In north-east Ulster the situation was different from that in the rest of the country. Here unionists were in a majority, and their cause enjoyed support from Protestants in all classes of society. The powerful, anti-Catholic Orange Order played a key role in fostering a sense of exclusive Protestant identity in opposition to Home Rule. At this time of crisis for unionists, they were led by two extremely able politicians, Edward Carson and James Craig.

The Campaign Against Home Rule

Sir Edward Carson (1854–1935) became leader of the Unionist Party in 1910. Born in Dublin, he attended Trinity College and then studied law. During the Plan of Campaign, he was one of the principal lawyers employed by Arthur Balfour to defend the interests of the British Government and the landlords. He later went to live in London, where he became one of the leading barristers in the country and featured in some famous court cases. Carson's main political ambition as a southern unionist was to keep all of Ireland directly under the Westminster Parliament. He had powerful allies within the British Conservative Party. From 1912 onwards he was to use his ability as a public speaker and his organisational skills to muster support in Ireland and throughout Great Britain in the struggle to prevent Home Rule.

Carson's leading assistant in the Ulster Unionist Party was Sir James Craig (1871–1940). Craig belonged to one of the leading industrialist families in Belfast. Like Carson, he hoped that the unionist campaign would prevent the introduction of Home Rule in any part of Ireland. However, whereas Carson was a southern unionist, James Craig was primarily a northern unionist. In effect, if he could not prevent the introduction of Home Rule in southern Ireland, he was determined to keep as much of Ulster as possible in the Union.

Carson and Craig threatened rebellion and claimed that if the Home Rule Bill were passed, unionists in Ulster would attempt to take over the running of the area themselves. Before Carson and Craig could reach this point, they had to demonstrate publicly the extent of their support and also to establish some military group that would carry out their aims. The response to these needs took the form of the Solemn League and Covenant and the Ulster Volunteers.

Edward Carson portrayed on an anti-Home Rule banner

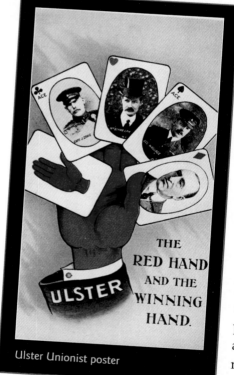

Ulster Unionist poster

The Solemn League and Covenant and the Ulster Volunteers

Unionist demonstrations took place throughout Ulster during 1912. Meetings also took place in London and other British cities. At these, Carson, Craig or other Unionist Party leaders were usually joined by members of the British Conservative Party, which was then in opposition. Its leader, Andrew Bonar Law, was descended from Ulster Protestants and had a deep interest in the cause of the unionists. Bonar Law and other Conservatives took the unusual step of actually saying that they would support unionists who broke the law in opposition to Home Rule.

On 28 September 1912 vast numbers of men throughout Ulster signed a pledge against Home

Rule. At the same time unionist women signed a similar declaration. Some people felt so strongly about the issue that they signed the pledge with their own blood. Known as the **Solemn League and Covenant**, it was based on the covenant, or agreement, between God and the Jewish people in the Old Testament of the Bible. The unionists regarded themselves as God's chosen people and believed that they were being threatened by their enemies, namely Catholics and nationalists in Ireland and the Liberal Party in Great Britain. In the Solemn League and Covenant, they refused to accept that Home Rule was being passed democratically by a majority in the British Parliament. Instead they regarded it as an illegal conspiracy against their Protestant way of life. In the Covenant, they pledged themselves to refuse to recognise the authority of any future Home Rule Parliament in Ireland.

Carson signing the Solemn League and Covenant in Belfast on 28 September 1912

To give substance to this threat, a military group known as the Ulster Volunteer Force was set up. The Volunteers began as local groups drilling and parading. Unionists discovered an old law that allowed Justices of the Peace to permit groups to arm and drill to defend the King. As most Justices of the Peace were unionists, they readily granted such permission. In early 1913 Carson and Craig took control of these local groups, which were united to form the Ulster Volunteer Force.

The founding of the Ulster Volunteers was an important turning point in Irish history. Since the defeat of the Fenian rising in 1867, violence for political aims had all but disappeared. Although the Irish Republican Brotherhood (IRB) remained in existence, it had little impact on public life. The decision of the Ulster unionists to take up arms altered the situation radically. Although professing loyalty to Great Britain, they now threatened to use violence against a law passed democratically by the British Parliament. This decision merely played into the hands of their greatest enemies – extreme nationalist separatists. If unionists were willing to arm themselves to prevent the introduction of Home Rule, then certain Irish nationalists would advocate the use of arms to ensure the success of Home Rule. Thus, in 1913 decisions were taken that paved the way for the following ten years of violence and division throughout Ireland.

The Formation of the Irish Volunteers

Irish Volunteers receiving military training in 1914

Throughout 1913, as the Ulster Volunteers grew in strength nationalists became more and more alarmed. They were also uneasy at the possibility that the British Government might exclude all or part of Ulster from Home Rule. In November 1913 Professor Eoin MacNeill called for the formation of an organisation of nationalist Volunteers to counter the pressure coming from the Ulster Volunteers. MacNeill was a nationalist from County Antrim, a founder of the Gaelic League and a professor of Irish history. In a famous article entitled 'The North Began', which appeared in the Gaelic League newspaper, *An Claidheamh Soluis*, he praised the

Ulster Volunteers for standing up for their principles and called on nationalists to form a Volunteer group of their own to put pressure on the British Government to introduce Home Rule for all of Ireland.

On 25 November 1913 the Irish Volunteers were founded at a meeting held at the Rotunda Hall in Dublin. Over 3,000 Volunteers joined on the first night, and Eoin MacNeill was elected leader, with a Provisional Committee to assist him. Unknown to MacNeill, most members of this committee were members of the Irish Republican Brotherhood. The secret society regarded the Irish Volunteers as offering an ideal opportunity to plan a rebellion against British rule in Ireland. This aim was at variance with the objectives of MacNeill and most ordinary Volunteers, who were prepared to accept the granting of Home Rule. The Irish Volunteers grew rapidly and had over 70,000 members by June 1914.

The British Government now faced a worsening crisis in Ireland. Two sets of Volunteers faced one another with diametrically opposed aims. In this situation Asquith set about attempting to reach a compromise between unionists and Home Rule nationalists.

The Search for a Compromise

In attempting to avoid civil war in Ireland between unionists and nationalists, the British Government focused on the possibility of special treatment for Ulster. Two main difficulties presented themselves: namely, the definition of Ulster and whether exclusion from Home Rule should be a temporary measure or a permanent arrangement.

Although Ulster was traditionally regarded as a bastion of unionism, not all of the province's nine counties were dominated by unionists. Three counties – Donegal, Cavan and Monaghan – had overwhelming nationalist majorities. Four other counties – Antrim, Armagh, Down and Londonderry – had clear unionist majorities. Two counties, however – Fermanagh and Tyrone – were divided almost equally, although they had slight nationalist majorities.

By 1914 John Redmond had come to accept that Antrim, Armagh, Down and Londonderry would have to be excluded in some way from Home Rule. Similarly, Carson agreed that Donegal, Cavan and Monaghan would be included under Home Rule. However, both sides were determined to keep all of Fermanagh and Tyrone. Redmond's suggestion of 'Home Rule within Home Rule', i.e. that Ulster could have special treatment within a Home Rule settlement, was rejected outright by unionists, who wished to remain under the Westminster Parliament. Redmond then offered a six-year period of exclusion for Ulster, but Carson rejected this too, remarking that it was like a death sentence with a six-year stay of execution. As the political situation remained deadlocked, both sets of Volunteers in Ireland continued to strengthen their position.

The Crisis Deepens

In March 1914 unionist morale received a huge boost from an incident known as the 'Curragh Mutiny'. Most British army officers had conservative and unionist political sympathies, and unionists hoped that they would refuse to obey orders to march into Ulster to enforce Home Rule. In March 1914 fifty-eight British army officers in the Curragh offered to resign their commissions. They mistakenly believed that they were about to be ordered to march against the Ulster Volunteer Force. The British Government assured them that no such operations were planned. The incident greatly weakened the position of Asquith's Government in its dealings with unionists.

Ulster Volunteers landing guns at Donaghadee, Co. Down

On board the *Asgard* during the Howth Gun-Running, 1914

Many nationalists took the view that they would have to rely more and more on their own resources in order to achieve a degree of self-government.

On 24 April the Ulster Volunteers succeeded in landing vast quantities of arms, which had been imported from Germany, at Larne, Bangor and Donaghadee. The incident was known as the Larne Gun-Running, and the British Government made no attempt to arrest or punish those involved.

In June 1914 John Redmond moved to gain control of the Irish Volunteers. He was alarmed that such a powerful organisation was outside his control. MacNeill and other leaders agreed to allow Redmond to appoint twenty-five members to the Provisional Committee, in order to avoid a split in the Volunteers.

On 26 July 1914 the Irish Volunteers landed arms and

Thousands lined the streets for the funerals of the three people killed at Bachelor's Walk in Dublin following the Howth Gun-Running

ammunition in Co. Dublin in an incident known as the Howth Gun-Running. The arms had been transported on Erskine Childers's yacht, the *Asgard*. Unlike in Ulster, where the authorities took no action, the police and British army attempted to intervene in this case. Later in the day, British troops opened fire on jeering crowds in Bachelor's Walk in Dublin city, killing three people. Nationalists contrasted this with the attitude of the authorities to the Larne Gun-Running.

Failure to Agree

As the deadline when Home Rule would become law (September 1914) approached, the British Government made one last effort to find a compromise. King George V offered Buckingham Palace as a setting for a conference between the British Government, the Conservative Opposition, and unionist and nationalist representatives. Asquith and Lloyd George for the Liberal Government were joined by the Home Rule leaders, Redmond and Dillon. On the other side sat the Conservative leaders, Bonar Law and Lord Lansdowne, and Carson and Craig for the Unionist Party. The speaker of the House of Commons chaired the meeting. No agreement whatever could

be reached on Fermanagh and Tyrone. As a result, the Buckingham Palace Conference broke up in complete failure on 24 July.

By then, however, Europe was on the road to war. Within ten days World War I had broken out, with Great Britain joining in on 4 August 1914.

The Outbreak of World War I

When war broke out, the British Government decided to pass the Home Rule Bill but to suspend its coming into effect until the end of hostilities. This partly pleased both unionists and nationalists. Unionists were given a guarantee that when the war was over, the situation of Ulster would be looked at again. For nationalists, the passing into law of Home Rule on 18 September 1914 was a victory of sorts. They expected the war to be over soon, and then, after nearly fifty years of struggle, Home Rule would finally come into operation.

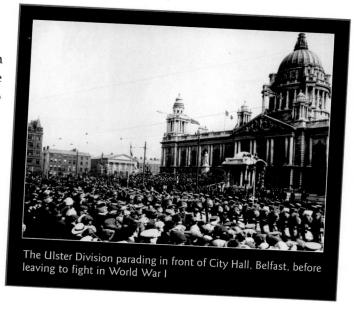

The Ulster Division parading in front of City Hall, Belfast, before leaving to fight in World War I

For Carson, Craig and other unionist leaders, the war was an opportunity to show their loyalty to King and country. They advised the Ulster Volunteers to join the British forces, and many answered this call. As the leaders of the British army were sympathetic to the unionists, they allowed the Ulster Volunteers to join in groups and to retain certain badges and emblems. A special division of the British army, the 36th (Ulster) Division, consisted largely of recruits from the province.

With the outbreak of war, John Redmond had a much more difficult decision to make than Carson or Craig. Although he was personally sympathetic to the British cause, many nationalists would be reluctant to become involved in fighting on Britain's side. However, in August and September 1914 there was a wave of sympathy for Belgium throughout Ireland. Britain had gone to war over the issue of Belgian neutrality, and the British press highlighted German atrocities against this small Catholic country. Against this background and because he hoped that a grateful Britain would grant Ireland Home Rule as a result, Redmond took the momentous decision to advise his followers to join the British forces. In a speech at Woodenbridge in Co. Wicklow in September 1914, Redmond strongly advised members of the Irish Volunteers to join the British army.

His speech caused a bitter split in the Irish Volunteers. A huge majority, consisting of around 170,000 members, followed Redmond and became known as the National Volunteers. They were now

Irish soldiers looking after wounded comrades in France during World War I

commanded by Colonel Maurice Moore, and around 25,000 of them joined the British army. The leader of the Irish Volunteers, Eoin MacNeill, and around 11,000 of his followers refused to follow Redmond. They kept the title Irish Volunteers and declared that World War I was England's quarrel and no direct concern of theirs.

For the IRB the outbreak of war in 1914 meant the arrival of a long-awaited opportunity. Basing their policy on the old slogan 'England's difficulty is Ireland's opportunity', its leaders now set about planning an armed rebellion in Ireland. The split in the Volunteers suited their purposes admirably. They could manipulate the smaller group of 11,000 much more easily than the larger group, which had been nominally under Redmond's control. At the outbreak of hostilities, as in other countries, the war was popular in Ireland. However, as the prolonged conflict developed, conditions soon changed to the detriment of Redmond and his Home Rule followers and to the advantage of more extreme nationalists of the republican tradition.

Ireland and World War I

As an integral part of the United Kingdom, Ireland was fully involved in World War I. Protestants and unionists supported the war effort without reservation from the outset. Indeed, many Protestant families suffered severely when the only son in the house was killed. This led many of them to leave Ireland for Great Britain after the war.

For Catholics and nationalists, the decision to join the army or navy was usually based on one of two motives. Many followed the advice of John Redmond and believed that they were fighting for Ireland's cause, as the British Government would be more likely to grant Home Rule because of their sacrifice. For others, the motivation was purely economic. For poorer soldiers, the separation allowance paid to their wives and children was an incentive to join up at a time when unemployment and low wages were rife throughout most of Ireland.

A British army recruitment poster featuring Lord Kitchener, Secretary of State for War, 1914–15

As the war continued and the number of casualties increased, recruitment levels declined in Ireland. Whereas 43,000 enlisted between the outbreak of war and the end of 1914, this number had declined to 12,000 between September 1915 and March 1916.

Some sectors of the Irish economy prospered during the war. Because of food shortages in Britain due to German submarine activity, the price of Irish food exports rose rapidly. Heavy industry flourished in the Belfast region, as there was a huge wartime demand for shipping and armaments.

However, because of inflation during World War I, people on fixed incomes, especially white-collar workers such as civil servants, clerks and teachers, suffered as their salaries failed to keep pace with inflation. As a result, there were a number of strikes in these sectors.

During the war, Irish soldiers took part in many varied operations. However, they were particularly prominent in two memorable engagements. During 1915 Irish regiments such as the Royal Dublin Fusiliers, the Inniskilling Fusiliers and the Royal Munster Fusiliers suffered heavy casualties in the ill-fated Gallipoli campaign in Turkey. During the following year, the Battle of the Somme, which began in July 1916, involved very heavy casualties for the 36th (Ulster) Division. Indeed, right to the end of the war in November 1918, Irish regiments remained in the thick of the fighting and suffered heavy casualties.

Historians have difficulty estimating the precise number of Irish recruits and casualties during World War I. This is partly because many Irish emigrants in Great Britain joined various regiments of the British army, and largely 'Irish' regiments contained people without any Irish connection. However, an estimate of around 300,000 Irish involved in the fighting and around 30,000 casualties has been reached.

Of all the consequences of World War I in Ireland, one of the most significant was the opportunity the war created for more extreme separatists to fill the political vacuum left by the declining influence of John Redmond and the Home Rule Party.

Opposition to World War I

Despite the difficulties involved, a small minority of Irish separatists began to voice their opposition to Irish involvement in World War I. Although the Defence of the Realm Act (DORA) imposed strict restrictions on freedom of speech, this did not deter determined protesters. Arthur Griffith, the leader of Sinn Féin, publicly voiced his opposition to the war. James Connolly and the Irish Citizen Army were also opposed. The banner at their headquarters at Liberty Hall declared, 'We serve neither King nor Kaiser but Ireland'. The Irish Volunteers, under the leadership of Eoin MacNeill, continued to recruit members, to drill and to discourage people from joining the British army. Unknown to MacNeill, practically all his headquarters staff were members of the IRB. These men had one purpose in mind – the planning of an armed rising as soon as possible.

An anti-Redmond cartoon showing opposition to Irish involvement in World War I

Liberty Hall, the Dublin headquarters of the Irish Transport and General Workers Union, with the banner 'We serve neither King nor Kaiser, but Ireland'

Planning a Rising

For the Supreme Council, or governing body, of the IRB, the planning of a rising was a matter of extreme urgency. They did not know how long the war was going to last, and it was essential from their point of view to attack British rule in Ireland while Britain was involved in a world war. Thomas Clarke, Seán Mac Diarmada, Joseph Plunkett and other leaders of the Supreme Council approached their task at two levels. On the surface, they would encourage anti-British feeling and exploit the difficulties encountered by Redmond. By the middle of 1915 Redmond's popularity had fallen considerably. Casualties were high in the war, and there was no immediate prospect of Home Rule. In June 1915 he refused an invitation to join a coalition government in Britain. Although this decision was supported in Ireland, Redmond's position was weakened because Carson joined the Government at the same time. From then on, unionists had a strong influence right at the heart of the British Government. For the IRB, this was further proof that the peaceful attainment of Home Rule was a distant prospect.

At a hidden level, members of the Supreme Council plotted an actual rising. They initially planned a rising for the autumn of 1915 but later changed this to Easter 1916. Eoin MacNeill and other non-IRB members of the Irish Volunteers were kept in the dark concerning these plans. The IRB men sent Sir Roger Casement as their secret agent to Germany to enlist the Kaiser's help. Casement had been a British diplomat until 1912 and had been knighted by the King for his humanitarian work. He had highlighted the horrific exploitation of native peoples in Africa and South America. By 1914 he had abandoned his loyalty to Britain and had joined the IRB. His mission to Germany was only partly successful. He tried but failed to persuade Irish prisoners of war in the British army to obtain their release from German prisoner-of-war camps by joining him to fight against Britain. The German authorities did not believe that the IRB had the capacity to stage a serious rising in Ireland. As a result, they only agreed to send a shipload of arms and ammunition to Ireland instead of the large numbers of troops and weapons that Casement had hoped for.

In planning the rising, the IRB decided to recruit two highly influential, talented, but vastly different men – Patrick Pearse and James Connolly.

Patrick Pearse and the Irish Nation

By 1914 Patrick Pearse was one of the leading public figures in Ireland spreading the belief that Ireland was a separate nation with its own ancient culture and that it was entitled to complete independence.

Born in Dublin in 1879, the son of an English stonemason, Patrick Pearse attended the Christian Brothers' school at Westland Row; he then went on to the Royal University and King's Inns, where he qualified as a barrister. While growing up, he was deeply influenced by the Irish cultural revival, most especially by the Gaelic League. He wrote books in the Irish language and edited the Gaelic League newspaper, *An Claidheamh Soluis*. Pearse was convinced that the language was at the heart of Ireland's identity and remarked that a country without its language was a country without a soul. His deep interest in education led him to study the school systems of different countries and to found his own school, St Enda's, in Dublin. Here, great emphasis was placed on the Irish language and on Irish history and culture.

Patrick Pearse (left) with his brother Willie in the grounds of St Enda's, the school he founded in Rathfarnham, Co. Dublin

In his writings, Pearse often returned to the theme of a hero who was willing to die for his country. He frequently used religious imagery to portray love of country as a sacred duty. He even compared a hero dying for his country to Christ dying on the cross to save the human race.

By 1915 Pearse had become convinced that only the shedding of blood could restore Ireland's honour. He believed that English influence in the country was destroying Irish identity and that if patriots died for Ireland, it would change the outlook of the Irish people. This idea is known as **blood sacrifice**. Whereas other leading members of the IRB concentrated on staging a successful rising, Pearse believed that even if the rising failed, the blood shed by the rebels would encourage future generations to rise against British rule. At a time when many people in Europe glorified sacrifice during World War I, Pearse was quite explicit in his views. He praised the war, remarking:

> It is good for the world that such things should be done. The old heart of the earth needed to be warmed by the red wine of the battlefields.

Although he had supported Home Rule in 1912, Pearse changed his mind when the emergence of the Ulster Volunteers appeared to threaten its implementation. He enthusiastically joined the newly formed Irish Volunteers in November 1913 and was sworn in to the IRB at around the same time. From then on, his writings became more and more dominated by the need for blood sacrifice. In July 1915, during a famous oration over the grave of the old Fenian Jeremiah O'Donovan Rossa, Pearse expressed the view that a risen Irish nation could only come as a result of armed rebellion:

> Life springs from death, and from the graves of patriot men and women spring living nations.

He concluded the speech with the observation that 'Ireland unfree shall never be at peace'. The British authorities in Dublin Castle regarded this as a typical speech by an extreme separatist with limited public appeal. They little realised that a major rebellion was already at an advanced stage of preparation.

While Pearse was expressing romantic and idealistic notions of Irish freedom, James Connolly was also committed to armed rebellion, but for much more practical reasons.

James Connolly and the Citizen Army

As a socialist, James Connolly had hoped that workers in different European countries would refuse to fight one another in World War I. When this hope failed to materialise, he concentrated on the notion that Irish workers could never be properly treated under British rule. In his view, a successful rising against Britain would be a prelude to a more equal society in Ireland.

After the departure of James Larkin to America in 1914, Connolly came to control the Irish Transport and General Workers' Union as well as the Citizen Army. By 1915 there were about 200 members of the Citizen Army, and Connolly grew more anxious and appeared willing to lead them on their own in a rebellion. This would interfere dangerously with the plans of the IRB and possibly lead the authorities in Dublin Castle to imprison hundreds of leading separatists because of the threat they posed to the war effort against Germany. To prevent this, the IRB recruited Connolly in early 1916 and made him a member of the Military Council, the small group which was planning the rising. In the months leading up to Easter 1916, therefore, the plotters hoped to involve both the Irish Volunteers and the Citizen Army in the rising.

Preparing for the Rising

For the leaders of the IRB on the Military Council, Eoin MacNeill was a serious obstacle to success. MacNeill only believed in a rising if it had a serious hope of succeeding. This depended on significant assistance from Germany, including the landing of German troops in Ireland. Right until the final days before the rising, the IRB kept MacNeill in the dark about their plans.

The authorities in Dublin Castle were deceived by the secrecy of the Military Council of the IRB. Aware that previous rebel movements had been full of British spies, Clarke, Mac Diarmada and the other leaders kept strict control over information. The Irish Chief Secretary, Augustine Birrell, and the Under-Secretary, Sir Matthew Nathan, did not regard the Irish Volunteers as a serious threat. They believed that the Volunteers had insufficient arms to stage a rebellion. John Redmond had advised them not to move against the Irish Volunteers, as this would only make them more popular and damage recruitment to the British army.

On Wednesday, 19 April 1916, the Military Council published a forged note known as the 'Castle Document' in the newspapers. It was written on official Dublin Castle notepaper and contained a list of people that the British authorities were supposedly planning to imprison. As the names included leading members of the Irish Volunteers, MacNeill at once gave orders to his followers to resist arrest.

On Thursday, 20 April, Pearse admitted to MacNeill that a rising was planned.

On the following day, Good Friday, 21 April, Patrick Pearse, Seán Mac Diarmada and Thomas McDonagh visited MacNeill and told him about the imminent arrival of a German ship with arms and ammunition. MacNeill now realised that a conflict could not be avoided and repeated his orders of the previous Wednesday on the need to resist imprisonment. On the same day, the German ship the *Aud* arrived in Tralee Bay in Co. Kerry. When it failed to rendezvous with Irish Volunteers, the captain sailed to Cork Harbour and sank the ship with all the armaments on board. When Roger Casement landed from a German submarine at Banna Strand near Tralee, he was almost immediately arrested. Ironically, he was coming to try to stop the rising because in his view the arms sent by the Germans were totally inadequate.

Having learned of the fate of the *Aud*, MacNeill tried to prevent a rising. On Easter Sunday, 23 April 1916, he published a notice in the *Sunday Independent* cancelling all Volunteer manoeuvres planned for that day. On Sunday evening the members of the IRB Military Council met in Liberty Hall in Dublin. Despite the loss of German arms, they were determined to go ahead and planned the rising for the following day, Easter Monday, 24 April 1916.

The 1916 Rising Breaks Out

As groups of Irish Volunteers and members of the Citizen Army moved to various positions around Dublin city on the morning of 24 April 1916, few onlookers believed that anything unusual would happen. People were used to seeing both groups engage in marches and drills. However, this time they were intent on real fighting. A number of strategic buildings were occupied, including the General Post Office (GPO) on Sackville Street (now O'Connell Street), which the rebels chose as their headquarters. At noon the Tricolour flag was raised over the GPO, and Patrick Pearse, who had been chosen as Commander-in-Chief, came outside to read the Proclamation of the Irish Republic.

A letter from Eoin McNeill to a priest, Fr Eugene Nevin, Easter Sunday 1916, authenticating his orders which had appeared in that day's *Sunday Independent*

Because of all the confusion of the previous days, the Easter Rising was mostly confined to Dublin, although some Volunteer activity also occurred in areas such as Ashbourne, Co. Meath, Galway and Wexford.

In Dublin, the Volunteers and Citizen Army seized seven strongpoints throughout the city: these were the GPO, the Four Courts, the South Dublin Union, the Mendicity Institute, the Royal College of Surgeons, Jacob's Factory and Bolands Mills. An attempt to capture Dublin Castle failed, although – unknown to the Volunteers – it was very poorly defended at the time.

The British soon rushed in reinforcements from Athlone, the Curragh Camp and Britain. General Sir John Maxwell was sent to take control with full powers to put down the rebellion. Gradually, British forces encircled the city centre and moved on the rebel positions. A gunboat, the *Helga*, sailed up the River Liffey to shell the GPO and Liberty Hall.

POBLACHT NA H EIREANN.
THE PROVISIONAL GOVERNMENT
OF THE
IRISH REPUBLIC
TO THE PEOPLE OF IRELAND.

IRISHMEN AND IRISHWOMEN: In the name of God and of the dead generations from which she receives her old tradition of nationhood, Ireland, through us, summons her children to her flag and strikes for her freedom.

Having organised and trained her manhood through her secret revolutionary organisation, the Irish Republican Brotherhood, and through her open military organisations, the Irish Volunteers and the Irish Citizen Army, having patiently perfected her discipline, having resolutely waited for the right moment to reveal itself, she now seizes that moment, and, supported by her exiled children in America and by gallant allies in Europe, but relying in the first on her own strength, she strikes in full confidence of victory.

We declare the right of the people of Ireland to the ownership of Ireland, and to the unfettered control of Irish destinies, to be sovereign and indefeasible. The long usurpation of that right by a foreign people and government has not extinguished the right, nor can it ever be extinguished except by the destruction of the Irish people. In every generation the Irish people have asserted their right to national freedom and sovereignty; six times during the past three hundred years they have asserted it in arms. Standing on that fundamental right and again asserting it in arms in the face of the world, we hereby proclaim the Irish Republic as a Sovereign Independent State, and we pledge our lives and the lives of our comrades-in-arms to the cause of its freedom, of its welfare, and of its exaltation among the nations.

The Irish Republic is entitled to, and hereby claims, the allegiance of every Irishman and Irishwoman. The Republic guarantees religious and civil liberty, equal rights and equal opportunities to all its citizens, and declares its resolve to pursue the happiness and prosperity of the whole nation and of all its parts, cherishing all the children of the nation equally, and oblivious of the differences carefully fostered by an alien government, which have divided a minority from the majority in the past.

Until our arms have brought the opportune moment for the establishment of a permanent National Government, representative of the whole people of Ireland and elected by the suffrages of all her men and women, the Provisional Government, hereby constituted, will administer the civil and military affairs of the Republic in trust for the people.

We place the cause of the Irish Republic under the protection of the Most High God, Whose blessing we invoke upon our arms, and we pray that no one who serves that cause will dishonour it by cowardice, inhumanity, or rapine. In this supreme hour the Irish nation must, by its valour and discipline and by the readiness of its children to sacrifice themselves for the common good, prove itself worthy of the august destiny to which it is called.

Signed on Behalf of the Provisional Government,

THOMAS J. CLARKE,
SEAN Mac DIARMADA,   THOMAS MacDONAGH,
P. H. PEARSE,   EAMONN CEANNT,
JAMES CONNOLLY.   JOSEPH PLUNKETT.

The Proclamation of the Irish Republic

There was massive loss of life, injury and damage to property, especially in the O'Connell Street area. Over 450 people, including nearly 300 civilians, were killed. Appalled at the suffering of civilians, Pearse agreed to an unconditional surrender on Friday, 28 April. His instructions were then carried to the other garrisons, ordering them to surrender as well.

Reaction in Ireland and Britain

At first people in Dublin and throughout Ireland were very confused. Because of the disruption to newspaper production and censorship by the British army, very little concrete information was in circulation. As a result, wild rumours, such as that of a German invasion, were in circulation. Once the Rising was over, however, people began to discover what had really happened. There were different reactions to this knowledge. While some nationalists admired the rebels, many were appalled at the death and destruction. Volunteer prisoners were jeered by local crowds on the streets of Dublin. Unionists were extremely angry, as they regarded the Rising as a stab in the back while Britain was engaged in a life-and-death struggle against Germany.

The British Government similarly condemned the Rising in Parliament and was determined to punish the leaders severely. For John Redmond, it was a devastating shock. It flew in the face of his efforts to gain Home Rule by supporting the British war effort. He condemned it in Parliament as a German plot. However, another leading member of the Home Rule Party, John Dillon, had been trapped in Dublin during Easter Week. He wrote to Redmond to warn him to advise the British Government against a wholesale shooting of rebels. In Dillon's view, public opinion was against the Rising but could easily change if the British reaction were excessive. His observations were to prove prophetic.

Executions and Imprisonment

General Maxwell, once the Rising was crushed, immediately set about punishing those involved. About 1,800 rank-and-file Volunteers and Citizen Army members were sent to prison in England and Wales. The leading 170 were tried by court martial, and 90 were sentenced to death. The executions began on 3 May with the shooting of Patrick Pearse, Thomas Clarke and Thomas McDonagh. They continued over the next week in groups of two or three.

John Dillon rushed to London and praised the bravery of the rebels in the House of Commons. He called on Asquith to stop the executions, warning him: 'You are washing our whole life work in a sea of blood.' By this Dillon meant that the peaceful Home Rule movement might be replaced by physical force republican organisations. Asquith decided to go to Dublin and call a halt to the executions. The shooting of Seán Mac Diarmada and James Connolly on 12 May marked the end of this policy. The remaining death sentences were commuted to life imprisonment. Included in this group were Countess Markievicz and Éamon de Valera. In all, fifteen had been executed, including all seven signatories of the Proclamation of the Irish Republic.

As a result of the executions, public opinion began to swing around in favour of the rebels. Huge crowds attended Requiem masses for the dead leaders. As Pearse had prophesied, the executed rebels were seen as martyrs and were held up as examples to be followed by future generations.

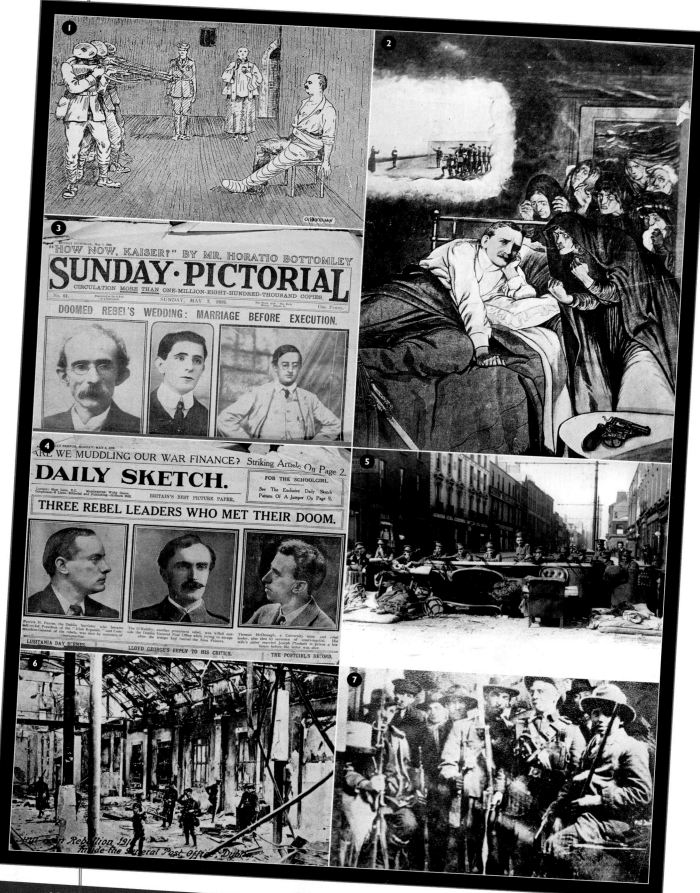

1. Postcard depicting the execution of the wounded James Connolly

2. A republican postcard (1917) depicting General Maxwell being haunted by the widows of the executed 1916 leaders

3. Newspaper coverage of the executions of the 1916 leaders

4. Newspaper coverage of the executions of the 1916 leaders

5. British troops barricade a Dublin street

6. British troops in the ruins of the GPO

7. A group of Irish rebels inside the GPO during Easter week, 1916

8. The shell of the GPO (right) after the Rising

9. Roger Casement is led from court in London after being sentenced to death for treason in 1916

10. The British Prime Minister H.H. Asquith visiting Dublin after the Rising

11. Dubliners survey the destruction around O'Connell Bridge after the city centre was shelled by British forces

The Legacy of 1916

The 1916 Rising was undoubtedly one of the most controversial events in Irish history. Unionists and many supporters of Home Rule condemned it. Home Rulers argued that Ireland already had democratically elected MPs and that even the delay in granting Home Rule did not justify violence. They also pointed out that a tiny minority in the IRB decided on the Rising without any mandate from the people. Later revisionist historians supported these viewpoints. In a famous article published in 1972, the Jesuit priest Fr Shaw strongly criticised the 1916 Rising and especially the attempts by Patrick Pearse to link it with the Christian faith. Fr Shaw objected strongly, for example, to the connection between Christ rising from the dead at Easter and the Irish people rising in rebellion in search of freedom. Another factor that led to a revision of attitudes to 1916 was the violence in Northern Ireland from 1968 onwards. Certain commentators believed that the central message of 1916 had been the glorification of violence for political ends.

The supporters of the 1916 Rising, on the other hand, argued that Irish people were entitled to take up arms in a struggle for freedom. They pointed to the fact that Home Rule was effectively killed off by the unionists and the Ulster Volunteers. Echoing Patrick Pearse's beliefs, they argued that Home Rule was inadequate; that only a fully independent republic was desirable; and that this could never be achieved without violence.

As history students, we are entitled to examine and consider all the various viewpoints. However, in studying the 1916 Rising, we must always ensure that we study it in the context of the time. For example, during World War I, the notion of dying for one's country had a different meaning from the same concept today. Above all, we must avoid allowing present-day ideas to distort our vision of the past. When guided by sound historical principles, the 1916 Rising can be a good test of a student's ability to be objective about past events.

KEY PERSONALITY: PATRICK PEARSE (1879–1916)

Patrick Pearse was born in Dublin in 1879, the son of an Irish mother and English father. He was educated by the Christian Brothers at Westland Row and then went on to study at University College, Dublin, and King's Inns, where he trained as a barrister. After practising law for a short period, Pearse became actively involved in the Gaelic revival. He joined the Gaelic League in 1895 and became editor of the League's journal, *An Claidheamh Soluis*, in 1903. He used its pages to attack the increasing anglicisation of Ireland and to promote the revival of the Irish language. He was a prolific writer of articles, poems and plays.

As well as being a writer, Pearse was an educationalist. He condemned the Irish education system as 'the Murder Machine' and opened a school – St Enda's – at Rathfarnham, in order to put his own ideas into practice. His school was bilingual, and he implemented a broad curriculum that included drama and nature study. He strongly promoted Irish history and culture and taught his pupils about legendary, heroic characters such as Cúchulainn.

Although Pearse initially supported the cause of Home Rule, he soon became disillusioned with parliamentary politics and believed that full Irish independence could only be achieved by armed rebellion. The Gaelic League played an important part in Pearse's path to extreme nationalism. He became a founder member of the Irish Volunteers in 1913. Shortly afterwards, he joined the IRB and became a member of the Military Council, which planned the Easter Rising of 1916.

As a revolutionary, Pearse was an idealist and a visionary. In his writings he blended nationalist and Christian imagery: just as Christ had died on Calvary to save mankind, he believed his own martyrdom would advance the cause of Irish freedom. Pearse believed in 'blood sacrifice' – the view that the spilling of blood for the cause of freedom was a necessary and cleansing act.

Pearse commanded the Easter Rising of 1916 from his headquarters in the GPO and read the Proclamation of the Irish Republic from its steps. He surrendered on 28 April because of the high number of civilian casualties. Pearse – revolutionary, educationalist and poet – was executed on 3 May 1916.

EXERCISES

ORDINARY LEVEL

1. How did the Parliament Act (1911) pave the way for the passing of the Third Home Rule Bill?

2. Outline the main provisions of the Third Home Rule Bill (1912).

3. Explain the political, economic and religious grounds of unionist opposition to Home Rule.

4. Examine the pictures concerning unionism on pages 120 and 121, and answer the following questions.

   (i) What is the common theme found in all three pictures?

   (ii) How does the poster of Sir Edward Carson on page 120 convey the determination of unionists to resist Home Rule?

   (iii) Do you think that the poster on page 120 conveys the unionist message effectively? Explain your answer.

   (iv) Describe the scene of the signing of the Solemn League and Covenant as illustrated by the photograph on page 121.

5. The following is an account of the Buckingham Palace Peace Conference of July 1914. Read it carefully, and answer the questions that follow.

   The Prime Minister (H.H. Asquith) indicated that in his opinion, the two serious outstanding points were (1) the area of exclusion, and (2) the time limit . . . the Prime Minister suggested that the question of area should be discussed first.

Sir Edward Carson strongly argued that the question of a time limit be discussed in the first place . . . Mr Redmond strongly dissented. Finally it was decided to take the question of area first.

Sir Edward Carson then made a strong appeal to Mr Redmond and Mr Dillon to consent to the total exclusion of [nine-county] Ulster in the interest of the earliest possible unity of Ireland. He argued that if a smaller area were excluded, the reunion of the whole of Ireland would be delayed . . .

The Irish Party only consented to negotiate on the basis of exclusion because the leaders of the Ulster Unionists repeatedly and emphatically refused to consider any other proposal . . .

Eventually Sir Edward Carson substituted, for his demand for the exclusion of the whole of Ulster, the exclusion of a block consisting of the six counties . . . all to vote as one unit.

Mr Redmond intimated that he could not seriously consider this proposal, any more than the proposal for the total exclusion of Ulster.

It became apparent that deadlock had arisen, and the question was raised as to whether it was of any value to continue the Conference.

National Library of Ireland, Redmond Papers, cited in D. Gwynn, The History of Partition, Dublin: Browne and Nolan 1950, 119–31

(i) What were the two outstanding points at issue between the parties concerning the implementation of Home Rule in Ireland?

(ii) Which issue did Carson want discussed first?

(iii) What appeal did he make to Redmond and Dillon?

(iv) Why did the Irish Parliamentary Party agree to discuss exclusion of some areas from Home Rule?

(v) What was Carson's final offer?

(vi) Did Redmond accept it? Explain your answer.

6. Write a paragraph on Irish involvement in World War I.

7. Examine the poster, cartoon and photograph concerning Ireland and World War I on pages 125 and 126, and answer the questions that follow.

(i) How do we know that the poster of Lord Kitchener on page 125 is a recruitment poster?

(ii) Do you think that the cartoon on page 126 favours or opposes Irish involvement in World War I? Explain your answer.

(iii) What message is conveyed in the slogan on Liberty Hall in the picture on page 126?

8. Write an account of the life and political ideas of Patrick Pearse.

9. Write an account of the British response to the Easter Rising of 1916.

HIGHER LEVEL

1. Analyse in detail unionist opposition to Home Rule up to the outbreak of war in 1914.

2. Account for the outbreak of a rebellion in Dublin at Easter 1916.

3. Read the Proclamation of the Irish Republic (1916) on page 130, and answer the following questions.

(i) What organisations, according to the Proclamation, prepared the Rising?

(ii) What rights does the Proclamation declare in the third paragraph?

(iii) What does the Proclamation state about freedom, equality and democracy?

(iv) Give examples of religious references contained in this document. What message do they convey?

(v) 'Honour and self-sacrifice are important themes in this document.' Would you agree?

4. Discuss the Easter Rising of 1916 and its immediate aftermath.

5. Write an essay on Patrick Pearse (1879–1916).

10. THE STRUGGLE FOR INDEPENDENCE

The Aftermath of the Rising

After the defeat of the Rising, the British Prime Minister, Asquith, made one further attempt to reach a compromise between unionists and nationalists. He did not want the Irish Question to continue absorbing the undue attention of the British Government in the middle of its titanic struggle on the Western Front. He also hoped to entice the neutral United States of America to join the war on the Allied side. A successful policy in Ireland would influence opinion in America in Britain's favour. Asquith therefore gave his most able minister, David Lloyd George, the task of seeking a compromise in Ireland. Having negotiated separately with

Crowds in Dublin welcoming the release of Countess Markievicz and other republican prisoners

Redmond and Carson, Lloyd George got both to agree that the area in Ulster to receive special treatment would consist of six counties. These included Fermanagh and Tyrone, which had nationalist majorities. However, whereas Redmond understood that the exclusion of the six counties from Home Rule would be only temporary, Lloyd George promised Carson that it would be permanent. By agreeing to the exclusion of Fermanagh and Tyrone and by being tricked by Lloyd George, Redmond lost a lot of his remaining popularity in Ireland. His apparent acceptance of partition alienated nationalists throughout the country, but especially in Ulster.

In December 1916 Asquith was forced out of office, and Lloyd George became Prime Minister at the head of a coalition government. His initial challenge was to lead Great Britain to victory in World War I. However, he was to remain in power until October 1922 and to make decisions that would have a deep impact on the future development of Ireland, north and south. On becoming Prime Minister, Lloyd George decided to implement a friendly gesture towards Ireland. He ordered the release of most of the 1,800 participants in the 1916 Rising who had not been considered important enough to be put on trial. After their release from prison camps in England and Wales, the prisoners returned to Ireland to huge demonstrations. Most of them were determined to continue the struggle for an independent Ireland. The continuing decline of the Home Rule Party and the actions of the British Government in Ireland during 1917 and 1918 were to facilitate greatly the growth of more extreme nationalism. This was represented by two organisations – the revived Irish Volunteers and a new Sinn Féin.

The Re-emergence of the Irish Volunteers

Among those Volunteers imprisoned after 1916, the determination to continue the struggle for independence remained strong. As the senior surviving commandant from the Rising, Éamon de Valera could expect to play a leading role on his release from prison. However, other leaders began to emerge as well. Michael Collins, who had been a rank-and-file Volunteer during Easter Week, showed leadership qualities during his imprisonment. In particular, he argued that the old-style open fighting between two forces was a thing of the past. In fighting the superior forces of the British Empire, he argued, the Irish should adopt guerrilla warfare, whereby the Volunteers would attack and then escape into the countryside. Collins also believed that the IRB should be revived, and he succeeded in dominating it from 1917 onwards. His views were shared by other Volunteers such as Richard Mulcahy, who had been prominent in the Rising in Ashbourne, Co. Meath.

Cathal Brugha, who had been badly wounded during the Easter Rising, was another key figure in the rebuilding of the Irish Volunteers. Totally committed to an Irish republic, he believed that it could be achieved only by force. Unlike Collins, he believed that the continued existence of the IRB would lead to a divided leadership. In his view, there should be only one united movement, openly committed to the achievement of an Irish republic.

Unlike the Volunteers before 1916, however, the revived Irish Volunteers in the changed circumstances from 1917 onwards were willing to work closely with a political party – the newly revived Sinn Féin.

Count Plunkett campaigning in the Roscommon by-election, 1917

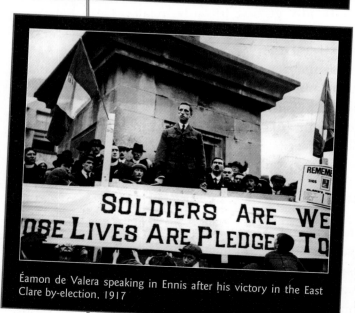
Éamon de Valera speaking in Ennis after his victory in the East Clare by-election, 1917

The Revival of Sinn Féin

Although Arthur Griffith and Sinn Féin had nothing to do with planning the 1916 Rising, he was arrested and interned after the Rising. Because the British mistakenly called the rebels 'Sinn Féin' Volunteers, people came to associate them with the party. The Rising was widely referred to as the 'Sinn Féin rebellion'. On his release from prison in December 1916, Griffith began to re-organise the party. Initially, he revived his old policy of dual monarchy, but Sinn Féin's policy would change radically as vast numbers of Volunteers and their supporters flocked to join the party.

In February 1917 Count Plunkett, the father of the executed signatory of the 1916 Proclamation, Joseph Plunkett, won a by-election in North Roscommon. He defeated the candidate of the Home Rule Party. Although not a member of Sinn Féin, Count Plunkett received support from the party and followed the Sinn Féin policy of **abstention**, that is, of refusing to take his seat in the British Parliament at Westminster.

In June 1917 de Valera was freed from prison when Lloyd George ordered the release of the remaining prisoners, who were serving life terms. He returned to Ireland to contest a by-election in East Clare as a Sinn Féin candidate. The vacancy occurred owing to the death of John Redmond's brother, Major William Redmond, who was killed fighting on the Western Front. De Valera's victory in the East Clare by-election strengthened his position and his claim to lead the Sinn Féin Party.

At an Ard-Fheis of Sinn Féin in October 1917, Arthur Griffith agreed to step aside and allow de Valera to become leader of Sinn Féin. The party abandoned the notion of dual monarchy and became a republican party. The delegates also supported the policy of abstention from Westminster and of appealing to a post-war peace conference to recognise Irish independence.

This revived Sinn Féin Party is usually known as the Second Sinn Féin Party (1917–22). Unlike the small first Sinn Féin, which effectively existed between 1905 and 1910, the new Sinn Féin was to become a mass political movement. It would be closely allied to the Irish Volunteers and contained people of vastly differing views, from old dual monarchists such as Arthur Griffith to determined republicans such as Cathal Brugha. As long as the struggle for independence continued, the Second Sinn Féin Party would remain united. Once this ended and choices had to be made, serious differences of opinion would surface.

A Sinn Féin group in 1917, including Arthur Griffith, Éamon de Valera and Michael Collins

The Irish Volunteers and Sinn Féin

Once the Sinn Féin Ard-Fheis was over, the Irish Volunteers held a convention in October 1917. Many Volunteers were members of Sinn Féin also. De Valera, the new president of Sinn Féin, was elected president of the Volunteers as well. He was assisted by a twenty-member Executive Committee that included Cathal Brugha, Michael Collins and Richard Mulcahy. From then on, Sinn Féin and the Volunteers co-operated closely in the struggle for independence. Their initial aim was to replace the Home Rule Party as the main force in Irish nationalism. When this had been achieved, they would then confront the British Government and demand independence. However, the achievement of both of these aims depended upon the conclusion of World War I. Its continuation and the pressing need for soldiers would lead the British Government to commit a serious political error in Ireland in 1918, when it attempted to introduce conscription against the wishes of the vast majority of the population.

The Conscription Crisis, 1918

In the spring of 1918 Lloyd George's Government was engaged in a further futile attempt to introduce Home Rule on the basis of agreement between nationalists and unionists. This took the form of the Irish Convention, which met in Dublin under the chairmanship of Sir Horace Plunkett between July 1917 and April 1918. All political groups were invited, but Sinn Féin boycotted the Convention. Carson and the Ulster unionists would not compromise on the permanent exclusion of six counties from Home Rule. Although John Redmond and Lord Midleton, the leader of the southern Irish unionists, made strenuous efforts to reach agreement, their efforts failed. Redmond died in March 1918, and John Dillon succeeded him as leader of the Irish Parliamentary Party. In April the Irish Convention broke up without reaching any agreement. This further weakened the prestige of the Irish Party and strengthened the position of Sinn Féin. At the same time, Sinn Féin was about to receive a massive boost in popularity from the British Government's handling of the conscription issue.

Although conscription – compulsory entry to the armed forces – was introduced in Great Britain in 1915, it was not extended to Ireland. After the 1916 Rising, this situation became increasingly unpopular in England, Scotland and Wales. In the spring of 1918 the British Government was under intense pressure to extend conscription to Ireland. Due to the withdrawal of Russia from the war, the Germans were able to divert troops to the Western Front and launch a spring offensive. Desperately in need of more troops and forced to increase the level of conscription in Britain, Lloyd George finally decided to introduce a Conscription Bill for Ireland. Despite the objections of John Dillon and his party, the bill was passed by the British Parliament. As a result, Dillon led his fellow Home Rule MPs out of Parliament and home to Ireland. The struggle against conscription now moved to Ireland.

The Conscription Crisis was eagerly taken up by Sinn Féin as a golden opportunity to advance the party's popularity. The failure of the Home Rule Party to prevent its introduction and the withdrawal of the Home Rule MPs from Parliament seemed to prove that Sinn Féin's argument in favour of abstention was correct. Under the leadership of de Valera, Sinn Féin soon assumed control of a mass movement of protest throughout Ireland. Practically all nationalists in Ireland were outraged at the introduction of conscription. Even those who supported joining the British army during the war believed that it should be on a voluntary basis. The Catholic bishops met at Maynooth and condemned conscription. Trade unions organised a general strike in protest. It was Sinn Féin and the Irish Volunteers who gained most, however. The Volunteers pledged to resist conscription by force, if necessary, and thousands of new recruits joined their ranks. In the middle of the crisis in May 1918, the British Government claimed it had uncovered a 'German plot' to start a new rebellion and arrested around a thousand Sinn Féin members, including de Valera and Arthur Griffith. The Government also banned Sinn Féin, the Gaelic League and other nationalist organisations.

Most nationalists in Ireland did not believe in the existence of a 'German plot' – in their view, it was a ploy used in order to crack down on Sinn Féin. Such actions by the British Government merely served to increase the popularity of the party. By the summer of 1918, with the collapse of the German offensive on the Western Front, the British Government abandoned its plans to introduce conscription in Ireland. The episode had served to discredit the British Government further among nationalists in Ireland. It also seriously undermined the position of the Home Rule Party. In 1917–18 the party had won three by-elections and had begun to challenge Sinn Féin once again. The Conscription Crisis totally reversed this trend. For Sinn Féin, the Conscription Crisis was of fundamental importance. Many people in Ireland believed that the threat of the Irish Volunteers to resist conscription forcibly had influenced the British Government's decision. As the leading party involved in the successful opposition to conscription, Sinn Féin was in a position to prepare for the forthcoming general election with confidence.

The 1918 General Election in Ireland

World War I finally ended on 11 November 1918. Shortly afterwards, Lloyd George called a general election throughout the United Kingdom. As no election was held during wartime, this was the first general election since December 1910. In Britain Lloyd George, in coalition with the Conservatives, won a huge victory. He campaigned on his success in winning the war and on his promise 'to make Germany pay'. However, although he was to continue as Prime Minister, his Liberal followers only held 136 seats, compared with 338 held by his Conservative allies. This dependence on Conservative support influenced his policy towards Ireland, especially as the Conservatives were close allies of the unionists.

In Ireland the 1918 general election was fought on a totally different basis from that in the rest of the United Kingdom. Here, there were two main contests. In Ulster there was the traditional struggle between unionists and nationalists, whereas in the rest of the country the contest was between the Home Rule Party and Sinn Féin. Because of favourable boundary changes, the number of Unionist MPs increased from 18 to 26. The Unionist Party was still led by Sir Edward Carson and still totally opposed to Home Rule. In eight seats in Ulster with nationalist majorities, the Home Rule Party and Sinn Féin agreed to contest only four each. They did this to avoid splitting the nationalist vote and letting a unionist candidate in. However, their choice of the Catholic Archbishop of Armagh, Cardinal Logue, as a mediator between both parties merely served to deepen unionist suspicions concerning the links between the Catholic Church and nationalist politicians.

Throughout most of the country, the 1918 election was a straightforward contest between the Home Rule Party under John Dillon and Sinn Féin under Éamon de Valera. Sinn Féin persuaded the Irish Labour Party not to contest the election in order to avoid splitting the more radical vote and allowing Home Rule candidates to be elected. Sinn Féin enjoyed many advantages facing into the 1918 election:

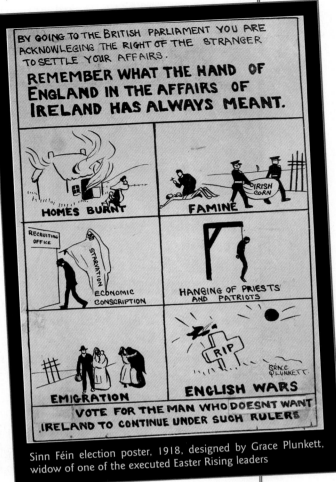

Sinn Féin election poster, 1918, designed by Grace Plunkett, widow of one of the executed Easter Rising leaders

- Most of its candidates and members were young and enthusiastic.
- It had built up a huge network of branches throughout the country.
- It had the active support of the Irish Volunteers and their women's section, Cumann na mBan.
- Sinn Féin members claimed to be the heirs of the martyrs of 1916 and to want to complete the work that the 1916 rebels had started.
- Changes in the electoral law ensured that many young voters were now voting for the first time. All men over twenty-one and all women over thirty could now vote. Many of these first-time voters had no tradition of voting for the Home Rule Party.
- Sinn Féin was credited with taking the lead in preventing the introduction of conscription into Ireland.
- Most leading members of the Home Rule Party were old by contrast with Sinn Féin leaders. John Dillon himself was almost seventy.

Map of Ireland showing the results of the 1918 general election, with Sinn Féin seats shown in dark green and unionist seats in orange

- The local branch structure of the Home Rule Party had declined. In twenty-five constituencies the party did not run a candidate.
- Many people believed that Redmond in particular had been too favourable to the British Government and that he had been outmanoeuvred by the British and the unionists.
- For a majority of Irish nationalists, Home Rule no longer offered a sufficient degree of autonomy from Great Britain.
- The British 'first past the post' system of voting favoured Sinn Féin because it gave the party far more seats than its proportion of the votes warranted.

When all the votes were finally counted in December 1918, Sinn Féin emerged with 73 seats, the Unionists with 26 and the Home Rule Party with 6. In terms of votes, however, the two nationalist parties were much closer.

1918 GENERAL ELECTION	
Sinn Féin	485,105 votes
Home Rule Party	237,393 votes

The 1918 election was historic in another sense. For the first time, women in the United Kingdom were allowed to vote and to stand for election. One Sinn Féin female candidate, Countess Markievicz, became the first woman elected to the Westminster Parliament. However, because of the Sinn Féin policy of abstention, she refused to take her seat.

For those searching for a solution to the Irish Question, the results of the 1918 general election appeared ominous. Unionists remained implacably opposed to any form of Irish self-government. They were now opposed not, as before, by a constitutional Home Rule Party prepared to accept Home Rule within the British Empire. Instead they faced Sinn Féin, which had close links with the Irish Volunteers and which demanded complete separation from Britain in the form of an Irish republic. As a first step in their struggle to achieve that aim, the newly elected Sinn Féin MPs proposed to abstain from going to the Westminster Parliament and to set up their own parliament in Dublin instead.

De Valera addressing a meeting of the first Dáil in April 1919

The First Dáil: 21 January 1919

In January 1919 Sinn Féin invited all 105 Irish MPs to a meeting in the Mansion House, Dublin, on 21 January. As expected, the 26 Unionist and 6 Home Rule MPs ignored this summons and continued to attend the Westminster Parliament. However, 27 Sinn Féin MPs attended and formed the First Dáil. The remaining members were either in prison or 'on the run' from the British authorities. This meeting of the First Dáil was extremely significant. The existing Irish Republic traces its existence back to that meeting.

The First Dáil conducted its business in the Irish language. The Declaration of the Republic of Easter 1916 was read out and approved. The Dáil then sent a message to the Paris Peace Conference, which met after World War I. It asked the nations of the world to recognise Irish independence. Seán T. O'Kelly was chosen as the Dáil's delegate to the Conference. Although Sinn Féin hoped to gain the support of the US President, Woodrow Wilson, this was highly unlikely. The British Government would be sure to prevent any hearing being given to O'Kelly at the Peace Conference.

The First Dáil also passed the **Democratic Programme**. This was a commitment to improve facilities for the poor, to invest in health and education and to develop trade and industry in order to create employment. It was included partly at the behest of the Labour Party leader, Thomas Johnson, in return for Labour's agreement not to contest the 1918 general election. Although the aims of the Democratic Programme were admirable, they were merely aspirations and did not commit the Dáil to any concrete proposals.

As de Valera was in prison in England, Cathal Brugha was elected as temporary President, or leader, of the Dáil Government. On his escape, de Valera returned to Dublin and attended a meeting of Dáil Éireann on 1 April. He was elected President of the Dáil by the fifty-two Sinn Féin TDs present. As members of the Dáil, they abandoned the old British letters MP (Member of Parliament) in favour of the Irish form TD (Teachta Dála, or Member of the Dáil). De Valera then appointed a Cabinet that included the following ministers:

Sean T. O'Kelly rebuffed when calling to the Paris Peace Conference on behalf of the Dáil

Arthur Griffith	Vice-President and Minister for Home Affairs
Michael Collins	Minister for Finance
Cathal Brugha	Minister for Defence
Countess Markievicz	Minister for Labour
Count Plunkett	Minister for Foreign Affairs
Eoin MacNeill	Minister for Industries
W.T. Cosgrave	Minister for Local Government
Robert Barton	Minister for Agriculture

The Sinn Féin ministers were to face immense difficulties in the years ahead. The British Government immediately declared the Dáil and the Sinn Féin Government illegal and sought to arrest those involved. However, despite these difficulties, the various departments endeavoured to function throughout the country over the following three years.

On the day on which Dáil Éireann first met, 21 January 1919, its political approach towards achieving independence was to be matched by a military endeavour. A group of Irish Volunteers in Co. Tipperary attacked a police convoy and thereby began the War of Independence.

The War of Independence: The Outbreak of Hostilities

Whereas some Sinn Féin members, such as Arthur Griffith, favoured a policy of passive resistance to British rule, the Irish Volunteers favoured armed attacks on the police and British army. Although key Volunteer leaders such as de Valera, Collins, Brugha and Mulcahy were also leaders of Sinn Féin, the Volunteers had their own independent structures. In January 1919 the most pressing problem for Volunteer units throughout the country was a shortage of arms and ammunition.

On 21 January 1919 a local group of Volunteers under the leadership of Seán Treacy shot dead two policemen in Soloheadbeg, Co. Tipperary, and captured their guns and the explosives they had been guarding. Although these Volunteers were acting on their own authority, their actions were not condemned by Volunteer headquarters. Other units soon followed suit and began to attack police barracks in search of arms.

Because they were loyal to Dáil Éireann and the Declaration of the Irish Republic, the Volunteers now changed their name to the Irish Republican Army (IRA). At first, the Dáil was slow to accept responsibility for the actions of the IRA members, over whom it had no control. However, later on, in April 1921, Dáil Éireann accepted full responsibility for all such actions up to that date.

While individual Volunteers around the country were arming themselves as best they could, in Dublin Michael Collins was assuming a decisive role in the prosecution of the armed struggle.

Michael Collins's Decisive Role

While de Valera was in America gathering support and financial backing for the Irish cause between June 1919 and December 1920, Arthur Griffith took his place as acting President of Dáil Éireann. He presided over the underground Sinn Féin system of government until his arrest in November 1920. As Minister for Finance, Michael Collins raised a loan through public subscription in order to keep the government system functioning and to purchase arms for the IRA.

Michael Collins as Minister for Finance

Collins's main function, however, was his successful deployment of counter-intelligence against British rule in Ireland. All previous rebellions in Ireland had been characterised by the presence of British spies at the heart of the revolutionary movements. In 1919 Collins was determined to turn the tables on the British and to infiltrate their headquarters in Dublin Castle. With the help of numerous spies, he had detailed information about British plans and intended troop movements. He used these to warn the IRA of imminent attacks and to plan successful ambushes.

While successfully spying on the British, Collins was also determined to eradicate British attempts to spy on the IRA. In July 1919 he formed an elite 'Squad' of twelve IRA men, who were used to assassinate British detectives, spies and those who informed on the IRA to the British authorities. Members of the 'Squad' operated in broad daylight. As a result of their activities, the flow of information to the British authorities in Dublin Castle decreased considerably.

Michael Collins (right) as military commander

The Response of Lloyd George

Throughout 1919 the situation continued to deteriorate for British forces in Ireland. The members of the police force (Royal Irish Constabulary) came in for special attack. Although the RIC's officer corps was mainly English and Protestant, most of the rank-and-file members were Irish Catholics. As attacks on them continued, many resigned or turned a blind eye to IRA activity. Some even passed secret information to the IRA. By the end of 1919, most small barracks had been burned out by the IRA, and the police were concentrated in larger population centres.

In response to this challenge, Lloyd George decided on a twofold approach. On the one hand, he would try to introduce Home Rule and give adequate guarantees to the unionists. At the same time, however, he was determined to crush Sinn Féin, Dáil Éireann and the IRA. He appointed a new, tough Chief Secretary, Sir Hamar Greenwood, and placed General Neville Macready in charge of the British army in Ireland. Where possible, he refused to use the British army against the IRA. Lloyd George refused to recognise the IRA as a real army, describing it instead as a gang of murderers. As such, he wished to use the police against it. As the RIC was weakened and demoralised, he proposed to strengthen it by recruiting new officers and men in England – the Auxiliaries and the 'Black and Tans'.

The 'Black and Tans' and the Auxiliaries

In order to strengthen the deeply demoralised RIC, Lloyd George recruited policemen in England for duty in Ireland. As unemployment was high, many former soldiers were glad to join the new force, which offered a chance of adventure and higher-than-average wages. The first recruits arrived in Ireland in March 1920 and soon became known as the 'Black and Tans' because they dressed in a combination of the RIC's dark green uniform and the khaki brown of the British army. By the end of 1920, there would be over 5,000 of them in Ireland.

Auxiliaries ready for action

In August 1920 the Black and Tans were joined by a newly recruited force of police officers known as the Auxiliaries. The latter were mostly former British army officers and soon numbered around 1,500 men. They were given more freedom of action than the RIC or Black and Tans, were extremely ruthless and were detested by the local population.

The arrival of the Black and Tans and Auxiliaries marked the beginning of a new phase in the War of Independence. They travelled from place to place, usually in Crossley tenders, and carried out reprisals in areas where IRA ambushes had taken place. The civilian population had to bear the brunt of their activities as they engaged in drunken sprees, robbed premises and burned buildings.

Black and Tans controlling pedestrians in Dublin

The response of the leaders of Sinn Féin and the IRA to the activities of the Black and Tans was both political and military. While the IRA engaged in armed attacks, Sinn Féin made strenuous attempts to influence world opinion in favour of Ireland's right to independence by various propaganda methods.

Terence MacSwiney's Hunger Strike and Death

Throughout 1920 Sinn Féin secretly published its account of events in Ireland, with its printing presses under constant threat of raids by British forces. Desmond Fitzgerald and Erskine Childers were in charge of the propaganda department. They published a newspaper, the *Irish Bulletin*, and sent reports on Black and Tan atrocities to foreign newspapers. In the autumn of 1920, however, the republican side achieved its most significant propaganda victory when worldwide attention was centred on the hunger strike and death of Terence MacSwiney, the Lord Mayor of Cork.

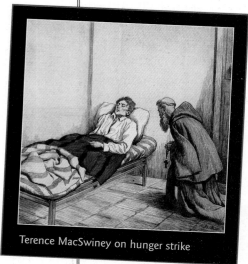

Terence MacSwiney on hunger strike

Terence MacSwiney was a leading member of Sinn Féin and the IRA in Cork and became Lord Mayor of the city in March 1920, following the death of his friend and predecessor, Tomás Mac Curtain. Mac Curtain had been shot dead in his home by a group of RIC men on 18 March 1920. His death led to an increase in anti-British feeling and an increase in tension throughout the Cork area.

When Terence MacSwiney was arrested in August 1920, he refused to recognise the British-controlled court and immediately went on a hunger strike. He was transferred to Brixton Prison in London, where he died on 25 October 1920. He believed that by sacrificing his life for Ireland, he would help bring about independence, remarking that it was not those who inflicted the most, but those who could suffer the most, who would win in the end. Lloyd George and the British Government had refused all pleas to release him. Both his hunger strike and his funeral in Cork received extensive coverage in Ireland and Britain and further afield.

'Bloody Sunday', 21 November 1920

On the day on which Terence MacSwiney was buried, 1 November 1920, Dublin city was the centre of another significant event in the War of Independence. Kevin Barry, an eighteen-year-old medical student and IRA Volunteer, was hanged for his part in an ambush. In the attack on a bakery that supplied British forces, a seventeen-year-old soldier was killed. During his imprisonment Barry was ill-treated, and all appeals for mercy because of his age were ignored. His execution became a signal for anti-British demonstrations, and a ballad kept his memory alive as a republican martyr.

Crowds in silent protest outside Mountjoy Jail in Dublin on the morning of Kevin Barry's execution

On Sunday, 21 November 1920, Michael Collins's hit squad shot dead eleven British spies. That afternoon, a group of Auxiliaries drove into Croke Park, where a football match between Dublin and Tipperary was taking place. They opened fire on the crowd, killing twelve and wounding around sixty. One of those killed was Michael Hogan, the goalkeeper on the Tipperary team.

That evening, three IRA prisoners in Dublin Castle, Peadar Clancy, Conor Clune and Dick McKee, were shot. The official account claimed that it happened while 'they were trying to escape'.

Events such as the deaths of Terence MacSwiney and Kevin Barry and the shootings in Croke Park turned public opinion in Ireland more and more against the British Government and in favour of Sinn Féin and the IRA. This made it easier for republican fighters to conduct their campaign of guerrilla warfare throughout the country.

An IRA flying column

Guerrilla Warfare – The Flying Columns

As the Black and Tans and Auxiliaries proved a more difficult enemy than the traditional RIC, the IRA in the countryside adopted special tactics to attack them. They continued with their guerrilla warfare, which involved ambushes on lorries from behind ditches and random attacks on individual policemen in city streets. However, IRA forces were now gathered into special units known as **flying columns**. These were small groups of Volunteers, heavily armed and under the leadership of a single powerful individual. They usually consisted of about thirty men, who could rarely go home; instead, they stayed in safe houses provided by sympathetic people in the countryside. There were flying columns in various parts of the country under leaders such as Seán MacEoin, Ernie O'Malley and Liam Lynch. One of the most ruthless of all was the one in West Cork under the leadership of Tom Barry. Barry, who had served in the British army during World War I, was an extremely capable and ruthless guerrilla leader.

The most famous ambush involving Tom Barry's flying column took place at Kilmichael in Co. Cork on 28 November 1920. An entire group of Auxiliaries travelling in two lorries was wiped out. The circumstances of their deaths were controversial, as Barry later claimed that one of them had given a false sign of surrender and that this led to the killing of the whole group. This view was disputed by other members of the flying column. Although the Kilmichael ambush was regarded as a victory by the IRA, it led to a significant British reaction.

An IRA attack on British forces in a train in Co. Cork

On 8 December 1920 four of the counties with the highest level of IRA activity – Cork, Limerick, Tipperary and Kerry – were placed under martial law. In effect, the British army replaced the ordinary courts in these areas. On 11 December the Black and Tans and Auxiliaries wreaked a terrible vengeance on Cork city. In the aftermath of the Kilmichael ambush and following an ambush near the Victoria Barracks in the city some hours earlier, groups of drunken Black and Tans and Auxiliaries set fire to important buildings in the city centre. Although the

The centre of Cork city in ruins after it was burnt in December 1920

Chief Secretary, Sir Hamar Greenwood, claimed in the House of Commons that the people of Cork set fire to their own city, the British Government later paid £3 million in compensation for the damage caused by its forces.

In December 1920, while the War of Independence was still at its height, the British Parliament passed a law that was to have a profound impact on the future of Ireland, north and south.

The Government of Ireland Act (1920)

The Government of Ireland Act (1920) went through the British Parliament during 1920 and finally became law on 23 December. Its most important provision was the **partition**, or division, of Ireland into two states: Northern Ireland, consisting of six counties, namely, Antrim, Armagh, Down, Fermanagh, Londonderry and Tyrone; and Southern Ireland, consisting of the remaining twenty-six.

There were to be two Home Rule parliaments in Ireland, with one based in Belfast and the other in Dublin. All members of these parliaments would have to swear loyalty to the King of England. The King's representative, the Viceroy, would sign the laws passed by these parliaments. They would have no control over war and peace, foreign affairs, the army and navy, coinage or the post office.

The Government of Ireland Act also provided for a Council of Ireland, to be made up of representatives of both parliaments. Not since the Act of Union (1800) had a law been passed that was to have such a profound effect on the lives of people in Ireland.

The Act was very favourable to the Ulster unionists. They had succeeded in persuading Lloyd George's Government to include all of Fermanagh and Tyrone and Derry city, areas with nationalist majorities, in the new state of Northern Ireland. At the time, their allies in the Conservative Party were part of the Coalition Government in London and gave the unionist case strong support. In contrast, nationalist Ireland was very poorly represented at Westminster. With the Sinn Féin MPs refusing to take their seats, only a few remaining Irish Home Rule MPs objected to the partition of Ireland contained in the Government of Ireland Act.

Lloyd George pressed ahead with the Government of Ireland Act, however, despite the massive opposition to it from nationalists throughout Ireland. Having satisfied unionist demands, he hoped to reach a settlement with Irish republicans based on recognition of partition and the inclusion of all of Ireland within the British Empire.

The Return of de Valera

In December 1920 de Valera returned to Ireland from America after an absence of more than a year. Although on the run from the British authorities, he began to exert an influence on the course of the War of Independence. He believed that peace negotiations should be opened with the British Government. He also disapproved of some of the guerrilla

De Valera inspecting an IRA unit in 1921

tactics of the IRA. He supported the Minister for Defence, Cathal Brugha, who wanted more large-scale attacks against the British. This was opposed by Michael Collins, who believed that such attacks would lead to serious loss of life on the part of the IRA Volunteers. There was considerable personal rivalry between Brugha and Collins. Brugha, as Minister for Defence, believed that he was Collins's superior, but Collins refused to acknowledge this. De Valera's support for Brugha was part of the growing rivalry between himself and Michael Collins.

In May 1921 de Valera persuaded the IRA to launch a large-scale attack on the Customs House in Dublin, the centre in which British local government records were stored. Although the Customs House was burned, the IRA suffered serious casualties, with over eighty men killed, wounded or captured. This episode contributed to the desire on the part of IRA leaders for a truce. Throughout the period between January and July 1921, the British

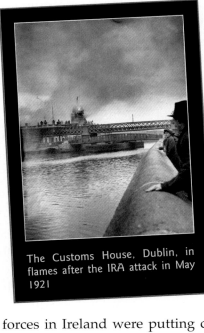

The Customs House, Dublin, in flames after the IRA attack in May 1921

forces in Ireland were putting considerable pressure on the IRA. The balance of casualties began to shift, with more IRA men and civilians being killed, compared with Crown forces. Many of the captured Volunteers were being executed, and the IRA was powerless to stop the executions. With stocks of arms and ammunition at a low level, even the most militant IRA commanders began to consider the advantages of de Valera's policy of negotiations with the British Government. At the same time, for reasons of its own, Lloyd George's Government began to consider the advantages of peace in Ireland.

IRA Volunteers surrender to British troops at the Custom House, leaving their dead on the ground

Towards a Truce

In the spring of 1921 the British Government was coming under increasing pressure from world opinion over atrocities by the Black and Tans, the Auxiliaries and other Crown forces in Ireland. Influential figures in the United States of America and in British dominions such as Canada, Australia and South Africa voiced their concerns. So too did Protestant and Catholic church leaders in England, Scotland and Wales.

In May 1921 developments in Ireland pointed the way towards a cessation of hostilities. Elections were held to the parliaments of Northern Ireland and Southern Ireland under the Government of Ireland Act. In the South, Sinn Féin candidates were not opposed. Voting took

ELECTION RESULTS, MAY 1921		
	Northern Ireland	Southern Ireland
Total No. of Seats	52	128
Unionists	40	4
Nationalists	6	0
Sinn Féin	6	124

place only in Trinity College, Dublin, where four Unionists were elected. Sinn Féin candidates refused to take their seats in the Parliament because they would have to take an oath of loyalty to the King, because the Parliament had limited powers and because of the partition of Ireland.

In Northern Ireland, Unionist candidates achieved an overwhelming victory and went on to form a government under the leadership of James Craig as Prime Minister. The fact that the unionists were satisfied with this solution enabled Lloyd George to consider dealing with Sinn Féin to end the hostilities and determine the future of the rest of Ireland.

In May 1921 the Viceroy, Lord French, was replaced by the first Catholic Viceroy, Lord Fitzalan. This was regarded as a conciliatory gesture towards Irish nationalists. With the refusal of Sinn Féin to consider involvement in the southern Parliament elected in May 1921, the British Government now faced the prospect of continuing with direct rule in most of Ireland against the wishes of the vast majority of the population. This would involve committing huge resources in terms of soldiers, armaments and finance. At a time of financial depression and rising unemployment in Great Britain, Lloyd George could ill afford to make this commitment. Consequently, his Government edged its way towards a truce with the IRA.

In June 1921 the South African Prime Minister, General Smuts, while visiting London, strongly urged the British Government to move towards a peaceful, diplomatic solution of the conflict in Ireland. On 22 June King George V came to Belfast to open the first session of the Parliament of Northern Ireland. In his speech he made a strong plea for peace throughout Ireland. Three days later, Lloyd George wrote to de Valera, suggesting that peace talks should take place between them.

The Anglo-Irish Truce, July 1921

Lloyd George wished to open talks with both de Valera and Craig in London. However, de Valera considered himself President of the Irish Republic, including the six northern counties, and refused to regard Craig as his equal; he also demanded a ceasefire as a prelude to talks. The British Government agreed, and on 8 July 1921 de Valera met Sir Neville Macready, the Commander-in-Chief of British forces in Ireland, to discuss a cessation of hostilities. It was agreed that a truce would come into effect on 11 July and that the IRA could continue to hold on to its arms. At noon on that day, the truce came into effect, bringing to an end a period of violence that had lasted for two and a half years.

By agreeing to the truce, Lloyd George had made certain concessions. He had agreed to allow the IRA to hold on to its arms; he recognised implicitly that the Government of Ireland Act (1920) did not go far enough in giving freedom to southern Ireland; he also faced the prospect of negotiating with men such as Michael Collins whom he had condemned as murderers.

However, de Valera, Sinn Féin and the IRA also had to make concessions. By agreeing to the truce, they had accepted that they could not inflict a complete military defeat on the British forces in Ireland. In these circumstances they would have to compromise on two crucial areas of concern: the degree of independence from Great Britain and the treatment of Northern Ireland. Despite these difficulties, the willingness of Great Britain, one of the biggest world powers, to accept a truce with a largely guerrilla movement represented a considerable achievement for Sinn Féin and the IRA.

The War of Independence: An Assessment

The War of Independence (1919–21) is undoubtedly one of the most controversial episodes in Irish history. The ruthlessness of the targeting of civilians by both sides and the widespread intimidation suppressed critical voices at the time. The treatment of the minority Protestant community by sections of the IRA in many parts of the country led to a widespread departure for England. The vague relationship between Dáil Éireann and individual IRA units for most of the war led to questions concerning the legitimate use of force. The ill-treatment and shooting of hostages, prisoners and informers by both sides was a marked feature of the struggle.

Until the 1960s, historical discussion in the Republic of Ireland was largely favourable to the republican side in the War of Independence. The war was seen as a necessary fight in the struggle for independence. However, from the 1970s onwards, partly because of the violence in Northern Ireland, historians began to re-examine the issues. Certain revisionist historians have argued that Irish nationalists could have achieved freedom by peaceful means within the British Parliament.

When discussing the War of Independence, it is important to assess people and events by the standards and values of the time and not by those of later generations. Whatever position one adopts having considered the evidence, it is hard to deny that the truce of July 1921 was an important turning point in the country's development towards full independence.

KEY PERSONALITY: CONSTANCE MARKIEVICZ (1868–1927)

Constance Gore-Booth was born in London on 4 February 1868 and was educated privately at the family home in Lissadell, Co. Sligo. She studied painting in London and Paris, where she met the Polish aristocrat Count Casimir Markievicz. She married him in 1900, thereafter assuming the title Countess Markievicz.

On settling in Dublin in 1903, Countess Markievicz became actively involved in the various cultural revival movements of the time, including the Gaelic League, the Abbey Theatre and Sinn Féin. She joined Maud Gonne's Inghinidhe na hÉireann and in 1909 founded Fianna Éireann, which inculcated nationalist ideals in the young. She took the side of the workers during the 1913 strike and lockout and maintained a soup kitchen at Liberty Hall.

Countess Markievicz joined the Citizen Army and was second-in-command at the College of Surgeons during the Easter Rising of 1916. She was sentenced to death for her part in the Rising, but the sentence was later commuted to life imprisonment. However, she was released in 1917 and immediately resumed her involvement in extreme nationalism. She was elected Sinn Féin MP in the general election of 1918. Although she did not take her seat, she was the first woman elected to the Westminster Parliament.

Countess Markievicz was appointed Minister for Labour in the First Dáil. She strongly opposed the Anglo-Irish Treaty of 1921 and campaigned against it at home and abroad. She was a founder member of Fianna Fáil in 1926. She died in Dublin on 15 June 1927.

ORDINARY LEVEL

1. Write an account of the revival of the Irish Volunteers and Sinn Féin between 1916 and 1918.

2. Write a paragraph on the Conscription Crisis (1918).

3. Write an account of the 1918 general election in Ireland.

4. Examine the Sinn Féin election poster on page 141. What images of British rule in Ireland are conveyed here? Is it a biased portrayal? Explain your answer.

5. Write a paragraph on the First Dáil (1919).

6. Write a detailed account of the role of Michael Collins in the War of Independence.

7. Write a paragraph on the Black and Tans and Auxiliaries.

8. Explain the term 'guerrilla warfare', and give examples of it from the War of Independence.

9. Write paragraphs on the following.

    (a) The Government of Ireland Act (1920)

    (b) The Anglo-Irish truce (1921)

HIGHER LEVEL

1. Analyse the revival of the Irish Volunteers and Sinn Féin between 1916 and 1919.

2. The following are newspaper accounts from the London *Times* concerning the death of Tomás Mac Curtain and the funeral of Terence MacSwiney. Read them carefully, and answer the questions that follow.

    (a) The death of Tomás Mac Curtain
    During the early hours of Saturday Alderman Thomas Mac Curtain, the recently elected Lord Mayor of Cork, was murdered in his own house in mysterious circumstances . . . He and his family were in bed when they were awakened by a loud knocking on the door. Mrs Mac Curtain, believing that the police were about to arrest her husband, who was a prominent Sinn Féiner, opened the door. She was immediately brushed aside by two men with blackened faces who carried revolvers. These were followed by two others, similarly disguised, who carried rifles. Four other men rushed into the shop. The first four men rushed upstairs and called upon Alderman Mac Curtain to come out of his room . . . When he made his appearance two revolver shots were fired at him . . . His assailants made off, leaving nothing apparently likely to lead to their identification . . . before help could reach him the Lord Mayor died of his wounds.

    The Times, 22 March 1920

    (b) The funeral of Terence MacSwiney
    The body of the late Lord Mayor of Cork [Terence MacSwiney] was yesterday borne in procession through the streets of London to Euston Station, thence to be taken to Cork for burial. The coffin was wrapped in the yellow, white and green of Sinn Féin; the flag of Sinn Féin waved over the procession; men of the Irish Republican Volunteers acted as escort. Many thousands of Londoners looked on in silence. There was no disturbance . . . The body had lain in state in St George's Roman Catholic Cathedral . . . Irish people came from all parts of the kingdom to be present . . . The predominance of youth in the crowd was very noticeable . . . It was a very long procession – a mile was a low estimate – and though it walked briskly, took quite half an hour to pass . . . The London crowd, so huge in its entirety . . . said nothing, and did nothing but pay its tribute to the dead.

    The Times, 24 October 1920

    (i) How was the Mac Curtain family awakened during the night?

    (ii) Describe the appearance of the first two men who entered the house.

    (iii) Where did Tomás Mac Curtain die?

(iv) How does the reporter describe the coffin of Terence MacSwiney?

(v) What was the reaction of ordinary Londoners?

(vi) What was noticeable about the mourners at the funeral procession?

(vii) Would you regard these primary sources as unbiased? Explain your answer.

3. Write an essay on the role of Michael Collins in the War of Independence.

4. Account for the decline of the Home Rule Party and the rise of Sinn Féin between 1916 and 1918.

5. Outline the main developments in the War of Independence between 1919 and 1921.

6. Read the following assessment of Michael Collins during the War of Independence by Richard Mulcahy and answer the questions that follow.

> He was the person who, by his approach and by the contacts he made, prised open the whole system of the British Intelligence and enabled it to be destroyed; in that his character has its place...His clarity of mind and his whole manner and demeanour, together with his power of concentration on the immediate matter in hand, gave him a very great power over men. There was little doubt that his position in the IRB and what he apparently wished to make of the IRB and its tradition gave him, in relation to those people that he was most responsibly and closely dealing with in matters of high secrecy, some kind of mystique which was a kind of cement in matters of loyalty and service; it probably helped particularly to penetrate, and to make effective as it was, the group of his associates inside the detective force and the police.
>
> *Richard Mulcahy quoted in Risteárd Mulcahy, Richard Mulcahy (1886–1971), A Family Memoir, Dublin: The Aurelian Press, 1999, 100*

(i) What effect had Michael Collins on the British Intelligence system in Ireland?

(ii) According to Mulcahy, what traits of character gave Michael Collins 'a very great power over men'?

(iii) How did Mulcahy estimate the significance of Michael Collins's position in the IRB?

(iv) What useful group did Collins have inside the British detective force and the overall British police force in Ireland?

(v) Mention one instance where Michael Collins ordered an attack against British spies in Ireland during the War of Independence.

(vi) Would you regard this as a biased or an unbiased source of information? In your answer refer to the overall impression that the extract makes upon you.

Negotiations Begin – de Valera and Lloyd George

Soon after the Anglo-Irish War ended with the truce of 11 July 1921, de Valera went to London for a series of meetings with the British Prime Minister, David Lloyd George. De Valera, with the backing of Dáil Éireann, demanded an independent 32-county republic. The British Government was unwilling to grant this. However, Lloyd George did offer a considerable improvement on the 'Home Rule' type of autonomy offered to southern Ireland under the Government of Ireland Act (1920). This was the type of government that had recently been set up in Northern Ireland. Instead, the British Government now offered the twenty-six counties of southern Ireland a type of independence known as **dominion status**. This would give southern Ireland the same degree of autonomy as dominions in the British Commonwealth, such as Canada, Australia and New Zealand. In Ireland's case, however, this autonomy would be restricted by provisions that free trade should continue to exist with Great Britain and that the British navy should have unhindered access to Irish ports.

The Cabinet of Dáil Éireann formally rejected these proposals. Although Lloyd George threatened a renewal of war if agreement could not be reached, both he and de Valera were anxious for a resumption of negotiations. During August and September 1921, the Irish and British sides were in constant communication in an effort to open up negotiations on a basis that would be acceptable to them both. Whereas the British insisted on Ireland's remaining within the Empire, de Valera and Dáil Éireann claimed that Ireland was an independent republic. Lloyd George eventually produced a formula that enabled both sides to enter formal negotiations. He wrote to de Valera, inviting an Irish delegation to come to a conference in London on 11 October 1921,

> with a view to ascertaining how the association of Ireland with the community of nations known as the British Empire may be reconciled with Irish national aspirations.

De Valera and his Cabinet agreed to this proposal and set about choosing a delegation to attend the conference.

De Valera and Lloyd George held talks in London after the truce began in July 1921

Choosing the Irish Delegation

When the Cabinet met to pick a delegation, de Valera caused a shock by refusing to lead it himself. It had been assumed by most Sinn Féin TDs that he would do so. However, he gave two main reasons for refusing to go to London. Firstly, that as the President of the declared Irish Republic, he could best influence more extreme republicans if he remained in Ireland. He also declared that by remaining in Ireland he could ensure that the conference delegates would have to refer matters back to him and could not, therefore, sign anything under pressure from the British Government. De Valera's momentous decision not to lead the Irish delegation was one of the most controversial in his long political career. Opinion at the time and since has been sharply divided on this point. Whereas his supporters accepted his stated reasons for remaining in Ireland, his critics have strongly condemned him because, in their view,

- He was the most experienced politician on the Irish side and had already been to London the previous July.
- He realised that compromise was inevitable and did not want to take responsibility for accepting less than a full Irish republic.

With the refusal of de Valera to join the delegation, Arthur Griffith, the Vice-President of Dáil Éireann, was chosen to lead it. Two hardline republican members of the Cabinet, Cathal Brugha and Austin Stack, refused to join the delegation. Michael Collins agreed very reluctantly to join the delegation. Although de Valera insisted on this, Collins himself believed that he would have been more useful back in Ireland as a threat if negotiations broke down. Three other delegates were then chosen – Robert Barton, Éamonn Duggan and George Gavan Duffy. As members of the Cabinet, Collins, Griffith and Barton were recognised as chief negotiators, with Gavan Duffy and Duggan termed legal advisers. Finally, Erskine Childers was appointed as secretary to the Irish delegation. An Englishman who had become an Irish nationalist, Childers was distrusted by Collins, who regarded him as a type of spy for de Valera.

The members of the Irish delegation were given written instructions by the Cabinet. Although they were termed 'plenipotentiaries', a word which implied that they had full power, any agreement reached would have to be communicated to the Cabinet in Dublin before they signed it. Their instructions also stated, 'It is understood that the Cabinet in Dublin will be kept regularly informed of the progress of the negotiations.'

In early October 1921, the Irish delegates travelled to London to prepare for the opening of the talks with the British Government.

The Irish delegation in London during the Treaty negotiations

THE BRITISH DELEGATION

The members of the British delegation at the Treaty negotiations were much more experienced than their Irish counterparts. They were led by the Prime Minister, Lloyd George, who had been a Cabinet minister since 1906 and leader of the Government since 1916. Widely experienced in administration both in peacetime and during World War I, he was known as the Welsh Wizard because of his cunning and political ability. Also included was the Secretary of State for War, Winston Churchill, who, like the Prime Minister, had spent many years in government. The delegation's other principal negotiators were two leading members of the Conservative Party: Lord Birkenhead, an accomplished lawyer, and Austen Chamberlain. These were very influential because although Lloyd George was a member of the Liberal Party, the majority of MPs supporting his Coalition Government were Conservatives. As the Conservatives were very close to the Ulster unionists and were strongly in favour of the British Empire, their influence limited Lloyd George's ability to offer significant concessions to the Irish delegation. The difficulty of his position can be seen in a debate in the House of Commons during which right-wing Conservatives opposed any negotiations with Sinn Féin (Document 1).

Lloyd George succeeded in defeating the challenge to his decision to negotiate with Sinn Féin when the Commons voted by 439 votes to 43 to support him on 31 October 1921. Nevertheless, the possibility of a Conservative revolt if he conceded too much in the negotiations was constantly on his mind.

THE CONFERENCE OPENS

The Conference began its first session on 11 October 1921, three months to the day since the truce came into operation. From the outset it was clear that there was a vast gulf between the aims of both sides. The British were very clear in their objectives. Their priority was the defence of British territory. Recalling the landing of Spanish and French troops in Ireland in centuries past, they feared that an independent Ireland could be used by an enemy to attack Britain in a future war. To avoid this, they were determined to prevent Ireland becoming an independent republic. In the last analysis, Lloyd George's Government would have been prepared to return to war rather than allow Ireland to leave the British Empire. The British Government was also anxious to protect the

---

Document 1

Lloyd George defends his decision to negotiate with Sinn Féin

Now I come to the Motion, which divides itself into two parts. The first is an expression of grave apprehension that the government should have entered into negotiations . . . with men who at the same time were engaged in a conspiracy against the authority of the crown . . . The second point is that those negotiations ought to have been preceded by the sanction of Parliament to the actual proposals made inside the Conference . . .

No pact entered into in the course of these negotiations can come into effect without the authority of Parliament. Every detail will have to be submitted to Parliament . . . If you enter into negotiations, you must have some latitude . . . otherwise there is no use in having a conference . . . There was the Act of Parliament of 1920. That was not a conference . . . it was Parliament making a proposal. That did not accomplish its purpose. I was always in favour of a conference, if I could get it . . .

I have repeatedly at this box stated . . . that the Government were prepared to meet in discussion any representatives of the Irish people who could – I used the phrase – 'deliver the goods', that is, who were in a position to make good a bargain when it was made . . . The House of Commons must either trust its negotiators or replace them . . .

It is not the first time that Britain has treated with rebels and it is not the first time that Britain has treated with rebels with good effects for the Empire . . .

But I cannot conceal from the House the possibility that I may have to make the grim announcement that it is impossible to settle without danger or without dishonour.

House of Commons Debates; 31 October 1921

Ulster unionists but was willing to put pressure on them if they stood in the way of an overall agreement. In the context of the times, the Government believed that the unity of the Empire would be clear only if Irish office-holders had to swear allegiance to the King.

In contrast to the clear aims of the British delegation, the Irish delegates had not worked out an exact strategy that reflected their aspirations. Although committed to an Irish republic and a restoration of Irish unity, they were unclear as to how they should compromise on these aspirations. Recognising the British demand for security guarantees, de Valera had developed a proposal known as external association, which involved close co-operation with the British Empire. However, the Irish delegates did not have an alternative plan to put forward if, as seemed likely, the British side rejected this. On the question of the Ulster unionists, the Irish side was even more vague. Various possibilities were considered, such as a Northern Ireland Parliament under overall Dublin rule, but a clear strategy on dealing with the issue was not worked out (Document 2).

A British cartoon expressing a desire for peace between Britain and Ireland

TWO MINDS WITH BUT A SINGLE THOUGHT —— NOW!

Michael Collins in London during the Treaty negotiations

DE VALERA AND POPE BENEDICT XV

An incident occurred in October 1921 that showed clearly the difference between British and Irish aspirations concerning the relationship between both countries. Soon after the Treaty negotiations began on 11 October, Pope Benedict XV sent a message to King George V of England to wish the talks a successful outcome (Document 3a). De Valera, however, objected because the Pope appeared to regard the King as the supreme authority in Ireland.

Document 3a

Pope Benedict XV to King George V

We rejoice at the resumption of the Anglo-Irish negotiations and pray to the Lord with all our heart that He may bless them and grant to Your Majesty the great joy and imperishable glory of bringing to an end the age-long dissension.

F. Pakenham, *Peace by Ordeal*, London: Sidgwick & Jackson 1972, 136–7

Document 2

The Treaty negotiations open

At the opening session on 11 October, Griffith, the leader of the Irish delegation, remarked that

England's policy in the past has been to treat Ireland as a conquered and subject country. If there is a change in the policy of subordinating Ireland to English interests, then there appears to be possibility of peace.

Lord Longford, in his study of the Treaty negotiations, *Peace by Ordeal* (pp 121–2), remarked that 'Griffith in a few words had placed Ireland on a negotiating equality. He would acquiesce in the intellectual effort of reconciliation, but only if there went with it on the British side a change of heart.' When Griffith remarked that the six conditions that the British Government attached to its offer of dominion status implied British desire to keep Ireland under military control, Lloyd George replied,

We certainly don't desire that, we seek nothing in the way of military domination of Ireland.

When members of the Irish delegation stated that Britain had broken treaties with Ireland in the past, Lloyd George made the interesting reply:

You have never made a treaty with the people of this country before. Treaties in the past have been with oligarchies ruling this country.

When the discussion turned to economic matters, the British side appeared particularly willing to compromise. Lloyd George spoke strongly in favour of free trade between both countries, and Lord Birkenhead remarked,

Nothing is intended to prevent the economic development of Ireland.

The first session of the conference ended with an impression among the delegates that some of the tension had eased. However, none of the most contentious topics had yet been reached.

Treaty Debates, 11 October 1921, cited in Pakenham, *Peace by Ordeal*, 121–2

Document 3b

George V to Pope Benedict XV

I have received the message of your Holiness with much pleasure and with all my heart I join in your prayer that the Conference . . . may achieve a permanent settlement of the troubles in Ireland, and may initiate a new era of peace and happiness for my people.

Pakenham, *Peace by Ordeal*, 136–7

The editor of the London *Times* objected strongly to de Valera's action, and that paper carried a leading article condemning him on 21 October 1921 (Document 3d).

Document 3c

President de Valera to Pope Benedict XV

The people of Ireland have read the message sent by your Holiness to the King of Great Britain, and appreciate the kindly interest in their welfare and the paternal regard which suggest it . . . They are confident that the ambiguities in the reply sent in the name of King George will not mislead you into believing that the troubles are in Ireland, or that the people of Ireland owe allegiance to the British King. The independence of Ireland has been formally proclaimed . . . The trouble is between England and Ireland and its source that the rulers of Britain have endeavoured to impose their will on Ireland.

Pakenham, *Peace by Ordeal*, 136–7

Document 3d

The Times criticises de Valera

Mr De Valera has sent a telegram to the Pope. Towards the Pope himself it is an act of impertinence; and towards the King it is unmannerly to the point of churlishness. What value can attach to Mr De Valera's assurance that 'we long to be at peace and in friendship with the people of Britain', when he deliberately flouts the settled convictions of the British people upon the only terms on which peace and friendship between the British and Irish peoples are possible?

The Times, 21 October 1921

On reading the Pope's message and the reply of George V (Document 3b), de Valera decided to express the Irish point of view in a public letter to the Pope (Document 3c).

Clearly this public row reflected the very issues which were at the heart of the Treaty negotiations. By 24 October seven plenary sessions had been held. Although there was a meeting of minds over issues such as trade and finance, there was no conclusive result on the key issues of the position of Ireland in the Empire and the Ulster Question.

THE IDEA OF A BOUNDARY COMMISSION

On 26 October the format of the negotiations changed, with the introduction of sub-conferences between smaller groups of delegates. At one such meeting, Griffith assured Lloyd George that if the 'essential unity' of Ireland were guaranteed, he would recommend a free partnership between Ireland and the other dominions in the British Commonwealth,

Document 4

Tom Jones's account of the origins of the Boundary Commission

7 November 1921: From 5.00 to about 6.20 Sir James Craig was with the Prime Minister. About 6.30 the Prime Minister sent for me and I had about half an hour with him alone during which time he paced up and down the Cabinet room, more depressed than I had seen him at all since the negotiations began. He said – 'Craig will not budge one inch . . . This means a break on Thursday' . . . He then said – 'There is just one other possible way out. I want to find out from Griffith and Collins if they will support me on it; namely that the twenty-six counties should take their own dominion parliament and have a Boundary Commission'.

9 November 1921: I told Griffith that the Prime Minister was prepared to play the Boundary Commission as an absolutely last card, if he could feel sure that Sinn Féin would take it, if Ulster accepted. Griffith replied, 'We would prefer a plebiscite, but in essential a Boundary Commission is very much the same. It would have to be, not for Tyrone and Fermanagh only, but for the six counties' . . . About 5.45 I saw the Prime Minister alone. He was perfectly satisfied with what I reported but pointed out that the Boundary Commission would be for the nine counties.

T. Jones, *Whitehall Diary*, III: *Ireland 1918–25*, London: OUP 1971, 154–7

with recognition by Ireland of the King as head of the proposed association of states. Lloyd George, for his part, agreed to attempt to persuade the Prime Minister of Northern Ireland, Sir James Craig, to allow Northern Ireland to come under the overall control of an all-Ireland Parliament. Lloyd George's secretary, Tom Jones, has left a clear account of his part in these events (Document 4).

For Griffith and Collins the idea of a Boundary Commission had both advantages and disadvantages. They believed that such a Commission would move predominantly nationalist areas such as Fermanagh, Tyrone, South Armagh and Derry city out of Northern Ireland. They also hoped that the threat of such a Commission would force Craig to compromise on the issue of recognising an all-Ireland Parliament. However, in two crucial respects acceptance of the idea weakened their position. By agreeing to a Boundary Commission, they were recognising the permanence of partition. They were also making sure that if the talks broke down, it would not be on the question of Ulster.

THE CULMINATION OF THE TREATY NEGOTIATIONS

With the issue of Ulster sidelined, Lloyd George and the British delegates concentrated on putting pressure on the Irish negotiators to accept dominion status. Refusing to accept external association, the British did, however, grant some minor concessions concerning the role of the King and the Oath of Allegiance to him. On 3 December the Irish delegates returned to Dublin with a copy of the British proposals. In the Cabinet discussion that followed, deep divisions emerged. De Valera, Cathal Brugha and Austin Stack rejected dominion status and wanted the delegates to return to London and argue for external association once again. Griffith replied that the British had rejected this several times and would do so again. At the end of the meeting, the delegates returned to London, agreeing not to sign any treaty until its terms had been referred back to Dublin.

On arrival in London on 4 December, the Irish delegation once again proposed external association. The British side rejected this, and the talks broke down in disagreement. Lloyd George then made contact with Griffith and Collins and persuaded them to return to the talks. Both men were under considerable pressure to reach an agreement. Arthur Griffith had never been a doctrinaire republican and was willing to accept a settlement which would give Ireland a substantial degree of independence. Michael Collins was keenly aware of how ill equipped the IRA was to resume war against superior British forces. Lloyd George's secretary, Tom Jones, recalled the pressure which both men were under shortly before the Treaty was signed (Document 5).

Document 5
Griffith and Collins before the Treaty was signed – Note from T. Jones to Lloyd George, 5 December 1921

I saw Arthur Griffith at midnight for an hour alone. He was labouring under a deep sense of the crisis and spoke throughout with the greatest earnestness and unusual emotion. One was bound to feel that to break with him would be infinitely tragic. Briefly his case was:

1. That he and Collins had been completely won over to belief in your desire for peace and recognised that you had gone far in your efforts to secure it.
2. This belief was not shared by their Dublin colleagues and they had failed to bring them all the way, but were convinced they could be brought further. In Dublin there is still much distrust and fear that if the 'Treaty' is signed they will be 'sold'.
3. They are told that they have surrendered too much ('the King' and 'association') and got nothing to offer the Dáil in return. Cannot you . . . get from Craig a conditional recognition, however shadowy, of Irish national unity in return for the acceptance of the Empire by Sinn Féin? . . .
4. Without something to offer the Dáil on these lines Arthur Griffith and Michael Collins could not carry more than about one-half of them.

Jones, *Whitehall Diary*, III: *Ireland 1918–25*, 160

At the meeting on 5 December, Lloyd George presented the Irish delegates with an ultimatum. He stated that he must let the Northern Ireland Prime Minister, Sir James Craig, know of their decision immediately. As a last-minute concession, he offered total fiscal autonomy – the Irish Free State could place protective tariffs on goods entering the country if it wished. This had been a long-term policy of Arthur Griffith. Lloyd George also agreed to modify the Oath of Allegiance by requiring Irish TDs to swear allegiance to the Constitution of the Irish Free State first and then to the King as head of the British Commonwealth.

Having made his final concessions, Lloyd George insisted that the Irish delegates sign the treaty there and then, or there would be 'immediate and terrible war'. He refused to allow them to refer the terms of the agreement back to Dublin.

Arthur Griffith was the first to accept the Treaty, followed by Michael Collins and Éamonn Duggan. After a few hours of persuasion, Robert Barton and George Gavan Duffy agreed to sign. At 2.10 a.m. on the morning of 6 December, the Irish delegates returned to 10 Downing Street and signed the agreement known as 'The Articles of Agreement for a Treaty between Great Britain and Ireland'.

THE ANGLO-IRISH TREATY

The Treaty contained eighteen articles in all and included the provisions shown in Document 6. Compared with Home Rule, the dominion status offered in the Treaty of 1921 was a huge advance. The British army would leave the Irish Free State and be replaced by an Irish army. The Free State Government could conduct its own defence and foreign policies. It would have complete control over taxation and other financial matters. The King's representative in Ireland, the Governor-General, would be a figurehead with very little power.

However, two aspects of the settlement were extremely contentious. First, it failed to reverse effectively the partition of Ireland introduced under the Government of Ireland Act a

> **Document 6**
> **The Anglo-Irish Treaty (1921)**
>
> 1. Ireland shall have the same status in the Community of Nations known as the British Empire as the Dominion of Canada, the Commonwealth of Australia, the Dominion of New Zealand, and the Union of South Africa, with a Parliament having powers to make laws for the peace, order and good government of Ireland, and an Executive responsible to that Parliament, and shall be styled and known as the Irish Free State.
> 2. The representative of the Crown in Ireland shall be appointed in like manner as the Governor-General of Canada and in accordance with the practice in making such appointments.
> 4. The oath to be taken by Members of Parliament of the Irish Free State shall be in the following form:
> I . . . do solemnly swear true faith and allegiance to the Constitution of the Irish Free State as by law established and that I will be faithful to H.M. King George V, his heirs and successors by law, in virtue of the common citizenship of Ireland with Great Britain and her adherence to and membership of the group of nations forming the British Commonwealth of Nations.
>
> *Articles of Agreement for a Treaty between Great Britain and Ireland, 1921*

year earlier. Second, the inclusion of the Oath of Allegiance, which marked the failure to secure an independent republic, was to prove the most contentious issue of all.

COMPREHENSION

1. Why were some Members of Parliament against Lloyd George negotiating with Sinn Féin? (Document 1)

2. Which body would have the final say on every detail of the settlement? (Document 1)

3. In Lloyd George's view, was the Act of 1920 a success? (Document 1)

4. What did he mean by the phrase 'deliver the goods'? (Document 1)

5. In Document 2, what, according to Arthur Griffith, was 'England's policy in the past'?

6. In Document 2, what did Lord Birkenhead say about the attitude of the British Government to economic development in Ireland?

7. Why did Pope Benedict XV rejoice? (Document 3a)

8. What was the main wish of King George V in Document 3b?

9. Why did de Valera thank the Pope? (Document 3c)

10. In Document 4, who spent half an hour with the Prime Minister?

11. Why was Lloyd George depressed? (Document 4)

12. In Document 4, what attitude did Arthur Griffith display towards a Boundary Commission?

13. Describe the condition of Arthur Griffith as outlined at the start of Document 5.

14. Explain the meaning of Point 4 in Document 5.

15. In Document 6, what is the King's representative in the Irish Free State known as?

16. According to Document 6, who will have to take an Oath of Allegiance to the King?

COMPARISON

1. Compare Documents 1 and 5. In both cases, people are compromising. List those who are prepared to compromise and the opponents of this in each case.

2. Contrast Documents 3a and 3b, on the one hand, with Documents 3c and 3d on the other. What is the main point of contrast?

3. Compare the situation of Lloyd George in Document 4 with that of Arthur Griffith in Document 5.

4. Contrast the approach of Arthur Griffith in Document 2 with his approach in Document 5.

CRITICISM

1. From the evidence of Document 1, would you agree that Lloyd George was a persuasive parliamentary debater?

2. Assess critically the comments of the British delegates in Document 2.

3. How effective is Document 3c as a piece of propaganda, in your opinion?

4. From the evidence of Documents 4 and 5, how influential would you consider their author to be?

5. Would you agree that Document 5 is biased in favour of Griffith and Collins?

6. Analyse in detail the provisions of Article 4 of the Treaty (Document 6).

CONTEXTUALISATION

1. Write an account of the main events between the truce and the signing of the Anglo-Irish Treaty in December 1921.

2. Assess the role of Éamon de Valera between July and December 1921.

3. Compare and contrast Home Rule and dominion status.

4. Write a paragraph on the part played by the Ulster Question in the Treaty negotiations.

5. Outline and discuss the British aims in the Treaty negotiations.

The Treaty Split

The immediate public reaction in Ireland to the signing of the Anglo-Irish Treaty was one of widespread relief and joy. For many ordinary people, it signalled the guarantee of peace and the removal of the British army, the Black and Tans and the Auxiliaries from the country. Convinced republicans, however, were dismayed at the failure of the delegates to achieve an independent republic, despite the fact that the British Government had no intention of conceding this.

When the Dáil Cabinet met, de Valera expressed his opposition to the Treaty and his annoyance that the delegates had signed it without referring it back to Dublin for approval. Although he himself, together with Austin Stack and Cathal Brugha, wished to reject it immediately, they were overruled by the other four Cabinet members – Arthur Griffith, Michael Collins, Robert Barton and William T. Cosgrave – who insisted that Dáil Éireann must decide. Before the Dáil met, de Valera issued a public statement condemning the Treaty, and Michael Collins got the support of the IRB leadership for the Treaty at a secret meeting.

The Treaty Debates: 14 December 1921 to 7 January 1922

When the Dáil met to debate the Treaty, positions began to polarise for or against the proposals. De Valera rejected it and instead put forward his own recommendations in what became known as Document No. 2, which proposed his idea of external association. However, as Document No. 2 omitted the Oath of Allegiance and any reference to the Governor-General, it was clear that the British Government would never accept it. When the Dáil failed to support this, de Valera withdrew his proposal.

Arthur Griffith and Michael Collins made powerful speeches in favour of the Treaty. Collins used the stepping-stone argument. In his view, the Treaty did not represent full independence, but 'it gives us freedom, not the ultimate freedom that all nations desire and develop to, but the freedom to achieve it'. Richard Mulcahy, the Chief of Staff of the IRA during the War of Independence, argued strongly in favour of the Treaty, pointing out that the IRA could not defeat the British in a renewed war. Other pro-Treaty speakers, such as Kevin O'Higgins, pointed to the advantages of dominion status and the huge advance it represented compared with Home Rule.

Arthur Griffith and others listen as the Dáil debates the Treaty

The anti-Treaty speakers concentrated on the Oath of Allegiance, which they regarded as a betrayal of the republic and of all those who had died for it from Easter Week 1916 onwards. Significantly, all six women TDs were anti-Treaty republicans: they included Patrick Pearse's mother, Terence MacSwiney's sister, Mary, and Countess Markievicz. They argued strongly that the members of the Dáil had no right to abandon their allegiance to the republic.

Most of the speakers concentrated on the constitutional issue of the conflict between dominion status and the republic. The Oath of Allegiance was the most contentious issue in this regard. Few dwelled on the question of partition and the right of Northern Ireland to remain in the United Kingdom. Seán MacEntee, an anti-Treaty republican and future government minister, argued strongly against the Treaty because of the continuation of partition.

Historians have estimated that opinion among TDs in the Second Dáil was more evenly divided than opinion in the country as a whole. When TDs returned home to their constituencies during the Christmas break, they discovered that a clear majority of the people favoured the Treaty. This may have influenced some wavering TDs towards voting for the Treaty. When, after a few weeks of bitter debate, the decisive moment arrived on 7 January 1922, the Dáil approved the Treaty by 64 votes in favour to 57 votes against. Although the margin was small, it was decisive and in democratic terms should have been accepted. However, as soon as the vote was declared, republicans protested that they would not accept the result.

De Valera and his followers, including Cathal Brugha and Countess Markievicz, withdrawing from the Dáil on 10 January 1922

The New Pro-Treaty Government

After losing the vote on the Treaty, de Valera resigned from the office of President and Arthur Griffith was elected in his place. Griffith appointed a Cabinet that included Michael Collins (Minister for Finance), George Gavan Duffy (External Affairs), Éamonn Duggan (Home Affairs), Kevin O'Higgins (Economic Affairs), Richard Mulcahy (Defence) and W.T. Cosgrave (Local Government). On 10 January 1922 de Valera led his anti-Treaty followers out of the Dáil, accusing the new Government of undermining the republic.

In order to take over from the British administration, the pro-Treaty side had to form a Provisional Government. As part of the Treaty, the British agreed to hand over power gradually until 6 December 1922, when the Irish Free State would formally come into existence. In the meantime, the British would hand over power to a Provisional Government consisting of TDs who had been elected to the Parliament of southern Ireland in May 1921 under the Government of Ireland Act. This Parliament met just once, on 14 January 1922, and was attended only by pro-Treaty Sinn Féin TDs and the four Unionists elected by Trinity College. It elected Michael Collins as head of the Provisional Government, and he then appointed a Cabinet.

On 16 January 1922 Michael Collins, as head of the Provisional Government, took power from the British administration in Dublin Castle. It was a symbolic occasion:

Collins addressing a rally at College Green in Dublin in March 1922

British troops leaving Limerick in 1922

after more than seven hundred years, British rule was coming to an end in most of Ireland. However, huge challenges now faced Griffith, Collins and the other pro-Treaty leaders as they sought to form a stable government in a deeply divided society.

The Drift Towards Civil War

The split among Sinn Féin TDs over the Treaty was accompanied by a split in the IRA throughout the country. In the early months of 1922, as the British army evacuated barracks in different parts of the country, groups of pro-Treaty and anti-Treaty IRA members vied with one another for control in local areas.

While a majority of the headquarters staff of the IRA, including the Chief of Staff, General Richard Mulcahy, followed Michael Collins, some prominent IRA leaders, including Rory O'Connor, Liam Lynch and Liam Mellowes, rejected the Treaty. Ordinary Volunteers throughout the country were split on the issue. Many supported the Treaty out of loyalty to Michael Collins.

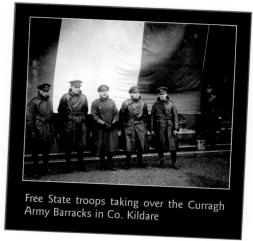

Free State troops taking over the Curragh Army Barracks in Co. Kildare

Many of the anti-Treaty IRA members distrusted the Dáil and were prepared to use force to achieve a republic. In order to preserve unity in the IRA, the Minister for Defence, General Richard Mulcahy, agreed to hold an Army Convention in March 1922. However, when it became obvious that a majority of the IRA might be anti-Treaty, he cancelled the Convention. In defiance of Mulcahy's order, over 200 anti-Treaty officers met under the leadership of Rory O'Connor and Liam Mellowes. They repudiated the authority of the Dáil and prepared to rebel against the pro-Treaty Government.

On 14 April the situation deteriorated seriously when Rory O'Connor and a group of anti-Treaty IRA men captured the Four Courts in Dublin. In order to avoid immediate civil war, Michael Collins did not take action to remove them. At the time, the Government was busy founding a new police force, the Garda Síochána, and creating a national army composed of former IRA members who accepted the Treaty.

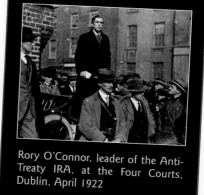

Rory O'Connor, leader of the Anti-Treaty IRA, at the Four Courts, Dublin, April 1922

De Valera also contributed to the growing bitterness and hostility between the Government and its anti-Treaty opponents. He declared that 'the majority has no right to do wrong' and made inflammatory speeches in which he stated that Irish people might have to 'wade through rivers of blood'.

In a further effort to bring about a reconciliation, Michael Collins agreed with de Valera to postpone a general election until June 1922. Historians have criticised this decision, as an earlier verdict by the people on the Treaty might have had the effect of calming political passions.

The Treaty Election, June 1922

A month before the election Collins and de Valera agreed to form a 'pact'. They would advise their supporters to vote for both pro- and anti-Treaty candidates, and they would form a coalition government later. Although Collins entered into this pact to avoid a drift towards civil war, his own supporters, including Griffith and O'Higgins, condemned it as undemocratic. Yet from Collins's point of view, such co-operation would have been useful as part of his policy on Northern Ireland. He hoped that if the pro- and anti-Treaty wings of the IRA co-operated in acting against Northern Ireland, the organisation would avoid a damaging split in the South. At the time, he was pursuing a devious policy on the North. Appalled at the widespread attacks on northern Catholics, he sent arms secretly to the IRA in the North. However, at the same time, he was engaging in talks with the northern Prime Minister, Sir James Craig, urging him to protect Catholics in Belfast and throughout the state.

Two days before the general election in June 1922, Collins cancelled the pact with de Valera and advised pro-Treaty voters not to vote for anti-Treaty candidates. Just before the election, the Constitution of the Irish Free State, drawn up largely by Michael Collins and Arthur Griffith, was published.

The result of the general election was a decisive victory for supporters of the Treaty. All parties favoured it, apart from anti-Treaty Sinn Féin. Many of those voting for smaller parties or Independents transferred their votes on to pro-Treaty Sinn Féin. The results of the general election signified a clear mandate by the people in favour of the Treaty. In normal, democratic circumstances this would have been decisive. However, in June 1922 Ireland had not known peaceful conditions for the previous eight years. Ten days after the people cast their votes, violence would come to the fore in a dramatic manner once again.

1922 GENERAL ELECTION	
Pro-Treaty Sinn Féin	58
Anti-Treaty Sinn Féin	35
Labour	17
Farmers	7
Unionists	4
Independents	7

The Outbreak of Civil War

The decisive verdict of the electorate strengthened the position of Michael Collins in dealing with the threat to the authority of the Government posed by the anti-Treaty IRA. Shortly after the election, two events occurred that forced him to act. On 22 June two IRA members shot Sir Henry Wilson dead in London. A leading figure in the British army, Wilson had been a long-term enemy of Irish nationalism and had recently been acting as an adviser to the Unionist Government in Northern Ireland. It later emerged that Collins may have ordered the shooting, but at the time the British Government assumed it was carried out by the anti-Treaty IRA. The British Government then threatened to take action against the garrison in the Four Courts if Collins failed to do so. On 27 June the anti-Treaty forces in the Four Courts captured J.J. O'Connell, the deputy Chief of Staff of the Free State army. At this point Collins finally acted. He ordered the garrison

The shooting of Sir Henry Wilson in London. June 1922

in the Four Courts to surrender. When it failed to do so, the Free State forces began to bombard the building, using guns provided by the British army. The bitterness and divisions of the previous six months had finally erupted into open warfare. Sinn Féin and the IRA, which had been united throughout the War of Independence, were now irrevocably split into two warring factions, fighting a civil war in which members of the same family frequently found themselves on opposing sides.

The Fighting in Dublin and the 'Munster Republic'

The fighting between the Free State army and its republican enemies in Dublin was over within a week. On 30 July the garrison of around two hundred men in the Four Courts was forced to surrender. In the course of the fighting the building was destroyed, together with the adjoining Public Records Office, which housed priceless historical sources dating back hundreds of years.

Much of the area around O'Connell Street was destroyed in fighting and burning that recalled the destruction of Easter Week 1916. The leading republican Cathal Brugha died from wounds received when emerging from a hotel; he had chosen to die rather than surrender. At the end of a week's fighting, the republicans were defeated in Dublin, and their struggle was taken up in the country.

1. Republican funeral procession in the ruins of O'Connell Street
2. Explosions destroy the Four Courts in Dublin, June 1922
3. Free State troops under attack in Co. Limerick
4. The battle for the Four Courts in Dublin, June 1922

In Munster, an area stretching from Limerick to Waterford was controlled by the republicans and was known as the 'Munster Republic'. The Free State forces set about capturing the main cities there. In July 1922 they succeeded in taking Limerick, Waterford and Tralee. On 12 August government troops, who had travelled by sea from Dublin, succeeded in capturing Cork city. At that stage de Valera called for peace but was overruled by General Liam Lynch, the commander of the republican forces. These forces now became known as the 'Irregulars' because they were in rebellion against the Free State, or 'regular', army.

With the main towns in government hands, the Civil War continued to be fought in the countryside, with both sides engaging in ambushes and reprisals. After the capture of Cork by his forces, Michael Collins decided to tour the area to inspect army units and to explore the possibilities of peace. However, this tour was dramatically interrupted by news from Dublin of the death of Arthur Griffith.

1. Anti-Treaty IRA (Irregulars) manning a roadblock during the Civil War
2. Free State soldier with Irregular prisoner
3. The body of Cathal Brugha lies in the Mater Hospital, Dublin
4. Free State troops in front of a tank in Limerick in 1922

The Deaths of Griffith and Collins

Arthur Griffith died suddenly from a brain haemorrhage on 12 August 1922. Although he was only fifty-one years of age, the stress and strain of the previous months and weeks had undermined his health. Michael Collins was chosen to succeed him as President of the Dáil. After Griffith's funeral, he returned to Munster on a tour of inspection. His death at the hands of a republican in Béal na mBláth in Co. Cork on 22 August came as a profound shock to the country.

The funeral of Michael Collins on 28 August was one of the largest seen in Dublin since Parnell's, thirty years previously. Like Parnell, he had been a larger-than-life figure who had a profound impact on the history of the country. After his death the Civil War became even more bitter, as both sides were determined to fight it out to the end.

The Civil War Continues

After the deaths of Arthur Griffith and Michael Collins, William T. Cosgrave was elected President. He immediately united the Dáil Government and the Provisional Government. His choice of the dynamic Kevin O'Higgins for the key post of Minister for Home Affairs was of immense significance. In this position O'Higgins was responsible for justice and law and order. As such, he was determined to crush all challenges to the authority of the Government.

Although the Irregular forces continued to fight the Civil War, their position weakened considerably. During the War of Independence, public support for the guerrilla fighters ensured that they had many 'safe houses' to hide in, but most people now supported the Free State Government. In October 1922 the Catholic bishops met at Maynooth and issued a very strong statement in support of Cosgrave's Government. They condemned the Irregulars for 'waging a war of wanton destruction, of murder and assassination against the people and the people's government'. People refusing to abandon their rebellion would be **excommunicated**, or excluded from membership of the Catholic Church.

The Free State Government introduced strict emergency legislation, with military courts and the death penalty for those found with illegal weapons. On 24 November 1922 Erskine Childers was shot by firing squad for this offence. He claimed that the pistol had been given to him by Michael Collins before the split over the Treaty.

On 8 December 1922 the Government acted in a ruthless manner to suppress the challenge of the Irregulars. In response to the shooting dead of the pro-Treaty Cork TD Seán Hales, four Irregular prisoners were executed without trial. These were four leading republicans from different parts of Ireland – Rory O'Connor, Liam Mellowes, Joseph McKelvey and Dick Barrett. Rory O'Connor had been the best man at the wedding of Kevin O'Higgins, who now voted for his execution. The Government's action was criticised on moral grounds by the Catholic Archbishop of Dublin, Dr Edward Byrne, among others. He conveyed his dismay privately to W.T. Cosgrave. However, Cosgrave and his colleagues argued that their first duty was to defend the state. In all, seventy-seven republican prisoners were executed during the Civil War.

By April 1923 around 13,000 republican prisoners were imprisoned. Any protests, such as hunger strikes, were ignored by the Government. As the fighting continued, some appalling atrocities were committed by both sides, especially in Co. Kerry. On 10 April 1923 General Liam Lynch was killed in action in the Knockmealdown Mountains. He was succeeded as Chief of Staff of the Irregular forces by Frank Aiken, who almost immediately ordered a ceasefire. On 24 May de Valera, who had been overshadowed by the military leaders during the Civil War, issued a statement to his followers calling on them to lay down their arms:

> Soldiers of the Republic, Legion of the Rearguard: the Republic can no longer be defended successfully by your arms. Further sacrifice of life would now be in vain . . . Military victory must be allowed to rest for the moment with those who have destroyed the Republic.

According to republicans, they never finally surrendered but only hid their arms. For the Free State side, however, the Civil War ended in a victory and gave supporters of the Treaty the opportunity to reconstruct and develop the newly independent state.

The Impact of the Civil War

The Civil War had profound consequences for the development of Ireland in the decades ahead:

- It created deep bitterness and resentment, which lasted for many years.
- It resulted in the deaths of talented men on both sides, including Arthur Griffith, Michael Collins, Harry Boland, Rory O'Connor and Cathal Brugha.
- It resulted in significant destruction of property and damage to the infrastructure, such as the transport system, throughout the state.
- It greatly strengthened the position of unionists in Northern Ireland as their nationalist opponents fought one another.
- The Civil War was a distraction from serious social problems such as poverty, bad housing, unemployment and emigration.
- The two main political parties to emerge in the Irish Free State can trace their origin back to the split in Sinn Féin between pro- and anti-Treaty factions.
- Unlike in other European countries, where politics was divided along right- and left-wing lines, in Ireland Civil War divisions predominated.

By the time the Civil War came to an end in the spring of 1923, Ireland had experienced conflict of one kind or another for nearly nine years. The challenges facing any government of a newly independent state would have been formidable. The Civil War ensured that the Free State Government would have to overcome serious obstacles in order to establish law and order and justify Ireland's claim to rule itself in the years ahead.

KEY PERSONALITY: ARTHUR GRIFFITH (1871–1922)

Arthur Griffith was born in Dublin in 1871. A printer by trade, he emigrated to South Africa in 1896. He returned to Ireland in 1899 and became editor of the weekly newspaper *United Irishman*. Considering Home Rule to be insufficient, he favoured instead the Austro-Hungarian model of 'dual monarchy'. This concept, which he proposed in *The Resurrection of Hungary* (1904), advocated the withdrawal of Irish MPs from Westminster and the establishment instead of a separate Irish parliament in Dublin.

With regard to economic policy, Griffith advocated self-sufficiency and the protection of Irish industry behind tariff barriers. In these matters he was greatly influenced by the German economist Friedrich List. In order to propagate his political and economic ideas, he established in 1905 a new organisation called Sinn Féin ('We Ourselves').

From its foundation in 1905 until 1918, Sinn Féin enjoyed minimal electoral success and was largely irrelevant. Griffith himself supported the formation of the Irish Volunteers and opposed recruitment to the British army at the outset of World War I. Although Sinn Féin as an organisation had no involvement in the Easter Rising of 1916, the British Government erroneously blamed Sinn Féin for instigating the Rising. Griffith himself was arrested after the Rising, although he had not been involved.

Sinn Féin became the focal point for the newly resurgent nationalism that developed after the Rising. The new Sinn Féin was a revolutionary, republican organisation that bore little resemblance to Griffith's original movement. Griffith himself was elected to Parliament for Sinn Féin in a by-election in Cavan in 1917. Following the resounding victory of Sinn Féin in the 1918 general election, the Sinn Féin MPs followed Griffith's original proposal of abstaining from Westminster and established instead the First Dáil.

In the First Dáil, Griffith became Vice-President and Minister for Home Affairs. He was responsible for setting up the Sinn Féin courts, which took the place of the British courts in many parts of the country. He led the Irish delegation that negotiated the Treaty settlement with Britain in 1921. He strongly defended the Treaty in the Dáil and, following the resignation of de Valera, became President of the Dáil. He now faced the huge task of establishing and consolidating the new Irish Free State in the face of a bitter civil war. Griffith's health had been failing for some time, and he died on 12 August 1922.

KEY PERSONALITY: MICHAEL COLLINS (1890–1922)

Michael Collins was born in Clonakilty, Co. Cork, in 1890. At the age of fifteen, he went to work in the British Post Office and lived in London until 1916. During his years in London, he became involved in Irish cultural organisations, including the GAA and the Gaelic League. He joined the IRB and fought in the GPO during the Easter Rising of 1916. He was arrested after the Rising and was interned for a period in Frongoch Camp in Wales.

On his release from Frongoch in 1917, Collins quickly became a key figure in the revitalised independence movement. In the 1918 general election, he was elected Sinn Féin MP to the Westminster Parliament in the South Cork constituency but instead took his seat in the First Dáil, which met on 21 January 1919. On the same day, the first shots of the War of Independence were fired.

During the War of Independence, Collins revealed his abilities as a strategist and organiser. As Minister for Finance in the Government established by the First Dáil, he helped raise money to pay for the activities of the Dáil. As Head of Intelligence during the War of Independence, he orchestrated the activities of the IRA. He used his own select group, known as 'the Squad', to infiltrate the British intelligence network in Ireland and assassinate many of its key operatives.

Following the declaration of a truce in July 1921 and the subsequent breakdown of talks between Lloyd George and de Valera, full negotiations between the British and Irish delegations commenced in October. Despite his protestations, Collins was chosen by de Valera to be a member of the Irish delegation appointed to negotiate a Treaty settlement.

Collins believed that the negotiated Treaty, which granted dominion status to Ireland, was the best that could be achieved in the circumstances. He vehemently defended the Treaty in the Dáil and argued that it was a stepping stone to greater independence in the future. Although the Treaty was accepted by a small majority in the Dáil, the divisions within the country, the Dáil and the IRA formed the prelude to the outbreak of civil war.

During the Civil War, Collins became Commander-in-Chief of the forces of the newly created Irish Free State. It was a bloody and bitter conflict, culminating in his own death at the hands of anti-Treaty forces in an ambush at Béal na mBláth, Co. Cork, on 22 August 1922.

Collins was a leader of exceptional ability and energy. As an outstanding organiser and strategist, he played a pivotal role during the War of Independence and the Civil War. In accepting, defending and implementing the Treaty settlement, Collins proved to be a realist who had made the successful transition from revolutionary to politician.

EXERCISES

ORDINARY LEVEL

1. Why did de Valera refuse to lead the Irish delegation during the Treaty negotiations in London? How did his critics view this refusal?

2. Explain 'dominion status'.

3. State two arguments in favour of the Anglo-Irish Treaty and two against during the debates on the Treaty in the Dáil.

4. What arrangements were made for the transfer of power from the British to the new pro-Treaty Government?

5. Write a paragraph on the split in the IRA over the Treaty.

6. Write a paragraph on the general election of 1922.

7. Explain in detail the causes of the Civil War.

8. Write an account of the main developments during the Civil War.

9. Outline the results of the Civil War.

HIGHER LEVEL

1. Consider in detail the role of de Valera between the truce of July 1921 and the outbreak of the Civil War in June 1922.

2. Assess the provisions of the Anglo-Irish Treaty (1921), and consider the principal arguments for and against it.

3. Write an essay on the causes of the Civil War.

4. 'The Irish Civil War had serious implications for the future of the independent Irish state.' Discuss.

5. Write an essay on the contribution of Arthur Griffith to the movement for Irish independence up to 1922.

6. Assess the role of Michael Collins in Irish affairs.

The Establishment of the Irish Free State

The Irish Free State was established on 6 December 1922, a year after the signing of the Anglo-Irish Treaty. The political structures of the new state were set out in a written constitution, which was based on the Treaty settlement. The following were the main provisions of the Constitution of the Irish Free State.

- The **Irish Free State** was a dominion in the British Commonwealth, with the King as head of state.
- The Governor-General represented the King in Ireland.
- All laws were passed by the **Oireachtas**, which contained two Houses, the Dáil and the Senate, whose members had to swear an Oath of Allegiance to the King.
- The Dáil elected the head of government, known as the President of the Executive Council. He then appointed ministers to the Executive Council, or Cabinet.
- Members of the Dáil (Teachtaí Dála), or TDs, were elected by all men and women over twenty-one years of age under the voting system of proportional representation (PR).
- The Senate, consisting of sixty members, had far less power than the Dáil and was elected by citizens over thirty years of age.
- The Constitution guaranteed basic rights such as freedom of expression, assembly and religion.

For the first time in its history, most of Ireland now had a written constitution which set down the basic laws of the country and the rights of its citizens. While the King of England was the official head of state, real power was in the hands of the elected Dáil and Government. The first Governor-General was Timothy Healy, a former member of the Home Rule Party. Whereas in other Commonwealth countries the Governor-General was usually a British nobleman, the Government of the Irish Free State insisted on the appointment of an Irishman and a commoner to that role.

Continuity and Change

The new political structures of the Irish Free State were modelled closely on the British system of government. Government ministers were responsible to the Dáil and presided over departments that were modelled closely on those of Britain. These government departments were run by civil servants who, in most cases, had also trained and worked in the British administration in Ireland.

Under the **Ministers and Secretaries Act** of 1924, government departments were re-organised. Whereas a permanent civil servant, known as a Secretary, was in charge of the administration of each department, ultimate responsibility and authority lay with the government minister. The most powerful department was the Department of Finance. Like its counterpart in Britain, the Treasury, this department controlled the money available to all other departments. From 1923 to 1932, the Minister for Finance in the Irish Free State was Ernest Blythe. Joseph Brennan was Secretary to the Department of Finance until 1927, when he was replaced by J.J. McElligott. McElligott held this powerful position until his retirement in 1953.

Other government departments included Home Affairs (Justice), Education, Local Government and Public Health, Defence, Agriculture, Industry and Commerce, and External Affairs. In most cases, the civil servants in these departments had years of experience in public administration. Although providing a high degree of continuity and stability, they were conservative and resistant to change. In the early years of the Irish Free State, members of the civil service provided much-needed guidance and support for politicians who were inexperienced in running a government.

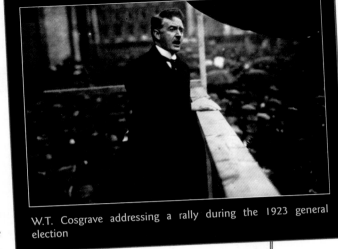
W.T. Cosgrave addressing a rally during the 1923 general election

Political Parties in the Irish Free State

The first general election under the new Constitution of the Irish Free State took place in August 1923. Although the Civil War had ended, political divisions in the new state continued to be dominated by attitudes towards the Treaty. The main political parties that contested the 1923 election were as follows.

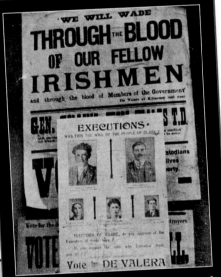
A pro-de Valera poster pasted on top of an anti-de Valera poster during the general election of 1923

- **Cumann na nGaedheal**: This consisted of pro-Treaty TDs who came together to form the new party in April 1923. It was led by W.T. Cosgrave and took its name from an organisation founded by Arthur Griffith prior to the foundation of Sinn Féin. Its main political position was support for the Treaty and the restoration of law and order.

- **Sinn Féin**: Although Sinn Féin had split over the Treaty, de Valera and the anti-Treatyite followers decided to contest the 1923 election under the name of Sinn Féin. They opposed the Treaty and were committed to abstaining from the Dáil. During the election campaign, de Valera was arrested and imprisoned.

- **The Labour Party**: Founded in 1912, Labour was the oldest political party contesting the election. Its members were mostly trade unionists, and it campaigned for improved living and working conditions. Under the leadership of Thomas Johnson, the party accepted the Treaty settlement.

- **The Farmers' Party**: This was a sectional party that supported the interests of farmers. It strongly supported the Treaty and favoured free trade and tight control of public expenditure.

After more than a decade of political turbulence, the 1923 general election was the first since 1910 to be held in relatively peaceful conditions. With 153 seats to be filled, the election yielded the results shown below. Although Cumann na nGaedheal did not have an overall majority, it formed the Government because the Sinn Féin TDs refused to take their seats in the Dáil. W.T. Cosgrave, as leader of Cumann na nGaedheal, was elected President of the Executive Council. As the Farmers' Party generally supported the Government, the Labour Party became the official Opposition within the Dáil. The new Cumann na nGaedheal Government was deeply conservative in outlook. In the immediate aftermath of the Civil War, its most pressing concern was the restoration of law and order.

RESULTS OF 1923 GENERAL ELECTION	
Cumann na nGaedheal	63
Sinn Féin	44
Farmers' Party	15
Labour	14
Independents	17

Law and Order

The Cumann na nGaedheal Government faced major challenges in restoring order and stability throughout the state. Although the Civil War had ended, acts of violence continued to take place, as many of the anti-Treaty republicans refused to recognise the authority of the Dáil. The minister responsible for dealing with the issue of law and order was Kevin O'Higgins. He was Vice-President of the Executive Council, or second-in-command to Cosgrave, and Minister for Home Affairs (Justice). He tackled this situation in three main ways:

- Public Safety Acts.
- Foundation of the Garda Síochána.
- Reform of the court system.

O'Higgins introduced a number of strict Public Safety Acts that gave extensive powers to the Government in the area of law and order. They increased the powers of arrest and detention and were effective in dealing with armed attacks and robberies. One of the most lasting achievements of Cosgrave's Government was the establishment in September 1922 of a new, unarmed police force, the Garda Síochána, which replaced the Royal Irish Constabulary. The Garda Síochána wore a distinct blue uniform. Their first Commissioner was

Members of the newly formed Garda Síochána

Michael Staines, but he was soon replaced by Eoin O'Duffy, who remained as Garda Commissioner until 1933. The Gardaí were drawn largely from the ranks of the pro-Treaty IRA, and they soon established a high level of public support for the force. The Garda Síochána played a critical role in restoring law and order throughout the land.

In 1924 Kevin O'Higgins introduced the Courts of Justice Act, which reformed the legal system. Both the old British and the Sinn Féin courts were abolished, and in their place a new court system was established, consisting of four main courts:

- Supreme Court.
- High Court.
- Circuit Court.
- District Court.

Minor matters were dealt with by paid judges in the District Court. This replaced the old British system of unpaid magistrates. The Circuit Court dealt with more serious civil and criminal matters. The two highest courts were the High Court and the Supreme Court, which dealt with serious cases and with appeals from lower courts. Although a new system of courts had been established, there was more continuity than change in the legal system. Old British laws remained in force, and both the training and dress of the legal profession were modelled closely on British practice.

The Garda barracks at Rathfarnham, Co. Dublin, which was blown up by the IRA

Through his various reforms, O'Higgins had played a key role in restoring stability to the country. However, the most serious threat to the security of the Government was to emerge not from anti-Treatyite republican sources but from within the army of the Irish Free State.

The Army Mutiny

After the Civil War, the Government set about transforming the army from a wartime to a peacetime force. This inevitably involved the extensive demobilisation of troops from the army, which consisted of 55,000 soldiers and 3,500 officers by the end of the Civil War. Many soldiers deeply resented this policy at a time of high unemployment. By early 1924 only 13,000 men and 2,000 officers remained.

Richard Mulcahy, Minister for Defence, inspecting troops

Many soldiers who had fought in the War of Independence and had remained loyal to Michael Collins during the Civil War had a particular grievance. Known as the 'Old IRA', they felt that they were undervalued and were being dismissed, whereas colleagues who had previously been in the British army were being kept on. The Old IRA members were also disappointed at the lack of progress towards the fulfilment of Collins's hope that the Treaty would form a stepping stone towards an Irish republic.

Matters came to a head on 6 March 1924, when two army officers and Old IRA members, Liam Tobin and Emmet Dalton, sent an ultimatum to the Cosgrave Government. In it they outlined the grievances of the army and made the following demands:

- An immediate halt to demobilisation.
- The removal of the Army Council.
- An assurance from the Government regarding progress towards a republic.

The Government immediately denounced the ultimatum and ordered the arrest of Dalton and Tobin. In the absence of Cosgrave, who was ill, Kevin O'Higgins took charge of the crisis. He strongly opposed the existence within the army of secret groups such as the IRB, which was controlled by the Minister for Defence, Richard Mulcahy. O'Higgins and other Cabinet members distrusted Mulcahy's motives. They therefore appointed the Garda Commissioner, Eoin O'Duffy, as supreme commander of the army over the head of Mulcahy. The mutineers were assured that an enquiry into the army would be set up and that they would not be victimised. However, on 18 March 1924 a small group of army officers met in a Dublin public house to plot further action. A senior army officer arrested the group, having consulted Richard Mulcahy but not Eoin O'Duffy. Fearful that the crisis was about to worsen once again, O'Higgins persuaded the Cabinet to take decisive action. They demanded the resignation of Mulcahy and the Army Council. Mulcahy, however, had resigned before this message reached him.

The main consequence of the Army Mutiny was the strengthening of control of the army by the elected Government. O'Higgins was determined to wipe out the influence of secret societies in the army. From 1924 onwards, members of the Irish army had to swear an oath, declaring that they did not belong to any secret society. However, the incident had serious consequences for the Cumann na nGaedheal Government. Two ministers – Richard Mulcahy and Joseph McGrath, Minister for Industry and Commerce – resigned, and eight TDs withdrew their support from the Government. While Cosgrave's Government had successfully surmounted the challenge posed by the Army Mutiny, it did so at considerable political cost.

Economic and Social Policy of Cumann na nGaedheal

The Anglo-Irish Treaty of 1921 provided the Irish Free State with full economic independence. However, in practice the new state was heavily dependent on the British market, which remained the main consumer of Irish exports. In addition, the banking systems of both countries were closely connected.

The partition of Ireland in 1920 resulted in the loss of the most industrialised part of the country. Furthermore, the War of Independence and the Civil War had serious economic consequences for the new state, with widespread destruction of property and disruption of transport. In the wake of years of unrest and economic disruption, the demands of restoring law and order placed a considerable strain on the economy.

The Irish Free State, therefore, was born in difficult economic circumstances. From the outset, the Cumann na nGaedheal Government pursued a conservative economic policy. Under the direction of Ernest Blythe, Minister for Finance from 1923, this policy was characterised by a desire to keep taxation and government expenditure at a low level. The Department of Finance modelled itself on the British Treasury and exercised strict control over the expenditure of the other government departments. Balancing the budget remained a high priority for the Cumann na nGaedheal Government.

Many historians have pointed out the contrast between the economic conservatism of the Irish Free State and the political revolution that brought it into being. Although Cumann na nGaedheal was the political heir of the founder of Sinn Féin, Arthur Griffith, the party did not implement his economic policies of tariff protection and self-sufficiency. In contrast, they implemented a policy of free trade, which involved minimal protection of industry on the part of the Government. This policy suited larger farmers exporting to Britain and export-oriented industries such as brewing and distilling. Smaller industries, however, looked for tariff protection from cheap imported goods. In 1923 the Government set up a **Fiscal Inquiry Commission** to examine the issue, but it concluded that very little change was needed. However, in a largely rural society such as Ireland, agriculture rather than industry remained the principal economic concern of the Cosgrave Government.

AGRICULTURE

During the 1920s agriculture was the greatest source of employment in the Irish Free State and accounted for over 80 per cent of total exports. The Minister for Agriculture, Patrick Hogan, summed up the importance of agriculture when he stated that agriculture was and would remain by far the most important industry in the Free State and that the touchstone by which every economic measure must be judged was its effect on the prosperity of the farmers.

As part of the Government's programme to advance the development of agriculture, Hogan and his department took a number of initiatives:

1 In order to improve the quality of agricultural exports, grading and inspection were introduced for butter, meat and eggs.
2 Land purchase was completed by the Land Commission, which replaced the Congested Districts Board in 1923.
3 Greater emphasis was placed on agricultural instruction, with an improved system of advisers and evening classes.
4 In order to encourage farmers to borrow for investment in their land, the Agricultural Credit Corporation (ACC) was established in 1927.

These policies had a limited success. Agricultural output increased gradually during the 1920s. Conditions in Great Britain rather than domestic policies determined the slow pace of expansion. During the 1920s prices for agricultural goods continued to fall on the British market. A combination of the British cheap food policy, depression, unemployment and tough competition from other countries kept prices low for Irish agricultural exporters. The only sector of farming to prosper at the time was cattle production, as prices here held up better than in other sectors.

The agricultural policies of the Cumann na nGaedheal Government mostly favoured the larger farmers, who in turn were among the Government's strongest supporters. The vast majority of farmers, however, lived on small, uneconomic holdings. Both they and landless labourers gained little from government policies, and emigration from rural Ireland remained high during the 1920s. Although agriculture accounted for half the jobs in the Irish economy in the 1920s, it contributed only one-third of the national income. Therefore, Hogan's assumption that the economic welfare of the state depended on the prosperity of agriculture was open to question. In this context, industrial development was central to the progress of the young state.

Cattle hides being exported to England during the 1920s

INDUSTRIAL DEVELOPMENT

Industrial development in the Irish Free State was impeded by a number of difficulties. These included lack of capital investment, absence of raw materials such as coal and iron, and intense competition from cheaper British imported goods. Smaller industries, such as clothing, footwear and furniture-making, were dependent on the home market and suffered the most from foreign competition. Although many of them saw tariff protection as the solution to their difficulties, in reality they were often inefficient, badly managed and slow to innovate.

Larger industries, on the other hand, were represented by thriving export-oriented firms, such as Guinness and Jacobs. They strongly favoured a policy of free trade with minimal government interference or protection. However, in response to pressure from the smaller industries, the Minister for Finance, Ernest Blythe, placed tariffs, or duties, on imported goods such as shoes, glass bottles, soap, candles and motor bodies. The Government also set up a Tariff Commission in 1926 to assess applications for tariff protection. This three-man Commission was chaired by J.J. McElligott, a senior civil servant who was later to become Secretary of the Department of Finance. It was heavily weighted in favour of free trade and granted few tariff applications.

The most dramatic economic achievement was the establishment of a hydroelectric station at Ardnacrusha on the River Shannon in 1929. This addressed the need for a major source of electricity for industrial and domestic use. The Shannon Scheme was the brainchild of Irish engineer T.A. MacLaughlin and enjoyed the full support of the Minister for Industry and Commerce, Patrick McGilligan. The contract for constructing the scheme was awarded to the German electrical firm Siemens and involved an investment of £5 million. During the construction period between 1925 and 1929, the Shannon Scheme provided employment for 4,000 Irish construction workers. Despite strong opposition both from within the Government and from sections of the business community, the Shannon Scheme was an outstanding success and was seen as one of the greatest achievements of the Cumann na nGaedheal Government.

The Shannon Hydro-Electric Scheme under construction

In 1927 the Government established a semi-state body, the Electricity Supply Board (ESB), to oversee the production and distribution of electricity. The ESB vastly increased the output of electricity and totally transformed living and working conditions in the countryside in the decades ahead. The ESB was the model for subsequent semi-state bodies, such as the Agricultural Credit Corporation (ACC), the Irish Sugar Company and Bord na Móna, in the decades ahead.

While the Shannon Scheme and the ESB were outstanding successes, on the whole, industrial progress during the 1920s was gradual. Between 1925 and 1930, the numbers employed in industry increased by 5,000. Although this increase may be attributed partly to tariff protection, it was more likely due to improving economic conditions in the worldwide economy. However, this modest economic improvement was to come to a dramatic halt with the onset of world depression after 1929.

SOCIAL POLICY

The social policy of the Cumann na nGaedheal Government was in line with its economic policy. The same principles of limited government intervention in the economy and balanced budgets applied. The Government continued to implement schemes inherited from the British administration, but made little attempt to improve them. In fact, in an effort to balance the budget, old-age pensions were actually reduced by a shilling a week by Ernest Blythe in 1924. Unemployment insurance was limited to a small proportion of workers, who only received payments for the first six months after losing their jobs. After this, they had to depend on a means-tested home assistance allowance, which was difficult to obtain. As a result, emigration remained the only viable option for many unemployed people.

Although a Department of Local Government and Public Health was established in 1924, public healthcare during the 1920s had not advanced since the nineteenth century. Poorer people who were old or sick were frequently cared for in county homes, which were old workhouses. In order to obtain any assistance at home, the poor had to undergo a humiliating means test during which their homes were examined and their goods valued. Indeed, without the involvement of religious organisations of priests, brothers and nuns in healthcare and education, the condition of the poor would have been much worse.

Education and the Irish Language

The Irish Free State inherited an extensive system of education from the British administration. Under the direction of Eoin MacNeill, the Minister for Education, some important changes were introduced. A new Department of Education was set up and took over the functions of the old National and Intermediate Boards of Education. While most primary and secondary schools remained under the control of the churches, the new Department of Education attempted to improve attendance and introduced reforms in the curriculum. In 1926 the School Attendance Act introduced compulsory school attendance for children between the ages of six and fourteen. Despite this, many children continued to leave school before the age of fourteen. During the 1920s about 90 per cent of children did not go beyond primary school.

At secondary level, significant changes were introduced. The old Intermediate examinations were abolished and replaced by the Intermediate and Leaving Certificate examinations. Payment by results was abolished, and schools were given grants by the Department of Education instead. As with primary schools, Department of Education inspectors had the task of visiting and improving secondary schools.

During the 1920s the need for a better system of vocational – or technical – education was clear. Technical schools had been set up in 1899, but they were under-funded and poorly attended. In 1930, therefore, the Government introduced the Vocational Education Act to reform technical education. This established thirty-eight Vocational Education Committees (VECs) to organise and oversee the provision of vocational education. Because vocational schools did not prepare students for the Leaving Certificate, many parents regarded them as inferior to secondary schools.

The most important innovation introduced into the education system of the Irish Free State was undoubtedly the promotion of the Irish language. In 1922 all primary schools were instructed to teach Irish for at least an hour each day. From 1926 onwards all infant classes were to be conducted through the medium of Irish. Special summer schools in Irish were organised to improve teachers' knowledge of the language. At second level, Irish was also given an important place in the curriculum. Schools which taught all subjects exclusively through Irish were given increased grants. Irish became a compulsory subject for entry to the civil service.

The position of Irish in the education system reflected government support for the revival of the Irish language. The policy of using schools as the main vehicle for the restoration of the language was not a successful one. In particular, the element of compulsion alienated many young people and turned them against the Irish language.

Culture and Society

After the cultural and political ferment of the Gaelic revival and revolutionary struggle, the Irish

Free State by contrast was culturally conservative and inward-looking. As a result of partition, the southern state was overwhelmingly Catholic in composition, and the Catholic Church exercised great power and influence over people's lives. The predominantly rural nature of society also contributed to its conservatism. Indeed, because of the level of emigration, many rural areas lost the younger and more dynamic elements of the population. As a recently independent country, the Irish Free State was anxious to establish its own distinct cultural identity and was sensitive to any criticism both at home and abroad.

The controversy over divorce in 1925 was typical of the cultural climate in the Irish Free State. In that year the Cosgrave Government, at the behest of the Catholic bishops, banned divorce in the Irish Free State. A number of prominent Protestants, including the poet and senator William Butler Yeats, protested in vain against this measure.

A bishop blessing flags for the Irish army during the 1920s

The position of women in society disimproved during the 1920s. Between 1914 and 1923 many women, including Countess Markievicz and Maud Gonne, played prominent roles in the struggle for independence. A separate women's organisation, Cumann na mBan, was attached to Sinn Féin and the IRA. However, during the 1920s women played little part in public affairs. Women at work usually earned less than their male counterparts, and they usually left their positions on getting married. At the time, the dominant roles played by women were those of wives and mothers, with very little opportunity outside the home.

One of the more controversial aspects of official policy in Ireland from the 1920s onwards was the existence of censorship. In an effort to protect the morals of its citizens, the state appointed censors to check books and films, with the power to edit them or to ban them outright. Whereas the system of censorship was strongly supported by the Catholic Church, it was deeply resented by writers and other artists. Many famous books by Irish and foreign authors were banned, and several writers emigrated as a result. More than any other facet of life, the strict censorship laws epitomised the conservative, inward-looking and insecure nature of Irish society at that time.

Foreign Policy

ESTABLISHING AN INDEPENDENT FOREIGN POLICY

Under the Anglo-Irish Treaty of December 1921, the Irish Free State became a dominion in the British Commonwealth, with the same rights as other dominions such as Canada, Australia, New Zealand and South Africa. However, unlike the other dominions, which grew out of British colonial settlement in different parts of the Empire, the Irish Free State had achieved dominion status as a result of revolution. From its inception, the Cumann na nGaedheal Government was anxious to vindicate Michael Collins's view of the Treaty as a stepping stone to greater freedom. As part of this approach it was anxious to follow an independent foreign policy from the beginning. The first example of this policy was the successful application to join the League of Nations in 1923. The Irish Free State insisted on having the Treaty registered at the League in Geneva as an agreement between two states. The British objected to this and regarded it as an internal matter within the Empire.

In October 1924 the Government sent a representative to the United States. This was a further advance towards greater autonomy, as before this, members of the Commonwealth had depended on the British ambassador in other countries. The Free State followed this initiative by sending representatives to France and Germany. By 1932 the Irish Free State had established diplomatic links with many countries abroad.

THE BOUNDARY COMMISSION

One of the outstanding issues that dominated relations with Great Britain during the early years of the Irish Free State was the issue of Northern Ireland. According to the Anglo-Irish Treaty, a Boundary Commission was to be set up to revise the border between Northern Ireland and the Irish Free State. During the Treaty debates, Griffith and Collins had presumed that large areas of Northern Ireland would be transferred to the South. However, the words of the Treaty on this point were open to different interpretations. The Civil War delayed the establishment of the Boundary Commission, which was eventually set up in 1924. The Minister for Education, Eoin MacNeill, was nominated to represent the Irish Free State; a South African judge, Richard Feetham, was appointed chairman by the British Government; and when James Craig, the Northern Ireland Prime Minister, refused to nominate a representative, the British Government appointed a Belfast lawyer, J.R. Fisher, to represent Northern Ireland.

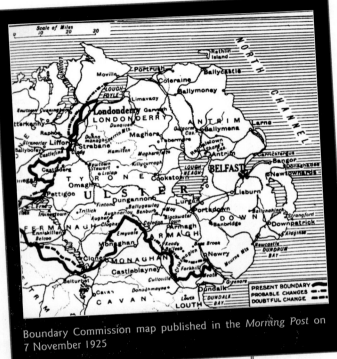

Boundary Commission map published in the *Morning Post* on 7 November 1925

The Boundary Commission heard legal submissions and visited border areas to hear the views of local inhabitants. The members had to decide whether to redraw the border completely or to make small alterations. They also had to decide whether to give greater weight to the wishes of local inhabitants or to economic and geographic conditions. As chairman, Justice Feetham's views carried great weight. He favoured minimal change. Whereas Fisher kept the Northern Ireland Government well informed, it appears that Eoin MacNeill failed to make Cosgrave familiar with developments.

On 7 November 1925 a British newspaper, the *Morning Post*, carried a leaked report on the work of the Boundary Commission. According to the report, minimal alterations were to be made to the border: the Free State was to gain small areas of Armagh and Fermanagh but was to lose part of Donegal to Northern Ireland. A huge controversy broke out, as few in the South had expected the Free State to actually lose territory to Northern Ireland. Eoin MacNeill resigned from the Boundary Commission and then from the Government. As a published finding would be binding on all parties, Cosgrave rushed to London to prevent the publication of the report. Under an agreement between the Irish Free State and Great Britain, the report of the Boundary Commission would not be published and the border would remain unchanged. The part of the British war debt owed by the Free State was cancelled.

The Boundary Commission episode was a political fiasco for the Cosgrave Government. This was seen as a triumph for Craig and the Government of Northern Ireland, as partition now became permanent.

Ireland in the Commonwealth

In the course of the 1920s the Irish Free State and other members of the British Commonwealth sought to redefine and expand the concept of dominion status. They sought equal status with Great Britain within the Commonwealth. These developments evolved at imperial conferences held at regular intervals to discuss Commonwealth affairs. From 1923 onwards, the Irish Free State played an important role in advancing the cause of equality within the Commonwealth. At these conferences the Irish Free State was represented in turn by Kevin O'Higgins, Desmond Fitzgerald and Patrick McGilligan.

One of the most significant advances took place at the 1926 Conference, with the issuing of the Balfour Declaration. This declared that the dominions were

> Autonomous (i.e. self-governing) communities within the British Empire, equal in status, in no way subordinate one to another in any aspect of their domestic or external affairs, though united by a common allegiance to the Crown and freely associated as members of the British Commonwealth of Nations.

The Balfour Declaration enshrined the concept of 'co-equality' between Great Britain and the other dominions. It also paved the way for the 1930 Imperial Conference, which led to the passing of the Statute of Westminster. This law declared that:

- Britain would no longer pass laws binding on dominions without their consent.
- Dominion parliaments could change laws passed by Britain on their behalf.

The Statute of Westminster marked the high point of the independent foreign policy pursued by the Cosgrave Government. It gave practical expression to Collins's view of the Treaty as a stepping stone towards greater independence. It marked the end of British involvement in the internal affairs of the Irish Free State. However, Cosgrave's Government remained committed to friendly relations with Great Britain and regarded Commonwealth membership as an advantage for Ireland.

Delegates, including Ireland's W.T. Cosgrave (far left) at the Imperial Conference in London in October 1926. Other heads of government attended from South Africa, Canada, Britain and Australia.

Political Developments in the Irish Free State, 1926–32

De Valera and the Foundation of Fianna Fáil

After the Civil War, the Irish Free State was firmly established. As a pragmatic politician, de Valera felt isolated and powerless as long as he remained outside the Dáil. At a Sinn Féin Ard-Fheis in March 1926, de Valera proposed that the party should enter the Dáil if the Oath of Allegiance were abolished. When this motion was narrowly defeated, de Valera used the opportunity to leave Sinn Féin, bringing many followers with him. In May 1926 he founded a new political party, Fianna Fáil. Its main aims were:

- The restoration of the Irish language.
- The achievement of a 32-county Irish republic.
- Economic self-sufficiency.

Most Sinn Féin TDs joined the new party, and many republicans gave it their support. The new party set up a local cumann, or branch, in most areas throughout the country.

The first electoral test for Fianna Fáil came in the general election of June 1927. Beforehand, de Valera went on a fund-raising trip to America. The outgoing Cumann na nGaedheal Government had become unpopular for a number of reasons. The reduction in the old-age pension and public service salaries caused resentment. So too did severe law-and-order measures. Kevin O'Higgins's proposal to reform the drink licensing laws in February 1927 encountered wide-spread opposition and contributed further to the falling popularity of Cumann na nGaedheal.

JUNE 1927 ELECTION RESULTS	
Total no. of seats	153
Cumann na nGaedheal	47
Fianna Fáil	44
Labour	22
Farmers' Party	11
National League	8
Sinn Féin	5
Independents	16

In the June 1927 election Cumann na nGaedheal lost 16 seats and was reduced to 47 seats. It was closely followed by Fianna Fáil, which won 44 seats in its first general election. However, Fianna Fáil TDs did not take their seats because of the requirement to take the Oath of Allegiance. Cosgrave was therefore able to form a government once again. However, the political scene was to be transformed in July 1927 with the assassination of Kevin O'Higgins.

A group of Fianna Fáil TDs, led by Éamon de Valera, leaving the Dáil in June 1927, having refused to take the Oath of Allegiance

FIANNA FÁIL ENTERS THE DÁIL

On Sunday, 10 July 1927, Kevin O'Higgins was assassinated as he walked home from Mass. Although nobody was ever arrested for the murder, it was presumed to be the work of the IRA. Cosgrave and the Government reacted vigorously to this challenge to their authority. Two important laws were passed by the Dáil:

- **The Public Safety Act**
  This gave the Government the authority to set up a special court that could impose the death penalty on those found with illegal weapons.
- **The Electoral Amendment Act**
  Candidates for the Dáil or Senate would have to swear that if elected they would take the Oath of Allegiance.

The Electoral Amendment Act was to prove highly significant. In the aftermath of Kevin O'Higgins's death, it was designed to force Fianna Fáil to enter the Dáil and pursue normal parliamentary politics. This was a courageous decision on the part of Cosgrave, who

Kevin O'Higgins, who was assassinated on 10 July 1927

realised that Fianna Fáil's entry into the Dáil would be likely to force another general election.

On 11 August de Valera and the other Fianna Fáil TDs entered Dáil Éireann. They described the Oath of Allegiance, which they had to sign, as an empty formula. Fianna Fáil's entry into the Dáil radically changed the political landscape. Having barely survived a motion of confidence, Cosgrave called an election for September 1927. As politics became more polarised, support for the two main parties increased. In the process, Labour, the smaller parties and independent candidates lost out. Cosgrave and

SEPTEMBER 1927 ELECTION RESULTS	
Total no. of seats	153
Cumann na nGaedheal	62
Fianna Fáil	57
Labour	13
Farmers' Party	6
National League	3
Independents	12

Cumann na nGaedheal formed a government, with Fianna Fáil as the official Opposition. From 1927 until 1932 the Cosgrave Government depended on the Farmers' Party and some Independents to survive. From the outset, it was a considerably weakened administration.

THE ADVANCE OF FIANNA FÁIL, 1927–32

Between 1927 and 1932 Fianna Fáil vigorously opposed the Government over a wide range of constitutional, social and economic issues. As a republican party, it campaigned for the abolition of the Oath of Allegiance to the King of England. Although Fianna Fáil had entered the Dáil in 1927, the party maintained close links with the IRA, especially at local level. This practice of maintaining connections with republican dissidents while participating in parliamentary politics is reflected in Seán Lemass's description of Fianna Fáil in 1928 as 'a slightly constitutional party'. Fianna Fáil combined a republican political programme with a radical social and economic agenda. The party campaigned for an end to the payment of land annuities (repayments of loans given to Irish farmers for land purchase); for better housing and healthcare; and for the encouragement of Irish industries through extensive tariff protection.

Between 1927 and 1932 Fianna Fáil grew in popularity as Cumann na nGaedheal declined. This may be attributed to a number of factors.

- Fianna Fáil had a highly developed and efficient local organisation centred around the party branch, or cumann, of which there was one in almost every parish. The cumann selected candidates for elections and pioneered an annual church-gate collection for the party. In 1931 Fianna Fáil founded the *Irish Press* newspaper to spread its views and to combat the pro-Cumann na nGaedheal stance of existing newspapers. Cumann na nGaedheal, by contrast, had a very poor local organisation. It depended largely on committees of local volunteers at election time.
- Fianna Fáil's social and economic programme appealed to various sectors of the electorate, especially small farmers and a wide range of workers in the towns. In contrast, Cumann na nGaedheal's support base was much narrower. It drew its main support from larger farmers and the professional and business sectors of society.
- Fianna Fáil's republican programme was widely popular. By contrast, Cumann na nGaedheal was seen as a pro-British or pro-Commonwealth party. The harsh public safety measures introduced by the Cumann na nGaedheal Government were

especially unpopular. These culminated in the Public Safety Act of October 1931, which provided for the death penalty for republican violence.

- Among his own supporters, de Valera was a charismatic leader who inspired personal loyalty and deep commitment. Cosgrave, by contrast, was seen as a less inspiring leader.

The Cumann na nGaedheal Government faced major difficulties with the onset of worldwide economic depression following the Wall Street Crash in October 1929. Agricultural exports declined sharply, factories closed and unemployment increased. The Government responded to the crisis by cutting public expenditure, which involved unpopular measures such as reducing the salaries of teachers and Gardaí. The deteriorating economic situation rendered the Cumann na nGaedheal Government increasingly unpopular with the electorate.

The political test for both Cumann na nGaedheal and Fianna Fáil was to occur in the general election of February 1932.

The 1932 General Election

A Cumann na nGaedheal election poster, 1932

Cumann na nGaedheal fought the 1932 general election on the basis of its record in government over the previous decade. The party emphasised its role in restoring stability to the country and maintaining law and order. It defended its careful management of the public finances.

Fianna Fáil, not wishing to alarm wide sections of society, presented a cautious programme of reform to the electorate. The party downplayed its republicanism: although promising the abolition of the Oath of Allegiance and the release of republican prisoners, the actual word 'republic' was not used in its programme. Fianna Fáil campaigned for social and economic reform, including increased dole payments, a house-building programme and the economic protection of industry and agriculture by means of tariffs.

The election campaign was fought in an atmosphere of great tension and bitterness. Cumann na nGaedheal campaigners stressed the links between Fianna Fáil and the IRA. They also used 'red scare' tactics against their opponents. This involved the accusation that a Fianna Fáil government might pave the way for the introduction of communism into Ireland. Peadar O'Donnell, an IRA member, had set up a left-wing group called Saor Éire in 1931. This group had been banned, and O'Donnell was imprisoned under the Public Safety Act. During the general election, Cumann na nGaedheal tried to link the small communist element in the IRA with de Valera and Fianna Fáil.

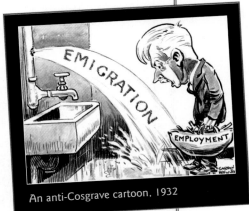

An anti-Cosgrave cartoon, 1932

Fianna Fáil, on the other hand, accused Cumann na nGaedheal of being pro-British and serving the interests of the better off. When de Valera's newspaper, the *Irish Press*, was prosecuted by the Government during the election campaign, Fianna Fáil gained more sympathy, as many people saw this as an attempt to interfere with the democratic process.

When the results of the election were declared, Fianna Fáil had made a major advance. It now had 72 seats out of a total of 153. Cumann na nGaedheal's share of the total declined to 57 seats, and Labour, the Farmers and the Independents lost seats as well. In the highly polarised circumstances of the election, it is not surprising that Labour, the smaller parties and the Independents lost support.

Fianna Fáil was now in a position to come to power with the support of Labour. Those who had been defeated in the Civil War a decade earlier were now about to take over the running of the country. The peaceful transfer of power was a strong sign of the democratic stability and political maturity of the young Irish Free State.

1932 ELECTION RESULTS	
Total no. of seats	153
Cumann na nGaedheal	57
Fianna Fáil	72
Labour	7
Farmers' Party	3
Independents	14

KEY PERSONALITY: WILLIAM T. COSGRAVE (1880–1965)

W.T. Cosgrave was born in Dublin on 6 June 1880. He joined Sinn Féin in 1905 and was elected to Dublin Corporation as a Sinn Féin councillor in 1909. In 1913 he joined the Irish Volunteers and served as adjutant to Éamonn Ceannt at the South Dublin Union during the Easter Rising of 1916. He was sentenced to death for his part in the Rising, but this was later commuted to a sentence of life imprisonment.

After his release from jail in 1917, Cosgrave became actively involved in the new, resurgent Sinn Féin and won a seat for the party in the Kilkenny by-election. He was arrested in May 1918 during the 'German plot' episode. He subsequently won a seat for the party in the 1918 general election. He was appointed Minister for Local Government in the First Dáil and played a key role in persuading most of the county councils to accept the authority of the Dáil. He supported the Treaty and became President of the Provisional Government of the Irish Free State after the deaths of Michael Collins and Arthur Griffith.

When Cosgrave assumed the reins of power, the Civil War was still in progress. He felt an unflinching duty to protect the new state against those who had taken up arms against it. He therefore succeeded in getting the Special Powers Act passed in the Dáil: this Act established a military tribunal and allowed the death penalty for certain offences.

After the Civil War, Cosgrave, as leader of Cumann na nGaedheal and President of the Executive Council, was committed to securing and consolidating the Irish Free State. In the early years of his Government, the restoration of law and order was a priority. In economic and social matters, the Cosgrave Government was cast in a conservative mould. It was committed to low taxation, low government expenditure and free trade. However, among the most enduring of the Government's economic achievements was the hydroelectric scheme at Ardnacrusha on the River Shannon and the subsequent establishment of the Electricity Supply Board.

Cosgrave and his ministers played an important role in establishing an increasingly independent voice for Ireland in foreign affairs during the 1920s: Ireland joined the League of Nations, appointed representatives to foreign countries and played a major part in the imperial conferences that redefined the relationship between Britain and the other members of the Commonwealth.

The Cumann na nGaedheal Government, under the leadership of W.T. Cosgrave, remained in power until 1932. One of Cosgrave's greatest achievements lay in facilitating the smooth transfer of power to Fianna Fáil after the 1932 general election, thus demonstrating the political maturity of the young democracy. When the Blueshirts, Cumann na nGaedheal and the Centre Party joined together in 1933 to form a new party, Fine Gael, Cosgrave handed over the leadership of the new party to Eoin O'Duffy. However, Cosgrave became leader of Fine Gael in 1935, when the party broke its links with O'Duffy and the Blueshirts. He was to remain leader of Fine Gael until his resignation in 1944.

ORDINARY LEVEL

1. Write an account of the main provisions of the Constitution of the Irish Free State (1922).

2. Write a paragraph on the following.

   (i)   Cumann na nGaedheal in the 1920s

   (ii) Sinn Féin between 1922 and 1926

   (iii) The Labour Party in the 1920s

3. Write an account of the political career of Kevin O'Higgins.

4. Explain the economic and social policy of Cumann na nGaedheal, 1923–32.

5. Write a paragraph on Patrick Hogan's policy on agriculture.

6. Write a paragraph on the establishment of the Shannon Hydroelectric Scheme.

7. Write an account of the foundation of Fianna Fáil, its main policies and its entry to the Dáil in 1927.

8. Explain the meaning of censorship, and write a short account of censorship in Ireland in the 1920s.

9. Write a paragraph on the Boundary Commission.

10. Write a detailed account of the Irish Free State and the British Commonwealth between 1922 and 1931.

11. What do you regard as the achievements of the Cumann na nGaedheal Government?

12. Write a detailed account of the general election of 1932.

13. Choose two election posters in this chapter and state (i) the election involved and (ii) the message conveyed.

HIGHER LEVEL

1. Consider the social and economic policies of the Cumann na nGaedheal Government between 1923 and 1932.

2. Outline the steps taken by the Cumann na nGaedheal Government to increase the autonomy of the dominions in the British Commonwealth.

3. Account for the rise of Fianna Fáil and the party's success in the general election of 1932.

4. Consider both the achievements and shortcomings of the Cumann na nGaedheal Government, 1923–32.

5. Write an account on the various steps taken by the Cumann na nGaedheal Government in the area of law and order between 1923 and 1932.

6. Assess the contribution of W.T. Cosgrave in the development of the Irish Free State between 1922 and 1932.

7. 'The year 1927 was of critical importance in the development of democratic politics in the Irish Free State.' Discuss.

A New Government Is Formed

On 9 March 1932 the new Dáil assembled to elect a government. With the support of the Labour Party, Fianna Fáil formed the Government, and Éamon de Valera was elected President of the Executive Council. Fearing that members of the Cumann na nGaedheal Government would be reluctant to hand over power to those whom they had defeated in the Civil War, some Fianna Fáil TDs carried guns in their pockets. However, W.T. Cosgrave was determined to uphold the democratic will of the people, and he arranged a peaceful transfer of power. He advised the army, the Garda Síochána and the civil service to co-operate with the new Government. Despite the desires of many of his followers, de Valera did not dismiss soldiers or civil servants who had opposed him during the Civil War and subsequently.

Within a few months of its formation, the Fianna Fáil Government was given an opportunity to enhance its reputation, when the Eucharistic Congress took place in Dublin in June 1932.

The Fianna Fáil Government, 1932

Case Study: The Eucharistic Congress (1932)

THE CATHOLIC CHURCH IN IRELAND

To understand the significance of the Eucharistic Congress, it is necessary to examine the role of the Catholic Church in early twentieth-century Ireland. Before the granting of independence in 1922, the Catholic Church had become quite powerful under the British administration. As the power of landlords declined, the local priests became more powerful throughout the country. At a time when only one person in every ten went beyond primary school, people often depended on priests for guidance to a far greater degree than in modern times. Unlike in most countries in Europe, where the Catholic bishops had been associated with the rich and powerful, in Ireland they had been far closer to the ordinary people. The leaders of the Church had usually been sympathetic to nationalist movements, as long as these did not involve violence.

Through the extensive involvement of Catholic priests and religious orders in healthcare and education from the 1850s onwards, the Church catered for people who often were not provided for by the state. The Church's control over education, in particular, gave it a powerful influence in turning the minds of future generations in its favour. With the widespread decline of the Irish language, many people valued their Catholic religion as one of the main signs of their Irish identity. In this way, being Catholic and being Irish were often closely connected, and this linkage was encouraged by the Catholic bishops. With the rising number of priests, brothers and nuns, and the high numbers of Catholics attending church regularly, the Irish bishops frequently declared that Ireland was one of the most Catholic countries in the world.

Between 1916 and 1922 the Catholic bishops had to balance condemnation of IRA violence with denunciations of British atrocities. However, after the signing of the Anglo-Irish Treaty (1921), they spoke out decisively in favour of the Free State. During the Civil War, they condemned those fighting on the republican side and excommunicated them (excluded them from membership of the Church). Once peace was restored in 1923, the bishops confidently expected to be highly influential in the new state, with its predominantly Catholic population.

In Northern Ireland, the Catholic Church faced problems of a different kind: being a minority church in a largely Protestant state. Its approach to this dilemma will be one of the themes of Chapter 15.

THE ROLE OF THE CATHOLIC CHURCH IN THE IRISH FREE STATE

During the 1920s in the Irish Free State, the power of the Catholic Church was strong, but on occasion other influences prevailed. For example, the Free State Government ignored the objections of the Catholic Archbishop of Dublin, Dr Edward Byrne, when ordering the execution of republican prisoners in December 1922. W.T. Cosgrave showed his concern for the views of the Protestant minority when he nominated a large number of Protestants to the first Senate of the Irish Free State.

1. De Valera welcoming the Papal Legate, Cardinal Lauri, on his arrival in Ireland for the Eucharistic Congress
2. Religious ceremonies took place on O'Connell Bridge in Dublin during the Eucharistic Congress
3. College Green, Dublin, specially decorated with an imitation Round Tower for the Eucharistic Congress

However, many citizens of the Free State in the 1920s regarded the granting of independence as a triumph for the long-suffering Catholic Irish against an officially Protestant British state. This narrow view of the independence struggle, which downplayed the involvement of Protestant nationalists, was frequently propagated in Catholic schools. Hence, it is not surprising to find that elaborate commemorations were organised in 1929 to celebrate the centenary of Catholic Emancipation. The identification of Catholic with Irish identity, which had developed strongly from O'Connell's time onwards, was now widely accepted as the natural order of life. In the same year, the Pope finally agreed to send a nuncio (papal diplomatic representative) to Dublin and to receive an Irish ambassador at the Vatican.

While strongly supportive of the Catholic Church on most matters, the Government of W.T. Cosgrave had taken an independent line on occasion. Nevertheless, most bishops strongly supported the Cumann na nGaedheal Government. The arrival of de Valera to power in 1932 along with many followers who had been condemned by the Catholic Church during the Civil War caused apprehension among certain Catholic bishops and priests. They need not have worried, however, as de Valera and the Fianna Fáil Government were strongly influenced by the teachings of the Catholic Church and the views of the bishops. One of de Valera's ways of seeking acceptance as a suitable government leader was to secure the approval of the Catholic Church. It was his good fortune that a major Catholic event took place three months after his election as Taoiseach. This was the Eucharistic Congress of 1932, and it gave him an ideal opportunity to prove to Ireland and the outside world that he was worthy to rule the largely Catholic Irish Free State.

THE EUCHARISTIC CONGRESS

The Eucharistic Congress was a religious festival that took place in different countries throughout the world every few years. It celebrated the Catholic belief in the real presence of Christ in the Eucharist and consisted of masses, processions, conferences and receptions. Pope Pius XI (1922–39) decided that it should take place in Dublin in 1932 because it was 1,500 years since the arrival of St Patrick in Ireland in AD 432.

The Congress began with the arrival at Dún Laoghaire Harbour, Co. Dublin, of the Pope's representative, or legate, Cardinal Lauri (Document 1).

Document 1

The arrival of the papal legate and his entry into Dublin

The coming of the Papal Mission was eagerly awaited at Dún Laoghaire. Elaborate preparations had been made by the local authorities, by the State, and by the Congress officials, to give the Legate a reception worthy of the Holy Father's representative and worthy of the great occasion. The people, on their part, joined enthusiastically in the work of preparing a royal reception. The whole town of Dún Laoghaire was decorated with festoons and garlands and flags. The Papal colours were everywhere in evidence. A battery of guns had been mounted at the East Pier to fire a royal salute in honour of the Legate's arrival . . .

By two o'clock more than 50,000 people had gathered round Dún Laoghaire Harbour to greet the Legate's arrival. The weather was perfect. The order of the multitude was excellent. The gorgeous sunshine, the vividly bright flags and festoons gently moving in the breeze, the sea of eagerly watching faces – everything combined to make a beautiful and memorable scene . . .

At 2.55 p.m. the booming of a gun announced that the *Cambria* was in sight. A squadron of aeroplanes flying in perfect cross formation had gone out to meet the *Cambria* and escort it into harbour. As the steamer and the aeroplanes approached the harbour a royal salute was fired from the battery on the East Pier, and a thunderous cheer of welcome was raised by the assembled multitude. Dún Laoghaire had often received royalties, but never had it given such a royal reception as the representative of the Holy Father received on 20 June . . . As the steamer came to its moorings at the Pier everyone was deeply moved, and the Cardinal Legate must have felt that no representative of Christ's Vicar had ever received a more genuine, gladdening and splendid welcome than this typically Irish welcome of Dún Laoghaire . . .

As soon as the *Cambria* was moored, His Grace the Archbishop of Dublin went on board. He was followed by Mr De Valera, President of the Free State Executive Council and members of his cabinet . . .

Thirty-first International Eucharistic Congress, Dublin 1932 – Pictorial Record, Dublin: Veritas 1932

Having disembarked at Dún Laoghaire, Cardinal Lauri, accompanied by Mr de Valera and Archbishop Byrne of Dublin, was driven through the streets on the way to the centre of Dublin. After being formally welcomed to the city by the Lord Mayor, Alderman Alfred Byrne, Cardinal Lauri replied in English (Document 2).

The journey between Dún Laoghaire and the Catholic Pro-Cathedral in the centre of Dublin was described as follows by a visiting journalist from the French newspaper *Revue des Deux Mondes* (Document 3).

Document 2

Cardinal Lauri's response to the Lord Mayor's address of welcome

I feel honoured to be the Pontifical Legate of His Holiness, Pope Pius XI, and to preside as his Ambassador at the Thirty-First International Eucharistic Congress now about to meet in this historic city of Dublin, the centre, heart, and capital of Ireland so justly renowned in all the world for the strong practical faith and the special attachment to the Holy See which have ever been characteristic of her noble people.

I confide the success of the Congress to Divine Providence, and to the intercession of your great Apostle, St Patrick, who fifteen centuries ago planted the Catholic faith so deeply in Irish hearts . . .

In accordance with your desire I shall at once very willingly communicate with the Holy Father, and inform His Holiness of your sincere cordiality and exquisite kindness, and of the very warm welcome which the great and good Irish people has given to the Representatives of the Pope.

Thirty-First International Eucharistic Congress, 48–9

Document 3

From Dún Laoghaire Harbour to the Pro-Cathedral, a distance of ten kilometres, there was an unbroken mass of people, compact, deep, on both sides of the route. In the city the pavements and the squares were completely covered by the multitude. Nor are to be forgotten the bouquets of heads in all the windows, and the daring spectators seated on the roofs of the houses. Without exaggeration, five hundred thousand persons! And what joy was in these people! Yes, joy was the dominant note. Oh without any doubt, there was an ardent enthusiasm which found expression in acclamation as the procession approached, a profound veneration, expressed in bowed heads and bended knees at the blessing of the Papal Legate . . . One felt, there was here the happiness of a large family welcoming their father.

Thirty-First International Eucharistic Congress, 149–50

Many contemporary observers were impressed by the decorations in the poorest areas of Dublin. Most of the poor were very sincere Catholics. In addition, the Congress was a welcome period of colour and excitement in the difficult struggle of their everyday lives. Documents 4 and 5 contain tributes to their efforts.

Document 4

Decorations in poorer areas

The Decorations Committee had spared no pains to make the great roads about Dublin and the chief streets of the city fit for the occasion . . . But quite outside the sphere of the influence of the Congress Committees and the Corporation a scheme of city decoration on a vast scale had been carried out unofficially by the very poorest of Dublin's folk. Away from the great centres and arteries of traffic and business, down in the back streets and the alleys and slums the faith of the poorest of Dublin's people had, of itself, and without any expert guidance, produced schemes of decoration huge in extent, brilliant in colouring, and often most touching in effect . . .

The poorest streets were the richest in colour. Shrines and altars had been set up in dingy nooks and alley-ways by loving hands, and the sordidness of grim poverty was hidden away behind the brightness of well chosen colour schemes.

To purchase materials for their Congress decorations the poor working people had deprived themselves, in many instances for months, of certain kinds of food, or certain pleasures, or little recreations. There probably was not one scrap of bunting or one solitary flag in the slums and backstreets, the procuring of which had not meant some serious self-denial for some poor worker. But the joy of helping to make Dublin fit for the coming of Our Lord was, for the poor people, a complete recompense for every self-denial and sacrifice.

Thirty-First International Eucharistic Congress, 28

Document 5

G.K. Chesterton's impression of the Dublin poor

Men who could not paint had painted pictures on their walls; and somehow painted them well. Men who could hardly write had written up inscriptions; and somehow they were dogmas as well as jokes. Somebody wrote, 'Long live St Patrick', as hoping that he might recover from his recent indisposition. Somebody wrote, 'God Bless Christ the King', and I knew I was staring at one of the staggering paradoxes of Christianity.

I went through all this glow and glory of poverty quite bewildered. . . One nameless impecunious person, in a slum, heard that the Legate was coming and laid down a red carpet on his doorstep.

G.K. Chesterton, *Christendom in Dublin*, Dublin: Sheed & Ward 1932, 16–17

In his official address to Cardinal Lauri, the head of government, Éamon de Valera, stressed the close connection between Ireland and the popes of Rome through the centuries (Document 6).

> **Document 6**
>
> **De Valera's official address of welcome**
>
> The records of centuries past bear eloquent testimony to that loving zeal with which the Apostolic See has ever honoured our nation. That special affection was ever the more amply given, in proportion to the sufferings of Ireland.
>
> Repeatedly over more than 300 years, our people, ever firm in their allegiance to our ancestral faith, and unwavering even to death in their devotion to the See of Peter, endured in full measure unmerited trials by war, by devastation, and by confiscation.
>
> They saw their most sacred rights set at naught under an unjust domination. But repeatedly also did the Successors of Peter most willingly come to our aid, in the persons of Gregory XIV, Clement VIII, Paul V, Urban VIII, Innocent X and many others of the line of Roman Pontiffs down to the present day.
>
> Today with no less favour and goodwill, His Holiness Pope Pius XI has turned his august regard to our country, our Metropolitan City, in this present year, a year of deep significance for our people . . .
>
> There is also for us a further cause of public rejoicing. At this time, when we welcome to Ireland this latest legation from the Eternal City, we are commemorating the Apostolic Mission to Ireland, given fifteen centuries ago to St Patrick, Apostle of our Nation.
>
> Who can fail on this day to recall to mind the utterance of our Apostle, recorded in the Book of Armagh. 'Even as you are children of Christ, be you also children of Rome.'
>
> *Thirty-First International Eucharistic Congress, 54–5*

In this address de Valera clearly identified the Irish nation with the Catholic people, whose ancestors had suffered persecution for their loyalty to their faith. Indeed, one of the main themes of the Eucharistic Congress in Dublin was to emphasise the contrast between the freedom of Catholics in independent Ireland and the sufferings of their ancestors under British rule.

THE OPEN-AIR MASS IN THE PHOENIX PARK

At the conclusion of a week of religious functions and celebrations, the highlight of the Congress was an open-air Mass in the Phoenix Park, followed by a procession of the Blessed Sacrament through the streets of Dublin (Document 7).

> **Document 7**
>
> **The Mass in the Phoenix Park, Sunday, 26 June 1932**
>
> The last and greatest day of the Congress dawned with promise of perfect weather. While it was yet scarcely day streams of pilgrims could be seen converging from every direction on the Phoenix Park . . .
>
> The whole ceremony was broadcast. The loud-speakers in the 'Fifteen Acres' functioned excellently, and the immense multitude of worshippers were able to follow the High Mass as easily as if they were in a comparatively small church . . .
>
> At the Offertory Count McCormack, who wore the very distinctive robes of a Knight of Malta, sang the *Panis Angelicus* of César Franck. The great singer sang the beautiful and delicate composition with an intensity of devotion, and a glorious perfection of voice and artistry that befitted the great occasion. As Count McCormack stood quietly for an instant before the beginning of the Motet and looked up at the Altar, one felt that the privilege now given to the singer of using his great gifts for the praise of God in the Congress Mass, in the name as it were, of the Irish race, was for him one of the greatest triumphs of his career . . .
>
> Just before the Blessing . . . the voice of Padre Granfranceschi, SJ, the radio expert of His Holiness the Pope, was heard announcing from the Vatican: Attention, the Holy Father is about to address you! Almost immediately the clear quiet voice of the Holy Father was heard by the whole congregation in words of fatherly greeting and apostolic blessing . . .
>
> It was the first time that an International Eucharistic Congress was directly addressed by the Holy Father, and the vivid realisation by all who were present at the Mass that the Pope himself had been listening to the Mass, and that his own voice was now addressing them, produced an atmosphere of profound emotion.
>
> *Thirty-First International Eucharistic Congress, 182–8*

In all, over a million people attended the ceremonies in the Phoenix Park. The Congress concluded with a procession of the Blessed Sacrament through the streets of Dublin from the Phoenix Park to O'Connell Bridge. On the bridge a temporary altar had been set up, and a service of Benediction was held. That night the legate, Cardinal Lauri, sent a telegram to Pope Pius XI in which he declared that the Irish people were united in uttering 'the cry which sums up the tradition, the faith, the very life of the whole nation: God Bless the Pope'.

The success of the Eucharistic Congress in Dublin was clearly appreciated at the Vatican. The official papal newspaper, *L'Osservatore Romano*, carried a highly favourable report (Document 8). The connection made on this report between Irish identity and the Catholic religion had been clearly evident throughout the Eucharistic Congress. Historians have used the word 'triumphalism' to describe the self-congratulation and assertion of power displayed by the Catholic Church during the Congress. This power, together with the close connection between Catholic clergy and laity, ensured that the Catholic Church remained an extremely influential force in Irish society for decades to come.

Document 8
The comments of *L'Osservatore Romano* on the Eucharistic Congress
Every sphere of life is affected by the great event – from schools, which are closed, to the business houses, which have given their employees a short holiday. The newspapers from the first page to the last are full of notes and comments on the religious events. Politics are suspended and the Government administration interrupted. The Government, the Army, the University and the County Councils, the Town Councils – all bow down in adoration at the feet of Jesus Christ in the Blessed Eucharist. Here there are no spectators – everyone from the highest to the lowest is an actor and plays his part in the great event with all the fervour and energy that is in him . . .

Everyone is at his post from the Bishop to the clerical student, from the President of the State to the policeman on the street . . . It is really nothing short of the miraculous – for here we see, after a century and a half of attempted laicisation, an entire people proud of its name, but prouder still of its Roman religion.

Cited in D. Keogh, *Ireland and the Vatican*, Cork: Cork University Press 1995, 98

1. Children's Mass in the Phoenix Park during the Eucharistic Congress
2. A souvenir commemorating the Eucharistic Congress
3. One of many commemorative postcards of the Eucharistic Congress

COMPREHENSION

1. Where did the Cardinal legate land in Ireland? (Document 1).

2. Describe how the people had decorated the town (Document 1).

3. How was the 'royal salute' to be given? (Document 1)

4. What was the purpose of the aeroplanes in the welcome given to the papal legate? (Document 1)

5. Who were the first two people to go on board ship to greet the papal legate? (Document 1)

6. Why, according to Cardinal Lauri (Document 2), was Ireland 'so justly renowned in all the world'?

7. Explain the message that Cardinal Lauri promised to make (Document 2).

8. Describe the crowds that watched the journey of the papal legate from Dún Laoghaire to Dublin city centre (Document 3).

9. How did they respond to the blessing of the legate?

10. What evidence is there of the deep faith of the poorest of Dublin's people? (Document 4)

11. What sacrifices had the poor made, according to the author of Document 4, in order to buy decorations?

12. According to de Valera (Document 6), why had the Irish people suffered for more than three hundred years?

13. Who came to their assistance?

14. Why did de Valera refer to 'this present year' as 'a year of deep significance for our people'?

15. Who was the solo singer at the Congress Mass in the Phoenix Park, and what hymn did he sing? (Document 7)

16. Explain the radio broadcast that took place at the end of the Mass.

17. List three activities that were suspended during the Eucharistic Congress (Document 8).

18. How does the author of Document 8 link the Irish people with the Catholic religion at the end of the account?

COMPARISON

1. Compare Cardinal Lauri's comments on the links between the Irish people and the Catholic faith (Document 2) with de Valera's observations on the same theme in Document 6.

2. Would you agree that the enthusiastic tone adopted by the author of Document 1 is also evident in Document 3? Support your answer by reference to both documents.

3. Identify the main theme that is common to Documents 4 and 5.

4. Both Document 2 and Document 7 contain references to Pope Pius XI. Compare these references.

CRITICISM

1. What evidence is there that the author of Document 1 strongly supports the events that are described?

2. List at least one advantage and one disadvantage of Document 4 as a primary source.

3. What does Document 6 reveal about de Valera's tendency to identify the Irish nation with the Catholic faith?

4. Is Document 8 an unbiased account? Explain your answer.

CONTEXTUALISATION

1. Write a paragraph on the role of the Catholic Church in Ireland during the 1920s.

2. Explain why de Valera and Fianna Fáil welcomed the holding of the Eucharistic Congress in Dublin in 1932.

3. Write an account of the main events of the Eucharistic Congress in Dublin in 1932.

4. Explain the meaning of 'Catholic triumphalism', and discuss the growing identification of the Irish nation with the Catholic religion from 1922 onwards.

Dismantling the Treaty

ABOLISHING THE OATH

On coming to power, de Valera was determined to increase the independence of the Irish Free State, in order to move Ireland closer to the status of a republic. He himself took charge of the Ministry of External Affairs and set about gradually dismantling the Anglo-Irish Treaty. In April 1932 the Dáil passed a bill abolishing the Oath of Allegiance. However, the Senate, still under the control of Cumann na nGaedheal, rejected the measure. As a result, the Oath was not finally abolished until May 1933. Although the British Government objected to this action, de Valera had acted legally and in accordance with the Statute of Westminster (1931).

DOWNGRADING THE OFFICE OF GOVERNOR-GENERAL

De Valera now proceeded to downgrade the office of Governor-General, the King's representative in the Irish Free State. From 1928 this position had been held by James MacNeill. Functions and ceremonies attended by the Governor-General were boycotted by the Government, and he had not received an official invitation to the Eucharistic Congress. In November 1932 MacNeill was dismissed and replaced by Dónal Ó Buachalla, a loyal follower of de Valera. Ó Buachalla co-operated with de Valera in further demeaning the office of Governor-General; he lived in a modest suburban house rather than in the Vice-Regal Lodge; he received a reduced salary; and he did not attend public ceremonies or functions. These measures paved the way for the eventual abolition of the office in June 1937.

De Valera took a further step towards a republic by abolishing the right of appeal from Irish courts to the British Privy Council. The Fianna Fáil Government also abolished the Senate in May 1936. They had long regarded it as an obstacle on the road to a republic because of its anti-Fianna Fáil majority. The removal of the Senate facilitated further constitutional changes.

THE EXTERNAL RELATIONS ACT (1936)

The abdication of King Edward VIII of England in 1936 provided de Valera with another opportunity to weaken the link between Great Britain and the Irish Free State. The Government introduced the Constitutional Amendment Bill (1936), which removed all references to the King from the Constitution of the Irish Free State. A second measure, the External Relations Act (1936), marked the end of any involvement by the King of England in the internal affairs of the Irish Free State. In future, the King would be recognised as a symbol of Commonwealth unity and could act in foreign affairs on the advice of the Government. This situation was very close to the idea of external association proposed by de Valera as an alternative to the Treaty in 1921. These two important measures prepared the way for the introduction of a new constitution in 1937.

A New Constitution

In 1937 de Valera introduced a new constitution – **Bunreacht na hÉireann**. This replaced the Free State Constitution of 1922, which was based on the Anglo-Irish Treaty. The new Constitution was passed by the Dáil in June 1937 and subsequently ratified by a narrow majority of voters in a referendum held on 1 July. Unlike its predecessor, it contained no reference to the King of England or to the British Commonwealth. De Valera stopped short of declaring an Irish republic because of the continuing existence of the Northern Irish state.

De Valera with ministers and judges at the formal signing of the 1937 Constitution

The Constitution of 1937 contained the following main points:

- The Irish Free State now became known as Éire and was defined as an independent, democratic state.
- Although Article 2 claimed jurisdiction over the whole island of Ireland, Article 3 limited the laws of the State to the twenty-six counties pending future reunification.
- The Houses of Parliament, or Oireachtas, consisted of a Dáil and a Seanad. A system of proportional representation (PR) was to be used in elections. The new Seanad had limited powers and could only delay a bill for up to ninety days.
- The head of government, or Taoiseach, was elected by the Dáil.
- The head of state was the President (Uachtarán na hÉireann), who was elected by the people to a seven-year term of office. Although it was largely a ceremonial office, the President signed bills into law and dissolved the Dáil on the advice of the Taoiseach.
- Although Article 44 recognised the main Christian religions and the Jewish community, it gave special recognition to the Catholic Church 'as the Faith professed by the great majority of the citizens'.
- The Constitution also gave special recognition to the family. Divorce was banned, and the Constitution stated that women should be supported in their work in the home.
- The Constitution could only be amended or changed by a referendum of the people.

The new Constitution came into effect on 29 December 1937. Although de Valera was its main architect, he had consulted widely during the drafting of the document. He sought the advice of the leaders of the main Christian churches on the article dealing with religion. One of his leading advisors was the president of Blackrock College, Fr John Charles McQuaid, who became Archbishop of Dublin in 1940. Although Pope Pius XI had wanted the Constitution to declare the Catholic Church to be the 'one true church', de Valera had resisted this demand. Nevertheless, the influence of the Catholic Church was very strong in the new Constitution. The preamble recognising the authority of the Blessed Trinity, the articles on the family and the prohibition of divorce reveal a strong Catholic influence.

Although the British Government did not object to the new Constitution, Ulster unionists condemned Articles 2 and 3, which contained a territorial claim over Northern Ireland.

The Constitution of 1937 had created an Irish republic in everything but name. It represented the culmination of de Valera's efforts to dismantle the Treaty and create a sovereign, independent state. Side by side with the strong Catholic influence, the Constitution contained liberal and democratic principles, such as guarantees of basic rights and freedoms, and limits on the powers of government. Although later generations criticised various aspects of the Constitution, it accurately reflected the values of Irish society at the time and can be regarded as one of de Valera's most enduring achievements.

The inauguration of Douglas Hyde as President of Ireland in 1938

Although constitutional issues dominated Irish political life and relations with Great Britain during the 1930s, deep division arose also over economic matters. This division took the form of the **Economic War (1932–8)** between Britain and the Irish Free State.

The Economic Policies of Fianna Fáil

AGRICULTURE AND THE ECONOMIC WAR

The guiding principle of Fianna Fáil's agricultural policy was self-sufficiency based on economic protection. Under the Minister for Agriculture, James Ryan, there was a considerable increase in state intervention in the farming sector. The Land Commission was responsible for the division of large estates and redistribution of land to poorer farmers. A return to tillage was encouraged by a system of guaranteed prices and restrictions on foreign imports. However, the state of agriculture was largely determined by the worldwide economic depression that began in 1929. Even before Fianna Fáil came to power, a huge decrease had taken place in both the volume and value of agricultural exports to Britain. In response to the crisis, the British Government introduced measures to protect British agriculture from competition from foreign imports.

The most controversial aspect of Fianna Fáil's agricultural policy was the refusal to continue paying land annuities to the British Government. These payments, amounting to £3 million per year, were collected from Irish farmers as repayment of loans received from the British Government for land purchase.

A typical harvesting scene from the 1930s

On 1 July 1932 de Valera's Government withheld payment of the annuities. The British Government retaliated immediately by placing a 20 per cent duty on Irish agricultural exports. The Fianna Fáil Government then imposed similar duties on British imports. This tariff war between Britain and the Irish Free State became known as the Economic War.

The Economic War was to have disastrous consequences for the Irish economy. It added greatly to the difficulties experienced by Irish agriculture at a time of deep international depression. At this time, the British market accounted for 98 per cent of all Irish agricultural exports. As a result of the Depression and the Economic War, the value of Irish agricultural exports fell from £36 million in 1931 to £13.9 million by 1935. The cattle industry was the worst affected: cattle exports to Britain fell from 750,000 in 1930 to 500,000 in 1934. The collapse in cattle prices led to the widespread slaughter of animals throughout the countryside as farmers failed to sell their stock.

The Fianna Fáil Government used the Economic War to press ahead with its policy of economic self-sufficiency. There was a strong campaign to persuade farmers to move from livestock farming to tillage. Farmers were given guaranteed prices for wheat, and restrictions were placed on the import of agricultural products.

Although the main burden of the Economic War fell on the Irish Free State, it also damaged the British economy. At a time of economic depression, Britain could ill afford to suffer losses in one of the country's main export markets. The British Government became alarmed at the prospect of the Irish Free State boycotting British coal and importing coal instead from Germany and Poland. Therefore, the first compromise in the Economic War was reached with the signing of the **Coal–Cattle Pact** in January 1935. In return for an agreement by the Irish Free State to buy British coal, the British Government agreed to increase the quota of imported Irish cattle by one-third.

De Valera in Downing Street, London, to sign the Anglo-Irish Agreement of 1938

The Economic War came to an end with the signing of the Anglo-Irish Agreement of 1938. The Irish Government agreed to pay Britain £10 million as a final settlement of the annuities issue. The special duties introduced by both governments during the Economic War were withdrawn. As part of the settlement, Britain agreed to return the three Treaty ports to the Irish Free State. The Anglo-Irish Agreement was a significant achievement for de Valera and Fianna Fáil. Not alone did it mark the ending of the Economic War, it was also an important landmark on the road to greater independence.

Despite the successful Anglo-Irish Agreement, the agricultural policy of Fianna Fáil was largely unsuccessful. By and large, farmers did not switch from livestock to tillage. Indeed, cattle accounted for a higher proportion of Irish exports in 1939 than they had in 1932. However, in contrast to its performance in agriculture, the Fianna Fáil Government was to be more successful in the area of industrial development.

INDUSTRIAL DEVELOPMENT

As with agriculture, the industrial policy of Fianna Fáil was based on economic self-sufficiency. The Minister for Industry and Commerce, Seán Lemass, was faced with the major challenge of developing industry in Ireland at a time of deep, worldwide economic depression. His task was made more difficult by the Economic War, which reduced the incomes of farmers and their ability to purchase goods.

The basis of Fianna Fáil's industrial policy was the encouragement of native Irish industries, which were to be protected from foreign imports by high tariffs. Tariffs were placed on over a thousand separate items entering the state, and new Irish-owned industries were encouraged. This policy of extensive economic protection contrasted with the policies pursued by the previous Government. Although the Cumann na nGaedheal Government had favoured free trade, it had been compelled to introduce some tariff protection with the onset of economic depression. Fianna Fáil, on the other hand, was committed to economic protection for largely political reasons: economic self-sufficiency was another expression of independence from Great Britain.

As well as promoting economic protection, Seán Lemass encouraged the development of Irish industry in other ways. He introduced the **Control of Manufacturers Acts** (1932 and 1934), which stated that Irish people must be involved in the ownership and management of new industries. In response to a shortage of capital investment in Irish industry, Lemass set up the

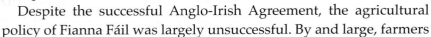

The Economic Policies of Fianna Fáil

Industrial Credit Company in 1933 to provide loans for the establishment of new businesses. He also established a number of new semi-state bodies, including the **Irish Sugar Company** (1933), **The Turf Development Board** (1934) and **Aer Lingus** (1936). Because of the limited size of the Irish market, some companies were given monopolies, or exclusive access to the Irish market. Although this lack of competition helped industries to survive, it also led to high prices and poor-quality goods.

Against an extremely unfavourable background of economic depression, the Fianna Fáil industrial policy was remarkably successful. Employment in industry rose from 110,000 in 1932 to 166,000 by 1938, representing an increase of 50 per cent in six years. Despite this achievement, the rates of unemployment and emigration remained high. One of the main concerns of Fianna Fáil's social policy was to deal with the widespread poverty that continued to exist throughout the country.

New houses under construction in Dublin in the 1930s

The Social Policy of Fianna Fáil

Under the direction of Seán T. O'Kelly, Minister for Local Government and Public Health, a vast scheme of house building and renovation took place. This was the first serious attempt to clear the slums of cities and replace them with new houses. Under the **Housing Act** (1932), the Government provided around half the cost of local authority house building. As a result, 132,000 houses were built or renovated between 1932 and 1942. This huge programme of slum clearance was one of the main successes of de Valera's Government in the area of social policy.

Fianna Fáil also attempted to alleviate the conditions of the poor by increasing and extending certain benefits. In 1933 the level of unemployment assistance was increased, and benefits were extended to include small farmers and farm labourers. Pensions for the elderly and the blind were improved, and widows and orphans received pensions for the first time in 1932. Although the rates of payment remained small, they constituted a certain advance for the poorest in society.

Despite the efforts of the Fianna Fáil Government, poverty remained widespread in towns and countryside alike.

Political Challenges to de Valera and Fianna Fáil

TENSION AND RIVALRY

We have already seen that the general election that brought Fianna Fáil to power in 1932 was a bitterly fought campaign. Tensions between Fianna Fáil supporters and the followers of Cumann na nGaedheal were heightened considerably following the release of IRA prisoners and the onset of the Economic War. In these circumstances, Civil War rivalry and bitterness surfaced again. In the autumn of 1932, a new party under the leadership of Frank MacDermot and James Dillon was founded – the National Centre Party. Consisting of Independents and former members of the Farmers' Party, the new party called for an end to the Economic War with Britain and for the healing of Civil War rivalries between the two main parties.

De Valera saw the new party as a threat and an effort to form a united opposition against him.

In order to catch the opposition off guard and secure an overall majority, he called an unexpected – or snap – general election in January 1933. He also sought a mandate from the people for the Economic War and for the moves he had made to dismantle the Anglo-Irish Treaty. The 1933 election was even more bitter and violent than that of the previous year. Whereas Cumann na nGaedheal denounced the constitutional and economic policies of Fianna Fáil, the Government in turn defended its policies of seeking greater freedom from Great Britain. The 1933 election resulted in an overall majority for de Valera and Fianna Fáil. This result was a significant advance for Fianna Fáil, which increased its representation from 72 to 77 TDs, and a setback for Cumann na nGaedheal, which declined from 57 seats to 48. However, despite its electoral victory, de Valera's Government faced major political challenges in the years ahead. These came from the IRA on the one hand, and a new organisation called the Blueshirts on the other.

RESULTS OF 1933 GENERAL ELECTION	
Total no. of seats	153
Cumann na nGaedheal	48
Fianna Fáil	77
Centre Party	11
Labour	8
Independents	9

The IRA

One of the first actions of the Fianna Fáil Government on coming to power in 1932 was to release republican prisoners and lift the ban on the IRA. However, de Valera hoped to reduce support for the IRA: he pursued republican policies, such as dismantling the Treaty, and recruited IRA members into the Free State army and the Garda Síochána. However, some more extreme leaders in the IRA remained determined to continue with their activities.

When the ban on the IRA was lifted, its members began an extensive campaign against Cumann na nGaedheal. Peadar O'Donnell, a leading figure in the IRA, advocated this in his newspaper, *An Phoblacht*, with the slogan 'No free speech for traitors'. This called for violent disruption of Cumann na nGaedheal political meetings throughout the country. Some in the IRA also demanded expensive economic and social changes, such as the breaking up of large farms and their division among small farmers. Their opponents in Cumann na nGaedheal accused them of being communists and of wishing to turn the Irish Free State into a dictatorship on the model of communist Russia. As Cumann na nGaedheal meetings continued to be disrupted by IRA men and the Gardaí failed to restore order, the supporters of the former government party decided to take steps to protect themselves.

The Blueshirt Movement

THE ORIGINS OF THE BLUESHIRTS

Just before the general election of 1932, former soldiers from the Free State Army had formed the Army Comrades Association (ACA). In the beginning, its main aim was to promote the welfare of its members. In August 1932 T.F. O'Higgins, a brother of Kevin O'Higgins, became its leader. The ACA then began providing stewards for Cumann na nGaedheal meetings and declared that its members would oppose communism and defend freedom of speech. As a result, clashes broke out between the ACA and the IRA at public meetings, and rioting and personal attacks increased greatly, especially during the general election of January 1933.

The return to power of de Valera and Fianna Fáil with an overall majority was a great blow to Cumann na nGaedheal and the ACA. Shortly after his re-election as head of government in February 1933, de Valera dismissed Eoin O'Duffy from his post as Garda Commissioner. Cosgrave and Cumann na nGaedheal took this as an indication that their followers could no longer rely on the Gardaí to protect them from the IRA. In March 1933 members of the ACA started to wear a uniform of blue shirts and black berets. They then invited General Eoin O'Duffy, the former Garda Commissioner, to take charge of the organisation. As a friend and associate of Michael Collins and an opponent of de Valera, O'Duffy was seen as the ideal leader. He took charge of the ACA in July 1933 and renamed the organisation the National Guard. Because of the blue uniform worn by its members, the organisation soon became widely known as the Blueshirts.

THE IDEAS OF O'DUFFY AND THE BLUESHIRTS

The Blueshirt programme, as outlined by O'Duffy, included the following main points:

- The Blueshirts supported the abolition of political parties.
- They supported reform of the Dáil – TDs should be elected by vocational groups such as workers and farmers, instead of in territorial constituencies.
- They had a strong sense of nationalism and emphasised the aim of a united Ireland.
- They had a strongly Catholic outlook – the group's social programme was heavily influenced by the views of Pope Pius XI (1922–39), and Jews were excluded from membership.
- They were totally opposed to communism.

O'Duffy was deeply influenced by the Italian Fascist dictator, Benito Mussolini, and his Blackshirt movement. O'Duffy saw the Blackshirts as a strong anti-communist force in Italy. The Blueshirts imitated the Fascist practice of dressing in uniform and saluting the leader. When O'Duffy announced a Blueshirt march in Dublin in August 1933 to commemorate Arthur Griffith, Michael Collins and Kevin O'Higgins, the Fianna Fáil Government feared that he was trying to imitate Mussolini's seizure of power in Italy following his march on Rome in 1922.

Eoin O'Duffy and Blueshirt supporters

THE CLASH BETWEEN DE VALERA AND O'DUFFY

Although no evidence exists that O'Duffy intended to seize power, de Valera took firm action against the Blueshirts. He banned the proposed Blueshirt march and used Garda reinforcements to prevent disorder. These Gardaí were known as the **Broy Harriers**, after Colonel Ned Broy, O'Duffy's replacement as Garda Commissioner. Many of them were former members of the IRA.

Rather than break the law, O'Duffy cancelled the march, but local marches were held a week later. The Government then moved to outlaw the National Guard. This represented a serious setback for the Blueshirt movement, whose members deeply resented the fact that the ban was not extended to the IRA.

THE FOUNDATION OF FINE GAEL

The events of August 1933 alarmed the enemies of Fianna Fáil, who feared that de Valera was about to establish a dictatorship. As a consequence, three groups united to form a new political party in opposition to Fianna Fáil. These were Cumann na nGaedheal, led by W.T. Cosgrave; the Centre Party, led by Frank MacDermot and James Dillon; and the Blueshirts, under Eoin O'Duffy. The new party was called the United Ireland Party or **Fine Gael**, and O'Duffy was elected as its first leader.

Fine Gael called for a united Ireland within the British Commonwealth and for an end to the Economic War.

The founding of Fine Gael in September 1933. Seated from left are Eoin O'Duffy (Blueshirts), James Dillon and Frank MacDermot (Centre Party) and W.T. Cosgrave (Cumann na nGaedheal).

THE DECLINE OF THE BLUESHIRT MOVEMENT

Although O'Duffy was now the president of Fine Gael, he continued to lead the Blueshirt movement within the new party. After the National Guard was banned, it was replaced by the Young Ireland Association, whose members continued to wear the Blueshirt uniform and to engage in public marches and demonstrations.

The Blueshirt movement drew its strongest support from larger farmers whose incomes fell considerably during the Economic War. O'Duffy encouraged farmers to refuse to pay land annuities to the Government. As a result, the Gardaí seized animals and farm equipment and auctioned them to recover the money due. The Blueshirts supported the farmers in resisting the actions of the Gardaí, and widespread violence followed.

Many leading figures within Fine Gael became increasingly alarmed by the violent tactics of the Blueshirts. They were horrified by the unpredictable and inflammatory speeches of O'Duffy, who called for the violent ending of partition. They warned him to moderate his speeches, but he refused to change his stance. A leading member of Fine Gael, Professor James Hogan, resigned from the Fine Gael Executive in protest. At the annual conference of Fine Gael in September 1934, Eoin O'Duffy was forced to resign as leader of the party. He was replaced by W.T. Cosgrave. O'Duffy attempted to keep the Blueshirts going as a separate movement. However, they became increasingly irrelevant and declined in popularity. O'Duffy's final public action was to lead a group of his followers to fight in the Spanish Civil War. He formed an Irish Brigade to fight on the side of General Franco, whom he regarded as the defender of Catholic Spain against communism.

Certain parallels existed between the Blueshirts and some fascist movements on the Continent of Europe. The Blueshirts adopted the outward signs of fascism, such as uniforms, salutes and marches. However, unlike continental fascists, the Blueshirts supported democracy and did not engage in extreme violence. They owed far more to the divisive politics of the Civil War than to European fascism. They emerged out of the tensions between the former Civil War adversaries during the general elections of 1932 and 1933.

While de Valera had taken decisive action against the Blueshirt movement, in the end it was

O'Duffy's own colleagues in Fine Gael who distanced themselves from the movement and contributed to its decline. Whereas by 1935 the Blueshirts were a spent force, the IRA now posed a serious ongoing challenge to the authority of the Fianna Fáil Government.

De Valera Moves Against the IRA

De Valera was initially reluctant to take action against the IRA, as many of its members had fought on his side during the Civil War. However, he became increasingly concerned during 1935, when the organisation resumed a violent campaign. Its members were involved in a number of murders throughout the country. As a result, de Valera banned the IRA on 18 June 1936, and some of its leaders were imprisoned.

De Valera at an election rally in 1938

The General Elections of 1937 and 1938

In June 1937 the Fianna Fáil Government faced the verdict of the people in a general election. The party won exactly half of the seats, 69 out of a total of 138. Fianna Fáil then formed a government with the support of the Labour Party, and as in 1932, de Valera waited for a chance to call another general election. However, de Valera's position was strengthened by the continued weakness of Fine Gael.

RESULTS OF 1937 GENERAL ELECTION	
Total no. of seats	138
Fianna Fáil	69
Fine Gael	48
Labour	13
Independents	8

A year later, in June 1938, de Valera – anxious to form a majority government – called another election. Fianna Fáil campaigned on its success in negotiating the Anglo-Irish Agreement, which brought the Economic War to an end. The election resulted in a triumph for de Valera and Fianna Fáil. The party achieved its highest ever vote and was in a particularly strong position to guide the Irish Free State as the threat of World War II approached.

RESULTS OF 1938 GENERAL ELECTION	
Total no. of seats	138
Fianna Fáil	77
Fine Gael	45
Labour	9
Independents	7

KEY PERSONALITY: J.J. McELLIGOTT (1893–1974)

J.J. McElligott was born in Tralee, Co. Kerry, in 1893. He was educated at University College, Dublin, where he studied Classics and Economics. He entered the civil service in 1913 and worked on the Local Government Board. He joined the Irish Volunteers and fought in the GPO during the 1916 Rising. He was sacked from the civil service for his part in the Rising and was interned in various jails in England until his release in 1917.

After his release from jail, McElligott earned his living as a financial journalist and became editor of *The Statist*. He was recruited into the Free State civil service in 1923 and was appointed Assistant Secretary in the Department of Finance. He succeeded Joseph Brennan as Secretary in the Department of Finance in 1927, a position he held until 1953. He was governor of the Central Bank from 1953 to 1960 and was subsequently a director. He was president of the Institute of Bankers in 1956 and was the first president of the Economic Research Institute (now known as the ESRI).

As Secretary in the Department of Finance, J.J. McElligott was the most powerful figure in the Irish civil service from 1927 until his retirement in 1953. He played a key role in the formation of the economic policies of the new state. As chairman of the Tariff Commission (1926–30), he was strongly against economic protection. While recognising the need for major developments such as the establishment of the ESB in 1927, McElligott was economically conservative, favouring low government expenditure and low taxation.

His achievements in the Department of Finance include the launching of the first national loan; his role in guiding politicians and civil servants successfully through the first change of government in 1932; and his support for the establishment of the Central Bank, which was set up in 1932.

EXERCISES

ORDINARY LEVEL

1. How did W.T. Cosgrave uphold democracy in 1932?

2. Write a note on the abolition of the Oath of Allegiance by de Valera's Government.

3. How did the Fianna Fáil Government downgrade the office of Governor-General?

4. Explain the External Relations Act (1936).

5. How did the Constitution of 1937 reflect the influence of the Catholic Church?

6. Why did Ulster unionists condemn the new Constitution?

7. Explain the reasons for the outbreak of the Economic War in 1932.

8. What was the effect of the Economic War on

   (i)   the Irish Free State

   (ii) Great Britain?

9. Write an account of industrial development in Ireland between 1932 and 1939.

10. In what ways did the Fianna Fáil Government try to improve the conditions of the poor during the 1930s? Were these efforts successful?

11. Explain the origins of the Blueshirt movement.

12. Outline the main ideas of Eoin O'Duffy and the Blueshirts.

13. Write a paragraph on the foundation of Fine Gael.

14. Account for the decline of the Blueshirt movement.

15. What action was taken by de Valera against the IRA during the 1930s?

16. Examine the tables on page 203, and compare the results of the 1937 and 1938 general elections.

HIGHER LEVEL

1. Consider de Valera's relations with Britain between 1932 and 1939.

2. Assess the reasons for the development and decline of the Blueshirt movement.

3. Discuss the agricultural and industrial policies of Fianna Fáil between 1932 and 1939.

4. Account for the electoral success of de Valera and Fianna Fáil between 1932 and 1939.

5. Consider the role of the Catholic Church in Ireland during the 1930s, with special reference to the Eucharistic Congress.

6. Write an account on the causes, course and resolution of the Economic War between 1932 and 1938.

7. Consider the Irish Constitution of 1937 as a reflection of de Valera's beliefs concerning the Irish nation and Irish society.

8. Outline the various stages in the development of the Fianna Fáil Government's relationship with the IRA between 1932 and 1939.

The Irish army at the Curragh Camp in 1939

De Valera and the League of Nations

By 1939 Éamon de Valera had firmly established the sovereignty of the Irish Free State. As well as weakening Ireland's links with Great Britain, he wanted the country to have an independent voice in world affairs. The Irish Free State under de Valera played an active role in the League of Nations: as President of the League in 1938, de Valera was very outspoken concerning the growing threat of war. He supported the League's call for disarmament and highlighted the plight of small nations in the event of future conflict between the great powers.

The Outbreak of World War II

On the outbreak of World War II in September 1939, de Valera immediately declared that the Irish Free State would remain neutral. He proclaimed this policy for a number of reasons:

> 1 In view of the continued existence of partition, the state would not enter the war on the side of Britain.
> 2 Neutrality in a war was seen as the ultimate symbol of independence.
> 3 As a small nation, Ireland would be vulnerable to attack, and it would therefore be safer to remain outside the conflict.

The policy of neutrality was made possible by the return of the Treaty ports under the Anglo-Irish Agreement of 1938. Had these ports remained under British control, German attacks on them would have brought Ireland into the war. Declaring neutrality was a relatively easy step; maintaining it through the six years of World War II would be a far more difficult task.

As soon as war was declared, de Valera convened a meeting of the Dáil to declare a state of emergency. The Government was given wide powers to deal with any threats that might emerge from inside or outside the state:

> • Strict censorship was introduced covering all books, newspapers and radio broadcasts. The purpose of this was to prevent the publication or broadcasting of opinions in favour of one side or the other in the war.
> • Weather forecasts were stopped in order to avoid giving help to ships or aeroplanes from either side.
> • The size of the army was increased, and volunteer corps such as the Local Defence Force (LDF) were established.

While these measures were enacted to deal with threats to Irish neutrality from abroad, the first major challenge to the Government's policy came from within the state, in the form of the IRA.

The IRA Threat to Irish Neutrality

With the appointment of Seán Russell as Chief of Staff in 1938, the IRA entered a more active phase. They began a bombing campaign in Britain in January 1939 in order to bring about a British withdrawal from Northern Ireland. The worst atrocity in this campaign occurred at Coventry in August, when five people were killed. The bombing campaign ended in failure – the British Government refused to end partition, and anti-Irish feeling increased in Britain.

Alarmed by the resurgence of the IRA, the Fianna Fáil Government introduced the **Offences Against the State Act** in June 1939. This law gave the Gardaí wide powers of arrest and interrogation. It also allowed internment without trial of IRA members.

When war broke out in September 1939, the IRA approach was based on the old Fenian slogan 'England's difficulty is Ireland's opportunity'. It adopted an anti-British stance and set about making contact with Nazi Germany. Russell went to Germany in order to persuade Hitler's Government to send arms and soldiers to Ireland. Several German agents landed in Ireland in an effort to join up with the IRA. Most were soon arrested, but one agent, Hermann Goertz, did succeed in making contact with the IRA and avoided capture for over a year and a half.

De Valera was most concerned by the danger posed to neutrality by the IRA. He feared that the IRA's pro-German activities might provoke a British invasion of the Irish Free State. Consequently, ruthless action was taken against the organisation. IRA members were interned without trial. Six were executed, and three others died on hunger strike. As a result of de Valera's policy, the IRA was weakened considerably and did not emerge as a threat again for the duration of the war.

Wartime Diplomacy

During the war, the neutral Irish Free State continued to maintain diplomatic relations with Britain and the USA on one side and Germany on the other. The safeguarding of Irish neutrality depended in part on the relationship that the Government established with the representative of each of these wartime powers in Dublin.

RELATIONS WITH BRITAIN

The British representative in Ireland during the war was Sir John Maffey. Maffey developed a good working relationship with de Valera. Once war broke out, strong pressure came from London for port facilities to be provided for the British navy in the Irish Free State. Maffey understood and carefully conveyed to the British Government the strength of Irish objections to this proposal. In May 1940, when Winston Churchill became Prime Minister of Great Britain, the pressure on de Valera increased considerably. After the conquest of France by the Germans, Britain stood alone on the Allied side, and it appeared that a German invasion was imminent. Churchill urged de Valera to abandon neutrality and join in the war on Britain's side. As an incentive, he offered to work towards Irish unity. De Valera rejected this offer. As well as wishing to maintain Irish neutrality, he did not believe that the British Government would force the Ulster unionists into a united Ireland after the war.

Volunteer soldiers being trained in the use of rifles and machine guns in Clontarf, Dublin, in 1939

While adhering strictly to neutrality in public statements and actions, de Valera's Government showed favour to the Allies in a number of ways. The Irish army passed on information to Britain; British airmen and soldiers who landed in the Free State were quietly sent back over the border to Northern Ireland, while their German counterparts were arrested and interned; and vital information regarding the weather was passed on to British shipping.

RELATIONS WITH GERMANY

The German Minister in Ireland during the war was Dr Eduard Hempel. He was sympathetic to Irish neutrality and disapproved of German contacts with the IRA, which could have resulted in a British invasion of the Irish Free State.

During 1940 the possibility existed of a German invasion of Ireland. However, this danger passed after the German invasion of Russia in June 1941. Hempel was aware that the de Valera Government was sympathetic to the Allies. However, he did not believe that this stance warranted German retaliation against the Irish Free State.

RELATIONS WITH THE UNITED STATES OF AMERICA

Searchlights were concentrated on coastal artillery positions

The American representative in Dublin during World War II was David Gray, a relative of President Roosevelt. From the outset, he was strongly pro-British and was unsympathetic to Irish neutrality. Even before the USA entered the war, Gray believed that Irish ports should be made available to the British navy. After the entry of America to the war in December 1941, Gray urged President Roosevelt to put pressure on de Valera to enter the war on the Allied side. Relations worsened after the arrival of American forces in Northern Ireland. The Americans reacted angrily when de Valera claimed that he should have been consulted. In the spring of 1944 the US Government placed strong pressure on the Irish Free State to expel the representatives of Germany and Japan from Ireland, claiming that their embassies were engaged in spying. De Valera refused and pointed out that he had already insisted on the removal of radio transmitters from the German legation. De Valera's defence of Irish neutrality in the face of American pressure enhanced his popular support.

In addition to preserving Irish neutrality by diplomatic means, the de Valera Government faced the formidable task of coping with the social and economic challenges of life in Ireland during the war years.

Life in Ireland During the Emergency

A cartoon on postal censorship during the Emergency

The war years in Ireland became popularly known as **the Emergency** because the Government declared a state of emergency on the outbreak of war in 1939. The war had serious economic implications for the Irish Free State. With major disruption to shipping, the supply of imported goods and raw materials was drastically reduced. In order to manage the wartime economy at a time of major shortage, the Government set up a new department, known as the Ministry of Supplies. It was led by the very able Minister for Industry and Commerce, Seán Lemass.

Rationing was the main method used to distribute scarce commodities in a fair manner. Sugar, tea and fuel were the first items to be rationed. The Government issued ration books for all citizens, adults and children alike. These had to be brought to the shops in order to buy rationed items. Later in the war, bread and clothes were also rationed.

Anti-aircraft defences in Dublin

Fuel shortages became widespread during the Emergency. Because little imported coal was available, turf was widely used. This was much less efficient than coal: when it was used in trains, journeys were very slow and unpredictable. A train could take twelve hours to travel between Dublin and Cork. Electricity and gas were rationed, and petrol for private cars was practically unobtainable.

Before the war, almost all Irish imports were brought into the country by British ships. Under severe pressure to import food for their own use, the British began to limit the number of ships importing goods into the Irish Free State. To meet the demands of the Irish economy, Seán Lemass founded a new semi-state company called the **Irish Shipping Company** in 1941. The company began by buying light ships in which vital supplies could be imported. Merchant sailors risked their lives in the submarine-infested waters to ensure that the country was supplied with food.

A German war aircraft which crash-landed in Co. Waterford after it was attacked by British forces over the Welsh coast

Because of the food shortages during the Emergency, compulsory tillage was introduced. Although the amount of land used to grow wheat more than doubled, yields were disappointing because of the lack of imported fertilisers, which were unobtainable by 1942. The livestock industry also suffered because imported animal feed was unobtainable. The British Government kept strict control over the prices paid for Irish agricultural exports. During World War II, therefore, Irish farming did not experience the boom that it had enjoyed during World War I.

Like agriculture, industry also went through major difficulties during the Emergency. Imported raw materials and parts were in short supply, and many factory workers became unemployed or had to work on a short-term basis. Living standards fell as prices rose and the Government kept wages down by a **Wages Standstill Order**.

Three women were killed when a German bomb hit this creamery in Co. Wexford in 1940.

As a result of the economic stagnation, the number of Irish emigrants to Britain increased. Many obtained jobs in armaments factories and other industries, where they contributed significantly to the British war effort. Around 50,000 people from the Irish Free State fought in the British forces during World War II. They were found at every level in the army, navy and air force, from the top generals to the ordinary service men and women.

One of the lookout posts which were built around the Irish coast. Each one was numbered and the 'Eire' sign was to warn military aircraft that they were flying over neutral territory.

The only direct experience, however, that the people of the Irish Free State had of the violence of warfare was a number of bombings by German aircraft. Most were small-scale incidents that were possibly due to mistakes by German pilots. However, in May 1941 German bombs killed twenty-seven people, injured eight and caused widespread devastation at the North Strand in Dublin. For many years, it was believed that the pilots had mistaken Dublin for Belfast. However, documents found in Germany over fifty years after the event show that the raid was intended as a warning to the de Valera Government because it had sent fire brigades to Belfast after German attacks there. For the people of Dublin, the North Strand bombings were a vivid reminder of the suffering being endured by civilians throughout war-torn Europe.

Politics in Ireland During the War Years and After

Neutrality was widely popular in the Irish Free State. It enjoyed the support of all political parties. The only politician who spoke out publicly against neutrality was James Dillon, the deputy leader of Fine Gael. He called for Irish entry to the war on the side of Britain and was expelled from the party in 1942.

Cross-party support for neutrality helped to heal some of the Civil War divisions. Former Civil War adversaries served in the defence forces together, and both Fianna Fáil and Fine Gael politicians spoke from the same platforms in favour of neutrality. It was therefore difficult for opposition parties to contest general elections successfully during the Emergency.

Despite the popularity of the policy of neutrality, de Valera and Fianna Fáil lost 10 seats in the general election of 1943. The reasons for this decline can be found in discontent over the economic hardships of wartime conditions, with widespread shortages and rationing. Fine Gael did very badly, losing 13 seats. It seemed in danger of being overtaken by the Labour Party,

RESULTS OF 1943 GENERAL ELECTION	
Total no. of seats	138
Fianna Fáil	67
Fine Gael	32
Labour	17
Clann na Talmhan	14
Independents	8

which increased its representation to 17 seats. However, Fianna Fáil and Fine Gael lost many of their seats to a new farmers' party called Clann na Talmhan. Led by Michael Donnellan, it was largely confined to Galway, Mayo and Roscommon. It represented the interests of small farmers, who it claimed were being neglected by Fianna Fáil.

After the 1943 general election Fianna Fáil lacked an overall majority, and de Valera was elected Taoiseach only with the help of Clann na Talmhan. Unhappy with his minority position, de Valera awaited an opportunity to call another general election. This opportunity arrived in May 1944. After defeat on a minor issue in the Dáil, de Valera called a general election.

Circumstances favoured Fianna Fáil during the 1944 general election. De Valera's popularity increased when

Seán Lemass campaigning for Fianna Fáil during the 1943 general election

he refused in early 1944 to accept a request by the British and American representatives in Dublin to break off diplomatic relations with Germany and Japan. Fianna Fáil also benefited from a weak and divided opposition. Fine Gael had recently changed its leader: W.T. Cosgrave had retired, and the new leader, Richard Mulcahy, was not a member of the Dáil at the time. The party's electoral progress was hampered by poor organisation and an unenthusiastic campaign. Internal divisions in the Labour Party – centring on the conflict between the leader, William O'Brien, and James Larkin – damaged its electoral prospects.

The general election of 1944 resulted in a victory for Fianna Fáil. With 76 seats, Fianna Fáil was the only party to increase its number of TDs since the 1943 election, and with a clear overall majority, de Valera was once again elected Taoiseach. He was now given a mandate to continue leading the Irish Free State through the difficult circumstances of the Emergency.

RESULTS OF 1944 GENERAL ELECTION	
Total no. of seats	138
Fianna Fáil	76
Fine Gael	30
Labour	8
Clann na Talmhan	11
National Labour	4
Independents	9

The End of the War

In the face of mounting pressure from Great Britain and the United States, de Valera maintained Irish neutrality to the end. When the President of the USA, Franklin D. Roosevelt, died on 12 April 1945, de Valera called on the American representative to express his sorrow. However, when Hitler committed suicide on 30 April, de Valera once again observed the strict protocol of neutrality by calling on the German minister, Dr Hempel, to express his condolences. He did this against the advice of his officials, and his action was deeply resented in America and Great Britain.

Tensions between the British and Irish governments over the policy of neutrality were reflected in Winston Churchill's victory speech on 13 May 1945. In his broadcast Churchill strongly criticised de Valera:

> Had it been necessary we should have been forced to come to close quarters with Mr De Valera . . . With a restraint and poise to which, I venture to say, history will find few parallels, His Majesty's Government never laid a violent hand upon them, though at times it would have been quite easy and quite natural, and we left the De Valera government to frolic with the German and later with the Japanese representatives to their heart's content.

De Valera's reply three days later was widely regarded as one of his finest speeches:

> Mr Churchill makes it clear that in certain circumstances he would have violated our neutrality and that he would justify his action by Britain's necessity. It seems strange to me that Mr Churchill does not see that this, if it be accepted, would mean that Britain's necessity would become a moral code . . . It is indeed hard for the strong to be just to the weak. But acting justly always has its rewards . . . Could he not find in his heart the generosity to acknowledge that there is a small nation that stood alone, not for one year or two, but for several hundred years against aggression . . . a small nation that could never be got to accept defeat and has never surrendered her soul?

De Valera's restrained response to Churchill was widely acclaimed – it expressed the widespread support that neutrality enjoyed throughout the country.

Irish Neutrality: An Assessment

The successful pursuit of Irish neutrality was a powerful expression of the independence and sovereignty of the Irish Free State. Neutrality had many short-term and long-term consequences:

> - Although the Irish Free State was spared the worst ravages of war, living standards were almost at subsistence level, and the economy remained stagnant for many years to come.
> - During the Emergency the widespread support for neutrality from people of different political views helped to heal some of the Civil War divisions.
> - Although neutrality acted as a unifying force in the South, it had the effect of deepening divisions between North and South. The widely different experiences of war in both parts of the island reinforced partition.
> - Although neutrality marked Ireland's pursuit of an independent foreign policy, Allied resentment ensured diplomatic isolation in the immediate post-war years. Ireland's application to join the United Nations was vetoed by the USSR in 1946, and the country remained largely marginalised in world affairs.

Despite many difficulties both within and outside the state, de Valera had successfully maintained Irish neutrality. In the view of many historians, this arguably constituted his greatest achievement.

Ireland After the Emergency, 1945–9

Although World War II ended in May 1945, the economic difficulties associated with the Emergency continued. Due to the shortage of fertilisers during the war, most of the land was unproductive, and farming was at a very low ebb. Weather contributed further to the worsening situation: a wet summer in 1946 was followed by a severe winter in 1947. Grain production fell, and a fuel crisis occurred. Bread rationing was re-introduced in 1947, and food prices rose. With the Government continuing to control wages and with prices rising, the standard of living fell. As soon as goods became available abroad after the war, the level of imports increased, while the level of exports fell. This resulted in a balance of payments problem for the Government. In these circumstances of economic hardship, discontent with Fianna Fáil increased. The party had been in power continuously since 1932 and was seen to be out of touch with the realities of everyday living.

Against this background of discontent, a new political party emerged to challenge the political dominance of Fianna Fáil.

The Rise of Clann na Poblachta

On 6 July 1946 Clann na Poblachta was founded in Dublin. It grew out of committees formed to help IRA prisoners. Many republicans, frustrated by the futility of an armed campaign to end partition, joined the new party to pursue their aims by political means. From the beginning, therefore, Clann na Poblachta pursued a strongly republican agenda.

The leader of Clann na Poblachta was Seán MacBride. He was the son of Major John MacBride, who was executed in 1916, and of Maud Gonne, a prominent republican supporter. MacBride himself had been Chief of Staff of the IRA between 1936 and 1938 but left it in 1939 because he disagreed with the bombing campaign in England. Although as a barrister he continued to defend republican prisoners, he himself now decided to follow the path of constitutional politics.

As well as pursuing republican policies, Clann na Poblachta called for radical social and economic reforms. They advocated a massive house-building programme, improved educational services and increased investment in the health service.

Seán MacBride, leader of Clann na Poblachta, at an early meeting of the new party

Clann na Poblachta appealed to several different sections of the community. These included those who were disillusioned by the old Civil War division between Fianna Fáil and Fine Gael. The party also gained the support of many primary school teachers in the wake of a bitter teachers' strike in Dublin in 1946. As discontent with Fianna Fáil grew, Clann na Poblachta saw its popularity increase. The party won a number of by-elections, including the election of its leader, Seán MacBride, to the Dáil.

De Valera, fearing the electoral challenge posed by Clann na Poblachta, called a snap general election for February 1948, before the new party had an opportunity to prepare its organisation.

The 1948 General Election

The election of February 1948 was the most exciting since 1933. The wave of support enjoyed by Clann na Poblachta posed the first serious threat to Fianna Fáil. Clann na Poblachta ran a very enthusiastic campaign and had high expectations of major electoral success. However, the party's lack of experience, together with the radical nature of some of its policies, impeded its success. In putting forward too many candidates, Clann na Poblachta's resources were overstretched. When the votes were counted, the new party won 10 Dáil seats, including 6 in the Dublin area – far fewer than expected.

RESULTS OF 1948 GENERAL ELECTION	
Total no. of seats	147
Fianna Fáil	68
Fine Gael	31
Labour	14
Clan na Poblachta	10
Clann na Talmhan	7
National Labour	5
Independents	12

Although Fianna Fáil had declined to 68 seats, it was still the largest party in the Dáil. It appeared highly unlikely that de Valera would lose his position as Taoiseach. However, this was exactly what occurred, as the other parties in the Dáil reached an agreement among themselves to exclude Fianna Fáil and form an Inter-Party Government.

A Fianna Fáil banner on display during the 1948 general election

Fine Gael posters in Connemara during the 1948 general election

The First Inter-Party Government included a wide array of parties and Independents:

- **Fine Gael**
- **Labour**
- **Clann na Poblachta**
- **Clann na Talmhan**
- **National Labour**

In the course of negotiations, it became clear that the leader of Fine Gael, Richard Mulcahy, would not be accepted as Taoiseach by Clann na Poblachta because of his Civil War record. Mulcahy agreed to stand aside in favour of John A. Costello, an eminent barrister who had been Attorney-General in the Cumann na nGaedheal Government. The leader of the Labour Party, William Norton, became Tánaiste and Minister for Social Welfare. The Fine Gael leader, Richard Mulcahy, became Minister for Education, and Seán MacBride, leader of Clann na Poblachta, was appointed Minister for External Affairs. Clann na Poblachta was given a second ministry, which was filled by Noël Browne, who became Minister for Health. James Dillon represented the Independents who supported the Government and became Minister for Agriculture.

As it was composed of so many parties with vastly different policies, the new Government was not expected to last very long. However, it worked quite well, and Costello succeeded in leading the Government with a sense of unity and purpose.

The Declaration of an Irish Republic, 1949

The most dramatic development during the term of office of the First Inter-Party Government was the declaration of a republic in 1949. A decision to leave the British Commonwealth was taken in principle shortly after the 1948 general election. Although Fine Gael had traditionally been a pro-Commonwealth party, Costello agreed with Seán MacBride and William Norton, the Labour leader, that the External Relations Act (1936) should be repealed, thereby breaking the remaining link with the British Commonwealth. Costello believed that making the country completely independent would 'take the gun out of Irish politics'.

Costello announced his intention to declare an Irish republic under controversial circumstances. In September 1948, while on an official visit to Canada, the Taoiseach announced the Government's intention to repeal the External Relations Act. While de Valera and Fianna Fáil criticised the making of such an important announcement outside the state, they did not oppose it in the Dáil, even though some believed that it would make the ending of partition more difficult.

The First Inter-Party Government. Seated from left are Noël Browne and Seán MacBride (Clann na Poblachta), William Norton (Labour and Tánaiste), John A. Costello (Fine Gael and Taoiseach), Richard Mulcahy (Fine Gael) and other ministers.

The formal declaration of an Irish republic took place on Easter Monday 1949. Although there was nothing to prevent a member state leaving the Commonwealth, the British Government was annoyed with the Irish action. The Labour Prime Minister, Clement Atlee, claimed that he had not been consulted in advance. The British response was contained in the **Ireland Act**, passed at Westminster in 1949. Under this Act, Irish emigrants to Britain continued to enjoy the rights of British citizens, and freedom of travel continued to exist between the two countries. The position of Northern Ireland in the United Kingdom was further strengthened by this Act. Its constitutional status could only change with the consent of the Parliament of Northern Ireland.

Both the Republic of Ireland Act and the Ireland Act reinforced partition, and neither succeeded in taking the gun out of Irish politics. In the years ahead, the IRA conducted violent campaigns to end partition. The declaration of a republic brought an end to a period of ambiguity and uncertainty in Anglo-Irish relations. It greatly diminished the importance of constitutional issues in Irish electoral politics. From then on, social and economic issues would assume greater importance in Irish political life.

The period between the Anglo-Irish Treaty (1921) and the Republic of Ireland Act (1949) had thus witnessed the gradual and steady transformation of southern Ireland from dominion of the Empire to republic.

Key Personality: Éamon de Valera (1882–1975)

Éamon de Valera was born in New York on 14 October 1882. His father, Vivion de Valera, was a Spaniard, while his mother, Kate Coll, was an immigrant from Co. Clare. Following the death of his father when he was less than three years old, his mother sent the young Éamon home to Ireland to be brought up by relatives in Bruree, Co. Limerick. He was educated at Bruree National School, the Christian Brothers' school in Charleville, Co. Cork, Blackrock College and University College, Dublin, where he studied Mathematics. He became Professor of Mathematics at Carysfort College.

De Valera joined the Gaelic League in 1910 and became a member of the Irish Volunteers in 1913. He reluctantly became a member of the IRB and was commander of the rebel forces at Bolands Mills during the Easter Rising of 1916. He was arrested after the Rising and sentenced to death. He was reprieved, primarily because of his American citizenship, and he was sentenced to life imprisonment instead.

As the most senior surviving figure of the 1916 Rising, de Valera became the undisputed leader of the resurgent independence movement. With the aid of Michael Collins, he escaped from Lincoln Gaol in February 1919. As Príomh-Aire, or Prime Minister, of the republican government set up by the Dáil, he appointed a Cabinet of ministers. From June 1919 to December 1920, in the midst of the War of Independence, de Valera toured the United States seeking money and recognition for the new republic.

When a truce was declared in July 1921, De Valera went to London for discussions with Lloyd George. Although the talks did not produce a settlement, both sides agreed to appoint a delegation for negotiations, which would begin the following October. De Valera made one of the most controversial decisions of his career in choosing not to be part of the Irish delegation appointed to negotiate a treaty.

De Valera led the opposition to the Treaty in the Dáil. He saw it as a betrayal of the Irish republic and objected particularly to the Oath of Allegiance to the British Crown. He also believed that the Irish delegation did not have the right to sign the Treaty without the prior approval of the Cabinet and Dáil. When the Treaty was accepted by a small majority of the Dáil, de Valera led the anti-Treaty Sinn Féin representatives in opposition to it.

De Valera became marginalised during the ensuing Civil War, which was fought between the forces of the new Irish Free State and the anti-Treatyite IRA. Once the institutions of the Irish Free State were set up and began to function, de Valera became increasingly frustrated by the abstentionist policies of Sinn Féin, whose elected representatives refused to enter the Dáil. In 1926 he resigned from Sinn Féin following the defeat of his motion calling on the party to enter the Dáil if the Oath of Allegiance were abolished. He immediately set up a new political party, Fianna Fáil.

Describing the Oath of Allegiance as an empty formula, Fianna Fáil TDs entered the Dáil in June 1927. Their combination of good organisation, radical social policies and republican credentials, coupled with the political and economic difficulties besetting the Cumann na nGaedheal Government, ensured electoral success in the 1932 general election.

Fianna Fáil, under the leadership of de Valera, was in government continuously from 1932 to 1948. During this period, the de Valera Government dismantled the Anglo-Irish Treaty and enacted a new constitution. The Economic War with Britain in the 1930s proved disastrous for Irish agriculture. However, the agreement that ended the Economic War paved the way for Irish neutrality during World War II by allowing the return of the three Treaty ports to Ireland. The maintenance of Irish neutrality through six years of war was arguably one of de Valera's finest achievements. It was the ultimate symbol of Irish sovereignty.

The First Inter-Party Government held power from 1948 to 1951. De Valera was Taoiseach again in 1951–4 and 1957–9. He resigned in 1959 and was replaced by the very able Seán Lemass. He was President of Ireland for two consecutive terms, from 1959 to 1973. He died in the care of the Franciscan Order in 1975.

De Valera was the dominant political figure in twentieth-century Ireland. He was a revolutionary in constitutional terms, presiding over the dimantling of the Anglo-Irish Treaty and the enactment of a new constitution. However, in social and economic terms, he was deeply conservative, with a distinctly rural and traditional vision of Irish society.

KEY PERSONALITY: EVIE HONE (1894–1955)

Evie Hone – Ireland's foremost stained glass artist – was born in Dublin on 22 April 1894. She began her formal training as an artist at the Byam Shaw School of Art in London shortly before the outbreak of World War I. She then moved to Paris, where she studied under André Lhote and Albert Gleizes. With her close friend and fellow student, Mainie Jellett, she first exhibited her abstract paintings in Dublin in 1924.

Evie Hone soon developed an interest in stained glass and in 1933 began work with Sarah Purser at An Túr Gloine to develop the Irish stained glass industry. Her first commission was for a window in St Naithi's Church, Dundrum, Co. Dublin. During her lifetime she completed forty-eight windows, the most famous being the east window for Eton College Chapel, completed between 1948 and 1952. Irish examples of her work include windows in the Jesuit seminary at Rahan, Co. Offaly, and St Mary's Church, Kingscourt, Co. Cavan.

Evie Hone's work was greatly influenced by George Rouault, medieval Irish carvings and the work of contemporary French artists. She died at her home in Rathfarnham, Co. Dublin, on 13 March 1955.

EXERCISES

ORDINARY LEVEL

1. Write a paragraph on de Valera's reasons for adopting a policy of neutrality during World War II.

2. Write an account of threats to Irish neutrality during World War II.

3. Write a paragraph on de Valera's relations with each of the following during World War II.

   (i)   Great Britain

   (ii) Germany

   (iii) The United States of America

4. Examine the tables on the general elections of 1943 and 1944 on pages 210 and 211, and compare the results.

5. Outline the economic difficulties that existed in the years after the Emergency.

6. Write a paragraph on the rise of Clann na Poblachta.

7. Write an account of the general election of 1948.

8. How did the British Government react to the declaration of an Irish republic in 1949?

HIGHER LEVEL

1. Analyse the reasons for Irish neutrality during World War II, and assess the implementation of this policy.

2. In a St Patrick's Day radio broadcast in 1941, de Valera explained his position on Irish neutrality for American listeners. Read the following extract from that broadcast and answer the questions that follow.

   > Some twenty years ago, when, in the cause of Irish freedom, I addressed many public meetings in the United States, I pointed out that the aim of the overwhelming majority of the Irish people of the present generation was to secure for Ireland the status of an independent sovereign state which would be recognised internationally as such and could pursue its own life and develop its own institutions and culture in its own peaceful way outside the hazards of imperial adventure – if possible with its neutrality internationally guaranteed like the neutrality of Switzerland. A small country like ours that had for centuries resisted imperial absorption, and that still wished to preserve its national identity, was bound to choose the course of neutrality in this war. No other course could secure the necessary unity of purpose and effort among its people, and at a time like this we heed the warning that a house divided against itself shall not stand the continued existence of partition, that unnatural separation of six of our counties from the rest of Ireland, added in our case a further decisive reason.

   De Valera, radio broadcast, 17 March 1941, quoted in J. Lee and G. Ó Tuathaigh (eds.), The Age of De Valera, Dublin: Ward River Press 1982, 78–9

   (i)   When he was in America in 1920 what was the main point which de Valera made at public meetings?

   (ii) What is meant by the phrase 'outside the hazards of imperial adventure'?

   (iii) Why did de Valera aspire to a neutrality according to the Swiss model for Ireland?

   (iv) What argument did he make concerning Ireland's status as a small country?

   (v)   Explain de Valera's view concerning unity among the Irish people.

   (vi) Identify the final reason for neutrality as stated by de Valera.

3. Consider the role of Éamon de Valera as Taoiseach between 1939 and 1948.

4. 'Keeping Ireland neutral has been described as de Valera's finest hour.' Discuss.

5. Discuss the declaration of an Irish republic in 1949, and assess the consequences.

The Establishment of the State of Northern Ireland

King George V leaving Belfast City Hall after the opening of the Northern Ireland Parliament on 22 June 1921

Northern Ireland was set up under the Government of Ireland Act (1920). As we saw in Chapter 10, this Act was passed by the Westminster Parliament in December 1920 as Lloyd George's solution to the Irish Question. Because of the failure of unionists and nationalists to reach agreement on the future of Ireland, Lloyd George implemented partition. Fearing that their majority would be very small in a nine-county Ulster, unionists agreed to accept six counties instead, where they would outnumber nationalists by a ratio of 2 to 1.

The Government of Ireland Act provided for the establishment of the state of Northern Ireland with a parliament in Belfast. In effect, it was a Home Rule Parliament for the Northern Ireland area alone. The state of Northern Ireland remained within the United Kingdom, and the Westminster Parliament continued to have supreme authority over its territory. The Parliament was to contain two houses – a House of Commons with fifty-two members, and a Senate. The House of Commons would elect the Government. Originally, the King of England was represented by the Viceroy in Dublin, but when southern Ireland became the Irish Free State, the King's representative in the North became known as the Governor of Northern Ireland.

Sir James Craig, Prime Minister of Northern Ireland, chairing a government meeting

Although the Parliament in Belfast could make laws for internal matters in Northern Ireland, its powers were quite limited. The Westminster Parliament continued to control taxation, the currency, the post office and foreign affairs. The people of Northern Ireland elected twelve MPs to represent them at Westminster.

The First Parliament of Northern Ireland

The state of Northern Ireland was due to come into existence in June 1921. Elections were therefore held for the new Parliament in May. Out of 52 seats, the Unionists won 40, with Sinn Féin and the Nationalist Party (the old Home Rule Party) winning 6 seats each. Sir James Craig, who succeeded Edward Carson as leader of the Unionist Party, became the first Prime Minister of Northern Ireland. The new Parliament was opened by King George V on 22 June. Both the Nationalist and Sinn Féin MPs boycotted the opening of Parliament and refused to recognise the new state. The first major challenge facing the new Unionist Government was to deal with a serious threat to law and order.

Violent Unrest in Northern Ireland

The northern state was born in an atmosphere of sectarian violence and tension. In response to IRA attacks, the Ulster Volunteer Force was revived in 1920 under the leadership of Basil Brooke. The level of sectarian violence increased drastically, especially in Belfast. The shooting of policemen by the IRA provoked attacks on ordinary Catholics. In circumstances of economic depression, 5,000 Catholics were driven from their jobs in the Belfast shipyards in July 1920, and anti-Catholic riots occurred in various towns in Ulster. Thousands of Catholics were also driven from their homes, and many moved to southern Ireland. In the violence of the years 1920–22, two-thirds of those killed were Catholics, although they constituted only one-third of the population of Northern Ireland. In the autumn of 1920 Dáil Éireann encouraged a boycott of goods produced in Belfast because of the treatment of nationalists. This measure created further bitterness between unionists and nationalists.

With serious levels of violent unrest, the Unionist Government took strong measures to defeat the IRA and to establish law and order throughout the province.

Nationalists in Belfast calling for a boycott of British goods in 1920

An Orange Order Parade passing through the streets of Portadown in the 1920s

Law and Order

Craig appointed Sir Richard Dawson Bates as the Minister for Home Affairs with responsibility for law and order. His approach involved strengthening the police and giving the Government strong emergency powers.

Even before the establishment of Northern Ireland, a special force of police officers had been set up to support the regular police. This was the Ulster Special Constabulary, established in the autumn of 1920. Class A Specials were full-time policemen; B Specials were part-time, fully armed police; and C Specials were unpaid reservists. Many Ulster Volunteers joined these forces, which were composed almost entirely of Protestants. Whereas the A and C Specials were disbanded, the B Specials remained and were to be a major target for IRA attacks.

In May 1922 the Royal Irish Constabulary (RIC) was replaced by a new police force called the Royal Ulster Constabulary (RUC). It was an armed police force with 3,000 members. Although one-third of the places in the RUC were reserved for Catholics, few of them joined. In the years ahead the RUC became associated with the Protestant community.

In March 1922 Dawson Bates introduced the Civil Authorities (Special Powers) Act to deal with violent

B Specials in the 1920s

threats to the authority of the Government. This law gave extensive powers to the Minister for Home Affairs to deal with threats to peace in Northern Ireland. The Special Powers Act imposed the death penalty for throwing bombs and flogging for carrying weapons. It also allowed the Minister to introduce internment without trial. In the beginning, the Act had to be renewed regularly. However, in 1933 it became a permanent feature of government in Northern Ireland. Because it was used almost exclusively against nationalists, it was deeply resented by the minority Catholic community in the decades to come.

Relations Between North and South, 1921-5

While the new state of Northern Ireland experienced internal challenges to its authority, it also had to face a serious threat to its existence from the south. During the Treaty negotiations in London in the autumn of 1921, the Irish delegates argued strongly for some recognition of Irish authority over the Parliament of Northern Ireland. Sir James Craig, the Prime Minister of Northern Ireland, refused to participate in the Treaty negotiations. In the event, the Anglo-Irish Treaty contained three important provisions relating to Northern Ireland:

> 1 The Parliament of Northern Ireland had the power to vote to remain outside the Irish Free State.
> 2 A Council of Ireland consisting of politicians from North and South was to be established to co-operate in areas of common concern such as agriculture and industry.
> 3 A Boundary Commission was to be set up to decide on the final border between Northern Ireland and the Irish Free State.

The Boundary Commission posed a serious threat to the northern state: any extensive loss of territory could undermine the economic survival of the province. Fortunately for the Unionist Government, divisions between Irish nationalists over the Treaty postponed the establishment of the Boundary Commission. In order to ease North–South tensions and promote co-operation, Sir James Craig met Michael Collins three times between January and March 1922. Collins agreed to end the southern boycott of northern goods, and Craig undertook to reinstate Catholics who had been expelled from their jobs in the Belfast shipyards. However, neither leader had the power to fulfil these promises, and the so-called pact between them soon broke down. With the outbreak of civil war in the south in June 1922, the security of Northern Ireland improved significantly. The threat from the IRA was removed, as republicans were engaged in conflict with the pro-Treaty forces in the south. Because of the Civil War, the work of the Boundary Commission was postponed until October 1924.

The final outcome of the Boundary Commission in 1925 was quite favourable to Northern Ireland. The border remained unchanged, and the northern Government was allowed to keep the land annuities payments collected from farmers in the province.

By the end of 1925, therefore, the Government of Northern Ireland had consolidated its authority and

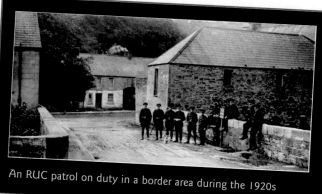

An RUC patrol on duty in a border area during the 1920s

had successfully surmounted both internal and external threats to its security. However, Northern Ireland remained a deeply divided society in which sectarian conflict continued to be a dominant feature of life.

Political and Religious Divisions in Northern Ireland

The unionist majority in Northern Ireland was almost totally Protestant. As unionists comprised two-thirds of the population, they were guaranteed permanent control over the Government. Almost all Unionist Party politicians were members of the Orange Order. The Order united Protestants of all social classes in a common defence of Protestant supremacy in Northern Ireland. The annual Orange marches on 12 July were an expression of the strong attachment of Protestants to their heritage and identity. Despite their dominant position in Northern Ireland, unionists did not feel secure: they regarded the Catholic majority on the island of Ireland as a potential threat to their position. In particular, they regarded the Catholic minority within Northern Ireland as a dangerous, disloyal force that sought to undermine the state.

The partition of Ireland was a major setback for members of the Catholic nationalist minority in Northern Ireland. They felt isolated and abandoned in a state that was dominated by unionists. These feelings were strengthened by the anti-Catholic violence in Northern Ireland between 1920 and 1922. In the beginning, most Catholics refused to recognise the new state of Northern Ireland. They hoped that partition would only be temporary as they awaited the findings of the Boundary Commission.

Whereas unionists were strongly united, striking divisions existed among nationalists. The Nationalist Party, led by Joseph Devlin, engaged in peaceful, parliamentary politics, whereas Sinn Féin was committed to ending partition by force. Up to 1925, all nationalist MPs refused to take their seats in the Belfast Parliament. However, following the failure of the Boundary Commission in 1925, Joseph Devlin led his Nationalist Party into Parliament. Sinn Féin, on the other hand, continued to abstain from attending Parliament. From the outset, the position of the Nationalist Party was extremely weak. With only a handful of MPs, the party exercised little influence in Parliament. Its MPs could not function as a real Opposition and had no chance of replacing the Unionist Government.

With a permanent Unionist Party majority in Parliament and deep sectarian divisions, normal political life could not prevail in Northern Ireland. While general elections took place at regular intervals, the sectarian divide ensured that there was never a change of government.

Unionist Control of the Electoral System

In an effort to give the Catholic minority in the North a greater voice in local and parliamentary elections, the British Government introduced proportional representation (PR). This was fairer to minorities than the British 'first past the post' system. Under the PR system, nationalists won a majority of seats in Counties Fermanagh and Tyrone and in Londonderry city in the elections of 1920. When Northern Ireland was established, these councils refused to recognise the new

The new Parliament Building at Stormont, on the outskirts of Belfast, which was opened in 1935

state and remained loyal to Dáil Éireann. As a result, the Unionist Government dissolved them in 1922.

Under the direction of Richard Dawson Bates, the Unionist Government set about ensuring Unionist Party victories in areas with nationalist majorities. This was achieved by the following means:

> - PR was abolished, and the British 'first past the post' voting system, which was more favourable to the Unionist Party, was restored.
> - Electoral boundaries were redrawn to ensure Unionist Party victories in areas with nationalist majorities. This practice is known as gerrymandering.
> - In local elections, only people who owned property could vote. In addition, people with a number of properties had more than one vote. Because Protestants were generally better off than Catholics, this measure served to strengthen Unionist control of local government.

The Unionist-controlled councils throughout Northern Ireland engaged in discrimination against Catholics. They favoured Protestants in areas such as employment and the allocation of council housing.

Having abolished PR in favour of the straight vote in local elections, in 1929 the Unionist Government also abolished it in parliamentary elections in Northern Ireland. Although the change in the electoral system at parliamentary level did not have as significant an impact as the changes in local government, it nevertheless revealed the determination of the Unionist Government to maintain its position of dominance.

Education in Northern Ireland

Education, like politics, was characterised by deep divisions between Protestants and Catholics. Practically all primary and secondary schools were managed by either Protestant clergy or Catholic priests, brothers and nuns. When the state of Northern Ireland was established, the Prime Minister, Sir James Craig, was committed to raising the standard of education. To achieve this, he appointed Lord Londonderry to head the new Ministry of Education. Londonderry set up a committee to examine the education system. He was disappointed when he failed to persuade the Catholic bishops to take part. At the time, Catholic clergy and teachers did not recognise the new Ministry of Education and would take no part in discussions. In the event, the committee declared that the education system was in serious need of investment and reform.

In 1923 Lord Londonderry introduced an **Education Act**, based largely on the

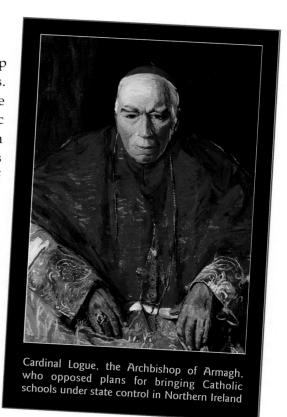

Cardinal Logue, the Archbishop of Armagh, who opposed plans for bringing Catholic schools under state control in Northern Ireland

recommendations of the committee. Under the Act, local Protestant and Catholic clergy would be replaced as managers of primary schools by committees in which the churches and local councils would be represented. Schools known as 'transferred schools', which agreed to accept pupils of all religions, would receive higher grants from the state. Those retaining independent management would be eligible for smaller grants.

The Catholic Church decided to remain outside the new system. Many Protestant schools transferred to the new system, although members of the clergy objected to the removal of religion as a mainstream subject. The Protestant churches and the Orange Order then conducted a campaign to have the Education Act changed. They succeeded in persuading the Government to allow increased clerical control and Bible reading in the 'transferred schools'. When Lord Londonderry resigned in 1925, his plans for a non-denominational system of primary education remained largely unfulfilled. From then onwards the state system of education was largely under Protestant control. Because Catholics remained outside the state system, their schools continued to receive lower grants. Although Catholics resented this situation, they were partly responsible because they had refused to enter into discussions with the Ministry of Education.

At second level, the schools were also controlled by the different churches. As in the rest of Ireland, most pupils did not go beyond primary level. However, between the foundation of the state in 1921 and the outbreak of war in 1939, the numbers attending secondary school showed a slow but steady improvement. Expenditure on schools rose from £51,000 to £200,000, and the number of pupils between ages eleven and nineteen rose from 6,200 to 11,500.

Northern Ireland also contained a university – Queen's University, Belfast – and separate teacher-training colleges for Catholics and Protestants. Whereas the Irish language was one of the major issues in education in the Irish Free State, in Northern Ireland religious divisions dominated the debate on education.

Social and Economic Policy

The limited self-government allowed under the **Government of Ireland Act** (1920) meant that the state of Northern Ireland had very little financial independence. Most taxes were set by the British Government at Westminster. The British Treasury wished to prevent the use of British taxpayers' money to raise living standards in Northern Ireland above those in Britain itself. As a result, 'the principle of parity' was introduced: this meant that taxation and government expenditure should remain the same throughout the United Kingdom. This system greatly limited the scope of the Northern Ireland Government and reduced its capacity to spend on areas of need such as health, education and housing.

AGRICULTURE

Despite the existence of heavy industry in Northern Ireland, about a quarter of all workers were still employed in agriculture in the 1920s. Many similarities existed between farming north and south of the border. However, farm sizes were generally smaller in the North. During the 1920s the Department of Agriculture in Northern Ireland, like its counterpart in the Irish Free State, sought to improve farming through a number of initiatives, including agricultural education, the establishment of co-operatives, the provision of credit and the introduction of quality control.

INDUSTRY

When Northern Ireland was established in 1921, two-thirds of all Irish industrial workers were concentrated in north-east Ulster. The major heavy industries, such as shipbuilding, engineering and linen manufacturing, had prospered during World War I. However, demand decreased in 1920, around the time the new state was established. During the 1920s and 1930s, industrial employment fell throughout the United Kingdom because of failure to modernise and falling prices. Northern Ireland's industries were to experience the same problems as those in the rest of the United Kingdom. The numbers working in the shipyards fell from 15,000 in 1913 to 7,500 in 1924. Those employed in the linen industry fell from 74,000 in 1924 to 55,000 by 1930. By the mid-1920s nearly a quarter of the workforce in Northern Ireland was unemployed.

A ship under construction at the Harland & Wolff shipyard in Belfast

Women making shirts at a Belfast linen mill

HEALTH, HOUSING AND WELFARE

Expenditure in the areas of housing, health and welfare was low in Northern Ireland during the 1920s and 1930s. There was little investment in healthcare: many hospitals were old and inadequate, and the old, nineteenth-century structures remained in place. Between 1921 and 1939, fewer than 8,000 houses were built by local authorities throughout Northern Ireland. Welfare payments were extremely low. Unemployment assistance was introduced only in 1934, and many benefits were strictly means tested. The already low standard of living for many people in Northern Ireland deteriorated further during the depression of the 1930s.

The 1930s – A Period of Depression

After the Wall Street Crash in New York in 1929, economic depression spread from the United States to the rest of the world. During the 1930s in Northern Ireland, economic activity declined and unemployment, already high, soared to new levels. In 1935 Belfast's second-largest shipyard – Workman, Clark & Co. – closed, and by 1937 the level of unemployment in Northern Ireland was the highest in the United Kingdom. Between 1926 and 1937, over 50,000 people emigrated from Northern Ireland. With the deepening economic crisis, sectarian divisions came to the fore.

In August 1931 serious anti-Catholic riots occurred in various towns after the IRA attacked an Orange Order meeting in Co. Cavan. A new Protestant organisation, the **Ulster Protestant League** (UPL), was formed to protect Protestants. Like Unionist leaders, the UPL advised Protestants to employ fellow Protestants in preference to Catholics. Throughout 1932, tension between Catholics and Protestants remained high, owing partly to unionist fears of the newly elected Fianna Fáil Government under de Valera in the Irish Free State. A cut in welfare rates in

1932 brought about a temporary alliance between Protestant and Catholic trade unionists. However, this was to be short-lived, and sectarian divisions soon re-asserted themselves. During the summer of 1935, serious rioting between Protestants and Catholics broke out in Belfast. The RUC failed to prevent the destruction of Catholic property by Protestant mobs. As a result, the British army was called in to restore order, although tensions between the two communities remained high.

It is clear, therefore, that in Northern Ireland, loyalties and allegiances were formed along religious and political rather than class lines: Protestant workers looked to their employers for protection and regarded Catholics as their political and religious enemies.

The Onset of War

By 1939 it was clear that Northern Ireland was characterised by deep religious and political divisions. It was governed by a permanent unionist majority, and most Catholics remained implacably opposed to the state. The Prime Minister, Lord Craigavon, had once declared, 'Ours is a Protestant government and I am an Orangeman.' Under such a regime, Catholics considered themselves to be second-class citizens. They experienced discrimination in both housing and employment.

Once the state of Northern Ireland had been established, successive British governments did not become involved in its internal affairs, thus facilitating its development along sectarian lines. However, with the onset of war in 1939, Northern Ireland assumed a strategic importance for the British Government. The involvement of Northern Ireland in World War II would strengthen its links with Great Britain and separate it even further from the Irish Free State, which was to remain neutral.

KEY PERSONALITY: JAMES CRAIG (1871–1940)

James Craig was born in Belfast on 8 January 1871, the son of a millionaire businessman. He was educated in Belfast and Edinburgh, before setting up his own stockbroking business. On returning from the Boer War, he became interested in politics and was elected Unionist MP for East Down in 1906.

Craig, along with Carson, played the leading role in organising resistance to the Third Home Rule Bill, and his home at Craigavon became a meeting place for unionists. He decided on the wording of the Solemn League and Covenant, played a key role in the formation of the Ulster Volunteer Force and contributed to the success of the Larne Gun-Running in April 1914.

When World War I broke out in August 1914, Craig saw it as an ideal opportunity for Ulster to demonstrate loyalty to Britain. While a special Ulster division of the British army was created, Craig continued to serve in parliament and held a minor position in the government during the war. He participated in the Buckingham Palace Conference and the Irish Convention, seeking to ensure a good deal for Ulster.

When the northern state was established in 1920, James Craig became its first Prime Minister. His priority in 1920–22 was to restore order to a state beset by violence. He appointed Richard Dawson Bates as Minister for Home Affairs, and Dawson Bates proceeded to introduce very harsh security measures under the Civil Authorities (Special Powers) Act. Craig's determination that the border would not change was seen in his refusal to appoint a representative to the Boundary Commission, which was set up in 1924. His Government also ensured Unionist Party domination of county councils by abolishing PR and redrawing electoral boundaries. Indeed, he made no efforts to reassure the Catholic nationalist minority, on one occasion insisting that Northern Ireland was 'a Protestant state for a Protestant people'.

In social and economic terms, Northern Ireland was beset by depression in the 1930s. Although reforms were introduced, especially in the areas of health and education, unemployment and poverty were widespread. However, he did succeed in securing an agreement with the British Government in 1938 that guaranteed equality of taxation and social services in all parts of the United Kingdom.

Craig (who became Lord Craigavon in 1927) continued as Prime Minister of Northern Ireland until his death in 1940. Although he had succeeded in establishing the Northern Ireland state, he presided over a period of economic difficulty and sectarian division.

KEY PERSONALITY: RICHARD DAWSON BATES (1876–1949)

Richard Dawson Bates was born in Belfast on 23 November 1876. He was educated at the Coleraine Academical Institution and was a solicitor by profession.

He was a staunch unionist and was secretary of the Ulster Unionist Council from 1906 to 1921. He was one of the main organisers of the Ulster Solemn League and Covenant in 1912 and a founder member of the Ulster Volunteer Force in 1913. Richard Dawson Bates was a prominent member of the Ulster Unionist Party and was MP at Stormont for East Belfast from 1921 to 1929 and for Victoria from 1929 to 1943.

He was Minister for Home Affairs in the Government of Northern Ireland from 1921 to 1943. In March 1922 he introduced the Civil Authorities (Special Powers) Act to deal with the violence that had erupted in Northern Ireland. This Act imposed the death penalty for certain offences and allowed the Minister to introduce internment without trial. As Minister for Home Affairs, Dawson Bates also set about ensuring Unionist Party election victories in areas with nationalist majorities. He did this by abolishing PR and redrawing electoral boundaries.

EXERCISES

ORDINARY LEVEL

1. Explain why the state of Northern Ireland consisted of six counties.

2. (i) Name the two houses in the Northern Ireland Parliament.

    (ii) List four areas which remained under the control of the Westminster Parliament.

3. Write a short account of the first election to the Northern Ireland Parliament and its opening in 1921.

4. Describe the sectarian tension in Belfast in 1920–22.

5. Write an account of the foundation of the Royal Ulster Constabulary (RUC) and the B Specials.

6. Write a paragraph on the Special Powers Act.

7. Outline the steps taken by Michael Collins and Sir James Craig to ease North–South tensions in the early months of 1922.

8. Explain 'sectarianism', 'discrimination' and 'gerrymandering' and give practical examples of each.

9. Write a paragraph on primary education in Northern Ireland during the 1920s.

10. What were the problems faced by industry in Northern Ireland during the 1920s?

11. Explain the divisions among nationalists in Northern Ireland during the 1920s.

12. Describe the economic depression in Northern Ireland during the 1930s.

13. Write an account of the Ulster Unionist Party and the Orange Order during the 1920s and 1930s.

14. Write a paragraph on the role of Sir James Craig as Prime Minister of Northern Ireland.

HIGHER LEVEL

1. 'The foundation and early years of the state of Northern Ireland were marked by violence and turmoil.' Discuss.

2. Consider social and economic developments in Northern Ireland between 1921 and 1939.

3. Assess the role of the Unionist Party in Northern Ireland between 1921 and 1939.

4. Analyse the contribution of Sir James Craig to the foundation, survival and political development of the state of Northern Ireland.

5. Discuss the experience of the minority Catholic nationalist community in Northern Ireland between 1921 and 1939.

6. Write an account on educational developments in Northern Ireland between 1921 and 1939.

The Outbreak of World War II

When war was declared between Britain and Germany in September 1939, the Unionist Government and people of Northern Ireland regarded it as an opportunity to show their loyalty to the British Crown. In contrast to the neutral Irish Free State, Northern Ireland, as part of the United Kingdom, was fully involved in the British war effort from the beginning. The return of the Treaty ports to the Irish Free State in 1938 greatly increased the strategic importance of Northern Ireland. In the absence of port facilities in the South, the ports of Northern Ireland were vitally important for the British navy. Ships sailed from ports such as Londonderry and Belfast to protect convoys carrying essential supplies from the United States. The Royal Air Force also had important bases in Northern Ireland.

Although conscription was introduced in Great Britain, it was not extended to Northern Ireland. Unionists were divided on this issue: whereas some strongly supported the introduction of conscription, others argued that it would be unwise to train members of the Catholic minority in the use of arms. In the event, many people from Northern Ireland, both Protestant and Catholic, volunteered to join the British forces during the war.

The Wartime Economy of Northern Ireland

The outbreak of World War II transformed the economy of Northern Ireland. Under government supervision, both agriculture and industry were mobilised to meet the war effort, and the depression of the 1930s was replaced by growth and expansion.

At a time of rationing and food shortages in Britain, Northern Ireland was an important source of food. To increase food production, the government introduced compulsory tillage, which resulted in a vast increase in the acreage of land used for growing crops. Farmers in Northern Ireland prospered during the war years because the British Government guaranteed good prices for the produce.

Even before the outbreak of war in 1939, industry in Northern Ireland benefited from British rearmament. The Harland & Wolff shipyard received orders from the British navy, whereas aircraft factories such as that of Short Bros. & Harland expanded to meet the increased demand. Textile factories were commissioned to provide shirts, uniforms, parachutes and tents.

The war brought prosperity to Northern Ireland and brought the economic depression of the 1930s to an end. Unemployment declined sharply from around 25 per cent of the workforce during the 1930s to 5 per cent by the end of the war. This improvement

Bomber aircraft production line at Short Bros. & Harland in Belfast on the eve of World War II

was due to a number of factors, including the expansion of industry, enlistment in the armed forces and migration of workers to factories in Britain.

Between 1940 and 1944, Belfast shipyards produced 140 warships and 123 merchant ships. Employment in shipbuilding increased from 7,200 in 1938 to 20,600 by 1945. During the war the numbers employed in engineering almost doubled to reach 28,000, and the number of aircraft industry employees rose from 6,000 to 23,000.

Wages rose in Northern Ireland during the war. Whereas during the 1930s the average industrial wage there was only 60 per cent of that in Britain, by 1945 it had risen to 75 per cent. Despite this, a certain amount of industrial unrest arose during the war. Although strikes were illegal, over 250 occurred, and 6,000 workers were imprisoned for interfering with the war effort. While World War II affected life in every part of Northern Ireland, the city of Belfast was the centre of most wartime activity.

Aldergrove Airport outside Belfast, which was built for the local aircraft building industry

Case Study: Belfast During World War II

When war broke out in September 1939, Belfast was an important city in terms of producing war materials for the British forces. The Harland & Wolff shipyard – the largest in the United Kingdom – was rapidly increasing its production of warships; at the same time, the Short Bros. & Harland aircraft factory was engaged in a massive expansion of its operations. Engineering works also engaged in the manufacture of armaments for the British forces. Despite the obvious fact that the city was a major target for enemy attack, it was very poorly defended. Whereas Glasgow had eighty-eight anti-aircraft guns, Belfast possessed a mere twenty-four. Furthermore, the fire brigade and other civil defence services had not been developed to meet the challenges of warfare.

Failure to anticipate devastating attacks on the city of Belfast can be traced to the Northern Ireland Government itself. Shortly before the outbreak of war, a junior minister wrote a report for the Cabinet that seriously underestimated the threat from the German airforce.

Document 1

Memorandum by Edmond Warnock, 19 June 1939

[Belfast] is the most distant city of the United Kingdom from any possible enemy base. It is 535 miles from the nearest point in Germany. An attack on Northern Ireland would involve a flight of over 1,000 miles. For aeroplanes of the bombing type, loaded, this is a very big undertaking. To reach Northern Ireland and to get back again, the enemy aeroplanes must twice pass through the active gun, searchlight and aeroplane defences of Great Britain . . . In coming to Northern Ireland the attacking plane would pass over targets which would appear to be more attractive than anything the North of Ireland has to offer. Bearing these facts in mind, it is possible that we might escape attack altogether. But if Northern Ireland is attacked, the above factors would suggest that at least we shall not be subject to frequent attack or to attack by large concentrations of enemy aircraft.

Edmond Warnock, 'Civil Defence Memorandum', 19 June 1939, Public Record Office of Northern Ireland, Cabinet Papers 4/408/12

The predictions of Edmond Warnock were to be proved completely unreliable by the tragic fate that would overtake the city of Belfast.

The German conquest of France in June 1940 transformed the military situation. Belfast was now vulnerable to attacks by German aircraft, which could fly from France and travel up the Irish Sea, thus avoiding Great Britain on the way. With cities in Britain under constant attack, there was little anti-aircraft material to spare to strengthen the defences of Belfast. In effect, the city was a prime target for enemy attack. In November 1940 the German *Luftwaffe* sent out reconnaissance flights that took photographs of the city, including its main factories.

THE BOMBING OF BELFAST

The first attack on Belfast took place on 7 April 1941. It was carried out by six German bombers and resulted in the deaths of thirteen people and started seventeen fires in the city. Although a relatively small-scale attack, it was a warning of what lay in store.

A week later, on the night of 15 April, the *Luftwaffe* carried out a mass raid on Belfast. The attack involved 180 aircraft and lasted some five hours, between 11.00 p.m. and 4.00 a.m. It resulted in huge loss of life and destruction to property. An Irish civil defence expert, Major Seán O'Sullivan, arrived in the city from Dublin on the morning of Wednesday 16 April. He prepared a detailed report on the event.

In the event, the number of casualties was almost midway between O'Sullivan's higher and lower estimates: the death toll was around 900, and 600 were seriously injured.

Scenes of devastation following German bombing raids on Belfast in April and May 1941

Document 2
Major Seán O'Sullivan's description of conditions in Belfast – 16 April 1941

In the Antrim Road and vicinity the attack was of a particularly concentrated character and in many instances bombs from successive waves of bombers fell within 15–20 yards of one another . . . In this general area scores of houses were completely wrecked, either by explosion, fire or blast, while hundreds were damaged so badly as to be uninhabitable . . . In suburban areas, many were allowed to burn themselves out and during the day wooden beams could be heard passing throughout the night . . . During the night of 16–17, many of these smouldering fires broke out afresh and fire appliances could be heard passing throughout the night . . . It is estimated that the ultimate number of dead may be in the neighbourhood of 500, and final figures may even approach 2,000 . . .

The greatest want appeared to be the lack of hospital facilities . . . At 2.00 p.m. on the afternoon of the 16th (nine hours after the termination of the raid) it was reported that the street leading to the Mater Hospital was filled with ambulances waiting to set down their casualties . . . There were many terrible mutilations among both living and dead . . . In the heavily 'blitzed' areas people ran panic-stricken into the streets and made for the open country . . . During the day, loosened slates and pieces of piping were falling in the streets and as pedestrians were numerous, many casualties must have occurred.

Major Seán O'Sullivan, Report on a visit to Belfast, 16–17 April 1941, National Archives, Dublin, Department of the Taoiseach, S 14993

For those attending to the dead and the injured, the experience was a traumatic one. Those who had experience of World War I found this even worse because civilian casualties were involved. One such person was Emma Duffin, who had been a nurse on the Western Front during the war of 1914–18. She recalled her impressions of the scene in Belfast during the bombing blitz.

Families being evacuated from Belfast to the countryside during Word War II

Document 3
Emma Duffin's description of casualties in Belfast

All the way to the place I told myself I was bound to see horrible sights, but only when seen could the full horror be realised. I had seen death in many forms, young men dying of ghastly wounds, but nothing I had ever seen was as terrible as this . . . [World War I casualties] had died in hospital beds, their eyes had been reverently closed, their hands crossed to their breasts. Death had to a certain extent been . . . made decent. It was solemn, tragic, dignified, but here it was grotesque, repulsive, horrible. No attendant nurse had soothed the last moments of these victims, no gentle reverent hand had closed their eyes or crossed their hands. With tangled hair, staring eyes, clutching hands, contorted limbs, their grey-green faces covered with dust, they lay, bundled into the coffins, half-shrouded in rugs or blankets, or an occasional sheet, still wearing their dirty, torn, twisted garments. Death should be dignified, peaceful; Hitler had made even death grotesque. I felt outraged, I should have felt sympathy, grief, but instead feelings of revulsion and disgust assailed me.

Emma Duffin, Diary, pp 86–111, Public Record Office of Northern Ireland, D2109/13

The immediate reaction of many Belfast people was to leave the city. Although before the raid the Government had estimated that 10,000 people might be rendered homeless in an attack, in the immediate aftermath of the actual attacks about 100,000 people were made temporarily homeless. The destruction of their homes and fear of future attacks led to a mass exodus from the city.

Document 4

Major Seán O'Sullivan's account of the exodus from Belfast

From the early morning of the 16th and all throughout the day there was a continuous 'trek' to railway stations. The refugees looked dazed and horror-stricken and many had neglected to bring more than a few belongings – I saw one man with just an extra pair of socks stuck in his pocket. Any and every means of exit from the city was availed of and the final destination appeared to be a matter of indifference. Train after train and bus after bus were filled with those next in line. At nightfall the Northern Counties Station (in York Street) was packed from platform gates to entrance gates and still refugees were coming along in a steady stream from the surrounding streets . . .

Open military lorries were finally put into service and even expectant mothers and mothers with young children were put into these in the rather heavy drizzle that lasted throughout the evening. On the 17th I heard that hundreds who either could not get away or could not leave for other reasons simply went out into the fields and remained in the open all night with whatever they could take in the way of covering.

Major Seán O'Sullivan, Report on a visit to Belfast, 16–17 April 1941, National Archives, Dublin, Department of the Taoiseach, S 14993

The evacuation of people from the slums revealed the terrible conditions that many of these people had to live in. Moya Woodside, a surgeon's wife from the prosperous south Belfast area, recorded her impressions of the condition of the poor in her diary.

Document 5

The condition of the poor in Belfast

My mother telephoned to say that she took in eight evacuees last night, two mothers and six children. She says that one mother is about to have another baby any minute, that they are all filthy, that the smell in the room is terrible. They refuse all food except bread and tea; the children have made puddles all over the floor etc. She is terribly sorry for them and kindliness itself but finds this revelation of how the other half live rather overpowering . . .

Belfast slum dwellers are pretty far down and to those not used to seeing poverty and misery at close quarters the effect is overwhelming. 'The smell is terrible,' said my sister-in-law . . . She said she had been given the job of finding private billets for the evacuees and she was ashamed to have to ask decent, working people with clean houses to take in such guests. More are 'scared out' than 'bombed out' too.

Moya Woodside, Diary, 17–18 April 1941, Tom Harrisson Mass-Observation Archive, MO 5462, University of Sussex, Brighton, England, cited in B. Barton, *Northern Ireland in the Second World War*, Belfast: Ulster Historical Foundation 1995, 49

The conditions endured by people in the slums of Belfast shocked other sections of society. As in Great Britain, the evacuation of poverty-stricken people led to calls for better healthcare, education and housing for all when the war was over.

HELP ARRIVES FROM DUBLIN

At the height of the bombing attack on the night of 16 April, the Northern Ireland Minister for Security, John McDermott, sent a message to Dublin requesting assistance in fighting the fires in Belfast. The Town Clerk and City Manager of Dublin, P.J. Hernon, made the following notes of the circumstances surrounding the request.

In agreeing to send assistance to Belfast, de Valera was in breach of strict neutrality. The Dublin fire-fighters were shocked at the conditions they witnessed in Belfast. Having worked all day, they returned home as night fell in order to avoid being caught up in a possible further bombing. The Government and people of Northern Ireland were extremely grateful for their assistance. This is reflected in the coverage of the event in contemporary newspapers.

Document 7a

The Northern Whig

News that fire brigades from Éire helped at certain places to deal with conflagrations started by the bombers deserves the fullest publicity. Without reserve our thanks are due for this assistance, not only because of its real usefulness, but because of the neighbourly spirit that it signifies. Northern Ireland is grateful and appreciative.

Cited in Redmond, *Belfast Is Burning*: 1941, 18

Document 7b

The Belfast Telegraph

The people will remember the magnificent spirit which prompted fire brigades from Éire to rush to the assistance of their comrades of the North. This is the good neighbour policy in action, worth months of speeches and assurances. Suffering can be a great leveller; cutting through all petty prejudices.

Cited in Redmond, *Belfast Is Burning*: 1941, 18

Document 6

De Valera agrees to send fire brigades to Belfast

16 April 1941. 5.10 a.m. Meeting of Public Security requested urgent assistance from Dublin Fire Brigade in fighting fires in Belfast. Supervisor Public Telephones phones Major Comerford and he got in touch in Belfast with Major O'Sullivan. Phoned An Taoiseach at the same time and informed him of this communication. He said a serious matter and he would get experts to advise him.

5.50 a.m. Phone message from An Taoiseach said to go ahead and give every assistance possible . . .

6.10 a.m. Phoned Comerford who said he would send three crews (two Fire Brigade and one Auxiliary Fire Service) men to volunteer. Rang Belfast regarding the message and was advised by the Supervisor Telephones there that Commissioner of Police there was asked by Minister of Public Security.

9.30 a.m. Rang An Taoiseach and informed him that three pumps with crews had gone – two more getting ready. One from Dún Laoghaire going and one from Dundalk gone.

P.J. Hernon, Notes, 5 May 1941, Dublin City Council Archives, cited in S. Redmond, *Belfast Is Burning*: 1941, Dublin: IMPACT 2002, 21

Both the *Northern Whig* and *Belfast Telegraph* were unionist newspapers. It is interesting to note their emphasis that Northern Ireland and Éire were neighbours, each in its own territory. The nationalist *Irish News* stressed the links between Irish people throughout the country.

The devastating raid of 15–16 April was followed by two further severe raids during the first week in May 1941. It has been estimated that, as a result of all the raids, around 1,100 people died in Belfast, over 56,000 houses were destroyed or damaged, and over £20 million worth of damage was done to property. Although some Government members feared that public anger over the lack of preparation for bombing attacks would lead to riots, this situation never materialised. The widespread destruction in the heart of Belfast would require a massive programme of reconstruction. However, this would have to await the conclusion of the war.

Document 7c

The Irish News

A word of high praise is due to the unstinted assistance given by our countrymen in the neutral part of this island to this area. Not only have they been prompt in sending their fire fighting units: No trouble is too great for the citizens of Éire when it is a question of housing and sheltering refugees. Never was sympathy so manifest: Never, pity so practised. We in our day of sorrow thank our countrymen from the South.

Cited in Redmond, *Belfast Is Burning*: 1941, 19

CASE STUDY: QUESTIONS

COMPREHENSION

1. How long a flight would a German pilot have to undertake to reach Northern Ireland? (Document 1)

2. What obstacles would German pilots face, according to the writer? (Document 1)

3. What conclusion is reached by the writer at the end of Document 1?

4. In Document 2, how does the writer show that the damage was 'particularly concentrated'?

5. What problems were caused when houses were allowed to 'burn themselves out'? (Document 2)

6. What, according to the author of Document 2, was 'the greatest want'?

7. Describe the scene on the street leading up to the Mater Hospital (Document 2).

8. How did the people in the 'heavily blitzed areas' react? (Document 2)

9. What previous experience of death did the author of Document 3 have?

10. How does she describe the death in hospital of World War I casualties? (Document 3)

11. Give examples of her description of the dead during the Belfast blitz (Document 3).

12. Where did the 'continuous trek' described in Document 4 lead to?

13. List some evidence of the troubled state of the refugees (Document 4).

14. Describe the scene at nightfall at York Street Station (Document 4).

15. What action was taken by those who could not get away from Belfast? (Document 4)

16. What complaints did the writer's mother make? (Document 5)

17. What does the statement 'They refuse all food except bread and tea' reveal about the diet of the poor? (Document 5)

18. Explain the difficulty that the writer's sister-in-law had (Document 5).

19. What request reached Dublin in the early hours of 16 April 1941? (Document 6)

20. Explain the initial response of the Taoiseach, Éamon de Valera, to the request (Document 6).

21. What phone message was received from the Taoiseach at 5.50 a.m.? (Document 6)

22. In Document 7c, what is meant by 'the neutral part of this island'?

COMPARISON

1. Compare the tone of the writers in Document 2 and Document 3. Which one reads more like a newspaper account? Explain your answer.

2. Documents 3 and 5 are both in the first person. Compare them as primary sources, and list their strengths and weaknesses.

3. Contrast the approach to Éire of the authors of Documents 7a and 7b on the one hand, and the author of Document 7c on the other. Account for the difference in approach.

4. Contrast the speculation in Document 1 with the reality as described in Document 2.

CRITICISM

1. Analyse the argument in Document 1, and identify the false premise upon which it is based.

2. Would you agree that Document 2 is a good example of a clear, unbiased report? Explain your answer.

3. Document 3 is based on a fundamental contrast. Identify it, and comment on the strengths of this primary source as a personal response to the events.

4. Account for the strong impact that Document 5 makes on the reader.

5. Give examples to show that Document 6 is not a final statement but consists of the original notes taken at the time by the author.

CONTEXTUALISATION

1. Write an account of Northern Ireland during World War II.

2. List the main difficulties faced by the Government of Northern Ireland during the war.

3. Explain why Northern Ireland and the rest of the United Kingdom drew closer together during World War II.

4. Write a paragraph on each of the following.

   (i) Agriculture in Northern Ireland during World War II.

   (ii) Industry in Northern Ireland during World War II.

5. Compare and contrast the experiences of Northern Ireland and the Irish Free State during World War II.

Political Developments

The bombing blitz on Belfast led to increasing criticism of the Unionist Government. Already in 1940 the Government of Lord Craigavon had been criticised because Northern Ireland was slower to adapt to wartime conditions than the rest of the United Kingdom. When Craigavon died suddenly in November 1940, he was replaced by his deputy, J.M. Andrews. Andrews, who was seventy years of age, had been in government since 1921. He refused to introduce younger men into his Cabinet, and public dissatisfaction was evident when the Unionist Party lost a number of by-elections. Unionist MPs revolted in January 1943, calling for the appointment of new faces to the Cabinet, and Andrews resigned from his position as Prime Minister the following May. His successor was Sir Basil Brooke, who reshuffled the Cabinet, dismissing some older ministers and replacing them with younger people.

Sir Basil Brooke (later Lord Brookeborough) addressing the Northern Ireland Parliament

Brooke was a highly divisive figure because ten years previously he had advised Protestant employers to employ only Protestants wherever possible. Like his two predecessors, Craigavon and Andrews, he made no effort to involve the nationalist community in the war effort.

During the war the IRA remained active in Northern Ireland. It attacked military targets but had very little success. The Government used the Special Powers Act and the B Specials to counter the threat from the IRA. As in the Irish Free State, internment was introduced in Northern Ireland during the war. By 1943 the threat from the IRA was almost eliminated.

American Forces in Northern Ireland

Even before the entry of the United States into the war in December 1941, the British Government had been planning the building of bases for American troops in Northern Ireland. In January 1942 American troops began to arrive. They constructed vast facilities in the Londonderry area: between 1942 and 1943, over $75 million was expended. In various parts of Northern Ireland,

American bases generated high spending power and brought money to the local economy. During the preparation for the Allied landings in Normandy in June 1944, thousands of American and British troops used Northern Ireland as a training ground.

American troops highly praised the welcome they received in Northern Ireland both at Government level and among the ordinary people. The leader of the Allied invasion of Normandy, General Dwight D. Eisenhower, later paid tribute to the role of Northern Ireland when he remarked, 'Without Northern Ireland, I do not see how the American forces could have been concentrated to begin the invasion of Europe.'

US troops stationed in Northern Ireland during World War II with some local children

The War Ends

Having fully participated on the Allied side in the war, the people of Northern Ireland joined in celebrating victory in May 1945. People in Britain felt great appreciation for the solidarity displayed by the people of the province. Around 38,000 people from Northern Ireland had enlisted, and almost 5,000 had been killed in action. The agricultural produce from the farms of the province, as well as the ships, planes, textiles and other goods manufactured there, contributed considerably to the British war effort. In addition, the people of Northern Ireland experienced suffering and death at the hands of German bombers in the same way as the people of Britain. All of these factors helped to strengthen the bond between Northern Ireland and the rest of the United Kingdom.

In his victory speech, Winston Churchill paid tribute to the part played by Northern Ireland in protecting the essential Atlantic shipping routes. He also contrasted the involvement of the North with the neutrality of the South and stated that only for Northern Ireland's ports, Britain would have invaded the Irish Free State. In the aftermath of the war Northern Ireland, like the rest of the United Kingdom, was to experience far-reaching social and economic changes.

The Establishment of the Welfare State

In July 1945 a general election was held throughout the United Kingdom, including Northern Ireland. Because of the war, it was the first election to be held in ten years. Whereas in Northern Ireland most of the 13 Westminster seats were won by Unionists, in Great Britain the Labour Party won a landslide victory. By electing a Labour Government under Prime Minister Clement Atlee, the voters were signalling clearly that they demanded radical change once peace returned.

The Labour Party proceeded to nationalise – or place in state ownership – important industries, such as coal and steel, and the rail transport system. It also introduced sweeping changes in the area of health, education and social welfare. Because the state took over responsibility in these areas, the new system became known as the welfare state.

Unionist politicians in Northern Ireland were mostly conservative in outlook and opposed to the welfare state. However, as the northern state was part of the United Kingdom, they had no choice but to implement the measures decided by the Labour Government in London. In the years ahead, these measures would have a huge impact on the quality of life enjoyed by people throughout Northern Ireland.

Health and Social Welfare

By 1945 the provision of healthcare in Northern Ireland had not advanced seriously beyond the inadequate level of the 1920s and 1930s. Whereas the better off could afford private care, the poor had to rely on an underfunded, antiquated public system. This changed completely when the Labour Government introduced the welfare state. Large-scale social reform had been planned during World War II, when the Beveridge Report was published. This was an all-party report in Britain that recommended free healthcare and a system of insurance for all people, irrespective of their income. For the first time, rich and poor in Northern Ireland would be treated equally in the health system. People could attend a doctor of their choice, and all healthcare, including medicines, would be free. To pay for this, taxation increased. However, Northern Ireland did very well out of the new system: between 1945 and 1951, taxation there doubled, whereas payments from the British Exchequer increased sevenfold. In effect, the British taxpayers were paying a massive subsidy to extend the welfare state to Northern Ireland.

Along with a transformation in healthcare, social welfare was radically overhauled. The old system of outdoor relief, with its association with the workhouses, was abolished. Instead a system of national insurance for all workers was introduced. The unemployed, the sick, the elderly and the widowed received vastly improved welfare payments.

Improvements in Education

Under the Education Act (1947), all levels of education, from primary to university level, were reformed. At eleven years of age, students sat the '11 Plus' examination. Those who passed were given a free academic education in grammar schools. The remaining three-quarters went to secondary modern schools, which provided a more practical type of education. In effect, the vast majority of pupils from then on did not have to pay school fees. As a result, the numbers attending secondary school doubled between 1947 and 1952.

Queen's University, Belfast

The reforms in education had a major impact on the Catholic community. The building grants paid to Catholic schools were increased, and about 80 per cent of their pupils did not have to pay fees. For able Catholic students, both school and university education could now be free. This opened up new opportunities that had not existed in their parents' time. As a result, by the 1960s many well-educated and articulate Catholics were emerging from secondary schools and universities. They were no longer prepared to put up with discrimination under unionist rule, and they led campaigns for civil rights for all the citizens of Northern Ireland.

Post-War Reconstruction in Northern Ireland

Although traditional industries such as shipbuilding, engineering and linen manufacturing had done well during the war, the return of peace resulted in a decline in demand for their products. The Government therefore saw the need for diversification of Northern Ireland's industrial base.

In 1945 it passed the Industries Development Act, which introduced loans and grants for new enterprises, as well as providing them with factory sites.

Many jobs were created in the construction industry as the ruins in Belfast and elsewhere were cleared away and new homes and factories were built. Under the welfare state, new hospitals and schools were also built. As a result, 10,000 new jobs were created between 1945 and 1950. However, despite social reforms and economic progress, political life in Northern Ireland continued to be dominated by bitter disagreements over the Union with Great Britain.

Northern Ireland and the Declaration of a Republic in the South

The declaration of the Irish Republic in 1949 and the consequent departure of the Irish Free State from the British Commonwealth gave unionists a further opportunity to stress their loyalty to the British Crown. The northern Prime Minister, Sir Basil Brooke, called a general election in order to rally his followers. At the time, the nationalists in Northern Ireland were supported by an Anti-Partition League. This consisted of supporters of Irish unity in Ireland, Britain and America who hoped to end partition by using peaceful means such as propaganda and lectures to state their

An RUC border patrol during the 1940s

case and persuade people. It had the backing of the Minister for External Affairs in Dublin, Seán MacBride. However, in the election in Northern Ireland, the Unionist Government was returned to power with an increased majority, as Protestants who had voted for Independents or Labour candidates in the previous election now supported official Unionist Party candidates.

In response to the declaration of the Irish Republic in Dublin, the British Labour Government passed the Ireland Act (1949). Although this Act accepted the declaration of a republic in the South, it gave the unionists the strongest guarantee of their position that they had yet received:

> In no event will Northern Ireland or any part thereof cease to be part of His Majesty's dominions and of the United Kingdom without the consent of the parliament of Northern Ireland.

This appeared to copperfasten partition for the foreseeable future.

Hence, both World War II and the subsequent introduction of the welfare state in Northern Ireland deepened divisions between North and South. The Americans and British were grateful for the participation of Northern Ireland on the Allied side, whereas the neutral South suffered a certain degree of diplomatic isolation in the immediate post-war years.

Whereas during the 1920s and 1930s there had been widespread poverty North and South, the introduction of the welfare state in Northern Ireland opened up a huge gap between the two states. The Republic of Ireland could not afford to match the huge subsidies that Northern Ireland received from Britain to finance its health, education and social welfare systems. In the years ahead, therefore, unionists had another powerful argument in favour of remaining in the United Kingdom – namely, a welfare state that was vastly superior to the welfare provisions existing in the Republic of Ireland. Thus, by 1949 Northern Ireland was advancing socially and economically. However, the underlying structural problems of sectarianism and discrimination remained unresolved. They were to surface with tragic consequences in the decades ahead.

EXERCISES

ORDINARY LEVEL

1. Examine the photographs of Belfast after German bombing raids on page 230 and answer the following questions.

   (i) List four forms of transport in evidence.

   (ii) Describe the damage to houses and other buildings.

   (iii) On the evidence of these pictures, were many people made homeless as a result of the raids?

   (iv) How valuable are they as primary sources? Explain your answer.

2. How did the Unionist Government of Northern Ireland and its supporters react to the outbreak of World War II in September 1939?

3. Write a detailed account of industry and agriculture in Northern Ireland during World War II.

4. Explain why the German air force targeted Belfast for bombing during World War II.

5. Write an account of the German bombing of Belfast in 1941.

6. Outline the main changes which took place in the Unionist Government of Northern Ireland between 1940 and 1943.

7. Write a paragraph on American troops in Northern Ireland during World War II.

8. How did the participation of Northern Ireland in World War II affect its relationship with the rest of the United Kingdom?

9. Explain what is meant by 'the welfare state'.

10. Outline the main provisions of the welfare state in Northern Ireland.

11. Explain how reforms in education affected the Catholic community in Northern Ireland after 1945.

12. Write a paragraph on post-war reconstruction in Northern Ireland between 1945 and 1950.

13. Explain the reaction of the Unionist Government in Northern Ireland to the declaration of the Republic in Dublin in 1949.

14. Outline the main provisions of the Ireland Act (1949) regarding the constitutional position of Northern Ireland.

15. Explain how Northern Ireland and the South drifted further apart from 1939 onwards.

HIGHER LEVEL

1. Discuss the impact of World War II on government and society in Northern Ireland.

2. Assess the impact of the Belfast bombing blitz on the people of Northern Ireland.

3. Analyse the implementation of the welfare state in Northern Ireland.

4. Compare and contrast the impact of World War II north and south of the border.

KEY CONCEPTS

THE PURSUIT OF SOVEREIGNTY AND THE IMPACT OF PARTITION, 1912–49

In this section you became familiar with the following KEY CONCEPTS:

Sovereignty A sovereign state is a fully independent state.

Partition Partition is the division of a country into separate states.

Ulster Unionism This is the belief that Ulster should remain an integral part of the United Kingdom.

Allegiance This term means loyalty to a state or a belief – for example, loyalty to the Irish Republic or to the British Crown.

Physical Force This refers to the use of violence to achieve political aims.

IRB/IRA These two organisations promoted the use of physical force to achieve an independent Irish republic.

Blood Sacrifice This term refers to the belief that the spilling of blood in the pursuit of Irish independence was an admirable and justified act.

Dominion Status Dominion status referred to the rights and privileges held by member states, or dominions, of the British Commonwealth.

Republic A republic is a fully independent democratic state without a monarchy.

Free Trade This is an economic policy that opposes the placing of taxes on imported and exported goods.

Protectionism This is an economic policy that supports the placing of taxes on imports from abroad to protect home industry.

Neutrality This is a policy of not taking sides in a war between different countries.

Discrimination This is the unfavourable treatment of a section of society on the basis of race, religion or political allegiance.

Conformity This term refers to a tendency to accept rather than challenge the predominant view.

Censorship This is the control by Church or state of books and films and the banning of materials considered contrary to public morality.

PART 3:
GOVERNMENT, ECONOMY AND SOCIETY IN THE REPUBLIC OF IRELAND, 1949-89

The General Election of 1948

The general election of February 1948 brought to an end a sixteen-year period of Fianna Fáil rule. Although still by far the largest party, with 68 seats out of 147 in Dáil Éireann, Fianna Fáil failed to secure an overall majority. However, no other party had enough TDs to form a government on its own. Instead, the other parties and the Independents combined to exclude Fianna Fáil from office and set up a coalition government, known as the First Inter-Party Government.

Fine Gael, the largest party in the coalition, was led by Richard Mulcahy. It had been in decline for a number of years and was not in a position to challenge Fianna Fáil on its own. The Labour Party had suffered from deep divisions and in 1944 had split into two parties, Labour and National Labour. Labour, under the leadership of William Norton, was the larger of the two. Clann na Talmhan, a farmers' party based largely in the

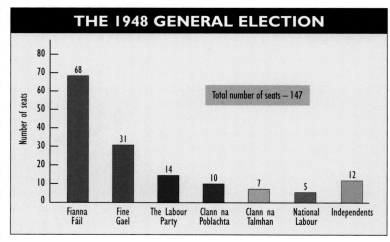

West, had seen its representation in the Dáil decline from eleven seats in 1944 to six in the 1948 election. However, the party that had made the greatest impact on the election campaign was the recently founded Clann na Poblachta. Led by Seán MacBride, the son of the executed 1916 leader John MacBride and Maud Gonne, Clann na Poblachta had been founded in 1946. It represented an effort by many republicans to strive for Irish unity through peaceful political means. Although its main political viewpoint was republicanism, it also advocated radical social reform, especially in the areas of health, housing and education. Despite conducting a vigorous campaign, Clann na Poblachta secured only ten seats in the general election.

When the final election results came in, all the parties except Fianna Fáil opened negotiations on the formation of an inter-party government. To succeed, the new initiative would need the support of Independent TDs as well. Although these parties and individual TDs represented vastly divergent viewpoints, they were united in their determination to keep Fianna Fáil out of power.

The Formation of the Inter-Party Government, 1948

When negotiations opened on the formation of the new Government, Seán MacBride and Clann na Poblachta objected to the Fine Gael leader, Richard Mulcahy, becoming Taoiseach because of his record during the Civil War. To facilitate the formation of the Government, Mulcahy agreed to stand aside in

John A. Costello of Fine Gael who succeeded Éamon de Valera as Taoiseach after the 1948 general election

favour of his party colleague, John A. Costello. Like Seán MacBride, Costello was an eminent barrister and had been Attorney-General in the Cumann na nGaedheal Government before 1932. The Labour Party leader, William Norton, was to become **Tánaiste**, or deputy Taoiseach, in the Government. The various parties were then allocated ministries according to their size in the Dáil, and James Dillon was chosen as Minister for Agriculture to represent the Independents in the Government. When the new Dáil met for the first time, Fianna Fáil proposed Éamon de Valera once again for the office of Taoiseach. However, the combined votes of the other parties and the Independents ensured his defeat and the election instead of John A. Costello as the new Taoiseach. This was the first time since the foundation of the state that the Government was not controlled by a single party. With the formation of the First Inter-Party Government, a new type of government emerged in Irish politics.

The Inter-Party Government, 1948

The posts in the new Government were distributed as follows:

Taoiseach:	John A. Costello (Fine Gael)
Tánaiste:	William Norton (Labour); also Minister for Social Welfare
Education:	Richard Mulcahy (Fine Gael)
Finance:	Patrick McGilligan (Fine Gael)
External Affairs:	Seán MacBride (Clann na Poblachta)
Agriculture:	James Dillon (Independent)
Defence:	T.F. O'Higgins (Fine Gael)
Justice:	Seán MacEoin (Fine Gael)
Industry and Commerce:	Daniel Morrissey (Fine Gael)
Posts and Telegraphs:	J. Everett (National Labour)
Health:	Noël Browne (Clann na Poblachta)
Lands and Fisheries:	Joseph Blowick (Clann na Talmhan)
Local Government:	T.J. Murphy (Labour)

The Government faced many difficult political and economic challenges. One particular danger was that an administration consisting of so many parties would be weak and divided. However, John A. Costello proved to be an effective leader who held the Government together and gave considerable freedom to his ministers to run their departments and develop new policies. On coming to power, the Inter-Party Government was faced with an economy that was badly in need of improvement and modernisation. It responded to the challenge by initiating important improvements in the areas of agriculture, industry and trade.

The Inter-Party Government with President O'Kelly when it took office. Seated in front, from left to right, are Richard Mulcahy (Fine Gael), John A. Costello (Taoiseach, Fine Gael), President O'Kelly, and William Norton (Tánaiste, Labour). Noël Browne and Seán MacBride (both Clann na Poblachta) are standing on the left.

Economic and Social Achievements

AGRICULTURE

Within a few months of entering government, the new Minister for Agriculture, James Dillon, negotiated the Anglo-Irish Trade Agreement with Great Britain. This agreement provided better prices for Irish agricultural produce and helped to increase both the volume and value of these exports. In particular, it provided for increased exports of poultry and eggs.

In 1949 a **Land Rehabilitation Project** was initiated in order to bring huge amounts of uncultivated land into production. Although the project required a huge injection of state capital, it did not prevent a continuing drop in the numbers working on the land. The Government also took steps to encourage forestry, which had been neglected in the past.

The development of forestry and wood products was encouraged by the first Inter-Party Government

As Minister for Agriculture, James Dillon was very concerned with the improvement of standards in farming throughout the country. He encouraged farmers to improve their incomes by exporting high-quality produce to the British market. He also believed that the agricultural sector should diversify and reduce its dependence on cattle in the export market. However, despite government policy, exports of cattle actually increased as a proportion of overall agricultural exports. Because of the dominance of pasture over tillage and the existence of many small, uneconomic farms, the numbers working on the land in Ireland continued to fall rapidly.

INDUSTRIAL DEVELOPMENT

When the Inter-Party Government came to power in 1948, an industrial recovery was already under way. As raw materials became available once again and as consumer spending increased after World War II, Irish manufacturing expanded by almost 50 per cent between 1946 and 1949. The increase in consumer spending was largely based on savings accumulated during the war years. Although the increased spending helped native industry, much of it was devoted to foreign imports, which rose sharply in the post-war period.

The Inter-Party Government believed that in order to strengthen native Irish industry, the state should become more involved in promoting industrial development. In line with the ideas of the economist John Maynard Keynes, ministers believed that the Government should invest in the economy to create more jobs in a period of economic difficulty. It was fortunate that money was then becoming available from the US Government for post-war recovery. The Marshall Plan was a

A pharmaceutical factory in Dublin built in the late 1940s

scheme for European economic recovery established by the United States in 1947. The Irish application for Marshall Aid was organised by Seán MacBride and the Department of External Affairs. As a condition of receiving such assistance, the Irish Government had to draw up an economic plan. Known as **Ireland's Long-Term Recovery Programme** and launched in January 1949, it was the first example of economic planning in Ireland. The application was successful, and between 1948 and 1951 the country received around $125 million, mostly in loans. Marshall Aid enabled the Government to implement new initiatives in both agriculture and industry.

Irish Free State stand at a London Trade Fair in the late 1940s

The Minister for Finance, Patrick McGilligan, was instrumental in setting up three new semi-state bodies – the Central Statistics Office, Córás Tráchtála and the Industrial Development Authority (IDA). The newly founded Central Statistics Office could now furnish governments with the detailed information necessary for economic planning. Córás Tráchtála was set up in order to promote Irish exports in Canada and the United States. The IDA was established in order to encourage and provide financial assistance for industrial development. In the years ahead, it became the most important organisation involved in attracting foreign investment to Ireland.

Employment in the building industry increased owing to a government-sponsored house-building programme. Under the direction of the Minister for Local Government, T.J. Murphy, the number of houses built annually by local authorities increased, reaching 12,000 in 1950. The modest industrial expansion of these years was accompanied by an increase in population. Between 1946 and 1951 the population of the southern state increased for the first time since the Famine. However, this trend was to be reversed during the 1950s.

The Declaration of an Irish Republic (1949)

One of the most significant actions of the First Inter-Party Government was the declaration of an Irish republic in 1949. When it came to power in February 1948, the new Government contained parties with different views on relations between Ireland and Great Britain. Clann na Poblachta clearly favoured taking the state out of the British Commonwealth and setting up a fully independent republic. However, during the election some members of Fine Gael had actually campaigned in favour of Ireland remaining in the Commonwealth. The Labour Party was sympathetic to the Clann na Poblachta position. The Taoiseach, John A. Costello, although a leading member of Fine Gael, saw advantages in leaving the Commonwealth. Since the External Relations Act of 1936, introduced by de Valera and the Fianna Fáil Government, the Irish Free State retained only a slender connection to the Commonwealth. Although the Free State now had a president, the King of England still had a role in receiving ambassadors to Ireland. Costello believed that this situation was unsatisfactory. He believed that if the country became a republic, it might 'take the gun out of Irish politics'. By this he meant that although the issue of Northern Ireland remained unresolved, the IRA would have no cause for grievance in the rest of the country.

On a visit to Canada by Costello in September 1948, he made public the intention of the Government to repeal the External Relations Act and take the country out of the British Commonwealth. Some commentators believe that he did this because he was angered by the behaviour of the Canadian authorities. At official functions, the King of England was toasted but

Celebrations in Dublin on Easter Monday, 18 April 1949, to mark the declaration of the Republic of Ireland

not the President of Ireland. On his return to Ireland, the Government prepared the law to declare an Irish republic.

The Irish Republic (Éire) came into existence officially at Easter 1949. Ceremonies were held outside the GPO in Dublin to celebrate the event. De Valera and Fianna Fáil, although in opposition in the Dáil, did not vote against the measure. Although de Valera attended the special Mass on Easter Sunday to mark the declaration of the Republic, he refused to attend any other functions because Northern Ireland still remained under British rule.

Strictly speaking, the departure of Éire from the British Commonwealth could have had adverse consequences, both in Ireland and for Irish people living in Britain. Because it suited both governments, however, favourable trading conditions continued to exist. Although some people in Britain wanted Irish people to be treated as aliens now that the country had left the Commonwealth, this did not in fact happen. The expanding British economy badly needed Irish workers, and Irish people continued to enjoy full citizenship rights in the United Kingdom.

The situation regarding Northern Ireland was more complicated. For years many people, even Fianna Fáil supporters, held the view that by remaining in the Commonwealth, the Free State would preserve a link with Northern Ireland. After the declaration of a republic, the British Labour Government, under Prime Minister Clement Atlee, gave the unionists of Northern Ireland a strong reassurance that their position within the United Kingdom was secure. The Ireland Act passed by the Westminster Parliament in 1949 stated that Northern Ireland would remain in the United Kingdom as long as a majority in the Parliament in Belfast favoured this. This guarantee appeared to strengthen partition still further.

In effect, the declaration of a republic had little effect on relations between both parts of Ireland or between the Irish Republic and Great Britain. Its main impact was within the Irish Republic itself. After almost thirty years, Michael Collins's statement that the Anglo-Irish Treaty was a stepping stone to greater freedom was proved correct. Northern Ireland apart, full sovereignty had now been achieved by the Irish people. The new republic was a fully sovereign, independent state. No longer would divisions between Commonwealth supporters and republicans over the constitutional issue feature in Irish elections. From 1949 onwards, as far as the Republic of Ireland was concerned, elections would be dominated by social and economic issues.

However, despite the achievement represented by the declaration of a republic in 1949, the issue of partition would continue to dominate Irish foreign policy.

Seán MacBride and the Department of External Affairs

As Minister for External Affairs in the First Inter-Party Government, Seán MacBride, the leader of Clann na Poblachta, took some important initiatives in foreign policy. In 1948 Éire became a founding member of the Council of Europe, a body set up to promote closer European co-operation. In April 1949 MacBride, acting on behalf of the Government, turned down an invitation to join the newly founded North Atlantic Treaty Organisation (NATO). He declared that as long as British rule continued in Northern Ireland, the Republic could not join a military alliance in which Britain was one of the main members. He also believed that as a small nation, Ireland was better off pursuing a policy of neutrality. While militarily neutral, however, Ireland was by no means ideologically neutral during the Cold War. The Irish Government and people were strongly anti-communist and favoured the United States and the West. They particularly objected to the persecution of the Catholic Church in the Soviet communist-controlled countries of Eastern Europe.

Although refusing to join NATO, the Republic of Ireland became a member of the Organisation for Economic Co-operation and Development (OECD) as a condition for receiving Marshall Aid from the US Government. Marshall Aid was of great assistance in the development of the Irish economy both under the Inter-Party Government and in the decades ahead.

Along with presiding over innovations in foreign policy, Seán MacBride devoted a lot of energy to the question of partition. In response to the British Government's Ireland Act (1949), the Irish Government began an anti-partition campaign. This involved meetings and rallies at home and assistance for nationalist candidates in elections in Northern Ireland. Irish diplomats abroad were instructed by Seán MacBride to raise the issue of partition at every available opportunity. This had very little effect and merely alienated the unionists of Northern Ireland and the British Government, whose determination to maintain partition remained as strong as ever.

The Minister for External Affairs, Seán MacBride, at a meeting of the Council of Europe in 1949

While Seán MacBride was making his mark on the Department of External Affairs, his party colleague Dr Noël Browne was proving himself to be an extremely dynamic Minister for Health.

Dr Noël Browne and the TB Crisis

When the Inter-Party Government was formed, the Health Ministry was given to Dr Noël Browne, a young member of Clann na Poblachta, on his first day in the Dáil. The department itself had only been created in 1947. Before that, health was the responsibility of the Minister for Local Government. This reflected a situation in which better-off patients attended private doctors, whereas others depended on the antiquated dispensary system based in local areas.

Dr Noël Browne, Minister for Health in the First Inter-Party Government

One of the worst diseases in Ireland at the time was tuberculosis, or TB. It attacked people of all ages, but especially those in their teens and twenties. Over half of those who contracted the disease died from it. It spread rapidly in the crowded conditions endured by the poorer sections of the community. Contracting TB was often considered a source of shame, and people tried to conceal the fact that family members suffered from the disease.

When Noël Browne became Minister for Health, he was determined to implement a Clann na Poblachta election promise to take action to eradicate TB. He himself had a tragic personal history – his parents and other family members had died from the disease. Having qualified as a doctor in Trinity College, Dublin, he went to

A sanatorium for TB patients in the 1940s

England to specialise in the area of TB treatment. As Minister for Health, he started a concerted campaign against the disease. The Government gave him full support and provided funds from the Hospital Sweepstakes for the purpose. Browne pursued an energetic programme of sanatorium building in various parts of the country. Sanatoria were special hospitals to cater for TB patients. Within two years, 5,500 special hospital beds had been provided in sanatoria. At the same time, new drugs were being developed to fight the disease. As a result of all these factors, the death rate from TB fell significantly from 124 per 100,000 of the

One of the new hospitals built during Browne's campaign to eradicate TB

population in 1947 to 73 per 100,000 in 1951. By 1957 it had fallen to 24 per 100,000.

Having successfully initiated a campaign against TB, Browne proceeded to tackle another area in need of reform, the healthcare provided for mothers and children.

The Mother and Child Scheme

When the Department of Health was established in 1947, the Fianna Fáil Government also introduced a Health Act. However, the party left office before the Act could be put into effect. One of the areas covered by the new Act was the care of mothers and children. At the time, partly because of widespread poverty, infant mortality was very high. More than 80 out of every 100,000 babies died during their first year. In addition, around a hundred women died in childbirth each year. In order to improve conditions for mothers and babies, the Health Act proposed to provide free medical care for all mothers and for children up to the age of sixteen.

A Department of Health brochure advertising the Mother and Child Scheme

Unknown to Noël Browne and the incoming Inter-Party Government, the Catholic bishops had secretly informed the Fianna Fáil Government of their objections to the Mother and Child Scheme as set out in the Health Act. When Browne attempted to implement it, a powerful campaign began to prevent him doing so.

THE OPPOSITION OF THE MEDICAL PROFESSION AND THE CATHOLIC BISHOPS

Most doctors were strongly opposed to the Mother and Child Scheme. They believed that free medical treatment should be available only to poorer people. A **means test** should, in their view, have been introduced to determine – on the basis of means, or income – whether people were eligible for free treatment or not. Doctors did not want to lose the fees paid by their private patients. They were also concerned by the introduction of the welfare state in Great Britain, with its free healthcare for everyone. Most Irish doctors did not want a British-style healthcare system in which they would be totally employed by the state. They saw the Mother and Child Scheme as a first step in this direction. On their own, however, they might not have been strong enough to defeat the Mother and Child Scheme. However, they had extremely powerful allies in the form of the Catholic bishops.

Like the doctors, the bishops stressed that they were in favour of a free scheme for poorer people. However, they believed that the country was too poor to pay for free healthcare for wealthy mothers and their children. The bishops were also deeply influenced by recent European history – both the totalitarian fascist states that existed before the war and the totalitarian communist governments that came to power in Eastern Europe afterwards. They argued that the state should not become too strong and should not provide care for people who could afford it themselves. They also regarded a free scheme for all mothers and children as a form of socialism, which they opposed.

Noël Browne and his supporters, on the other hand, believed that the **means test** would victimise poor people and that such care should be free for all mothers and children. They noted that the Catholic bishops in Northern Ireland and in Great Britain managed to accommodate themselves to free healthcare for all under the welfare state. When Browne refused to compromise on the proposals, a major clash with the Catholic bishops was inevitable.

THE CONTROVERSY DEEPENS

The Catholic hierarchy, led by the Archbishop of Dublin, Dr John Charles McQuaid, set out to prevent the introduction of the Mother and Child Scheme. McQuaid met Noël Browne, but they failed to reach an agreement. The archbishop then appealed to the Taoiseach, John A. Costello, to stop the scheme. In April 1951 matters came to a head. The other members of the Government refused to support the Mother and Child Scheme as proposed by Browne and called on him to amend it to meet the requirements of the bishops. By this stage Browne was involved in a deep quarrel with his party leader, Seán MacBride. MacBride convened a meeting of Clann na Poblachta delegates, only a handful of whom supported Browne. As party leader, MacBride then demanded that the Minister for Health resign, which Browne duly did on 11 April 1951. The Taoiseach, John A. Costello, remarked that had MacBride not acted, he himself would have demanded Browne's resignation.

Having resigned, Noël Browne published the correspondence on the Mother and Child Scheme involving the Taoiseach, the bishops and himself. A very acrimonious debate followed in the Dáil, during which Costello and other Government members stressed their loyalty to the Catholic Church. De Valera condemned Browne for publishing the secret correspondence. In his view, these matters should have been discussed in private meetings between bishops and politicians. The *Irish Times*, which was then a largely Protestant-supported paper, published an editorial in support of Noël Browne and claimed that the Catholic bishops were acting like the real government of the country.

In Belfast the Ulster unionists published the Mother and Child Scheme correspondence as a pamphlet and claimed that Rome Rule prevailed in the Republic. However, the reality was far more complex. The fact that Noël Browne was a young, inexperienced minister contributed to his downfall. His determination not to compromise and his refusal to take advice contributed to his political isolation. The existence of a coalition government and the split between Browne and MacBride also enabled the bishops to exercise greater influence.

Although they succeeded in defeating the Mother and Child Scheme, the Catholic bishops had overplayed their hand. Although most people accepted the outcome, there were expressions of discontent, especially in poorer areas. Never again would the bishops exercise such a high degree of power. Within a few years, a Fianna Fáil Government would quietly reach a compromise with the hierarchy and introduce a modified Mother and Child Scheme.

The immediate effect of the Mother and Child crisis, however, was to destabilise the Inter-Party Government. With rising prices due to the impact of the Korean War, the Government was becoming unpopular. When two farmer TDs withdrew support from the Government over the price of milk in May 1951, Costello decided to call a general election in order to seek a renewed mandate from the electorate. As the first election since the declaration of the Irish Republic, it would mark a new stage in the development of the Irish political system.

KEY PERSONALITY: ARCHBISHOP JOHN CHARLES MCQUAID (1895–1973)

John Charles McQuaid was born in Cootehill, Co. Cavan, on 28 July 1895 and was educated at St Patrick's College, Cavan, Blackrock College, Clongowes Wood College and UCD. Intending to become a missionary priest, he entered the Congregation of the Holy Spirit (the Holy Ghost Fathers) in 1913. However, after completing some postgraduate studies in Rome, he returned to Ireland and was appointed Dean of Studies at Blackrock College in 1928. He was President of Blackrock College from 1931 to 1939. In 1940 he was appointed Archbishop of Dublin, a position he held until his retirement in 1972.

John Charles McQuaid had a keen interest in educational and social matters. In 1931 he was elected chairman of the Catholic Headmasters' Association and was consulted by his predecessor as Archbishop of Dublin, Edward Byrne, on educational matters. He also strongly supported the Catholic social teaching advocated by Pope Pius XI. Éamon de Valera consulted McQuaid when the Government was drawing up the new Constitution in 1937.

As Archbishop of Dublin, John Charles McQuaid took a very strong interest in the social problems of Dublin. With the aim of alleviating poverty and hardship, he founded the Catholic Social Service Conference in 1941 and, the following year, formed the Catholic Social Welfare Bureau to look after the welfare of Irish emigrants. During the 1940s he frequently acted as a mediator during industrial disputes, and in 1946 he sympathised with the striking national school teachers in their unsuccessful dispute with the Fianna Fáil Government. In 1950 he led the Catholic bishops in opposing Noël Browne's Mother and Child Scheme.

He believed strongly in denominational education and persuaded orders of nuns and brothers to open new primary and secondary schools in the archdiocese. He established the Advisory Commission on Secondary Schools. He also emphasised his support for the ban on Catholics attending Trinity College without the permission of their bishop.

John Charles McQuaid was widely regarded as a very effective administrator. He oversaw the expansion of the diocese of Dublin and between 1940 and 1965 established 26 new parishes. The number of diocesan clergy increased substantially during his episcopacy. He exercised very strict control over the clergy and took a particular interest in their training at Clonliffe College.

Archbishop McQuaid was a deeply conservative man. On returning from the Second Vatican Council, he assured his flock that traditional values would remain unchallenged: 'No changes will worry the tranquillity of your Christian lives.' He remained unenthusiastic about the growing ecumenism of the time and was strongly at variance with the mood of change within the Church during the 1960s. He was very suspicious of the media and did not offer explanations for his decisions. He was increasingly portrayed by the media as a reactionary figure out of touch with his clergy and flock. He retired in January 1972 and was succeeded as Archbishop of Dublin by Dermot Ryan. He died on 7 April 1973.

ORDINARY LEVEL

1. Read the following account written by Mr J.G. Browne, Roscommon County Manager, of his impression of the Minister for Health, Dr Noël Browne.

> Early in 1948 I received a telephone message from the department saying that Dr Browne would like me to call to the Custom House the following Monday morning to discuss the question of Roscommon County Council taking over the mental hospital at Castlerea and opening it as a temporary, regional sanatorium, the first in the country, pending the building of a permanent regional sanatorium in Galway. The appointment was for 9.00 a.m. Naturally I was there in good time and was ushered into the Ministerial office promptly at nine o'clock. Dr Browne was already there and I can never forget my first impression.
>
> He sprang up from his desk and hurried across the room, shaking my hand warmly, and thanking me for attending so early, explaining that he had to leave for Cork at ten o'clock . . . He then set me a deadline: June 30th. It was tough going . . . I lost half a stone in weight in the process but it was a labour of love, because he was so enthusiastic and appreciative and was obviously working so hard himself.
>
> *J.G. Browne, Letter in the Irish Times,*
> *13 October 1967*

(i) What message did the author receive?

(ii) What was the topic of discussion?

(iii) Describe the author's first impressions of Dr Noël Browne.

(iv) Give two pieces of evidence to show that the Minister was hardworking.

(v) Why did the author describe his task as a 'labour of love'?

2. Write a short account of the Clann na Poblachta party.

3. State three important developments that took place in agriculture between 1948 and 1951.

4. Write a paragraph on the industrial policy of the First Inter-Party Government, 1948–51.

5. Describe the role played by Seán MacBride as Minister for External Affairs, 1948–51.

6. What was the Mother and Child Scheme? Explain the attitudes of the following groups towards the scheme.

(i) The Catholic bishops

(ii) The medical profession

7. What do you think was the significance of the Mother and Child Scheme?

8. Give an account of the decision to leave the British Commonwealth and the declaration of an Irish republic (1949).

9. Examine carefully the illustration on the Mother and Child Scheme on page 248 and answer the questions which follow.

(i) What is the main message being conveyed here?

(ii) How effective is the figure of the child in conveying this message?

(iii) What is the purpose of the St Brigid's Cross in the background?

(iv) Would you regard this as a well-designed example of an official document aimed at the general public? Explain your answer.

HIGHER LEVEL

1. Discuss the general election of 1948 and the formation of the First Inter-Party Government.

2. Discuss the industrial and agricultural policies of the First Inter-Party Government.

3. Analyse the causes, course and consequences of the Mother and Child controversy.

4. Assess the role of Seán MacBride in the First Inter-Party Government.

Political Developments, 1951-7

FIANNA FÁIL RETURNS TO POWER

The general election of May 1951 followed the fall of the First Inter-Party Government. After the declaration of the Irish Republic in 1949, election campaigns in the Republic were dominated by social and economic concerns rather than constitutional issues. Therefore, the main issues in the 1951 election were prices and wages. Although Fianna Fáil increased its first-preference vote by 4.4 per cent, the party secured only one extra seat. This unexpected outcome was due to 'strategic' voting in support of a coalition government by non-Fianna Fáil voters: they transferred their preferences to parties other than Fianna Fáil. Fine

Unemployed workers demonstrate outside the Dáil in the early 1950s

Gael's first experience in a coalition government benefited the party, as its number of Dáil seats increased from 31 in 1948 to 40 in the 1951 election. However, Fianna Fáil, with 69 seats, was in a position to form a minority government with the help of a number of Independents, including Noël Browne.

The Fianna Fáil Government, with Éamon de Valera as Taoiseach and Seán MacEntee as Minister for Finance, remained in power until 1954. At a time of severe economic difficulty, the Government pursued a policy of tight budgetary control, which required lower state expenditure and increased taxation. The Government's lack of popularity was evident when it lost a series of by-elections in the spring of 1954. When de Valera called a general election in the summer of that year, this downward trend was

Emigrants at the port of Dun Laoghaire in 1952

confirmed: Fianna Fáil lost 3 seats and, with 65 seats, returned its lowest number of TDs to the Dáil since 1927. Fine Gael, on the other hand, increased its representation from 40 to 50 TDs, whereas the Labour Party secured 18 seats.

THE SECOND INTER-PARTY GOVERNMENT, 1954–7

A Second Inter-Party Government was formed, consisting of Fine Gael, Labour and Clann na Talmhan. Although Clann na Poblachta did not join the new Coalition Government, the party's TDs supported the Government in the Dáil. John A. Costello of Fine Gael was elected Taoiseach once again. New, younger members of the Cabinet included Gerald Sweetman (Finance) and Liam Cosgrave (External Affairs) of Fine Gael and Liam Corish (Social Welfare) of the Labour Party. Although this Government was more united than the First Inter-Party Government (1948–51) had been, it lacked the innovation and enthusiasm of its predecessor and was faced with major social and economic difficulties.

The Second Inter-Party Government failed to halt the rising tide of unemployment and emigration. It lost the support of Clann na Poblachta in the Dáil when it took stern action against the IRA, which had started a campaign in Northern Ireland. Early in 1957 Costello was forced to call a general election in very unfavourable circumstances.

A DECISIVE VICTORY FOR FIANNA FÁIL

The general election of March 1957 saw a significant swing of 5 per cent to Fianna Fáil, which was returned to office with 78 seats, a comfortable overall majority. Fine Gael in turn lost 10 seats, and Labour lost 7. Clann na Poblachta was almost wiped out. However, Sinn Féin contested its first election since 1927 and won 4 seats in the Dáil. However, the Sinn Féin TDs refused to take their seats in the Dáil.

Fianna Fáil's return to power in 1957 marked the start of a long period of single-party government. The new Government faced serious challenges in its efforts to reverse the economic decline of the country. In seeking to understand the changes of government between 1948 and 1957 and the failure of any single party to achieve an overall majority in the Dáil, it is necessary to understand the deep social and economic crisis that the country faced in these years.

An Economy in Crisis

During the 1950s the Irish Republic experienced a period of severe economic depression and decline. This was in marked contrast to developments in many other European countries, where rapid economic growth and expansion occurred at this time. The economic slump in Ireland during the 1950s was due to both internal and external factors. There was a marked failure to increase agricultural exports and thereby generate income for the economy. Employment in the farming sector was declining rapidly, but unlike the rest of Europe, Ireland did not have enough industry to provide jobs for those leaving the land.

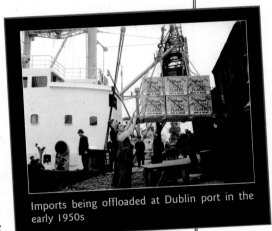

Imports being offloaded at Dublin port in the early 1950s

Irish industry had expanded between 1946 and 1951. However, from 1951 onwards it entered a period of stagnation. Most Irish companies had been established with tariff protection during the 1930s and had become inefficient, slow to change and uncompetitive. Unable to compete in foreign markets, they were largely dependent on the home market. This in turn was in a depressed state and grew very little during the 1950s.

A fundamental difficulty facing the Irish economy during the 1950s was the striking imbalance between the value of exports and imports. This factor was known as the **balance of payments**. An economic crisis occurred when the value of imports into Ireland substantially exceeded the value of Irish agricultural and industrial exports. The devaluation of sterling in 1949 and the outbreak of the Korean War in 1950 led to a rise in the prices of imported goods and raw materials. As a result, the balance of payments deficit increased from £30 million in 1950 to £62 million in 1951. In reaction to this, Seán MacEntee, the Minister for Finance in the Fianna Fáil Minority Government, introduced a severe budget in 1952. By reducing people's spending power, he hoped to reduce the consumption of imported goods. When another balance of payments crisis occurred in 1955, the Minister for Finance in the Inter-Party Government, Gerald Sweetman, adopted a similar approach, which depressed the economy and prolonged the recession.

Although external factors played an important part in the economic crisis of the 1950s, inappropriate government responses frequently exacerbated the situation. Both the Fianna Fáil Minority Government (1951–4) and the Second Inter-Party Government (1954–7), in responding to the situation by a series of cutbacks in government expenditure, failed to alleviate the problems caused by mass unemployment and emigration.

The Rising Tide of Unemployment and Emigration

The economic stagnation of the 1950s resulted in massive unemployment and emigration. At a time when vast numbers of people were leaving the land, the number employed in industry was also falling. Unemployment in Ireland reached a peak in 1957, with 78,000 out of work. Conditions were especially harsh for the unemployed – state benefits were very low and ceased after six months. For many people in the Ireland of the 1950s, emigration seemed the only viable option.

The true depth of the economic depression was reflected in the massive level of emigration. During the 1950s emigration averaged at around 40,000 a year, reaching a peak of 54,000 in 1957. Between 1951 and 1961, more than 408,000 people emigrated. Most went to Great Britain, where well-paid jobs were readily available, especially in the building industry. Emigration had far-reaching consequences for Irish society. Many rural areas were increasingly populated by an ageing community, as the young departed to seek work abroad. Emigration also affected towns and cities, where an atmosphere of widespread despair prevailed. By 1961 the population had declined to 2.8 million, more than 5 per cent below its level at the foundation of the state in 1922.

Although many politicians publicly questioned the need for emigration and accused people of emigrating in order to acquire a higher standard of living, they also understood that emigration contributed to a peaceful society at home. In this respect they viewed emigration as a type of safety valve, without which vast numbers of unemployed people at home could have engaged in violent protest against the Government. The continued electoral strength during these years of traditional parties such as Fianna Fáil and Fine Gael is partly explained by the emigration of so many young people, which gave more influence to older people, who tended to be more conservative. The economic stagnation of the 1950s, with soaring levels of unemployment and emigration, contributed significantly to the deeply conservative nature of Irish society.

Irish Society in the 1950s

Irish society in the 1950s had changed very little since the foundation of the state in 1922. It was predominantly rural and overwhelmingly Catholic. In 1950 more than half the men and over a quarter of the women at work were involved in agriculture. The vision of rural Ireland articulated by de Valera in his speech on St Patrick's Day in 1943 was still shared by many people in the 1950s:

> That Ireland which we dreamed of would be
> the home of a people who valued material

Dancing at Clogherhead pier in the 1950s. Many young people emigrated to England to find work.

wealth only as the basis of right living, of a people who were satisfied with frugal com
and devoted their leisure to the things of the spirit – a land whose countryside would
bright with cosy homesteads, whose fields and villages would be joyous with the soun
of industry, with the romping of sturdy children, the contests of athletic youths and tl
laughter of comely maidens, whose firesides would be forums for the wisdom of serer
age. It would in a word, be the home of a people living the life that God desires that
should live.

This ideal of a contented and self-sufficient rural society was far removed from the harsh realities of life in Ireland during the 1950s. Nevertheless, the traditional, conservative values that underpinned this worldview continued to be held by the leaders of both Church and state.

The Role of the Catholic Church

The Catholic Church maintained a dominant position in the Irish Republic during the 1950s. As the church of 95 per cent of the population, it exercised a strong influence both on government policies and on the lives of ordinary people. Catholic bishops were rarely criticised, and their writings and activities were widely reported in the newspapers. Governments frequently consulted the Catholic bishops concerning proposed legislation. For example, in 1952 the de Valera Government reached a compromise with the bishops over the Mother and Child Scheme, and a proposal containing a means test was introduced by the Government with the approval of the Church. In the same year an Adoption Act was passed, allowing for legal adoption for the first time in the state. It was introduced only after the bishops were given guarantees that children would be placed for adoption with parents of the same religion. Throughout the 1950s the Catholic Church successfully resisted all attempts to change the licensing laws and permit the later opening of public houses. The bishops suggested that it was a sin for Catholics even to campaign for such changes.

Crowds of women leaving a church in Dublin in the 1950s

The fact that many schools and hospitals were run by the Catholic Church strengthened its position further. Under the guidance of powerful bishops such as Archbishop John Charles McQuaid of Dublin, the Church ensured that teachers, doctors and nurses adhered to Catholic values in the course of their work.

The strength of the Catholic Church in Ireland during the 1950s was reflected in the high number of vocations. Each year, many young people began training to become priests, brothers or nuns. Although many embarked on a career in Ireland, many more were destined for missionary work overseas. Traditionally, Ireland had supplied many priests to the Catholic Church in English-speaking countries abroad. During the 1950s large numbers of Irish missionaries were working in Africa and Asia as well. This activity was supported financially by the Catholic community at home. Protestant missionary activity from Ireland, which had a long tradition, continued to flourish.

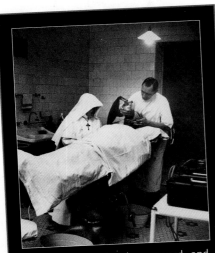

The Catholic Church managed and staffed many hospitals in the 1950s

Marriage and the Family

One of the strongest indications of the conservative nature of Irish society in the 1950s was the position of marriage and the family. In effect, marriage patterns had not changed since the 1880s: the rate of marriage was low, and the age of those marrying was high. By 1951 one person in four remained unmarried for life. This is partly explained by the social expectation that a man should be economically secure before marrying. There was no divorce, as it was forbidden by the Constitution. The majority of women gave up work when they married. In the civil service and in teaching, they had no choice in the matter, as a **'marriage ban'** – or regulation compelling married women to resign – was enforced in those occupations. Female participation in the workforce remained stagnant during the 1950s. For example, the number of women engaged in manufacturing in 1961 was practically unchanged since 1951. Generally, women were recruited into low-paid jobs, and their average wages remained significantly lower than those of men. Most of the jobs done by women were exclusively female occupations, with very little opportunity for promotion. Throughout the 1950s the main role model for women continued to be that of wife and mother, as laid down in de Valera's Constitution of 1937.

In the Catholic, male-dominated society of the 1950s, women who gave birth to children outside marriage were treated harshly. They were frequently abandoned by their families and were rarely able to keep their children. In most cases, such children were either given up for adoption or sent to orphanages. In certain cases, women who were condemned by society for immoral behaviour were confined to institutions run by nuns. The most noted of these were the Magdalen laundries, where women lived and worked in very harsh conditions. In attempting to cover up social problems by treating women in this way, both the state and the Catholic Church sought to promote the image of Irish society as a moral, God-fearing community that offered a model for other countries to follow.

Education

The condition of education in Ireland during the 1950s reflected the general atmosphere of economic depression. Most children did not go beyond primary education. They left school after completing the Primary School Certificate, an examination in Irish, English and arithmetic that was taken at the end of sixth class. Although there were 464,000 pupils in primary schools in 1950, only 47,000 attended secondary schools. The strikingly smaller number receiving second-level education reflected the poverty of the times. Most parents could not afford

A girls' secondary school in the late 1950s

the school fees in secondary schools, and many expected their children to begin earning money at fourteen years of age, the legal age at which they could leave school.

Of the small number of pupils entering secondary school, a large proportion failed to complete the full five-year course. In 1950, for example, 10,200 students sat the Intermediate Certificate examination, which was taken at the end of three years at secondary school. However, in the same year, only 4,500 sat the Leaving Certificate, which was taken after five years at secondary school.

As well as depriving thousands of students of a complete education, such drop-out rates were very bad for the Irish economy, which needed educated workers.

By the early 1950s the number of girls in secondary schools was slowly approaching the figure for boys. This represented an improvement on the situation in 1925, when boys had outnumbered girls in secondary schools by 14,200 to 8,800. However, the curriculum in Irish secondary schools was quite conservative. Irish, English, Latin and mathematics were the most important academic subjects; science subjects were only taken by a minority of students. Almost all secondary schools were controlled by the Catholic and Protestant churches, and in many of them, priests, brothers or nuns outnumbered lay teachers on the staff.

Most third-level education during the 1950s was provided in universities. The numbers involved were quite limited: in 1950 only 7,900 full-time students attended university. Of these, only a quarter were female. Even more than secondary schools, universities in the 1950s were for better-off, privileged members of society. Almost all students had to pay fees, except for a small group who had won scholarships that covered their fees. Yet despite the small numbers graduating from university during the 1950s, many could not find work at home because of the depressed state of the economy. Irish doctors and teachers joined other emigrants in the search for work in England and further afield.

The Irish Language, Music and Culture

One area that experienced new vibrancy during the 1950s was that of Irish culture. An example of this was the flowering of modern literature written in the Irish language by writers such as Máirtín Ó Cadhain, Seán Ó Riordáin and Máire Mhac an tSaoi. Other writers subsequently followed their example and showed that high-quality modern literature could be written in the Irish language.

Traditional Irish dancing in the 1950s

During the 1950s attitudes to the revival of the Irish language began to change. Census figures showed a continuing decline in the population of the Gaeltacht. In an effort to halt this decline, the Second Inter-Party Government set up a special department – **Roinn na Gaeltachta** – to provide economic assistance for people in these areas. More and more people came to realise that it was unrealistic to place all of the burden of reviving the language on schools and that compulsion was not the best way.

In 1953 a new organisation to support the Irish language was established. Known as **Gael Linn**, it adopted a practical approach to promoting Irish. It produced records of Irish music, organised Irish language courses and sponsored Irish debates in schools. It also produced two films, *Saoirse* and *Mise Éire*. These dealt with the struggle for Irish independence, and the music for them was written by the Irish composer Seán Ó Riada. By producing these films, Gael Linn was making good use of the cinema to spread the Irish language. In the pre-television era of the 1950s, Ireland had one of the highest rates of cinema attendance in the world.

A revival of Irish traditional music also began during the 1950s. In 1951 **Comhaltas Ceoltóirí Éireann** was set up in order to promote traditional Irish music. It organised festivals and competitions and enjoyed great success in the decades ahead as a revival of interest in Irish music took place. The revival of Irish music was helped by Radio Éireann, which broadcast traditional music and sponsored the collection of music throughout the country.

During the 1950s, in the absence of television, radio was extremely popular. In 1952 Radio

Éireann began broadcasting in the morning for the first time. Throughout the 1950s radio listenership remained extremely high, with news programmes being particularly popular.

Irish Involvement in International Affairs

Although Irish society in the 1950s was isolated and inward-looking, the first steps were being taken towards greater participation in international affairs. In 1948 Ireland had become a founder member of the Council of Europe. However, in the following year the First Inter-Party Government refused to join NATO. At the same time, the country became a member of the OECD as a condition for receiving Marshall Aid. Although not a member of NATO, the Irish Republic adopted a strongly pro-Western and anti-communist foreign policy during the Cold War. The USSR vetoed Irish entry to the United Nations between 1946 and 1955. When this veto was lifted, Ireland became a member of the UN in December 1955 and was represented there by the Minister for External Affairs, Liam Cosgrave. Ireland was to play an important role in UN peacekeeping forces in the years ahead. Irish entry to the UN was the most significant development in Irish foreign policy since the end of World War II. At a time of deep economic gloom, it represented the slow emergence of Ireland from a period of insularity and isolation.

While the Republic of Ireland was expanding its role on the world stage, at home an old problem was about to re-emerge. The IRA, which had been largely inactive since the early 1940s, initiated a campaign against the Unionist Government in Northern Ireland.

The IRA and the Border Campaign

During the 1950s public opinion in the Republic of Ireland was strongly against partition. This view was summed up in 1954 by John A. Costello, Taoiseach in the Inter-Party Government:

> The Ending of Partition is in the long run inevitable, because Ireland is one nation by history and tradition, by the facts of race and geography and economics.

Whereas political parties were committed to ending partition by peaceful means, the IRA believed in bringing about a united Ireland by the use of physical force.

During the 1950s many new recruits joined the IRA. Although some were deeply committed republicans, for others the organisation offered the prospect of adventure and escape from the economic gloom and unemployment of the time. In 1954 the IRA began a 'Border Campaign' in Northern Ireland. This involved attacks across the border from the South on RUC barracks in Northern Ireland in search of arms and ammunition.

The most significant incident of the Border Campaign occurred on 1 January 1957, when two young IRA men, Fergal O'Hanlon and Seán South, were killed during a raid on Brookeborough Barracks in Co. Fermanagh. The funeral of Seán South from the border to his native Limerick was a huge event attended by thousands of people. Although most people opposed the tactics of the IRA, many sympathised strongly with the republican cause.

The Northern Ireland border customs post at Killeen, Co. Down, which was bombed by the IRA in 1956

The Inter-Party Government of John A. Costello, alarmed by the threat to law and order posed by the Border Campaign, took strong measures against the IRA. Widespread arrests took place throughout the country, and soon most of the IRA leaders were in custody. However, government action against the IRA had important political consequences. Clann na Poblachta withdrew its support from the Government because of the measures taken against the IRA and the failure to make progress towards the ending of partition. As a result, Costello was forced to call a general election in the spring of 1957, after which Fianna Fáil returned to power with a majority of ten seats. This marked the beginning of sixteen years of continuous Fianna Fáil rule between 1957 and 1973.

A suspect is interrogated by the RUC Head Constable during the 1956 IRA campaign

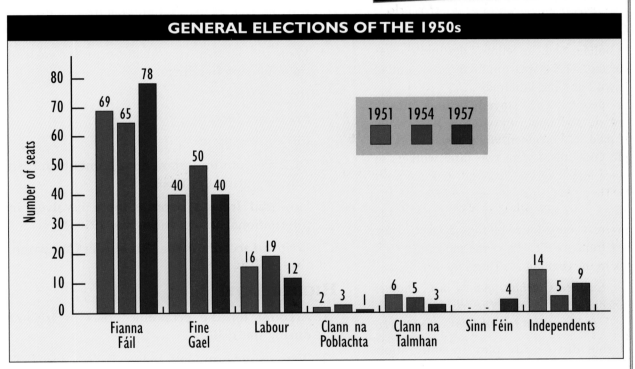

The Need for a New Direction

We have seen in this chapter that the 1950s were years of gloom and depression. With rising unemployment and emigration, some commentators began to question the economic performance of the Irish state three decades after independence. Before independence, many nationalists such as Arthur Griffith blamed the Union with Britain for Ireland's economic problems. Now, after more than thirty years of self-government, a radical reappraisal of economic policy was urgently required. By the late 1950s a new direction in economic policy was beginning to emerge. In the years ahead, this new approach would transform Irish society by inaugurating a period of growth and prosperity.

ORDINARY LEVEL

1. Read the following account of life in Ireland, written by Stephen Croghan, who emigrated to London.

   > I remember a man called Cuddy, from Athleague, who owned a racing stables. Cuddy arrived at the labour exchange in Roscommon and started to sign up men for Wimpey and McAlpine in England.
   >
   > He'd put a tag here on the coat, same as you'd tie a parcel, and up to the railway station with them. This fellow could be for Wrexby, so many fellows for London and so on. The name of the builder and the fellow's destination was on the tag. There was hundreds went out of this town like that, hundreds . . .
   >
   > The people who stayed behind mostly worked on the land, and it was hard work, badly paid. I remember, when I was working outside Cork, there were two farm workers in the place and they had to hand-milk eighteen cows. They were up at six o'clock in the morning . . . I remember that their wages at the time were twenty-four shillings a week. They worked from six o'clock in the morning to six o'clock in the evening . . . That's the way it was.
   >
   > *Stephen Croghan, quoted in C. Dunne,*
   > *An Unconsidered People: The Irish in London,*
   > *Dublin: New Island Books 2003, 116*

   (i) What role did Cuddy play in emigration from Roscommon?

   (ii) Explain the purpose of the tags on the men's coats.

   (iii) Describe the employment opportunities for those who stayed behind.

   (iv) Describe the work and pay of the two farm workers outside Cork.

   (v) Do you think this is a biased source? Explain your answer.

2. What issues dominated the general election of 1951, and what was the outcome of the election?

3. Write a paragraph on the Second Inter-Party Government, 1954–7.

4. Outline the main difficulties facing the Irish economy during the 1950s.

5. Write a paragraph on emigration from Ireland during the 1950s.

6. Describe the nature of Irish society in the 1950s.

7. In what ways did the Catholic Church dominate Irish society at this time?

8. Describe the marriage patterns in Ireland during the 1950s. What was the status of women at this time?

9. Write an account of education under each of the following headings.

   (i) Primary

   (ii) Secondary

   (iii) University

10. Describe four important developments in Irish culture during the 1950s.

11. How did Ireland become more involved in international affairs during the 1950s?

12. Write an account of the IRA Border Campaign.

HIGHER LEVEL

1. Account for the economic crisis in Ireland during the 1950s.

2. 'Various governments between 1948 and 1957 failed to resolve the serious economic problems facing Irish society.' Discuss.

3. Consider the role of the Catholic Church in Irish society during the 1950s.

4. Discuss cultural development in Ireland during the 1950s.

5. Discuss Ireland's increasing involvement in international affairs between 1948 and 1958.

From de Valera to Lemass

Following Fianna Fáil's victory in the general election of March 1957, de Valera was elected Taoiseach at the age of seventy-five. In appointing his government ministers, he recognised the need for a new direction. Seán Lemass was appointed Minister for Industry and Commerce, and James Ryan was chosen as Minister for Finance instead of the more conservative Seán MacEntee.

Seán Lemass, who became Taoiseach and leader of Fianna Fáil in 1959

In June 1959 de Valera resigned from the office of Taoiseach and contested the presidential election. He defeated the Fine Gael candidate, Seán MacEoin, and went on to serve two terms as President until 1973. Seán Lemass was chosen unopposed by Fianna Fáil TDs as their new leader, and he succeeded de Valera as Taoiseach in June 1959.

Seán Lemass was born in Dublin in 1899. He fought in the 1916 Rising and the War of Independence. He took the anti-Treaty side in the Civil War and became a founder member of Fianna Fáil in 1926. He served in successive Fianna Fáil governments as Minister for Industry and Commerce and took charge of the Department of Supplies during the Emergency. Although he was sixty years of age on becoming Taoiseach, Lemass was to bring a new, dynamic approach to government and politics in Ireland. Nowhere was this more evident than in his management of the Irish economy.

The Irish Economy Under Lemass: A Period of Progress and Prosperity

As Minister for Industry and Commerce during the 1930s and 1940s, Lemass had advocated and implemented a policy of economic self-sufficiency and protectionism. One of his great qualities was his openness to change, and by the 1950s he had come to realise that this policy was seriously impeding economic progress and that a new direction was urgently required.

Between 1959 and 1966, Lemass as Taoiseach was to preside over a period of unprecedented growth and expansion in the Irish economy. Although he provided the leadership and vision, Lemass was also greatly favoured both by external economic circumstances and by new thinking within the Irish civil service. The prosperity of the Lemass years was based on a plan for the development of the Irish economy known as the First Programme for Economic Expansion.

Case Study: The First Programme for Economic Expansion, 1958-63

Although the implementation of the First Programme for Economic Expansion is inextricably linked with the name of Seán Lemass, its origins can be traced to the Second Inter-Party Government of 1954–7. The Minister for Finance in that Government, Gerald Sweetman, began to encourage a greater degree of foreign investment in the Irish economy. He allowed the Industrial Development Authority (IDA) to attract investment from abroad and provide tax concessions and grants for export-oriented industries.

However, Sweetman's greatest contribution to economic progress was his appointment in 1956 of T.K. Whitaker as Secretary of the Department of Finance at the relatively young age of forty.

T.K. Whitaker and Economic Development

Whitaker was a leading advocate of the need for radical change in order to lift Ireland out of the depression of the 1950s. In 1957 the Department of Finance, under Whitaker's direction, prepared a comprehensive survey of the economy, including proposals for change and reform. Entitled *Economic Development*, it was completed in May 1958 and formed the basis for the subsequent White Paper outlining government policy, known as the **First Programme for Economic Expansion** and published on 12 November 1958.

One of the strengths of *Economic Development* was its accurate analysis of the social and economic failures of the 1950s. The following extract from *Economic Development* vividly portrays Whitaker's view of the state of Ireland in the 1950s.

Document 1

The condition of Ireland in the 1950s

A sense of anxiety is, indeed, justified. But it can too easily degenerate into feelings of frustration and despair. After 35 years of native government people are asking whether we can achieve an acceptable degree of economic progress. The common talk among parents in the towns, as in rural Ireland, is of their children having to emigrate as soon as their education is completed in order to be sure of a reasonable livelihood. To the children themselves and to many already in employment, the jobs available at home look unattractive compared with those obtainable in such variety and so readily elsewhere. All this seems to be setting up a vicious circle – of increasing emigration, resulting in a smaller domestic market depleted of initiative and skill, and a reduced incentive, whether for Irishmen or foreigners, to undertake and organise the productive enterprises which alone can provide increased employment opportunities and higher living standards. There is, therefore, a real need at present to buttress confidence in the country's future and to stimulate the interest and enthusiasm of the young in particular. A general resurgence of will may be helped by setting up targets of national endeavour which appear to be reasonably attainable and mutually consistent.

Economic Development, Dublin: Department of Finance 1958

One of the main arguments put forward in *Economic Development* and subsequently in the First Programme for Economic Expansion was that the old policy of economic protectionism had failed and that it should be replaced with free trade. Protectionism had sheltered inefficient, uncompetitive industries and was a major barrier to economic progress. This emphasis on the shortcomings of protectionism and the need for competitiveness can be clearly seen in Documents 2 and 3, also taken from *Economic Development*.

Document 2

The failure of economic protectionism

It is accepted on all sides that we have come to a critical and decisive point in our economic affairs. It is only too clear that the policies we have hitherto followed have not resulted in a viable economy. It is equally clear that we face economic decay and the collapse of our political independence if we elect to shelter permanently behind a protectionist blockade. For this would mean accepting that our costs must permanently be higher than those of other European countries, both in industry and in large sections of agriculture. That would be a policy of despair . . . The effect of any policy which entailed relatively low living standards here would be to sustain and stimulate the outflow of emigrants and make it impossible to preserve the 26 counties as an economic entity.

Economic Development, Dublin:
Department of Finance 1958

Document 3

The need to be competitive

If we do not expand our production on a competitive basis, we shall have failed to provide the economic basis for the political independence and material progress of the community. Indeed, if we expect to fail, it would be better to make an immediate move towards re-incorporation in the United Kingdom rather than to wait until our economic decadence became even more apparent.

For these reasons the importance of the next five to ten years for the economic and political future of Ireland cannot be over-stressed. Policy must be re-shaped without regard to past views or commitments.

Economic Development, Dublin:
Department of Finance 1958

The radical proposals advocated by T.K. Whitaker in *Economic Development* were widely acclaimed at the time. In a lecture given in 1959 an eminent economist, Patrick Lynch, praised the new approach.

Document 4

In praise of T.K. Whitaker

Mr Whitaker's *Economic Development* is the most important single survey of the Irish economic problem since the Banking Commission Reports of 1938. Deservedly, it has aroused wide interest and elicited the highest commendations. The qualities of mind revealed in his work are those of one who seeks to stimulate fresh ideas and expose false ones; he deserves enthusiastic applause . . .

What he has done, generally, is to isolate the main problems; to show how previous attempts to solve them have failed; to argue that solutions are possible if sought in a realistic manner; and to convince that realism demands radical change in a great deal of the thinking associated with Irish economic development in the past . . . He is explicit that past policies, though given a fair trial, have failed to secure maximum economic development. Mr Whitaker has pointed the way towards more effective development of the republic's resources. Former policies have failed, and their failure has been greater than is realised by many who give their assent to Mr Whitaker's analysis . . . Ireland has unused human and material resources, but there must be a change in the attitudes towards using them. More than anything else, new ideas count in the long run – provided they are the right ones.

Patrick Lynch, *The Economics of Independence*, Dublin: Cahill 1959, 1–2

THE LEADERSHIP OF SEÁN LEMASS

Whereas Whitaker's report, *Economic Development*, reflected the radical new thinking within the Department of Finance, it was Seán Lemass who provided the political leadership and drive to bring about real change in the Irish economy. As Minister for Industry and Commerce from 1957 onwards and then as Taoiseach between 1959 and 1966 he presided over a period of economic growth and prosperity. Free trade and the encouragement of export-oriented industries were central to the new approach. This was a major theme in the First Programme for Economic Expansion, 1958–63. Lemass's commitment to the development of strong, competitive industries within a European free trade area is evident in the following extract from the Programme.

Document 5

A commitment to free trade

It would be unrealistic, in the light of the probable emergence of a Free Trade Area, to rely on a policy of protection similar to that applied over the past 25 years or so. Assuming that a Free Trade Area is set up in Western Europe and that Ireland joins the Area, the Government will, of course, still be prepared, in suitable cases, to grant protection to worthwhile new industries up to the limits permissible under the rules of the Free Trade Area, but it must be expected that in future the criterion to be applied in determining what is 'worthwhile' will be very much stricter than hitherto. Bearing in mind that the only scope for substantial expansion lies in the production of goods for sale on export markets, it is clear that there can be no place for weak or inefficient industries. Even where only the home market is involved, it must be accepted that such industries place a burden on the economy generally and render other industries less able to meet foreign competition. Hence it must now be recognised that protection can no longer be relied upon as an automatic weapon of defence and it will be the policy in future in the case of new industries to confine the grant of tariff protection to cases in which it is clear that the industry will, after a short initial period, be able to survive without protection. The rules of the Free Trade Area will require a gradual and systematic reduction in existing tariffs.

T.K. Whitaker, *Interests*, Dublin: Institute of Public Administration 1983, 69–70

The First Programme for Economic Expansion was marked by a significant shift in government expenditure from social investment, such as housing, to productive investment in industry and agriculture. The Government set a target of 2 per cent growth per year for the Irish economy for the following five years. Export industries were given special support. The Industrial Development Authority (IDA) received increased resources to attract foreign investment. Many British, American and European companies were attracted to Ireland by means of grants and tax concessions. The Government also invested in agriculture to encourage export-oriented production. However, the performance of the agricultural sector remained disappointing by comparison with industry.

THE IMPACT OF THE FIRST PROGRAMME FOR ECONOMIC EXPANSION

The First Programme for Economic Expansion was highly successful. Instead of the projected 2 per cent annual growth rate in the Irish economy, an actual rate of 4 per cent per year was achieved for the duration of the Programme. The turnaround in the economy was quick and dramatic. Between mid-1959 and mid-1960 alone, the volume of national output rose by 8 per cent, and the value of the country's exports rose by nearly 35 per cent. The rapid expansion in Irish exports eliminated the balance of payments problems that had been a marked feature of the stagnant Irish economy earlier in the 1950s. During the years of the First Programme for Economic Expansion, from 1958 to 1963, unemployment fell by one-third. This in turn

Scenes of Irish industrial expansion in the 1960s

led to a reduction in emigration, which fell by 40 per cent in the early 1960s. One of the most significant indications of the success of the Irish economy appeared in the 1966 census. It showed a population increase of 66,000 over the historically low figure recorded in 1961.

LEMASS'S MINORITY GOVERNMENT, 1961–5

In October 1961, in the middle of the First Programme for Economic Expansion, Lemass contested his first general election as Taoiseach. Despite the country's economic progress, Fianna Fáil won only 70 seats. This represented a drop of 8 since 1957 and left the party just short of an overall majority. Fine Gael increased its representation from 40 to 47 seats, and Labour also improved from 12 to 16 seats. However, the failure of Fine Gael and Labour to co-operate helped Fianna Fáil to return to government. With the support of Independents, Lemass was re-elected as Taoiseach and led a minority government for the next four years. During this time, he continued to pursue the same progressive economic policies that had characterised his first two years in office.

In the early 1960s, therefore, Lemass and his ministers continued to use every opportunity to emphasise the need for competitiveness and openness to change. Speaking to the Institute of Public Administration in Killarney in April 1962, he spoke about the challenges facing industry and agriculture.

THE CONTRIBUTION OF LEMASS TO ECONOMIC GROWTH

Although the upsurge in international trade provided a favourable climate for Irish economic expansion, it is widely acknowledged by historians that Seán Lemass played a vital role in Ireland's economic transformation. He showed his openness to change and new ideas by appointing young, energetic ministers to his Cabinet. These included his own son-in-law Charles J. Haughey, Donogh O'Malley, Patrick Hillery and Brian Lenihan. T.K. Whitaker, in an interview given in 1986, paid tribute to the huge role played by Lemass in Ireland's economic recovery.

Undoubtedly, the First Programme for Economic Expansion ushered in an era of prosperity and rising expectations. It was followed by a Second Programme for Economic Expansion, which covered the years 1963 to 1970. This had targets even more ambitious than those of the First Programme. Although the Second Programme was not as successful as its predecessor, growth rates remained high throughout the 1960s.

Document 6
Lemass calls for modernisation
The industrial producer whose equipment, organisation and sales methods may have been good enough in the conditions of a protected market and who fails to adjust to the new conditions with sufficient speed and thoroughness; the farmer who still thinks of farming only as a traditional way of life and not as a business enterprise in which the maximum utilisation of resources, modern productivity techniques and new methods of marketing his output are as essential as in any other kind of competitive business; the trade union leader who is still thinking in terms of the defensive campaign of the Victorian era and not of labour's vital interest in productivity and expansion – all these by 1970 will have become anachronistic relics of a dead past.

Seán Lemass, Speech at Killarney on 26 April 1962, cited in Fergal Tobin, *The Best of Decades*, Dublin: Gill & Macmillan 1984, 71

Document 7
T.K. Whitaker's tribute to Seán Lemass
I must say it was a very pleasant surprise when the Fianna Fáil Government, committed so much to self-sufficiency and protection, abandoned it all so readily. There is no doubt that Lemass was the great moving dynamic spirit in all of this. There was grudging acquiescence, or recognition granted, that without Lemass's drive and also probably without de Valera's benevolent blessing, change would not have come about nearly as quickly.

Lemass was a pragmatic nationalist, and I put the emphasis on the two words. He was a nationalist in the sense of wanting to see Ireland have a respectable place in the world, but I don't think he was opposed to Dev's traditionalist outlook. He simply had some impatience with it in so far as it might be a hindrance to change, the change he wanted. He didn't have a programme of cultural change. His aim, as indeed my own, was focussed on improving the economic and social scene.

J.F. McCarthy (ed.), *Planning Ireland's Future: The Legacy of T.K. Whitaker*, Dublin: Glendale 1990, 52–3

COMPREHENSION

1. In Document 1, what is the danger of having 'a sense of anxiety' concerning Ireland's economy?

2. What question was being asked by people after thirty-five years of native government? (Document 1)

3. Why did young people have to emigrate, according to the common talk? (Document 1)

4. Why were 'productive enterprises' important? (Document 1)

5. What, according to Document 2, would be the consequences if people chose to 'shelter permanently behind a protectionist blockade'?

6. Explain the 'policy of despair' (Document 2).

7. What should the Irish Government do if it expects to fail in its economic policy, according to Document 3?

8. Explain the final sentence in Document 3.

9. What praise is given to *Economic Development* at the start of Document 4?

10. State three important achievements of T.K. Whitaker in *Economic Development*, according to Document 4.

11. What does the author of Document 4 have to say about 'new ideas'?

12. What type of area does the author of Document 5 expect to emerge in Europe?

13. Why can there be 'no place for weak or inefficient industries'? (Document 5)

14. Describe the unsuitable type of industrial producer as outlined by Seán Lemass (Document 6).

15. What criticism does Lemass make of old-fashioned farmers? (Document 6)

16. Explain his reference to the trade union leader (Document 6).

17. Explain the surprise expressed by T.K. Whitaker at the start of Document 7.

18. State the respective contributions of de Valera and Lemass to economic recovery (Document 7).

19. Explain the statement 'Lemass was a pragmatic nationalist' (Document 7).

COMPARISON

1. Compare Seán Lemass's own description of his views (Document 6) with T.K. Whitaker's description (Document 7).

2. Compare the problems outlined in Document 1 with the approach suggested in Document 4.

3. Read Documents 2 and 5. Compare the treatment of the theme of economic protectionism in both documents.

4. Both Document 4 and Document 6 were speeches. Pick out features common to both that strike you.

CRITICISM

1. Analyse the emotional method used by the author in Document 1 to convince the readers of the need for change in the Irish economy.

2. Do you think that Document 1 as a primary source gives a satisfactory impression of how people felt in 1958? Explain your answer.

3. Consider Documents 2 and 3 as arguments stating a case. Do they state this case well? Explain your answer.

4. Explain the main ways in which the author of Document 4 praises *Economic Development*. Would you regard this as an unbiased source?

5. Relate the views expressed by Seán Lemass in Document 6 to his overall approach to the economy. Would you agree that this document expresses these views very well?

6. Consider the value of Document 7 as a recollection set down several decades after the events described.

CONTEXTUALISATION

1. Write an account of the role of T.K. Whitaker in Ireland's economic recovery.

2. Explain the main changes of direction in economic policy that occurred at the time.

3. Write a paragraph on the targets set, and the economic performance achieved, under the First Programme for Economic Expansion, 1958–63.

4. Write a detailed account of Seán Lemass's economic policies between 1958 and 1966.

Emerging from Isolation

Under the leadership of Lemass, therefore, Ireland was emerging from economic isolation. By attracting increased foreign investment and promoting export-oriented industries, the country was forging new economic links with the outside world, especially Europe and Britain. This outward-looking approach was also evident in Ireland's greater participation in world affairs at this time and in efforts to establish better relations with the Northern Ireland Government.

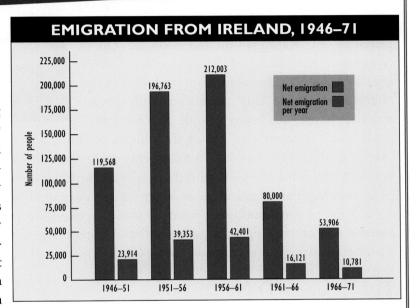

CLOSER ECONOMIC LINKS WITH EUROPE AND BRITAIN

Lemass believed that Ireland's future prosperity depended on closer ties with Europe. This pro-European outlook was clearly seen in Ireland's application to join the European Economic Community (EEC), which had been founded in 1957. Lemass believed that a small nation like Ireland would benefit greatly from closer economic ties with Europe. Ireland's application to join the EEC was linked with the British application. Both were vetoed by the French President, Charles de Gaulle, in January 1963. This had the effect of delaying Irish entry to the EEC for ten years.

In the meantime, Lemass promoted closer economic ties with Ireland's leading trading partner, Great Britain. In 1965 he and the British Prime Minister, Harold Wilson, signed the Anglo-Irish Free Trade Area Agreement (AIFTAA). Both countries agreed to reduce tariffs gradually on each other's imports and abolish them completely by 1975. The gradual establishment of free trade between the two countries was another milestone in Ireland's emergence from economic isolation.

IRELAND AND THE UNITED NATIONS

While the Irish Government was attempting to forge closer links with Britain and Europe, it was also expanding the country's role in international affairs by participation in the United Nations. Since joining the UN in 1955, Ireland had established an important role within the organisation.

Under the direction of Frank Aiken, Minister for External Affairs, Ireland played an important role in formulating UN policies on decolonisation, disarmament and international peacekeeping. In 1960 the Irish ambassador to the UN, F.H. Boland, was President of the General Assembly.

Ireland's most significant contribution to the UN was in the area of peacekeeping. The first major involvement of the Irish army in foreign peace-keeping duties took place in the Congo, in Africa, between 1960 and 1964. An Irish diplomat, Conor Cruise O'Brien, was UN representative in the province of Katanga in the Congo. On 9 November 1960 the Irish troops suffered their greatest loss when ten soldiers were killed in the Niemba ambush. This produced widespread shock at home, but many people also felt great pride that Irishmen had given their lives in the

Soldiers of the Irish army leaving for a tour of duty, under UN command, in the Congo in December 1961

cause of international peace. In all, twenty-six Irish soldiers were to die in the Congo operation between 1960 and 1964. Despite these casualties, Ireland continued to play a major role in UN peacekeeping, participating in seven out of twelve operations between 1960 and 1970.

As well as contributing to international peacekeeping operations, the Government of Seán Lemass was attempting to forge new relationships closer to home. Attempts were made to begin a process of dialogue with the Unionist Government of Northern Ireland.

THE LEMASS–O'NEILL TALKS

In his approach to Northern Ireland, Seán Lemass encouraged co-operation between North and South in non-political areas such as tourism and fisheries. His approach marked a departure from the old anti-partition outlook of earlier governments. As long as the hardline unionist Lord Brookeborough remained Prime Minister, there was little hope of better relations between the two governments. However, in 1963 Brookeborough retired and was replaced by a more moderate Unionist Party leader, Terence O'Neill. O'Neill invited Lemass to a meeting in Belfast on 14 January 1965. This was a landmark in North–South relations. Although reaction in the North was mixed, the meeting was generally welcomed in the South as a possible new beginning. A month later O'Neill visited Dublin. After this exchange of visits, other ministers in both governments met to discuss co-operation in areas of mutual concern such as agriculture, tourism and trade.

However, these first tentative steps towards greater co-operation were soon to be overtaken by the emergence of serious conflict in Northern Ireland from 1968 onwards.

Terence O'Neill, Prime Minister of Northern Ireland (left), and Seán Lemass meet in Belfast in January 1965

The End of the Lemass Era

We have seen how Lemass presided over a period of economic expansion and greater international involvement. It was not surprising, therefore, that Fianna Fáil chose the slogan 'Let Lemass Lead On' for the 1965 general election campaign. As well as having a strong record of economic achievement, Lemass and Fianna Fáil were fortunate in facing a divided opposition. The Fine Gael Party was itself divided over the **Just Society policy**, which was drawn up by Declan Costello, the son of former Taoiseach John A. Costello. Supporters of this policy advocated state action to bring about greater equality in Irish society. It was opposed by the party leader, James Dillon, and other conservative people in the party. Fine Gael had a poor election result, with the number of seats won by the party remaining unchanged at 47. The Labour Party, under Brendan Corish, was becoming more socialist in outlook. It increased its number of Dáil seats from 16 to 21. However, Labour's refusal to enter a coalition with Fine Gael helped Fianna Fáil. Fianna Fáil under Lemass increased its number of seats from 70 to 75 and emerged with an overall majority. This was a clear vindication of the successful economic policies pursued by the Lemass Government over the previous number of years.

In April 1966 Seán Lemass as Taoiseach, together with Éamon de Valera as President, presided over the commemoration of the fiftieth anniversary of the Easter Rising of 1916. In the presidential election held the following June, de Valera, the Fianna Fáil candidate and outgoing President, was re-elected for a second term of office. He narrowly defeated the Fine Gael candidate, T.F. O'Higgins.

Owing to increasing ill health, Seán Lemass retired in November 1966. During his period as Taoiseach between 1959 and 1966, he had made a remarkable impact on the Irish economy and on Irish society in general. He brought a new, pragmatic managerial style to the Irish economy. In encouraging competitiveness and openness to change, he moved the Irish economy away from the stagnation of the past. Although remaining strongly nationalist, he also believed that Ireland's future would be best served by developing closer links with the outside world.

Lemass believed firmly in the view that 'a rising tide would lift all vessels'. By this he meant that economic progress would benefit everybody in society. However, while Ireland did experience a period of unprecedented economic growth during the Lemass years, glaring inequalities persisted between rich and poor. The emergence of a more materialistic consumer society also threatened to undermine traditional beliefs and values.

The resignation of Seán Lemass marked the end of an era in Irish politics. A new, younger generation of politicians was now emerging to take over from those who had fought in the struggle for independence.

Jack Lynch Becomes Taoiseach

Following the resignation of Seán Lemass in November 1966, an intense leadership battle occurred within Fianna Fáil. Three ministers in particular competed to succeed Lemass – Neil Blaney, George Colley and Charles Haughey. In order to prevent a bitter contest between the favourite candidates, Colley and Haughey, Jack Lynch, the Minister for Finance, was put forward as a compromise choice. Blaney and Haughey then withdrew, and in a ballot by Fianna Fáil TDs, Lynch defeated Colley by 51 votes to 19.

Jack Lynch was born in Cork in 1917. After a short career in the civil service, he studied law and became a barrister. He was a brilliant sportsman, winning All-Ireland medals in both hurling and football for his native Cork. He was elected to the Dáil as a Fianna Fáil TD in 1948. He served as a Cabinet minister under both Éamon de Valera and Seán Lemass. In 1965, following the retirement of James Ryan, he was appointed Minister for Finance by Lemass.

As Taoiseach, Jack Lynch always gave the impression that he had not sought the position but had accepted in order to serve the party and country. He related very well to ordinary people and was especially popular in his native Cork. His first real test as leader of Fianna Fáil came with the general election of June 1969.

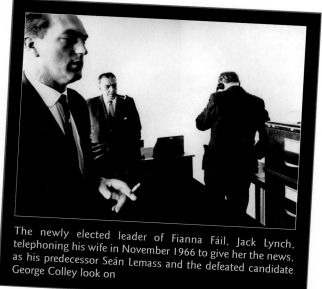

The newly elected leader of Fianna Fáil, Jack Lynch, telephoning his wife in November 1966 to give her the news, as his predecessor Seán Lemass and the defeated candidate George Colley look on

The 1969 General Election

The general election of June 1969 was keenly contested. Fianna Fáil campaigned on its record; it claimed that it provided strong single-party government and warned the electorate against the dangers of coalitions. Fine Gael fought its first election campaign with Liam Cosgrave as leader. It was the Labour Party under Brendan Corish, however, that dominated the campaign. The party had moved considerably to the left, a development summed up in its slogan 'The Seventies Will Be Socialist', and it completely ruled out participation in a coalition government. Labour's new, socialist agenda was associated with a group of intellectuals that included Conor Cruise O'Brien, Justin Keating and David Thornley. Fianna Fáil exploited the Labour Party's move to the left by means of a 'red scare' campaign that portrayed Labour as being a communist party. In rural Ireland particularly, Fianna Fáil candidates accused the Labour Party of threatening to take land from inefficient farmers.

Jack Lynch and Fianna Fáil introduced an American-style presidential campaign. Jack Lynch toured the country and campaigned in person in an effort to win votes. Contrary to expectations, Fianna Fáil, with 75 seats, secured an overall majority. The failure of Fine Gael and Labour to co-operate contributed to Fianna Fáil's success. Fine Gael increased its representation in the Dáil by 3 seats to 50. The election was a big disappointment for the Labour Party, which won 18 seats, a loss of 4 since the previous election. Gains made in Dublin by the Labour Party were more than offset by serious losses in the country, where Fianna Fáil's 'red scare' tactics had worked.

Victory in the 1969 general election strengthened the position of Jack Lynch, both as Taoiseach and leader of Fianna Fáil. He could now look forward to a comfortable period in office. However, soon after Lynch's re-election a new crisis erupted in Northern Ireland that was to have a dramatic impact on his Government.

Jack Lynch and the Crisis in Northern Ireland

In August 1969 serious rioting broke out in Belfast and Derry. Since a civil rights march had ended in violence in Derry in October 1968, events in Northern Ireland had been moving at a fast pace. Civil rights groups demanded justice and equal rights for the minority Catholic community. The

Jack Lynch and the Crisis in Northern Ireland

Prime Minister, Terence O'Neill, made certain concessions but was under pressure from Rev. Ian Paisley and from extreme unionists in his own party not to introduce reforms. Jack Lynch and the Government in the Republic advised the British Prime Minister, Harold Wilson, to take charge of the situation in Northern Ireland and insist on the implementation of reforms.

However, when violence appeared to be getting out of control in August 1969, Wilson had to send the British army into Northern Ireland. With nationalists in Belfast and Derry under attack from the RUC and Protestant loyalists, the Irish Government came under pressure to intervene. People in the Republic could see the violent scenes on the television every night. The arrival of Catholic families who had been burned out of their homes in Belfast evoked much sympathy in the South.

In this atmosphere of heightened emotions, Jack Lynch decided to address the nation on Wednesday, 13 August. He declared that partition was at the root of the Northern Ireland problem and criticised the Unionist Government for its treatment of the Catholic minority. He also promised to send troops to border areas to set up field hospitals for people who might want to flee from Northern Ireland. However, he stopped short of direct intervention. Although he declared that 'the Irish Government can no longer stand by and see innocent people injured and perhaps worse', he had no intention of sending Irish troops over the border. To have done so could have provoked civil war in Ireland and conflict between Ireland and Great Britain. Instead, Lynch, who strongly supported the peaceful unification of Ireland, concentrated on two main approaches to the problem of Northern Ireland. Firstly, he continued to advise the British Government to introduce reforms there. Secondly, he set out to do everything in his power to prevent the 'Troubles' in Northern Ireland from spilling over into the South and destabilising the Government and society of the Republic. This approach was soon to be challenged not only within the Fianna Fáil Party itself but also by members of Lynch's own Government.

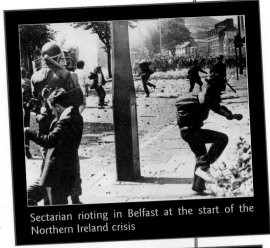
Sectarian rioting in Belfast at the start of the Northern Ireland crisis

Families salvaging property from their burnt-out homes in Belfast following a night of violence

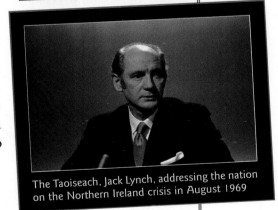
The Taoiseach, Jack Lynch, addressing the nation on the Northern Ireland crisis in August 1969

The Arms Crisis, 1970

Within the Fianna Fáil Government in 1969, strong differences of opinion existed concerning Northern Ireland. Whereas Jack Lynch and a majority of the Cabinet held moderate views, some ministers were of a strongly republican outlook. These included the Donegal TD Neil Blaney, who was Minister for Agriculture, and two Dublin-based ministers, Kevin Boland and Charles Haughey. Both Blaney and Haughey had hoped to succeed Lemass as leader of Fianna Fáil, but the success of Jack Lynch in the 1969 general election strengthened his position, and he appeared set to remain leader for a long time. Thus, personal resentment against Lynch was mixed with disagreement over the Government's Northern Ireland policy.

On 6 May 1970 there was profound shock when news broke that Jack Lynch had dismissed two of his senior ministers, Neil Blaney and Charles Haughey. The official statement said that it was because of their failure to support government policy on Northern Ireland. Another minister, Kevin Boland, resigned out of sympathy with Blaney and Haughey. The real reason for the dismissals, however, was an accusation that both Blaney and Haughey were using public money to import arms and ammunition from abroad for the use of nationalists in Northern Ireland. Jack Lynch finally acted when the leader of Fine Gael, Liam Cosgrave, came to him with information concerning this accusation. On 28 May Blaney and Haughey were arrested and charged with planning to import arms and ammunition illegally into the state.

However, both former ministers were found not guilty of the charges. In July the case against Neil Blaney was dismissed, and in October Charles Haughey was acquitted by a jury. Haughey then called on Lynch to resign, but Lynch refused and secured a vote of confidence in the Dáil.

Charles Haughey arriving at court during the Arms Trial

The Arms Crisis had a deep long-term impact on Fianna Fáil. Both Neil Blaney and Kevin Boland left the party and set up their own political organisations. Charles Haughey chose to remain within Fianna Fáil, however, and to work his way back slowly to a prominent position within the party. The 1970 Fianna Fáil Ard-Fheis witnessed scenes of violent disagreement between the supporters of Jack Lynch and his more republican opponents. One of Lynch's main defenders was the Minister for Foreign Affairs, Dr Patrick Hillery, who said that the rebellious minority would not be allowed to take over Fianna Fáil. Hillery also played a prominent role in the most significant economic initiative taken by the Government of Jack Lynch – Irish entry into the European Economic Community (EEC).

Dr Patrick Hillery, Minister for Foreign Affairs, strongly supporting the Taoiseach, Jack Lynch, during the Fianna Fáil Ard-Fheis in 1970

Ireland Joins the European Economic Community

In 1969 Georges Pompidou, de Gaulle's successor as President of France, withdrew French objections to British entry into the EEC. Britain and Ireland immediately applied once again to join. Under the leadership of the Minister for Foreign Affairs, Dr Patrick Hillery, the Irish negotiating team secured very favourable terms for the country. A referendum was called for May 1972 on the issue of joining the EEC. Both Fianna Fáil and Fine Gael were strongly in favour, pointing to the economic advantages of membership. So too were the farmers' organisations, as Irish farmers expected to do very well under the Common Agricultural Policy of the EEC. The Labour Party campaigned against Irish entry, arguing that jobs could be lost in traditional industries and that the EEC in Brussels would have too great a say in Irish affairs. When the referendum took place, a huge majority of 83 per cent voted in favour of joining

Newspaper headlines on the morning of Ireland's accession to the EEC, 1 January 1973

the EEC. This decision by the people confirmed the Treaty of Accession, which had been signed by Jack Lynch and Patrick Hillery in January 1972. Ireland was now set to become a full member of the EEC on 1 January 1973.

The End of an Era

Having successfully organised Irish entry into the EEC, Jack Lynch was about to seek the verdict of the people on his Government in a general election. Despite success in joining the EEC, the Fianna Fáil Government was beset by difficulties at home. The deep divisions in the party during and after the Arms Crisis made it appear divided in the eyes of voters. Its opponents could claim that some sections of Fianna Fáil were sympathetic to the IRA at a time when increasing violence in Northern Ireland was alarming most people in the Republic. Indeed, Dublin was to experience the direct impact of the northern Troubles during 1972. Following the shootings in Derry on Bloody Sunday, 30 January 1972, violent scenes took place in Dublin, including the burning of the British Embassy. In December two people were killed by bombs in the centre of Dublin city.

In an effort to gain popularity in the country, the Government introduced a generous budget in 1972. As unemployment increased from 6.7 per cent in 1968 to 8.1 per cent by 1972, the Minister for Finance, George Colley, refused to take corrective measures. Instead, for the first time since the foundation of the state, he failed to balance the current budget and borrowed to make up the difference between taxation and expenditure. Historians would later criticise this as the first step on a very dangerous road that would lead to a crisis ten years later.

Despite attempting to win over the electorate, however, the Government faced a severe challenge in the general election of February 1973. For the first time in sixteen years, Fianna Fáil's main political opponents, Fine Gael and Labour, joined forces in an attempt to remove them from power.

KEY PERSONALITY: T.K. WHITAKER (1916–)

T.K. Whitaker – public servant and economist – was born in Rostrevor, Co. Down, in 1916 and educated at CBS Drogheda. He obtained a BA degree in Mathematics, Economics and Celtic Studies and later went on to achieve a master's degree in Economics from London University. He entered the civil service in 1934 and four years later was attached to the Department of Finance. He rose rapidly within the ranks of the civil service, becoming Secretary of the Department of Finance in 1956 at the very young age of thirty-nine.

Whitaker took up his new position as Secretary of the Department of Finance at a time of deep economic gloom and depression in the country. He believed that economic protectionism should end and that Irish agriculture and industry should become more competitive in a free-market system. He also believed that jobs would have to be created by a shift from agriculture to industry and services. He advocated long-term planning to assist the development of the Irish economy.

Whitaker formed a team of officials within the Department who together carried out a detailed survey of the Irish economy. He set out his findings and proposals in a paper known as *Economic Development*. His proposals for the Irish economy were accepted by the Government and formed the basis of the First Programme for Economic Expansion, adopted in November 1958. This programme is widely regarded as a landmark in the development of the Irish economy, resulting in unprecedented growth rates, rising employment and population increase for the first time since the Famine. Whereas the dynamic T.K. Whitaker provided the plan for economic progress, it was the political drive of Seán Lemass as Taoiseach that transformed the plan into reality. Whitaker also played a key role in organising the historic meetings between Seán Lemass and the Prime Minister of Northern Ireland, Terence O'Neill, in 1965. He retired from the Department of Finance in 1969.

T.K. Whitaker was Governor of the Central Bank from 1969 until 1976. He was a senator from 1977 to 1982. Other appointments in an illustrious career included President of the Economic and Social Research Institute, Chairman of Bord na Gaeilge and Chancellor of the National University.

KEY PERSONALITY: SEÁN LEMASS (1899–1971)

Seán Lemass was born in Dublin on 15 July 1899 and educated by the Christian Brothers at O'Connell School. He joined the Irish Volunteers in 1914 and fought in the GPO during the Easter Rising of 1916 and subsequently in the War of Independence. He opposed the Anglo-Irish Treaty (1921) and was a member of the Four Courts garrison at the outset of the Civil War. He was elected to Dáil Éireann in 1922, but in line with Sinn Féin policy he refused to take his seat in the Dáil.

Lemass was a pragmatist who, like de Valera, believed that Sinn Féin should come in from the political wilderness. He followed de Valera in leaving Sinn Féin and was a founder member of Fianna Fáil in May 1926. Seán Lemass, together with Gerald Boland, played a key role in building up the organisation of the new party at local constituency level. When Fianna Fáil entered the Dáil in 1927, Lemass took a leading part in opposing the Cumann na nGaedheal Government. He famously described Fianna Fáil in March 1928 as 'a slightly constitutional party'.

Following the 1932 general election, Fianna Fáil entered government, and Lemass was appointed Minister for Industry and Commerce. At this time he advocated the old Sinn Féin policy of economic self-sufficiency and protectionism. During the 1930s he put in place a programme of tariff protection for Irish industry and state intervention to develop the country's resources. He established a number of semi-state bodies, including Bord na Móna, Aer Lingus and Irish Shipping. Despite the depression of the 1930s, Lemass's achievement in generating industrial growth was remarkable.

During World War II, Lemass was appointed Minister for Supplies. He had responsibility for rationing and controlling the distribution of limited resources such as petrol and foodstuffs. His energy, pragmatism and organisational ability made him well suited for this task.

During the 1950s Lemass was again appointed Minister for Industry and Commerce in the two de Valera governments of 1951–4 and 1957–9. He became increasingly convinced of the need for Irish industry to become competitive in a market economy based on free trade. He believed that the protectionist policies of the past were in need of radical review. Lemass strongly supported the economic policy proposed by T.K. Whitaker, Secretary of the Department of Finance. The Government adopted Whitaker's proposals in November 1958 in the First Programme for Economic Expansion. Lemass provided the political will to implement this programme when he succeeded de Valera as Taoiseach and leader of Fianna Fáil in 1959.

The First Programme for Economic Expansion was a watershed in the development of the Irish economy. It set targets for growth and attracted foreign industries to Ireland by means of generous grants and tax concessions. The results were spectacular: output increased by almost one-quarter, unemployment fell by one-third, and emigration declined sharply. Lemass believed that Irish industry should become more competitive within Europe, and he applied for Irish membership of the EEC in 1961, as part of a joint application with Britain. However, as a result of France's opposition to Britain's application for membership, Ireland did not become a member of the EEC until 1973. Nevertheless, Lemass sought to maximise Ireland's economic advantage abroad by joining the European Free Trade Association and concluding an Anglo-Irish Trade Agreement in 1965.

Lemass also brought new thinking to the problem of Northern Ireland. In 1965 he had two historic meetings with the Prime Minister of Northern Ireland, Captain Terence O'Neill. These meetings indicated a willingness to develop a more open relationship between the governments of North and South.

As Taoiseach from 1959 to 1966, Lemass presided over a period of unprecedented economic and social change in Ireland. A significant increase in prosperity was accompanied by the introduction of far-reaching social policies, including free secondary education. His most successful government was the minority Fianna Fáil Government from 1961 to 1965. Lemass retired as Taoiseach and leader of Fianna Fáil in November 1966 and was succeeded by Jack Lynch.

EXERCISES

ORDINARY LEVEL

1. Read the following account of the publication of the Programme for Economic Expansion, and answer the questions that follow.

> To anyone passing Leinster House that day, 11 November 1958 must have seemed drearily typical of Dublin's autumn. Rain splashed against the Irish Parliament building's mullioned windows and spattered its limestone façade. Inside, however, the atmosphere was aglow with unusual anticipation as Finance Secretary T. Kenneth Whitaker received congratulations on a project that had taken almost two years to complete. That afternoon, members of the Dáil had received copies of a White Paper entitled Programme for Economic Expansion. This White Paper was based on *Economic Development*, a 250-page study of the Irish economy which Whitaker had initiated and supervised. To mark the occasion, the Taoiseach, Éamon de Valera, had invited Whitaker to attend the parliamentary session. As members of the Dáil shook his hand, Whitaker's thoughts drifted back to 1956 when he had begun work on the study that was to revolutionise Ireland's economic thinking. Twenty-eight years later, Whitaker recalled his achievement with characteristic understatement. 'I knew I could put together a team of willing collaborators who would be very able,' he said. 'I knew there were people I could touch who would be glad of a release from the rather narrow confines of their own responsibilities. We had economists. In the Finance Department itself I brought in as many good officers as I could, no matter what their rank. One must try to transcend the hierarchical system.'
>
> *J.F. McCarthy, 'Ireland's Turnaround: Whitaker and the 1958 Plan for Economic Development' in J.F. McCarthy (ed.), Planning Ireland's Future: The Legacy of T.K. Whitaker, Dublin: Glendale 1990, 52–3*

(i) Describe the scene outside Leinster House on 11 November 1958.

(ii) Why was T.K. Whitaker being congratulated?

(iii) What was the new programme based on?

(iv) How did the Taoiseach, Éamon de Valera, mark the occasion?

(v) What had begun in 1958?

(vi) Explain Whitaker's recollections of the events twenty-eight years later.

2. Write a paragraph on the career of Seán Lemass before he became Taoiseach in 1959.

3. What kind of information was contained in the document *Economic Development*, which was completed in May 1958? Name its author, and outline the main ideas proposed in it.

4. Explain why economic policy shifted from protectionism to free trade in the late 1950s.

5. Write a paragraph on the First Programme for Economic Expansion.

6. Outline the efforts of the Government of Seán Lemass to create closer economic ties with Britain and Europe.

7. Discuss Irish involvement in United Nations peacekeeping operations during the 1960s.

8. Write a paragraph on Seán Lemass's approach to Northern Ireland when he was Taoiseach.

9. Account for the success of Fianna Fáil in the 1965 general election.

10. Write an account of the role of T.K. Whitaker in the economic development of Ireland between 1956 and 1966.

11. Explain how Jack Lynch became Taoiseach in 1966.

12. Write a paragraph on the 1969 general election.

13. Explain the policy of Jack Lynch concerning the Troubles in Northern Ireland.

14. Write an account of the origins, course and consequences of the Arms Crisis (1970).

15. Write a paragraph on Irish entry to the European Economic Community.

16. Examine carefully the illustrations covering industrial expansion in the 1960s on page 264 and answer the questions that follow.

   (i) Choose an example of highly skilled work. Would you think products such as this were likely to be exported? Explain your answer.

   (ii) Pick out an example of a native Irish product that was presented in a modern way.

   (iii) Can you identify examples of modern machinery in the illustrations? What does this tell you about the companies involved?

   (iv) Would you regard these pictures as unbiased sources? Explain your answer.

HIGHER LEVEL

1. Assess the contribution of Seán Lemass to Ireland's economic development between 1957 and 1966.

2. Analyse in detail the First Programme for Economic Expansion and its impact on the Irish economy.

3. Read the following criticism of Irish society in 1966 that was made by Patrick Lynch, a lecturer in economics in University College, Dublin and Chairman of Aer Lingus. Then answer the questions that follow.

   We would best honour 1916 by being honest with ourselves and in our attitudes towards 1916. As a people we have deliberately chosen not to realise many of the ideals of 1916. Neither Pearse nor Connolly contemplated a middle-class society of the kind that we have created over the last fifty years. Socially, we have become a conservative, self-satisfied people. To judge from the pictures in the evening papers, our middle class, which sets standards for all of us, is more concerned to be seen publicly rejoicing in material affluence than with idealisms of any kind.

   P. Lynch, February 1966,
   quoted in F. Tobin, The Best of Decades,
   Dublin: Gill & Macmillan 1984, 147

   (i) How would the people alive in 1966 best honour 1916, according to the speaker?

   (ii) What, in your view, were the ideals of 1916 which were not realised by 1966?

   (iii) How did Lynch characterise Irish society of the 1960s in social terms?

   (iv) In his view, what was the main concern of the middle class?

   (v) Would you agree that this passage accurately points to some of the weaknesses of Irish society during the Lemass years? Explain your answer.

4. Discuss the position of Jack Lynch as Taoiseach between 1966 and 1973.

5. Outline the impact of events in Northern Ireland on public life in the Republic up to 1973.

A Greater Sense of Freedom

The economic progress witnessed in Ireland during the 1960s was accompanied by extensive changes throughout society. To understand these changes, it is important to appreciate the significance of greater wealth throughout the community. In effect, higher incomes allowed ordinary

Dublin around 1960

people a greater degree of choice in their lives. They could socialise more, buy more consumer goods and form their own opinions on the basis of information received from the mass media, particularly from the newly established television service.

As more and more people found jobs in towns and cities, many of the traditional restrictions on their lifestyles were weakened. In country areas it was easier for parents and other older members of the community to monitor the lifestyle of the young. The greater anonymity of towns and cities meant greater freedom for the youth of the 1960s.

In addition to the growing affluence and urbanisation of Irish society during the 1960s, other strong forces were at work and were leading to greater choice and freedom for the individual. One of the most important of these was the radical transformation in education.

Education – A Period of Major Change

Glaring inadequacies in the Irish education system were revealed in an OECD report entitled *Investment in Education*, which was published in 1965. Using detailed statistics, the authors of the report highlighted a lack of resources in education and unequal provision throughout the country. Huge disparities in participation existed between different regions in the country and between different social classes. The report also drew a strong link between economic progress and the availability of an educated workforce. Reform in education became a priority for the Fianna Fáil governments of both Seán Lemass and Jack Lynch. Under a number of young and energetic ministers, the Department of Education assumed a central role in the direction and planning of educational policy. The Department made building grants available to schools and took steps to modernise the curriculum.

Donagh O'Malley, the minister who introduced free post-primary education

The most significant change of all came with the introduction of free post-primary education in 1967. This was the scheme of the Minister for Education, Donogh O'Malley. Most secondary schools

A new community school built after the introduction of free post-primary education

entered the Free Education Scheme and no longer charged fees to their pupils. Although the number of pupils in second-level schools had been increasing steadily during the 1960s, the introduction of free education led to a huge expansion in the sector. Enrolment in post-primary schools rose from 148,000 in 1966–7 to 185,000 in 1968–9, and by 1974 it had reached a figure of 239,000.

During the 1960s the state assumed a much more active role in education and challenged the control of the churches. This was clearly seen in the establishment of new, state-owned schools, known as community schools.

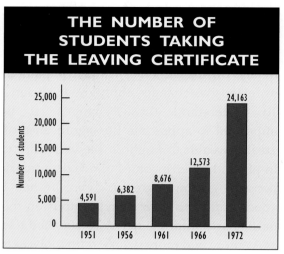

THE NUMBER OF STUDENTS TAKING THE LEAVING CERTIFICATE

Some significant reforms also took place in third-level education. New regional technical colleges (RTCs) established during these years offered a more practical and technological education than the traditional universities. In 1968 grants for third-level education were introduced for students whose parents' income was below a certain level. As with the introduction of free second-level education, the provision of university grants contributed to greater educational access in the years ahead.

The reforms in education led to the emergence of a more critical and questioning society in Ireland. This trend was also powerfully influenced by major reforms in the Catholic Church.

The Second Vatican Council, 1962–5

Kevin Street College of Technology in Dublin, which was modernised during the late 1960s

Because the population of the Republic of Ireland was about 95 per cent Catholic, any changes in that Church were bound to have a significant impact on Irish society. As we have seen in Chapter 18, the Catholic Church in Ireland remained deeply conservative throughout the 1950s. The last major public event of the traditional Catholic Church took place in the Patrician Year of 1961. This was the 1,500th anniversary of the death of St Patrick, and it was marked by the arrival of a papal legate and splendid ceremonies throughout the country. However, by then plans were in progress in Rome that would radically change the role of the Catholic Church in Irish society.

In 1958 the conservative Pope Pius XII died and was replaced by Pope John XXIII. To the surprise of many, this

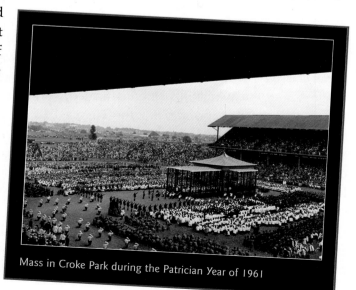

Mass in Croke Park during the Patrician Year of 1961

elderly Pope turned out to be one of the most radical in history. He believed that the Catholic Church needed to change and reform, and he called the Second Vatican Council (1962–5) to examine in detail the condition of the Catholic Church and to plan its role in the future.

The Council ordered the most detailed and thorough reform in the Church since the Council of Trent four hundred years previously. It stressed that the Church consisted of the whole people of God, not just of bishops, priests and nuns. It placed a new emphasis on the role of lay people. It ordered that the Mass be said in the vernacular, or ordinary, languages of the people instead of in Latin. Perhaps the most radical departure initiated by Vatican II was in its approach to other Christians. They were now to be regarded as brothers and sisters in Christ and treated with respect. This approach is known as ecumenism and stresses the agreement between Catholics and other Christians rather than their differences. The Council expressed the hope that all Christians would eventually become united in a spirit of peace and friendship.

These changes were to have a profound effect on the Catholic Church in Ireland. As lay people grew more confident, they began to criticise bishops and priests if they disagreed with them. This was practically unheard of in Ireland before the 1960s, where Church leaders were concerned. For the first time, priests, and later bishops, came on radio and television programmes to discuss religious issues with lay people. The downgrading of the Latin language would also affect the education system. Up to the 1960s knowledge of Latin was required for entry to most faculties in the universities. After this requirement was removed, most schools replaced Latin with modern continental European languages.

The decree of Vatican II on ecumenism led to better relations between the Catholic and Protestant churches in Ireland. Before this, the Catholic Church had very strict rules forbidding its members from attending services in Protestant churches. For example, when Douglas Hyde, a member of the Church of Ireland and the first President of Ireland, died in 1949, members of the Government had to stand outside St Patrick's Cathedral to pay their respects. During the 1960s these old attitudes changed. Catholics and Protestants were allowed to visit each other's churches and to conduct joint ecumenical services. These services took place especially during Church Unity Week between 18 and 25 January each year. The Catholic Church also relaxed its strict rules concerning mixed marriages, i.e. marriage between Catholics and members of other religions.

Despite the hope created by the Second Vatican Council, however, the Catholic Church faced certain difficulties during the 1960s. Higher incomes, greater job opportunities and more freedom led to a decline in the number of vocations to the priesthood and religious life from the middle of the 1960s onwards. Certain bishops and priests were slow to implement reforms at local level. In Ireland, as elsewhere in the Western world, controversy arose when Pope Paul VI (1963–78) issued *Humanae Vitae* in July 1968. This was a papal encyclical that condemned artificial methods of birth control. It sparked a lively debate among Catholics in Ireland as well as in other countries, with many Catholics rejecting the Pope's teaching on this matter. The traditional, authoritarian, united Catholic Church in Ireland had become a feature of the past.

Alongside the transformation of the Catholic Church in Ireland in the 1960s, and indeed contributing to that transformation, was another powerful force for change: the exciting new medium of television.

Case Study: The Impact of RTÉ, 1962–72

In 1958 the Government set up a commission to examine the possibility of setting up an Irish television service. At that time only a small number of people on the east coast tuned in to British television stations. The broadcasting commission issued a favourable report in May 1959, and in 1960 the Government passed the Broadcasting Authority Act. The Act set up the Radio Éireann Authority, which had power to operate both radio and television services. Overall control remained in the hands of the Minister for Posts and Telegraphs.

On 31 December 1961 the new Irish television service, called Telefís Éireann, broadcast for the first time.

Continuity announcer Kathleen Watkins at the opening of Telefís Éireann on 31 December 1961

Document 1

The inauguration of Telefís Éireann

Irish television went on the air for the first time on the last, cold, night of December 1961.

At Donnybrook, the celebrities picked their way through pools of mud to reach the half-completed studio building. In O'Connell Street, outside-broadcast cameras panned across the crowds near the Gresham Hotel. Inside the hotel, 'a tremendous party' was in progress under the observing eyes of another pair of cameras.

The festivities in O'Connell Street were 'live' and punctuated an evening's transmission of otherwise largely recorded material. The station opened with the Anthem at seven o'clock.

The traditional national proprieties were observed.

President Éamon de Valera inaugurated the service. The Taoiseach, Seán Lemass, and the Minister, Michael Hilliard, 'also spoke'. The Archbishop of Dublin, Most Rev. Dr McQuaid, gave Benediction. The actors added their *imprimatur*: Siobhán McKenna and Micheál Mac Liammóir.

The show was on.

Jimmy O'Dea, Maureen Potter, Mary O'Hara, Dermot O'Brien's Céilí Band gave a céad míle fáilte. The Newsroom contributed film of major events throughout the country. The three women continuity announcers led a tour to 'Meet the People'. Every so often the 300,000 audience at 35,000 sets were whisked back to the Gresham to see the spree.

To mark the occasion, there were no advertisements.

Among those who must have watched with special interest were Eamonn Andrews, Chairman of the Authority, Edward Roth, Jnr., Director-General, and Michael Barry, Controller of Programmes.

It was half past midnight before the little white dot shimmied from the screen. As the floor manager, Charlie Roberts, counted down the last few seconds to the New Year on the floor of the Gresham ballroom, the newspapers were preparing to tell a bemused and bedazzled television audience what they thought of the night's doings.

Lelia Doolan, Jack Dowling and Bob Quinn, *Sit Down and Be Counted: The Cultural Evolution of a Television Station,* **Dublin: Wellington 1969, 3**

After the successful opening night of Telefís Éireann, life in Ireland would never be the same again. Up to this time, most homes were dependent on a radio or wireless set for live news and entertainment. The Irish radio service had begun in 1926. However, even in 1960 it broadcast for only a limited number of hours each day, and the style of presentation was usually formal. Controversial discussions involving leaders of Church or state were unheard of.

One of the immediate effects of television was to bring distant persons and places into the living rooms of ordinary people. The religious affairs series *Radharc* was a good example of this. The programme won several awards and made a number of visits to missions in Africa and South America. Before this, most Irish people could only read about life in these countries. Now, through the medium of television, their horizons were broadened, and they could actually see what conditions were like for their fellow human beings in the developing world. One of the presenters of *Radharc*, Fr Joseph Dunn, has written of his experiences of film-making in Africa.

As well as introducing Irish viewers to foreign cultures, the new television service had a significant influence on the culture and values of the Irish people themselves. It is important to realise that from the 1960s onwards Telefís Éireann both expressed the values of Irish society and helped to bring about changes in these values. Many of the home-produced situation comedy programmes in particular attempted to show what life was like for ordinary people. The earliest of these was *Tolka Row*, which was set in Dublin and

A scene from *Tolka Row*, an early popular Telefís Éireann soap with a city setting

The Riordans was a soap set in rural Ireland

Document 2

Filming for *Radharc* in Africa

Our first big trip abroad was to Africa. There were several other visits in later years, but the memories of the first one have lasted the longest.

We prepared for about six months, reading everything from Elspeth Huxley to technical data on how to keep lenses and film from going mouldy in tropical countries.

Because we were going on the missions, however temporarily, we were entitled to go by Raptim, a Dutch charitable agency which subsidises missionary travel: This meant going Dublin/Amsterdam/Nairobi return for £66, a very good price even then.

One of the things that made the 1965 trip memorable is the fact that we were witnessing the beginning of the sudden transition of people like the Pokot and Turkana from a stone age to a high technological culture.

One day we recorded a group of Pokot women singing and then played it back. They had never seen or heard or imagined a tape recorder before.

Less than five years later, when I was next in Africa, I noticed a big change. Driving in East Pokot, we stopped the land-rover to talk to a young boy looking after grazing cattle. He had a few brown rags about his middle, a stick to goad the cattle and a small transistor. He told us that the first man had landed that day on the moon.

Radharc in Africa

Five programmes were eventually produced under this title. Two of them concerned themes which we would pick up again in other countries. 'New Voices' dealt with the struggles of a church which wants to be part of its own people, rather than a carbon copy of a European original. 'The Problems' dealt with the concerns of the church in a very new situation. Independence was a watershed in the history of the Kenya mission, and in 1965 missionaries were trying to come to terms with it.

The other programmes dealt with different areas of mission in which Irish people were involved: 'Kikuyu Country', homeland for the dominant tribe in Kenya, 'Forbidden Valley', where the Suk tribe lived, and 'Turkana'.

I remember looking at a print of 'Turkana' on Christmas morning 1965 in a flat in my mother's house where I was then living and working, and saying to myself aloud, 'You've made at least one interesting film.' The Turkana – a tall good-looking people untouched by the twentieth century; famine in the land; young Irish nuns flying aeroplanes here and there to bring them succour. It was sure-fire material and we didn't need to be great artists to put together a good story.

'Turkana' won the UNDA international award at Monte Carlo, and was shown on BBC, CBS (Canada) and in the USA, Belgium, West Germany, Holland and New Zealand.

Joseph Dunn, *No Tigers in Africa: Recollections and Reflections on 25 Years of Radharc*, Dublin: Columba 1986, 46, 55–6

Gay Byrne hosting a discussion on one of the first *Late Late Shows*

followed the lives of the fictional Nolan family and their friends and neighbours. This was followed a few years later by a series set in the countryside in Co. Kilkenny. Entitled *The Riordans*, it concerned the lives of members of a fictional farming family and their community.

However, one programme in particular had a profound and sustained impact on Irish society from the 1960s onwards. This was the *Late Late Show*, produced and presented by the accomplished broadcaster Gay Byrne.

The *Late Late Show*, which began in July 1962, six months after the opening of Telefís Éireann, was a chat show filmed before an invited audience. It frequently dealt with controversial topics that had rarely been discussed in public before. In his account of the first ten years of the show, Gay Byrne explained how it originated.

Document 3

The start of the *Late Late Show*

Tom McGrath contacted me and said he wanted to do a quiz on Saturday nights called *Jackpot* and would I act as compere and I agreed. Then shortly afterwards he again told me that he was placing a late-night talk show as a summer filler, something on the lines of the Jack Parr show in the States (Tom had come home from Canadian Television to RTÉ) and he wanted me to host that as well. This was all in the first year of RTÉ. We did a first dry-run of the show in June 1962. This went very well, and we decided to go into production on 6 July 1962, for a few months, as a summer filler only.

That was the first live *Late Late Show*, and that's how it all started.

In my opening announcement on that first night I told viewers roughly what we had in mind and what the show was about: *I warned them that because it was totally ad-lib and unscripted and off the cuff, they must expect the built-in disadvantages of such a format: we did not know what anyone was going to say at any particular time, so they must not expect 'balance'.* Sometimes, I warned them, the show would be interesting, informative, entertaining and amusing. On other occasions, it would bore them stiff. Some nights, they would hear gems of wit and wisdom, other nights they would be dropped into the middle of a holiday for clichés. Some nights, I warned them, they would love it, and on others it would be far better for all concerned if they took their cocoa with them and went to bed. *The one thing I asked them not to do was sit it out to the bitter end and then phone in to complain.* I reckon now that my opening announcement was remarkably prophetic and still pretty well applies after ten years. Not, of course, that anyone paid any attention to it.

Gay Byrne, *To Whom It Concerns: Ten Years of the Late Late Show*, Dublin: Gill & Macmillan 1972, 18–19

Two issues in particular were to prove extremely controversial on the *Late Late Show* – religion and the Irish language. Whenever they were discussed, the telephone lines were busy with people complaining, and the programme team received many critical letters. A typical example of a controversial *Late Late Show* occurred on 26 March 1966, when a Trinity College student, Brian Trevaskis, criticised the Catholic Bishop of Galway, Dr Michael Browne, for spending a vast sum on a new cathedral, which Trevaskis declared to be of poor architectural merit. *The Sunday Press*, on the following day, reported the controversy in detail.

Document 4

Late Late controversy

Audience joins heated debate

TE [Telefís Éireann] rumpus

There were heated interjections from the studio audience during the *Late Late Show* on Telefís Éireann last night, and at one stage a spectator said to Gay Byrne: 'I think it is up to you Mr Byrne to stop characters coming up here to slag the clergy.' Gay Byrne instantly replied: 'Wait a minute. I do not bring people in here to slag the clergy. We have a programme and we are proud of it as a programme on which you are allowed to say what you want.'

Dublin University student and playwright, Brian Trevaskis, who appeared as a member of the panel, referred to Galway's new cathedral as 'a ghastly monstrosity'. In a city which did not have such things as a theatre or art galleries the people were having to pay for this monstrosity.

He added: 'I don't blame the people of Galway – I would rather blame the Bishop of Galway.' Referring to the celebration of the fiftieth anniversary of the 1916 Rising, he added that the Constitution had guaranteed equal rights and equal opportunities for all our citizens. One man who tried to achieve this was Dr Noël Browne, but the Archbishop of Dublin had put back the image of Ireland from fifty to one hundred years.

Compere Gay Byrne interjected: 'We are getting into a hell of a belt at the clergy which goes on from time to time.' Wesley Burrowes of *The Riordans* television programme, who was a guest on the show, interjected to say that he also thought the cathedral was a monstrosity, but he thought Mr Trevaskis could not blame the Bishop for that – its design was a matter of architecture.

Mr Trevaskis: 'We are sending missionaries all over the world to convert people to Irish Christianity. I think it is about time we applied Christianity to our own country. We have just had another martyr chopped off a few months ago – John McGahern, and because he wrote a certain book with which a certain parish priest did not agree he lost his job, and this was right because His Grace said so.'

A member of the studio audience rose and said: 'The people from where I come from – Ballygarvan, County Cork, would not listen to you speaking so degradingly about our Churches and Bishops. I am glad to say at the moment that our clergy are renovating our cathedral and I have never heard anyone say that they would not contribute to the building or renovating of it, and we all hope to see a magnificent building when it is finished.' Another member of the audience said he thought Mr Trevaskis spoke a bit harshly, but he was glad to see he was not afraid to express his opinions.

Mr Byrne: 'In all fairness, we would agree with you when you say he was a bit harsh.'

Another spectator: 'I do not think it takes a lot of courage to smite at the clergy and the bishops from the privileged position in which this man (Mr Trevaskis) is at present. I think it is up to you (Mr Byrne) to stop characters coming up here to slag the clergy.'

Mr Byrne: 'Wait a minute. I do not bring people in here to slag the clergy. We have a programme and we are proud of it in which you are allowed to say what you want to say.'

Another member of the audience who said his name was Ronald Handcock from Cork then rose and said he thought Mr Trevaskis was right in his criticism, and he agreed that Ireland had developed very little since the Proclamation. 'I support Brian as a progressive member of the youth of Ireland,' he said.

The Sunday Press, 27 March 1966

As a result of the controversy some county councils throughout the country passed resolutions condemning the *Late Late Show*. Throughout the 1960s the show was frequently condemned from the pulpit by priests during Sunday sermons. Many churchmen found it hard to adjust to the new era in which people now questioned established rules and regulations.

The *Late Late Show* was often the first place where controversial topics such as divorce and family planning were openly discussed. On one famous occasion the Fine Gael TD for Laois–Offaly, Oliver J. Flanagan, remarked that there was no sex in Ireland before television, implying that there was no open discussion of the matter before the arrival of programmes such as the *Late Late Show*.

In reviewing the role played by the *Late Late Show* in Irish life during its first ten years between 1962 and 1972, Gay Byrne placed particular emphasis on the fact that it allowed the open expression of different points of view.

Document 5

The search for balance

They tell me, the historians and writers and people who know about such things, that when the history of Ireland for the next fifty years comes to be written, television in general and the *Late Late Show* in particular will be mentioned as having been a tremendous force for change in the community, although we in the *Late Late Show* were never supposed to come under the headings of 'information', 'education' or 'uplift'. Such lofty ideals are better left to those who know about them. 'Broadening the horizons' and 'letting in fresh air' are two of the phrases thrown around like snuff at a wake. I'm sure they are right, but I'd rather they said it and not me.

One of the things which this programme has done to me is to deprive me of the luxury of ever having only one point of view about anything; give me a man who has an opinion about something and by tomorrow morning I'll produce ten men who will disagree with him. And they will all fiercely resent the other being allowed to speak. I envy those who can make up their minds, and then get the head down and go for broke, looking neither left nor right and hearing not the voices of dissent on either side. When one is producing television programmes, one is reminded forcefully and regularly that there are two sides to every story, and the depressing thing is that when you try honestly to present those two sides, you very quickly discover that there are another two you hadn't dreamed of.

In fifteen years of radio and television I have never been able to find out what balance is. I only know that 'lack of balance' is when anyone gets up and says anything a politician disagrees with. When a Fianna Fáil man comes along and congratulates me on a job well done and tells me that I have achieved a 'balance', I know precisely what he means. He means thank God that shower from Fine Gael and Labour never got a chance to get a word in. The only trouble is that as soon as he's gone both of the other two are screaming at me about 'lack of balance' and about programmes which are a disgrace and an affront to Irish viewers. It is quite astonishing the number of people in this country who are firmly convinced that they have a God-given mandate to speak on behalf of the nation.

Gay Byrne, *To Whom It Concerns: Ten Years of the Late Late Show*, Dublin: Gill & Macmillan 1972, 158–60

It is clear, therefore, that between 1962 and 1972 the *Late Late Show* was one of the most influential and controversial of all television programmes on Telefís Éireann. Another important subject of controversy was the station's coverage of current affairs.

Under the terms of the Broadcasting Authority Act (1960), the station had to provide fair and unbiased coverage of current affairs. The Act declared that the national broadcasting service had to ensure that

> The broadcast treatment of current affairs, including matters which are either of public controversy or the subject of current public debate, is fair to all interests concerned and that the broadcast matter is presented in an objective and impartial manner and without any expression of the Authority's own views.

During elections, Telefís Éireann showed party political broadcasts by the various parties. It also ensured that the different parties were given fair representation on television programmes during election campaigns. The advent of television produced a gradual change in the methods of electioneering. The old-style mass meetings in towns and cities and the election addresses outside church gates became less important. Instead the voters could see the spokespersons for the political parties discussing the issues on television.

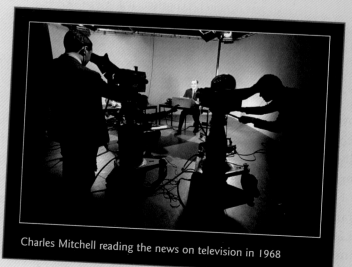

Charles Mitchell reading the news on television in 1968

The main current affairs programmes in the 1960s were news broadcasts and the *Seven Days* programme. It was in programmes such as these that government intervention was most likely. In 1966 the radio and television stations were renamed Radio Telefís Éireann (RTÉ). In the same year a memorable clash occurred between the television station and the Minister for Agriculture in the Fianna Fáil Government, Charles J. Haughey. At the time there was a serious dispute between the Department of Agriculture and the farmers, who were represented by the National Farmers' Association (NFA). Haughey objected to the coverage of the situation on the television news bulletin. The following is an account of the events from the point of view of RTÉ journalists.

Document 6

Charles J. Haughey and RTÉ

The telephone rang on 2nd October 1966 in the Newsroom.

Mr C.J. Haughey was on the line, complaining about the juxtaposition of a statement from the National Farmers' Association with one of his own. The NFA had advised the farmers to sell the cattle which Mr Haughey had advised them to hold.

The complaint was in vigorous terms, no doubt. Mr Haughey does nothing by three-quarters. Both statements had appeared in the main News bulletin. The Duty-Editor telephoned the Head of News at home and the NFA statement was deleted from the following bulletins. 'All hell' broke loose.

The National Union of Journalists met to discuss the incident which was reported in the following morning's papers. The Minister for Agriculture said that he had felt compelled in the public interest to protest that the NFA statement should have been carried immediately after his. 'I gave specific advice to farmers in reply to questions from Deputies in the Dáil . . . and I felt that to have my advice followed by a contradiction from a [farming] organisation could only lead to confusion and damage the industry.'

The NFA said it was amazed at the Ministerial intervention.

The *Irish Times* was amazed that Mr Haughey's telephone call had succeeded. It asked whether he had any right to ring the Newsroom at Montrose. RTÉ, it pointed out, had immediately complied with the request.

The NUJ was amazed. It was already considering what union action it could take.

Staff generally were not amazed. They were uneasy and disturbed.

Lelia Doolan, Jack Dowling and Bob Quinn, *Sit Down and Be Counted:
The Cultural Evolution of a Television Station*, Dublin: Wellington 1969, 85–7

The intervention by Charles Haughey was not an isolated incident. Because RTÉ was a public company, funded by the taxpayers, the Government had overall responsibility for it. Seán Lemass as Taoiseach had made this quite clear when he stated in Dáil Éireann:

> RTÉ was set up by legislation as an instrument of public policy and as such was responsible to the Government. The Government had overall responsibility for its conduct and especially the obligation to ensure that its programmes do not offend against the public interest, or conflict with national policy as defined in legislation . . .
>
> To this extent the Government reject the view that RTÉ should be, either generally or in regard to its current affairs programmes and news programmes, completely independent of Government supervision.

Normally, however, the Government exercised restraint when dealing with RTÉ in order to avoid being accused of exerting undue political pressure on the organisation. Nevertheless, in times of crisis the Government bore the ultimate responsibility for the actions of the broadcasters. This ultimate power was used in November 1972, when the Government of Jack Lynch sacked the RTÉ Authority as a result of the broadcast of an interview with Seán Mac Stiofáin of the Provisional IRA. The RTÉ journalist who interviewed him, Kevin O'Kelly, was sentenced to three months' imprisonment for refusing to identify his source. As the Troubles in Northern Ireland continued, the

Government of the Republic was careful to ensure that RTÉ radio and television did not broadcast the views of people who advocated the use of violence in Northern Ireland.

The expansion of television in Ireland in the first ten years of the new service had been remarkable. At the outset, in 1961, only 30,000 homes out of a total of 700,000 were believed to be watching British television channels. By 1966, 380,000 homes were receiving RTÉ, and this increased to 536,000 by 1971. As many of the programmes originated in England or the United States of America, the culture of these countries was increasingly influential in Ireland. Often the ideas broadcast were materialist and consumerist. In advertisements and in programmes, people were given the message that wealth and spending were glamorous. Influences such as these, together with greater freedom of expression, marked television out as a new and powerful force in Irish society.

CASE STUDY: QUESTIONS

COMPREHENSION

1. According to Document 1, when did Irish television first go on air?

2. How did the new station open at seven o'clock (Document 1)?

3. Who inaugurated the service (Document 1)?

4. What were the newspapers preparing to do, according to Document 1?

5. How did the author of Document 2 prepare for his first trip to Africa?

6. Why, according to the writer in Document 2, was the 1965 trip to Africa memorable?

7. Explain the change that the author of Document 2 experienced on returning to Africa five years after the first trip.

8. Explain why he considers 'Turkana' to be a good film (Document 2).

9. When was the *Late Late Show* first broadcast (Document 3)?

10. What has the author of Document 3 to say about 'balance'?

11. What was 'the one thing' that the author of Document 3 asked the television audience not to do?

12. What complaint was made by a spectator at the start of Document 4?

13. Outline the reply of Gay Byrne to this complaint (Document 4).

14. What complaint did Brian Trevaskis make concerning Galway (Document 4)?

15. Whom did he blame for this situation (Document 4)?

16. What had Trevaskis to say about the Catholic Archbishop of Dublin, Dr John Charles McQuaid (Document 4)?

17. What complaint did Brian Trevaskis make about the treatment of the author John McGahern (Document 4)?

18. Explain the views of the man from Co. Cork (Document 4).

19. What has Gay Byrne been told about how history would view the *Late Late Show* (Document 5)?

20. How has the programme influenced his belief concerning differing points of view (Document 5)?

21. How does Gay Byrne define 'lack of balance' (Document 5)?

22. Explain the final sentence in Document 5.

23. What was Charles Haughey's complaint to RTÉ in Document 6?

24. What action did the Head of News take following this complaint (Document 6)?

25. How did the Minister for Agriculture defend his actions (Document 6)?

26. What action did the National Union of Journalists (NUJ) take (Document 6)?

27. Explain the comments of the *Irish Times* (Document 6).

28. How did the staff at RTÉ react (Document 6)?

COMPARISON

1. Compare the description of the opening night of Telefís Éireann (Document 1) with that of a controversial *Late Late Show* (Document 4).

2. Both Document 2 and Document 6 are first-hand accounts of the experiences of broadcasters. Which do you find more interesting? Support your answer by referring to the documents.

3. Illustrate how the concerns of Gay Byrne in Document 5 relate to the controversy described in Document 4.

4. Compare the references to politics and politicians in Documents 5 and 6.

CRITICISM

1. Would you consider Document 1 to be a clear, well-ordered, factual account of events? Explain your answer.

2. Show how Document 2 is concerned with the theme of change. How well does the author convey this?

3. What is the effect of the repeated use of 'I' in Document 3?

4. How effective is Document 4 in conveying opposing points of view?

5. List three means used by Gay Byrne in Document 5 to make his points effectively.

6. Would you regard Document 6 as a biased account? Explain your answer.

CONTEXTUALISATION

1. Write an account of the foundation of Telefís Éireann.

2. Assess the contribution of the *Late Late Show* to the development of Irish society between 1962 and 1972.

3. Write a paragraph on the relations between the Government and RTÉ.

4. Compare the changes introduced by the Second Vatican Council with the changes facilitated by television in Ireland between 1962 and 1972.

Changing Lifestyles

One of the most significant developments in Irish society during the 1960s was the emergence of a distinctive youth culture. Modelled on the experience of young people in America and England, it featured a preference for pop music and the latest fashions in clothes. When the pop group The Beatles visited Dublin in November 1963, they received a rapturous welcome from their Irish fans. The most popular Irish music groups during the 1960s were the showbands. Stars such as Dickie Rock, Brendan Bowyer and Eileen Reid attracted thousands when they played for dances. They also performed on records, radio and on the new medium of television.

New fashions on the streets of Ireland during the 1960s

The new, more confident assertion of identity on the part of young people was not confined to leisure alone. As improvements in communication made them more aware of injustice throughout the world, they took to the streets in protest. One cause that attracted particular attention during the 1960s and 1970s was the abolition of apartheid in South Africa. Although older people were also involved in the Irish anti-apartheid campaigns, students and other young people were usually the mainstay of public demonstrations. Young people also protested against the destruction of Georgian Dublin by property developers and campaigned in favour of better educational opportunities. Their political importance was recognised when the electorate passed a referendum in 1972 that lowered the voting age from twenty-one to eighteen.

The Beatles in Dublin in 1963

The prosperity achieved during the 1960s allowed the Fianna Fáil Government to improve the provision of health and social welfare. The health service was re-organised, with the introduction of regional health boards, the building of new hospitals and the employment of more staff. The introduction of the medical card was a major improvement in health provision for the less well off. They were no longer compelled to go to a dispensary doctor but could choose their own general practitioner (GP) and receive free medical care and prescriptions. In the area of social welfare, the introduction of free travel for senior citizens by Minister for Finance Charles Haughey was a milestone in the provision of services for the elderly. Although of limited benefit in rural areas, it was widely availed of by pensioners in towns and cities.

Although significant advances towards equal treatment of women in Irish society only took place from the 1970s onwards, the position of women was

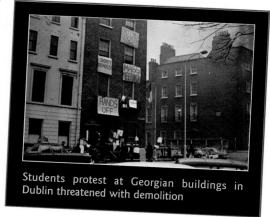
Students protest at Georgian buildings in Dublin threatened with demolition

The 1960s saw the development of large suburban estates on the outskirts of cities as more people became home-owners

beginning to improve during the 1960s. Greater wealth and the arrival of modern conveniences such as vacuum cleaners and washing machines lightened the workload of women in the home. Those who worked outside the home benefited from a gradual improvement in wages, although women's average wage still lagged behind that of men. With the gradual decline in the older, stricter notions of behaviour, women were less under the control of their fathers or husbands. One obvious sign of their newfound freedom was the widespread popularity of the miniskirt during the 1960s.

It was a period of rapid change in transport and travel, both domestic and foreign. At home many railway lines were closed down because they were considered uneconomic. As a result, both passengers and goods had to travel by road. The number of motor cars grew steadily throughout the 1960s as the country grew wealthier. Foreign travel became more widely available at the same time, as people could afford to fly to Spain and other sunny destinations. The national airline, Aer Lingus, symbolised the new confidence of Irish society during the 1960s. It greatly expanded its services, and its aeroplanes and staff were regarded as representatives of Irish hospitality abroad.

Whereas many of the social developments in Ireland during the 1960s were positive, others caused unease. Greater wealth often produced a materialistic outlook and the loss of a distinctive

An Aer Lingus plane being refuelled at Dublin Airport during the 1960s

Irish cultural identity. The continuing decline of the Gaeltacht at a time of economic expansion was a cause of concern. Many people also expressed the fear that, partly because of television, Irish people were becoming too heavily influenced by the cultures of America and England, to the neglect of their own traditions. Despite the unprecedented economic expansion and the significant growth in employment, many people continued to live out their lives in poverty, which was made all the more unbearable by the sight of prosperity all around them.

Even with these shortcomings, however, the 1960s are remembered as a time of exceptional prosperity and a period of greater choice and freedom in Irish society.

KEY PERSONALITY: GAY BYRNE (1934–)

Gay Byrne was born in Dublin on 5 August 1934 and educated by the Christian Brothers at Synge Street. He started his career in insurance but soon became involved in broadcasting, becoming a presenter on Radio Éireann in 1958. He did some work for Granada Television in Manchester and for the BBC, but after the establishment of RTÉ in 1961, he worked increasingly and eventually totally for the home station.

Gay Byrne became most famous as the producer and host of the *Late Late Show*, the longest-running live television chat show in the world. The first *Late Late Show* was broadcast on 6 July 1962. The programme was an important agent for social change in Ireland in the 1960s and 1970s. While reflecting the changing values of Irish society, it also acted as a catalyst for change and modernisation by providing a forum for the discussion of controversial topics previously considered off-limits for debate. Subjects of public and personal morality, including contraception, abortion and divorce, were aired for the first time on the *Late Late Show*. Although Byrne himself held conventional, conservative views on many subjects, his programme played an important role in creating a more open, outward-looking society in Ireland.

In addition to his work in television, Gay Byrne also made an important impact through his radio programmes. His most popular daily programme was the *Gay Byrne Show*, which began broadcasting in 1972. Many people, especially women, wrote to the programme about their personal and family problems, thus providing an insight into the lives of hardship endured by many ordinary people.

Gay Byrne has received numerous awards for his contribution to Irish broadcasting, including six Jacob's Awards, a Golden Award and, in 1988, an honorary doctorate from Trinity College, Dublin. He was TV presenter of the Rose of Tralee festival for seventeen years and is the author of two books: *To Whom It Concerns* (1972) and his autobiography, *The Time of My Life* (1988). Although he retired as host of the *Late Late Show* in 1999, he has continued to do some work in broadcasting, both on radio and on television.

KEY PERSONALITY: BREANDÁN Ó hEITHIR (1930–91)

Breandán Ó hEithir — writer and broadcaster — was born on the Aran island of Inishmore in 1930. A nephew of the writer Liam O'Flaherty, he was educated at Coláiste Éinde, Co. Galway, and at UCG. He began his career in journalism, becoming editor of the Irish-language section of the *Irish Press* from 1957 to 1973. He was also editor of an Irish magazine, *Comhar*.

Ó hEithir became best known as one of the main journalists working on the Irish-language politics programme, *Féach*, and played an important role in modernising Irish for television. An active participant in the Irish language movement, he helped it to shed its conservative and anti-British image. He had a lifelong interest in sport, especially Gaelic games.

Throughout his career Ó hEithir remained a prolific commentator on Irish life, and his many publications in Irish and English include *Lig Sinn i gCathú* (1977), *Over the Bar: A Personal Relationship with the GAA* (1984) and *The Begrudger's Guide to Irish Politics* (1986). He died in 1991.

ORDINARY LEVEL

1. Write an account of changes in education during the 1960s.

2. Outline the impact that the Second Vatican Council, 1962–5, had on the Catholic Church in Ireland.

3. Read the following description by Gay Byrne of Irish television viewers, and answer the questions that follow.

> I was beginning also to realise a startling truth about the Irish viewer. Many people had praised the *Late Late Show* for its quality of free speech; I was naïve enough to think they meant it – that what they wanted was free speech. But it now slowly began to dawn on me that free speech was all right as long as the talker was saying what they wanted to hear – anything else was some weird kind of licence or obscenity or just 'lack of balance'. Of course, one must realise that at that time television was a very new toy and Irish people generally were still attaching far more importance to it than the average British viewer, and, in my opinion, far more importance than it deserved. Now, ten years later, the medium had begun to find its own level and people have begun to live with it, accept it for what it is, and have become a little more discerning about what it portrays. Although still to far too many people the cursed box is the all-embracing drug they cannot do without, worse than drink or tobacco or gambling. It is as if, having paid the annual licence fee, they are hell-bent on getting the maximum value for money, and so the box is lit up at six o'clock and stays on until midnight and close-down. They will sit there in front of it in a state bordering on stupefaction and take anything it cares to dish up.
>
> *Gay Byrne, To Whom It Concerns:*
> *Ten Years of the Late Late Show, Dublin:*
> *Gill & Macmillan 1972*

(i) Did viewers really want free speech on the *Late Late Show*? Explain your answer.

(ii) What is meant by the phrase 'new toy'?

(iii) How has the situation changed ten years later, according to the author?

(iv) Why does he compare the television set to a drug?

(v) Describe the actions of people who leave the television set on all the time.

4. Explain how the Government set about establishing an Irish television service, and describe the opening night of Telefís Éireann.

5. Show how television broadened the experience of Irish viewers during the 1960s.

6. Write an account of the *Late Late Show* during the early years of Irish television.

7. What was the relationship between the Government and RTÉ? Give examples of conflict between government ministers and broadcasters.

8. How did the lifestyle of young people in Ireland change during the 1960s?

HIGHER LEVEL

1. Outline the changes in Irish education during the 1960s, and illustrate their connection with economic development.

2. Discuss the changes in the Catholic Church in Ireland following the Second Vatican Council, 1962–5.

3. Consider the part played by the *Late Late Show* in the transformation of Irish society during the 1960s.

4. Assess the impact of television on political developments in Ireland between 1962 and 1972.

5. 'The rapid transformation of Irish society during the 1960s contained both positive and negative elements.' Discuss.

The General Election of 1973

On 5 February 1973 the Taoiseach, Jack Lynch, took opposition parties by surprise by calling a general election for 28 February. The two main opposition parties, Fine Gael and Labour, had already been in talks for some time. The day after the election was called, Liam Cosgrave, the Fine Gael leader, and Brendan Corish, the leader of the Labour Party, met and agreed to fight the election on a common platform against Fianna Fáil. They offered the electorate an alternative government to Fianna Fáil. If successful, Cosgrave would be Taoiseach and Corish would be Tánaiste. Calling themselves the National Coalition, Fine Gael and Labour placed a Fourteen-Point Plan before the people. Fine Gael inserted commitments on law and order, a peaceful solution to the Northern Ireland problem, Ireland's position in the EEC and the abolition of compulsory Irish. The Labour Party insisted on social reforms, increased levels of house building and the control of prices.

The National Coalition's Fourteen-Point Plan, or manifesto, made public on 14 February, transformed the political situation. For the first time in sixteen years, the people were being offered a real alternative government to Fianna Fáil. This was the first time ever that opposition parties had agreed on a programme before the election and fought a joint campaign. The 1973 election campaign was dominated by economic issues. The public found the National Coalition's proposals attractive, especially the promises to control prices, reduce rates and abolish value-added tax (VAT) on food. Although Fianna Fáil tried to shift the debate to the question of Northern Ireland, most voters were more interested in economic issues. The Coalition parties conducted a very united campaign and enjoyed quite favourable coverage in the press. The Coalition election campaign got off to a flying start, and Fianna Fáil never succeeded in regaining lost ground. Many voters felt that a change was needed after sixteen years of Fianna Fáil Government.

Polling took place on 28 February 1973. The result was quite close. Although Fianna Fáil increased its share of first-preference votes compared with the 1969 election, the party's representation dropped by 6 seats to a total of 69. This was because of the high rate of vote transfers between Fine Gael and Labour candidates. Fine Gael won 54 seats – an increase of 4 – and Labour gained an extra seat to achieve a total of 19 seats. Although the combined total of 73 seats was no landslide victory, it gave the National Coalition an overall majority of 2 and thus enabled it to form a government and remove Fianna Fáil from power after sixteen years.

The New Government

The new Taoiseach, Liam Cosgrave, showed generosity to the Labour Party by offering it five ministries, more than the party was entitled to on the basis of its size. Fine Gael was to hold key ministries such as Finance, Foreign Affairs, Justice, Defence and Education. The Labour leader, Brendan Corish, became Tánaiste and Minister for Health and Social Welfare. Other Labour ministries included Posts and Telegraphs, Industry and Commerce, Local Government, and Labour. The following were the main ministers who served in the Coalition Government:

Taoiseach:	Liam Cosgrave (Fine Gael)
Tánaiste and Minister for Health and Social Welfare:	Brendan Corish (Labour)
Finance:	Richard Ryan (Fine Gael)
Foreign Affairs:	Garret FitzGerald (Fine Gael)
Industry and Commerce:	Justin Keating (Labour)
Justice:	Patrick Cooney (Fine Gael)
Agriculture:	Mark Clinton (Fine Gael)
Posts and Telegraphs:	Conor Cruise O'Brien (Labour)
Labour:	Michael O'Leary (Labour)
Defence:	Patrick Donegan (Fine Gael)
Local Government:	James Tully (Labour)
The Gaeltacht:	Tom O'Donnell (Fine Gael)
Education:	Richard Burke (Fine Gael)
Transport and Power:	Peter Barry (Fine Gael)
Lands:	Tom Fitzpatrick (Fine Gael)

The new Government was widely regarded as being highly talented. Although Fine Gael and Labour had been divided during the 1960s, their unity in the National Coalition was firmly based on the strong political relationship between Liam Cosgrave and Brendan Corish.

The Coalition Government's first few months in office were successful. Its first budget, introduced by the Minister for Finance, Richie Ryan, in April 1973, was regarded as being socially progressive. The harmonious relations between the two parties could be seen in Labour's support for the Fine Gael candidate in the presidential election in May. However, Fine Gael's

The Fine Gael–Labour Coalition Government elected in 1973, pictured with the President, Éamon de Valera. The new Taoiseach, Liam Cosgrave (Fine Gael) is seated on the President's right and the new Tánaiste, Brendan Corish (Labour), is on his left.

candidate, T.F. O'Higgins, was heavily defeated by the Fianna Fáil candidate, Erskine Childers. This was the first setback for the new Government. Later in the same year, it was to face further difficulties with the onset of a worldwide economic crisis.

The Irish Economy

The Arab–Israeli War of October 1973 led directly to a worldwide oil crisis. Oil was in short supply and very expensive. The huge increase in the price of oil in turn caused major economic difficulties in the Western world, including extremely high inflation and unemployment. This situation posed major economic problems for the Irish Government.

Inflation had already been a problem before the oil crisis and was running at 11 per cent during 1973. This was in part due to large wage increases. The rise in prices was greatly accelerated by the onset of the oil crisis. Rising to 17 per cent in 1974 and 21 per cent in 1975, inflation in Ireland

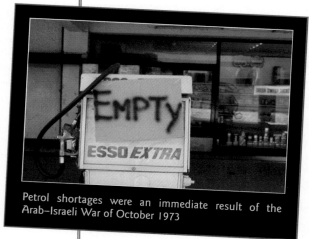

Petrol shortages were an immediate result of the Arab–Israeli War of October 1973

was far higher than in other European countries. To cope with the crisis, the Coalition Government resorted to borrowing from foreign banks. The result was a massive increase in borrowing, which rose from 8 per cent of Gross National Product (GNP) in 1973 to 16 per cent in 1975. During Richie Ryan's period as Minister for Finance, Ireland's foreign debt rose from £126 million in March 1973 to £1,040 million at the end of 1976. Unfortunately, most of the Government borrowing was not for productive purposes but served merely to sustain standards of living for those already in work.

Unemployment rose significantly during the economic crisis – from 71,000 in March 1973 (7.9 per cent) to 116,000 in March 1977 (12.5 per cent). The increase was due partly to the oil crisis but partly also to the failure of Irish-owned industries to perform successfully against competitors from within the EEC and from Third World countries.

One of the most controversial economic policies of the Coalition Government was the introduction of a wealth tax. This tax was intended to replace death duties, which had been abolished. These had been unpopular because widows or children were often left with large tax bills, irrespective of their ability to pay. The Minister for Finance, Richie Ryan, introduced a wealth tax in 1974. This affected the very wealthy, who had to pay a 1 per cent tax on incomes of over £100,000. This measure met with huge opposition from wealthy people. Fianna Fáil vigorously opposed the wealth tax and promised to abolish it once the party returned to power.

Queuing for the dole in the 1970s

In the midst of the economic difficulties of these years, there was some hope of future wealth from oil exploration off the Irish coast. The first serious exploration for oil took place under the direction of the Minister for Industry and Commerce, Justin Keating. He was determined to safeguard Irish interests, and he negotiated licensing laws that were favourable to the state. Under the agreement negotiated by Keating with oil exploration companies, the Irish Government had a 50 per cent stake in exploration profits, and all companies exploring for oil would have to operate from an Irish base. During the Coalition's term of office, oil exploration was still at an early stage, and the state did not benefit from any major generation of wealth.

While the Cosgrave Government faced a major economic crisis at home, membership of the EEC provided new opportunities for growth and modernisation.

Ireland and the EEC

When Ireland became a member of the EEC in January 1973, it immediately benefited from the Common Agricultural Policy (CAP). Under this policy Irish farmers enjoyed larger markets and better prices. Although the oil crisis led to a decline in industry and employment, agriculture generally prospered in these years as a result of membership of the EEC. The Minister for

Agriculture, Mark Clinton, achieved good terms for Irish farmers during various negotiations at the headquarters of the EEC in Brussels. By 1978 real incomes in agriculture had doubled compared with 1970. However, the large increase in agricultural prosperity of the mid-1970s would be short-lived. The Government concentrated on making short-term gains and failed to plan for the long-term future of Irish agriculture.

The Department of Foreign Affairs assumed a new role with Irish membership of the EEC. Garret FitzGerald was appointed Minister for Foreign Affairs in the Coalition Government. FitzGerald's ability, sense of idealism, capacity for hard work and fluency in French greatly impressed other foreign ministers within the EEC. As Foreign Minister, he represented Ireland on the powerful Council of Ministers in the EEC. In 1975, when Ireland held the EEC presidency for the first time, FitzGerald was President of the Council of Ministers. His role during this period greatly enhanced Ireland's reputation within the EEC. In addition to raising Ireland's profile within the EEC, FitzGerald, as Minister for Foreign Affairs, was instrumental in forging new links with Great Britain in relation to the problem of Northern Ireland.

Northern Ireland

The problems in Northern Ireland posed a major challenge for the Government of Liam Cosgrave. The violence of the Northern Troubles in the early 1970s led to a reassessment on the part of the Coalition partners, Fine Gael and Labour. The traditional view held by all parties in the South was that partition and the British presence in Northern Ireland were the main cause of the problem. Garret FitzGerald in Fine Gael and Conor Cruise O'Brien in the Labour Party argued strongly for a radical change in attitudes to Northern Ireland. They held the view that reconciliation between the two communities in Northern Ireland should be the priority and that there should be no change in the constitutional status of Northern Ireland without the consent of a majority of its citizens.

The new direction in northern policy was expressed by Liam Cosgrave in a speech he made in 1973, shortly after becoming Taoiseach:

> We must be prepared to recognise the right of the two communities in Northern Ireland
> to set aside their different views of the eventual shape of Irish political institutions and
> to establish institutions that will provide the North with a system of government designed
> to reconcile the two communities in peace and harmony.

This speech was welcomed by the leader of the Unionist Party in Northern Ireland, Brian Faulkner. It was also in line with the views of the British Government, which saw the need for power-sharing between Catholics and Protestants in Northern Ireland. This new approach by the British and Irish governments led to a historic development known as the **Sunningdale Agreement**.

The Sunningdale Agreement, 1973

In March 1972 the British Conservative Government under Prime Minister Edward Heath abolished the Parliament and Government of Northern Ireland and introduced direct rule from London. William Whitelaw was appointed Secretary of State for Northern Ireland and took charge of British rule in the province. Against a background of rising levels of violence, Heath and Whitelaw adopted a twofold approach to the problem of Northern Ireland. On the one hand, they used the British army and the RUC to defeat the IRA. However, they also wished to end direct rule and restore a local parliament in Northern Ireland.

Brian Faulkner, the Ulster Unionist leader (left), with Taoiseach Liam Cosgrave during talks at Sunningdale in 1973

By this stage the British Government had accepted the view of the Irish Government that there should be no return to Unionist majority rule. Instead, they proposed that Northern Ireland should be ruled by a power-sharing government, or executive, which would include both unionist and nationalist representatives. From then on, succeeding British governments refused to devolve power to Northern Ireland unless it was on the basis of power sharing. In 1973 many unionists were opposed to the idea of sharing power with nationalists. However, they were even more alarmed at the other main element of the proposals being discussed – a recognition of an 'Irish dimension', or a role for the Irish Republic in the affairs of Northern Ireland.

The twin elements of a power-sharing executive in Northern Ireland and of a Council of Ireland were the main features of an agreement worked out in December 1973. At a major conference held in Sunningdale Park in England, unionist and nationalist politicians from the North met with the British and Irish governments in an effort to bring peace and stability to Northern Ireland.

The Sunningdale Agreement established an eleven-member power-sharing executive in Northern Ireland, with the Unionist Party leader, Brian Faulkner, at its head. The executive – which consisted of six members of the Unionist Party, four members of the SDLP, including its leader, Gerry Fitt, and one member of the Alliance Party – was to take up office on 1 January 1974. The most difficult and controversial part of the Sunningdale Agreement was the proposed Council of Ireland. The recognition of any Irish role in Northern Ireland's affairs was opposed by most unionists. Northern nationalists and the Irish Government, on the other hand, insisted on the recognition of an Irish dimension in the affairs of Northern Ireland. The Council of Ireland in the Sunningdale Agreement was strongly opposed by unionists. In a subsequent meeting at Hillsborough in Co. Down in February 1974, its functions were defined. In effect it would involve co-operation between North and South in non-controversial areas such as drainage, fisheries and tourism. This did nothing to lessen the opposition of a growing number of unionists to the Sunningdale Agreement.

Members of the Northern Ireland Executive set up under the Sunningdale Agreement in December 1973, including from left, the Unionist leader Brian Faulkner, Gerry Fitt, leader of the SDLP, and his deputy leader John Hume

The Collapse of the Sunningdale Agreement

The high hopes of the Cosgrave Government that the Sunningdale Agreement would lead to a lasting solution to the problem of Northern Ireland were soon to be disappointed. In February 1974 a general election took place in Great Britain and Northern Ireland. Deep divisions emerged within Brian Faulkner's Unionist Party over the Agreement. Anti-Faulkner unionists and followers of the Rev. Ian Paisley had huge success in the general election, winning eleven out of the twelve Westminster seats in Northern Ireland. This greatly weakened the position of Brian Faulkner and the power-sharing executive.

The future of the Sunningdale Agreement was further threatened by a change of government in London. Edward Heath's Conservative Party was defeated by the Labour Party under Harold Wilson. In the face of mounting unionist opposition to the Sunningdale Agreement, Wilson's Labour Government soon abandoned the Agreement. The existence of the Council of Ireland and the continuing IRA campaign of violence hardened the attitudes of unionists against the Sunningdale Agreement.

In May 1974 Protestant workers in Northern Ireland took part in a massive strike organised by the Ulster Workers' Council in order to bring down the power-sharing executive. The British Government failed to stand up to the strikers and allowed the Sunningdale Agreement to collapse.

The short-lived Sunningdale Agreement may be seen as a lost opportunity. It marked a new development in co-operation between Britain and Ireland, between North and South and between unionists and nationalists within Northern Ireland. Its collapse postponed political progress in Northern Ireland for over a decade. However, the Sunningdale Agreement enshrined fundamental principles that were to characterise subsequent agreements on Northern Ireland. These principles included power-sharing, the Irish dimension and the need for majority consent to any change in the constitutional status of Northern Ireland.

Loyalist strikers confront the RUC during the Ulster Workers' Council strike against the Sunningdale Agreement

The Impact of Northern Ireland on Life in the Republic

During the Ulster Workers' Council strike against the Sunningdale Agreement, violence spread to the Republic of Ireland in a very dramatic way. On Friday, 17 May 1974, extreme unionists or loyalists bombed Dublin and Monaghan, killing 28 people instantly and injuring a further 137, several of whom later died. This was the worst terrorist outrage in Ireland or Great Britain during the Northern Ireland conflict. At the same time, the IRA stepped up its activities north and south of the border and posed a growing threat to the Republic itself. Security arrangements for government ministers were tightened considerably in the face of IRA threats to kidnap members of their families. One of the worst IRA atrocities of the period was the murder of Senator Billy Fox of Monaghan, a Fine Gael politician and a member of the Presbyterian Church. A wave of IRA violence appeared to be spreading throughout the country, with bank robberies and prison escapes.

The Cosgrave Government remained steadfast in its determination to uphold law and order and not to compromise in the face of IRA violence. Whereas the British Government negotiated with the IRA and established a temporary ceasefire during Christmas

Death and destruction in Dublin after the loyalist bombings of May 1974

1974, the Coalition Government in Dublin opposed any contacts with the IRA.

One of the most striking examples of the determination of the Cosgrave Government to oppose the IRA was its reaction to the IRA kidnapping of the Dutch industrialist Dr Tiede Herrema in 1975. The Government refused to accede to the demands of the kidnappers, who threatened to kill Herrema unless three IRA prisoners were released. He was released unharmed after a three-week Garda siege at a house in Monasterevin, Co. Kildare.

In July 1976 the IRA murdered the British ambassador, Sir Christopher Ewart-Biggs, by placing a bomb under his car at Sandyford in Co. Dublin. This atrocity shocked the nation and strengthened further the resolve of the Coalition Government to uphold law and order in the face of IRA violence.

The remains of the car in which the British ambassador to Ireland was killed by a booby-trap IRA bomb in 1976

The Security of the State

As part of the government response to IRA violence, the Minister for Posts and Telegraphs, Conor Cruise O'Brien, used Section 31 of the Broadcasting Act to ban members of Sinn Féin and the IRA from appearing on Irish radio or television. The ban extended to anyone advocating the use of violence for political purposes. Although journalists regarded this as an attack on free speech, successive Irish governments kept the ban in place until the IRA ceasefire in 1994.

The Minister for Justice, Patrick Cooney, pursued a vigorous policy against paramilitary groups. He strongly supported members of the Garda Síochána who were accused of rough treatment of IRA suspects. He also introduced a number of strict new laws to deal with the threat to the security of the state. After the killing of the British ambassador in July 1976, Cooney introduced the Offences Against the State Amendment Bill (1976), which allowed terrorist suspects to be detained for up to seven days before they were charged. Fianna Fáil opposed it strongly in the Dáil. After being passed in the Dáil and Seanad, it went to the President, Cearbhall Ó Dálaigh, for signing.

Cearbhall Ó Dálaigh had become President after the sudden death of Erskine Childers in 1974. A former Chief Justice, he was the agreed choice of all the political parties. He exercised his right as President

Conor Cruise O'Brien (right) being interviewed on RTÉ television when he was Minister for Posts and Telegraphs

to refer the Offences Against the State Amendment Bill to the Supreme Court to test whether it was in accordance with the Constitution or not. Although the Supreme Court judged the measure to be constitutional, President Ó Dálaigh's action had unforeseen political consequences.

The Resignation of the President

On 18 October 1976 the Minister for Defence, Patrick Donegan, attended a ceremony at Columb Barracks in Mullingar during which he attacked the decision of the President to refer the Offences Against the State Amendment Bill to the Supreme Court. He was reported as referring to the President as a 'thundering disgrace'. When he realised the implications of his statement, Patrick Donegan offered his resignation to the Taoiseach, Liam Cosgrave, who refused to accept it. The President sent a letter to the Government protesting at the Minister's remarks. In the Dáil, Fianna Fáil called on the Minister to resign. Cosgrave expressed regret over the incident, but he praised Donegan's record as Minister for Defence. The President responded to these developments by tendering his resignation. He was particularly offended that the speech was made to members of the army, because the President is the Commander-in-Chief of the Irish army. Ó Dálaigh believed that resignation was the only means open to him to defend the honour of the presidency.

Cearbhaill Ó Dálaigh making a phone call from his home following his resignation as President in October 1976

The Cearbhall Ó Dálaigh affair seriously damaged the reputation of the Coalition Government as it approached the next general election. Many political commentators were highly critical of the Taoiseach's refusal to accept Patrick Donegan's resignation when it was offered. That refusal was portrayed by Cosgrave's political opponents as placing loyalty to his Minister ahead of respect for the office of President.

The National Coalition, 1973–7: An Assessment

By the time it reached the end of its term of office in the summer of 1977, the National Coalition had a mixed record. By providing the electorate with an alternative after sixteen years of Fianna Fáil government, it had strengthened democracy in the state. It could also point to certain definite innovations in terms of policy. For example, the Minister for Education, Richard Burke, put an end to a long-standing grievance by abolishing compulsory Irish in state examinations. Before this, if students failed Irish in the Intermediate or Leaving Certificate, they failed the entire examination, regardless of how they performed in other subjects. Although criticised by many in the Irish language movement, Burke defended the implementation of this long-standing Fine Gael policy by stating that it was better to encourage people to learn Irish than to force them to do so. He further demonstrated his commitment to the language by deciding that an Honour in Leaving Certificate Irish would count as two out of the four Honours required for university grants. Burke's colleague Tom O'Donnell, the Minister for the Gaeltacht, also actively promoted the language and was quite popular in Gaeltacht areas.

Although the wealth tax introduced by the Coalition Government was criticised by better-off groups, it was regarded by many people as a fairer method of taxation than the old death duties. The performance of Garret FitzGerald as Minister for Foreign Affairs, the achievements of Mark Clinton in agriculture negotiations in Europe and the signing of the Sunningdale Agreement were also regarded as positive achievements.

However, the performance of the Cosgrave Government in economic matters was far less impressive. The decision to borrow to keep living standards from falling significantly during the oil crisis succeeded only in storing up trouble for the future. To the credit of the Minister for Finance, Richie Ryan, and his government colleagues, they risked annoying the voters by reducing the level of borrowing in their last year in office.

As the general election approached, two matters were causing unease among the voters: the Cearbhall Ó Dálaigh affair and the allegations that a 'Heavy Gang' operating in the Garda Síochána used violence to force confessions out of IRA suspects. Although the allegations were vigorously denied by Liam Cosgrave and the Minister for Justice, Patrick Cooney, many people were suspicious that all was not well.

After more than four years in office, Liam Cosgrave called an election on 25 May 1977. The voting was due to take place on 16 June. Without having taken any opinion polls, the members of the outgoing Government were reasonably confident as the campaign began. They were to experience a considerable shock when the electorate delivered its verdict.

KEY PERSONALITY: SYLVIA MEEHAN

A former school vice-principal, Sylvia Meehan came to prominence in the 1970s when she was involved in the establishment of the Commission for the Status of Women. Her national profile was consolidated when she was appointed Chief Executive of the Employment Equality Agency.

Since her retirement, Sylvia Meehan has actively publicised issues relating to ageing. She became a board member of the organisation Age & Opportunity and since 2000 has been president of the Irish Senior Citizen Parliament, the largest organisation of older people in Ireland. She was also nominated as Irish representative to the executive board of AGE, the European Older People's Platform, an umbrella organisation of groups working to promote the interests of older people in Europe.

EXERCISES

ORDINARY LEVEL

1. Read the following extract from Liam Cosgrave's speech in the Dáil on the day he was elected Taoiseach, 14 March 1973, and answer the questions that follow.

    > This Government was founded in a spirit of co-operation and I believe that spirit of co-operation will influence their work and guide their activities . . .
    >
    > I believe one of the clear decisions of the electorate in this election, whether they voted for the present Government or the outgoing Government, was that a majority of the people, irrespective of party, rejected voices from the past counselling extremism, doctrinaire solutions and violent ways as a method of solving the problems of the present or the future . . .
    >
    > This government has been described as one of many talents and commentators and informed writers have been unanimous in their speculation on at least a minority of the members who would form the team. They all agree that it is a talented team. I need hardly say that I am glad to have got a place on it.

    Dáil Debates, vol. 265, 14 March 1973

    (i) To what is Cosgrave referring when he uses the word 'co-operation'?

    (ii) Regarding Northern Ireland, what approach is rejected by a majority of the voters?

    (iii) To what period of time do violent solutions belong, according to the speaker?

    (iv) Explain the joke at the end of the extract.

    (v) Would you agree that this is a good primary source? Explain your answer.

2. Write a paragraph on the 1973 general election.

3. What caused an oil crisis in the autumn of 1973? Explain the main effect of the crisis in Ireland.

4. Outline the response of the National Coalition Government to the effects of the oil crisis.

5. Write a short account of the wealth tax introduced by Minister for Finance Richie Ryan in 1974.

6. How did the Minister for Industry and Commerce, Justin Keating, deal with the issue of oil exploration off the coast of Ireland?

7. Outline the impact of membership of the EEC on Irish agriculture between 1973 and 1977.

8. Write a short account of the achievements of the Minister for Foreign Affairs, Dr Garret FitzGerald.

9. How did the National Coalition change the traditional policy of Irish governments towards the problem of Northern Ireland?

10. Outline the terms of the Sunningdale Agreement (1973), and explain why it collapsed.

11. State the main activities of the IRA in the Republic of Ireland during the Coalition Government's term of office, and outline the reaction of the Government.

12. Write a paragraph on the resignation of President Cearbhall Ó Dálaigh in 1976.

HIGHER LEVEL

1. Assess the strengths and weaknesses of the Fine Gael–Labour National Coalition Government, 1973–7.

2. Analyse the economic policies of the National Coalition Government, 1973–7.

3. Discuss the place of the Sunningdale Agreement in Anglo-Irish relations.

4. Account for the decline in the popularity of the National Coalition Government, 1973–7, by the end of its term of office.

The 1977 General Election

The 1977 general election was dominated by the Fianna Fáil election manifesto. The party promised that if returned to power, it would abolish rates on private houses and also car tax. Jack

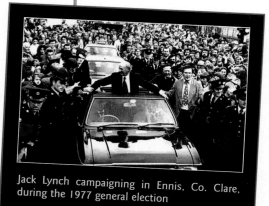

Jack Lynch campaigning in Ennis, Co. Clare, during the 1977 general election

Lynch toured the country, and the party ran a highly successful, professional campaign. The members of the outgoing Coalition, on the other hand, defended their record in government and did not attempt to match Fianna Fáil in terms of promises to the electorate. There were tensions within the Labour Party concerning the party's future role in a coalition government.

Fine Gael and Labour had another reason to be complacent. They believed that the re-organisation of the constituencies by the Minister for Local Government, James Tully, gave them an advantage over Fianna Fáil. The Fianna Fáil Minister for Local Government, Kevin Boland, had done the same for his party before the 1969 election and had helped the Government to be re-elected. Believing that Tully's redrawing of the constituencies was unfair, Jack Lynch promised that if Fianna Fáil returned to power, he would appoint an independent commission to redraw constituency boundaries in the future.

In the event, Tully's redrawing of the constituencies backfired on the Coalition parties and helped Fianna Fáil. Because of the massive swing in its favour, Fianna Fáil won two out of three seats in many areas where the party was expected to face difficulties. When the votes were counted, Fianna Fáil had won almost 51 per cent of the vote. Only once before, in 1938, had the party's share of the popular vote exceeded 50 per cent. Fianna Fáil also won 84 seats out of 144 in the Dáil, a huge majority of 23 seats.

Jack Lynch was elected Taoiseach once again and appointed George Colley as his Tánaiste and Minister for Finance. Other important appointments included that of the Trinity College economist Dr Martin O'Donoghue as Minister for Economic Planning and Development and that of Charles J. Haughey as Minister for Health. During the following two years, Dr O'Donoghue played a key role in the implementation of the Government's expansionary economic policies.

Jack Lynch watching Liam Cosgrave concede defeat on television as the results of the 1977 election come in

With his appointment as Minister for Health, Charles Haughey had finally been fully rehabilitated after the events surrounding the Arms Crisis. Under pressure from ordinary Fianna Fáil members throughout the country, Jack Lynch had appointed him as the front-bench spokesman on health in 1975. Then, when Fianna Fáil returned to power in 1977, he was chosen as Minister for Health. Haughey was an extremely able minister and performed well in the Department of Health, but by restoring him to office, Jack Lynch gave him a power base that he could use to achieve his ultimate ambition – the leadership of Fianna Fáil and the office of Taoiseach.

In contrast to the Fianna Fáil landslide victory, Fine Gael and Labour had a poor election. Whereas the Labour Party declined by 2 seats, from 19 to 17, Fine Gael dropped 11 seats, from 54 in 1973 to 43 in 1977. Both the Fine Gael leader, Liam Cosgrave, and the Labour Party leader, Brendan Corish, resigned shortly after the election. The Dublin TD Frank Cluskey narrowly defeated Michael O'Leary in the contest for the Labour Party leadership. There was no contest in Fine Gael, however, and Dr Garret FitzGerald was chosen unopposed to succeed Liam Cosgrave. He immediately set about building up the organisation of the Fine Gael party throughout the country. From the start his dynamic and energetic personality made him a high-profile leader of the Opposition in the Dáil and in the country. He challenged Fianna Fáil both inside and outside the Dáil as he prepared his party for electoral contests at local, national and European level.

Economic Expansion

After its election in June 1977, the Government of Jack Lynch set about implementing its electoral promises. Rates on private dwellings were abolished, although they were retained for business premises. Car tax was abolished, although it would be reintroduced within a few years.

The main thrust of the Government's economic policy was to combine high levels of public spending with increased borrowing. The Government justified this by claiming that if a consumer boom arose from these measures, it would lift the economy. However, this plan was to go disastrously wrong. In his budgets, George Colley reversed the attempts of his predecessor, Richie Ryan, to control government borrowing. His budget of February 1978 almost doubled the existing budget deficit and raised the exchequer borrowing requirement to 13 per cent of GNP.

Also in 1978, the Department of Economic Planning and Development under Dr Martin O'Donoghue produced a three-year plan to cover the years 1978 to 1981. As can be seen from the bar chart below, the Government completely miscalculated the economic outcome of its policies by 1981. Because of an increase in the number of public-sector workers and high wage increases, the country was spending more than it could afford. Ultimately, a country living beyond its means is forced to face reality. In the short term, unemployment fell from 106,000 in 1977 to 90,000 in 1979. However, in 1979 a second oil crisis occurred. The resulting rise in fuel costs and the effects of excessive government borrowing combined to cause massive unemployment during the 1980s.

In December 1978 the Government made the significant decision to apply for membership of the European Monetary System (EMS), a group of EEC currencies that were drawing closer together. The decision of Great Britain to remain outside the EMS meant that for the first time since 1826, British and Irish currencies were not equal in value.

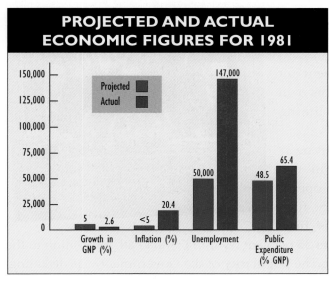

Source: J.J. Lee, *Ireland, 1912–1985: Politics and Society,* Cambridge University Press 1995, 488

Before the temporary prosperity of 1978 and 1979 disappeared, however, the Republic of Ireland was to experience a joyful occasion of a traditional nature when the Pope visited the country in September 1979.

The Visit of Pope John Paul II to Ireland

In September 1979 Pope John Paul II became the first pope ever to visit Ireland. When elected in September 1978, the Polish Cardinal Karol Wojtyła had been the first non-Italian to be elected pope in over 450 years. He had a great regard for Ireland, which, like his native Poland, was a largely Catholic country with a history of foreign occupation. His outgoing, charismatic personality made him extremely popular in Ireland, as in other countries.

During his visit to Ireland, Pope John Paul went to Dublin, Drogheda, Limerick, Knock and Galway. In Dublin over a million people attended his open-air Mass in the Phoenix Park. He celebrated a special Mass for young people at Galway. At Drogheda he made a special appeal to the IRA to give up violence. However, his appeal was ignored by that organisation.

The arrival of Pope John Paul II in Ireland in September 1979

In his sermons and speeches, the Pope stressed the traditional teachings of the Catholic faith and called on Irish people to support the family and to oppose divorce and abortion. He warned against the dangers of seeking material progress for its own sake.

Although huge crowds assembled to see the Pope and a great spirit of celebration existed in the country, his visit did not have a long-term impact on people's attitudes and everyday lives. Indeed, many historians see it as the last example of a strong traditional Catholic Irish influence rather than a factor influencing the future development of society.

Both President Patrick Hillery and Taoiseach Jack Lynch played a prominent and public role in the Pope's visit. However, this was one of the final important ceremonial occasions in which the Taoiseach participated. In just over two months' time, he would resign as Taoiseach and leader of Fianna Fáil.

Charles J. Haughey Becomes Taoiseach

Jack Lynch had been contemplating retirement for some time, but he wished to go at a time of his own choosing. However, political developments during 1979 hastened his departure.

In June 1979 direct elections to the European Parliament were held for the first time. In the Republic of Ireland, fifteen Members of the European Parliament (MEPs) were to be elected every five years. Fianna Fáil performed poorly in this first

The newly elected leader of Fianna Fáil, Charles J. Haughey, giving his victory press conference in December 1979

European election, with the party vote falling to 35 per cent. Within Fianna Fáil, opposition to the leadership of Jack Lynch gathered momentum. The popularity of the Government was declining, and many TDs elected in 1977 feared that they would lose their seats in the next election under

Lynch's leadership. Growing opposition to Lynch centred around Charles Haughey. Many of Lynch's critics within Fianna Fáil criticised his policy on Northern Ireland. They wanted the party to adopt a more republican stance.

When Fianna Fáil lost two by-elections in Cork – one in the Taoiseach's own constituency – Jack Lynch came under increasing pressure to resign. On 5 December 1979 he announced his resignation as Taoiseach and as leader of Fianna Fáil. In the contest among Fianna Fáil TDs to succeed him, two candidates emerged – George Colley and Charles J. Haughey. Lynch's own preferred choice was George Colley. However, when the vote was taken, Haughey defeated Colley by 44 votes to 38. This close result did nothing to heal the deep divisions within the Fianna Fáil Party. Intense rivalry continued to exist between the Haughey and Colley factions, and the party remained bitterly divided for many years to come.

Charles Haughey in Power

Charles Haughey's first Cabinet contained both supporters and opponents during the leadership election. His position within Fianna Fáil was not strong enough to allow him to govern without his adversaries within the party. He appointed George Colley as Tánaiste and Minister for Energy, and prominent Colley supporter Desmond O'Malley became Minister for Industry and Commerce. Among his own supporters, he appointed Michael O'Kennedy Minister for Finance, and Brian Lenihan became Minister for Foreign Affairs. The appointment of Máire Geoghegan Quinn as Minister for the Gaeltacht was historic: she was the first woman since Countess Markievicz to be appointed to a Cabinet post.

One of the major preoccupations of the new Government was the condition of the economy. Rising levels of public borrowing and the effects of the second oil crisis were a serious cause for concern. On the evening of 9 January 1980, Haughey addressed the nation on television and presented a gloomy picture of the Irish economy. He declared:

> As a community we are living way beyond our means . . . we have been borrowing enormous amounts of money, borrowing at a rate which just cannot continue. We will just have to reorganise government spending so that we can only undertake those things we can afford.

Haughey's diagnosis of the problems of the Irish economy was extremely accurate. Unfortunately, his Government did not take action to remedy the situation. In fact, with a general election due within two years, it moved in exactly the opposite direction. The budget at the end of January 1980 contained tax concessions and high increases in social welfare. The Government and private employers continued to pay high wage awards. As a result, a marked increase took place in inflation, unemployment and government borrowing. These trends intensified during the following year, 1981.

Whereas Charles Haughey's management of the economy between 1979 and 1981 was marked by a failure to control government spending, he was more successful in his management of relations with Great Britain. He achieved this by initiating a process of co-operation between the two governments over the future development of Northern Ireland.

Anglo-Irish Relations

Six months before Charles Haughey was first elected Taoiseach in December 1979, a new Conservative Prime Minister came to power in Great Britain – Margaret Thatcher, the country's first

British Prime Minister Margaret Thatcher and Taoiseach Charles Haughey at Dublin Castle in December 1980

female head of government. For the following eleven years, she would be closely involved with different Irish governments, mainly in efforts to seek a solution to the problem of Northern Ireland.

The first summit meeting between Haughey and Thatcher took place in London in May 1980. The Haughey Government's approach to Northern Ireland was based on the idea that the six-county state was a 'failed political entity' and that any solution would have to come from the two sovereign governments in London and Dublin. Although no important decisions were taken at this summit, the two leaders established a good working relationship.

At a summit in Dublin Castle in December 1980, Haughey and Thatcher held constructive discussions and agreed that the 'totality of relationships' between both countries would be examined in a number of joint studies. This implied that the British Government was willing to consider new approaches to all the relationships in the two countries: between Britain and Ireland, between Northern Ireland and the Republic and between both communities in Northern Ireland itself. The actions of the Haughey Government in relation to Northern Ireland paved the way for future progress and laid the foundation for the Anglo-Irish Agreement of 1985.

However, the positive working relationship between the British and Irish governments was to be placed under considerable strain by a hunger-strike campaign by IRA prisoners in Northern Ireland.

The IRA Hunger-Strike Campaign

During the spring of 1981, IRA prisoners in the Maze Prison in Northern Ireland started a hunger strike in order to be recognised as non-criminal, or political, prisoners. They demanded a number of concessions, including the right to wear their own clothing and to associate freely with each other. The British Government of Margaret Thatcher refused to compromise on any of the demands. The Irish Government seemed unable to influence the situation.

A protest in London in May 1981 calling on the British Government to concede the demand of the IRA hunger-striker Bobby Sands to be treated as a political prisoner

The General Election of 1981

Charles Haughey intended to call a general election in the spring of 1981. However, on 14 February that year, 48 young people died in the Stardust dancehall fire in his own constituency in Dublin, causing him to postpone his election plans. The hunger strikes in the North led to a further delay in calling the election. He eventually had the Dáil dissolved by the President on 21 May and called an election for 11 June.

The 1981 election centred around the presidential-style campaigns conducted by Charles Haughey and the Fine Gael leader, Dr Garret FitzGerald. Fianna Fáil promised more spending programmes, whereas Fine Gael promised cuts in taxation. This was the first general election held in the new constituencies established by the independent commission. The results showed a swing against Fianna Fáil and in favour of the opposition parties. The intervention of the hunger-strike candidates damaged the electoral prospects of Fianna Fáil by drawing votes away from the party. The election

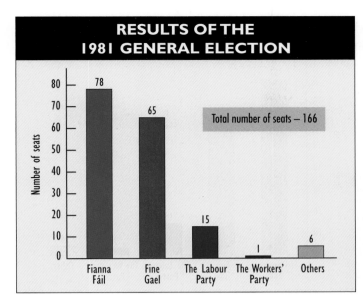

RESULTS OF THE 1981 GENERAL ELECTION

Total number of seats – 166

Party	Number of seats
Fianna Fáil	78
Fine Gael	65
The Labour Party	15
The Workers' Party	1
Others	6

of two hunger-strike candidates to the Dáil possibly deprived Fianna Fáil of its chance to return to government. The result was Fianna Fáil's worst in twenty years. Having enjoyed an overall majority of over twenty seats in 1977, Fianna Fáil now lost power and entered opposition.

Fine Gael campaigners backing Garret FitzGerald in the general election of 1981

The Fine Gael–Labour Coalition, 1981-2

Although the Fine Gael and Labour TDs combined outnumbered those of Fianna Fáil only by 80 to 78, the two parties were able to form a coalition government with the support of Independents. When the new Dáil met, Garret FitzGerald was elected Taoiseach, and Michael O'Leary, the leader of the Labour Party, became Tánaiste.

From the outset, the new Government was dominated by the state of the economy. On taking power, the Government claimed that the public finances were much worse than expected, and the Minister for Finance, John Bruton, immediately introduced a supplementary budget. This increased taxes in order to reduce the level of government borrowing, which was spiralling out of control.

In the first main budget of the Fine Gael–Labour Coalition in January 1982, further efforts were made to reduce the level of borrowing. One of the measures included in John Bruton's budget speech was a proposal to tax children's shoes. When Independents supporting the Government voted against the budget, it was defeated on 27 January 1982. Defeat on a budget leads to the immediate resignation of a government. Garret FitzGerald then proceeded to Áras an Uachtaráin to advise President Hillery to dissolve the Dáil and call a general election. In theory, the President could refuse to dissolve the Dáil on the advice of a Taoiseach who has lost the confidence of the Dáil. Indeed, members of Fianna Fáil made efforts to contact the President in order to persuade him not to dissolve the Dáil. However, President Hillery agreed to a dissolution, and a general election was called for 18 February 1982.

The General Election of February 1982

The Coalition Government of Fine Gael and Labour campaigned on its record of strict control of the public finances. Fianna Fáil accused the Coalition of spreading 'gloom and doom' and questioned the need for higher taxes and cutbacks in government expenditure. The election result was inconclusive, with neither the Coalition nor Fianna Fáil securing an overall majority. Although Fianna Fáil secured 47 per cent of the first-preference vote, the party was three seats short of an overall majority in the Dáil. Before the new Dáil met, a group of anti-Haughey TDs led by Desmond O'Malley tried to bring about a change in the leadership. This was the first of many attempts to topple Charles Haughey from the leadership of Fianna Fáil. It failed to receive sufficient support in the parliamentary party. When the new Dáil met, Charles Haughey was elected Taoiseach with the support of the Workers' Party and Independent TDs. One of these was Tony Gregory of Dublin Central, who was promised a major investment programme in his constituency (the 'Gregory Deal'). However, as a minority government, the new Haughey administration was unstable and faced serious difficulties from the beginning.

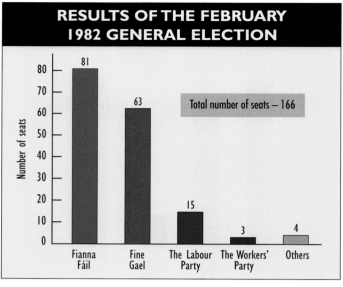

RESULTS OF THE FEBRUARY 1982 GENERAL ELECTION

Total number of seats – 166

Number of seats

Fianna Fáil	81
Fine Gael	63
The Labour Party	15
The Workers' Party	3
Others	4

Fianna Fáil in Power, March–December 1982

Although Charles Haughey had initially rejected the failed Fine Gael–Labour budget, he came to accept the scale of the economic problems facing the country.

In an effort to gain an extra Dáil seat for Fianna Fáil, Haughey offered the Irish commissionership in the EEC to the Fine Gael TD Richard Burke, who had earlier held the post during the 1970s. To take up this post, Burke would have to resign his seat in the Dáil, and Fianna Fáil expected to win the resulting by-election in the Dublin West constituency. Against the advice of Fine Gael, Richard Burke took up the position of European Commissioner. However, the Fianna Fáil candidate, Eileen Lemass, was defeated in Dublin West by Liam Skelly of Fine Gael. As a result, there was no change in the position of the parties in the Dáil, and Haughey's plan had backfired. This by-election defeat damaged the morale of Fianna Fáil. For Garret FitzGerald and Fine Gael, on the other hand, victory in Dublin West provided hope that the Fianna Fáil Government might fall from power before long.

A public scandal threatened Haughey's Government in August 1982, when a murder suspect, Malcolm MacArthur, was arrested in the apartment of the Attorney-General, Patrick Connolly. The Attorney-General was not involved, but MacArthur was later convicted of the murder of a nurse, Bridie Gargan, in the Phoenix Park in Dublin. The incident caused serious embarrassment to the Government, and Haughey described the events as 'grotesque, unbelievable, bizarre and unprecedented'. The press reported these words, and Conor Cruise O'Brien used them to construct the word 'GUBU' to describe Haughey's style of government during 1982.

On 1 October 1982 Haughey's enemies within the Fianna Fáil Party launched another attempt to remove him from the leadership. A motion of no confidence in Haughey was placed before the Fianna Fáil Parliamentary Party by the Kildare TD, Charlie McCreevy. Both Desmond O'Malley and Martin O'Donoghue resigned from the

Fianna Fáil leader Charles Haughey surrounded by supporters

Government and supported the motion. Haughey refused to allow a secret ballot in the parliamentary party, and after an open vote the motion against him was defeated by 58 votes to 22.

In October, the Government published a strategy document outlining its economic policy for the future. The document, entitled *The Way Forward*, proposed substantial spending cuts, and as a result the Workers' Party TDs and the Independent TD Tony Gregory withdrew their support. Fine Gael then tabled a motion of no confidence in the Government. On 4 November 1982 the Fianna Fáil Government lost the vote of no confidence by 82 votes to 80. A general election followed soon after.

From the beginning, this Government had been characterised by instability and controversy. Within the Fianna Fáil Party, deep divisions persisted between pro- and anti-Haughey factions. The main opposition parties also focused much of their attention on the controversial figure of Haughey. His record in government and, in particular, his personal style of leadership were to be central issues in the second general election of 1982.

KEY PERSONALITY: JACK LYNCH (1917–99)

Jack Lynch was born in Cork on 15 August 1917 and was educated at the North Monastery School, UCC and King's Inns. He qualified as a barrister while working in the civil service in Dublin. He was an outstanding sportsman, winning six All-Ireland medals for Cork in hurling and football during the 1940s. In 1948 he was elected a Fianna Fáil TD for Cork City and continued to represent Cork in the Dáil until his retirement in 1981.

Jack Lynch held a number of positions in Fianna Fáil governments during the 1950s and 1960s. He was a Parliamentary Secretary from 1951 to 1954 and joined the Cabinet as Minister for Education from 1957 to 1959. He was Minister for Industry and Commerce from 1959 to 1965 and was Minister for Finance in 1965–6. When Seán Lemass resigned in 1966, Jack Lynch emerged as a compromise candidate in the leadership contest that followed and succeeded Lemass as Taoiseach and as leader of Fianna Fáil.

Although Lynch was considered a 'reluctant' leader of the party, he led Fianna Fáil to victory in the 1969 general election. Almost immediately, however, he had to confront a major crisis in Northern Ireland as conflict between nationalists and unionists deepened. Lynch believed that a united Ireland could come about only through consent and not through violence. Some ministers with strong republican views within his own Government were critical of Lynch's cautious approach to the northern crisis. In 1970 he fired two of his ministers — Charles Haughey and Neil Blaney — for 'not subscribing fully' to government policy on Northern Ireland. A third minister, Kevin Boland, resigned in protest. The dismissed ministers were later acquitted in the courts on charges of conspiring to import arms illegally to aid the northern nationalists.

Jack Lynch successfully led Ireland into the EEC in 1973. However, his Government fell from power after the general election of March 1973, and he led his party in opposition from 1973 to 1977. Fianna Fáil secured a landslide victory in the general election of 1977, winning an unprecedented 84 seats. After a presidential-style election campaign, Lynch himself won over 20,000 first-preference votes in his Cork City constituency, prompting Liam Cosgrave to refer to him as the most popular Irish leader since Daniel O'Connell. However, within that victory lay the seeds of his political demise.

Within two years, the popularity of the Fianna Fáil Government had declined sharply. The extravagant promises made to the electorate during the election campaign resulted in economic policies that drove the economy deeply into recession. When the party lost two crucial by-elections in Lynch's native city in 1979, the political omens were not good for him. On 11 December 1979 he announced his resignation. Much to his dismay, he was succeeded as Taoiseach and as leader of Fianna Fáil by Charles Haughey, who defeated Lynch's preferred choice, George Colley, in a bitter leadership contest. Although Lynch retired from active politics, he continued to support Haughey's main rival — Desmond O'Malley — during the 1980s.

EXERCISES

ORDINARY LEVEL

1. What promises were contained in the Fianna Fáil election manifesto of 1977?

2. Explain why Fianna Fáil won a large majority of seats in the 1977 election.

3. Write an account of the economic policies of the Fianna Fáil Government between 1977 and 1979.

4. Describe the visit of Pope John Paul II to Ireland in September 1979.

5. Why did Jack Lynch come under pressure to resign in 1979?

6. Explain why Charles Haughey was elected leader of Fianna Fáil and Taoiseach in December 1979.

7. What warning did Charles Haughey give the Irish people in a television address in January 1980? Did his Government follow the course he proposed? Explain your answer.

8. Write a paragraph on relations between Charles Haughey and the British Prime Minister, Margaret Thatcher, during 1980.

9. Write an account of the general election of June 1981.

10. Explain why the Fine Gael–Labour Government fell from power in January 1982.

11. Outline the results of the general election of February 1982.

12. Write an account of the minority Fianna Fáil Government of Charles Haughey, March–December 1982.

13. Examine the charts of the general elections of June 1981 and February 1982 on pages 307 and 308 and compare the results.

HIGHER LEVEL

1. Assess critically the economic performance of Fianna Fáil in government between 1977 and 1981.

2. Account for the political instability in Ireland between June 1981 and November 1982.

3. Consider the economic priorities of Fine Gael between 1977 and 1982.

4. Analyse the role of Charles Haughey as Taoiseach between 1979 and 1981 and during 1982.

23. The Fine Gael-Labour Coalition, 1982-7

The November 1982 Election

When Irish voters went to the polls on 24 November 1982, they were voting in the third successive general election in less than eighteen months. Having lost a vote of confidence in the Dáil and leading a divided Fianna Fáil Party, Charles Haughey was on the defensive from the start of the campaign. He claimed that Fine Gael and Labour had caused an unnecessary election. He decided to accuse Garret FitzGerald in particular of being too pro-British and of being willing to allow the RUC in Northern Ireland to cross the border into the Republic in pursuit of IRA suspects. During 1982 Haughey had developed a more 'republican' stance on Northern Ireland while Taoiseach and had damaged relations with the British Prime Minister, Margaret Thatcher, by criticising British involvement in the Falklands War. In the course of the election campaign, he criticised Garret FitzGerald for meeting one of the leading members of the British nobility, the Duke of Norfolk. The attempt to portray FitzGerald as a type of British spy did not work for Fianna Fáil during the election, however.

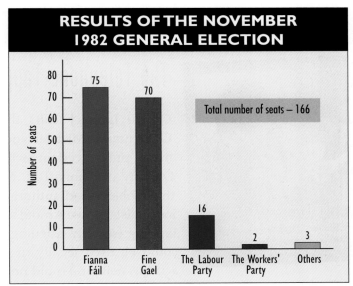

RESULTS OF THE NOVEMBER 1982 GENERAL ELECTION

Total number of seats – 166

Party	Number of seats
Fianna Fáil	75
Fine Gael	70
The Labour Party	16
The Workers' Party	2
Others	3

Fine Gael and Labour strongly criticised Haughey's record in government between March and November 1982 and promised progress on the economy and on Northern Ireland if elected to power. When the votes were counted, it was clear that there had been a swing against Fianna Fáil and towards Fine Gael. Fianna Fáil lost 6 seats and, with 75 TDs, went into opposition. Under Garret FitzGerald's leadership, the Fine Gael Party had achieved its best result ever. With 70 seats, it was now only 5 seats behind Fianna Fáil. When the Labour Party agreed to go into coalition with Fine Gael, a government with a comfortable overall majority in the Dáil could be formed. The Coalition Government of Fine Gael and Labour had every prospect of serving a full term of four or five years and thus brought an end to the period of political instability that had existed since June 1981.

The Fine Gael-Labour Coalition

When the new Dáil met, Garret FitzGerald was elected Taoiseach for the second time. The new Tánaiste was the leader of the Labour Party, Dick Spring. He had recently been elected leader of the party to replace Michael O'Leary, who had resigned and left to join Fine Gael because of disagreement with party policy. As well as becoming Tánaiste, Dick Spring was also Minister for the Environment. Alan Dukes of Fine Gael became Minister for Finance, and his party

Garret FitzGerald (right, Fine Gael) and Dick Spring (Labour), Taoiseach and Tánaiste in the Coalition Government between 1982 and 1987

colleague, Peter Barry, was appointed Minister for Foreign Affairs. In all, Labour held four ministries: as well as Dick Spring, Labour ministers included Barry Desmond (Health and Social Welfare), Liam Kavanagh (Labour) and Frank Cluskey (Commerce and Tourism).

The first memorable event in the life of the new Government was not of its own making, however, but concerned the public exposure of secret developments that had taken place under the previous Haughey Government.

The Telephone-Tapping Scandal

Journalists Geraldine Kennedy and Bruce Arnold reading a government statement confirming that their telephones had been tapped

On 20 January 1983 the Minister for Justice in the Coalition Government, Michael Noonan of Fine Gael, held a press conference to make public certain activities of his predecessor in office, Seán Doherty of Fianna Fáil. Noonan told the crowded press conference that Doherty had authorised the Gardaí to tap the telephones of two journalists, Bruce Arnold and Geraldine Kennedy. Although telephone tapping (secretly listening to and recording telephone conversations) could be used legally in the struggle against crime or paramilitary activity, neither Arnold nor Kennedy were involved in such activities. The Commissioner and Deputy Commissioner of the Gardaí resigned because of the scandal.

It appeared that the tapping of both telephones on the instruction of Seán Doherty was an attempt to stop 'leaks' – or the unauthorised disclosure of information to journalists – by members of the Fianna Fáil Government. Most commentators claimed that the affair was connected to the internal divisions in Fianna Fáil and had nothing to do with crime or threats to national security.

The public exposure of telephone tapping by the previous Government gave the Coalition a boost early in its term of office. It further discredited Charles Haughey and his close followers in the eyes of many observers. Within Fianna Fáil, it provoked a further crisis and yet another attempt to oust Haughey as leader of the party. After a few weeks of unprecedented turmoil within Fianna Fáil, however, Haughey won a vote of confidence in a secret ballot of TDs by 40 votes to 33. Despite the revelations surrounding telephone tapping, he had survived as leader and proceeded to concentrate on opposing the Coalition Government at every possible opportunity.

One issue that generated deep political divisions soon emerged – the highly sensitive issue of the life of the unborn child.

A pro-life referendum poster in a church porch in 1983

The Pro-Life Referendum, 1983

The coming to power of the Fine Gael–Labour Government in 1982 coincided with the emergence of the abortion issue as a significant factor in Irish politics. At that time three highly controversial 'social' topics caused divisions among politicians and among the Christian churches, which took a leading part in public debates on these topics. These issues were:

- Family planning and contraception.
- Divorce.
- Abortion and the life of the unborn child.

The first of the three to be tackled by the Government of Garret FitzGerald was the right to life of the unborn child.

During the political instability of 1981–2, pro-life, or anti-abortion, groups succeeded in obtaining commitments from Fianna Fáil and Fine Gael to hold a referendum on the issue. The pro-life groups believed that only when the people voted in a referendum to safeguard the life of the unborn child would abortion be completely banned in Ireland. They cited two examples to support their case. In the USA abortion was legalised in 1973 by a decision of the Supreme Court, and in Ireland it was the courts that established the right of married people to have access to contraceptives. Although an old law of 1861 outlawed abortion in Ireland, pro-life groups feared that it could be overturned in the courts. They wanted to add an amendment to the Constitution that would make it impossible for the courts to change this law.

An anti-abortion rally outside the Dáil

Before leaving office in November 1982, the Fianna Fáil Government had come up with a form of wording for the amendment that guaranteed the right to life of the unborn child and the equal right to life of the mother. Garret FitzGerald's Government obtained legal advice that this wording could actually be interpreted as permitting abortion. However, it was supported by the Catholic Church, by most in Fianna Fáil and by a considerable section of Fine Gael. When TDs voted on the issue in the Dáil, this was the wording that they chose to put to the people.

Some groups expressed strong opposition to the pro-life amendment. The Labour Party and Workers' Party opposed the idea of an amendment entirely. The more liberal wing of Fine Gael opposed it. Many women's groups feared that if passed, it would threaten the lives of mothers in cases of very difficult births. Most Protestant church leaders also opposed the amendment.

The referendum campaign was extremely bitter and acrimonious. Supporters of the proposed amendment claimed that they were the only people who were pro-life and that their opponents threatened the lives of innocent unborn children. Anti-amendment campaigners claimed that women would be at risk if the amendment succeeded and that the Catholic Church was too influential in Irish life. Both sides claimed to be concerned about the number of women going to England each year for abortions: both sides, in their different ways, wished to help women with crisis pregnancies.

When the referendum took place in September 1983, it was carried by a two-thirds majority. Unfortunately, this was not the end of the controversy. Ten years later abortion would dominate the political agenda in Ireland once again.

Family Planning and Divorce

Although the sensitive issue of abortion and the life of the unborn child caused divisions in families and political parties alike, it was an extremely difficult problem to resolve, either in law or in the Constitution. Compared with abortion, the other two 'social' issues, family planning and divorce, seemed easier to resolve.

Garret FitzGerald had a particular interest in tackling these questions. He launched a 'constitutional crusade' in an attempt to modernise the Irish Constitution and to make it more acceptable to northern unionists. His mother came from a northern Protestant background, and he had a lifelong commitment to the reconciliation of the two traditions, Protestant and Catholic, on the island of Ireland. Although the more conservative wing of Fine Gael was suspicious of social change, FitzGerald had strong support from politicians on the more liberal wing of his party, including dynamic female TDs such as Gemma Hussey, the Minister for Education, Nuala Fennell and Monica Barnes. Within the Labour Party, support for changing the laws on family planning and divorce was almost unanimous.

In 1985 the Minister for Health, Barry Desmond, introduced a bill to liberalise the law on the sale of contraceptives. They had been banned in the state for many decades. During the 1970s, however, the courts ruled that married people could legally acquire them. The first attempt at legalisation was defeated when a number of Fine Gael TDs, including the Taoiseach, Liam Cosgrave, voted against the Coalition Government's measure in 1974. In 1978 Charles Haughey, as Minister for Health, introduced a bill allowing access to contraceptives for married people only. Barry Desmond's 1985 bill finally abolished the distinction between married and single people regarding access to contraceptives and permitted their public sale. It brought to an end the political controversy on the issue, which had lasted for almost twenty years.

Because divorce was prohibited by the Constitution, any change would have to be approved by the people in a referendum. In June 1986 the Coalition Government held a referendum on the issue. Almost all Labour Party representatives and most Fine Gael TDs campaigned in favour of change. So also did private lobby groups that supported the legalisation of divorce. Supporters of change argued that there were many broken marriages in Ireland and that people in this situation should have a chance to remarry on a legal basis.

Posters during the divorce referendum campaign of 1986

Opposition to the introduction of divorce was led by the Catholic bishops. Although Fianna Fáil was officially neutral, the party leader, Charles Haughey, and most of the party's TDs campaigned strongly against the referendum. Defeat of the measure would discredit the Fine Gael–Labour Government. The main arguments against divorce were that it was against the law of God, that its introduction would weaken family life in Ireland and that women would be left to raise families on their own. In rural areas, opponents of change played on fears that the family farm could be divided in the event of divorce.

When the referendum was put to the people on 26 June 1986, it was decisively rejected by a majority of 63 per cent. The defeat of the divorce referendum was a blow to the liberalising plans of the Government and to the 'constitutional crusade' of the Taoiseach, Garret FitzGerald. However, the Government's efforts to deal with the problem of Northern Ireland were to meet with greater success.

The New Ireland Forum

Following the IRA hunger strike of 1981, Garret FitzGerald was extremely concerned about the rising level of support for the IRA and Sinn Féin, particularly among nationalists in Northern Ireland. He believed that if a peaceful solution was to be found there, it was essential to strengthen the other major nationalist party, the non-violent, constitutional Social Democratic and Labour Party (SDLP). As part of his strategy to achieve this, he invited the SDLP to Dublin to attend meetings of all the constitutional nationalist parties on the island of Ireland. These meetings took place under the auspices of a body known as the **New Ireland Forum**, which was established in 1983. The four most influential figures in the Forum were the Taoiseach, Garret FitzGerald; the Tánaiste, Dick Spring; the leader of the Fianna Fáil Opposition, Charles Haughey; and John Hume, the leader of the SDLP. In May 1984 the Forum issued its report, which offered three solutions to the problem of relations between Northern Ireland and the Republic:

The first meeting of the New Ireland Forum in 1984, including (from left) Dick Spring, Charles Haughey, John Hume and Garret FitzGerald

- A unitary state.
- A federal state.
- Joint authority in Northern Ireland by the British and Irish governments.

To the annoyance of the other parties, Charles Haughey almost immediately repudiated the agreed report and stated that a unitary state was the only possible solution.

In London, the Prime Minister, Margaret Thatcher, dismissed the three options in her famous 'Out, Out, Out' speech. However, the Irish Government began a long and arduous campaign of diplomacy to convince her to take a fresh approach to the problem of Northern Ireland.

The Anglo-Irish Agreement

In November 1985 the Irish Government negotiated a major agreement on Northern Ireland with the British Conservative Government of Margaret Thatcher. Entitled the **Anglo-Irish Agreement**, it was the most significant advance since the Sunningdale Agreement of 1973. It built upon the foundations laid by Haughey and Thatcher at the 1980 summits, which stressed the central role of the British and Irish governments in providing a solution to the conflict in Northern Ireland. By placing both governments at the centre of the process, the Anglo-Irish Agreement avoided the weaknesses of the Sunningdale Agreement and ensured that the new arrangements could not be brought down by strikes in Northern Ireland.

Garret FitzGerald and Margaret Thatcher signing the Anglo-Irish Agreement in 1985

In order to achieve greater Irish co-operation on security matters in the fight against the IRA, Margaret Thatcher was prepared to give the Irish Government a role in the administration of Northern Ireland. Anxious to lessen support for the IRA, the Irish Government claimed to be defending the rights of Catholics and nationalists in Northern Ireland. The Irish Foreign Minister, Peter Barry, considered that he was in the tradition of Michael Collins in this regard.

Under the Anglo-Irish Agreement, both governments agreed to co-operate much more closely on the question of Northern Ireland. A formal inter-governmental conference was established involving the British Secretary of State for Northern Ireland and the Irish Minister for Foreign Affairs. At civil service level, there was to be a permanent secretariat in Northern Ireland involving both British and Irish civil servants. Therefore, although Britain retained sovereignty over Northern Ireland, the Irish Government had gained a formal right to be consulted over its administration.

Unionists outside Belfast City Hall protesting against the Anglo-Irish Agreement

Public opinion in Britain and in the Republic of Ireland was extremely favourable to the Agreement. Unionists reacted with fury, however, and condemned what they regarded as interference by the Republic in the affairs of Northern Ireland. However, the Thatcher Government stood firm in the face of unionist protests and continued to implement the Agreement.

In the Republic, the Agreement was the greatest and most enduring achievement of the 1982–7 Fine Gael–Labour Coalition. It laid the foundation for further progress in Northern Ireland after the IRA declared a ceasefire in 1994. Indeed, the decision of successive British governments to support the Anglo-Irish Agreement helped to bring about that ceasefire.

The reaction of Charles Haughey and Fianna Fáil to the signing of the Anglo-Irish Agreement was completely negative. Indeed, Haughey had greatly angered influential Irish-Americans by sending his Foreign Affairs spokesman, Brian Lenihan, to Washington to lobby against its provisions while it was still being negotiated. His opposition to the Agreement in November 1985 was a step too far in the view of his leading critics within Fianna Fáil. Before the end of the year they would break away and form a new party – the Progressive Democrats.

The Founding of the Progressive Democrats

By 1985 Desmond O'Malley had almost reached the parting of the ways with Fianna Fáil, which remained under the domination of Charles Haughey. On three occasions O'Malley had tried and failed to remove Haughey as leader of the party. In February 1985 he refused to vote with Fianna Fáil against Barry Desmond's bill legalising the sale of contraceptives. He declared in the Dáil:

> The politics of this would be very easy. The politics would be to be one of the lads, the safest way in Ireland. But I do not believe that the interests of this State or our Constitution and of this Republic would be served by putting politics before conscience in regard to this. There is a choice of a kind that can only be answered by saying that I stand by the Republic and accordingly, I will not oppose this Bill.

By using the phrase 'stand by the Republic', O'Malley meant that true republicans should be in favour of greater separation of Church and state. He was also aware of the impression that unionists in Northern Ireland would form if the bill was defeated. As a result of this action, Haughey had O'Malley expelled from the Fianna Fáil Parliamentary Party.

When the Anglo-Irish Agreement was announced in November 1985, it was immediately supported by O'Malley, by the former Fianna Fáil Taoiseach Jack Lynch, and by Mary Harney, a Fianna Fáil TD who joined O'Malley in voting for it in the Dáil. She was immediately expelled from the Fianna Fáil Parliamentary Party. Harney strongly urged O'Malley to form a new party.

Discussions among interested individuals had been taking place for months. Eventually, on 21 December 1985 the new party, led by Desmond O'Malley, was launched. It was named the Progressive Democrats

Desmond O'Malley and Mary Harney, founders of the Progressive Democrats, in December 1985

and initially contained only two TDs, Desmond O'Malley and Mary Harney. Three policy areas of the new party stood out:

- *Political*: It favoured private enterprise, low taxation, reduced government spending and less public borrowing.
- *Economic policy*: It took a liberal approach, favouring the introduction of divorce and greater separation of Church and state.
- *Northern Ireland*: It supported the Anglo-Irish Agreement and the reconciliation of unionists and nationalists.

The new party inspired a wave of enthusiasm during the first months of its existence. Public meetings drew huge numbers of enthusiastic supporters. Three more sitting TDs joined the Progressive Democrats – Bobby Molloy and Pearse Wyse of Fianna Fáil and Michael Keating of Fine Gael. Two extremely able supporters from outside the Dáil also joined: Michael McDowell, a barrister and former member of Fine Gael, and Pat Cox, a broadcaster and former member of Ógra Fianna Fáil. Both men were to play a leading role in the development of the PDs in the years ahead.

Although formed initially by anti-Haughey members of Fianna Fáil, the PDs appealed to a much wider constituency than this group. One of the reasons for this was the appalling state of the economy and the apparent inability of the Fine Gael–Labour Coalition to remedy the situation.

Economic Stagnation

The poor record of the Government on the economy undermined its achievements in other areas. From the outset it was riven by tensions between the left-wing social policy of the Labour Party on the one hand and the conservative economic instincts of Fine Gael ministers such as Alan Dukes and John Bruton on the other. In an effort to reduce public borrowing, the Government had to increase taxes and cut back on public spending. Areas of high government spending, such as health and education, bore the brunt of the cutbacks. In education, despite the achievement of Minister Gemma Hussey in introducing curricular reforms, the period is recalled as one of cutbacks. Pupil–teacher ratios worsened, and in 1986 the Government refused to implement a pay increase awarded to teachers, on the grounds of inability to pay.

In a reversal of the trend of the 1970s, emigration increased in a dramatic fashion. As unemployment levels soared, young people could not get jobs, and they emigrated as a result. As long as public borrowing remained at a high level, the proportion of tax revenue going to service the national debt was unacceptably high. Although unemployment began to fall in 1986, a sustained decline would follow only if strict limits were imposed on government spending.

In two areas of economic policy, the Government was successful. Inflation fell steadily throughout its term of office, and it succeeded in reducing pay settlements, thus paving the way for national pay agreements from 1987 onwards. However, given the economic problems faced by the Government, it is not surprising that it eventually fell over a dispute between Fine Gael and Labour over budget estimates.

Dick Spring leading the Labour ministers out of Government in January 1987

The Fall of the Coalition Government

By mid-December 1986 Fine Gael and Labour had reached a stalemate concerning the 1987 pre-election budget. Labour refused to countenance further cutbacks in government spending, particularly in the Department of Health. Fine Gael, on the other hand, would not agree to increases in taxation. Both parties agreed to break up the Coalition on 20 January 1987. The Labour ministers then announced that they were leaving the Government because they could not agree to the spending cuts proposed in the budget. Garret FitzGerald then advised President Hillery to dissolve the Dáil and call a general election for 17 February 1987.

As they faced the electorate, the parties of the outgoing Government left behind them a varied record in office. Though they had initiated a number of reforms and negotiated the Anglo-Irish Agreement, they would ultimately be judged by the voters mainly on the state of the economy and on the levels of unemployment and emigration.

KEY PERSONALITY: GARRET FITZGERALD (1926–)

Garret FitzGerald — economist and politician — was born in Dublin on 9 February 1926 and was educated at Belvedere College, Dublin, and UCD, where he obtained a degree in Economics. His father, Desmond FitzGerald, had taken part in the 1916 Rising and the War of Independence and was one of the leading members of the Irish Free State Government after 1922. Garret FitzGerald worked in Aer Lingus from 1947 to 1958 and then returned to UCD as a lecturer in Economics from 1959 to 1973. He entered politics in 1964 and served as a Fine Gael senator from 1965 until his election as TD in 1969. He was Opposition spokesman on education (1969–72) and then on finance (1972–3). Within Fine Gael, he was regarded as a radical voice, especially in the area of social and economic policy.

Garret FitzGerald was appointed Minister for Foreign Affairs by Liam Cosgrave in the Fine Gael–Labour Coalition Government that held power from 1973 to 1977. Ireland had recently become a member of the EEC, and FitzGerald greatly heightened the reputation and profile of Ireland within Europe, especially during his presidency of the Council of Ministers from January to June 1975.

Following the general election of 1977 and the fall of the Coalition Government, Liam Cosgrave resigned as leader of Fine Gael and was succeeded by FitzGerald, who immediately set about modernising the party. After the general election of 1981, FitzGerald led Fine Gael into another coalition government with Labour. The FitzGerald Government fell over a controversial budget proposal in 1982, and after two general elections in that year FitzGerald again led a Fine Gael–Labour Coalition Government, which lasted until 1987.

As Taoiseach, Garret FitzGerald hoped to implement his vision of a more pluralist society in Ireland. However, in 1986 the Government's attempt to have the constitutional ban on divorce lifted by referendum failed. His most noted successes related to policy on Northern Ireland. In 1983 the New Ireland Forum was established with the aim of bringing together representatives from North and South in an effort to bridge differences and seek common ground. Garret FitzGerald's efforts culminated in the signing of the Anglo-Irish Agreement in November 1985. This historic agreement recognised Ireland's interest in Northern Ireland and provided the basis for further progress in the years ahead. He also attempted to change attitudes to Northern Ireland in the South by engaging in a constitutional crusade to remove Articles 1 and 2 of the Irish Constitution.

FitzGerald's Government of 1982–7 was beset by economic difficulties. The mounting public debt required strict control of expenditure. Although he developed a very good relationship with Dick Spring, leader of the Labour Party, tensions between the coalition parties over economic policy led to the break-up of the Government in January 1987. After the general election in 1987, Fianna Fáil was returned to power, and Garret FitzGerald resigned as leader of Fine Gael. He retired completely from politics in 1992 and resumed a career in writing and lecturing.

EXERCISES

ORDINARY LEVEL

1. What was Fianna Fáil's strategy in the general election of November 1982?

2. Outline the results of this election.

3. Explain the telephone-tapping scandal that was revealed in January 1983.

4. How did the news of this scandal strengthen the new Government? What was the immediate effect of the scandal on the Fianna Fáil Party?

5. What were the main issues in the abortion referendum of 1983?

6. Write an account of the abortion referendum of 1983.

7. Explain what was meant by Garret FitzGerald's 'constitutional crusade'.

8. Outline the changes made by Minister for Health Barry Desmond in the area of family planning and contraception in 1985.

9. Write a paragraph on the divorce referendum of 1986.

10. What was the New Ireland Forum? List the three main solutions to the problem of Northern Ireland set forth in the final report.

11. Write an account of the Anglo-Irish Agreement (1985) under the following headings.

    (i) Origins of the Agreement

    (ii) Terms of the Agreement

    (iii) Immediate aftermath of the signing of the Agreement

12. Explain why Desmond O'Malley founded the Progressive Democrats in 1985, and list the main aims of the new party.

13. Read the following account of the foundation of the Progressive Democrats, and answer the questions that follow.

    The PDs dominated the headlines and the news bulletins and O'Malley sounded very confident as he went on radio asking for donations of £150,000 a year to make the PDs a viable prospect. In the early days of the new year the party took off. Advertisements were placed in the papers on 2 January seeking money and supporters, and the party headquarters was inundated with people wanting to get involved. By 6 January over 4,000 people had enrolled as members and £25,000 was contributed by public subscription. Over 1,000 people attended the first party constituency meeting at the Marine Hotel in Sutton and the major parties began to sit up and take notice. Haughey went on radio a few days later and expressed the view that the PDs were not acting in the national interest. But the crowds continued to flock to their public meetings . . . O'Malley's imposing presence and Mary Harney's abilities as a speaker contributed to the air of excitement generated at these meetings.

    S. Collins, The Power Game: Ireland Under Fianna Fáil, Dublin: O'Brien 2001

    (i) What appeal did Desmond O'Malley make on radio?

    (ii) What progress had the new party made by 6 January 1986?

    (iii) What event caused the major parties to 'sit up and take notice'?

    (iv) Describe the action that Charles Haughey took.

14. Write an account of the Irish economy under the Coalition Government, 1982–7.

15. Examine carefully the election and referendum posters in Chapter 23 and answer the questions that follow.

   (i)   Choose a poster and write a short account on how effectively it conveys its message.

   (ii) Slogans often appeal to people's feelings. Choose two examples of such slogans and comment upon the message which they convey.

   (iii) Would you regard the pro-life referendum slogans as biased sources? Explain your answer.

HIGHER LEVEL

1. Consider the Coalition Government's handling of social issues such as family planning, divorce and the right to life of the unborn.

2. Read the following account of the foundation of the Progressive Democrat Party in 1985 and answer the questions that follow.

   > The Progressive Democrats were finally launched on 21 December 1985. To begin with the party had just two TDs, Desmond O'Malley and Mary Harney. In acknowledgement of his work in establishing the party Michael McDowell was appointed chairman, which emphasised that the PDs were not simply a Fianna Fáil dissident rump...
   >
   > Gemma Hussey records in her Cabinet diaries how the involvement of McDowell came as a blow to Fine Gael. 'Dessie O'Malley's new party, the Progressive Democrats, was announced today. Will it hurt Fianna Fáil more than us? It is depressing that Michael did this; it must be hurtful to Garret...'
   >
   > Haughey went on radio a few days later and expressed the view that the PDs were not acting in the national interest, but the crowds continued to flock to their public meetings. At these early meetings O'Malley hammered home the core message of the party – that the state was strangling the economy through an involvement matched only by the communist countries of Eastern Europe. He committed the PDs to cutting taxes as the essential first step in putting the economy right.

   > *S. Collins, The Haughey File, Dublin: O'Brien 1992, 79–80*

   (i)   Name the first two TDs in the Progressive Democrat Party.

   (ii) Why was Michael McDowell appointed chairman of the new party?

   (iii) What is meant by the expression 'a Fianna Fáil dissident rump'?

   (iv) From reading the extract can you infer which political party Michael McDowell belonged to before joining the PDs?

   (v)   Describe Charles Haughey's reaction to the foundation of the Progressive Democrats.

   (vi) Explain the core message of the new party.

3. Account for the foundation and early popularity of the Progressive Democrats.

4. Analyse the Anglo-Irish Agreement (1985) and its importance both for Northern Ireland and for Anglo-Irish relations.

5. Discuss the performance of Charles Haughey as leader of the Opposition between 1982 and 1987.

6. Assess the economic policies of the Fine Gael–Labour Coalition Government between 1982 and 1987.

24. Fianna Fáil Enters Coalition

The 1987 General Election

The 1987 general election was dominated by the Fianna Fáil attack on the outgoing Government and the participation of the Progressive Democrats in their first major electoral contest. Fianna Fáil, under the leadership of Charles Haughey, campaigned under the slogan 'There Is a Better Way'. They conducted a nationwide poster campaign criticising the cutbacks in health spending of Garret FitzGerald's Government and promising to spend more on health if elected. Fine Gael and Labour defended their record in

Fianna Fáil poster from the 1987 general election

government, especially the successful negotiation of the Anglo-Irish Agreement. They claimed that a Haughey-led government could not be trusted on Northern Ireland. Many Fianna Fáil speakers agreed to implement the Agreement, although they had criticised it in opposition.

The Progressive Democrats, under Desmond O'Malley, advocated reduced government spending and lower taxes. They blamed Fianna Fáil, Fine Gael and Labour, who were all in government over the previous ten years, for causing serious damage to the economy by allowing government borrowing to get out of control. As an economically conservative party, the PDs drew a direct link between high borrowing and taxes on the one hand and high unemployment on the other. In social matters, however, the PDs were liberal in their views. They supported the introduction of divorce and greater separation of Church and state.

It was the state of the economy, however, that was of greatest concern to voters as they went to the polls in February 1987. Given the high levels of unemployment and emigration, it is not surprising that the outgoing Government of Fine Gael and Labour suffered a serious defeat. Fianna Fáil increased its number of seats from 75 (in November 1982) to 81. This left the party just three seats short of an overall majority. Labour's representation dropped from 16 seats to 12. However, the result was disastrous for Fine Gael, which saw its number of Dáil seats fall from 70 to 51. At their first general election, the Progressive Democrats succeeded in winning 14 seats in the Dáil. Two factors in particular explain the huge fall in the Fine Gael vote. Many voters deserted the party because of the economic crisis of the mid-1980s. In addition to this, the emergence of the Progressive Democrats was a serious blow to Fine

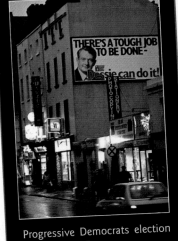

Progressive Democrats election poster in 1987

Gael. Many of their supporters, who would have been reluctant to vote for Fianna Fáil, could now turn to the Progressive Democrats instead. Thus, the 1987 election marked the start of a significant trend in Irish politics. Whereas the Progressive Democrats were founded largely by ex-Fianna Fáil members who were dissatisfied with Charles Haughey, in the long run they would do more damage to Fine Gael than to Fianna Fáil.

When the new Dáil met, Charles Haughey was narrowly elected Taoiseach at the head of a minority Fianna Fáil Government. Without an overall majority, he was faced with a choice between two strategies: he could attempt to reach an agreement with Independents, or he could follow the example of Seán Lemass between 1961 and 1965. At that time Lemass pursued his own policies and challenged the Independents to defeat him if they wished. Haughey chose to adopt the latter approach between 1987 and 1989 and presided over a spectacular reversal of Fianna Fáil's previous approach to dealing with the country's economic problems.

Fiscal Rectitude and the Tallaght Strategy

In two key areas Charles Haughey adopted the policies favoured by his political enemies in Fine Gael and the Progressive Democrats. He overcame his objections to the Anglo-Irish Agreement and worked within the institutions it had established, in the same way as the previous Coalition Government. However, it was in managing the economy that the minority Fianna Fáil Government made its most spectacular U-turn.

Haughey appointed the Sligo TD Ray MacSharry as his Minister for Finance, with a clear mandate to introduce stringent cutbacks in government spending. This was followed by a national wage agreement that applied to all workers and helped to prevent wage increases that were too large for the economy to bear. The policy of making difficult decisions in order to set the economy on the right footing was known as **fiscal rectitude**. After Ray MacSharry had finished his budget speech in 1987, the Fine Gael finance spokesman, Michael Noonan, remarked: 'I have great pleasure today in welcoming Fianna Fáil's acceptance of the Fine Gael analysis of the problem and of the targets which we have set down.' Because Fine Gael supported the Government's policy of fiscal rectitude, the party's new leader, Alan Dukes, made the momentous decision to adopt an approach known as the Tallaght Strategy.

Ray MacSharry, Minister for Finance, brings his budget statement to the Dáil

After the huge defeat sustained by Fine Gael in the 1987 general election, Dr Garret FitzGerald resigned as party leader and was replaced by the Kildare TD and former minister, Alan Dukes. In a speech made at Tallaght, Co. Dublin, Dukes promised that if the Government of Charles Haughey continued to follow the path of fiscal rectitude, then Fine Gael would not attempt to bring it down in the Dáil. This offer of conditional support became known as the Tallaght Strategy. It gave the Haughey Government support for difficult but necessary economic measures between 1987 and 1989. This type of co-operation between Fianna Fáil and Fine Gael had not been witnessed since the Emergency, when all-party co-operation helped to keep Ireland out of World War II. Alan Dukes's statesmanlike action was in the national interest and was widely appreciated. Within his own Fine Gael Party, however, it caused divisions, with many members preferring the traditional approach of outright opposition to the Fianna Fáil Government.

Historians consider that the radical changes in economic policy adopted by the Haughey Government in 1987, and supported by Fine Gael in the Tallaght Strategy, laid the foundations for a period of spectacular growth ten years later, when the Republic became known as the 'Celtic Tiger'.

In attempting to reduce the national debt and make the Irish economy more competitive, Ray MacSharry was keenly aware that the country's prosperity was bound up with its ability to remain competitive in world markets. As a member of the EEC, Ireland needed to be in a position to adapt to the changes taking place in Europe as a whole. One area where the need for change and adaptation was very apparent was fisheries.

Case Study: The Impact of the EEC on Fisheries

Compared with other European countries, the Irish fishing industry was slow to develop. Although a special semi-state body, Bord Iascaigh Mhara (the Irish Sea Fisheries Board), was set up in 1952, progress was slow during the 1950s because of the depressed state of the economy. In 1962 the Board was re-organised, and development of the industry became its main objective. As well as promoting the fishing industry itself, the Board also encouraged the creation of onshore employment in fish processing and other related activities.

When Ireland joined the EEC in 1973, its fishing industry still lagged behind those of many other countries. For example, Denmark, a country only half the size of Ireland, had a fish catch nearly twenty times as great. However, at that stage around 6,000 Irish fishermen, both full-time and part-time, were earning a living in the industry. Because of lack of investment, most Irish fishermen used small vessels and fished close to the shore. Fishing further out was left to foreign fishermen who had larger fishing boats. This situation was to change radically in the years ahead as Irish fishermen took full advantage of grants and other assistance available due to membership of the EEC.

Bord Iascaigh Mhara responded quickly to the changed situation, as can be seen from its official publication, *The Story of Sea Fishing*.

Document 1

Bord Iascaigh Mhara on the development of the fishing industry

In 1975 the Board opened a European office in Paris which has helped to expand established markets on the Continent and has developed new ones; major retail food outlets and food distributors were introduced to high added-value packs of Irish fish; among the newest of these are vac-packed smoked-eel products, mussel meat delicacies and canned herring and mackerel. Market information helps the exporter to get the highest price. Quality has to be attended to and improved, new products developed, and existing ones adapted to command a greater share of the consumer market.

In the past the vast bulk of Irish processed fish has been sent abroad for the final processing. This situation is giving way now to the development of more sophisticated processing in Ireland itself, with consequent benefits to the national economy.

The Board promotes investment from home and overseas sources so that developments at sea and on shore can keep pace with marketing opportunities.

There are further substantial benefits to be gained by setting up a healthy aquaculture sector alongside the traditional fishing industry. Significant species for development include rainbow trout, Atlantic salmon, oysters, mussels, scallops and turbot.

More efficient vessels, technological innovation, and the training of fishermen in the new skills involved, have changed not only the prospects of the young fishermen but the economic outlook and lifestyle of communities where fishing has been traditional for hundreds of years. Processing and freezing facilities, fishmeal manufacture, net making and repairing, marine engineering and the other back-up services created by the needs of the fishermen, their trawlers and their equipment, bring a welcome bustle and activity to the ports they are set up in. In Donegal, for instance, fishing is now the largest single industry and gives employment to 3,000 people, a figure which includes fishermen, fish plant and boatyard workers and those in ancillary industries.

The development of the fishing industry has transformed areas, which at the turn of the century were threatened and deprived, into flourishing and forward-looking communities.

The Story of Sea Fishing, Dublin: Bord Iascaigh Mhara [n.d.]

When Ireland joined the EEC on 1 January 1973, Brussels, as well as Dublin, became a centre of decision-making that would affect the lives of all those involved in the fishing industry. Many Irish fishermen had been disappointed with the agreement negotiated by the Minister for Foreign Affairs concerning Ireland's entry into the EEC. They felt that concessions had been made in the area of fisheries in order to gain better terms under the Common Agricultural Policy. However, once the people had voted overwhelmingly in a referendum to join the EEC, fishing interests in the country had to accept the new situation. Fishermen began to organise themselves into a representative body and to demonstrate publicly for their rights.

Document 2

The setting up of the Irish Fishermen's Organisation

The Irish Fishermen's Organisation was established in 1974 and is the representative body of Irish fishermen in the social, political and economic spheres at both national and international levels. The objectives include representing the interests of fishermen at national and international levels and to formulate proposals for fisheries development. It concerns itself with any developments which the organisation considers to be of interest or benefit to Irish fishermen.

The Story of Sea Fishing, Dublin: Bord Iascaigh Mhara [n.d.]

Under the leadership of its dynamic chairman, Joey Murrin from Donegal, the Irish Fishermen's Organisation soon established a national profile as a key lobby group in the fishing industry. One of its early, unsuccessful demands was for an exclusive 50-mile limit around the coast of Ireland that would be reserved for Irish fishermen only. The newly founded organisation soon engaged in public protest.

The early years of EEC membership were traumatic for fishermen, who now had to accept the right of other EEC countries to fish in the waters around Ireland. They continued to campaign for the 50-mile limit and eventually accepted defeat only in 1978. During 1977 the struggle had been intense, as the author of Document 4 makes clear.

Fishermen take action to protect their livelihood:
Fishing trawlers blockading Dublin port in 1975; soldiers on duty during the fishermen's blockade; fishermen protest outside Government Buildings in Dublin; fishermen demand special treatment for Ireland in the EEC.

Document 3

Fishermen protest in April 1975

In April 1975 Irish fishermen staged a temporary blockade of six major ports to try to force our government to put up a stronger fight on the question of fishing limits, and also to try to induce the government to institute a fuel subsidy and work out a coherent plan for development of our fishery resources. None of these aims was attained but the very widespread public sympathy for the protesters showed that the industry had at last won back the kind of place in the hearts of Irish people that it evidently held in our fishing ports in the Middle Ages, and never since.

**John de Courcy Ireland, *Ireland's Sea Fisheries:
A History*, Dublin: Glendale 1981, 149**

Document 4

The struggle for the 50-mile limit

Throughout the year the struggle continued to try to secure the 50-mile exclusive zone. Ministers were obviously influenced by the intensity of the feelings expressed and the cogency of the arguments advanced in favour of Irish exploitation of what the public now saw as an Irish natural resource. In particular, they saw the deficiencies of the quota systems proposed in Brussels. Who was going to supervise to see no trawler exceeded its quota? (Months later the Irish Fishermen's Organisation promulgated a plan for the planting of inspectors in each boat fishing within 50 miles of Ireland.) The country was virtually promised that there would be no backing down on the 50-mile demand. But by the end of the year it was evident that forces had built up which were making it impossible for the Irish government to hold out. Moreover the industry itself was suffering from loss of investment and decline in morale owing to continuing uncertainty.

Towards the end of the year Brian Lenihan accepted an interim zoning plan, and the two-day fishermen's strike and the Dublin demonstration in February 1978, coinciding as they did with the ruling of the European Court that the previous government's exclusion of large foreign trawlers from the 50-mile limit was invalid, marked the conclusion of this lengthy battle. If the battle itself was lost, the Irish people's interest in the fishing industry had been won and so at last had the authorities' realisation that our fisheries could no longer afford to be neglected. *The Irish Times* wrote in an editorial on 17 February 1978: 'Yet there is hope on the horizon, even for young trawler skippers with £300,000 boats to pay off. Europe's shrinking fishing fleets have few grounds left to them to make up a year's economic working, so that the run down of their fleets which is rapidly taking place is in Ireland's interest.'

John de Courcy Ireland, *Ireland's Sea Fisheries: A History*, Dublin: Glendale 1981, 157–8

At this point of crisis for the Irish fishing industry, the Vice-President of the European Commission, Finn Gundelach, visited Ireland. During a speech at Letterkenny, Co. Donegal, on 17 February 1978 he stressed the fact that membership of the EEC involved both give and take.

Document 5

Solidarity at European level

It is fair and reasonable, as the Commission has proposed, to reserve especially favourable treatment for the Irish fishing industry within Community policies and it is equally fair and reasonable to suggest that other Community fishermen, in whose markets and for whose assistance in other ways Ireland rightly claims equal treatment as a matter of Community law and solidarity, should continue to fish within strictly controlled limits in waters which have just recently come into Irish fisheries jurisdiction. Any other approach by the Commission would have been one-sided and unjust.

**Speech of Finn Gundelach at Letterkenny, 17 February 1978,
reported in the *Irish Times*, 18 February 1978**

As well as attempting to ensure that fishermen from all member states received fair treatment, the EEC authorities in Brussels were very concerned with the conservation of fish stocks. For example, because of over-fishing of herring, the EEC placed a complete ban on herring fishing between 1977 and 1982. This commitment to conservation was one of the cornerstones of the Community's Common Fisheries Policy, which was finally agreed in 1983. An ESRI report on the fishing industry contains a clear account of the new policy.

Document 6

The Common Fisheries Policy (1983)

This policy which was agreed by the EC Council of Ministers in January 1983 provides an overall regulatory framework for sea fishing within the Community. It has three principal elements:

(1) Fishing limits;

(2) Total allowable catches, quotas and other conservation measures; and

(3) Structural policy.

(1) *Fishing Limits:* These define rights of access to fish resources. Ireland has exclusive fishing rights in a zone up to 12 miles from the North-West and South-West coastlines. Along the remaining areas of the coast certain other member states (notably France, UK and the Netherlands) have retained their traditional fishing rights in the 6–12 mile zone, these rights being limited to specific fish varieties.

A major issue concerning access has to do with Spain's entry to the EC. According to the Act of Accession (EEC, 1985) Spain will not be allowed to fish inside the 50-mile Irish zone for a ten-year period commencing on 1 January 1986. The regulations state, however, that there will be orderly opening of the Irish zone to Spanish vessels from 1 January 1996. Fishing in the Irish zone after that date will be restricted to waters outside the 12-mile limit. Rights inside the Irish 12-mile zone have been formally relinquished by Spain but considering the level of illegal fishing in the past this relinquishment is likely to be more hypothetical than real.

Robert O'Connor, *The Irish Sea Fishing Industry*, Dublin: ESRI 1990, 32–3

Within three years of the introduction of the Common Fisheries Policy, the Irish fishing industry was to face a major challenge with the accession of Spain and Portugal to the EEC in 1986. Spain in particular had a large fishing fleet whose owners were eager to fish in Irish waters.

Document 7

The accession of Spain and Portugal to the EEC

Spain and Portugal, two coastal countries with large fishing industries, applied for membership of the EC. Prior to joining the EC, Spain had the fourth largest fishing fleet in the world. The Spanish fleet was equal to almost three quarters of the total fleet of the ten. On accession, nearly a third of all the fishermen in a community of twelve would be Spanish. When account was taken of the fact that three quarters of the 17,000 Spanish fishing vessels weighted over 100 grt. the magnitude of the problems arising from expansion became clear. On the positive side, Spain would open up valuable new markets because Spain had a per capita consumption of fish of 37 kilograms per year compared to an EC average of 16 kilograms per year.

The inclusion of Portugal and Spain opened up opportunities AND created an even greater awareness of the problems of managing a limited renewable resource with an expanding exploiting capacity. Revision of the CFP was required to accommodate such expansion.

Joan McGinley, *Ireland's Fishery Policy*, Teelin, Co. Donegal: Croaghlin Press 1991, 27

By 1986, after more than a decade of EEC membership, the Irish fishing industry had changed radically. The introduction of quotas under the Common Fisheries Policy undoubtedly prevented the industry from developing to its full potential. On a positive note, grants and loans made available by the EEC enabled fishermen to expand their concerns and invest in better boats and equipment.

The fishing industry continued to possess two vital elements that contributed positively to the Irish economy. It provided jobs in areas associated with the primary activity of fishing, and it was an important source of income in economically disadvantaged areas in the West of Ireland. In the mid-1980s almost 80 per cent of the total fish catch was landed at ports along the west coast of Ireland. An ESRI report outlined the importance of fishing in terms both of employment and of regional development.

Document 8

Fisheries: employment and regional development

The labour force in fisheries
In 1986 there were an estimated 12,100 people directly employed either in a full-time or part-time capacity in the fish catching, fish farming and fish processing sectors. This represents an increase of almost 50 per cent on the 1975 level and 8 per cent on the 1980 figure. The details of employment are given in Table 2.

TABLE 2 – EMPLOYMENT IN FISHERIES, FISH PROCESSING AND AQUACULTURE IN 1975, 1980 AND 1986

	1975	1980	1986
Full-time fishermen	2,275	3,486	3,800
Part-time fishermen	4,356	5,339	3,950
Aquaculture	-	500	1,370
Fish processing	1,500	2,080	2,930
Total	8,130	11,404	12,050

Source: BIM

In addition to the numbers engaged in fishing, fish farming and processing there is substantial employment in ancillary industries which service the primary industry such as transport, distribution, net making, boat building, servicing, etc. A study of the fishing industry in Donegal in 1982 (Drudy and Phelan, 1982) found that for every job at sea in the Donegal fishing industry there were two jobs ashore in the fish processing and ancillary industries. The multiplier in other areas is probably less than this since Donegal has a very well-developed on-shore industry.

Regional importance of sea fishing
The greatest concentration of employment in sea fishing is in the West and North-West coastal areas which together account for about 60 per cent of the total employment in the industry (O'Connor et al., 1980). The West coast has 25 per cent, the North-West coast 35 per cent, the South coast 30 per cent and the East coast 10 per cent of the total fishermen.

Though they form only a small proportion of the total national labour force fishermen form a relatively high proportion of the gainfully occupied in their respective regions. In many areas round the coast fishing is the main source of full or part-time employment while in recent times fish farming has opened up new opportunities for isolated communities. The combination of fishing and fish farming based, as they are, on natural resources, provides a source of employment which is compatible with the life styles of the people in those areas.

In 1987 as many as 14 ports situated mainly on the West and South coasts had fish landings in excess of £1.0 million each. Also as indicated above the total gross earnings of fishermen and fish farmers was £94 million in 1987. This sum gives an indication of the flow of income to the coastal regions with incomes to workers in fish processing and services providing additional sources of revenue.

Robert O'Connor, *The Irish Sea Fishing Industry*, Dublin: ESRI 1990, 8–9

By 1990, therefore, the fishing industry in Ireland was in a vibrant condition. Fishermen continued to protest about the activities of Spanish trawlers and to argue for the highest possible quota during the annual EEC fisheries negotiations in December each year. However, successive Irish governments have shown their commitment to the fisheries industry by sustaining a strong

Department of the Marine and by arguing the case of the industry during negotiations at Brussels. The development of aquaculture from the 1980s onwards was further evidence of the strength and resilience of the fisheries sector despite all the challenges and opportunities it has faced since Ireland joined the EEC in 1973.

CASE STUDY: QUESTIONS

COMPREHENSION

1. What action did Bord Iascaigh Mhara take in 1975? (Document 1)

2. How did market information help the fish exporter? (Document 1)

3. What changes were taking place in the final processing of fish? (Document 1)

4. What development does the author of Document 1 favour 'alongside the traditional fishing industry'?

5. Name some other activities associated with the fishing industry (Document 1).

6. How has fishing affected the economy in Donegal? (Document 1)

7. What were the objectives of the Irish Fishermen's Organisation? (Document 2)

8. What action did Irish fishermen take in April 1975? (Document 3)

9. Why did they take this action? (Document 3)

10. How did the public react to the protestors? (Document 3)

11. How did the Irish public regard the 50-mile zone in 1977? (Document 4)

12. What was evident by the end of 1977? (Document 4)

13. What did the European Court decide in February 1978? (Document 4)

14. Explain the main argument made by the author of Document 5.

15. List the three principal elements of the Common Fisheries Policy (Document 6).

16. What arrangement was made regarding Spain? (Document 6)

17. Give two examples from Document 7 to illustrate the extent of the Spanish fishing fleet.

18. What 'positive side' was there to Spain's entry to the EEC? (Document 7)

19. Why was revision of the Common Fisheries Policy necessary? (Document 7)

20. According to Document 8, how many people were employed in the Irish fishing industry in 1986?

21. Name four industries ancillary to fishing (Document 8).

COMPARISON

1. Documents 3 and 4 both concern fishermen. Compare them in terms of subject matter. Which conveys the concerns of fishermen more vividly? Explain your answer.

2. Compare the reference to Donegal in Documents 1 and 8.

3. Documents 6 and 7 both refer to Spain's entry into the EEC and the implications this had for fisheries policy. Compare the references to Spain in both documents.

4. Documents 4 and 5 contain an Irish and a wider European perspective on fisheries in the EEC. Compare the differing points of view.

1. Would you consider Document 1 to be a biased source? Explain your answer.

2. Where do the sympathies of the author of Document 4 lie in the struggle between the fishermen and the Irish Government? Refer to the document in your answer.

3. Would you agree that Document 5 is a carefully argued plea to Irish fishermen to change their views? Show how the author argues his case.

4. Assess the value of Document 7 in conveying the effect on fisheries of the entry of Spain and Portugal to the European Community.

5. Document 8 makes use of a number of important statistics. How effective do you find these in conveying the author's message?

CONTEXTUALISATION

1. Write an account of Irish fisheries in the EEC between 1973 and 1990.

2. Write a paragraph on the importance of fisheries in Co. Donegal.

3. Explain the role of Bord Iascaigh Mhara in Irish fisheries.

Agriculture: The Development of the Beef Industry

The trend towards larger commercial operations in fisheries during the 1980s was also evident in agriculture. The Taoiseach, Charles Haughey, took a particular interest in the development of the beef industry after his return to power in 1987. In June 1987 he announced a massive investment programme for the beef industry. The main beneficiary of this investment was the largest beef producer in the country, Larry Goodman, who agreed to invest £30 million as part of the programme. However, the original plan was never fully implemented.

One of the main foreign markets of the Goodman companies was Iraq, which was ruled by the dictator Saddam Hussein. Because of the dangerous political situation there and the possibility that companies would not be paid for their exports, the Irish Government had set up a system of insurance known as the Export Credit Insurance Scheme. However, in 1986 the Fine Gael Minister for Industry and Commerce, Michael Noonan, had withdrawn cover for exports to Iraq because of the risks of trading with that country. When Fianna Fáil returned to power, the Minister for Industry and Commerce, Albert Reynolds, restored the insurance cover for Iraq. The bulk of this went to Goodman companies. In 1987 export credit for beef exports to Iraq was £41.2 million; in 1988 this had risen to £78.5 million.

Opposition TDs questioned the close link between the Government and the Goodman companies and expressed serious concern about the vast amounts of

Businessman and beef producer Larry Goodman boarding his helicopter in 1990

taxpayers' money put at risk in the Export Credit Insurance Scheme. Charles Haughey vigorously defended the Goodman companies and the Government's support for the beef industry. These events were later to result in major controversy and became the subject of a tribunal of inquiry into the beef industry.

The 1989 General Election: Fianna Fáil Enters Coalition

While Charles Haughey's Minority Government was under pressure in the Dáil in relation to the beef industry, it also faced criticism for its continuing cutbacks in expenditure, especially in the area of healthcare. Opposition speakers constantly taunted the Government with Fianna Fáil's 1987 election slogan condemning cutbacks.

In May 1989 the Government was defeated in the Dáil on a motion by the Opposition calling for state compensation for haemophiliacs who had been infected with HIV, the virus that causes AIDS, as a result of receiving contaminated blood products from state agencies. Normally, such a defeat in the Dáil would not have led to a general election. However, Haughey was anxious to secure an overall majority, and he called an immediate general election. He believed that public support for the Government's reduction in borrowing would help him to achieve this. However, his decision to call the election turned out to be one of the greatest misjudgements of his political career.

In the general election of 15 June 1989, Fianna Fáil lost 4 seats, dropping to 77. Fine Gael improved marginally, increasing by 4 seats to 55. The parties of the left – Labour and the Workers' Party – gained at the expense of Fianna Fáil and the PDs.

When the new Dáil convened, it failed to elect a Taoiseach, and Charles Haughey had to continue as a caretaker Taoiseach while negotiations took place between the different political parties. Charles Haughey's own preference was to continue leading a minority Fianna Fáil government. However, with just seventy-seven seats, seven short of an

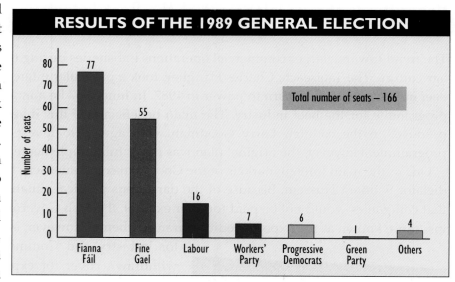

overall majority, this was not possible. Negotiations began between Fianna Fáil and the Progressive Democrats. The two parties had just enough seats between them to form a majority government. Although considerable opposition to coalition existed within Fianna Fáil, it was now the only way the party could stay in power. Charles Haughey and the Progressive Democrat leader, Desmond O'Malley, came to an agreement to form a coalition. As part of the arrangement, the PDs were to be allocated two senior ministries and one junior ministry: Desmond O'Malley became Minister for Industry and Commerce; Bobby Molloy was appointed Minister for the Environment; and Mary Harney became a Minister of State.

The Progressive Democrats approved of the economic policies pursued by Fianna Fáil since 1987, and the new Programme for Government committed the Coalition to maintain strict control of the public finances. The two parties also agreed to continue implementing the Anglo-Irish Agreement in Northern Ireland.

Entry into coalition for the first time was a major change of direction for Fianna Fáil. For decades the party had condemned coalitions as unstable and unreliable. Opposition to coalition was considered to be a 'core value' in the party. This principle had to be abandoned if the party was to remain in office. Many within Fianna Fáil deeply resented entering into coalition with the Progressive Democrats and blamed Charles Haughey for calling an unnecessary election. Despite bitter differences in the past, Haughey and O'Malley co-operated well in government. In 1990 Charles Haughey was to experience mixed fortunes. During Ireland's presidency of the European Union (EU), his international reputation was greatly enhanced. However, Fianna Fáil experienced political trauma during the presidential election campaign at home.

One of Mary Robinson's posters in the 1990 presidential election

Mary Robinson Is Elected President of Ireland

In November 1990 President Patrick Hillery's second term of office was due to come to an end. There had not been a presidential election since 1973, as presidents since then had been agreed candidates. From an early stage the Labour Party was determined to put forward a strong candidate for the presidency. The party leader, Dick Spring, persuaded a former Labour senator and eminent lawyer, Mary Robinson, to stand for the presidency. Fianna Fáil chose the Tánaiste and long-serving government minister, Brian Lenihan, as the party candidate. Fine Gael nominated the former SDLP politician, Austin Currie, to stand for the party.

From the outset, Mary Robinson carried out a dynamic campaign throughout the country. By contrast, the Fine Gael campaign was struggling from the beginning. It soon became evident that the election was a contest between Mary Robinson and Brian Lenihan. Lenihan's bid for the presidency suffered a major setback when a controversy erupted over attempts to influence President Hillery in 1982. Lenihan was accused of making a phone call to the President in an effort to persuade him not to dissolve the Dáil when Garret FitzGerald's Government fell in January 1982. Fianna Fáil hoped that Charles Haughey would be elected Taoiseach in the Dáil without a general election. Although Lenihan denied these allegations, the controversy that followed considerably lessened his chances of being elected President.

Meanwhile, Mary Robinson's campaign was going from strength to strength. When the election took place on 7 November 1990, she was elected President of Ireland. Although Brian Lenihan was ahead on the first count, he was overtaken by Robinson, who received a large number of transfers when Austin Currie was eliminated. For the first time in the history of the state, a Fianna Fáil candidate had been defeated in a presidential election.

The election of a woman to the highest office of the state was a momentous occasion. Her style of presidency was to be very different from that of previous presidents. She made the office of President accessible to more and more people by travelling extensively throughout the country. She also emphasised the wider Irish community abroad by referring to the important role of Irish emigrants throughout the world. As an ambassador for Ireland on her official visits abroad, Mary Robinson frequently spoke out in favour of the poor and the marginalised and enhanced Ireland's reputation within the international community.

Above all, Mary Robinson symbolised the emergence of a modern, confident and outward-looking Ireland during the final decade of the twentieth century.

KEY PERSONALITY: CHARLES HAUGHEY (1925–2006)

Charles Haughey was born in Castlebar, Co. Mayo, on 16 September 1925. He was reared in Dublin and was educated at St Joseph's CBS in Fairview and at UCD. He studied Law at King's Inns, but although called to the bar, he never practised law and concentrated instead on a career in accounting. He was a co-founder of the accountancy firm Haughey and Boland in 1950. He married Maureen Lemass, daughter of Seán Lemass, in 1951. He joined the Fianna Fáil Party in 1948, but his early attempts to get elected to Dáil Éireann failed. He was first elected to the Dáil as TD for Dublin North East in the general election of 1957.

After serving as Parliamentary Secretary to the Minister for Justice in 1960–61, he entered the Cabinet as Minister for Justice in 1961. He proved to be a talented, energetic and innovative minister. He introduced an important legislative reform in the Succession Act, which guaranteed financial entitlement for widows. He was Minister for Agriculture from 1964 to 1966 and Minister for Finance from 1966 to 1970. Highly ambitious, Haughey contested the leadership of the party after the resignation of Seán Lemass in 1966. However, he withdrew from the contest when Jack Lynch emerged as a compromise candidate.

Haughey held strong republican views and was increasingly critical of Jack Lynch's cautious approach to the Northern Ireland crisis in 1969–70. Haughey's ministerial career came to an abrupt end when, together with Neil Blaney, he was sensationally dismissed by Lynch from the Cabinet in 1970 for failing to support government policy on Northern Ireland. He was arrested and charged with conspiring to import arms illegally to aid northern nationalists. Although a jury acquitted him of all charges, he remained in the political wilderness for much of the 1970s.

During Fianna Fáil's years in opposition from 1973 to 1977, Haughey gradually built up a new power base within the party, and his rehabilitation seemed complete when Lynch appointed him Opposition spokesman on health in 1975. When Fianna Fáil returned to power after a landslide victory in the 1977 general election, Jack Lynch appointed Haughey Minister for Health and Social Welfare. With the party's popularity declining in the face of a deepening economic crisis, many of the newly elected TDs became anxious about holding their seats in the next general election. Under increasing political pressure, Jack Lynch resigned in December 1979. In the leadership contest that followed, Charles Haughey — who had built up considerable support among some of the new Fianna Fáil TDs — defeated his arch-rival, George Colley, by 44 votes to 38.

Haughey was elected Taoiseach after a very bitter Dáil debate that witnessed unprecedented attacks by the Opposition on his character and integrity. Despite commitments to curb public expenditure, Haughey's Government failed to come to grips with the worsening state of the public finances, and he lost office in 1981. However, the incoming Fine Gael–Labour Government soon ran into difficulty and fell from power in 1982, and after another general election, Haughey led a minority Fianna Fáil Government. In the midst of political controversy this Government also fell from power, and a second general election in November 1982 returned a Fine Gael–Labour government, which remained in office until 1987.

Haughey had an undistinguished period as leader of the Opposition from 1982 to 1987. Within his own party, his personal style of leadership antagonised many and resulted in a number of unsuccessful attempts to oust him as leader. Following the general election of 1987, Haughey once again led a minority Fianna Fáil Government. This administration is widely regarded as his most successful, as it succeeded in restoring balance to the public finances. However, he made a serious error of judgement when he called a snap general election in 1989 in the hope of gaining more seats. Instead Fianna Fáil lost seats, and for the first time in its history entered coalition government — this time with the Progressive Democrats, led by Desmond O'Malley.

Although Haughey skilfully led the Fianna Fáil–PD Coalition and maintained a good working relationship with Desmond O'Malley, some within Fianna Fáil were very critical of the party's entry into coalition government.

However, the pressure on Haughey's leadership came from an unexpected source. Early in 1992 his former Minister for Justice, Seán Doherty – previously an enthusiastic Haughey supporter – announced that Haughey had been aware of phone taps on two political journalists when he was Taoiseach for a short period in 1982. Although Haughey denied this, the controversy resulted in his resignation. He was succeeded as Taoiseach and as leader of Fianna Fáil by Albert Reynolds.

Haughey's long political career was dogged by controversy. Although a talented and reforming minister in a number of departments, his success as Taoiseach was more mixed. He remained a very controversial figure, evoking feelings of loathing among some and love and loyalty among others.

KEY PERSONALITY: MARY ROBINSON (1944–)

Mary Robinson – barrister, politician and President of Ireland – was born in Co. Mayo in May 1944. Both her parents were medical doctors. She was educated at Trinity College, Dublin, and obtained law degrees at King's Inns in Dublin and Harvard University in the USA. She was Reid Professor of Law at Trinity College from 1969 to 1975. She gained a very high reputation as a constitutional lawyer and was involved in many attempts in Irish and European courts to challenge and change the law in areas such as access to legal aid, the decriminalisation of homosexual activity and the right of women to serve on juries.

She was elected to the Seanad in 1969 and held her seat until 1989. As a senator, she introduced the first bill to make contraceptives available in the Republic, but it received little support. In 1976 she joined the Labour Party but failed in a number of attempts to be elected to the Dáil. She was a member of the New Ireland Forum, which was established in 1983, and of the Oireachtas Joint Committee on Marital Breakdown (1983–5). She resigned from the Labour Party after the signing of the Anglo-Irish Agreement (1985) in protest at the failure to involve unionists in the negotiations leading up to the Agreement.

In 1990 Dick Spring, leader of the Labour Party, asked Mary Robinson to accept a Labour Party nomination for the presidential election later that year. She agreed to accept the nomination on the condition that she would not have to rejoin the Labour Party or run strictly as a Labour candidate. She ran a highly successful nationwide campaign that resulted in her election as Ireland's first woman President. During her time in office from 1990 to 1997, she transformed the role of President. She visited communities throughout the country and took a special interest in poverty and human rights issues throughout the world. In 1996 she was the first Irish head of state to pay an official visit to Britain, where she was received by Queen Elizabeth II.

Mary Robinson did not seek a second term of office as President. She resigned in November 1997 to take up a new position as United Nations High Commissioner for Human Rights.

ORDINARY LEVEL

1. Explain the campaign strategies of Fianna Fáil and the Progressive Democrats in the 1987 general election.

2. Outline the results of the 1987 general election.

3. What was meant by 'fiscal rectitude'?

4. Explain in detail the Tallaght Strategy of Alan Dukes.

5. What were the main achievements of Ray MacSharry as Minister for Finance?

6. Write an account of the effect of Ireland's EEC membership on Irish fisheries.

7. Outline the main terms of the Common Fisheries Policy (1983).

8. What effect did the accession of Spain and Portugal to the EEC in 1986 have on Irish fisheries?

9. Write a paragraph on the beef industry under Fianna Fáil between 1987 and 1989.

10. Write an account of the 1989 general election and the formation of the Fianna Fáil–Progressive Democrat Coalition Government.

11. Write an account of the election of Mary Robinson as President of Ireland in 1990.

HIGHER LEVEL

1. Discuss in detail the economic policies of the minority Fianna Fáil Government between 1987 and 1989.

2. Assess the part played by the Tallaght Strategy in the economic development of Ireland after 1987.

3. Discuss the impact of EEC membership on Irish fisheries.

4. Account for the formation of the Fianna Fáil–Progressive Democrat Coalition Government in 1989.

5. Discuss the election of Mary Robinson as President of Ireland in 1990.

6. Contrast the economic policies of the Fianna Fáil 1987–9 Government and the Fianna Fáil–Progressive Democrat Coalition on the one hand with those of the Fine Gael–Labour Coalition of 1982–7 on the other.

7. 'During most of the 1980s political progress in Ireland was hampered by economic difficulties.' Discuss.

8. Assess the political career of Charles Haughey between 1957 and 1990.

GOVERNMENT, ECONOMY AND SOCIETY IN THE REPUBLIC OF IRELAND, 1949–89

During this section you became familiar with the following KEY CONCEPTS:

Economic Planning
The government decides economic goals and targets to be achieved over a set period of time.

Free Trade
This refers to an economic system in which goods and services can move freely from one country to another without the imposition of taxes or tariffs on imported goods.

Common Market
This refers to a free trade area in which goods and services can move freely between member countries.

Equality of Opportunity
This concept means that everyone, regardless of background, religion or race, will be given the same chance to succeed in life. It particularly refers to the areas of justice, employment and education.

Ecumenism
This movement emphasises the common beliefs and traditions rather than the differences between the various Christian churches and works for eventual unity among Christians.

Secularisation
This refers to the declining influence of religion in people's lives.

Balance of Payments
This refers to the difference between the value of exported goods and the value of imported goods in a country.

Discrimination
This refers to a bias against a person or group of people on the basis of factors such as race, religion, social class or age.

Censorship
This involves the banning by the state of books or films considered to be a danger mostly to the morals of the people.

Pluralism
This refers to the development of a society that accommodates people of different religions, races and points of view.

Liberalisation
This refers to the establishment of a more open and questioning society that accommodates different points of view, especially in areas such as divorce, contraception and other moral issues. In economic matters, it refers to a decrease in state control and the encouragement of private enterprise and competition.

PART 4:
POLITICS AND SOCIETY IN NORTHERN IRELAND, 1949-93

Northern Ireland Comes of Age

In April 1949, with the declaration of a Republic, the twenty-six counties of Southern Ireland finally achieved complete independence. The Southern state left the British Commonwealth and severed all connections with the King of England. However, this development did not weaken the connection between Northern Ireland and the rest of the United Kingdom. It actually strengthened the union between both.

In response to the decision of the Irish Government in Dublin to leave the British Commonwealth, the Labour Government in London, under Prime Minister Clement Atlee, gave a guarantee to the unionists in Northern Ireland. The British Government passed the Ireland Act (1949), which stated that Northern Ireland would remain part of the United Kingdom unless the parliament in Belfast voted against the union. As the unionists had a huge majority, this was extremely unlikely to occur. However, despite their strong position in Northern Ireland, unionists never felt secure and free from internal and external threats to their rule.

Northern Ireland: A Divided Society

Since 1921 the six counties of Northern Ireland had been ruled by the Unionist Party. Under the Government of Ireland Act (1920), passed by the Westminster Parliament, partition was introduced into Ireland. The six counties of Northern Ireland remained part of the United Kingdom. The Imperial Parliament in London retained control over war and peace, foreign affairs, taxation and other important matters. The Home Rule-style parliament in Belfast was responsible for the day-to-day running of the state and controlled areas such as law and order, education, health and local government.

Stormont Castle, Belfast. This was especially built to house the Parliament of Northern Ireland.

The Northern Parliament consisted of a Senate and a House of Commons. Out of the fifty-two MPs in the House of Commons, unionists usually accounted for at least forty. Because they made up two-thirds of the population, they always controlled the government.

From the foundation of the State of Northern Ireland in 1921, the nationalist minority was deeply resentful and longed for a united Ireland. As most unionists were Protestants and most nationalists were Catholics, religious and political divisions went hand in hand. To protect Northern Ireland and to secure its place within the United Kingdom, the Unionist Government took some controversial steps, including the following:

- The Special Powers Act, which gave extensive emergency powers to the government, including internment without trial.
- The establishment of the B Specials, part-time policemen who assisted the Royal Ulster Constabulary (RUC).
- The abolition of proportional representation (PR) in elections.

These official measures were deeply resented by nationalists. They complained that the Special Powers Act and the B Specials were always used against them. Proportional representation (PR) had been introduced by the British Government because it was fairer to minorities than the British straight vote system.

In addition to official measures, nationalists also complained of widespread discrimination in the areas of jobs and housing. The Northern Ireland Civil Service, local government bodies and private employers tended to favour Protestants over Catholics when allocating jobs and council housing. These issues were to fester and poison relations between Protestants and Catholics for decades, until violence erupted during the 1960s.

From Depression to Prosperity

During the 1920s and 1930s Northern Ireland suffered from serious economic depression. Under the rule of its first Prime Minister, Sir James Craig (Lord Craigavon from 1927), stability and law and order were established. However, Craig made no real effort to win over the Catholic nationalist minority. On one occasion he boasted that Northern Ireland was a 'Protestant state for a Protestant people'. During his time as Prime Minister, healthcare, housing and social welfare were at a very low standard. Because of serious unemployment, over 50,000 people emigrated from Northern Ireland between 1926 and 1937. During the 1930s there were riots in Belfast because of poverty and unemployment. In 1938 the average income of people in Northern Ireland stood at 56 per cent of the level in Great Britain. However, following the outbreak of World War II in September 1939, this situation was to change dramatically.

Sir James Craig, the first Prime Minister of Northern Ireland

Whereas the Irish Free State under the rule of Éamon de Valera remained neutral during World War II, Northern Ireland took a full part in the war as part of the United Kingdom. The economy of the northern state was geared to meet the needs of the British war effort. Farmers increased food production and got good prices on the British market. The Harland & Wolff shipyard went into full production, as did aircraft, engineering and textile factories. Unemployment declined sharply, from around 25 per cent during the 1930s to around 5 per cent by

Farmers ploughing land in the grounds of Stormont Castle during World War II as part of a campaign to grow more food for the war effort

the end of the war in 1945. Wages also rose during the war, leading to increased prosperity among ordinary people.

The people of Belfast suffered severely when the city was bombed a number of times in 1941. It has been estimated that around 1,100 people were killed, over 56,000 houses were destroyed or damaged and over £20 million worth of damage was done to property.

This suffering, together with the overall contribution of the people of Northern Ireland to the British war effort, strengthened the bond between the state and the rest of the United Kingdom. At the end of the war in May 1945 the British Prime Minister, Winston Churchill, paid tribute to the people of Northern Ireland when he declared that without the use of its ports, Great Britain would have had to invade the Irish Free State.

In July 1945 Churchill was overwhelmingly defeated in a general election and his government was replaced by a Labour Government under Prime Minister Clement Atlee. The measures introduced by this government were to have a profound impact on the people of Northern Ireland in the decades ahead.

The Welfare State

One of the main promises of the new Labour Government in Great Britain was to introduce a Welfare State. In the future, health care, social welfare and education would be radically changed to create a more equal society. In return for increased taxation, the state provided free health care, higher old-age and disability pensions and better educational opportunities for all sections of the population.

The leaders of the Unionist Party in Northern Ireland did not welcome the introduction of a welfare state. They were opposed to radical social change and were closely linked to the Conservative Party in Westminster. However, they were bound to implement the welfare state policies of the Government in London. In doing so, they obtained highly favourable measures for the people of Northern Ireland. The task of implementing the

Lord Brookeborough, Prime Minister of Northern Ireland from 1943 to 1963

welfare state in Northern Ireland lay with the Government of Sir Basil Brooke (later Lord Brookeborough), who became Prime Minister in 1943.

Under an agreement reached in 1946 between the governments in Belfast and London, Northern Ireland was to enjoy the same level of social services as the rest of the United Kingdom. In return for increased funding from the British Government, the Government of Northern Ireland accepted increased control by the British Treasury in London. The increased funding was used to bring about significant improvements in the areas of healthcare, social welfare and education.

Children receiving lunch in school as part of the improvements in education under the welfare state

A Transformation in Healthcare

Healthcare in Northern Ireland had not advanced significantly since the state was founded in 1921. By the 1940s healthcare in the province lagged behind the provisions in the rest of the United Kingdom. While the better-off sections of society could afford to pay for private healthcare, poorer people had to depend on an under-funded and inadequate public system of healthcare. This situation was radically changed in 1948 when a national health service was set up in Northern Ireland. Almost identical to the system enacted in Great Britain in the same year, it introduced a free medical service which was open to all. People could attend a doctor of their choice and all healthcare, including medicines, would be free.

Sustained efforts were made to tackle the devastating disease of tuberculosis (TB), which was responsible for almost half the deaths in the 15–25 age group during the 1940s. This problem was so serious in Northern Ireland that a Tuberculosis Authority was established in 1941. By means of an effective screening programme and the use of new drugs, the death rate from tuberculosis was considerably reduced. By 1954 it was reduced to the same level as in other parts of the United Kingdom.

Due to a totally inadequate health service in the past, the impact of the new National Health Service was more dramatic in Northern Ireland than in England, Scotland or Wales.

Improvements in Social Welfare and Housing

Along with the improvements in healthcare, there was a complete transformation in social welfare. Under the welfare state, a new system of national insurance was introduced. All workers paid regular contributions into a social insurance fund. In return, they received payments from the state after retirement or when unemployed. The sick, the elderly and the widowed received vastly improved levels of payment.

Advances also took place in the provision of public housing. Before World War II, the standard of housing for poorer sections of society was particularly low. This situation was clearly seen during the Blitz in Belfast in 1941, when there was a high level of death, injury and destruction among the closely packed, poor-quality terraced houses in the city. In 1945 the Minister for Health and Local Government, William Grant, set up the Northern Ireland Housing Trust with power to borrow money from the government in order to build houses. Between 1945 and 1963, around 113,000 new houses were built. Although the Housing Trust was fair in its allocation of houses, the same could not be said of the local authorities. Many of these, under unionist control, favoured fellow unionists and Protestants in the allocation of council housing. This was to be a source of much tension between unionists and nationalists in the years ahead.

New houses built by local authorities being opened in Belfast in November 1948

Reform in Education

As in the case of health and social welfare, educational reforms introduced in Great Britain were also implemented in Northern Ireland. Under the Education Act (1947), major changes were introduced at all levels, from primary to university. At the end of primary education, pupils sat for an examination known as the 11 Plus. The most able 20 per cent attended grammar schools which followed a strictly academic curriculum. The other 80 per cent attended intermediate or secondary schools which followed a more technical programme. The vast majority of pupils did not pay fees and there was a huge increase in state grants for all types of schools. As a result of these reforms, the numbers attending second-level schools in Northern Ireland doubled between 1947 and 1952.

As in the rest of the United Kingdom, third-level education became accessible to greater numbers of students. Grants were available to enable less well-off students to attend university.

Despite the improvements introduced by the 1947 Education Act, the changes met with strong opposition from sections of both the Catholic and Protestant communities. Catholic bishops complained that their schools still received lower grants than the largely Protestant state system. They also believed that the state was gaining too much control over education. Many Protestants were alarmed by the provisions in the Education Act that diminished the role of religious instruction in state schools. Their anger was directed at the Education Minister, Colonel Hall-Thompson. Although he successfully introduced the educational reforms, he resigned in 1949 when the Prime Minister, Lord Brookeborough, failed to support his plans concerning pensions for Catholic teachers.

Although introduced in controversial circumstances, the education reforms played a significant role in transforming society in Northern Ireland. Both Protestants and Catholics remained at school longer and attended university in greater numbers. The implications for the Catholic population were particularly profound. Within a short period, educated and articulate young Catholics emerged who were not prepared to put up with discrimination under unionist rule and went on to campaign for civil rights for all citizens of Northern Ireland.

The Economy of Northern Ireland

While the welfare state was being introduced into Northern Ireland after 1945, changes were also taking place in the economy. At this time, Northern Ireland remained the most disadvantaged region in the United Kingdom. The average rate of unemployment during the 1950s was 7 per cent, in marked contrast to the economic prosperity in Great Britain and much of Western Europe at the time.

Agriculture remained the single most important industry in the province at this time. About a quarter of the workforce was still engaged in agriculture in the late 1940s. The majority of these worked on small family farms. Although farmers enjoyed government subsidies and guaranteed prices on the British market, this did not

Farmers working on the land in Co. Down in the 1940s

prevent a decline in the numbers working in agriculture. During the 1950s the number of men working on the land declined by 27 per cent, largely due to the increased use of tractors and other forms of machinery.

The numbers working in traditional industries in Northern Ireland also declined after 1945. The linen industry experienced a rapid decline when linen became less popular on world markets. Synthetic materials like rayon and nylon had taken over much of linen's traditional trade. A large number of linen factories closed down and 27,000 jobs were lost in the industry between 1948 and 1964.

Another significant traditional industry, shipbuilding, also experienced difficulties. In the immediate post-war period it continued to prosper, but declined after 1955 due to increased competition from Germany and Japan.

In an effort to provide jobs for the increasing population, the government had to look beyond agriculture and traditional industries. A number of laws were passed to provide incentives to foreign companies locating in Northern Ireland. Largely as a result of these incentives, around 55,000 new jobs were created between 1945 and 1963.

Factory workers bleaching linen in 1948

Despite these achievements, unemployment remained high, especially in strongly nationalist areas such as Derry and Newry. In the early 1960s protests and demonstrations were organised by trade unions over the high levels of unemployment.

Whereas social and economic issues played a central role in people's lives, the underlying divisions between unionists and nationalists continued to dominate the political life of the province.

RELIGION AND UNEMPLOYMENT IN NORTHERN IRELAND IN 1961		
County	% Catholic	% Unemployment
Londonderry City	67.1	7.5
Co. Tyrone	54.8	12.3
Co. Fermanagh	53.2	9.8
Co. Armagh	47.3	12.8
Co. Londonderry	42.6	11.5
Co. Down	28.6	8.3
Co. Antrim	24.4	6.7
Belfast City	27.5	8.5

The Anti-Partition Movement

On 15 November 1945 nationalist MPs and senators were among 500 people who gathered in Dungannon, Co. Tyrone to set up the Irish Anti-Partition League. The aim of the new movement was to unite all nationalists into a solid bloc in order to campaign against partition. The league also hoped to gain support from the de Valera Government in Dublin and from Irish emigrants in the US and in other countries abroad. De Valera began an international campaign against partition. However, the First Inter-Party Government (1948–51), under the leadership of John A. Costello, continued the Anti-Partition Campaign. At the declaration of the Irish Republic in April 1949, the southern state severed all connections with the British Commonwealth. Costello declared at the time that his aim was 'to take the gun out of Irish politics'. He hoped to achieve Irish unity by peaceful means. A public relations campaign was begun under the direction of the Minister for External Affairs, Seán MacBride, to persuade the British Government to end partition. Very little effort was made to persuade the Ulster unionists of the advantages of entering a united Ireland.

Sean McBride (second from the left) waiting to speak at an anti-partition demonstration in London in 1951

While most Irish nationalists were committed to ending partition by peaceful means, the members of the IRA continued to take a different view.

The IRA and the Border Campaign

Between 1956 and 1962 the IRA engaged in a series of attacks on Northern Ireland from across the border in the Republic. This became known as the Border Campaign. The campaign, codenamed Operation Harvest, began in December 1956 with attacks on a number of police barracks in border areas. Most of these attacks ended in failure. The most famous episode in the Border Campaign took place on 31 December 1956 when twelve IRA men attacked the RUC barracks in Brookeborough, Co. Fermanagh. Two IRA men, Fergal O'Hanlon and Sean South, were killed in this operation. Their deaths gave rise to a wave of sympathy and huge numbers attended their funerals. In the general election in the Republic of Ireland in March 1957, four Sinn Féin TDs were elected. However, they refused to take their seats in the Dáil.

An RUC officer questioning the occupants of a car during the Border Campaign in December 1956

Although the Border Campaign continued until 1961, it achieved no tangible results. The Brookeborough Government took strict measures against the threat from the IRA. Security was improved at police barracks, the part-time B Special police reserve was called into action and internment without trial was introduced. At the same time, the

Fianna Fáil Government in the Republic of Ireland introduced internment without trial.

By the autumn of 1958 nearly all the leading IRA activists were either interned, in prison or dead. Internment came to an end in the Republic in March 1959 and in Northern Ireland in April 1961. On 26 February 1962 the IRA issued an official statement announcing the end of the Border Campaign. During the campaign, twelve IRA members and six RUC men were killed, thirty-two members of the security forces were injured and over 200 IRA members were convicted and sentenced for their

The funeral of Sean South in January 1957

role in the campaign. The Border Campaign did not bring Irish unity any closer and after its close in 1962 the IRA did not re-emerge as a force in Northern Ireland until after the outbreak of the Troubles in 1969.

The Close of the Brookeborough Era

With the exception of the Border Campaign, the 1950s and early 1960s were characterised by relative political stability in Northern Ireland. The IRA campaign posed little real threat to the security of the state. Most nationalists rejected violence and supported peaceful constitutional politics. Brookeborough's Government failed to take the opportunity to encourage Catholics to participate more in the institutions of the state. Instead, unionists continued to regard Catholics with deep suspicion and remained attached to the policy of Protestant supremacy.

The greatest difficulties facing the Brookeborough Government, therefore, emerged not over political divisions, but over economic concerns. As we have already seen, unemployment rates remained high in Northern Ireland. Trade unionists protested against the record of the Brookeborough Government, and in the general election of 1962 the unionists lost votes and seats to the Northern Ireland Labour Party. In the aftermath of this election, discontent grew among unionists with Lord Brookeborough, who had been Prime Minister since 1943. Eventually, leading members of the Unionist Party compelled the reluctant Prime Minister to resign in March 1963. He was succeeded in office by the Minister of Finance, Captain Terence O'Neill.

EXERCISES

ORDINARY LEVEL

1. What was the importance of the Ireland Act (1949)?

2. Who controlled the government of Northern Ireland after 1921?

3. What steps were taken by the Unionist Government of Northern Ireland to secure the position of Northern Ireland within the United Kingdom? How did nationalists respond to these measures?

4. Write a paragraph on the state of the Northern Ireland economy during the 1930s.

5. What impact did World War II have on the economy of Northern Ireland?

6. How did the Unionist Party in Northern Ireland react to the introduction of the welfare state?

7. Outline the main changes brought about in the area of healthcare in Northern Ireland as a result of the introduction of the welfare state.

8. What improvements occurred in social welfare and housing?

9. Outline the reforms brought about in education and explain their role in transforming society in Northern Ireland.

10. What changes occurred in agriculture at this time?

11. How did traditional industries perform in Northern Ireland in the 1950s?

12. What was the anti-partition movement?

13. Write an account of the Border Campaign.

14. What difficulties were facing the Brookeborough Government in the early 1960s?

HIGHER LEVEL

1. Explain how Northern Ireland was a divided society after 1921.

2. State why you think nationalists felt aggrieved.

3. Explain the economic and political impact of Northern Ireland's participation in World War II.

4. 'The introduction of the welfare state brought about a social and economic transformation in Northern Ireland.' Do you agree with this statement?

5. What were the main economic changes which took place in Northern Ireland between 1949 and 1963?

6. State how the IRA differed in aims and tactics from the Anti-Partition League.

7. 'The Border Campaign of the 1950s achieved no tangible results.' Discuss this statement.

Captain Terence O'Neill

Captain Terence O'Neill was forty-eight years of age when he succeeded Lord Brookeborough as Prime Minister of Northern Ireland in March 1963. A leading member of the Unionist Party, he had already served as Minister of Finance. Coming from a privileged, aristocratic background, he attended a private school and university in England. After this he served as an officer in the British army. Unlike some of his predecessors, he did not relate well to ordinary people.

Terence O'Neill (centre), Prime Minister of Northern Ireland from 1963 to 1969

Despite his privileged unionist background, O'Neill was committed to the modernisation of Northern Ireland for the benefit of all sections of the community. In this regard he represented a more liberal type of unionism, which was in marked contrast to the approach of Craigavon and Brookeborough, who saw Northern Ireland as a 'Protestant state for a Protestant people'. Speaking during a parliamentary debate at Stormont, O'Neill stated that his principal aims were 'to make Northern Ireland economically stronger and prosperous...and to build bridges between the two traditions within our community'.

Economic Transformation

During his seven years as Minister of Finance prior to becoming Prime Minister, Terence O'Neill had played a key role in attracting foreign industries to Northern Ireland. He was clearly convinced of the merits of economic planning, which was opposed by the more conservative Lord Brookeborough. O'Neill greatly admired the implementation of the Whitaker Report and the Programme for Economic Expansion by the Lemass Government in the Irish Republic. On becoming Prime Minister, O'Neill invited Professor Wilson of Glasgow University, a native of Northern Ireland, to draw up a report on the future direction of the economy. Published in February 1965 and entitled *Economic Development in Northern Ireland*, Wilson's report set high targets of economic expansion, just like the Whitaker Report in the South. The prevailing optimistic outlook in economic matters was expressed by Terence O'Neill in his opening speech as Prime Minister:

> It is a new motorway driving deeper into the province. It is a new airport which will match our position as the busiest air centre in Britain outside London. It is a new hospital in Londonderry–the most modern in the British Isles. It is new laboratories and research facilities at Queen's to carry us to the frontiers of existing knowledge and beyond. It is the replacement of derelict slums by modern housing estates.

In some respects, the Northern Ireland economy performed well during the O'Neill years. The annual growth rate of 4 per cent was higher than that in the United Kingdom as a whole. During the 1960s around 40,000 new jobs were created in Northern Ireland. At the same time, however, around 25,000 jobs were lost in older industries such as textiles and shipbuilding.

Another example of O'Neill's break with the past was his decision to recognise the Northern Ireland section of the Irish Congress of Trade Unions. This represented mostly Catholic workers, as the majority of Protestant trade union members belonged to British-based unions. A much more symbolic departure from the past occurred in 1965, when Terence O'Neill invited the Taoiseach of the Irish Republic, Seán Lemass, to visit Northern Ireland.

An oil rig being launched at the Harland & Wolff Shipyard, Belfast in November 1966

The Lemass-O'Neill Meetings

On 14 January 1965 Seán Lemass travelled to Belfast for a meeting with Terence O'Neill. This was a truly historic meeting, as it was the first time that a Prime Minister of Northern Ireland had met a Taoiseach of the Irish Republic. This meeting involved political risks for both men. Lemass was a lifelong republican dedicated to the reunification of Ireland. On arriving at Stormont, he stated, 'I shall get into terrible trouble for this.' However, the risks were much greater for O'Neill, who realised the existence of opposition within the unionist community to any contact with the Irish Republic. While leading civil servants were aware of the meeting, O'Neill kept it secret from his Cabinet colleagues until the last minute in case they refused to agree to it.

Captain Terence O'Neill welcoming the Taoiseach, Seán Lemass, to Belfast in January 1965

The main focus of the discussions between the two leaders centred on economic matters. The economic gap between both parts of Ireland had narrowed considerably and O'Neill admired the progress in the Republic under the leadership of Lemass. During the talks, both leaders explored the possibility of future co-operation in economic matters. On returning to Dublin that evening, Lemass declared:

> There is no question that this meeting was significant...its significance should not be exaggerated. I think I can say that a road block has been removed. How far the road may go is not yet known. It has been truly said, however, that it is better to travel hopefully than to arrive.

On the evening of the Lemass visit, O'Neill defended the meeting by observing on television that both parts of Ireland 'share the same rivers, the same mountains and some of the same problems'.

In February 1965 O'Neill returned Lemass's visit when he travelled to Dublin for talks with the Taoiseach. While the Lemass–O'Neill talks were largely uncontroversial in the South, they proved to be far more contentious in Northern Ireland. Some of O'Neill's own unionist colleagues resented his meetings with Lemass. The strongest opposition came from a small group of extreme Protestants led by the Rev. Ian Paisley, who was moderator of the Free Presbyterian Church. They handed in a letter of protest at Stormont and accused O'Neill of behaving like a dictator, as he had not consulted unionist members of parliament before inviting Lemass to Belfast. Although Ian Paisley had little influence in 1965, his power was to grow as O'Neill's difficulties increased in the years ahead.

Although O'Neill's contacts with Seán Lemass showed his modernising outlook, his more traditional unionism was seen in the controversial decision to establish a new university in the largely Protestant town of Coleraine.

The Rev. Ian Paisley, who protested at the visit of Seán Lemass to Northern Ireland

Case Study: The Coleraine University Controversy

A Second University for Northern Ireland

When Captain Terence O'Neill succeeded Lord Brookeborough as Prime Minister in 1963, Northern Ireland still contained only one major institution of third-level education, Queen's University Belfast. Founded as Queen's College in 1845, it became a fully independent university in 1908. In the 1960s it had a high reputation as a centre of learning where Protestants and Catholics mixed freely. The proportion of Catholic students at Queen's University had been increasing steadily and had reached a quarter of all students by the early 1960s.

As well as Queen's University in Belfast, there was a much smaller university college known as Magee College in Londonderry. This college had originally trained Presbyterian ministers and in the 1960s it provided the first two years of training for university students in certain subjects. They then finished their courses either at Queen's University or at Trinity College in Dublin.

When it became clear that more university places would be required in the future, the Northern Ireland Government was faced with a choice: either expand Queen's University or found a second, completely new university in the province. The decision to found a new university was to lead to a bitter public controversy during 1965.

The Lockwood Committee

In 1963 the Robbins Report on Higher Education in Great Britain recommended a huge expansion in the number of places in third-level education, especially in the area of science and technology. The expert authors believed that future economic prosperity depended on a better-educated workforce. They also believed that clever working-class students should receive more encouragement to go on to third-level education. The same was proposed in the Republic of Ireland, as witnessed by the highly influential report entitled *Investment in Education*, which was published in 1965.

Against this background, the Northern Ireland Government set up its own enquiry on third-level education. In November 1963 a committee was appointed under the chairmanship of Sir John Lockwood, the Master of Birbeck College in London. The eight members of the committee included education experts from Northern Ireland and Great Britain. However, not a single representative from the Catholic and nationalist community in Northern Ireland was included.

From the outset it was clear that the location of the new university would be of great interest to the general public. Three towns in particular were considered to be leading contenders: Londonderry, Armagh and Coleraine. As the second largest city in Northern Ireland, with a population of 54,000, Derry appeared to be in a strong position. Even before the Lockwood Committee was appointed, the city council set out its claims.

Statement of Derry Corporation concerning a new university

1. The demand for university places in the 1970s may well be double the present one. It has been represented by a substantial body of responsible opinion that the establishment of a second university is the best way of meeting this demand.

2. It is an obvious and logical step to use Magee College as the nucleus around which to build a second independent university. Magee, despite its past limitations, is today a flourishing institution with a well-qualified staff.

3. As a city, Derry is well situated geographically to support a university, and the establishment of a university in Derry would help to restore the equilibrium of Northern Ireland, educationally, economically and culturally. It is well served by communications with all parts of Northern Ireland and further afield.

4. There are several highly suitable sites in the vicinity of Derry capable of housing a university, either as a single unit or in a collegiate pattern.

5. Accommodation of students and staff presents no major problem. The city also offers excellent facilities for the cultural and recreational activities which form an important and necessary part of university life.

6. The possible establishment of a university in Derry has aroused the support of all sections of the community.

7. The Council...is prepared to make an annual contribution...towards the finances of the university for a period of ten years from the date of its foundation.

City and County Borough of Londonderry: Submission to the Government of Northern Ireland Promoting the Case for the Promotion of a University at Londonderry (Londonderry 1963)

The strong desire of the people of Derry to acquire the new university for their city was understandable. A university was a major source of employment in itself. Furthermore, it could attract more employment in the form of industries and services to the city. At the time, Derry and the western part of Northern Ireland were seriously underdeveloped compared to the east of the province. Around two-thirds of the population lived within a 30-mile radius of Belfast and most industrial development was located in this region. The fact that, apart from West Belfast, this area was predominantly Protestant led to resentment among nationalists. Areas in the south and west, including Newry, Strabane and Derry, had nationalist majorities but also much higher rates of unemployment. In 1963 nationalists were disappointed when the Unionist Government decided to build a new town called Craigavon in a strongly Protestant area near Portadown.

At the beginning of 1965 the majority nationalist community in Derry, supported on the university issue by most unionists in the city, waited anxiously for the publication of the Lockwood Report and the decision concerning the location of Northern Ireland's second university.

A DECISION IS TAKEN

After sixteen months of investigation and discussion, the Lockwood Committee Report was finally published in February 1965.

The members of the Lockwood Committee justified their decision to locate the new university at Coleraine on a number of grounds. They believed that the representatives of Coleraine had presented a better case than those from Derry or Armagh. They also believed that the availability of accommodation in the nearby seaside resorts of Portrush and Portstewart was another factor in Coleraine's favour, in contrast to Derry, where there was a chronic shortage of accommodation.

However, the recommendations of the Lockwood Committee were received with outrage by most sections of public opinion in Derry, where people set about persuading the government in Belfast to reject the Lockwood Report.

OPPOSITION AND PROTEST IN DERRY

A 'University for Derry' campaign was set up under the chairmanship of local schoolteacher John Hume, who was later to become one of the leading political figures in Northern Ireland. At this time he was pleased that the campaign for a university brought Catholics and Protestants together in a rare example of joint action.

Along with John Hume, the main figures in the campaign for a university in Derry were the city's unionist mayor, Albert Anderson, and the local MP, Eddie McAteer, who was leader of the Nationalist Party in the Northern Ireland Parliament at Stormont. At a protest meeting in the town hall of Derry, the Guildhall, McAteer declared, 'Stormont might ignore the people of Derry, or even the people of Londonderry; but when the people of Derry and Londonderry get together as one, surely they will have to listen.' The members of the action group decided that a delegation should visit the Prime Minister, Captain Terence O'Neill.

Document 4

Confronting Captain Terence O'Neill

It was decided that O'Neill must be confronted face to face, and on 11 February John Hume led a delegation to see the premier. Their mood was uncompromising, but O'Neill remained noncommittal. Hume was cogent and incisive, O'Neill sympathetic but silent. Hume told him he had a glorious opportunity to do something that would not only earn undiluted applause in Derry, but could have a revitalising effect towards general reconciliation in Northern Ireland, to which he had expressed himself ardently dedicated. Hume observed later that 'we did not know of course that even as he listened to our appeal, the decision against Derry had already been taken and his government was on the point of launching a white paper accepting the Lockwood Committee Report and its recommendation that the second university should be located in the small unionist town of Coleraine, thirty miles from Derry.'

F. Curran, 'Derry: Countdown to Disaster', Dublin: Gill & Macmillan 1986

TAKING THE CASE TO STORMONT

A week after the delegation met O'Neill at Stormont, a massive public protest was planned in Derry to take place on 18 February. Most shops and businesses in the city closed early and a huge motorcade travelled to Belfast to hand in a protest at Stormont. Leading the motorcade was the mayoral car, in which Eddie McAteer travelled with Mayor Albert Anderson. More than 20,000 people took part in the protest.

However, the government refused to change direction and arranged for the Lockwood Report to be debated in parliament.

A mass protest at Stormont on 18 February 1965 objecting to the decision to locate the new university at Coleraine instead of at Derry. In the forefront of the picture are the Mayor of Londonderry, Albert Anderson, together with Eddie McAteer and John Hume.

DEBATE AT STORMONT

The debate, which began on 3 March 1965, lasted fifteen hours and was one of the longest post-war debates in Stormont. O'Neill, opening the debate, stressed the importance of the Report's proposals for the economic future of Northern Ireland and defended the process by which the locational decision was made. After the debate, the result of the vote in the House of Commons at Stormont was a foregone conclusion. The Unionist Government imposed the party whip on its MPs: most of them followed this instruction, although two members abstained and two others voted with the Opposition. When the vote was called, the government won by twenty-seven votes to nineteen. All those voting in favour were unionists. Those voting against included eight nationalists, seven Labour MPs, the only Liberal MP, one independent and the two unionists who defied the party whip.

CONTINUING CONTROVERSY

Although the clear victory in parliament for the O'Neill Government appeared to decide the issue, controversy continued over the treatment of Derry. One of the unionists who had voted against the government, Dr Robert Nixon, MP for Co. Down, caused consternation when he alleged that a member of O'Neill's Government had told him that 'nameless faceless men from Londonderry had gone to Stormont and advised against the siting of Ulster's second university in the city or in settling industrial development there'. The names of those alleged to have been involved were later published and included prominent members of the loyal order, the Apprentice Boys of Derry.

Although Nixon was expelled from the unionist parliamentary party, his allegations were indeed correct. Years later, when archives at Stormont were opened to historians, details of such a meeting became available. It took place at Stormont on 19 February 1965, when the group met O'Neill and the Minister of Education, H.V. Kirk. They spoke up for Magee College and wanted the university to be shared between Coleraine and Derry. However, throughout the meeting, these unionists stressed their fear of losing control of Derry should Catholics become more prosperous. Despite the public co-operation between Protestants and Catholics to acquire a university for Derry, these members of the Unionist Party were prepared to undermine the campaign in case a university threatened their position by benefiting the Catholic community in Derry.

Document 5

A nationalist viewpoint

With the dramatic expansion of second-level education in the North, it was obvious that university provisions would have to be similarly expanded to accommodate the increasing demand for university places by the young people emerging from these new second-level schools. The North would need a second university. It was believed, indeed assumed, that even the Stormont Government could not be so arrogant as to locate such a university anywhere but in Derry. After all Derry was the second city and it already had the nucleus of a university in Magee College. Such a decision could be the springboard for the renaissance of the city... After some toing and froing, the Stormont Government formally accepted the Lockwood Report and decided to site the North's second university in Coleraine. It subsequently emerged that several prominent unionist figures, leading citizens in Derry, had not supported the city as the site for the second university. They were described as 'the faceless men'. There was outrage among much of the Derry population. The die had been cast. Things would never be the same again.

E. Daly, *Mister, Are You a Priest?*, Dublin: Four Courts Press 2000, 120–22

CONTRASTING VIEWPOINTS

Ever since the events of 1965, the Coleraine University Controversy has continued to evoke radically different viewpoints from nationalist and unionist observers. Dr Edward Daly, the Catholic Bishop of Derry, was very clear in his opinion, which he set forth in his memoirs.

On the other hand, unionist commentators continue to defend the decision of the Lockwood Committee to locate Northern Ireland's second university at Coleraine. A typical example of this viewpoint is to be found in the observations of Professor Thomas Wilson.

Document 6

A unionist viewpoint

At that time, I was engaged in the preparation of the development plan but not, of course, any of the meetings of the Lockwood Committee and saw none of the papers. It was arranged, however, for Sir John and myself to meet after the committee had reached its conclusions. It had never seemed at all likely that he would be influenced by sectarian prejudice that Ulster noses, sometimes, too readily, claim to be able to detect, and after the meeting I was quite sure of this... It is scarcely surprising that the committee was accused of acting as a tool of a Unionist Government that wanted to do down the predominantly Catholic city of Derry. I do not believe for a moment that Lockwood would have submitted to any such instructions from the unionist leaders, as he was alleged to have done. What is, however, beyond question is that the whole affair was grossly mishandled.

T. Wilson, *Ulster: Conflict and Consent*, Oxford: Blackwell 1989, 146–7

A MISSED OPPORTUNITY

The failure to locate a university in Derry can be seen in retrospect as a missed opportunity by the Unionist Government of Terence O'Neill. Instead of supporting those Protestants in Derry who wished to co-operate with the Catholic community, O'Neill followed the path recommended by the more extreme traditional unionists. By favouring the small Protestant town of Coleraine over the North's second city, he alienated the Catholic population throughout the province even further. John Hume aptly summed up the impact of O'Neill's choice in the controversy:

> The isolation of the west policy was to be continued under O'Neill as rigidly as under any of his predecessors. He lost all credibility in Derry as a crusading premier, and reinforced among the Catholic community all over the North the conviction that the unionist leopard could not change its spots, and that change would have to be wrested from them.

Far from settling the university question, the decision to locate the new institution in Coleraine influenced opinion so much that it became one of the principal grievances of the minority nationalist community in the years ahead. Indeed, by the time the new university opened in Coleraine with 400 students on 25 October 1968, events were unfolding in Derry which would lead to profound changes in the lives of the people of Northern Ireland.

CASE STUDY: QUESTIONS

COMPREHENSION

1. According to Document 1, what was the best way of meeting the demand for more university places in Northern Ireland?

2. Why should Magee College be used as the nucleus of a new university? (Document 1)

3. Mention three advantages Derry would have as the site of a new university, according to Document 1.

4. In what practical way did the Londonderry City Council offer to help a new university located in the city? (Document 1)

5. According to Document 2, what was the best location for a new university in Northern Ireland?

6. What did the Lockwood Committee recommend concerning Magee College, Derry? (Document 2)

7. What was the main idea of John Hume's speech? (Document 3)

8. How did his listeners react to the speech?

9. Describe Captain Terence O'Neill's reaction to the visit of the delegation from Derry (Document 4).

10. Did O'Neill deceive the delegation? Explain your answer (Document 4).

11. According to the author of Document 5, what would be the result of 'the dramatic expansion of second-level education'?

12. What advantages did Derry possess as a centre of third-level education, according to Document 5?

13. According to Document 5, how did most of Derry's population react to the location of the new university in Coleraine?

14. What impression did Sir John Lockwood make on the author of Document 6?

15. According to the author of Document 6, what fault was the Lockwood Committee accused of?

COMPARISON

1. How do Document 1 and Document 2 differ concerning the future of Magee College?

2. Both Documents 3 and 4 contain references to John Hume. What view of John Hume emerges from these references?

3. Explain how the authors of Document 5 and Document 6 differ in their views concerning the recommendations of the Lockwood Committee.

4. How do Documents 3 and 4 differ from the other documents as sources for the historian?

CRITICISM

1. Does the author of Document 3 admire John Hume? Give a reason for your answer.

2. Is Document 5 an unbiased account? Explain your answer.

3. State two pieces of evidence from Document 6 to show that it presents a unionist point of view.

CONTEXTUALISATION

1. Why was Northern Ireland in need of a second university?

2. Why was the Lockwood Committee established and what was contained in its report?

3. How did the people of Derry react to the recommendations of the Lockwood Committee?

4. How may the failure to locate the new university in Derry be seen as a missed opportunity by the O'Neill Government?

Unionist Reaction

Throughout his term as Prime Minister of Northern Ireland, Terence O'Neill faced continuous opposition to any measures of reform from certain sections of the unionist community. These included members of his own political party as well as the powerful Orange Order. Together with its sister organisations, the Apprentice Boys of Derry and the Royal Black Institution, the Orange Order was strongly opposed to any concessions to the Catholic minority. All members of the Northern Ireland Government, including O'Neill himself, were members of the Orange Order. Many belonged to the other two organisations as well.

An Orange Order parade on 12 July 1966

The loyal orders organised parades during the annual marching season from Easter to November which celebrated the triumph of William of Orange at the Battle of the Boyne (1690) and other Protestant victories. They frequently marched through largely Catholic areas supported by the police, the Royal Ulster Constabulary. Enjoying huge influence over government and society, the Orange institutions were determined to prevent any weakening in the unionist domination of Northern Ireland.

The Emergence of Ian Paisley

O'Neill also faced opposition to his attempts to reach out to the Catholic minority from another source – the Rev. Ian Paisley. Born in Armagh in 1926, Paisley had become a Presbyterian minister. Dissatisfied with the official Presbyterian Church and the Orange Order, he set up his own Free Presbyterian Church and Independent Orange Order. From the outset of O'Neill's period as Prime Minister, Paisley became his constant critic.

Paisley completely condemned ecumenism, the attempt to unite Christians by friendly discussions and understanding and by emphasising the common ground they shared. He reviled Pope John XXIII (1958–63), who called the Second Vatican Council which supported ecumenical dialogue between Christians. When Pope John died in 1963, Paisley led a crowd of around 1,000 followers to Belfast City Hall because the Union Jack was lowered to half mast as a mark of respect. A year later he was involved in a much more serious

The Irish republican candidate, Liam McMillan, holding the tricolour at his office in Divis Street, Belfast during the British general election campaign in October 1964

incident in West Belfast. He threatened to lead a group of followers into West Belfast to remove an Irish tricolour from the offices of a republican candidate during the British general election of October 1964. When the police seized the flag and its replacement, two days of violence followed. Known as the Divis Street Riots, the disturbances were the worst in the city since 1935.

This confrontation between nationalists and the largely Protestant RUC over the flying of a tricolour took place at a time when the nationalist minority was becoming increasingly impatient with the existing conditions of life in Northern Ireland.

Nationalist Grievances

By the early 1960s pressure for change was increasing in Northern Ireland. With the exception of the largely ineffectual Border Campaign of the IRA, society had been more stable since 1945 than in previous years. However, beneath the surface the profile of the nationalist community was being transformed. Because of the availability of free education under the welfare state, increasing numbers of young Catholics were graduating from college. Most of these were not prepared to accept the status of second-class citizens which their parents' generation had endured.

Northern Ireland remained a deeply sectarian society. Protestants and Catholics were educated separately, often lived in different areas and socialised with members of their own religion. Bigotry and religious intolerance were rife. Whereas Catholics tended to stereotype Protestants as

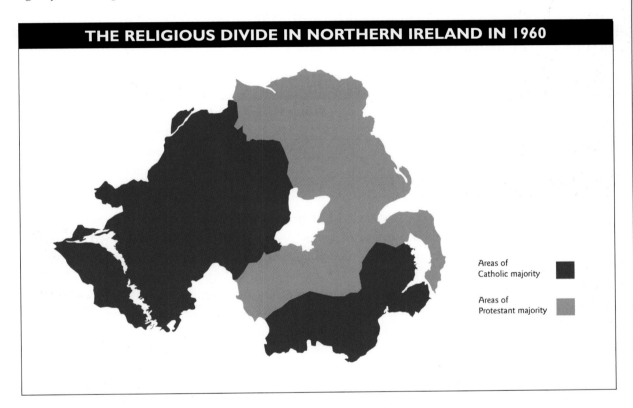

THE RELIGIOUS DIVIDE IN NORTHERN IRELAND IN 1960

Areas of Catholic majority

Areas of Protestant majority

sour and intolerant, many Protestants regarded all Catholics as socially inferior. Even Terence O'Neill betrayed this attitude in a notorious speech:

> It is frightfully hard to explain to Protestants that if they give Roman Catholics a good house they will live like Protestants, because they will see neighbours with cars and television sets. They will refuse to have eighteen children. But if a Roman Catholic is jobless and lives in the most ghastly hovel he will rear eighteen children on National Assistance. If you treat Roman Catholics with due consideration, they will live like Protestants in spite of the authoritarian nature of their Church.

Given the prevailing intolerant attitudes, many Protestant employers discriminated in favour of fellow Protestants when taking on new employees. Because there were far fewer Catholic employers, their employment of Catholic workers had a much smaller impact. In addition to discrimination in the private sector, Catholics were seriously under-represented in jobs in the civil service, where over 90 per cent of the higher posts were held by Protestants.

Problems in Local Government

Nationalists had two serious grievances in the area of local government:
- Gerrymandering.
- Multiple votes.

Gerrymandering was the practice of adjusting constituency boundaries to suit one party. The unionist-controlled government at Stormont did this in a number of areas with nationalist majorities. The most blatant example was in Derry city, where the electoral wards were fixed to ensure a permanent unionist majority in the corporation, despite the existence of a nationalist majority in the city. This was accomplished by including most of the nationalist voters in one ward and spreading the unionist electors over two wards.

GERRYMANDERING OF ELECTORAL BOUNDARIES IN DERRY CORPORATION, 1967			
	Catholic Voters	**Other Voters**	
North	2,530	3,946	8 Unionists
Waterside	1,852	3,697	4 Unionists
South	10,047	1,138	8 Non-Unionists
TOTAL	14,429	8,781	12 Unionists and 8 Non-Unionists

At the time, not every citizen could vote in local government elections. Only rate payers had the vote and businesses were given a number of votes. As most businesses were owned by unionist supporters, nationalists condemned the practice and called for 'one man, one vote' in all local government elections.

The focus on reform of local government had a twofold purpose: first to ensure fair nationalist representation in county councils and corporations, but secondly, and most importantly, to bring about a change in the housing allocation in Northern Ireland. For nationalists, the unfair and discriminatory allocation of public housing by unionist-controlled councils was the most glaring of all grievances. Indeed, it was to be the spark that ignited a protest movement which utterly transformed the nature of politics and society in Northern Ireland in the years ahead.

The Origins of the Civil Rights Movement

The housing shortage was particularly severe for Catholic families in areas west of the River Bann. In areas like Derry city, Dungannon and Enniskillen, unionist-controlled councils refused to build sufficient new houses for Catholics in case they endangered their control by upsetting the existing gerrymandered electoral boundaries.

The situation was at crisis point in Dungannon, Co. Tyrone. By 1963 no Catholic family had been allocated a permanent house by the local council in the previous thirty-four years. A group of local Catholics therefore joined together to set up the Homeless Citizens League. They decided to take direct action such as protests and squatting in houses which had been vacated by Protestant tenants who had moved to newly built houses. Prominent in the Homeless Citizens League were a local doctor and his wife, Dr Conn and Patricia McCluskey. During the protests in

Dungannon, the McCluskeys received requests from nationalists in other parts of Northern Ireland looking for help with housing problems. As a result they decided to broaden their concern to include all of Northern Ireland.

On 14 January 1964 at a meeting in Belfast, the McCluskeys established the Campaign for Social Justice in Northern Ireland. They made it clear in a press release that they rejected the main approach of nationalists in the past, namely to concentrate on the ending of partition and the achievement of a united Ireland. Instead, the Campaign for Social Justice concentrated on civil rights. If Catholics in Northern Ireland were full British citizens, then they were entitled to all the rights and freedoms which this involved. In particular, the movement demanded an end to discrimination and full equality for all citizens in Northern Ireland.

The Campaign for Social Justice in Northern Ireland was strongly inspired by the contemporary peaceful struggle of African-American people for civil rights in the United States of America. One of the banners during the protests in Dungannon stated: 'Racial discrimination in Alabama hits Dungannon'. In the years ahead, the link between the struggle for civil rights in America and in Northern Ireland was to figure prominently in the campaigns of the nationalist minority.

Publicising the Problem

One of the main functions of the Campaign for Social Justice was to gather information on the treatment of nationalists and to publicise it. They published a pamphlet entitled 'Northern Ireland – The Plain Truth' which contained facts and figures regarding various forms of discrimination. The campaign also drew attention to the huge subsidy which British taxpayers were paying each year to Northern Ireland. During 1964 they wrote a number of letters to the British Prime Minister, Sir Alec Douglas Home, but he refused to intervene in the affairs of Northern Ireland. He justified his actions by stating that since 1921 British governments had left the running of the province in the hands of the Northern Ireland Government.

Harold Wilson, the British Labour Prime Minister

When the Conservative Government of Sir Alex Douglas Home was defeated in the general election of October 1964, a Labour administration came to power under Harold Wilson. Because the Conservatives were allies of the Ulster unionists, many nationalists in Northern Ireland hoped for a more sympathetic hearing from a Labour Government. By and large they were to be disappointed, as Wilson's government had no intention of becoming involved in affairs in the province if they could possibly avoid doing so. However, in 1965 a group of backbench Labour MPs launched 'the Campaign for Democracy in Ulster' in the British House of Commons. This group called for an end to discrimination and the establishment of an enquiry into the administration of government in Northern Ireland. However, the group made little headway, as the British Government steadfastly refused to intervene. After his election as a Republican Labour MP for West Belfast in 1966, Gerry Fitt added his voice to calls for reform in Northern Ireland when he spoke in the British Parliament. He was ignored, however, and it became clear that the initiative for change would not come from books, pamphlets and speeches, but rather from direct action on the streets of Northern Ireland.

KEY PERSONALITIES: CONN AND PATRICIA McCLUSKEY

Dr Conn and Patricia McCluskey played an important role in highlighting discrimination against Catholics in Northern Ireland, especially in the area of public housing. Living in Dungannon, Co. Tyrone, they were founder members of the Homeless Citizens League, which they helped establish in response to the local discrimination in the allocation of public housing. This organisation decided on direct action, including protests and squatting in houses.

In response to requests from other nationalists in the North, the McCluskeys broadened their activity beyond Dungannon and as a result set up the Campaign for Social Justice in Northern Ireland on 14 January 1964. The aim of this new organisation, strongly inspired by the peaceful struggle of African-American people for civil rights in the United States of America, was to campaign for civil rights for Catholics in the North. As a means of highlighting discrimination against the minority community in Northern Ireland, they wrote a number of letters to the British Prime Minister, Sir Alec Douglas Home, and published a pamphlet entitled 'Northern Ireland – The Plain Truth' which highlighted the various forms of discrimination in operation.

The McCluskeys' efforts to campaign against discrimination in Northern Ireland was to provide the genesis of the civil rights movement in the late 1960s, which began with the establishment in 1967 of the Northern Ireland Civil Rights Association (NICRA).

EXERCISES

ORDINARY LEVEL

1. Read the following extract from the memoirs of a Catholic civil servant in Northern Ireland and answer the questions that follow.

   To many of my colleagues Catholics were strange animals of which they had astonishingly little knowledge...I had learned of their beliefs about the power of the Pope and his clergy and no words could persuade them that I was not subject to malevolent direction by black-robed priests to whom Rome had entrusted its master plan for world domination. I was astonished to meet youths of my own age who had never met a Catholic until I appeared in the office, who believed, as one of them told me, that in the event of their coming under a nationalist government the Pope would require his obedient Irish flock to banish the Protestants from the land.

   P. Shea, Voices and the Sound of Drums: An Irish Autobiography, Belfast: Blackstaff Press 1981, 113

   (i) How did many of the author's colleagues regard Catholics?

   (ii) What power did these colleagues think that Catholic priests had?

   (iii) What evidence is there in the passage to show that Protestants and Catholics did not mix much socially?

   (iv) Explain the extreme view of one of the author's colleagues regarding a united Ireland.

2. White a paragraph on the background of Captain Terence O'Neill and his main aims when he became Prime Minister of Northern Ireland in 1963.

3. Outline O'Neill's main economic policies.

4. White an account of the Lemass–O'Neill visits of 1965.

5. What was the Lockwood Report (1965) and why was it so controversial?

6. Name the three main Protestant loyal orders in Northern Ireland.

7. Write a paragraph on the Divis Street Riots (1964).

8. Explain the following terms.

   (i) Ecumenism

   (ii) Discrimination

   (iii) Gerrymandering.

9. Write an account on nationalist grievances in Northern Ireland during the 1960s.

10. Explain why Dr Conn and Patricia McCluskey set up the Campaign for Social Justice in Northern Ireland in 1964.

11. How did the British Prime Minister, Sir Alec Douglas Home, respond to the complaints of the Campaign for Social Justice in Northern Ireland?

12. Who launched 'the campaign for Democracy in Ulster' in 1965 and how effective was this movement?

HIGHER LEVEL

1. Read the following extract from the reminiscences of Dr Conn McCluskey and answer the questions which follow.

   > The most crushing handicap of working-class Catholics at the time was the housing shortage. The town's gerrymandered electoral system consisted of three wards, two of which were controlled by the unionists (Protestants). There was no points system for housing allocation, tenancies being assigned in the unionist wards by the unionists and in the one anti-unionist ward by the nationalist (Catholics) councillors. Since no new houses had been built in the Catholic ward, the only houses on offer there were re-lets...

   > The position was that to control voting strength, no Catholic family had been allocated a permanent house for thirty-four years. Young newly-weds were compelled to move in with in-laws and keep their wedding presents under the bed. This usually worked until the second child arrived when family tensions began to mount. In some cases families had been waiting as long as twelve years for a home. As a medical practitioner myself, I had close contact with several of these people and could clearly observe their suffering.

   > *C. McCluskey, Up Off Their Knees: A Commentary on the Civil Rights Movement in Northern Ireland, Dublin: Anna Livia Press 1989, 10*

   (i) According to the author, what was the 'most crushing handicap of working-class Catholics' at the time?

   (ii) How were tenancies of houses assigned?

   (iii) Why do you think no new houses had been built in the nationalist ward of Dungannon?

   (iv) Explain how the author graphically shows the effects of overcrowding.

   (v) What advantage do you believe the author's profession gave him as an observer?

   (vi) How would you evaluate this extract as a historical source?

2. Assess the political career of Terence O'Neill between 1963 and 1968.

3. Discuss the Coleraine University Controversy and its impact on nationalist political attitudes.

4. What were the main grievances of the nationalist community in Northern Ireland during the 1960s?

5. Outline the origins of the civil rights movement in Northern Ireland.

The Formation of the Civil Rights Association

In January 1967 the Northern Ireland Civil Rights Association was founded in Belfast. Its programme included demands for one man, one vote in local elections, no gerrymandering of constituency boundaries, a fair distribution of local council houses and a proper complaints procedure against local authorities. The association also called for the disbandment of the part-time police force, the B Specials, which it regarded as overwhelmingly Protestant and biased against the nationalist community. Finally, it called for the repeal of the Special Powers Act, which gave vast powers to the Northern Ireland Government, including internment without trial and the right to ban all demonstrations.

From the outset, the civil rights movement was highly controversial. While most nationalists strongly identified with its demands, many unionists believed that it was a front for the IRA. In their view, following the defeat of the Border Campaign in 1962, the IRA was now using other means to undermine the security of Northern Ireland.

The First Civil Rights March

In the summer of 1968 the Civil Rights Association and the Campaign for Social Justice joined forces to organise a protest march in Co. Tyrone. This arose out of a housing scandal in a small village called Caledon. Although many large Catholic families were on the waiting list, the local council allocated a house to a single nineteen-year-old Protestant woman who worked as a secretary to a unionist solicitor. The local MP, Austin Currie, a member of the Nationalist Party, raised the matter at Stormont on 19 June. When he got no satisfactory response, he squatted in the house in Caledon before being removed by police.

On 24 August 1968 a civil rights march, involving around 2,500 people, took place from Coalisland to Dungannon to protest against the Caledon affair and other forms of injustice. When the marchers reached the outskirts of Dungannon, they were blocked by a police barricade. Behind the RUC there was a crowd of around 1,500 loyalists taking part in a counter-demonstration. They regarded the centre of Dungannon as part of their territory and were

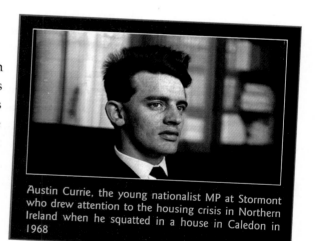
Austin Currie, the young nationalist MP at Stormont who drew attention to the housing crisis in Northern Ireland when he squatted in a house in Caledon in 1968

The first civil rights march which took place from Coalisland to Dungannon on 24 August 1968

determined to keep the civil rights marchers out of it.

When the civil rights marchers reached the police cordons, they sat on the road and listened to speeches. Betty Sinclair, a veteran communist and chairwoman of the Civil Rights Association, declared, 'What we have done today will go down in history and in this way we will be more effective in showing the world that we are a peaceful people asking for our own civil rights in an orderly manner.'

Some other participants were less calm, however. Austin Currie compared the police cordon to the Berlin Wall and Gerry Fitt declared that his blood was boiling and that he would not stop until full civil rights were won.

Soon after this first march, the Civil Rights Association agreed to the request of a number of activists to hold the next protest march in Derry. The event was planned for 5 October 1968.

The Derry Civil Rights March

Like Dungannon, the housing situation in Derry was appalling. The unionist-controlled corporation constantly refused to build houses for Catholics outside the overcrowded southern ward in case this threatened their control of the city. In September 1967 the Derry Housing Action Committee was formed to highlight the crisis by taking direct action such as marches and sit-ins. A young socialist journalist from Derry, Eamon McCann, was prominent in the movement. When the Northern Ireland Civil Rights Association began to organise protests, the Derry Housing Action Committee joined in.

When the date for the proposed civil rights march in Derry was announced, the loyal order, the Apprentice Boys of Derry, immediately announced a march of their own over the same route at the same time. Using his powers under the Special Powers Act, the unionist Minister of Home Affairs, William Craig, banned the civil rights march. Fearing violence, members of the Civil Rights Association wished to cancel the march, but they were persuaded to go ahead by the Derry Housing Action Committee.

Students demonstrating for civil rights at Belfast City Hall in October 1968

When the civil rights march took place in Derry on Saturday, 5 October, the marchers were attacked with batons by the RUC. Gerry Fitt was accompanied by three MPs from the British Labour Party. However, he was struck on the head by a baton, as were two Stormont nationalist MPs, Eddie McAteer and Austin Currie. In all, seventy-seven people, including marchers and bystanders, were injured by the police. In the aftermath of the march there were violent clashes between the police and nationalist youths for the following two days.

Members of the RUC baton-charging demonstrators at the civil rights march in Derry on 5 October 1968

World Attention

The events in Derry on 5 October 1968 were captured on television and shown around the world. Later that night, William Craig appeared on television and completely defended police behaviour. He accused the civil rights marchers of being communists, republicans and a front for the IRA. The television scenes from Derry attracted the attention of many Irish Americans in the United States. They also embarrassed the British Government of Harold Wilson. It appeared to the outside world that freedom of speech was being trampled on in a part of the United Kingdom by a violent and vindictive police force.

Ulster at the Crossroads

Events began to move quickly after the Derry civil rights march. Four days later, the Derry Citizens Action Committee was established in the city. On the same day in Belfast, students of Queen's University held a protest meeting and founded a new organisation called People's Democracy. This radical new organisation was to play a major role in the civil rights campaign in the months and years ahead. All over Northern Ireland, especially in towns with a large proportion of Catholics, new branches of the Civil Rights Association sprang up. As demonstrations continued in Belfast and Derry, the British Government decided to intervene in the situation.

The Prime Minister, Harold Wilson, summoned Terence O'Neill and two leading members of his Cabinet, Brian Faulkner and William Craig, to a meeting in London. Wilson and the British Home Secretary, James Callaghan, insisted that the Unionist Government introduce a programme of reforms in Northern Ireland. After several difficult Cabinet meetings at Stormont, O'Neill announced a five-point programme on 22 November:

- Londonderry Corporation was to be abolished and replaced by an appointed commission.
- Local councils would have to implement a points system to ensure fair housing allocation.
- Parts of the Special Powers Act would be suspended.
- An ombudsman would be appointed to investigate citizens' complaints.
- 'One man, one vote' in local elections would be considered.

In a few months, the civil rights campaign had gained more reforms than the minority community had gained since the establishment of Northern Ireland in 1921. These concessions produced totally different responses from unionists and nationalists. Many nationalists now believed that the civil rights campaign should keep up the pressure to gain more reforms. Many unionists, on the other hand, believed that the reforms had been introduced as a result of nationalists breaking the law. Ian Paisley expressed the fears of more extreme unionists and their determination to resist any concessions to nationalists. He organised counter-demonstrations in towns where civil rights marches were planned. Before one such meeting in Armagh on 30 November, his supporters put up posters with the following message: 'For God and Ulster...S.O.S. To all Protestant religions. Don't let the Republicans, IRA and Civil Rights Association make Armagh another Londonderry. Assemble in Armagh on Saturday 30 November.'

As the demonstrations and counter-demonstrations continued, Captain O'Neill made a famous television broadcast to the people of Northern Ireland on 9 December 1968. He began with the words 'Ulster stands at the crossroads' and reminded people of the financial support provided by the British Government. He then warned that if he did not introduce reforms, the British

Government would step in and take over the ruling of Northern Ireland. Having appealed to the civil rights leaders to end street demonstrations, he asked all the people of the province, 'What kind of Ulster do you want? A happy respected province...or a place continually torn apart by riots and demonstrations and regarded by the rest of Britain as a political outcast?'

The immediate response to O'Neill's speech was mostly positive. The Civil Rights Association agreed to call off street protests to allow time for the introduction of reforms. However, William Craig strongly attacked O'Neill's speech as a sell-out to nationalists. O'Neill then immediately sacked him from the government. Many letters of support poured into O'Neill's office and he appeared more secure as the year of 1968 came to an end. However, events early in the New Year were to shatter hopes for an early peaceful solution to the problems of Northern Ireland.

Violence at Burntollet Bridge, January 1969

Whereas the moderate leaders of the Northern Ireland Civil Rights Association were prepared to give Terence O'Neill time to implement reforms, other groups were not. Prominent among these was the students' group, the People's Democracy. They announced their intention to organise a civil rights march from Belfast to Derry early in the New Year. Each day, their route passed through some strongly loyalist districts. Eventually, on 4 January 1969 the group of around fifty marchers came under attack from loyalists at Burntollet Bridge, an isolated area in the middle of Co. Derry.

The Burntollet civil rights march in January 1969

The marchers were led into an ambush. Dozens were injured by a loyalist mob using sticks, stones and crowbars. Although the march was legal and had not been banned, the RUC did little to protect the members of the People's Democracy. Instead, many policemen were openly friendly to the loyalists. It later emerged from photographs that many of the attackers were local members of the reserve police force, the B Specials.

After the marchers reached Derry, they were again attacked with stones, sticks and petrol bombs. Later that night, members of the RUC invaded the Bogside, attacked local Catholics and damaged their houses and shops.

As intended by some of its radical young leaders, such as Michael Farrell and Bernadette Devlin, the People's Democracy march of January 1969 had broken the truce and put more pressure on the government of Terence O'Neill. However, it also greatly deepened sectarian bitterness between Protestants and Catholics. Protestants were outraged at the People's Democracy 'invasion' of their territory when the march had passed through loyalist districts. Catholics, on the other hand, were angry at the attack on the marchers and the undisciplined and biased behaviour of the police.

The focus of attention shifted clearly to Terence O'Neill as people in Northern Ireland waited to see how he would cope with the worsening situation.

The Fall of Terence O'Neill

In a television broadcast on 5 January 1969, O'Neill condemned the People's Democracy marchers and strongly praised the police for having 'handled this most difficult situation as fairly and firmly as they could'. However, most outside observers, including the British Government and the British media, had seen for themselves on television how badly the RUC had behaved. The Prime Minister, Harold Wilson, now increased pressure on the Northern Ireland Government to speed up the implementation of reforms. At the same time, civil rights marches in Newry and other towns became more violent as control passed from moderate leaders to more radical young republicans.

Civil rights demonstration in London in August 1969

Caught between pressure from the British Government and the civil rights movement on the one hand and his own more extreme unionist supporters on the other, O'Neill tried to follow the middle path. On 15 January 1969 he announced an enquiry into recent disturbances, to be chaired by a Scottish judge, Lord Cameron. As a result, Brian Faulkner resigned from the government in protest and twelve unionist MPs met and called for O'Neill's resignation. The Prime Minister then decided to appeal to the people and called a general election for 24 February.

In a bitter election, O'Neill had to campaign against opponents within his own Unionist Party and against Ian Paisley's Protestant Unionist Party. Although none of his party's candidates was elected, Paisley humiliated O'Neill by standing against him in the Bannside constituency and coming to within 1,414 votes of defeating him. Of the thirty-nine unionists elected, only twenty-seven were definitely pro-O'Neill. On the nationalist side, the old Nationalist Party under the leadership of Eddie McAteer lost out badly to younger civil rights activists such as John Hume, Ivan Cooper and Paddy Devlin.

The Rev. Ian Paisley campaigning in the Bannside constituency in February 1969, where he stood against Prime Minister Terence O'Neill

The 1969 election undoubtedly further weakened O'Neill's position because he could not trust many of the newly elected MPs in his own party. He had also failed to convince the nationalist community that he was seriously committed to introducing reforms.

In April 1969 unionists suffered a defeat in a by-election for the Westminster constituency of Mid-Ulster. Bernadette Devlin, a twenty-one-year-old final year student at Queen's University and a leading member of the People's Democracy, defeated the unionist candidate. Her maiden speech in the House of Commons was a devastating attack on the Unionist Government in Northern Ireland. She instantly became a media personality who spread the civil rights message far and wide.

However, Terence O'Neill had to face a more sinister threat from extreme unionists. During March and April 1969, a series of explosions took place at electricity stations and reservoirs across Northern Ireland. Although the IRA was immediately blamed, in reality the attacks were carried out by an extreme Protestant paramilitary group, the Ulster Volunteer Force (UVF), in an effort to remove Terence O'Neill from power and put an end to the reform programme. The plot was successful and such was the pressure on O'Neill that he resigned from office on 28 April 1969. O'Neill later claimed that the explosions 'quite literally blew me out of office'.

The Battle of the Bogside

Terence O'Neill was succeeded as Prime Minister of Northern Ireland by his cousin, Major James Chichester-Clark. He declared his commitment to continue to implement the reform programme. However, the situation on the streets was worsening all the time and there was rioting in several places during the Orange marches on 12 July 1969. Although the RUC was under severe pressure, its leaders refused help from the British army and claimed that they could cope with the security situation. Events in Derry in August were to prove otherwise.

Major James Chichester-Clark arriving at Downing Street, London for a meeting with the British Prime Minister, Harold Wilson, in August 1969

Despite several warnings, the Unionist Government refused to ban the Apprentice Boys of Derry parade scheduled for 12 August. The majority Catholic community in the city was still extremely angry over police behaviour during the civil rights march the previous October and after the Burntollet march in January. If the Apprentice Boys' march went ahead, it was quite likely to lead to a confrontation between the Catholics from the Bogside and members of the RUC who were protecting the Apprentice Boys. In the event, this is exactly what happened.

The Apprentice Boys' parade approaching the walls of Derry on 12 August 1969

Over the next two days, the RUC tried in vain to enter the Bogside but were driven back by locals who had erected barricades and were using petrol bombs to halt the police advance. CS gas, officially described as 'tear smoke', was used by the police for the first time in Northern Ireland.

As the street fighting raged, the Taoiseach of the Irish Republic, Jack Lynch, made a famous television broadcast concerning the situation in Northern Ireland.

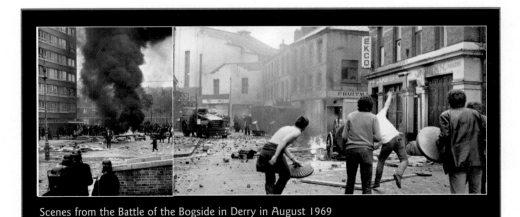

Scenes from the Battle of the Bogside in Derry in August 1969

Jack Lynch Intervenes

Ever since the civil rights marches began, the Irish Government had been observing events in Northern Ireland with increasing alarm. Lynch's own political party, Fianna Fáil, called itself a republican party and had the reunification of Ireland as one of its main aims. Indeed, supporters of all political parties in the Republic strongly sympathised with the Catholic minority in Northern Ireland and fully supported the civil rights campaign.

Jack Lynch, Taoiseach of the Irish Republic

In his momentous television broadcast, Lynch strongly criticised the Northern Ireland Government:

> It is evident that the Stormont Government is no longer in control of the situation. Indeed the present situation is the inevitable outcome of the policies pursued by decades of successive Stormont governments. It is clear also that the Irish Government can no longer stand by and see innocent people injured and perhaps worse.

Despite these words, the Taoiseach had no intention of sending Irish troops across the border. However, he did send army medical teams to treat people who might not have wished to go to hospital in Northern Ireland in case they were questioned by the RUC. He also rejected the deployment of British troops on the streets of Northern Ireland and called instead for a United Nations peacekeeping force. However, the British Government would never allow this, as they regarded Northern Ireland as an integral part of the United Kingdom.

Jack Lynch's speech did not calm the situation in Derry. It failed to meet the Catholic expectations that Irish troops would cross the border, while simultaneously angering Protestants by criticising the Unionist Government and the RUC.

The Arrival of British Troops in Derry

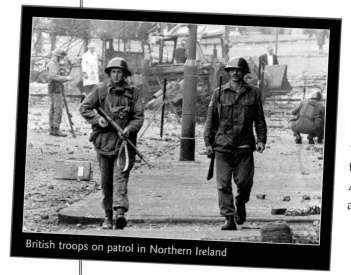

British troops on patrol in Northern Ireland

As the RUC had ground to a halt in Derry, the Northern Ireland Government of Chichester-Clark had no choice but to request the deployment of British troops. On 14 August 1969 the first group of soldiers arrived in Derry and replaced the RUC. The arrival was clear proof that the local people had won the Battle of the Bogside and they were welcomed by most Catholics, who looked to them for protection against the RUC and the B Specials. As the situation calmed down in Derry, events were about to take a very serious turn in Belfast.

Sectarian Riots in Belfast

As Catholics rioted in several towns across the North to overstretch police resources and take pressure off the Bogside in Derry, the most horrific events occurred in Belfast. By 14 August 1969 tension was extremely high throughout the city. Catholics were happy that the police had lost the Battle of the Bogside. Protestants, however, were resentful and fearful. They believed that the Unionist Government was losing control over certain areas of Northern Ireland and they were outraged by Jack Lynch's speech, which they regarded as outside interference in the affairs of Northern Ireland.

A scene of destruction in Northern Ireland as sectarian riots spread throughout the province

British soldiers standing guard outside houses which have been destroyed during riots in Belfast

Massive rioting took place over several nights, with Protestant mobs burning out whole streets of Catholic homes. Fully armed groups of B Specials supported these mobs. During or immediately after the riots in Belfast, 1,850 families fled from their homes; 1,505 of these were Catholic.

Soon working-class areas of Belfast resembled a war zone, with barricades, walls of corrugated iron and barbed wire separating Catholic and Protestant areas. As in Derry, the British troops were also initially welcomed by the local Catholic population in Belfast, who regarded them as protectors.

Because the IRA was very weak after the defeat of the Border Campaign, it was not present in Belfast to defend nationalists from attack in August 1969. Some local people chalked up the slogan 'IRA = I Ran Away' on walls at this time. However, the IRA had not disappeared but would re-emerge in a new and more ruthless form the following year. With this development, the honeymoon period of friendship between Belfast nationalists and the British army would come to an end.

Republican slogans on walls in West Belfast during the Troubles

KEY PERSONALITY: TERENCE O'NEILL (1914–90)

Terence O'Neill was born in Co. Antrim in 1914. He was educated at Eton College in England. He joined the British army and served in the Irish Guards during World War II. In 1946 he was first elected as a Unionist MP for the Bannside constituency in the Stormont Parliament. He served as Minister of Finance in the Brookeborough Government from 1956 to 1963. During this period, he was quite successful in attracting industries and foreign investment to Northern Ireland.

Terence O'Neill succeeded Lord Brookeborough as Prime Minister of Northern Ireland in 1963. One of his key aims was to improve relations between the Protestant and Catholic communities in the North. He also wished to advance the industrial development of Northern Ireland and admired the economic progress of the Irish Republic under the leadership of Seán Lemass. In January 1965 O'Neill invited Lemass for talks in Belfast. He returned the visit to Dublin later in the year. These meetings met with strong opposition within the Unionist Party and from more extreme unionists such as Ian Paisley.

In 1968 the Northern Ireland Civil Rights Association demanded an end to discrimination against Catholics, especially in the areas of housing, employment and local government. In November 1968 O'Neill announced a five-point programme of civil rights. While nationalists welcomed these measures, there was growing criticism of O'Neill's conciliatory approach within the unionist community.

Matters came to a head when a march organised by the People's Democracy in January 1969 was accompanied by violence at Burntollet Bridge. There was public demand for an investigation into the conduct of the police and, under pressure from the British Government, O'Neill announced the establishment of the Cameron Commission. Brian Faulkner, deputy leader of the Unionist Party, resigned in protest.

In an attempt to avert a challenge to his leadership and unify the party, O'Neill called a general election for 24 February 1969. He was nearly defeated in his own Bannside constituency by Ian Paisley. Under mounting pressure, he resigned as leader of the Unionist Party and as Prime Minister of Northern Ireland in April 1969. He retired from politics in January 1970. In the same year he was created a life peer as Baron O'Neill of Maine, and died in England in 1990.

KEY PERSONALITY: BERNADETTE DEVLIN (1947–)

Bernadette Devlin was born in Co. Tyrone in 1947 into a Catholic nationalist family. As a student at Queen's University, Belfast in 1968, she played a prominent role in the People's Democracy, a student-led civil rights organisation. She was one of the leaders of the People's Democracy march in January 1969 which received worldwide publicity because of the violence at Burntollet.

In the general election of 1969, Bernadette Devlin opposed James Chichester-Clark. She subsequently won a by-election and, at the age of twenty-one, was the youngest MP in the Westminster Parliament at the time. She represented the Mid-Ulster constituency in the Westminster Parliament from 1969 to 1974.

She was convicted of incitement to riot in December 1969 for her role in the Battle of the Bogside and served a short period in prison. Later she was temporarily suspended from parliament when she slapped Reginald Maudling, the British Home Secretary, who had made a statement that the army had acted in self-defence when they fired on the marchers on Bloody Sunday.

As a socialist republican, Bernadette Devlin helped form the Irish Republican Socialist Party in 1974 but subsequently left the party. She condemned the Peace People as dishonest in 1976. She supported the prisoners' protests at Long Kesh and stood as an independent candidate in the European Elections in 1979 in support of their demands. She was a leading spokesperson for the Smash H Block campaign which supported the hunger strikes of 1981. In the same year, she and her husband, Michael McAliskey, were shot and seriously injured by loyalist terrorists who broke into their remote Co. Tyrone home.

Throughout the 1980s and 1990s, Bernadette Devlin remained an active commentator on Northern politics. She was to strongly oppose the Good Friday Agreement and was to be especially critical of Sinn Féin's decision to enter into government in Northern Ireland.

EXERCISES

ORDINARY LEVEL

1. Read the following extract from *The Price of My Soul* by Bernadette Devlin and answer the questions that follow.

The Civil Rights Association had been in existence for two years, during which it had been doing ordinary constitutional things like writing to Members of Parliament, and getting nowhere by these methods. There was only one thing to do, they decided, and that was to take the movement to the people, so on August 24th, 1968, they organised a civil rights march from Coalisland to Dungannon, a distance of some three miles. I read about it in a newspaper and thought to myself, 'Civil rights march! Excellent idea! It's about time somebody did something about the situation in Northern Ireland.' And I set off to join it with my young brother and a friend... At Coalisland there were masses of people milling around, selling civil rights rosettes, eating oranges, and generally behaving as if they were at a carnival... We had been told this was a non-sectarian, non-political march – for all that the demands we were making were political... It was the first civil rights demonstration that Northern Ireland had ever seen, and we were all jogging along happily, eating oranges and smoking cigarettes, and people came out of their houses to join the fun...

Then we got to Dungannon and the carnival feeling faltered. There was a police cordon across the road. We weren't going to be allowed into the town...

At first the marchers only got half-heartedly annoyed...but when the officer in charge came over and said that in the interests of peace the march was being rerouted into the Catholic section of Dungannon, the whole atmosphere changed... I do believe that then for the first time it dawned on people that Northern Ireland was a series of Catholic and Protestant ghettos. The meeting got very angry... Some men were calling that we should force our way through, and the lines of the march were breaking formation, and crowding up to the police...

In spite of their 'civil rights' label, the politicians had demanded Catholic equality and majority rule for Catholic areas. People like myself had not come to support such demands. We had come because we wanted to be involved – we were not quire sure in what. We knew something was wrong with a society where the rate of unemployment rarely fell below ten per cent; where half the houses lacked at least one basic amenity... I also thought about the strength of feeling the march had shown, the amount of frustration people felt, and their readiness to release this frustration in wanton violence.

Bernadette Devlin, The Price of My Soul,
London: Random House 1969, 91–2

(i) According to the author, what kind of activity did the Civil Rights Association engage in during the first two years of its existence?

(ii) What took place on 24 August 1968?

(iii) Describe the atmosphere in Coalisland at the start of the march. What does this reveal about people's initial attitude to the occasion?

(iv) What happened when the march reached Dungannon?

(v) What did the officer in charge tell the crowd and how did the marchers react to this?

(vi) What, according to the author, dawned on people for the first time?

(vii) What change came about in the mood of the marchers?

(viii) Can you detect from the passage any difference between the views of the politicians and those of the author?

(ix) What, according to the author, had the march illustrated?

2. Outline the main demands of the Civil Rights Association.

3. How did many unionists view the civil rights movement?

4. Explain why a protest march took place from Coalisland to Dungannon in August 1968.

5. Write an account of the civil rights march in Derry on 5 October 1968.

6. What was the People's Democracy?

7. Outline the five-point programme of reform introduced by the Unionist Government.

8. How did nationalists react to the reforms?

9. What was the reaction of unionists to the reforms?

10. What message was conveyed by Terence O'Neill in his television broadcast to the people of Northern Ireland on 9 December 1968?

11. Write a note on the actions of the People's Democracy in January 1969. What were the reactions of nationalists and unionists to these events?

12. What difficulties did Terence O'Neill face in the early months of 1969?

13. Write an account on the Battle of the Bogside.

14. What was the view of the Irish Government on events in Northern Ireland?

15. How did most people in Derry initially regard the arrival of the first British troops in the city in August 1969?

16. Describe the events that occurred in Belfast in August 1969.

HIGHER LEVEL

1. Read the following extract from Terence O'Neill's television broadcast to the people of Northern Ireland on 9 December 1968 and answer the questions that follow.

> Ulster stands at the crossroads. I believe you know me well enough by now to appreciate that I am not a man given to extravagant language. But I must say to you this evening that our conduct over the coming days and weeks will decide our future. And as we face this situation, I would be failing to you in my duty as Prime Minister if I did not put the issues, calmly and clearly, before you all...
>
> For more than five years now I have tried to heal the divisions in our community. I did so because I could not see how an Ulster divided against itself could hope to stand. I made it clear that a Northern Ireland based upon the interests of any one section rather than upon the interests of all could have no long-term future...
>
> In Londonderry and other places recently, a minority of agitators determined to subvert lawful authority played a part in setting light to highly inflammable material. But the tinder for that fire, in the form of grievances real or imaginary, had been piling up for years.
>
> And so I saw it as our duty to do two things. First, to be firm in the maintenance of law and order, and in resisting those elements which seek to profit from any disturbances. Secondly, to ally firmness with fairness, and to look at any underlying causes of dissension which were troubling decent and moderate people. As I saw it, if we were not prepared to face up to our problems, we would have to meet mounting pressure both internally, from those who were seeking change, and externally from British public and parliamentary opinion, which had been deeply disturbed by the events in Londonderry.
>
> That is why it has been my view from the beginning that we should decide – of our own free will and as a responsible

government in command of events – to press on with a continuing programme of change to secure a united and harmonious community. This, indeed, has been my aim for over five years.

Moreover, I knew full well that Britain's financial and other support for Ulster, so laboriously built up, could no longer be guaranteed if we failed to press on with such a programme... I make no apology for the financial and economic support we receive from Britain. As part of the United Kingdom, we have always considered this to be our right. But we cannot be a part of the United Kingdom merely when its suits us...

A sound custom has grown up that Westminster does not use its supreme authority in fields where we are normally responsible. But Mr Wilson has made it absolutely clear to us that if we did not face up to our problems the Westminster Parliament might well decide to act over our heads. Where would our Constitution be then? What shred of self-respect would be left to us?...

What I seek...is a swift end to the growing civil disorder throughout Ulster. For as matters stand today, we are on the brink of chaos, where neighbour could be set against neighbour... We must tackle root causes if this agitation is to be contained. We must be able to say to the moderate on both sides: come with us into a new era of co-operation, and leave the extremists to the law...

Television broadcast on BBC and ITA networks, 9 December 1968

(i) What do you think Terence O'Neill meant when he stated 'Ulster stands at a crossroads'?

(ii) What, according to O'Neill, had he tried to do over the previous five years? Do you agree with this claim?

(iii) What did he consider to be the duty of his government?

(iv) What pressures did the Prime Minister anticipate if his government failed to confront the problems of Northern Ireland?

(v) How important was pressure from the British Government? Give evidence from the broadcast in support of your answer.

(vi) Which sections of society in Northern Ireland was Terence O'Neill most appealing to in this broadcast? How did he believe the extremists should be dealt with?

(vii) What insights into Terence O'Neill do we gain from this broadcast?

2. In what respects was the civil rights movement controversial from the beginning?

3. How significant were events in Derry on 5 October 1968?

4. What role was played by the People's Democracy in the early history of the Troubles?

5. 'The reforms announced by Terence O'Neill on 22 November 1968 met with varying reactions from different sections of the community.' Discuss this statement.

6. What role was played by unionist opposition to O'Neill in his fall from power?

7. What were the achievements and failures of Terence O'Neill as Prime Minister of Northern Ireland from 1963 to 1969?

The View from London

The deployment of British troops on the streets of Northern Ireland in August 1969 radically altered the security situation. Although technically present to assist the RUC and the Northern Ireland Government, their presence inevitably brought about greater involvement in the affairs of the province by the British Prime Minister, Harold Wilson, and his Home Secretary, James Callaghan.

When Chichester-Clark met Harold Wilson at his official residence on Downing Street on 19 August, both men issued a statement promising equality of treatment for all citizens in Northern Ireland but also reaffirming that the province would remain part of the United Kingdom as long as the majority of the people living there so wished. Despite public displays of support for the Northern Ireland Government, the British Government had every intention of pulling out the extra troops as soon as the security situation improved. In order to restore calm, the British Home Secretary, James Callaghan, decided to visit Northern Ireland to convince the people there that the British Labour Government was determined to assist the Northern Ireland Government in bringing about reforms and in restoring law and order.

During visits to troubled parts of Derry and Belfast, Callaghan promised reforms to nationalists and assured unionists that his government was committed to the Union between Northern Ireland and Great Britain. The process of reform got a boost on 12 September when the Cameron Report was published. It contained a detailed and comprehensive condemnation of the anti-Catholic discrimination which existed in Northern Ireland. A month later, Lord Hunt's report on the police was published. He recommended that the RUC be disarmed and that the part-time B Specials be fully disbanded. They were to be replaced by a new part-time police force, which became known as the Ulster Defence Regiment (UDR). This new force would be under the control of the British army.

The British Home Secretary, James Callaghan, addressing a crowd during his visit to the Bogside area of Derry in August 1969

Loyalists reacted with fury to the recommendations in the Hunt Report. There were serious riots in Belfast's Shankill Road, during which the first policeman to be killed in the 'Troubles' was shot. In quelling the outbreak, the British army killed two rioters. Chichester-Clark then went on television and called for calm and appealed to Protestants not to oppose the British army.

Although peaceful conditions returned towards the end of 1969, it was a case of the calm before the storm. Towards the end of December, a split occurred in the IRA which was to be of huge significance for the future of Northern Ireland.

The Birth of the Provisional IRA

Contrary to the public declarations of unionist politicians that the IRA was behind the civil rights movement, the reality was far different. Secret police reports confirmed that the IRA had been caught unprepared and that it was in a very weak state. During the 1960s, the IRA and its political wing, Sinn Féin, had been moving in a socialist direction. This was opposed by many traditional members who had no time for socialist policies but who believed that the republican movement should concentrate on opposing the British presence in Northern Ireland.

A loyalist mob on the streets of Belfast in October 1969

In December 1969 at a secret meeting in Dublin, the army convention of the IRA voted to end abstentionism and to recognise the de facto existence of the two existing states in Ireland. This was too much for the traditionalists. They withdrew and formed their own group, naming it the Provisional Army Council. The Belfast republican Joe Cahill and the British-born Seán Mac Stíofáin were leading figures in the new movement. On 10 January 1970 Sinn Féin also split and Ruairí Ó Brádaigh became president of Provisional Sinn Féin, which was linked to the Provisional IRA. Although they stated that the 'provisional' or transition period was over ten months later, the name continued to be used to describe the new movement for many years to come.

The older IRA and Sinn Féin became known as the Officials and their members continued to have a strong presence in parts of Northern Ireland. Soon after its establishment, the Provisional IRA gained support in the Catholic housing estates of Belfast. In the early stages, the Provisionals had to be cautious because the locals regarded the British army as their protectors from attacks of loyalist mobs. However, the Provisionals gradually became involved in confrontations between local youths and the British army. During rioting following Orange marches in the summer of 1970, the Provisional IRA stepped up its involvement and began shooting loyalists. However, the event which did most to boost its standing in West Belfast was the Falls Road Curfew of July 1970.

Ruarí Ó Brádaigh, who became President of Provisional Sinn Féin after the split in the republican movement in 1970

The Falls Road Curfew

After police and troops uncovered a cache of arms in a house in the Falls Road on 3 July, the British army sealed off the area for thirty-five hours and conducted house-to-house searches. Many houses were ransacked and four men were killed by the army. Although over a hundred weapons were found, the operation had drastic political consequences. It turned many local Catholics completely against the British army and led to a huge surge of recruitment to the Provisional IRA. By this stage the paramilitary movement had also received support from certain people in the Republic of Ireland in the form of arms and financial assistance.

The British army arresting a suspect during the Falls Road Curfew in July 1970

The Arms Trial

The Provisionals looked to supporters in the Republic for support to build up and equip their movement. Interest in events in Northern Ireland was at a high level in the South. Despite Jack Lynch's determination to prevent violence from spilling over the border into the Republic, his government kept a close watch on events in Northern Ireland. On the day after the ending of the Falls Curfew in Belfast, the Irish Minister for External Affairs, Dr Patrick Hillery, paid an unannounced visit to the area, much to the annoyance of the unionists and the British Government. However, some other members of the Fianna Fáil Government had a more direct involvement with affairs in Northern Ireland.

Certain rich businessmen in the Republic were more sympathetic to the new Provisional IRA, which claimed to defend the nationalist community, than to the Official IRA and Sinn Féin, which promoted left-wing ideas in the Republic as well as in Northern Ireland. The same approach applied to two ministers in the Fianna Fáil Government, Neil Blaney and Charles Haughey. Blaney had actually urged that the Irish army should cross into Northern Ireland.

On 6 May 1970 the Taoiseach, Jack Lynch, dismissed both Blaney and Haughey from the government and they were charged with conspiracy to smuggle arms into the country for use by the Provisional IRA. Blaney was discharged in July, as the state believed he had no case to answer, and Haughey was found not guilty by a jury the following October.

Neil Blaney at the Arms Trial in 1970

Although the exact course of events is still unclear, money voted for humanitarian aid by Dáil Éireann vanished to pay for arms for the Provisional IRA. From the outset, the Provisionals also received money and weapons from supporters among Irish emigrants in the United States of America. As a result, within a short period the movement was well supplied with arms and was even in a position to launch a limited bombing campaign in the summer of 1970.

Political Developments

THE ADVANCE OF PAISLEY

As the levels of violence increased during 1970, political representatives were responding to the unfolding events. Unionist resentment at the inability of Chichester-Clark's Government to cope with the worsening security situation played into the hands of the Rev. Ian Paisley. As a result, he was elected to the Stormont Parliament as MP for the Bannside constituency in April 1970 when Terence O'Neill resigned from the parliament at Stormont to take up a seat in the House of Lords in London. An ally of Paisley's, the Rev. William Beattie, was elected in another by-election held on the same day. The following June, during the British general election, Paisley was elected MP for North Antrim in the British Parliament at Westminster.

THE FORMATION OF THE ALLIANCE PARTY

On 21 April 1970, four days after Paisley's election victory, a new political party was launched in Northern Ireland. Known as the Alliance Party, it was committed to reaching out to both sections of Northern Ireland's divided community. Although the Alliance Party supported the continuation of the Union between Northern Ireland and Great Britain, it also advocated the full involvement of the minority nationalist community in the running of Northern Ireland. Given the deep sectarian divisions in the province, the Alliance Party was destined to remain relatively small. However, in the years ahead it attracted support from both Catholics and Protestants and was constantly looking for opportunities to heal divisions.

A recruitment poster for the Alliance Party

A NEW GOVERNMENT IN BRITAIN

In June 1970 the Labour Government in Britain was defeated in a general election by the Conservatives under Edward Heath. As soon as he became Prime Minister, Heath and his Home Secretary, Reginald Maudling, encouraged the British army in Northern Ireland to take a strict line with anyone causing violence. Despite this, the activities of both the Official and Provisional IRA on the one side and of Protestant paramilitaries on the other continued to expand.

Edward Heath, the leader of the Conservative Party who became British Prime Minister in June 1970

Reginald Maudling, the British Home Secretary, speaking to soldiers during a visit to Northern Ireland in July 1970

The Birth of the SDLP

The leading members of the SDLP (from left to right, Austin Currie, Gerry Fitt, John Hume and Paddy Devlin)

In August 1970 a major realignment took place on the nationalist side of Northern Ireland politics. The old Nationalist Party under Eddie McAteer was out of touch and rapidly losing support. In its place, a new party, called the Social Democratic and Labour Party (SDLP), was formed. It marked a coming together of Catholic politicians in the Labour tradition, such as Gerry Fitt and Paddy Devlin from Belfast, and more traditional conservative nationalists such as Austin Currie and John Hume. Gerry Fitt, the Westminster MP for West Belfast since 1966, became leader of the party. Although the SDLP had a small number of Protestant members, from the start it was the main political party of the Catholic nationalist community. Unlike the old Nationalist Party, it did not support abstention but advocated full participation in the political life of Northern Ireland. As well as standing for greater equality and a fairer society, the principal hallmark of the SDLP was its total condemnation of violence and its commitment to purely peaceful means to bring about a united Ireland. This struggle against violence was to characterise the SDLP in the months and years ahead as the province descended into a nightmare of terror and bloodshed.

The Pressure Mounts

From the start of 1971, pressure mounted on the Chichester-Clark Government as armed violence grew in intensity, especially in the city of Belfast. On 6 February the first British solider to die in the 'Troubles' was shot in West Belfast. The Provisional IRA launched a bombing campaign throughout the province. Having failed to persuade the British Government to allow him to introduce stronger security measures, Chichester-Clark resigned as Prime Minister on 20 March 1971. He was succeeded by Brian Faulkner, who had long held an ambition to hold the post. Under the new Prime Minister, the violence intensified further.

Tensions increased with the arrival of the traditional Orange marching season in July. The Provisional IRA stepped up its bombing campaign and there were riots in several areas of the province. There was bitter division in the parliament at Stormont when the SDLP walked out because Faulkner's Government refused to order an enquiry into two men shot dead by the British army in Derry. Witnesses had claimed that the men were innocent.

Brian Faulkner, who became Prime Minister of Northern Ireland in March 1971

Against this background of mounting pressure, Brian Faulkner persuaded the Conservative Government in London to allow him to introduce internment without trial in Northern Ireland. It was to be an extremely costly mistake on the part of the Unionist Government.

A scene of devastation in the centre of Belfast as the IRA stepped up its bombing campaign

Internment without Trial

In the early morning of 9 August 1971, in an exercise known as Operation Demetrius, the British army rounded up 342 men all over Northern Ireland and interned them without trial. All but one of the internees were Catholics.

Faulkner justified the action by referring to the success of internment when used against the IRA during the Border Campaign of 1956–62. However, the situation was completely different back then. At that time, the Republic had introduced internment as well. In 1971

British troops searching a civilian in Belfast shortly after the introduction of internment in August 1971

Internment without Trial

there was no prospect of internment in the South and the IRA members who were not picked up could escape across the border. The numbers involved in the Border Campaign had been small compared with the surge of membership in the Provisional IRA by 1971. Finally, in August 1971 most of the young active IRA members were unknown to the British security forces and escaped internment.

Violence soared on the day internment was introduced, with thirteen people killed on that day alone. So bad was the police intelligence that one-third of the internees had to be released within two days because they had no connection with the IRA.

The introduction of internment led to outrage among the Catholic community for a number of reasons. Despite the fact that loyalist paramilitaries in the UVF had murdered over 100 Catholics by that time, no loyalist terrorists were interned until February 1973. Two months after the introduction of internment, it became known that internees had been tortured by members of the British army and the RUC by means of beatings, noise, sleep deprivation and starvation. All levels of the Catholic community reacted with horror. A united front consisting of Catholic bishops and priests, community leaders, the

Two wrecked buses after a night of violence in Belfast in August 1971

SDLP, Sinn Féin and the GAA condemned the actions of Faulkner's Government. On the streets, violence escalated at an alarming rate. Twenty-nine people were killed in 1970; this figure rose to 180 in 1971.

The Provisional IRA went from strength to strength as recruitment rose rapidly following the introduction of internment. In the midst of this turmoil, two important new organisations were established by extreme Protestants dissatisfied with the efforts of the Unionist Government to defeat the IRA. In September 1971 Ian Paisley launched a new political party, the Democratic Unionist Party (DUP), which would challenge the leading position of the Ulster Unionist Party in the years ahead. In the same month, a new loyalist paramilitary organisation, the Ulster Defence Association (UDA), was formed in Protestant working-class areas.

By the end of 1971 it appeared that before long the British Government would have to dismiss Faulkner and assume direct control over Northern Ireland as the violence intensified at a shocking rate. The final breaking point was reached in tragic circumstances in Derry at the end of January 1972.

Bloody Sunday

On Sunday, 30 January 1972 the Civil Rights Association organised a mass protest against internment in Derry, despite the fact that the march had been banned by the Unionist Government. By the time the marchers had passed by the Bogside area, they numbered at least 15,000. Shortly after four o'clock in the afternoon, soldiers from the Parachute Regiment in the British army began firing into the crowd. Although they claimed that they had been fired on, members of the crowd claimed that the

Fr. Edward Daly attending to the wounded on Bloody Sunday

The burning of the British Embassy in Dublin

soldiers were the first to open fire. By the time the firing ended, the soldiers had killed thirteen men, seven of them under nineteen years of age. Fr Edward Daly, a priest from the Bogside who later became Bishop of Derry, attended to the dead and wounded, as did a local doctor, Dr Raymond McClean.

After the initial shock, there was outrage among Irish nationalists in Northern Ireland, in the Republic and in the United States of America. There were several protests in the days and weeks ahead throughout Northern Ireland. In the House of Commons in London, Bernadette Devlin slapped the face of the British Home Secretary, Reginald Maudling.

The reaction in the Republic of Ireland was extremely serious. The Taoiseach, Jack Lynch, condemned the shootings as 'unbelievably savage and inhuman' and recalled the Irish ambassador from London. Three days after the shootings in Derry, a crowd of 30,000 people marched to the British Embassy in Dublin and burned it down. The British Prime Minister, Edward Heath, refused to accept the criticisms of the Irish Government and declared that events in Derry were purely a British responsibility because Northern Ireland was part of the United Kingdom. Therefore, the aftermath of Bloody Sunday marked one of the lowest points in the relations between the British and Irish governments during the Troubles in Northern Ireland.

An official enquiry was set up to look into the events in Bloody Sunday under the chairmanship of Lord Widgery. When he issued his report, most nationalists condemned it as a cover-up and indeed a new tribunal of enquiry was to be set up into Bloody Sunday over twenty years later.

The Fall of Stormont

Bloody Sunday marked the final stage in the existence of the unionist-controlled government in Northern Ireland. In the weeks after this event, republicans carried out bombings in Northern Ireland and in England. On 24 March 1972 Faulkner and his government ministers were called to London to meet the British Prime Minister, Edward Heath. Heath informed them that he was transferring control of security from them to the British Government. When the Northern Ireland Government resigned in protest, Heath progrogued, or dissolved, the Northern Ireland Parliament for a year and instituted direct rule from London. The period of unionist self-rule which had begun in 1921 had now come to an end. While nationalists were triumphant at the fall of the Stormont Government, unionists were outraged and blamed the IRA campaign for the loss of the parliament they had controlled.

A unionist demonstration at Stormont, led by Brian Faulkner, in protest at the decision of the British Government to abolish the Northern Ireland Parliament and impose direct rule from London

The British Government in London now faced two main challenges: to end the violence by restoring law and order in the short term and to return power to the local politicians in the longer term.

The Fall of Stormont

ORDINARY LEVEL

1. Read the following account of Bloody Sunday by Edward Daly, Bishop of Derry, and answer the questions that follow.

The week before the march...was a bad week. Loyalists threatened to attack or disrupt the march. On Thursday of that week, two RUC officers were cruelly murdered in a fierce IRA ambush just up the street from the cathedral. Police and army saturated our entire area for many hours after the ambush. The atmosphere became ugly and frightening... We waited for the weekend with a little foreboding, but no more than usual on the eve of a big march...

Sunday, 30 January 1972, was a cold and crisp day... I assisted at the various morning masses in the cathedral... I was scheduled as celebrant for the 12 noon mass. After the Communion ended...Father Bennie O'Neill, administrator of the cathedral, came to me on the altar. He told me that, within the previous fifteen minutes, large numbers of heavily armed paratroopers had moved into position around the cathedral and into all the adjoining streets. He asked me to appeal to the people to remain calm and to make their way home without getting into any confrontation with the new arrivals...

Around 2.15 p.m. I left the parochial house...to take a funeral to the city cemetery... When I returned from the funeral, I decided to go to Rossville Street to ensure the elderly and housebound were alright. This was my usual practice when there was a possibility of serious confrontation or of CS Gas being used... I went on past the junction of William Street and Rossville Street. The crowd had built up. The army had erected a barrier further down William Street... There was a crowd backed up some distance from the barricade... I was on the point of going back to Rossville Street when there was an outbreak of jeering and catcalling. Originally it was good humoured, and then, after a short time, missiles were thrown by some members of the crowd in the direction of the Army barrier. The firing of the missiles intensified and the Army responded with water-cannon and CS gas... Some of the crowds eventually dispersed...and the biggest majority went across Rossville Street with the main body of the march...

Some time after this, I heard two or three shots ring out... With others, I moved close to the wall at the end of Kells Walk for cover...

Some minutes after I returned to Rossville Street, the revving up of engines, motor engines, drew my attention... I noticed three or four Saracen armoured cars moving towards me at increasing speed, followed by soldiers on foot... Simultaneously everyone in the area began to run in the opposite direction...

As I was entering the courtyard, I noticed a young boy running beside me... He seemed about 16 or 17... I heard a shot and simultaneously this young boy, just beside me, gasped or groaned loudly... I glanced around and the young boy just fell on his face... A woman was screaming. The air was filled with the sound of panic and fear... Then there was a burst of gunfire that caused terror... I took a handkerchief from my pocket and waved it for a few moments...and I went to the boy... There was a substantial amount of blood oozing from his shirt...the other men in the group then said that if I was prepared to go before them with a handkerchief, they would be prepared to carry this young man somewhere he could receive the necessary medical attention... We got up first of all from our knees and I waved the handkerchief, which, by now, was heavily bloodstained... We made our way into Chamberlain Street...

At that point he appeared to be dead...

We waited until the ambulance arrived...and then I made my way...to the area of Block Two of the Rossville Flats in front of the shops. I was thunderstruck by the scene which met my eyes... There were dead and dying and wounded everywhere...

Edward Daly, Mister, Are You A Priest?,
Dublin: Four Courts Press 2000, 188–96

(i) Describe the atmosphere in the city of Derry in the days preceding the march.

(ii) What news did the administrator of the cathedral convey to the author?

(iii) Why did the author visit Rossville Street?

(iv) Describe the scene he witnessed when he went past the junction of Rossville Street and William Street.

(v) What happened when he returned to Rossville Street?

(vi) Describe the events following the shooting of the young boy.

(vii) What was the author's reaction when he entered the area of the Rossville Flats?

(viii) State one advantage and one disadvantage of this account as a source for the historian.

2. Why did James Callaghan, the British Home Secretary, visit Northern Ireland? What message did he have for nationalists and unionists?

3. What were the findings of (i) the Cameron Report and (ii) the Hunt Report?

4. Why was there a split in the IRA in December 1969?

5. What was the Falls Road Curfew and what effect did this have on the Provisional IRA?

6. Why did Jack Lynch dismiss two of his government ministers on 6 May 1970?

7. How did Rev. Ian Paisley benefit from the worsening security situation in 1970?

8. What new political party was launched in Northern Ireland in April 1970 and what were its aims?

9. Write a note on the formation and aims of the Social Democratic and Labour Party (SDLP).

10. Why did the government of Brian Faulkner introduce internment without trial in August 1971?

11. Why did the introduction of internment lead to outrage among the Catholic community?

12. Write a paragraph on the events of Bloody Sunday, 30 January 1972.

13. How did most nationalists react to the report of Lord Widgery?

14. What were the reactions of nationalists and unionists to the fall of Stormont?

HIGHER LEVEL

1. Read the following account by the British Home Secretary, James Callaghan, of his meeting with Ian Paisley and answer the questions that follow.

> Paisley's view was that the leaders of the civil rights movement were really interested in subverting the constitution. He knew Protestant grass-roots opinion because he had the largest Protestant church in the United Kingdom, with an attendance of over two thousand every Sunday evening. The defence of the constitution was what people were really concerned about. Bread-and-butter issues, even unemployment, did not count. I asked him what his attitude was to the programme of reforms. He said he did not like the word reform but he did not object to change provided it did not affect the fundamentals of the constitution. Did he agree with one man one vote in local government elections? He said he did, but he considered that everyone who had a vote should pull his weight in the State... Then he went on to say something that I found very odd. He said the real truth was that in many ways discrimination existed not against Catholics but against Protestants. He based this, so far as I could see, on the case of a lady who lived in the Protestant district of Sandy Row and whose home had been ransacked by the military. He made great play of this, I said it sounded a little far-fetched to base such a far-reaching conclusion on such slender grounds. However, I asked him whether he would welcome the establishment of machinery to make discrimination against either Protestant or Catholic impossible in the allocation of housing and jobs? He is honest in discussion and, driven by the logic of his own argument, he had to say that he would.
>
> *James Callaghan, A House Divided: The Dilemma of Northern Ireland, London: Collins 1973, 81*

(i) What was Ian Paisley's view of the civil rights movement?

(ii) What, according to Paisley, was the main concern of people in Northern Ireland? Do you think he was correct in this view?

(iii) What view did Ian Paisley express on reform?

(iv) What did Paisley have to say about discrimination? Why do you think James Callaghan found this view to be very odd?

(v) What do we learn about Ian Paisley and James Callaghan from the above account?

2. What policy was pursued by the British Government towards Northern Ireland in the latter half of 1969?

3. Explain the changes that occurred within the IRA at this time.

4. What major realignment took place on the nationalist side of Northern Ireland politics in August 1970?

5. Was the policy of internment a success or a failure? Explain your answer.

6. Was Bloody Sunday a turning point in the history of the Troubles in Northern Ireland? Explain your answer.

7. What led to the fall of Stormont? Explain the significance of this development.

William Whitelaw Becomes Secretary of State for Northern Ireland

When Edward Heath's Conservative Government suspended the parliament and government of Northern Ireland in March 1972, a member of the British Cabinet known as the Secretary of State took over the running of the province. The first Secretary of State appointed under direct rule was a leading member of the Conservative Party, William Whitelaw. Along with two junior ministers, he was responsible for all the government departments at Stormont. His greatest challenge, however, was dealing with the continuing violence from both republican and loyalist sources.

William Whitelaw, the new Secretary of State for Northern Ireland, speaking to British soldiers on his arrival in the province

Scene of destruction after a bomb exploded in a public house in Belfast in 1971

Unionist fury at the abolition of Stormont led to widespread protests and an increase in loyalist violence. Three days after Whitelaw arrived to take up his position in Belfast, unionists held a huge protest rally at Stormont. A crowd of over 100,000 was addressed by Brian Faulkner and William Craig. They made defiant speeches and condemned the British Government for introducing direct rule. Some people feared that Craig would use his extreme Vanguard Movement to try to take control of Northern Ireland. However, Faulkner urged the crowd to confine themselves to peaceful protest. Nevertheless, the new loyalist paramilitary group, the UDA, built up its strength throughout 1972. As well as engaging in bomb attacks and shooting Catholic civilians, it held marches in Belfast with its members wearing masks and paramilitary uniforms.

In an effort to regain the support of the Protestant community, Whitelaw attempted to stop the violence and sent the British army and the RUC into Catholic 'no go' areas. These were places like the Bogside in Derry and parts of West Belfast where the security forces did not venture in

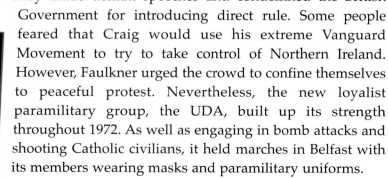

William Craig addressing a rally of the Vanguard Movement outside Belfast City Hall

and which appeared to be under the control of republican paramilitaries.

To win the approval of the Catholic community, the new Secretary of State hoped to control the actions of the British army and eventually put an end to internment without trial. However, Whitelaw's chances of making progress would ultimately depend on the reactions of the paramilitaries.

The IRA Campaign Continues

The result of continued IRA violence

Although the Provisional IRA was pleased with the fall of the Stormont Government and claimed credit for bringing it about, the organisation continued with its campaign of violence. Its aim was the complete withdrawal of the British from Northern Ireland and direct rule from London was totally rejected by its members. Following the imposition of direct rule, leading members of the Provisional IRA met in the Irish Republic and issued a statement which declared that 'the war goes on'. In fact, they stepped up their bombing campaign and on 14 April 1972 thirty bombs exploded in various parts of Northern Ireland.

In reaction to the rising level of violence, groups of concerned citizens pleaded for an end to the IRA campaign. These included a peace group known as Women Together and the Belfast-based Central Citizens' Defence Committee. This group collected 50,000 signatures on a petition calling on both the Official and Provisional IRA to end their campaigns. Although the Provisionals flatly refused, on 29 May the Official IRA announced a ceasefire. Whitelaw then attempted to see if he could persuade the Provisional IRA to do likewise.

Catholic and Protestant women in Derry marching for peace in Northern Ireland

Whitelaw Meets the IRA

In preparing the ground to bring about a ceasefire by the Provisional IRA, Whitelaw had removed the ban on marches and had released hundreds of internees. He then used members of the SDLP as mediators to establish contact with the Provisionals. John Hume then met leading members of the Provisional IRA to discuss the possibility of a ceasefire.

On 20 June 1972 representatives of William Whitelaw met with two leading members of the Provisional IRA, Gerry Adams and Daithi O Conaill. Two days later it was announced that the Provisional IRA would begin a ceasefire on 26 June. However, shootings and bombings continued right up to the time of the agreed ceasefire.

Almost two weeks into the ceasefire, on 7 July a number of leading members of the Provisional IRA met William Whitelaw in London for

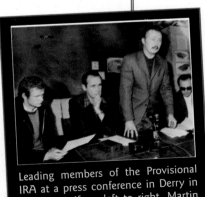

Leading members of the Provisional IRA at a press conference in Derry in June 1972 (from left to right, Martin McGuinness, Daithi O Conaill, Seán Mac Stíofáin and Seamas Tuomey)

negotiations. The IRA delegation, which was led by the movement's Chief of Staff, Seán Mac Stíofáin, laid down conditions which the British side found impossible to meet. Mac Stíofáin insisted that all IRA prisoners be released and that the British would promise to leave Northern Ireland by 1 January 1975. Whitelaw realised that there was no prospect of reaching an agreement with the Provisional IRA.

Two days after the talks in London, the ceasefire collapsed when fighting broke out between the Provisionals and the British army at Andersonstown in West Belfast.

Bloody Friday – Belfast, 21 July 1972

One of the worst atrocities during the Troubles was to take place in Belfast on Friday, 21 July 1972. In the space of an hour during the afternoon, twenty bombs were detonated by the Provisional IRA in the city centre. There were scenes of horrific carnage and suffering. Men, women and children were victims of these indiscriminate attacks. Nine people were killed and over 130 seriously injured. Police and rescue workers had to carry plastic bags to recover the scattered remains of the dead. Ambulance crews and fire brigade workers risked their lives and ignored the possible existence of

Rescue workers lifting the remains of a body into a bag following an explosion on Bloody Friday in Belfast on 21 July 1972

further bombs in order to help the injured and to recover the remains of the dead.

As night fell on the city, prolonged gun battles took place between the Provisional IRA and the British army. One of the immediate results of the horrific slaughter of Bloody Friday was the decision by William Whitelaw to allow the British army to enter the 'no go' areas in Northern Ireland.

Operation Motorman

On 31 July 1972 the British army launched Operation Motorman, an exercise designed to put an end to 'no go' areas. Despite the fears of Prime Minister Edward Heath that there would be hundreds of casualties, the operation went very smoothly.

The army was careful to include Protestant 'no go' areas as well as Catholic ones. Huge special tanks demolished barricades without any difficulty in areas like the Bogside in Derry. Apart from the deaths of two people who were shot in Derry, Operation

British troops entering a 'no go' area in Derry on 31 July 1972

Motorman was a complete success from the British Government's point of view.

The ending of 'no go' areas was a serious blow to the Provisional IRA and to loyalist paramilitaries. With the British army patrolling all areas, they found it more difficult to hide weapons and explosives and to organise attacks. However, both groups of paramilitaries were far from defeated and continued their campaigns of violence in the years and months ahead.

The Threat from Loyalists

Loyalist violence continued to pose a serious challenge for the British Government. Paramilitary groups like the UVF and the UDA had begun a campaign of regular assassinations of innocent Catholics in April 1972. Regular battles took place between the British army and loyalist gunmen in areas like the Shankill in West Belfast. Sometimes loyalists carried out attacks against innocent civilians across the border in the Republic in areas like Cavan or Donegal.

Masked members of the UDA manning a barricade on the Shankill Road in Belfast in June 1972

In December 1972 UVF bombs exploded in Dublin, causing the deaths of two people and injuring 127 others. As a result of the huge increase in loyalist violence, the first loyalists were interned by the British Government in March 1973.

Thus, by the end of 1972 it was clear that the year had been by far the worst since the Troubles began, with 497 dead and hundreds more injured. The increasing level of violence also had a profound impact on both government and society south of the border in the Irish Republic.

A UVF explosion in Dublin on 4 December 1972

Reaction in the Republic

The Fianna Fáil Government under Jack Lynch and most people in the Irish Republic supported the civil rights campaign and had been horrified by the events in Derry on Bloody Sunday. However, they were strongly opposed to the violent campaign of the Provisional IRA. Both government and people did not wish to see violence extend from Northern Ireland into the Republic.

In the Cabinet reshuffle around the time of the Arms Trial in 1970, Jack Lynch had appointed Desmond O'Malley, an able young Fianna Fáil TD, to be the new Minister for Justice. O'Malley took a strong stand against the Provisional IRA and their political wing, Sinn Féin.

As the violence in Northern Ireland intensified in the autumn of 1972, stronger measures were taken in the Republic. On 6 October the government closed down the offices of Provisional Sinn Féin and the following month the IRA Chief of Staff, Seán Mac Stíofáin, was sentenced to six months' imprisonment for membership of an illegal organisation. When an interview with Mac Stíofáin was broadcast on Irish radio, the government dismissed the RTÉ Authority, which was responsible for the state-run radio and television channels.

While Dáil Éireann was discussing tough new emergency laws to deal with the IRA, loyalists planted bombs in Dublin, killing two people and injuring over a hundred on 1 December 1972. When the bombs went off, the main opposition party, Fine Gael, was having a heated discussion on whether to support the new law. The party leader, Liam Cosgrave, was nearly removed because he favoured supporting the law, while a majority of his followers thought it was too strict.

Liam Cosgrave (left), Taoiseach of the Coalition Government in the Republic from 1973 to 1977, and Dr Garret Fitzgerald (right), the Minister for Foreign Affairs

When the bombs went off, the party supported Cosgrave's view; he survived as leader and went on to win a general election and become Taoiseach a few months later.

When Fianna Fáil lost power in the general election of February 1973 it was replaced by a Fine Gael–Labour coalition government with Liam Cosgrave as Taoiseach. Cosgrave was strongly committed to law and order and to tough measures against the IRA. The Minister for Foreign Affairs in the new government, Dr Garret FitzGerald of Fine Gael, had a lifelong interest in Northern Ireland. His mother came from a Protestant background in Co. Down and he was committed to bringing about reconciliation between unionists and nationalists. Another member of the government, Dr Conor Cruise O'Brien of the Labour Party, was a stern critic of the IRA and sympathetic to the position of Northern unionists. During his term as Minister for Posts and Telegraphs, he introduced a law to prevent members of violent organisations from appearing on Irish radio or television.

Dr Conor Cruise O'Brien, Minister for Posts and Telegraphs from 1973 to 1977, was a severe critic of the IRA

The main policy of the new government in the Republic regarding Northern Ireland was to co-operate with the British Government to end the violence and to encourage the local parties to reach an agreement on the future government of the province. At this time, the British Government was moving in the same direction.

CASE STUDY: THE SUNNINGDALE AGREEMENT AND THE POWER-SHARING EXECUTIVE, 1973-4

PREPARING THE GROUND

In September 1972 William Whitelaw invited political parties from Northern Ireland to roundtable talks in Darlington, Co. Durham to explore the possibility of a political agreement. While the Unionist Party, Alliance Party and the Northern Ireland Labour Party attended the talks, the SDLP boycotted them because of the continued existence of internment without trial. However, both the SDLP and the Taoiseach of the Republic went to meet the British Prime Minister, Edward Heath. They were pleased when the British Government agreed that any new arrangement should be 'so far as possible, acceptable to and accepted by the Republic of Ireland'. This recognition by the British that there was 'an Irish dimension' to the problems in Northern Ireland was an important matter both for the Irish Government and for the nationalist minority in Northern Ireland.

In order to reassure unionists, the British Government's proposals included a referendum on the existence of the border. The referendum took place on 8 March 1973. With nationalists advised to boycott it, the result was 97.8 per cent in favour of keeping the Union, which represented 57 per cent of the voters. Having assured the unionist majority that their position in the United Kingdom was safe, the British Government went on to publish its detailed proposals two weeks later.

THE WHITELAW PROPOSALS

Published on 20 March 1973, the proposals of the British Government included the restoration of power to an assembly in Northern Ireland. An assembly would be elected using the proportional representation (PR) voting system and it in turn would elect an executive to control matters handed over by the British Government. However, the British Government would only agree to this on the basis of power-sharing between unionists and nationalists. This insistence on power-sharing was to be maintained by every British Government from that time forward.

The second key element in the proposals was a Council of Ireland. This body would allow representatives from both Northern Ireland and the Republic to meet to discuss matters of joint concern.

Document 1

The Conservative Government's proposals

I believe that the initial British idea had been simply that there should be a coalition government in Northern Ireland, in which both unionists and nationalists would take part, in proportion to their electoral strength. But John Hume – without whose approval the idea would not have the requisite nationalist support – stipulated that there should be an All-Ireland dimension in the shape of a Council of Ireland, felt to be the precursor of a united Ireland, and cherished for that reason by those who cherished it.

When the matter came before the cabinet for discussion I warmly welcomed the idea of a bipartisan government in Northern Ireland. But I thought the Council of Ireland with the implication of progress towards a united Ireland, might be a bridge too far. On that issue, the unionist population might desert Brian Faulkner, and the Northern Ireland government would then collapse. I therefore urged that the idea of a Council of Ireland be re-examined.

C.C. O'Brien, *Memoir: My Life and Themes*, Dublin: Poolbeg 1998, 348–9

REACTION IN NORTHERN IRELAND

Conor Cruise O'Brien's fears, as seen in Document 1, were about to be realised. While most constitutional nationalists welcomed the proposals, the Provisional IRA completely rejected them as being merely the continuation of British rule under another form in Northern Ireland. The organisation committed itself to continuing its campaign of bombing and shooting.

On the unionist side, the response was more mixed. Paisley, Craig, the Orange Order and the loyalist paramilitaries rejected the proposals completely. They called for a return to the old system of the Stormont Government, with majority rule by the unionists. Brian Faulkner and the Ulster Unions were divided in their responses and decided to wait and see how events proceeded.

On 28 June 1973 elections were held to the new assembly in Northern Ireland. When the results came in they showed deep divisions on the unionist side. Anti-power-sharing unionists outnumbered Faulkner's unionists by twenty-six to twenty-four in the seventy-eight-seat assembly. The Alliance Party won eight seats and the SDLP captured nineteen. Whitelaw underestimated the determination of the anti-agreement unionists. He had hoped to build an agreement by combining the strength of the Faulkner unionists, the SDLP and the Alliance

Party. Brian Faulkner and his followers were willing to co-operate with the Secretary of State at this stage, but they would come under strong pressure from anti-agreement unionists in the months ahead.

THE SUNNINGDALE AGREEMENT

Agreement was finally reached in November 1973 between the Faulkner Unionists, the Alliance Party and the SDLP to form a power-sharing executive. There were to be six Unionists, four SDLP members and one Alliance member in the new executive. Brian Faulkner was to be chief executive with the leader of the SDLP, Gerry Fitt, as his deputy. There were

Unionist and nationalist leaders during talks at Sunningdale in December 1973 (from left to right, Brian Faulkner, Gerry Fitt, John Hume and Paddy Devlin)

violent scenes in the assembly as Vanguard and DUP members attacked unionists who supported power-sharing.

On 6 December talks began at Sunningdale in England between the British and Irish governments and the power-sharing parties from Northern Ireland. The British Prime Minister, Edward Heath, and the Taoiseach, Liam Cosgrave, were both in attendance. After four days of negotiation, consensus was finally reached and on 9 December 1973 the Sunningdale Agreement was signed. The Agreement incorporated the positions of the various parties.

Document 2

Extracts from the Sunningdale Agreement

- The people of the Republic together with a minority in Northern Ireland as represented by the SDLP delegation, continue to uphold the aspiration towards a united Ireland. The only united Ireland they wanted to see was unity established by consent.
- The desire of the majority to remain part of the United Kingdom, as represented by the unionist and Alliance delegations, remained firm.
- The Irish Government fully accepted and solemnly declared that there could be no change in the status of Northern Ireland until a majority of the people of Northern Ireland desired a change in status.
- The British Government solemnly declared that it was, and would remain, their policy to support the wishes of the majority of people in Northern Ireland. The present status of Northern Ireland is that it is part of the United Kingdom. If in the future the majority of the people of Northern Ireland should indicate a wish to become part of a united Ireland, the British Government would support that wish.

The Sunningdale Agreement, 9 December 1973

DIFFERENCES OVER THE COUNCIL OF IRELAND

Although the Irish and British governments had high hopes for the success of the power-sharing arrangement, it was deeply unpopular among large sections of the unionist population. While the element of power-sharing was contentious, the Council of Ireland was to prove even more controversial. Realising this, Brian Faulkner had tried to reduce its powers during the Sunningdale negotiations. He later attempted to play down its significance.

Document 3
Brian Faulkner's view on the Council of Ireland
The Council of Ministers had a valuable practical role in formalising co-operation on security and social and economic matters. In a very real sense getting the Dublin Government to treat Northern Ireland representatives as equals on an inter-governmental body underlined the acceptance of partition... The other appendages of the Council – the Consultative Assembly, the Permanent Secretariat, the executive functions of the Council of Ministers – fell in my mind into the 'necessary nonsense' category. They were necessary to get the co-operation of the SDLP and the Dublin Government. But nothing agreed at Sunningdale infringed on the powers of the Northern Ireland Assembly by which everything would have to be approved and delegated. Given the overwhelmingly unionist composition of the body and the unanimity rule in the Council of Ministers we were satisfied that the constitutional integrity of Northern Ireland was secure.

Brian Faulkner, *Memoirs of a Statesman*, London: Weidenfeld & Nicholson 1978, 236–7

In contrast to Faulkner, the SDLP tried to emphasise the significance of the Council of Ireland.

Document 4
The SDLP view on the Council of Ireland
[The general approach of the SDLP to the talks] was to get all-Ireland institutions established which, with adequate safeguards, would produce the dynamic that could ultimately lead to an agreed single State for Ireland. That meant, of course, that SDLP representatives would concentrate their entire efforts on building up a set of tangible executive powers for the Council which in the fullness of time would create and sustain an evolutionary process. All other issues were governed by that approach and were aimed generally at reducing loyalist resistance to the concepts of a Council of Ireland and a power-sharing executive.

Paddy Devlin, *The Fall of the Northern Ireland Executive*, Belfast 1975, 32

OPPOSITION TO THE SUNNINGDALE AGREEMENT

On 1 January 1974 the new power-sharing executive began to function in Belfast. Three days later, the Ulster Unionist Council, the governing body of the Unionist Party, met and voted against 'the proposed all-Ireland Council settlement' by a majority of eighty votes. Faulkner had to resign immediately as leader and he and his followers withdrew from the party. He was replaced as leader of the Official Unionists by Harry West.

When Heath called a British general election for 28 February 1974, the unionist parties opposed to Sunningdale joined together to form the United Ulster Unionist Council (UUUC). Having fought the election with the slogan 'Dublin is just a Sunningdale away', the UUUC candidates won eleven out of twelve of Northern Ireland's Westminster seats. The other seat in West Belfast was won by Gerry Fitt of the SDLP. Just over half the electorate voted for candidates who opposed Sunningdale. Although the executive still continued to function, it was now clear that it did not have the support of a majority of the voters.

THE ULSTER WORKERS' COUNCIL STRIKE, MAY 1974

As a result of the general election of February 1974, Edward Heath's Conservative Government lost power and was replaced by the Labour Party under the leadership of Harold Wilson. Merlyn Rees was appointed as Secretary of State for Northern Ireland and on 18 April Wilson visited Belfast and declared that the Sunningdale Agreement was the only way forward.

British soldiers manning a petrol station in Belfast during the Ulster Workers' Council strike in May 1974

Having failed to destroy the Sunningdale Agreement by political pressure, leaders of the unionist parties opposed to the settlement entered into talks with loyalist paramilitaries such as the UVF and the UDA. A group of loyalist workers then formed the Ulster Workers' Council with the intention of using strikes to bring Northern Ireland to a standstill in an effort to destroy the agreement.

The Ulster Workers' Council Strike began on 14 May 1974. Control of electricity and oil supplies was to be a powerful weapon in the hands of the strikers. The UDA commander, Andie Tyrie, later recalled plans to use power supplies as a strike weapon.

Roadblocks were set up and manned by paramilitary groups to control the movement of goods. Widespread intimidation was used to ensure that workers complied with the strike. The strike gradually brought the economy of Northern Ireland to a halt. At the end of its first week on Friday, 17 May, loyalist paramilitaries planted bombs in Dublin and Monaghan, causing the greatest loss of life on a single day in the whole history of the Troubles.

Document 5

Use of power supplies as a strike weapon

What happened that particular night was this. Billy Kelly said power could be brought right down within a couple of hours and I replied, 'Why not say that power could be brought down within twelve hours, giving yourself some room to move?'

I had been listening to him [Kelly] earlier on saying that...you have to be very careful in case you destroy the machinery... If you took the power too low, it could destroy the coils and put the machinery out of action for three months, or even a year.

Some said 'What about the hospitals? The public will kick up.' I said they won't. They'll blame it on the government because that's the way their minds are thinking. They'll say everything that's happening is the government's fault.

A. Tyrie, cited in D. Anderson, *Fourteen May Days: The Inside Story of the Loyalist Strike of 1974*, Dublin: Gill & Macmillan 1994, 72

The Collapse of the Power-Sharing Executive

Faced with massive civil disobedience and a clear challenge to its authority, Harold Wilson's British Government failed to take decisive action. The Secretary of State, Merlyn Rees, and the British army commanders in Northern Ireland stood aside as paramilitaries imposed their will on society. Wilson did, however, denounce the strike in a famous television broadcast on 25 May.

A loyalist victory parade led by the Rev. Ian Paisley after the collapse of the power-sharing executive in May 1974

Document 6

Wilson denounces the strikers

It is a deliberate and calculated attempt to use every undemocratic and unparliamentary means for the purpose of bringing down the whole constitution of Northern Ireland so as to set up there a sectarian and undemocratic state... British taxpayers have seen the taxes they have poured out, almost without regard to cost... Yet people who benefit from all this now viciously defy Westminster, purporting to act as though they were an elected government; people who spend their lives sponging on Westminster and British democracy and then systematically assault democratic methods. Who do these people think they are?

H. Wilson, Broadcast, 25 May 1974

Wilson's comments caused outrage in Northern Ireland, where people deeply resented his use of the word 'sponging'. Despite the widespread intimidation, the strike was supported by most people in the unionist community, including members of the RUC who were on friendly terms with the strikers.

In the absence of support from the British Government and given the deep-seated opposition within the unionist community, the ministers in the power-sharing executive, including Chief Minister Brian Faulkner, resigned within a fortnight of the start of the strike. This signified the end of the power-sharing arrangement and a return to direct rule from London. Unionists were jubilant at this outcome and there were bonfires in Protestant districts in celebration of the end of the Sunningdale Agreement.

Nationalist Responses to the End of the Sunningdale Agreement

In contrast to unionist celebrations, nationalists were outraged at the success of the Ulster Workers' Council strike. It reinforced their belief that the Northern state was still based on unionist domination. They were shocked at the failure of the British Government to confront the strikers and looked on with disbelief at the weak response of the Secretary of State, Merlyn Rees.

The response of the Irish Government was one of deep disappointment, as they believed that Sunningdale was a missed opportunity to bring peace to Northern Ireland. The Irish Foreign Minister, Dr Garret FitzGerald, later recalled his reaction to these events.

Document 7

Garret FitzGerald recalls the end of Sunningdale

The end came on Tuesday 28 May. The failure of the British government to give adequate support to the Executive that it had caused to be established by a democratic process, and its incapacity to maintain essential services, led to a complete collapse of self-confidence amongst the pro-Assembly unionists.

At this time Faulkner felt obliged as a result of pressure from his unionist colleagues to propose the appointment of a mediator to negotiate with the political-cum-paramilitary leadership of the UWC. This was more even than the British government was prepared to concede at that point. Faulkner, together with his unionist colleagues, then resigned, following which Merlyn Rees announced that there was no longer any statutory basis for the Executive, and reinstalled direct rule.

Irish nationalists, North and South, believed at the time that had the British army been willing to take prompt action against road blocks, barricades and overt intimidation when these features first made their appearance, the strike could have been broken. Nationalists also believed that it had been totally irresponsible and indefensible to have allowed, through tolerating discrimination in public employment, a situation to develop and to persist that put control of power supplies into the hands of extremists from one section of the community.

G. FitzGerald, *All in a Life*, Dublin: Pan Macmillan 1991, 243

THE SIGNIFICANCE OF SUNNINGDALE

Although the Sunningdale Agreement ended in failure, it was an historic attempt to bring the two communities together. For the first time, unionists and nationalists were to share power in the government of Northern Ireland. The concept of power-sharing at the heart of the Sunningdale Agreement was to be an essential element in all future attempts to reach a settlement in Northern Ireland.

The Sunningdale Agreement was signed by both the British and Irish governments in recognition of the central role played by the Irish Republic in negotiating a settlement in Northern Ireland. Acceptance of the 'Irish dimension' by the British Government was to remain a key feature in later attempts to reach agreement on the future of Northern Ireland.

Despite its failure, the principles enshrined in the Sunningdale Agreement, such as consent, power-sharing and the Irish dimension, were to remain central to the quest for peace and stability in Northern Ireland.

CASE STUDY: QUESTIONS

COMPREHENSION

1. According to Document 1, what was the initial British idea concerning power-sharing in Northern Ireland?

2. How did John Hume differ from this view? (Document 1)

3. What concerns did the author of Document 1 express about the proposal to establish a Council of Ireland?

4. Which aspiration of the minority in Northern Ireland was stated in the Sunningdale Agreement? (Document 2)

5. What was accepted by the Irish Government in the Sunningdale Agreement? (Document 2)

6. What declaration was made by the British Government? (Document 2)

7. According to the author of Document 3, what underlined an acceptance of partition by the Irish Government?

8. What view of the Council of Ireland is portrayed in Document 3?

9. According to the author of Document 3, why was the constitutional integrity of Northern Ireland secure?

10. Why did the SDLP want to establish all-Ireland institutions? (Document 4)

11. According to Document 5, who will people blame for the loss of electricity power during the loyalist strike?

12. What is Harold Wilson's opinion of the loyalist strikers? (Document 6)

13. Why does he refer to them as 'spongers'? (Document 6)

14. According to the author of Document 7, what led to the collapse of the Sunningdale Agreement?

15. In the view of nationalists, what would have helped to break the strike? (Document 7)

COMPARISON

1. Compare the views on the Council of Ireland expressed in Documents 3 and 4.

2. Did Brian Faulkner (Document 3) share Conor Cruise O'Brien's views concerning the Council of Ireland?

3. What were the aspirations of the SDLP (Document 4) expressed in the Sunningdale Agreement? (Document 1)

4. Were the views of unionists (Document 3) reflected in the Agreement? (Document 1)

CRITICISM

1. Does the author of Document 1 attempt to understand the unionist point of view? Explain your answer.

2. What is the value of Document 5 as a primary source?

3. Point out two examples in Document 6 which reveal a strong condemnation of the loyalist strike by the British Prime Minister.

4. Does Document 7 present a balanced view on the reasons for the fall of the Northern Ireland Executive? Explain your answer.

CONTEXTUALISATION

1. State two key aspects of the Sunningdale Agreement and name the parties to the agreement.

2. How did nationalists in Northern Ireland react to the agreement?

3. What was the reaction of unionists?

4. Write an account of the Ulster Workers' Council strike.

5. Why did the power-sharing executive collapse?

6. What was the significance of the Sunningdale Agreement?

KEY PERSONALITY: BRIAN FAULKNER (1921–77)

Brian Faulkner was born in Co. Antrim in 1921. After receiving his early education in Northern Ireland, he then attended St Columba's College at Rathfarnham in Dublin. In 1939 he entered Queen's University to study law but returned to work in the family shirt-making business when World War II broke out.

In 1949 he was elected Unionist MP for East Down in the Stormont Parliament. He was appointed Minister of Home Affairs in the Brookeborough Government in 1959 and was subsequently appointed Minister of Commerce by Terence O'Neill in 1963.

As a traditional unionist, he opposed O'Neill's conciliatory politics and resigned from the Cabinet in protest at the decision to appoint the Cameron Commission to investigate police conduct during the People's Democracy march in 1969. He returned to serve as Minister for Development under James Chichester-Clark, who succeeded O'Neill as Prime Minister in May 1969. He stated that he now favoured a policy of reform.

Amid mounting violence, Chichester-Clarke resigned as Prime Minister and was succeeded by Brian Faulkner on 23 March 1971. In response to the worsening security situation, Faulkner introduced internment without trial on 9 August 1971. This policy proved to be a disaster and, instead of reducing the violence, it led to an escalation of violence.

During an anti-internment march in Derry in January 1972, British paratroopers shot and killed thirteen civilians. The events of Bloody Sunday were to mark the end of Faulkner's Government. When the British Government decided to take over responsibility for security in Northern Ireland, Faulkner and his Cabinet resigned. The Stormont Parliament was dissolved and direct rule was imposed.

Faulkner supported the power-sharing arrangement established under the Sunningdale Agreement and became Chief Minister in a power-sharing executive with the SDLP and the moderate Alliance Party. Unionist opposition to the Sunningdale Agreement resulted in the loyalist strike in May 1974 which brought down the power-sharing executive.

In 1974 Faulkner lost the leadership of the Ulster Unionist Party and was succeeded by Harry West. He established a new party, the Unionist Party of Northern Ireland, but this fared badly in the Convention election of 1975. In 1976 Faulkner retired from politics. In 1977 he was appointed a life peer and acquired the title Baron Faulkner of Downpatrick. He died as a result of a horse riding accident in 1977 at the age of fifty-six.

ORDINARY LEVEL

1 What arrangements were made for the government of Northern Ireland following the fall of Stormont?

2. How did unionists react to the introduction of direct rule?

3. What efforts did William Whitelaw make to regain the support of the Protestant community?

4. How did the IRA react to the imposition of direct rule?

5. What steps were taken by William Whitelaw to bring about a ceasefire by the Provisional IRA?

6. Was the meeting between William Whitelaw and the Provisional IRA successful? Explain your answer.

7. Describe the events of Bloody Friday, 21 July 1972.

8. What was Operation Motorman?

9. Write a paragraph on the threat posed by the loyalist paramilitary organisations.

10. What measures were taken by Jack Lynch's Government in the Irish Republic to deal with the Provisional IRA?

11. What policy towards Northern Ireland was pursued by the coalition government under the leadership of Liam Cosgrave?

HIGHER LEVEL

1. Read the following extract from a speech by Brian Faulkner following the announcement of direct rule in March 1972 and answer the questions that follow.

> On Wednesday Senator Andrews and I travelled to London for what we well knew would be a crucially important meeting with Mr Heath and his colleagues. We were determined to do anything we could reasonably do to restore peace and stability to Ulster and confident that we would hear from Mr Heath realistic proposals to help end violence and find a new way forward for this community.
>
> Even as we sat at the Cabinet table at 10 Downing Street, news reached me of yet another massive explosion in the centre of Belfast, with further casualties to innocent civilians who were once again the victims of foul and callous terrorism. We were deeply conscious, too, of the appalling situation in such places as Londonderry, a city of the United Kingdom which includes enclaves of total lawlessness, from which come those who day and daily wreck more and more of the business and commercial centre of that city.
>
> ...We went to Downing Street fully prepared to acknowledge that, in defeating the violence, military means would have to be buttressed by realistic political proposals, designed to unite the communities and detach them from any sympathy or support for violent men.
>
> ...The proposition put to us was that all statutory and executive responsibility for law and order should be vested in the United Kingdom Parliament and Government.
>
> ...Of course, chief amongst those who have sought the emasculation and ultimately the downfall of Stormont have been the IRA terrorists themselves. And when it was made clear to me that the United Kingdom Government could not give an assurance of

any further positive measures against terrorism, I felt bound to ask whether the end of violence was being sought, not – as we have always asserted – by defeating the terrorists, but by surrendering to them.

...It was made clear to us, however, that the United Kingdom Cabinet at its meeting the next day was likely to reaffirm the decision to transfer all law and order responsibilities. I then informed Mr Heath and his colleagues that...the Government of Northern Ireland would not accept this situation. I told him that it would be widely construed as an acceptance of totally baseless criticism of our stewardship; that it would be seen by the IRA and others as a first and major step on the road to a terrorist victory; and that it would leave the Government of Northern Ireland totally bereft of any real influence and authority by removing the most fundamental power of any Government.

I said clearly that we were not interested in maintaining a mere sham, or a face-saving charade.

Cited in D. Bleakley, Faulkner – Conflict and Consent in Irish Politics, London and Oxford: Mowbrays 1974, 139–41

(i) What did Brian Faulkner expect from the meeting with Mr Heath?

(ii) How did Brian Faulkner believe the violence in Northern Ireland could be defeated?

(iii) What proposition did the British Government put to the unionist delegation?

(iv) According to Faulkner, how would the decision of the British Government be interpreted?

(v) What do you think he meant by the last sentence of the passage?

2. 'Following his appointment as Secretary of State for Northern Ireland, William Whitelaw attempted to win the support of both the Protestant and Catholic communities.' Do you agree with this statement?

3. Examine the main developments within republican and loyalist paramilitary organisations at this time.

4. 'Successive governments of the Irish Republic in the early 1970s showed a determination to deal strongly with the Provisional IRA.' Discuss this statement.

Political Stalemate

With the failure of the Sunningdale Agreement, the British Government restored direct rule in Northern Ireland. The Secretary of State, Merlyn Rees, took over the day-to-day government of Northern Ireland. Like the previous Conservative Government of Edward Heath, the Labour Government of Harold Wilson favoured a power-sharing arrangement. Although a number of efforts were made to restore a power-sharing arrangement in Northern Ireland, none were successful in the short term. The main obstacles in the way were political opposition by a majority of unionists and violent resistance by loyalist and republican paramilitaries.

In the British general election of October 1974, the anti-power-sharing United Ulster Unionist Council (UUUC) won ten out of the twelve Northern Ireland seats in the Westminster Parliament. During the early months of 1975 the British Government decided to set up an elected convention in the hope of restoring power-sharing to the province. However, in the convention election in May 1975 the unionists opposed to power-sharing won 58 per cent of the vote, resulting in forty-seven seats out of seventy-eight. Brian Faulkner's pro-power-sharing unionists only won five seats, Alliance won eight, the SDLP seventeen and the Northern Ireland Labour Party one seat. As a result, the convention was doomed to failure from the outset.

At this time of political stagnation and continuing paramilitary violence, Northern Ireland also faced deep economic problems.

Economic Failure

During the 1970s Northern Ireland was beset by serious economic difficulties. Between 1973 and 1979 the economy only grew by around 2 per cent a year and most of this growth was due to subsidies from the British Government. After reaching a peak in 1973, the numbers employed in the manufacturing industry fell rapidly. The big employers of the past, such as the shipbuilding and engineering

Workers leaving a Belfast factory which has just closed down

MANUFACTURING INDUSTRIAL EMPLOYMENT IN NORTHERN IRELAND			
	1979	1986	% change
Engineering and allied trades	41,600	29,650	-28.7
Textiles	30,000	11,030	-63.3
Food, drink and tobacco	22,600	18,720	-17.2
Clothing	18,900	16,220	-14.2
Other	26,900	22,650	-15.8
TOTALS	140,000	98,270	-29.5

Source: TSB Business Outlook & Economic Review, Sept. 1986
From *Ulster: An Illustrated History* by C. Brady, M. O'Dowd and B. Walker (eds.), London 1989

industries, were in serious decline.

The Oil Crisis of the mid-1970s had a severe impact on Northern Ireland. By 1974 the province had become more dependent on cheap oil than any other region in the United Kingdom. Therefore the huge increase in energy prices had a particularly severe impact on the local economy and contributed to rising levels of unemployment.

As well as suffering a decline based on economic factors such as the Oil Crisis, the economy of Northern Ireland was seriously damaged by the effects of political unrest and violence. The sustained bombing campaigns of both loyalist and republican paramilitaries resulted in massive destruction to factories, shops and homes. Furthermore, the widespread violence discouraged foreign companies from locating industries in Northern Ireland.

Unemployment rates among Catholics remained extremely high – they were almost three times as likely to be unemployed as Protestants. In order to lessen the inequalities, the British Parliament passed the Fair Employment Act in 1976. This set up a Fair Employment Agency in Northern Ireland and made it illegal for employers to discriminate on the basis of a person's religion or politics. Although this measure brought about little practical improvement, it was a significant first step which paved the way for more effective change in fair employment in the future.

A row of bombed houses in Belfast in October 1971

The Troubles also had a serious impact on the housing situation in Northern Ireland. By 1976 around 25,000 houses had been either destroyed or damaged in Belfast alone. The Northern Ireland Housing Executive had been established in 1971 to provide public housing. It faced serious challenges from the outset. Not only did it have to deal with years of neglect in the provision of maintenance of housing, it also had to confront the problems of violence and intimidation. During the Troubles there was a huge population movement as both Catholics and Protestants were forced to flee from their homes. As a result, the community became more polarised and most localities were either overwhelmingly Catholic or Protestant.

Against this background of sectarian tension and economic stagnation, both the British Government and the Provisional IRA were preparing for a long struggle.

The Long War

With the failure of the Sunningdale Agreement (1973) and the Convention (1975), the British Government concentrated on defeating the IRA. They felt let down by the failure of the IRA ceasefire in 1975 and there was widespread outrage at the assassination of the British ambassador in Dublin, Christopher Ewart-Biggs, in July 1976.

Meanwhile, the IRA had been reviewing

The assassination of the British ambassador, Christopher Ewart-Biggs, in Dublin in July 1976

Young members of the IRA in Long Kesh internment camp

their approach. A group of IRA members inside Long Kesh prison, including Gerry Adams, concluded that the struggle to achieve Irish unity was going to be slow and long lasting. They hoped to wear down the British resolve to remain in Northern Ireland by a long campaign of bombing and shooting. The group also set about radically reforming the structures of the IRA. The old structures were to be replaced by a system of active service units, each consisting of four members. This was done to reduce the risk of infiltration by informers. In future, IRA activities in Northern Ireland would come under the control of a Northern Command consisting of local young IRA members. A very important innovation was the decision by the IRA to build up Sinn Féin as a political organisation to campaign for British withdrawal from Northern Ireland.

By the mid-1970s violence had become a way of life in many working-class areas of Northern Ireland. Both the IRA and loyalist paramilitaries controlled areas and carried out acts of violence, robbery and intimidation. During the winter of 1975–76 a gang of UVF members known as 'The Shankill Butchers' roamed the streets kidnapping, torturing and murdering innocent Catholics. Their leader, Lenny Murphy, was also feared in Protestant areas because he shot anybody who quarrelled with him.

A youth tarred and feathered and tied to a lamppost by the IRA in the Falls Road area of Belfast

Against this background of constant violence and sectarian attacks, a movement sprang up demanding an end to violence and a return to peace in Northern Ireland.

The Peace Movement

In August 1976 two women founded the peace movement, one a Protestant named Betty Williams and the other a Catholic named Mairead Corrigan. Betty Williams had just witnessed an accident in which Mairead Corrigan's sister Anne was injured and three of her four children were killed when a gunman's getaway car crashed into them. The two women founded the Peace People and organised rallies and marches to promote peace and reconciliation. Unlike previous efforts, the Peace People attracted widespread cross-community support, with some of their rallies being attended by over 20,000 people.

Directed by the journalist Ciaran McKeown, the peace

A rally by the Peace People outside the City Hall in Belfast in August 1976 to welcome home Mairead Corrigan and Betty Williams, who had just won the Nobel Peace Prize

Leaders of the Peace Movement, seen here in London with the singer Joan Baez and Mrs Jane Ewart-Biggs, the widow of the assassinated British ambassador to Ireland (from left to right, Betty Williams, Joan Baez, Ciaran McKeown, Jane Ewart-Biggs and Mairead Corrigan)

movement attracted widespread support both at home and abroad. However, in a deeply divided society, the movement was opposed by extremists on both sides in Northern Ireland. After seven years of violence, the leaders of the peace movement found it difficult to bring about any great change in existing attitudes and the violence continued throughout the province.

A New Secretary of State: Roy Mason Arrives in Northern Ireland

In September 1976 a new Secretary of State arrived in Northern Ireland. Roy Mason was appointed by James Callaghan, who had replaced Harold Wilson as British Prime Minister the previous April. From the outset, he was determined to defeat the IRA. His strong statements supporting law and order and condemning republicans won favour with unionists but made him unpopular among nationalists. Mason believed that the North's problems were primarily due to massive unemployment and poverty. If the IRA could be defeated, economic prosperity would result in a more stable society.

Roy Mason, who was appointed Secretary of State in Northern Ireland in September 1976

Due to his hardline approach to republican violence, Mason faced accusations of turning a blind eye to brutality by members of the British army and the RUC. He refused to take action over complaints of brutality by RUC interrogators against IRA suspects at a specially built interrogation unit at Castlereagh outside Belfast.

A few months before Mason's arrival in Northern Ireland, the British Government had ended the Special Category Status for paramilitary prisoners.

Under this status, IRA members and loyalists had been treated as political prisoners with permission to wear their own clothes. Under the new regulations they would be treated as ordinary criminals and would have to wear special prison clothing. The resistance of the IRA prisoners to the new prison regime was to lead to major convulsions in Northern Ireland, the Republic and Great Britain in the years ahead.

Prison Protests

The abolition of Special Category Status met with an immediate response by the IRA prisoners in the Maze Prison (the former Long Kesh). They refused to wear prison clothes and covered themselves instead with a blanket in their cells. By 1977 over 150 republican prisoners were on the blanket protest. When these tactics failed to result in concessions, the prisoners began the dirty protest, which involved spreading their excrement on the walls of their cells. The

A scene from the 'dirty protest' in the Maze Prison in November 1980

Secretary of State, Roy Mason, ignored this protest as well and believed that he could eventually force the prisoners into submission. He was encouraged in this approach by declining levels of violence in 1977 and 1978.

Mason's tough approach towards the IRA appealed to the unionists, who felt more secure than at any stage since the outbreak of the Troubles in 1968. However, his preoccupation with crushing the IRA in the absence of any political initiatives further alienated nationalists. Therefore, when Roy Mason left office on the defeat of the Labour Government in May 1979, bitter tensions and divisions continued and the difficulties within the prisons remained unresolved.

Margaret Thatcher Becomes Prime Minister

In May 1979 the Conservative Party under the leadership of Margaret Thatcher won the general election in Great Britain. The new Prime Minister, known as the 'Iron Lady', already had a reputation as a strong and tough personality. While in opposition, Mrs Thatcher and her friend and Northern Ireland spokesman Airey Neave had been sympathetic to the unionists. She later remarked in her autobiography, 'My own instincts are profoundly Unionist...Airey Neave and I felt the greatest sympathy with the Unionists while we were in Opposition.'

Both Thatcher and Neave strongly believed that the solution to the problems in Northern Ireland lay in the military defeat of the IRA. However, in March 1979 – two months before the general election – Airey Neave was killed by a car bomb in the grounds of the House of Commons at Westminster. The bomb was planted by members of a small breakaway republican paramilitary group called the Irish National Liberation Army (INLA).

Margaret Thatcher campaigning during the general election in May 1979

On coming to power as Prime Minister, Margaret Thatcher appointed Humphrey Atkins as the new Secretary of State for Northern Ireland. On 27 August 1979 the IRA carried out two bombing attacks on the same day. In Mullaghmore, Co. Sligo, a bomb blew up the boat of Earl Mountbatten, a cousin of the British royal family. He and four other people were killed, including his fourteen-year-old grandson, Nicholas. Meanwhile, eighteen British soldiers were killed by an IRA double bomb at Warrenpoint in Co. Down.

Margaret Thatcher immediately flew to Belfast and announced an increase of 1,000 members to the police force. These atrocities had clearly shown the new Prime Minister the ruthlessness and the destructive capacity of the IRA.

The assassination of Airey Neave at Westminster in March 1979

A scene of destruction after the IRA bombing at Warrenpoint, Co. Down on 27 August 1979

Margaret Thatcher speaking to British troops during a visit to Northern Ireland

The Pope's Plea for Peace

In September 1979 Pope John Paul II paid an historic trip to Ireland. He spent a few days in the Republic but did not visit Northern Ireland because of the security situation. However, tens of thousands of Catholics from the North were present during the Pope's visit to Drogheda on 29 September. He made a passionate plea to all men and women engaged in violence: 'On my knees I beg you to turn away from the paths of violence and return to the ways of peace.'

Pope John Paul II on his way to Drogheda, where he pleaded for an end to violence in Northern Ireland

The vast majority of people, North and South, supported the Pope's plea. However, three days later, on 2 October, the IRA rejected his plea and pledged a continuation of their campaign.

Attempts to Break the Deadlock

The new Conservative Government under Margaret Thatcher continued to adopt a hardline approach against the IRA. However, like previous Conservative and Labour governments since the introduction of direct rule in 1972, the Thatcher Government also attempted to find a political solution in Northern Ireland. The Secretary of State for Northern Ireland, Humphrey Atkins, proposed a roundtable conference involving the four main political parties in the province.

The attempt met with almost total failure. On the unionist side, Rev. Ian Paisley, leader of the DUP, flatly rejected Atkins's proposal and called on the British Government to defeat the IRA. Paisley was in a strong position because he headed the poll in the first-ever election for the European Parliament in June 1979. The new leader of the official Ulster Unionist Party, James Molyneaux, was also opposed to the initiative. He had succeeded Harry West as leader of his party in 1979. He favoured the continuation of direct rule and believed that Northern Ireland should be integrated more closely with the rest of the United Kingdom.

The moderate Alliance Party favoured Atkins's attempt to reach a political consensus. However, the main nationalist party, the SDLP, was divided on the issue. The party leader, Gerry Fitt, was in favour of the proposed roundtable talks. However, a majority of his party colleagues opposed the proposal because it lacked an Irish dimension. As a result, Fitt resigned as leader in November 1979 and was replaced by John Hume.

Although the parties were willing to talk separately to the Secretary of State, they refused to participate together in a roundtable conference. Eventually Atkins abandoned the initiative in March 1980. Together with the attempts to initiate all-party talks in the North, the British Government also engaged in discussions with the Irish Government in Dublin.

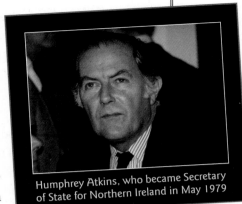

Humphrey Atkins, who became Secretary of State for Northern Ireland in May 1979

Haughey and Thatcher Meet

In May 1980 the Taoiseach of the Irish Republic, Charles Haughey, met Prime Minister Margaret Thatcher in London. Mrs Thatcher's main priority was to secure increased co-operation from the Irish Government in the struggle against the IRA. For its part, the Irish Government was hoping for greater co-operation between the two governments regarding Northern Ireland. To the alarm of Ulster unionists, both governments issued a joint statement which contained the phrase 'totality of relationships'. This signified that the British Government appeared to be recognising an Irish interest in the affairs of Northern Ireland.

In December 1980 Margaret Thatcher and her leading ministers attended a summit in Dublin Castle. The two governments announced the establishment of joint studies to explore the possibility of greater co-operation in areas such as the economy and security. In Northern Ireland, Ian Paisley organised a mass rally to protest against the Anglo-Irish talks.

Margaret Thatcher and Charles Haughey outside 10 Downing Street in May 1980

However, Margaret Thatcher was furious when members of the Irish Government exaggerated the significance of the talks. Soon, however, the relationship between the British and Irish governments was to come under severe strain as a result of a crisis in the prisons of Northern Ireland.

The H Block Hunger Strikes

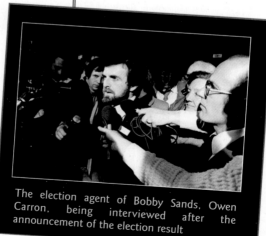

A republican poster supporting the prisoners in the H Blocks

With the failure of the blanket and dirty protests, certain IRA prisoners in the Maze Prison decided to go on hunger strike in order to be classified as special category or political prisoners. These prisoners were located in new single-storey brick units known as the H Blocks.

The first hunger strike began in October 1980 when seven IRA prisoners refused food. This protest was called off two months later. However, in March 1981 a new hunger strike began led by the IRA commander in the prison, Bobby Sands. This time the prisoners were determined to continue until the British Government conceded their demands. Unless this occurred, they were willing to die. Despite the concerns of the families of the hunger strikers and the opposition of Catholic bishops and priests, the hunger strike continued. Outside the prison, Sinn Féin was to organise a massive propaganda campaign aimed at glorifying the prisoners and placing pressure on the British Government of Margaret Thatcher.

Bobby Sands, the IRA leader in the Maze Prison, who was elected to the British Parliament and who died on hunger strike in May 1981

Bobby Sands Elected MP for Fermanagh-South Tyrone

During the hunger strike, the independent nationalist MP for Fermanagh-South Tyrone, Frank Maguire, died. Sinn Féin decided that the leading IRA hunger striker, Bobby Sands, should contest the ensuing by-election. Other nationalists interested in contesting the election withdrew and the contest was between Bobby Sands and the unionist candidate, Harry West.

The election campaign was extremely bitter as unionists and nationalists had totally opposing views on the hunger strikes. Most unionists regarded the IRA as murderers and supported the refusal of Margaret Thatcher to grant any concessions to the prisoners. Many nationalists, on the other hand, regarded the British Prime Minister as unfeeling and uncompromising. While they did not necessarily support the IRA, they sympathised with the plight of the hunger strikers and believed that a compromise should be reached. When the by-election took place on 9 April 1981 Bobby Sands defeated his unionist opponent by margin of 1,446 votes. He secured over 30,000 votes and had been on hunger strike for forty days when the election took place.

The election agent of Bobby Sands, Owen Carron, being interviewed after the announcement of the election result

The election of Bobby Sands to the Westminster Parliament did not alter Margaret Thatcher's determination to defeat the hunger strikers. Unionists were outraged that over 30,000 people had voted for a member of the IRA. Sinn Féin, the political wing of the IRA, had won a huge propaganda victory and were encouraged by the result to become more involved in politics in the future.

The Hunger Strikes Continue

On 5 May 1981 Bobby Sands was the first of the hunger strikers to die in the Maze Prison. His funeral was attended by over 100,000 people and attracted worldwide attention. By the time the hunger strike ended in October 1981, ten men had died. It came to an end when the families of prisoners began to intervene to prevent further deaths.

The funeral of Bobby Sands in Belfast on 7 May 1981

During the hunger strikes there was widespread rioting in nationalist areas in the North. The hunger strikes also had a huge impact on the Republic of Ireland. There were marches, rallies and black flags throughout the country. The Irish Government tried in vain to persuade Margaret Thatcher to compromise. Irish-Americans also campaigned for a resolution to the issue and Pope John Paul II sent Monsignor John Magee as his envoy to visit the Maze Prison.

During the crisis, a general election took place in the Irish Republic in June 1981. Two republicans were elected as TDs, including Ciaran Doherty, a hunger striker who died soon after his election.

Although the hunger strikers were defeated, these events marked a turning point in the development of Northern Ireland. They had further polarised the two communities. Unionists believed that because nationalists supported a compromise, they were sympathetic to the IRA. Nationalists in turn felt totally alienated and turned in increasing numbers from the moderate SDLP to Sinn Féin. Sinn Féin itself learned valuable lessons concerning the powerful weapon of political agitation. The Irish Government was particularly concerned at the alienation of the nationalist minority in Northern Ireland. This concern lay at the heart of a new initiative called the New Ireland Forum.

A march in Dublin in support of the H Block campaign

The New Ireland Forum

The New Ireland Forum, which first met in Dublin in May 1983, was a gathering of constitutional nationalists from Ireland, North and South. It was convened by the Taoiseach, Dr Garret

Pictured at the first meeting of the New Ireland Forum in May 1983 were, from left to right, Dick Spring, Charles Haughey, Garret FitzGerald and John Hume

FitzGerald, who was anxious to strengthen constitutional nationalists and to draw support away from Sinn Féin and the IRA. He particularly wanted to strengthen the position of the SDLP as the main constitutional nationalist party in Northern Ireland.

The most influential figures in the forum were the Taoiseach, Dr FitzGerald, the Tánaiste and leader of the Labour Party, Dick Spring, and the leader of the SDLP, John Hume. The aim of the forum was to explore ways of achieving Irish unity by consent and to protect the identity of northern Protestants in a new Ireland. They also wished to show that Irish unity could be achieved by peaceful means.

The forum issued its report in May 1984, which offered three solutions to the problem of relations between Northern Ireland and the Republic:

- A unitary state.
- A federal state.
- Joint authority in Northern Ireland by the British and Irish governments.

A unitary state would involve a completely united Ireland under a government in Dublin. In a federal state, Northern Ireland would maintain its own parliament within a united Ireland. Under joint authority, the state of Northern Ireland would continue to exist but would function under equal British and Irish rule.

The IRA bombing of the Grand Hotel, Brighton in October 1984

To the annoyance of the other parties, Charles Haughey, leader of Fianna Fáil, almost immediately repudiated the agreed report and stated that a unitary state was the only possible solution. The unionist parties in Northern Ireland totally rejected the report of the New Ireland Forum. However, the most dramatic rejection of the report was to come from the British Prime Minister, Margaret Thatcher.

Margaret Thatcher Rejects the New Ireland Forum

In October 1984 the IRA attempted to kill Margaret Thatcher and members of her government during the Conservative Party Conference in Brighton. A massive bomb exploded in the Grand Hotel during the conference. Although Margaret Thatcher, the target of the attack, was uninjured, five people were killed and many more were seriously injured. The IRA claimed responsibility and stated, 'Today we were unlucky, but remember we only have to be lucky once.' Margaret Thatcher, however, refused to allow the Brighton bombing to divert her attention from confronting the problems of Northern Ireland.

In the aftermath of the Brighton bombing, Dr Garret FitzGerald travelled to London for a meeting with Mrs Thatcher. Although the talks were positive and friendly, controversy emerged during the press conference at the conclusion of the joint discussions. When asked about the New Ireland Forum, the British Prime Minister categorically dismissed all of the suggestions put forward: 'I have made it quite clear...that a unified Ireland was one solution that is out. A second solution was confederation of two states, that is out. A third solution was joint authority – that is out.'

Despite this obvious setback in Anglo-Irish relations, both leaders remained committed to closer co-operation in an effort to achieve a political solution to the problem of Northern Ireland.

ORDINARY LEVEL

1. Read the following extract on the hunger strike from the memoirs of Margaret Thatcher and answer the questions that follow.

> To the outside world the issue at stake must have seemed trivial. But both the IRA and the Government understood that it was not. The IRA and the prisoners were determined to gain control of the prison and had a well-thought-out strategy of doing this by whittling away at the prison regime. The purpose of the privileges they claimed was not to improve prisoners' conditions but to take power away from the prison authorities. They were also keen to establish once again, as they felt they had in 1972, that their crimes were 'political', thus giving the perpetrators a kind of respectability, even nobility. This we could not allow. Above all, I would hold fast to the principle that we would not make concessions of any kind while the hunger strike was continuing. The IRA were pursuing with calculated ruthlessness a psychological war alongside their campaign of violence: they had to be resisted at both levels.
>
> *Margaret Thatcher, The Downing Street Years, London: HarperCollins 1993, 389–90*

(i) According to Margaret Thatcher, what were the IRA and the prisoners determined to do?

(ii) What did the Prime Minister see to be the purpose of the privileges claimed by the prisoners?

(iii) According to the extract, what would the granting of political status give to the IRA?

(iv) State the approach the Prime Minister determined to follow.

(v) What do you think she meant by the phrase 'psychological war'?

2. What main obstacle remained in the path of a restoration of power-sharing in the North?

3. Write an account on the economic difficulties facing Northern Ireland in the 1970s.

4. What impact did the Troubles have on the housing situation in Northern Ireland?

5. How was the IRA changing their approach at this time?

6. Who were 'The Shankill Butchers'?

7. Write a note on the peace movement.

8. What policies were pursued by Roy Mason on his appointment as Secretary of State for Northern Ireland?

9. What new regulations did the British Government introduce for paramilitary prisoners?

10. What was the immediate response of IRA prisoners to these new regulations?

11. In Margaret Thatcher's view, what was the best means of solving the problems in the North?

12. What happened on 27 August 1979? How did Margaret Thatcher respond to these events?

13. What plea was made by Pope John Paul II on his visit to Ireland? How did the IRA respond to this?

14. Why did proposals by Humphrey Atkins for a roundtable conference in Northern Ireland meet with almost total failure?

15. What was the significance of the meeting between Charles Haughey and Margaret Thatcher in May 1980?

16. Why did IRA prisoners decide to go on hunger strike?

17. Write a note on the Fermanagh-South Tyrone by-election campaign.

18. What was the impact of the hunger strikes in the Republic of Ireland?

19. In what respects may the hunger strikes be regarded as a turning point in the development of Northern Ireland?

20. Write an account of the New Ireland Forum.

21. What was Margaret Thatcher's reaction to the report of the New Ireland Forum?

HIGHER LEVEL

1. Read the following extract from Dr Garret FitzGerald's speech at the opening of the New Ireland Forum and answer the questions that follow.

> All of the political parties in the New Ireland Forum will in effect for a period of months be sacrificing some of their interests and some of their independence. In deciding to do so, our parties have demonstrated an awareness of the deepening crisis in Northern Ireland and a willingness to put country before party. This is an encouraging augury for the success of our work. By this decision our parties, which are supported by the votes of well over 90 per cent of the nationalist people on this island, demonstrate on behalf of those we represent a powerful collective rejection of murder, bombing and all other cruelties that are being inflicted on the population of Northern Ireland in an attempt to secure political change by force. Let the men of violence take note of this unambiguous message from the nationalist people of Ireland: the future of the island will be built by the ballot box alone.

(i) According to Dr FitzGerald, what have the political parties demonstrated by their participation in the New Ireland Forum?

(ii) How can you tell from the extract that this is a forum for constitutional nationalists?

(iii) Explain the meaning of the message he gives to the 'men of violence'.

(iv) What did Dr FitzGerald hope to achieve by the establishment of the New Ireland Forum?

2. What political initiative was made by the British Government in the early months of 1975 in the hope of restoring power-sharing in Northern Ireland? What was the result of this initiative?

3. 'The economy of Northern Ireland in the 1970s was beset by internal and external difficulties.' Do you agree with this point of view? Explain your answer.

4. What changes occurred in the structures of the IRA in the mid-1970s and how significant do you think these changes were?

5. What were the strengths and weaknesses of Roy Mason as Secretary of State for Northern Ireland?

6. What was Margaret Thatcher's approach to the problems of Northern Ireland on becoming Prime Minister?

7. What was the significance of the phrase 'totality of relationships' contained in the joint statement issued by both governments after the Haughey–Thatcher meeting in May 1980?

8. Assess the significance of the H Block hunger strikes.

9. 'The New Ireland Forum failed to achieve any tangible results.' Do you agree with this statement? Explain your answer.

The Anglo-Irish Agreement

Despite Margaret Thatcher's public rejection of the New Ireland Forum Report in November 1984, secret talks continued between the British and Irish governments in an attempt to break the deadlock in Northern Ireland. These talks culminated in the Anglo-Irish Agreement which was signed by both governments at Hillsborough Castle, Co. Down on 15 November 1985.

Margaret Thatcher and Garret FitzGerald after the signing of the Anglo-Irish Agreement at Hillsborough Castle in November 1985

The most important feature of the agreement was the establishment of the Inter-Governmental Conference under the leadership of the Secretary of State for Northern Ireland and the Irish Minister for Foreign Affairs. The conference would meet regularly and deal with cross-border co-operation on a wide range of issues. The conference provided an official forum where Irish representatives could raise grievances of concern to the Catholic minority in Northern Ireland.

The Inter-Governmental Conference was serviced by a permanent secretariat containing civil servants from Northern Ireland and the Republic. The headquarters of the secretariat was at Maryfield outside Hollywood, Co. Down.

Margaret Thatcher hoped that the new agreement would lead to much greater security co-operation between Northern Ireland and the Republic. She believed that she was strengthening the Union because the Irish Government accepted that no change could come about in the status of Northern Ireland without the consent of the majority.

For Dr Garret FitzGerald, the signing of the Anglo-Irish Agreement was a major achievement. Because of the Inter-Governmental Conference, Irish governments would have a significant role in the affairs of Northern Ireland. FitzGerald hoped that in championing the cause of the minority in Northern Ireland, he would help reduce the level of support for the IRA and Sinn Féin.

The Anglo-Irish Agreement was the most important political initiative in Northern Ireland since the Sunningdale Agreement of 1973. By placing the British and Irish governments at the centre of the process, the new agreement, unlike Sunningdale before it, could not be brought down by strikes in Northern Ireland.

The reaction to the Anglo-Irish Agreement was mixed. The main opposition party in the Irish Republic, Fianna Fáil, under the leadership of Charles Haughey, condemned it as an abandonment of the principle of Irish unity. The IRA and Sinn Féin completely rejected the agreement and insisted that their armed campaign would continue. In contrast, the SDLP, under the leadership of John Hume, welcomed the agreement as a huge advance for the nationalist community in Northern Ireland.

However, unionists in Northern Ireland were outraged and set about organising a massive campaign of protest to undermine the agreement.

Ulster Says No

Throughout the talks leading to the Anglo-Irish Agreement, unionists had been kept in the dark. They accused Margaret Thatcher of a complete betrayal, especially given her strong unionist beliefs in the past. They found it difficult to believe that having refused to compromise during the hunger strikes and having survived the Brighton bombing, she would sign such an agreement. Unionists rejected out of hand any role for the Irish Government in the affairs of Northern Ireland and began a widespread and long-lasting series of protests.

On Saturday, 23 November 1985 a massive unionist rally took place at the City Hall in Belfast. Using the slogan 'Ulster Says No', the leaders of the two main unionist parties, James Molyneaux and Ian Paisley, made defiant speeches pledging their complete opposition to the Anglo-Irish Agreement. The unionists withdrew all support from the British Government and unionist MPs resigned their seats and fought by-elections to demonstrate public support for their stance.

A unionist rally protesting against the Anglo-Irish Agreement at Belfast City Hall

Although unionist protest continued for a number of years, Margaret Thatcher refused to yield to violence or threats of violence against the Anglo-Irish Agreement.

Loyalist Violence

As well as political opposition to the Anglo-Irish Agreement, Northern Ireland experienced widespread and repeated violent incidents as loyalists reacted with fury at their inability to destroy the Anglo-Irish Agreement. Much of the loyalist anger was vented at the RUC because without police co-operation, the agreement could not have been enforced. During the first meeting of the Anglo-Irish secretariat at Maryfield on 11 December 1985, crowds of loyalist workers battled with police in an attempt to tear down the gates. On the same day, the homes of fifteen police officers were attacked. By May 1986, 368 members of the RUC and their families had been attacked by loyalists. Throughout 1986 the loyalist paramilitary organisations, the UDA and the UVF, continued to attack the homes of police officers. They also increased sectarian attacks against Catholics throughout Northern Ireland.

Loyalist protesters clash with RUC officers outside the gates of the Anglo-Irish Secretariat at Maryfield

Despite the violence of loyalists, by the end of 1986 it was clear that the Anglo-Irish Agreement would not be removed.

The IRA and Sinn Féin – New Directions

While the unionist opposition to the Anglo-Irish Agreement dominated the political scene in Northern Ireland after 1985, significant changes were taking place within Sinn Féin and the IRA. After the failure of the hunger strikes in 1981, a number of young republicans under the leadership of Gerry Adams attempted to expand the political role of the republican movement. They remained committed to the continuation of the campaign of violence but also attempted to build up a political movement side by side with this.

In June 1983 Gerry Adams was elected as a Sinn Féin MP for West Belfast, and the following September he became president of the party. In local council elections in Northern Ireland in May 1985 the party won fifty-nine seats. At the Sinn Féin annual conference, or Ard Fheis, in November 1986 in Dublin, an important decision was reached. From now on, Sinn Féin TDs elected to Dáil Éireann would take their seats rather than abstain, as they had done in the past. This caused a split in the party when a minority under Ruairí Ó Brádaigh left and formed their own party, Republican Sinn Féin.

RESULTS OF LOCAL GOVERNMENT ELECTIONS, MAY 1985			
Party	First Preference Votes	% Valid Poll	Number of Seats
Ulster Unionist Party (UUP)	188,497	(29.5%)	190
Democratic Unionist Party (DUP)	155,297	(24.3%)	142
Social Democratic & Labour Party (SDLP)	113,967	(17.8%)	101
Sinn Féin (SF)	75,686	(11.8%)	59
Alliance Party of Northern Ireland (APNI)	45,394	(7.1%)	34

A Sinn Féin election conference presided over by the party leader, Gerry Adams. To his left sat Danny Morrison.

Under the direction of Gerry Adams and the Derry republican Martin McGuinness, Sinn Féin was committed to a twofold strategy: continuation of the armed campaign on the one hand and involvement in politics on the other. This approach was summed up in the phrase of leading republican Danny Morrison as 'an Armalite in the one hand and a ballot box in the other'.

During 1987 the IRA carried out a series of high-profile attacks. In April they killed Northern Ireland's second most senior judge, Lord Justice Gibson, and his wife in a bomb attack near the border. In November, the French coast guard captured a ship called the *Eksund* which was carrying

IRA explosion which killed Lord Justice Gibson and his wife

French policemen unloading arms and ammunition from the *Eksund*, a ship carrying weapons for the IRA

The IRA explosion at Enniskillen on Remembrance Day, 8 November 1987

Minister. These contacts continued for three years between 1990 and 1993.

While these contacts were ongoing, Sir Patrick Mayhew, who succeeded Peter Brooke as Secretary of State in April 1992, engaged in talks with political parties in Northern Ireland except Sinn Féin. The British Government, however, through its secret contacts, kept Sinn Féin informed of the progress of the Mayhew talks, which ended without agreement in November 1992.

While Sinn Féin continued its secret contacts with the British Government, the IRA had no intention of calling off its campaign as long as Sinn Féin was excluded from talks and the British refused to withdraw from Northern Ireland. Indeed, while Sinn Féin was engaged in contacts with both John Hume and the British Government, the IRA, in a show of strength, intensified its bombing campaign.

In March 1992 a series of IRA bombings took place at railway stations in London. A month later a massive bomb destroyed the Baltic Exchange in London, causing around £1 billion worth of damage. In April 1993 an IRA bomb at Bishopsgate in London caused millions of pounds worth of damage. At the same time,

The aftermath of an IRA bomb in London in April 1992

the IRA bombing campaign continued in Northern Ireland itself.

Side by side with the IRA's continuing campaign of violence, efforts were being made in Ireland and England to bring about a political settlement in Northern Ireland.

The IRA bombing at Bishopsgate in London in April 1993

Towards Agreement

From an early stage, the Irish Government was supportive of the Hume–Adams contacts. John Hume believed that both the British and Irish governments should make a joint declaration which could provide the basis for an IRA ceasefire. In October 1991 Hume drew up a document entitled 'A Strategy for Peace and Justice in Northern Ireland'. He presented it to the Irish Government, which amended it. The document envisaged a declaration by the British Government that it had no 'selfish, strategic, political or economic interest in Northern Ireland'. It also required the Irish Government to accept that a change in the status of Northern Ireland depended on the will of the majority there.

Both the Irish Government as well as John Hume and Gerry Adams hoped to convince the British to persuade the unionists to accept a united Ireland. This approach was also followed by Albert Reynolds, who succeeded Charles Haughey as Taoiseach in January 1992. However, the British Prime Minister, John Major, absolutely refused to accept this, as he believed it to be unrealistic and undemocratic.

When news of the Hume–Adams talks became public, unionists were alarmed. Their suspicions of a nationalist conspiracy were further confirmed when statements by the Irish Government closely resembled those made by the SDLP and Sinn Féin leaders. The UDA referred to this as a 'Pan-Nationalist Front' and stepped up the levels of paramilitary violence.

In October 1993, amid increasing violence, the IRA killed nine Protestants on the Shankill Road in Belfast in an unsuccessful attempt to blow up the UDA leadership. A week later, loyalist gunmen shot dead seven Catholics and one Protestant in the Rising Sun bar at Greysteel, Co. Derry – it was the highest number of deaths for a single month since October 1976.

These atrocities convinced both John Major and Albert Reynolds of the need to intensify their efforts to achieve peace.

A scene of destruction following the IRA bombing at the Shankill Road, Belfast in October 1993

The Downing Street Declaration, December 1993

At a European conference in Brussels in December 1993 the two Prime Ministers met and decided to drive the peace process forward themselves. Discussions began between both governments and led to an agreed statement known as the Joint Declaration or the Downing Street Declaration of 15 December 1993.

This declaration consisted of a set of principles regarding the future of Northern Ireland agreed by both governments. The British Government formally declared that it had no 'selfish, strategic or economic interest in Northern Ireland'. This was an attempt to remove the principal republican justification for violence, namely, the existence of British imperial rule in Northern Ireland.

The declaration stated that the primary interest of the British Government was 'to see peace, stability and reconciliation established by agreement among all the people who inhabit the island'. Their role would be 'to encourage, facilitate and enable the achievement of such agreement over a period through a process of dialogue and co-operation based on full respect for the rights and identities of both traditions in Ireland'. While the British Government did not see its role as that of a persuader for Irish unity, it accepted in the declaration that agreement within the island of Ireland might eventually lead to such an outcome.

The Taoiseach, on behalf of the Irish Government, accepted that it would be wrong to attempt to impose a united Ireland without the consent of the majority of the people of Northern Ireland. He also stated that 'every effort must be made to build a new sense of trust' between the two traditions on the island. As part of this process, the Taoiseach also agreed to examine any aspects of life in the Irish Republic which might be a threat to the unionist ethos and way of life.

Both governments accepted that 'Irish unity would be achieved only by those who favour this outcome persuading those who do not, peacefully and without coercion or violence, and that, if in future a majority of people in Northern Ireland are so persuaded, both governments will support and give legislative effect to their wish'.

In the declaration, both governments repeated that the achievement of peace would only come about with the permanent end of paramilitary violence. Any political party wishing to participate in talks regarding the future of Northern Ireland would have to demonstrate 'a commitment to exclusively peaceful methods'.

The Downing Street Declaration of December 1993 was an important milestone on the road to peace. It made it clear that Irish unity would only be possible with the consent of the people of

The British Prime Minister, John Major (left), and the Taoiseach, Albert Reynolds, at the launch of the Downing Street Declaration on 15 December 1993

Northern Ireland. While the tone of the document was quite nationalist with references to Irish unity and self-determination, many unionists welcomed the principle of consent that was enshrined in the document.

While Sinn Féin accepted that the British had no 'selfish, strategic or economic interest in Northern Ireland', they were very critical of the Downing Street Declaration. They objected to the principle of consent based on two parts of the island rather than on the island as a whole. They were also disappointed that the British Government did not become a persuader for Irish unity. While Sinn Féin formally rejected the declaration in July 1994, Gerry Adams nevertheless described it as a step in the peace process. He stated that Sinn Féin was now looking forward to the next steps.

ELECTION RESULTS IN NORTHERN IRELAND, 1973 – 92						
Party	OUP	DUP	OTHER UNIONISTS	ALLIANCE PARTY	SDLP	SINN FÉIN
1973 Assembly Election	29.3	8.5	22.0	9.2	22.1	
1974 (Feb) General Election	32.3	8.2	24.0	3.2	22.4	
1974 (Oct) General Election	36.5	8.5	22.0	6.3	22.0	
1975 Convention Election	25.8	14.8	21.9	9.8	23.7	
1979 General Election	36.6	10.2	12.3	11.9	19.7	
1979 European Election	21.9	29.8	7.3	6.8	24.6	
1982 Assembly Election	29.7	23.0	5.7	9.3	18.8	10.1
1983 General Election	34.0	20.0	3.1	8.0	17.9	13.4
1984 European Election	21.5	33.6	2.9	5.0	22.1	13.3
1987 General Election	37.9	11.7	5.3	10.0	22.1	11.4
1989 European Election	22.2	29.9		5.2	25.5	9.1
1992 General Election	34.5	13.1	3.0	8.7	23.5	10.0

The IRA Ceasefire

On 31 August 1994 the IRA decided to call 'a complete cessation of military operations' in the belief that an opportunity existed to create a 'just and lasting settlement'. They believed that this was an opportunity to create a strong nationalist consensus embracing Sinn Féin and the SDLP in Northern Ireland, the Irish Government and supportive Americans, including President Bill Clinton.

Although nationalists regarded the IRA ceasefire as a great opportunity for political progress, the British Government and unionists were much more cautious. They demanded to know if the ceasefire was permanent and spoke of the need to hand over weapons or decommissioning. This issue was to be one of the main obstacles in the peace process over the following years.

Nationalists celebrating the declaration of the IRA ceasefire on 31 August 1994

Although the IRA ceasefire broke down for a short period later on with the denotation of a massive bomb at Canary Wharf in London in February 1996, it created the circumstances for the development of a lasting peace in Northern Ireland.

Towards a Lasting Peace

By the first anniversary of the IRA ceasefire in August 1995, republicans were furious that they had not been invited to participate in talks. In an effort to advance the peace process, President Bill Clinton visited Belfast in November 1995 and endorsed American Senator George Mitchell, who had been appointed to head an international body to resolve the decommissioning issue.

Bill Clinton, President of the US, visiting Belfast on 30 November 1995

Mitchell recommended that decommissioning and all-party talks should proceed at the same time. However, progress was slow until the Conservative Government in Great Britain was succeeded by a new Labour Government in May 1997 under the leadership of Tony Blair. In the following month, a new Taoiseach, Bertie Ahern, was elected in the Irish Republic. Both leaders were to personally invest huge amounts of time and energy in advancing the peace process.

In April 1998 an historic agreement was signed in Belfast. Known as the Good Friday Agreement, it established a power-sharing executive and Assembly in Northern Ireland. It also set up a decommissioning body to oversee the decommissioning of weapons and provided for a referendum north and south of the border in order to ratify the agreement. David Trimble, leader of the Ulster Unionist Party, became First Minister and Seamus Mallon, deputy leader of the SDLP, was appointed Deputy First Minister. While this agreement was supported by the Ulster Unionists, the Alliance Party, the SDLP and Sinn Féin, it was opposed by the Democratic Unionist Party under the leadership of Ian Paisley.

While obstacles still remained in the peace process, the Good Friday Agreement was to provide the basis for a lasting settlement in Northern Ireland.

Bertie Ahern, the Irish Taoiseach (left), and Tony Blair, the British Prime Minister, at the signing of the Good Friday Agreement at Stormont on 10 April 1998

KEY PERSONALITY: JAMES MOLYNEAUX (1920–)

James Molyneaux was born in Killead, Co. Antrim in 1920. He served in the Royal Air Force during World War II. In 1970 he was elected Ulster Unionist Member of Parliament for South Antrim and in October 1974 he became leader of the Ulster Unionists in the House of Commons. He became leader of the Ulster Unionist Party in 1979, a position he held until 1995.

Molyneaux was a strong opponent of the Anglo-Irish Agreement and in 1985 he, along with his unionist colleagues, resigned his seat in the Westminster Parliament in protest at the agreement. He was re-elected in a subsequent by-election. He joined with Ian Paisley in protesting against the Anglo-Irish Agreement and on 23 April 1986 both men unveiled a twelve-point plan of civil disobedience.

James Molyneaux opposed any political initiatives involving all-party talks or power-sharing in the North. He referred to such political initiatives as 'high-wire acts'. He was content with the continuation of direct rule and personally favoured full integration with the United Kingdom, which he believed was the best way to secure the Union.

After the 1992 general election, the British Prime Minister and leader of the Conservative Party needed the support of the Ulster Unionist MPs to help push through his policy on Europe. Molyneaux hoped to use his new bargaining position to bring a halt to talks between the British Government and republicans. He also expected the Anglo-Irish Agreement 'to wither'. He welcomed the Downing Street Declaration of 1993 and was confident that the constitutional position of Northern Ireland within the United Kingdom was not under threat.

Molyneaux had miscalculated British intentions to continue with the peace process. Doubts began to arise within the Unionist Party concerning Molyneaux's judgement and, under increasing pressure, he resigned as leader in 1995 and was replaced by David Trimble. He was knighted in 1996 and created a life peer in 1997 with the title Baron Molyneaux of Killead. As a traditional unionist, he remained very critical of the peace process. He was openly critical of his successor David Trimble and strongly opposed the Good Friday Agreement.

KEY PERSONALITY: IAN PAISLEY (1926–)

A Protestant clergyman and unionist politician, Ian Paisley was born in Armagh in 1926. He was the son of an independent Baptist preacher and was brought up in Ballymena. He was co-founder of the Free Presbyterian Church in 1951, with himself as moderator. Even in his teens he had a reputation as a very effective preacher. He came to prominence first in the 1950s as a result of his strident opposition to Catholicism. He was a strong opponent of ecumenism and visited Rome to protest against the Second Vatican Council.

Paisley fiercely opposed the conciliatory policies toward nationalists pursued by Terence O'Neill, whom he denounced as a traitor for meeting Seán Lemass in 1965. He believed that the Northern Ireland Civil Rights Association was really a front for the IRA. In 1969 he was imprisoned for a short period for organising an illegal counter-demonstration against a civil rights march in Armagh.

In the 1970 general election, Paisley was elected to the Westminster Parliament as MP for the North Antrim constituency. The following year he founded a new political party, the Democratic Unionist Party (DUP), and became its leader. He opposed the fall of Stormont and the imposition of direct rule in 1972. Paisley strongly opposed the Sunningdale Agreement, which established a power-sharing executive and set up a Council of Ireland. In 1979 he was elected a Member of the European Parliament in the first direct elections to the parliament.

Paisley fiercely opposed the Anglo-Irish Agreement of 1985 and, along with the leader of the Ulster Unionist Party, James Molyneaux, organised public protests against the meeting. Using the slogan 'Ulster Says No', he addressed a crowd of around 200,000 unionists who had gathered outside Belfast City Hall to protest against the agreement.

Throughout the 1990s Paisley strongly opposed the peace process and particularly objected to any talks with Sinn Féin until full decommissioning of IRA weapons had taken place. He condemned the Good Friday Agreement (1998), which established an Assembly and power-sharing executive in Northern Ireland. In November 2003 Paisley's DUP became the largest unionist party in Northern Ireland.

After a period of much turmoil and instability, the DUP entered into a power-sharing executive with Sinn Féin in May 2007, with Ian Paisley as First Minister and Martin McGuinness of Sinn Féin as Deputy First Minister.

KEY PERSONALITY: JOHN HUME (1937–)

John Hume was born in the city of Derry in 1937. He was educated at St Columb's College, Derry, St Patrick's College, Maynooth, and Queen's University, Belfast. He was a founder member of the credit union movement in Derry in the 1960s and was president of the Credit Union League of Ireland from 1964 to 1968. Having been involved in the campaign to have a university located in Derry, he became a leading member of the civil rights movement in the late 1960s. As a pacifist and nationalist, he was co-founder of the Derry Citizen's Action Committee, which was set up to campaign peacefully for an end to discrimination against the nationalist population in Derry.

John Hume was elected as an independent member to the Stormont Parliament in 1969 and played a leading role in the prevention of rioting in Derry on 16 November 1969. He was a founding member of the Social Democratic Labour Party (SDLP) and was elected to the short-lived Northern Ireland Assembly in 1973. For a brief period in 1974 he served as Minister of Commerce in the power-sharing executive which had been enacted under the Sunningdale Agreement. He succeeded Gerry Fitt as leader of the SDLP in 1979 and in the same year was elected as a Member of the European Parliament. He was elected to the Westminster Parliament in 1983.

The New Ireland Forum, which opened in Dublin in May 1983, was essentially John Hume's idea and was a gathering of constitutional nationalists with the aim of exploring ways of achieving nationalist aspirations by peaceful means. Hume was a strong supporter of the Anglo-Irish Agreement (1985), which he believed was capable, 'without changing a word of it', of major developments along the road to peace. He had underestimated the strength of unionist opposition to the agreement.

John Hume is widely credited as one of the main architects of the peace process in Northern Ireland. The Hume–Adams talks, which commenced in 1988, were instrumental in eventually bringing Sinn Féin to the negotiating table. He played a major role in the negotiations which led to the Good Friday Agreement (1998).

John Hume was awarded the Nobel Peace Prize in 1998 along with the leader of the Ulster Unionist Party, David Trimble, for the contribution both men had made to the achievement of peace in Northern Ireland. He retired from the leadership of the SDLP in 2001 and completely from politics in 2004.

KEY PERSONALITY: GERRY ADAMS (1948–)

Gerry Adams was born in West Belfast in 1948 into a strongly republican family. He was educated at St Mary's Christian Brothers' Grammar School and, after leaving school, worked as a bartender. Following the Divis Street riots, he became actively involved in the republican movement, joining Sinn Féin and Fianna Éireann in 1964. He joined the Northern Ireland Civil Rights Association in 1967.

Following the split in the IRA in 1970, Adams joined the more militant Provisional wing and was interned for a period in 1972 under the policy of internment without trial introduced by Faulkner's Government. He was released to take part in negotiations with the British Government for a truce. However, talks failed and he went on to play an organising role in the events known as Bloody Friday. He was then imprisoned in Long Kesh internment camp.

Adams played a key role during the hunger strikes of 1981. He became a leading advocate of increased political activity by the republican movement. He was appointed President of Sinn Féin in 1983. In this role he was the main architect of the strategy of pursuing the dual tactics of armed struggle and political activity – 'the Armalite in one hand and the ballot box in the other'.

Gerry Adams and Sinn Féin were dismissive of the Anglo-Irish Agreement, stating that it institutionalised the British presence in Ireland and pledged Dublin's acceptance of partition. Despite the continuing violence, the beginnings of the peace process occurred when secret talks commenced between Gerry Adams and John Hume in 1988. These talks opened the door to contacts between the British Government and Sinn Féin.

While Sinn Féin under the leadership of Gerry Adams sought initial clarification of aspects of the Downing Street Declaration, the party formally rejected the Declaration in July 1994. However, Gerry Adams importantly described it as a 'step' in the peace process. The next step took place on 31 August 1994 when the IRA, after a briefing from Adams, announced a ceasefire.

Gerry Adams played a key role in the negotiations which led to the Good Friday Agreement (1998). After many difficulties relating to policing and the decommissioning of IRA weapons, Sinn Féin and the DUP entered a power-sharing arrangement on 8 May 2007. Adams had successfully brought the republican movement into the realm of constitutional politics.

KEY PERSONALITY: MARGARET THATCHER (1925–)

Margaret Thatcher was born in the town of Grantham, Lincolnshire, England in 1925. She graduated with a degree in Chemistry from Oxford University. She then studied law and qualified as a barrister in 1953. She became active in the Conservative Party in the 1950s and was elected to the Westminster Parliament in the general election of 1959. In 1970 she was appointed Secretary of State for Education and Science. In 1979 she became Prime Minister of Britain, a position she held until 1990.

During her eleven years as Prime Minister of Great Britain, Margaret Thatcher was to have a formative influence on political and economic developments in Northern Ireland. At the outset, she declared herself a unionist and her sympathies thus lay strongly with the unionist community.

Margaret Thatcher was determined to defeat the IRA militarily and evoked much criticism within the nationalist community and further afield for her uncompromising policy towards the H Block hunger strikes in 1981. In the face of escalating violence, including the Brighton bombing in October 1984, she remained steadfast in her determination to defeat the IRA.

Alongside this military strategy, Margaret Thatcher was also seeking a political solution to the difficulties in Northern Ireland. To this effect, she had two meetings with the Irish Taoiseach, Charles Haughey, in May and December 1980. However, Anglo-Irish relations reached a low ebb when she rejected the recommendations of the New Ireland Forum in her famous 'Out, Out, Out' speech in November 1984.

Despite this setback, negotiations between the two governments continued and resulted in the signing of the Anglo-Irish Agreement in 1985. She hoped that this agreement would reassure unionists and lead to enhanced security co-operation between North and South. She had miscalculated the wrath of unionists but remained resolute in her commitment to the agreement.

The economy of Northern Ireland fared poorly during Margaret Thatcher's period as Prime Minister. While there was huge investment in the security forces during the 1980s, there were cutbacks in expenditure in the areas of health and education as part of an overall policy she was pursuing in the United Kingdom as a whole.

On the political side, however, the Anglo-Irish Agreement, together with the contacts between the British Government and Sinn Féin from the late 1980s, played an essential part in the development of the peace process.

EXERCISES

ORDINARY LEVEL

1. **Read the following extract from a speech made in the House of Commons by the unionist MP Harold McCusker in reaction to the Anglo-Irish Agreement and answer the questions that follow.**

The agreement deals with my most cherished ideals and aspirations. On three occasions in the week prior to the signing of the agreement...I stood in the House, having been told in essence by foreign journals what the agreement contained, and it was denied to me that an agreement existed, or had even been reached.

I went to Hillsborough on the Friday morning... I stood outside Hillsborough, not waving a Union flag – I doubt whether I will ever wave one again – not singing hymns, saying prayers or protesting, but like a dog and asked the Government to put in my hand the document that sold my birthright. They told me that they would give it to me as soon as possible. Having never consulted me, never sought my opinion or asked my advice, they told the rest of the world what was in store for me.

I stood in the cold outside the gates of Hillsborough Castle and waited for them to come out and give me the agreement second hand. It is even more despicable that they could not even send one of their servants to give it to me...

I felt desolate because as I stood in the cold outside Hillsborough Castle everything that I held dear turned to ashes in my mouth.

Cited in J. Bower Bell, The Irish Troubles: A Generation of Violence 1967–1992, Dublin: St Martins Press 1993, 709–10

(i)   What does Harold McCusker say the agreement deals with? What do you think he means by this?

(ii) Does he feel that he was kept informed about this agreement? Explain your answer by reference to the extract.

(iii) Why did he go to Hillsborough on Friday morning?

(iv) What do you think he means when he refers to 'the document that sold my birthright'?

(v)   What are his views on the Anglo-Irish Agreement?

2. What was the most important feature of the Anglo-Irish Agreement?

3. What did Margaret Thatcher hope to achieve by signing the Anglo-Irish Agreement?

4. What was the significance of the agreement from the Irish point of view?

5. How did unionists react to the signing of the Anglo-Irish Agreement?

6. What efforts were made by loyalist paramilitaries to destroy the agreement?

7. What changes took place within the IRA and Sinn Féin following the failure of the hunger strikes in 1981?

8. Explain the twofold strategy adopted by Sinn Féin under the leadership of Gerry Adams and Martin McGuinness.

9. Write a note on events at Enniskillen on 8 November 1987.

10. Explain how the Hume–Adams talks were initiated.

11. Why was John Hume criticised for talking to Sinn Féin and how did he justify these contacts?

12. State two important developments contained in speeches by Peter Brooke in November 1989.

13. What contacts existed between Sinn Féin and the British Government?

14. What was the view of unionists concerning the Hume–Adams talks?

15. What did the UDA mean by their reference to a 'Pan-Nationalist Front'?

16. Write a paragraph on the Downing Street Declaration.

17. What was Sinn Féin's reaction to the declaration?

18. What announcement was made by the IRA on 31 August 1994 and what were the reactions to it?

19. Write a paragraph on (i) John Hume and (ii) Gerry Adams.

HIGHER LEVEL

1. Read the following extract from the memoirs of Margaret Thatcher concerning the Anglo-Irish Agreement and answer the questions that follow.

> At two o'clock on the afternoon of Friday 15 November Garret FitzGerald and I signed the Anglo-Irish Agreement at Hillsborough Castle in Northern Ireland. It was not perfect from either side's point of view. Article 1 of the agreement affirmed that any change in the status of Northern Ireland would only come about with the consent of a majority of the people of Northern Ireland and recognised that the present wish of that majority was for no change in the status of the province. I believed that this major concession by the Irish would reassure the Unionists that the Union itself was in no doubt...I was wrong about that. The tactics which they used to oppose the agreement – a general strike, intimidation, flirting with civil disobedience – worsened the security situation and weakened their standing in the eyes of the rest of the United Kingdom.
>
> ...The agreement allowed the Irish Government to put forward views and proposals on matters relating to Northern Ireland... But I was clear that there was no derogation from the sovereignty of the United Kingdom. It was for us, not the Irish, to make the decisions...
>
> The real question now was whether the agreement would result in better security. The strong opposition of the Unionists would be a major obstacle... Above all, however, we hoped for a more co-operative attitude from the Irish Government, security forces and courts. If we got this the agreement would be successful...
>
> In dealing with Northern Ireland, successive governments have studiously refrained from security policies that might alienate the Irish Government and Irish nationalist opinion in Ulster, in the hope of winning their support against the IRA. The Anglo-Irish Agreement was squarely in this tradition. But I discovered the results of this approach to be disappointing. Our concessions alienated the Unionists without gaining the level of security co-operation we had a right to expect.
>
> *Margaret Thatcher, The Downing Street Years, London: HarperCollins 1993, 402–15*

(i) What concession by the Irish Government did Margaret Thatcher believe would reassure unionists?

(ii) What was the effect of unionist tactics in opposing the agreement?

(iii) What concession was made to the Irish Government? How did she view this?

(iv) What criteria would Margaret Thatcher use to judge the success of the agreement?

(v) Why was she disappointed with the results of the Anglo-Irish Agreement?

(vi) Did she see the Anglo-Irish Agreement as consistent with the approach of previous British governments towards Northern Ireland? Explain your answer.

2. Assess the significance of the Anglo-Irish Agreement.

3. Why did unionists reject the agreement?

4. Explain the Sinn Féin policy of 'an Armalite in one hand and a ballot box in the other'.

5. Why were the Hume–Adams talks a significant development in the history of Northern Ireland?

6. Assess the contribution of Peter Brooke as Secretary of State for Northern Ireland.

7. What did the British Government accept in the Downing Street Declaration?

8. What was accepted by the Irish Government in the declaration?

9. In what respect was it an important milestone on the road to peace in Northern Ireland?

10. What contribution did John Hume make towards the achievement of peace in Northern Ireland?

32. The Impact of the Troubles on the Economy and Society of Northern Ireland

The Economy

At the height of the Troubles during the 1970s and 1980s the economy of Northern Ireland went through a phase of prolonged crisis and decline. This was a complete reversal of the economic progress during the 1960s. Factories closed, foreign investment declined severely and industrial employment fell sharply.

The decline in manufacturing industry was due to a number of factors, including worldwide depression following the various oil crises and decline in demand for various products such as textiles. However, the situation was worsened considerably by the bombing campaigns of the paramilitaries. The violence not only resulted in widespread damage to commercial property, but also created an atmosphere of uncertainty which deterred outside industries from locating in Northern Ireland. Between 1966 and 1971 foreign industries had created 11,600 manufacturing jobs in the province. In contrast, between 1972 and 1976 only 900 jobs were created by foreign companies.

Workers protesting in Belfast over rising rates of unemployment

However, these developments did not lead to an immediate decline in the total numbers in employment. During the 1970s there was a massive expansion of government services in the areas of health, education and security. There was increased investment on the part of the British Government in health and education in an attempt to bring social services there into line with the rest of the United Kingdom. Both Labour and Conservative governments during the 1970s believed that better standards of healthcare and education would reduce poverty and lessen support for violence.

The conflict resulted in a huge expansion in the security services in Northern Ireland. In the beginning troops arrived from Britain in large numbers but from the mid-1970s a policy of 'Ulsterisation' was followed. This involved an increased role for locally recruited security forces in the policing of the province. Numbers in the RUC, the police reserve force the UDR and the prison service expanded greatly.

PERCENTAGE OF PEOPLE UNEMPLOYED IN NORTHERN IRELAND		
	1971	1981
Male		
Catholic	17.3	30.2
Non-Catholic	6.6	12.4
AVERAGE	10.3	19.1
For comparison:		
Great Britain	5.5	11.3
Female		
Catholic	7.0	17.1
Non-Catholic	3.6	9.6
AVERAGE	4.7	12.6
For comparison:		
Great Britain	4.7	7.4

The Economy

Most of these jobs were filled by members of the Protestant community.

Under Margaret Thatcher's Conservative Government, between 1979 and 1990 investment was increased in security forces. However, expenditure on social services such as health and education was restricted as part of cutbacks in the United Kingdom as a whole.

During the peace process from 1990 onwards the state of the Northern Ireland economy was high on the agenda of the various parties. The words 'peace dividend' were used to indicate that social and political stability would lead to economic progress. The British and Irish governments, the US Government, individual investors and the European Union were all committed to investing in the economy of Northern Ireland in the event of a peaceful resolution of the conflict there.

Security forces on duty in Northern Ireland in 1991

Religion and Population Change

As well as discouraging investment in Northern Ireland, the Troubles also had a major impact on population distribution. As a result of violence and intimidation, thousands of people, both Catholics and Protestants, were forced out of their homes. In working-class parts of Belfast, people lived mostly in either Protestant or Catholic ghetto areas with a huge barrier known as the peaceline separating them. In Derry, Protestants almost completely abandoned the Cityside area west of the River Foyle, which contained areas such as the Bogside and Creggan, and transferred east to the Protestant Waterside or to Protestant towns in Co. Derry such as Limavaddy and Coleraine. According to the 1991 census, most people in Northern Ireland lived in areas which were either 90 per cent Catholic or 90 per cent Protestant. As a result of the Troubles, Northern Ireland had become one of the most segregated societies in Europe.

The peace wall separating Catholic and Protestant areas of West Belfast

There was a steady rise in the proportion of Catholics in the population of Northern Ireland from the 1960s onwards. Catholics had traditionally formed about one-third of the population, but by 1991 they made up 42 per cent of the total population in the province. As a result there were significant Catholic populations in largely Protestant and unionist towns such as Lisburn and Portadown.

These increases in Catholic population had important political implications. Unionists felt increasingly insecure as the two main nationalist parties, the SDLP and Sinn Féin, increased their electoral support. In the city of Belfast, for example, nationalist councillors accounted for nearly half of the overall membership of the corporation by the 1990s. This was a huge transformation from the situation that existed in the past, where unionists had always dominated the Belfast Corporation.

Education in a Divided Society

Education in Northern Ireland was almost completely segregated at first and second level. Practically all primary and secondary schools were attended almost exclusively by Catholics or Protestants. While nearly all Catholic parents decided to send their children to Catholic schools, most Protestants attended state schools.

Pupils at Hazelwood Integrated College in North Belfast

Although the vast majority of parents in Northern Ireland wished to have their children educated separately, a small minority thought differently. These people believed that children of different faiths or of no faith at all should be educated together in integrated schools. They hoped that this would lead to greater respect, tolerance and mutual understanding. The movement for integrated education faced many challenges, such as attracting sufficient funding and pupil numbers. While the movement received support from the British Government, education continued to remain deeply segregated in Northern Ireland.

The British Government believed that education had an important role to play in bringing about a more tolerant society in Northern Ireland. In 1982 they issued a Department of Education circular which stated that mutual understanding was both a duty and a responsibility for everyone in education. With the introduction of the National Curriculum in 1989, pupils in all types of schools followed the same programme of study. As a result of this initiative it was no longer possible for some schools to avoid the study of Irish history or to neglect the study of British history. Within the curriculum there were compulsory sections on cultural heritage and education for mutual understanding.

While integration was largely absent at primary and secondary level in Northern Ireland, the third-level sector presented a different picture. Apart from separate Protestant and Catholic primary teacher training colleges, practically all third-level colleges contained a mixture of Catholics and Protestants. The increasing Catholic participation in third-level education since the introduction of the welfare state provided many of the leaders in nationalist politics during the Troubles.

The new University of Ulster at Coleraine

The continuing violence in Northern Ireland had a serious impact on the proportion of Protestants attending third-level education in Northern Ireland. Many Protestant students chose to attend university in Great Britain from the 1970s onwards. They often remained in Britain to work after graduation. This trend became known as the 'Protestant brain drain' as the province lost some of its most capable young people. This contributed to the increased proportion of Catholics in the higher education sector in Northern Ireland.

Conflicting Identities

At the heart of the conflict in Northern Ireland was the existence of two separate traditions or identities – the Protestant/unionist identity on the one hand and the Catholic/nationalist identity on the other. This division was seen in many areas of life. The separate traditions attended different

A young Celtic supporter cheering on his team in a match against Glasgow Rangers at Celtic Park, Glasgow

churches and schools, supported different political parties, played different sports and supported different teams. A glaring example of this division was the overwhelming Protestant support for Glasgow Rangers and the Catholic support for Glasgow Celtic soccer teams.

Rangers supporters at a match in Glasgow

The divisions in Northern Ireland stretched back centuries. However, memories of past triumphs were kept alive and fuelled conflict and division during the Troubles.

The Unionist Identity

As a result of the Troubles, many unionists felt threatened and insecure. In these circumstances they supported traditional expressions of their cultural identity, such as the Orange Order. Landmark events such as the Fall of Stormont, the IRA campaign and the Anglo-Irish Agreement further deepened their siege mentality or belief that their way of life was under threat.

The whole issue of identity was a major dilemma for many unionists. While their main identity was British, before the Troubles, many would have described themselves as Irish as well. Against a

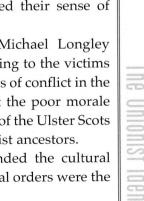

Michael Longley

background of IRA violence to promote the cause of Irish unity, many unionists emphasised their British identity and downplayed their sense of Irishness.

Poets from the unionist tradition such as Michael Longley responded to the Troubles by writing poetry relating to the victims of the violence. He graphically described the effects of conflict in the province. Another poet, Tom Paulin, argued that the poor morale among Protestants was reflected in the low status of the Ulster Scots language, which was the language of their unionist ancestors.

Organisations such as the loyal orders defended the cultural identity of Protestants. Included among these loyal orders were the Orange Order and the Apprentice Boys of Derry.

Tom Paulin

The Unionist Identity

THE LOYAL ORDERS

Commemorating the past plays a very important part in the cultural identity of Protestants in Northern Ireland. Each year, they remember Ulster Protestants who died fighting in the British forces during World War I (1914–18) and World War II (1939–45). However, the main focus of their commemorations lies much further back in history, namely the War of the Three Kings (1688–91), when the Protestant William of Orange defeated the Catholic King James II, who was assisted by his cousin, King Louis XIV of France. The defeat of James II paved the way for a secure Protestant Ascendancy or control throughout Ireland. In Northern Ireland, the Protestant Ascendancy continued down to recent times.

A group of Apprentice Boys of Derry during a tradional march

To keep the memory of historical victories alive and to organise annual commemorations, three Protestant loyal orders were established. The most powerful, the Orange Order, was founded in 1795. The Orange Order organised parades each year to commemorate the victory of William of Orange at the Battle of the Boyne in July 1690. Although Orange parades took place at various times of the year, the main events were on 12 July, the anniversary of the Battle of the Boyne.

In 1797, two years after the foundation of the Orange Order, the Royal Black Institution was established. Those wishing to join the Royal Black had to be members of the Orange Order first. In general, the Royal Black catered for more better-off sections of the Protestant community. Like the Orange Order, it organised parades throughout Northern Ireland.

The third loyal order, the Apprentice Boys of Derry, founded in 1813, was the last to be founded. Its main function was to commemorate the Protestant victory during the Siege of Derry (1688–9).

THE SIEGE OF DERRY

The Siege of Derry, which lasted from December 1688 to August 1689, was the longest in the history of Great Britain or Ireland. It began when the Catholic forces of James II arrived outside the walls of the town. Inside the population was swollen by the arrival of Protestant refugees from all over Ulster. When the governor, Colonel Robert Lundy, wished to surrender, thirteen apprentice boys defied him and closed the gates in the face of the Catholic army. Lundy's replacement as governor, the Rev. George Walker, became one of the heroes of the siege.

After a harrowing 105-day experience involving gunshot, cannon balls, hunger and disease, the siege was broken by the arrival of relief ships from Britain. Ever since then, Protestants in Northern Ireland have drawn inspiration from the victory.

Document 1

Commemorating the Siege of Derry

At the centre of Ulster Protestant culture lies a cycle of myths concerning the seventeenth-century struggle between Protestant and Catholic, settler and native, for supremacy in Ireland. The high point of the Protestant calendar is the Twelfth of July, the anniversary of the Battle of the Boyne (1690), still kept as a bank holiday in Northern Ireland. By comparison, the parades held to commemorate the shutting of the gates of Derry (18 December 1688) and the relief of the city (12 August 1689) are local affairs. It is the Siege of Derry, however, which is the key episode for loyalists... The Siege of Derry carries an emotional charge that the more famous Battle of the Boyne lacks. In part this is simply because the 'Maiden City', unlike the River Boyne, is situated within the six Ulster Counties which became Northern Ireland in 1921. Ulstermen and women participated in the defence of Derry, and their descendants still live there... The story serves to reinforce the social cohesion and political resolve of Ulster Protestants by recalling the unchanging threat to their faith and liberties posed by the Catholic majority in Ireland; 'No Surrender', the watchword of the defenders of Derry, has become the arch-slogan of loyalism.

I. McBride, *The Siege of Derry in Ulster Protestant Mythology*,
Dublin: Four Courts Press 1997, 9–12

THE FOUNDATION OF THE APPRENTICE BOYS OF DERRY

Although the relief of Derry was commemorated regularly during the eighteenth century, there was no specific organisation set up to take charge of the celebrations. This situation changed when the Apprentice Boys of Derry organisation was founded. On 7 December 1813 the first Apprentice Boys club was formed in Dublin by fourteen Derrymen. Shortly afterwards, a club was formed in the city of Londonderry itself. In 1824, with the formation of the 'No Surrender' club, the Apprentice Boys took charge of the annual ceremonies in the city. In 1856 a General Committee of the Apprentice Boys was formed to co-ordinate the siege celebrations.

These celebrations took place each year around 18 December and 12 August. On 18 December the ceremony of the closing of the gates occurred. This involved young members of the Apprentice Boys dressed in seventeenth-century costumes re-enacting the shutting of the gates against the

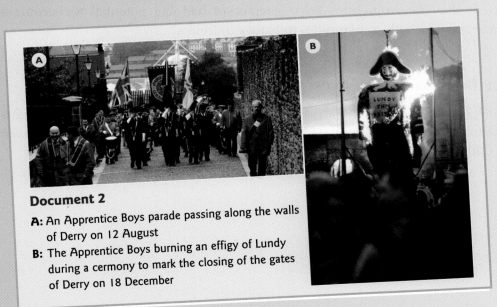

Document 2

A: An Apprentice Boys parade passing along the walls of Derry on 12 August

B: The Apprentice Boys burning an effigy of Lundy during a cermony to mark the closing of the gates of Derry on 18 December

Catholic army in December 1688. Afterwards an effigy of Robert Lundy was burned.

On 12 August the main Apprentice Boys commemorations took place. After a religious service in the Protestant Cathedral, the Apprentice Boys, complete with banners, wearing sashes and to the accompaniment of bands, marched around the walls of Londonderry. These ceremonies were to mark the anniversary of the relief of Londonderry in August 1689.

A Divided City

After the implementation of partition and the creation of Northern Ireland in 1921, the city of Londonderry became the second largest in the new province after Belfast. However, its Protestant population felt far from secure. There had been strong nationalist pressure to have it included in the South because of its Catholic majority. Under these circumstances, local Protestants welcomed the annual Apprentice Boys celebrations, when their co-religionists from all over Northern Ireland came to the city to join them in recalling a Protestant victory. This feeling was expressed by the preacher at the Apprentice Boys cathedral service in August 1947, the Rev. J.G. Mac Manaway. He also happened to be the unionist MP for Londonderry City in the Northern Ireland Parliament.

> **Document 3**
>
> **Ulster's Protestant shrine**
>
> We in Ulster have our own Holy Place, our own religious shrine to which our history as Protestants forever joins us. The Protestant shrine of Protestant Ulster is forever Derry. We do not meet together to provoke anybody or criticise any man's faith. But, just as our forefathers before us, we are resolved that we shall not be driven out of this country by political pressure or economic measures to deprive us of our freedom and our faith.
>
> **Rev. JG. MacManaway as reported in Belfast Newsletter, 13 August 1947**

However, for the majority Catholic community in Derry, the annual Apprentice Boys parade was a source of provocation. A statue of Governor Walker had been placed on a column overlooking the largely nationalist Bogside area. As the Apprentice Boys marched along the section of the walls overlooking nationalist areas, they frequently exchanged insults with the local inhabitants. Such exchanges would normally not lead to serious unrest, but as tension mounted in Derry in the 1960s it became clear that the Apprentice Boys ceremonies had the potential to become a flashpoint of violence between both communities in Northern Ireland.

The Apprentice Boys of Derry and the Battle of the Bogside

In the summer of 1969 the city of Derry was in a highly tense state. Ever since the civil rights march there on 5 October 1968, when police had baton-charged the marchers, relations between the Protestant and Catholic communities in the city had deteriorated.

Document 4

Trouble expected

On 12 July [1969] the Orange Parade was stoned in Derry and rioting between the Bogsiders and the RUC lasted for three days, with an RUC man shooting and wounding two civilians...

Everyone knew the crunch would come on 12 August. That was the day of the Apprentice Boys parade in Derry, when thousands of Orangemen from all over the North would come to Derry, and parade through the city and around the walls overlooking the Bogside to commemorate the siege. It was virtually a direct celebration of the plantation and the Protestant Ascendancy and served as a yearly reminder to the Catholic population of who was master even in this Catholic city.

After a year of civil rights marches banned from the centre of every town and batoned off the streets of Derry, the Catholics were in no mood to be reminded of their inferiority. If the march went ahead there was bound to be a riot... The Stormont government turned down all appeals to ban the march.

M. Farrell, *Northern Ireland: The Orange State*, London: Pluto Press 1976, 258–9

With the Northern Government under James Chichester-Clark refusing to ban the Apprentice Boys march, efforts were made at a local level to persuade the organisers to call it off. One such attempt was made by a Catholic community leader in the Bogside, Paddy Doherty.

With the refusal of the Apprentice Boys to cancel their proposed march, it was clear that conflict could erupt between the marchers and the local Catholics. This in turn could lead to serious violence between the Catholic inhabitants of the Bogside and the RUC. Journalists and television crews made their way to Derry in anticipation of such events. One of the young Apprentice Boys who took part in the march in Derry on 12 August 1969, Billy McFetridge, has written an account of his experiences that day.

The Battle of the Bogside between local Catholics and the RUC which followed the Apprentice Boys parade in Derry in August 1969 is seen by many historians as the real start of 'the Troubles in the province. It led immediately to the deployment of British troops in Northern Ireland, which radically altered the political situation and paved the way for direct rule from Westminster in the future.

Document 5

An attempt to avert trouble

We passed a slogan 'Give Peace a Chance', daubed in large white letters on the tarmac, as we made our way up Fahan Street towards the Apprentice Boys' Hall in the walled city... Our principal purpose was to make the controlling body of the Apprentice Boys aware of the possibility of serious trouble if the parade were allowed to take place. Their granite Scottish baronial building with its turrets and high, square battlemented tower, dominated its surroundings. It had been constructed on the site of the old monastic settlement which dated from the sixth century and was the world headquarters of the Apprentice Boys of Derry.

The meeting was chaired by Doctor Abernathy who remained silent during the proceedings, leaving the talking to Jim Guy, the Secretary, and Reverend Dickenson, the chaplain. Politely, they explained the precautions they had taken to ensure that the march would pass off peacefully. We Bogsiders insisted that the only way to ensure that there would be peace would be to call off the parade. They flatly refused.

Returning to the Bogside, we saw two boys with pots of black paint busily obliterating the white plea for peace from the tarred roadway. No one slept that night. Residents scoured the area for material for barricades. The Bogside was now on a war footing.

P. Doherty, *Paddy Bogside*, Cork: Mercier Press 2001, 127

Document 6

An Apprentice Boy's account

It happened in 1969 when I was twenty. I had joined with my mates and had become an Apprentice Boy – a thing all young men in Ulster are encouraged to do. Although I wasn't particularly religious or patriotic, I felt proud to take the solid oaths of allegiance to God, the Order and my country. It was during the mass parade in Derry, while the bands marched and we were about to be made Apprentice Boys inside the Guild Hall there, that they reckon the so-called recent troubles began. I'd noticed an unusually heavy police presence throughout the day, but I took no special notice until after the ceremony when we were parading through the Diamond in Derry. Suddenly a mob of teenaged boys pressed in close, cursing and laughing at us. A police cordon was formed to keep us apart. Within seconds all us lads were being pelted by stones and missiles launched by a gang the police said had come from Roman Catholic Bogside.

I remember a lad in our own parade broke rank, and charged through the crowd trying to get his hands on one of the troublemakers. But before he could turn down the passage where they had retreated, a big police sergeant reached out a massive hand and grabbed him by the collar and shouted, 'Hey where are you going?' The newly-made Apprentice Boy replied that he was going after the retreating Catholics. 'Aye, that's just what they want you to do. Don't you know that if you go down there you'll not be coming back?' I was shocked by his words. Did he really mean that the boys meant to kill him? Instantaneously, shock gave way to anger that the police didn't chase them. They had insulted our banner. They had injured us with rocks. Indeed they meant to murder any one of us. I wondered why the police were letting them get away with this.

Billy McFetridge, 'An Apprentice Boy 1969' in S.H. King and S. McMahon (eds.), *Hope and History –Eyewitness Accounts of Life in Twentieth-Century Ulster*, Belfast: Friars Bush Press 1996, 150–2

THROUGH CONFLICT TO CONSENSUS

Like its sister loyal orders the Orange Order and the Royal Black Institution, the Apprentice Boys organisation had a turbulent history during the conflict in Northern Ireland. In 1970 and 1971 a ban was imposed on the Apprentice Boys' parades and between 1972 and 1974 they were restricted to the Protestant Waterside district of the city. In 1973 the IRA blew up the Walker monument where the effigy of Lundy had traditionally been burned during the December commemorations of the closing of the city gates. The Apprentice Boys were not allowed to march around the city walls again until 1995.

Like the other loyal orders, the Apprentice Boys frequently found themselves in conflict with local nationalist residents over the right to march. Feeder parades were also a source of conflict with nationalist communities. This involved groups of Apprentice Boys marching in various parts of the province before getting on buses to travel to the main parade in Derry. The British Government appointed a Parades Commission to adjudicate on contentious marches. However, a satisfactory solution was not reached until the Apprentice Boys agreed to discuss marches with the local residents in the late 1990s. When they did so they reached a compromise acceptable to all sides at a time when the Orange Order had still not accepted the need for this approach.

During 1989 there were special celebrations to mark the tercentenary of the siege. Some of these were organised by the nationalist-controlled Derry City Council, which believed that the siege and relief of Derry were part of the heritage of all its citizens. However, these events obviously mattered most for the Protestant community and the Apprentice Boys of Derry continued to have members in all parts of the world. At a time when many Northern Ireland Protestants felt insecure facing the challenge of conceding equality to their Catholic fellow citizens, the memory of past victories still had a role to play.

COMPREHENSION

1. According to the author of Document 1, what lies at the centre of Ulster Protestant culture?

2. Why has the Siege of Derry remained a key episode for loyalists? (Document 1)

3. What watchword has survived to become a slogan of loyalism? (Document 1)

4. Pick out two symbols of the British and Protestant identity of the Apprentice Boy marchers in Document 2A.

5. Why is the effigy of Lundy being burned? (Document 2B)

6. Where is Ulster's Protestant shrine? (Document 3)

7. What are unionists resolved to prevent? (Document 3)

8. According to the author of Document 4, what was celebrated each year in Derry on 12 August?

9. Why did the residents of the Bogside want the Apprentice Boys to call off their march scheduled for 12 August 1969? (Document 5)

10. What response did the 'Bogsiders' get from the Apprentice Boys? (Document 5)

11. How did the author of Document 6 feel on becoming an Apprentice Boy?

12. How did trouble begin on the march? (Document 6)

13. Why was the young Apprentice Boy shocked and angry? (Document 6)

COMPARISON

1. How do Documents 1 and 4 differ from the other documents as sources for the historian?

2. Contrast the portrayal of the Apprentice Boys' yearly commemorations in Document 3 and Document 4.

3. Were the fears expressed in Document 5 realised according to the account in Document 6?

CRITICISM

1. Does Document 3 present a unionist or a nationalist perspective? Explain your answer.

2. Does Document 4 present a fair and balanced account? Give a reason for your answer.

3. Why should historians treat Documents 5 and 6 with a degree of caution?

CONTEXTUALISATION

1. Give three examples of how commemorating the past plays an important part in the cultural identity of Protestants in Northern Ireland.

2. Name three Protestant loyal orders established in Northern Ireland.

3. Why were the Apprentice Boys of Derry established?

4. Describe the role played by the Apprentice Boys of Derry in the Battle of the Bogside.

5. How did relations between the Apprentice Boys and the Catholic Community in Derry improve in the late 1990s?

The Nationalist Identity

The identity of nationalists in Northern Ireland was defined in terms of being Irish and Catholic. At the outbreak of the Troubles in 1968 they were united by a common sense of grievance against unionist majority rule. Their focus was primarily on achieving an end to discrimination and securing equality of access to housing and employment.

A Gaelic football match between Antrim and Derry at Casement Park, Belfast

While the general political aspiration among nationalists was a united Ireland, there were deep divisions within the Catholic community over the role of violence in achieving this. As the Troubles progressed there were conflicting loyalties in nationalist areas between supporters of the constitutional SDLP and Sinn Féin, the political wing of the IRA.

The distinct cultural identity of nationalists was seen in their sporting activities. They were deeply involved in the Gaelic Athletic Association (GAA), an all-Ireland sporting organisation. In contrast to the Republic of Ireland, there was a very close link between politics and the GAA in Northern Ireland. Under the association rules, members of security forces in the North were not permitted to join GAA clubs.

Irish language supporters holding a protest in Belfast

The Irish language was another important element in the cultural identity of Northern nationalists. It was taught in Catholic schools and an Irish-speaking area developed in West Belfast. Irish-speaking nationalists in Northern Ireland called on the British Government to provide greater funding and support for the language. Unionist support for the Ulster Scot language was largely in response to nationalist attempts to promote the Irish language.

Brian Friel

Just as poets and writers from the unionist tradition reflected the fears and aspirations of their community during the Troubles, writers also emerged from the nationalist tradition. In 1980 the playwright Brian Friel founded the Field Day Theatre Company in Derry. From the beginning, Field Day had a nationalist political agenda. Its plays were performed in Derry's Guildhall, a huge symbol of the British Empire. Stephen Rea, one the directors of the company, observed that there was an irony 'in us doing plays there which maybe undermine that position and certainly come from a different point of view'. As well as producing plays, Field Day also published pamphlets that explored various cultural issues.

One of the founding directors of Field Day was the Nobel Prize-winning poet Seamus Heaney. His sense of nationalist identity was made clear in a verse he wrote in a Field Day pamphlet:

> My passport's green
> No glass of ours was ever raised
> To toast The Queen
> ...[whose] reign
> Of crown and rose
> Defied, displaced, would not combine
> What I'd expose

Heaney sometimes used the Northern Ireland Troubles as a theme in his poetry. While his writings are not openly political, his poetry reflects the traditions and way of life of the nationalist community in Northern Ireland.

Towards Greater Understanding

With the advent of the peace process, there was a greater awareness of the need to accommodate the two traditions in Northern Ireland. There was a growing recognition that a stable society would need to take account of diversity and difference. This more open attitude was seen in the increased willingness within local communities to arrive at an agreed resolution to the contentious issue of marches. As new structures were being developed for the future of Northern Ireland, there was an increased willingness among both unionists and nationalists to heal the divisions of the past.

KEY PERSONALITY: SEAMUS HEANEY (1939–)

Seamus Heaney was born in Co. Derry in 1939, the son of a farmer and the eldest of nine children. He was educated at St Columb's College, a Catholic boarding school in Derry, and at Queen's University, Belfast, where he studied English. In 1963 he became a lecturer at St Joseph's Teacher Training College in Belfast.

Heaney started publishing poetry in the early 1960s and came into contact with other poets in Northern Ireland, such as Michael Longley. In 1972 he moved to Dublin and lectured at Carysfort College. He left Dublin in 1981 and returned to Belfast, where in 1983, along with Brien Friel and Stephen Rea, he co-founded Field Day Publishing, which had a strongly nationalist political agenda.

While Heaney's poems have universal themes, they often deal with the local rural surroundings where he grew up in Derry. While not overtly political in nature, his poetry is in the nationalist tradition and allusions to sectarian differences and violence can be found in his poems. His Gaelic heritage is a central part of his work, both culturally and politically. Seamus Heaney was awarded the Nobel Prize for Literature in 1995.

ORDINARY LEVEL

1. Why was there a decline in manufacturing industry in Northern Ireland in the 1970s and 1980s?

2. What impact did the Troubles have on foreign investment?

3. Why did these developments not result in an immediate decline in the total numbers in employment?

4. What impact did the peace process have on the economy of Northern Ireland?

5. Explain the effect of the Troubles on population distribution in Northern Ireland.

6. What was integrated education and what did its advocates hope to achieve?

7. Name some government initiatives in education which aimed at increasing the sense of mutual understanding in Northern Ireland.

8. What impact did the violence have on the proportion of Protestants attending third-level colleges in Northern Ireland?

9. Name the two traditions or identities which existed in Northern Ireland.

10. What landmark developments in Northern Ireland deepened the unionist belief that their way of life was under threat?

11. What was the initial focus of the nationalist community at the outbreak of the Troubles?

12. Explain the deep divisions that existed within the nationalist community over the role of violence in achieving a united Ireland.

13. Write a paragraph on Seamus Heaney.

HIGHER LEVEL

1. Read the following reflection written by Seamus Heaney in the week after the declaration of the IRA's ceasefire of 31 August 1994 and answer the questions that follow.

The announcement by the Provisional IRA last Wednesday changed everything for the better. I listened to the radio all afternoon, hoping to hear words that would be up to the magnitude of what was happening. But while the political leaders and the commentators were (with predictable exceptions) elated, the sheer volume of the talk began to have an almost claustrophobic effect.

So I went outside to try to recollect myself, and suddenly a blind seemed to rise somewhere at the back of my mind and the light came flooding in. I felt twenty-five years younger. I remembered again what things had felt like in those early days of political ferment in the late '60s. How we were all brought beyond our highly developed caution to believe that the effort to create new movement and new language in the Northern Ireland context was a viable project.

But as well as feeling freed up, I felt angry also. The quarter century we have lived through was a terrible black hole, and the inestimable suffering inflicted and endured by every party to the conflict has only brought the situation to a point that is politically less promising than in 1968.

At that time there was energy and confidence on the nationalist side and a developing liberalism – as well as the usual obstinacy and reaction – on the unionist side. There was a general upswing in intellectual and social activity; the border was more pervious than it had been, the sectarian alignments less determining.

I remember in particular feeling empowered by a week on the road with David Hammond and Michael Longley in May 1968 when we brought a programme of songs and poems to schools and hotels and libraries in unionist and nationalist areas all over Northern Ireland.

As a member of the 11-Plus generation of Catholic scholarship boys, just recently appointed to the faculty of Queen's University, I knew myself to be symptomatic of a new confidence in the nationalist minority...and I was conscious that an Irish dimension was at last beginning to figure in the official life of the North.

In a few years' time, of course, to have read 'Requiem for the Croppies' in such venues would have been taken as a direct expression of support for the IRA's campaign of violence. And this was only one tiny instance of the way in which, during the 1970s, artistic and cultural exercises got peeled away from the action of politics...

What I felt last Wednesday, however, was that there was now an opportunity for everybody to get involved again.

...The refusal to consider any move that might erode the Britishness of the Ulster Protestant way of life is totally ingrained in the loyalist community, and after the past twenty-five years it would be stupid and insulting to expect them to renege on their sense of identity.

But it is neither stupid nor insulting to ask them to consider consenting to some political adjustments that would give the nationalist minority equally undisputed and uncontested rights to the grounds of their Irish identity.

Seamus Heaney, 'Light Finally Enters the Black Hole', Sunday Tribune, 4 September 1994

(i) What positive memories did Seamus Heaney have of developments in Northern Ireland in the late 1960s?

(ii) Why did he have feelings of anger when he looked back over the previous twenty-five years?

(iii) In what respect was he himself symptomatic of the new confidence in the nationalist community?

(iv) What occurrence empowered Seamus Heaney in May 1968 and why do you think he experienced that feeling?

(v) What changes had come about during the 1970s?

(vi) In the last paragraph, Heaney refers to the conflicting identities of nationalists and unionists. How does he define these identities?

(vii) Does he believe that the situation is better in Northern Ireland in 1994 than it was in 1968? Refer to the passage in support of your answer.

2. What was the effect of the Troubles on the economy and population of Northern Ireland?

3. 'The education system in Northern Ireland remained almost completely segregated.' Give your view on this statement.

4. 'At the root of the problems in Northern Ireland was a clash between two conflicting identities.' What were the characteristics of these identities?

POLITICS AND SOCIETY IN NORTHERN IRELAND, 1949–93

During this section you became familiar with the following KEY CONCEPTS:

Civil Rights	The belief that all citizens, irrespective of class, race or religion, should be treated equally by the state.
Gerrymandering	The fixing of electoral boundaries to favour the ruling unionist party during elections in Northern Ireland.
Terrorism	The use of violence to achieve political objectives.
Power-sharing	Joint participation by unionists and nationalists in the government of Northern Ireland.
Sectarianism	Division and hostility within society on the basis of religious difference.
Bigotry	Intolerance and prejudice towards other beliefs.
Tolerance and Intolerance	Tolerance involves respect and accommodation for the beliefs of others. Intolerance is the lack of respect or understanding for different points of view.
Cultural Traditions	Customs and practices that express the identity of particular groups in society.
Cultural Identity	The distinguishing features which define the way of life of particular groups in society, e.g. nationalists and unionists.
Ecumenism	The attempt to achieve unity among Christians by exploring the common ground between the various Christian churches.
Propaganda	A biased or exaggerated version of events in order to further a political aim.

Appendix. Working with Evidence: Using Documents and Preparing the Research Study

History and the Role of the Historian

History is concerned with the experience of human life in the past. It is based on the understanding and interpretation of evidence. The word 'history' has a broader meaning than this, however. It can refer to:

- The past itself.
- Surviving evidence from the past.

However, we are concerned here with the third meaning of the word, namely:

- An interpretation of human life in the past based upon the scientific use of evidence.

In seeking evidence upon which to base their investigation of the past, historians turn to **sources**. Sources can be either **primary** or **secondary**:

- *Primary sources* are surviving documents, monuments or artefacts from the period under consideration.
- *Secondary sources* are works that date from a later period, usually narratives or interpretative studies written by historians.

Both primary and secondary sources play an important part in the historical studies of Leaving Certificate students. The documents-based Case Studies contain examples of both, and students must become familiar with the skills necessary to use sources with confidence. Students gain further practice in this area while studying the syllabus topics, which have been specially designed for a documents-based approach. In preparing their Research Study projects, students will become familiar with different types of sources. The syllabus states that the sources used in Research Studies 'should be either primary or specialist secondary'.

Primary sources can take many forms, ranging from ancient and medieval manuscripts to modern government records such as census returns. They are frequently to be found either in archives, museums and libraries or in private ownership. When large organisations such as government departments or churches had a collection of documents that they no longer required on a day-to-day basis, they usually stored the documents away for safekeeping in collections known as archives. Documents in archives are usually subject to a time limit – a period during which the documents are not released to historians. The time limit is usually thirty or fifty years after the document has been archived, although some sensitive documents may not be examined for up to one hundred years. In choosing a Research Study, students should be aware that a thirty-year rule applies to government archives in the Irish Republic and in Northern Ireland. Many primary sources, particularly those covering local topics, are stored in local libraries and museums. Students should understand that libraries and museums are not only concerned with recording the achievements of the past: they are also actively involved in providing scholars with the sources they require to pursue their studies.

For Leaving Certificate students, gaining access to sources is just the first step in a rewarding enquiry into some aspect of human life in the past. Using these sources properly will contribute enormously to the writing of an impressive Research Study.

Working with Historical Sources

Whether engaged in documents-based work under one of the syllabus study topics or in the preparation of the Research Study, students should always engage actively with their sources. They should be aware that evidence needs to be derived, or drawn out, from sources. To do this successfully, a thorough knowledge of the background, or context, of the subject being investigated is necessary. When evaluating the evidence contained in sources, students will find it helpful if they learn to categorise sources according to type, for example public records, letters, interviews, newspaper accounts, memoirs or maps. Students should also attempt to discover the purpose for which a given source was written. This is important when trying to form judgements about whether particular sources are trustworthy or not. Sometimes the motives of the person who produced a source can be questionable, as in the case of propaganda.

Having collected historical information from various sources, students should then be in a position to evaluate its strengths and weaknesses and to choose the most relevant information as a basis upon which to write up the results of their research. They will find it helpful to approach their material by asking a number of key questions, such as why, who, where and when. Students should also be aware when using sources of the importance of proceeding from cause to result, always using evidence to support their conclusions.

Finally, when using sources, students should be aware of the presence of bias, or partisan feeling. They should try to detect this and should reflect differing viewpoints in their own writing and try to be as objective – or unbiased – as possible. Before embarking on individual research, they can practise using these skills when working with documents in the study of history.

Case Studies and Documents

In preparing to engage in independent historical research, students can develop their skills by using documents either in the Case Study sections of the various topics or in the topic specifically designated for documents-based study. In particular, they should develop the **evidence-handling skills** laid out in the History syllabus and develop the ability to:

- Recognise different types of historical source material.
- Extract information from source materials to answer historical questions.
- Evaluate the usefulness of particular sources and their limitations.
- Detect bias.
- Identify propaganda.

Regular practice with documents and, in particular, experience in answering the four main types of document question should enable students to acquire these skills. Documents-based questions are divided into the following four categories:

1 *Comprehension*: In answering questions of this type, students should try to focus on the point of information that is required and should be as accurate as possible in their answers.
2 *Comparison*: Here the student is frequently asked to distinguish between two different documents concerning the same event and to pass judgement on their relative merits.

Students should look out here not merely for different types of authors, but for different types of documents.

3 *Criticism*: Here students are expected to assess critically the usefulness of documents as sources and to be on their guard for the presence of bias or propaganda.

4 *Contextualisation*: These questions test the ability of students to relate the events described in the documents to the wider historical background. An ability to cope well with Contextualisation questions is particularly important at Higher Level.

The importance of regular practice at answering documents-based questions will be apparent to students when they begin preparation for the Research Study.

The Research Study

As part of their Leaving Certificate assessment in History, all students must submit a written report on a Research Study topic, as well as taking a terminal written examination. The report must be submitted a few months before the written examination and counts for 20 per cent of the total marks. Marks are allocated for the report as follows.

Outline plan	3
Evaluation of sources	5
Extended essay	12

Each student will choose the subject of his or her Research Study, under the direction of the teacher. The History syllabus states that 'the subject for investigation must be clearly defined. Its focus should be narrow rather than broad so as to allow for depth of investigation.' Therefore, when choosing a subject, students should consider the following:

- An aspect of local history.
- A person in history who was not of major significance.
- An episode in a wider historical process, such as a single battle in a war or an important event during a revolution.
- A person from the world of art, music or science.

The syllabus also states that the subject chosen 'should not be obscure or trivial' and that 'it should be based on information that may be readily authenticated'. In effect, students should choose subjects where historical processes such as change and development can be discussed. The requirement that subjects should be based on information that can be checked is extremely important. As history is based on evidence, it is essential that students present their findings in such a way that the examiners can readily check the sources of information. In choosing sources for the Research Study, students should be aware of the minimal limits set out in the syllabus:

- At Ordinary Level, a minimum of two sources should be used.
- At Higher Level, three (or more) should be used.

The syllabus further requires that the sources used should be either primary or specialist secondary sources. 'Specialist secondary' refers to studies on particular topics and would rule out general textbooks or narratives of events.

When writing a report on the results of the Research Study, each student must include three sections:

1 The Outline Plan.
2 The Evaluation of Sources.

3 The Extended Essay.

In the Outline Plan, students are expected to state clearly the scope of their study and to give reasons explaining why they chose it. They must also describe their aims, how they intend to approach the topic and the sources upon which it is based. It is vital that students write clearly and to the point in this section and avoid a discussion of matters that belong in the other two sections.

Under the heading Evaluation of Sources, students are expected to show how relevant their chosen sources are to the subject of the study. They must also comment on the strengths and weaknesses of the sources.

At the end of the study, the Extended Essay sets out the main findings and conclusions arrived at by the student. It must outline and comment on the process of investigation and relate it to the aims as set out in the Outline Plan. In addition to text diagrams, the student might well include illustrations and charts in this section of the study. In order to write a good Extended Essay, students must prepare it carefully and pay particular attention to structure. It should include a clear introduction, a well-developed and logical discussion of the topic and a strong conclusion based on the main findings of the study.

Above all, in the course of the report on the Research Study, students should demonstrate that they were engaged in their own personal enquiry into a historical topic and should show clearly how the process led to the conclusions that they have reached.

Conclusion

In the various aspects of historical study, including reading and research, students should bear in mind that the study of history is constantly changing. New evidence and new insights constantly challenge the students of history to reassess previously held viewpoints. The cultivation of a dynamic approach to history based on this understanding will develop the critical judgement of students. A tolerance of differing points of view and a commitment to the critical analysis of historical change should inform the approach of Leaving Certificate History students not merely to documents and research, but to the entire experience of history itself.

Sample Research Study for Higher Level
Recruitment of Irishmen to the British Army during World War I

OUTLINE PLAN

It is estimated that over 300,000 Irishmen volunteered to fight in the British army during World War I. In this research study I intend to examine the issue of recruitment, including the reasons for joining the army and the methods of enlistment adopted. I shall also place my study in the wider context of Irish political developments of the time, including the Home Rule Crisis and the 1916 Rising.

WHY I CHOSE THIS TOPIC

This topic interests me because I feel that in the past the Irish contribution to World War I has been overshadowed by the attention given to the 1916 Rising and the subsequent struggle for independence. I believe that this topic is of major historical significance because far more Irishmen were involved in World War I than in the struggle for independence. In addition, it provides me with an insight into the differing perspectives of nationalists and unionists on the British war effort.

AIMS OF THE RESEARCH STUDY

I hope that this study will provide me with a deeper insight into the motivation of the many Irishmen who joined the British army during World War I. I also hope to gain an understanding of the methods used by the British Government to enlist recruits during World War I. I hope through my research study to practise the skills of the historian in gathering, collating and interpreting historical information. I also hope that this study will deepen my awareness of the existence of diverse traditions in the Ireland of the time and thereby arrive at a balanced view of the period in question.

MY INTENDED APPROACH TO THE RESEARCH STUDY

I will begin by reading general accounts of Irish history in the period. I will follow this by consulting specialist primary and secondary sources on Irish involvement in World War I. In all cases I will take detailed notes from the sources which will form the basis of my extended essay.

SOURCES

A. General histories
B. Specialised sources

General histories
J.J. Lee, *Ireland, 1912–1985* (Cambridge, 1989)
F.S.L. Lyons, *Ireland Since the Famine* (London, 1971)

Specialised sources
D. Fitzpatrick (ed.), *Ireland and the First World War* (Dublin, 1986)
H.E.D. Harris, *The Irish Regiments in the First World War* (Cork, 1968)
A.C. Hepburn (ed.), *Ireland 1905–25, Vol. 2: Documents and Analysis* (Newtownards, 1998)

P. Hogarty, *The Old Toughs – A Brief History of the Royal Dublin Fusiliers 2nd Battalion* (Dublin, 2001)

T. Johnstone, *Orange, Green and Khaki: The Story of the Irish Regiments in the Great War 1914–1918* (Dublin, 1992)

EVALUATION OF THE SOURCES

J.J. Lee, *Ireland 1912–1985* (Cambridge, 1989)

This is a general history of the period but it contains more discussion than *Ireland Since the Famine*. It contained some very useful statistics on the recruitment figures in Ireland during World War I.

F.S.L. Lyons, *Ireland Since the Famine* (London, 1971)

This is also a general textbook which gives very useful background information on the political situation at the time. I found it particularly helpful for researching the issue of Home Rule between 1912 and 1914 and for its coverage of the Conscription Crisis of 1918.

D. Fitzpatrick (ed.), *Ireland and the First World War* (Dublin, 1986)

I found this secondary source very useful in preparing my study. It is a collection of essays on various aspects of World War I. The essay on recruiting posters was very interesting. It contained primary sources in the form of copies of original posters. I relied a lot on this book when preparing my paragraph on recruiting techniques during the war.

H.E.D. Harris, *The Irish Regiments in the First World War* (Cork, 1968)

Although this is the oldest of my secondary sources, it was essential reading for me. It is clear, well-written and very easy to follow. In the earlier chapters the author gives the history of Irish regiments in the British army and the situation in July 1914 just before the outbreak of war. The book also contains charts on the various regiments, useful maps and many photographs.

A.C. Hepburn (ed.), *Ireland 1905–25, Vol. 2: Documents and Analysis* (Newtownards, 1998)

I used this source – a reproduction of original documents – in order to get a reliable version of John Redmond's important Woodenbridge speech of September 1914.

P. Hogarty, *The Old Toughs – A Brief History of the Royal Dublin Fusiliers 2nd Battalion* (Dublin, 2001)

This recently published book is the first study on a regiment from southern Ireland to appear for many years. It gives a detailed picture of the lives of the soldiers in the last few years of peacetime and of their experiences on the Western Front during World War I. It also contains many photographs from the time.

T. Johnstone, *Orange, Green and Khaki: The Story of the Irish Regiments in the Great War 1914–1918* (Dublin, 1992)

Although I found this book too detailed at times, it contains much useful information. When using it, I had to be careful to focus on the relevant information and extract it by means of using the index and taking notes.

Extended Essay: The Report

TITLE: THE RECRUITMENT OF IRISHMEN TO THE BRITISH ARMY DURING WORLD WAR I

Between August 1914 and November 1918 it is estimated that over 300,000 Irishmen fought in the British army during World War I. Unlike Great Britain, France or Germany where conscription existed, all of those joining the army in Ireland were volunteers. At a time of deep political divisions in Ireland, it was remarkable that so many men volunteered to fight. In this study I intend to examine the reasons for these developments, the recruitment methods adopted and the decline in the numbers volunteering as the war went on.

As part of the United Kingdom of Great Britain and Ireland, the whole country was involved in World War I. From the outset the British Government looked to Ireland as a valuable source of recruits for the war effort. This was not surprising given the large numbers of Irishmen in the British forces even before the war broke out. In July 1914 there were thirteen Irish regiments in the British army. They included famous ones like the Irish Guards, the Connaught Rangers, the Dublin Fusiliers, the Munster Fusiliers and the Inniskilling Dragoons. Many Irish regiments had depots in towns like Galway, Tralee and Clonmel and they recruited among the local population. While many ordinary soldiers joined the British army because of poverty and unemployment, at officer level there was also a significant Irish contribution, particularly from Anglo-Irish Protestant families. Indeed, the most powerful man in the British army in 1914, Lord Kitchener, came from an Anglo-Irish background.

When war broke out in August 1914 Ireland was on the verge of civil war. The Buckingham Palace Peace Conference, involving unionist and nationalist politicians together with members of the British Government, had broken up without agreement over the future of Home Rule. Once war was declared, the British Government and the leaders of the British army were to make clever use of the conflicting aims and objectives of both unionist and Home Rule party leaders, in order to persuade them to encourage their followers to join the British army.

When Britain joined World War I in protest against German violation of Belgian neutrality, the attack on the 'small nation' Belgium was used for propaganda purposes. Because Belgium, like Ireland, was a mainly Catholic country, Irishmen were encouraged to join the British army to rescue Belgium. Once war was declared most county councils and corporations, most Catholic bishops and all Church of Ireland bishops called on Irishmen to join the British army. However, in this regard the position of the two leaders of political opinion would be crucial. Both the Home Rule party leader, John Redmond, and the Ulster unionist leader, Sir Edward Carson, had vital decisions to make regarding the advice they would give to their followers concerning joining the British army. Redmond was the first to act. Although Home Rule was passed at Westminster, its operation was postponed until the end of the war. As well as this, many of Redmond's Catholic and nationalist followers were traditionally hostile to England. However, in the hope that Irish involvement in the fighting would persuade a grateful British Government to fully implement Home Rule, John Redmond encouraged his supporters to join the British army. In a speech at Woodenbridge, Co. Wicklow, on 20 September 1914, he remarked:

> Go on drilling and make yourselves efficient for the work, and then account yourselves as men, not only in Ireland itself, but wherever the firing line extends, in defence of right, of freedom, and of religion in this war.

Throughout the war until his death in March 1918, Redmond was never to withdraw his support for Irish involvement in the British army. Although his position was to prove controversial later in the war, he was undoubtedly a major influence in encouraging Irish recruits to join up, many of them from the ranks of the nationalist volunteers, the Redmond-controlled group which had split from the Irish Volunteers over the issue of fighting in World War I.

Like Redmond, Carson too had a difficult decision to make. On the outbreak of war, Lord Kitchener, the new Secretary of State for War, made it clear to him that he expected the Ulster Volunteers to join the British army in huge numbers. After all, throughout the Home Rule Crisis between 1912 and 1914 Ulster unionists had proclaimed their loyalty to King George V and to Great Britain. However, Carson hesitated because he feared that if most of the Ulster Volunteers marched off to war, Home Rule might be imposed on the people back home against their will. Having received guarantees from the British Government in late September 1914, Carson advised his followers to join the British army. From then on Ulstermen were to play a prominent role in the war effort. About half of all recruits in Ireland came from the province, with a quarter from Leinster and the rest from Munster and Connaught. This higher figure from Ulster reflected the greater level of commitment to the British war effort among Protestants and unionists in Ireland. To consolidate this trend the authorities in the British army provided for the formation of a special Ulster Division in addition to the two other Irish divisions already in existence.

There were three divisions of the British army raised in Ireland during World War I. The Tenth Division was the second of all the new British army divisions to be formed for the war. It was almost wholly Irish in membership and would see action in Gallipoli and the Middle East. Shortly afterwards a second division was formed – the Sixteenth (Irish) Division. It recruited throughout Ireland and served throughout the war on the Western Front in France and Belgium. The third division to be formed was the 36th (Ulster) Division, drawn largely from the Ulster Volunteer Force. It recruited mainly in Ulster and served on the Western Front where it suffered severe casualties during the Battle of the Somme in 1916. The three Irish divisions were formed during a wave of enthusiasm for the war in August and September 1914. This mood would not last long, however. Between August and December 1914, 43,000 men enlisted in Ireland, to be followed by a further 37,000 between January and August 1915. Between September 1915 and April 1916 only 12,000 volunteered. Faced with this challenge to recruit more soldiers, the authorities made use of various propaganda techniques in order to boost recruitment figures.

In the opening months of the war the recruiting posters in Ireland did not have any specific Irish content. They mainly appealed to loyalty to King and Empire such as the famous poster with Lord Kitchener declaring 'Your country needs you'. However, this changed early in 1915 when the Central Council for the Organisation of Recruiting in Ireland (CCORI) was established. New posters were designed with specific Irish elements such as 'Join an Irish regiment today' or 'To the young women of Ireland: won't you help and send a man to join the army today?' Sometimes verse was used as a means of getting the message across:

> For if in Ireland's glory
> Each soldier may claim his share,
> So he who would shirk his duty
> His burden of shame must bear.
> You who are strong and active,
> You who are fit for the fray,
> What have you done for Ireland,
> Ask of your heart today!

The poster campaign reached a peak in 1915, faded during 1916 and 1917 and then revived somewhat in 1918 when there was an urgent need for soldiers to counter the German spring offensive of that year. Despite widespread opposition to recruitment in the later stages of the war, the British authorities continued to attempt to attract volunteers and it has been estimated that around two million recruitment posters were circulated in Ireland between 1914 and 1918.

The anti-recruitment movement in Ireland during World War I came from a number of sources. A section of the labour movement associated with James Connolly, the Irish Citizen Army and the Irish Transport and General Workers' Union was strongly opposed to the British war effort. This attitude was summed up in the banner hanging on the front of the union's headquarters, Liberty Hall in Dublin. Its slogan read: 'We serve neither King nor Kaiser, but Ireland.' A small group of pacifists, such as Francis Sheehy-Skeffington, genuinely opposed the war on grounds of conscience. However, by far the most significant group to oppose the recruitment of Irishmen to the British army was advanced nationalists such as the Irish Volunteers under the leadership of Eoin McNeill or Arthur Griffith and Sinn Féin. When protestors such as Arthur Griffith carried out demonstrations against recruitment, they were imprisoned under the strict provisions of the Defence of the Realm Act. The efforts of these objectors were assisted by the duration of the war. The early enthusiasm soon waned; indeed the number of volunteers in the first year of the war exceeded that of the following three years combined. During 1915 there were huge casualties among Irish regiments serving in Gallipoli, in a campaign that had to be abandoned within a year of its beginning. Therefore by the end of 1915 such losses were already leading to a marked decline in the number of Irishmen volunteering to join the British forces.

During the following year of 1916 the hope of the British army recruiters in Ireland was to be dashed by two critical events – the Easter Rising in Dublin in April and the Battle of the Somme which began on the Western Front in July. The reaction of the British authorities to the Easter Rising, especially the execution of its leaders, led to a fundamental change in public opinion throughout nationalist Ireland. The message emanating from the leaders of 1916 and from the revived Sinn Féin and Irish Volunteers from 1917 onwards was that the British army was an enemy force of occupation. This created serious difficulties for Irishmen fighting on Britain's side in the war. It also led to a reduction in recruitment levels throughout the country, except in north-east Ulster. Massive casualties were endured by various Irish regiments in the Battle of the Somme but particularly by the 36th (Ulster) Division. This in turn led to war weariness and a decline in the number of volunteers. The response to a similar situation in Great Britain was the introduction of conscription. Eventually the Government of Lloyd George, desperate for more soldiers and under pressure from public opinion in England, began to consider the introduction of conscription in Ireland as well.

Whereas historians usually discuss the Conscription Crisis in Ireland in 1918 in terms of the rise of Sinn Féin, I would like to examine it in the context of the recruitment of Irishmen to the British army throughout the war. Lloyd George had hoped that the Irish Convention of 1917–18 would reach agreement on Home Rule for Ireland and that he could then introduce Home Rule together with conscription. When the Irish Convention failed to reach agreement he pressed ahead with his plan to introduce conscription in Ireland in April 1918. This marked the final abandonment by the British Government of its policy of persuading Irishmen to enlist voluntarily in the British army during World War I. The confrontational attitude adopted was completely at variance with the earlier recruitment campaigns which stressed co-operation between Ireland and England within the British Empire. It was also a reversal of the hopes which Redmond had placed on such co-operation. Following his death in March 1918 he was succeeded as leader by John Dillon. During the debates on the Conscription Bill at Westminster, Dillon warned Lloyd George: 'All Ireland will rise against you.' When the bill was passed he then led his party out of Parliament and home to Ireland.

In planning a campaign of passive resistance to conscription, the Irish Party was joined by the labour movement, the Catholic bishops and Sinn Féin. However, Sinn Féin, under the leadership of Éamon de Valera, dominated the campaign and gained most of the credit when the British Government backed down and changed its mind. In the anti-conscription campaign some of those who had been prominent supporters of Irishmen volunteering to join the British army, such as the Irish Party and Catholic bishops, were now on the opposite side. By its disastrous handling of the conscription issue in Ireland, Lloyd George's Government further undermined the Irish Parliamentary Party and strengthened the up-and-coming Sinn Féin movement. In the process it was further undermining the future of Irishmen in the British army as Sinn Féin was bitterly opposed to their participation in the war.

When World War I finally ended in November 1918, Irishmen returned home to a political situation which had totally transformed from the conditions prevailing in 1914. The expectations of both unionists and nationalists who joined for different reasons were to be sadly disappointed. On the unionist side the bravery of the Ulster Volunteers in the 36th (Ulster) Division did not succeed in maintaining all of Ireland within the United Kingdom. Many returned home to unemployment and poverty in the new state of Northern Ireland. In a falsification of history the participation of vast numbers of Ulster Catholics in the British army was deliberately ignored and the sacrifices of the Ulster Division were linked with the Orange Order and the Protestant identity. The situation in nationalist Ireland was even more imbalanced. Many men had volunteered in the belief that they were fighting for Ireland and for the early implementation of Home Rule. On returning home after the war, they were frequently targeted by republicans as being pro-British and their contribution was mostly quietly forgotten. The new Irish Free State from 1922 onwards chose to honour those who died in the 1916 Rising and the War of Independence and pointedly ignored the Irishmen who died in World War I. However, the participation of Irishmen of both major traditions in World War I is worthy of study not only because it is interesting in its own right, but also because of the light it shines on the world in which they lived and on the attitudes of subsequent generations.

A REVIEW OF THE RESEARCH PROCESS

I began by reading general textbooks such as F.S.L. Lyons's *Ireland Since the Famine*. I took notes from these textbooks and drew up a time chart of the main events of the period. Having completed a general overview by consulting general histories of the period, I then went to the library to search for more specialised works on the topic. Having consulted the library catalogue, I succeeded in locating a number of relevant books. I then took detailed notes from them, using the table of contents and index in each book in order to access the most relevant information.

When I had gathered my information I then structured it on the basis of a thematic plan. I decided to cover a number of themes in my study and structured my work accordingly. I then wrote the first draft and showed it to my teacher, who made a number of helpful suggestions such as the need for a certain number of quotations. I returned to my notes and did some re-ordering of my material for the next draft of the study.

I was satisfied that I had succeeded in achieving the aims set out in my outline plan. I had taken due care to present my study within the wider context of Irish history by showing the relevance of issues such as unionism, Home Rule and the 1916 Rising. I showed clearly the completely divergent hopes of unionist and nationalist recruits, with one group fighting in the war to strengthen the link between Ireland and Great Britain and the other fighting to guarantee the introduction of Home Rule for Ireland. I believe that in my paragraph on recruitment posters I gained an insight into the methods used to recruit volunteers in Ireland during World War I. It was particularly rewarding to work with primary sources and to analyse the actual pictures and slogans used at the time. I also found that throughout my preparation of the study I was constantly aware of the different traditions on the island of Ireland during World War I.

Throughout the research process I practised many skills of the historian. I found it difficult at first to choose between various pieces of information but I always came to a decision by referring to the subject matter of the paragraph in question and the general aims of the study. As I had to do most of the work on my own, I gradually got used to taking decisions and accepting responsibility for my own conclusions. I tried to be as objective as possible and to respect the different points of view expressed by various people at the time. I felt at the end of the process that the research was interesting and worthwhile. It enabled me to fulfil my stated aims and to shed light on a topic which is frequently neglected in mainstream Irish historical writing.

Note: Ordinary Level students – the Research Study for Ordinary Level follows the same pattern as Higher Level except for a shorter extended essay and report.

Extended Essay: The Report

Picture Credits

Picture research by Sinead McCoole and Helen Thompson.

For permission to reproduce photographs and other material, the author and publisher gratefully acknowledge the following:

68, 90R, 102, 110R, 121B, 123R, 126 both, 132TL, 132 third from TL, 132 second from TL, 133TR, 134, 145B, 149B, 164B, 166TR, 169, 175B, 189TL, 189R © The Allen Library; 219T, 247T © Anna MacBride White Collection; 231, 288T © Belfast Telegraph; 132CR, 133B, 133C, 142, 144B, 242, 250, 298T, 309 © Camera Press Ireland; 53 © Christies Images Ltd. 2004; 252B, 270, 272C, 299, 302T, 306T, 311, 332 © Colman Doyle; 66, 147T © Crawford Municipal Art Gallery; 294B, 300, 304 both, 308, 312 both, 313, 314, 316B, 321 both, 322, 324 all, 331 © Derek Speirs/Report; 204 courtesy of The Economic and Social Research Institute; 180 © Felix Rosentiel's Widow & Son Ltd., London on behalf of the Estate of Sir John Lavery 2004/courtesy of the Hugh Lane Gallery; 219C, 222 © Felix Rosentiel's Widow & Son Ltd., London on behalf of the Estate of Sir John Lavery 2004. Photograph reproduced with the kind permission of the Trustees of the National Museums and Galleries of Northern Ireland; 9B, 31, 32T, 40, 105, 108T, 111T, 112, 118, 121T, 123B, 138B, 148, 157R, 163C, 164T, 173T, 182, 183B, 186, 196, 197T, 198, 201, 202, 210, 213 both, 214 both, 215, 236, 245, 259, 296 both, 306B, 307 © Hulton Archive; 109T, 220 © Illustrated London News; 230BL © Imperial War Museum; 8, 9T, 10T, 16, 25T, 42, 46 all, 49, 67, 78, 83, 108B, 132BL, 133TR, 145T, 149T, 163B, 166BL, 166TL, 167TL, 167TR, 167BR, 175T, 203, 256, 264 second right, 277T, 277B, 278T, 289 both © The Irish Picture Library; 124B, 177, 178, 189BL, 193TL, 197B, 206, 244T, 247B, 248 both, 255 both © Fr. Browne S.J. Collection/The Irish Picture Library; 12T, 20B, 25B, 26T © Leland Duncan Collection/The Irish Picture Library; 272T, 297 both, 302B © Irish Times; 23B, 95, 104, 119, 127, 130, 132BR, 132TR, 137, 141T, 147B, 151, 163T, 170 © Kilmainham Gaol Collection; 246 © Irish Press PLC/courtesy of Kilmainham Gaol; 247C, 252T, 253, 257, 261, 264L, 264 second left, 264R, 268T, 273, 277C, 278B © Lensmen Press; 244B © Mairin Hope and Hope Trust; 79 © Mander & Mitchenson Theatre Collection; 19T, 23T, 28, 30, 33, 34, 37, 43, 48, 54 both, 57L, 62, 81, 85TR, 97, 101, 125, 146T, 147C, 154, 155, 157L, 165, 166BR, 173B, 193R, 193BL © Mary Evans Picture Library; 129 EM(BMH CD 288/4)/Military Archives; 208T, 208C, 209 all © Military Archives; 50 courtesy of the National Gallery of Ireland; 216 © Hilda van Stockum/courtesy of the National Gallery of Ireland; 15 © Aloysius O'Kelly/courtesy of the Artist's Estate/National Gallery of Ireland; 11, 19B, 29, 38B, 77, 99, 141B, 185T © National Library of Ireland; 272B © Independent Newspapers/National Library of Ireland; 26B, 32B, 38T, 139 © National Museum of Ireland; 12B, 13, 84, 85TL, 221, 224L, 229, 237, 271T © National Museums & Galleries of Northern Ireland, Ulster Folk & Transport Museum; 271C © Belfast Telegraph/National Museums & Galleries of Northern Ireland, Ulster Museum; 10B, 98, 107, 109B, 110L, 113, 120 both, 123L, 124T, 218T, 224R, 230T, 230C, 230BR, 258 © National Museums and Galleries of Northern Ireland, Ulster Museum; 58B, 144T, 174 © National Photographic Archive; 316T © Pacemaker Press International; 315T, 315B, 317, 318, 329, 333 © Photocall Ireland; 218B, 225, 235 © Public Record Office of Northern Ireland; 90L, 94, 111B, 138T, 146B, 167BL, 183T, 188, 271B, 280, 281 both, 282, 284, 288C, 288B, 290 both, 293, 294T, 298B © RTÉ Stills Library; 243 © Irish Press PLC/RTÉ Stills Library; 268B © Belfast Telegraph/RTÉ Stills Library; 228 © Shorts PLC; 162, 226, 238, 274 © Topham Picturepoint; 70 courtesy of Alma Mater (UCD), Summer 1994; 254 courtesy of the Head of the Department of Irish Folklore, University College, Dublin; Alamy: 339R © Popperfoto, 402T © Homer Sykes Archive, 422T © David Mansell; 377T © Alliance Party; 308B, 356B, 375T, 384TR, 385T, 393, 401B © Belfast Telegraph; Corbis: 338L, 348, 366B, 408B © Bettmann, 404B © Vittoriano Raestelli; 362B from We shall Overcome-the History of the Struggle of Civil Rights in Northern Ireland 1968-1978 (NICRA,1978); 338R, 339L, 341, 342, 344, 347T, 356T, 366T, 367T, 367C, 367BL, 367BR, 368B, 369C, 369B, 375CL, 375B, 377CL, 377CR, 378T, 378B, 379T, 380T, 384B, 385B, 387T, 388T, 390, 392, 400L, 405B, 414BC, 420L, 429TR, 429TL © Getty Images; 387B The Irish Times; 363T, 365, 379B, 385C, 399, 401T, 402B, 404TL, 404TR, 406TR, 406B, 407T, 412, 413T, 413B, 414T, 414BL, 414BR, 415TL, 415TR, 415C, 416B, 418T, 419, 420R, 421T, 426, 427T, 427B, 428T, 428B, 429BR, 430, 431, 436T, 436C, 436B © Pacemaker Press International; 407B, 408T © Photocall Ireland; 347B © PRONI; 429BL, 437 © Rex Features; 362T, 363B, 376, 400R © RTÉ Stills Library; 406TL © Sinn Féin; Topfoto: 359, 375CR, 377B, 386T, 386B, 401C, 403B, 415B, 416T, 417R, 417L, 421B © PA Photos, 337, 340, 343T, 343B, 346, 369T, 370T, 370B, 374, 378C, 384TL, 388B, 396, 402C, 403B, 405T, 416C, 418B, 422B, 423, 431R © Topfoto.

The author and publisher have made every effort to trace all copyright holders, but if any has been inadvertently overlooked we would be pleased to make the necessary arrangements at the first opportunity.